AMERICAN FOREIGN POLICY

THEORETICAL ESSAYS

FIFTH EDITION

G. JOHN IKENBERRY

EDITOR

PRINCETON UNIVERSITY

PEARSON
Longman

New York • Boston • San Francisco
London • Toronto • Sydney • Tokyo • Singapore • Madrid
Mexico City • Munich • Paris • Cape Town • Hong Kong • Montreal

Vice President and Publisher: Priscilla McGeehon
Acquisitions Editor: Edward Costello
Senior Marketing Manager: Elizabeth Fogarty
Managing Editor: Bob Ginsberg
Production Manager: Joe Vella
Project Coordination, Text Design, and Electronic Page Makeup:
    Thompson Steele, Inc.
Senior Cover Design Manager: Nancy Danahy
Cover Design Manager: John Callahan
Cover Designer: Laura Shaw
Cover Photo: Courtesy of Getty Images, Inc.
Manufacturing Manager: Mary Fischer
Manufacturing Buyer: Lucy Hebard
Printer and Binder: R.R. Donnelley & Sons
Cover Printer: Coral Graphics Services

Library of Congress Cataloging-in-Publication Data
American foreign policy : theoretical essays / G. John Ikenberry, editor.— 5th ed.
        p. cm.
      ISBN 0-321-15973-X (alk. paper)
      1. United States—Foreign relations. I. Ikenberry, G. John.
JZ1480.A96 2005
327.73—dc22

                                                                    2004009409

Please visit our website at http://www.ablongman.com

ISBN 0-321-15973-X

2 3 4 5 6 7 8 9 10—DOC—07 06 05

Contents

ꙮPART THREEꙮ

Capitalism, Class, and Foreign Policy
137

ꙮPART FOURꙮ

National Values,
Democratic Institutions, and Foreign Policy
213

☙PART FIVE❧

Public Opinion, Policy Legitimacy, and Sectional Conflict
311

☙PART SIX❧

Bureaucratic Politics and Organizational Culture
401

✤PART SEVEN✤

Perceptions, Personality, and Social Psychology
461

✤PART EIGHT✤

American Foreign Policy After the Cold War and 911
539

Preface

The purpose of this book is to provide students with representative statements of the major, contending explanations of American foreign policy. The idea is to showcase the variety of theoretical perspectives that scholars have pursued in attempting to make sense of policy. I have gathered these essays together in the hope that students will become more familiar with the avenues of inquiry that are available and the debates they engender. Left only to the textbook or the occasional popular book on the subject, students and teachers alike can all too easily overlook the very real controversies at the heart of the study of American foreign policy: What political, economic, and cultural forces shape policy? What is the realm of choice and what is the realm of necessity in making policy? What types of language and levels of analysis are most useful in our search to explain policy? My hope is that after reading the essays in this volume, the student can achieve more clarity in answering these questions.

The theoretical traditions that these essays represent are of long standing. Scholars over many generations have worked within them and drawn on many of them, although the specific formulations presented in most of the essays are quite original. Because the effort is to present theoretical approaches and not analysis of current foreign policy events, the essays themselves range in vintage as widely as they range in content. This is a virtue; it reinforces the notion that scholarly endeavor springs from theoretical traditions. We build on some and react to others. Through this process we create new traditions.

In the introduction I present an overview of the challenge of explanation in foreign policy. The problem in the study of American foreign policy is that we have too many ways of explaining policy—we have an overabundance of theory. In this introductory essay I explore some of the methods whereby students can deal with this problem of overdetermination. Part One, "The Problem of Explanation," presents discussions of analytical choice in the study of foreign policy. These essays help us develop a set of tools to explore more specific types of explanation. Each of the following parts represents an alternative route to explanation. Taken together, the book provides a sort of compendium of maps for the study of foreign policy. It is the readers who must judge which map is most useful.

Many of the categories of explanation and some of the essays that are presented here were used in a course I taught for many years at Princeton University and the general focus on the problem of explanation has remained useful in my teaching at the University of Pennsylvania and Georgetown University. Over the years this course was taught and passed along to several professors. Its organization, with a focus on explanation, was given shape by Miles Kahler and Kenneth Oye as well as myself. Its original inspiration, if oral history is correct, came from James Kurth when he taught Government 179, Comparative Foreign Policy, at Harvard. As it turns out, the teaching of American foreign policy also has its traditions.

I wish to thank the following reviewers: Andrew Bennett, Georgetown University; Robert H. Donaldson, University of Tulsa; David Hendrickson, The Colorado College; Steven Livingston, State University of New York at Albany; Michael Mastanduno, Dartmouth College; John M. Owen, IV, University of Virginia; Roy Pateman, University of California at Los Angeles; Gene Rainey, University of North Carolina; Shilby Telhami, University of Maryland; and Shelton L. Williams, Austin College.

I thank Thomas Wright for his extraordinary research assistance.

G. JOHN IKENBERRY

Introduction

G. John Ikenberry

Few areas of American political life have attracted more commentators, critics, and interpreters than United States foreign policy. Popular views of the proper direction and aims of American foreign policy are as ubiquitous and wide-ranging as the policies themselves. The end of the Cold War has only widened and intensified the public debate. 911 and the American wars in Afghanistan and Iraq have also intensified the debate on the sources of American action abroad. Scholarly analysis of American foreign policy is no less diverse. Schools of thought that claim to explain the sources and purposes of foreign policy are scattered across the academic landscape. This is scarcely surprising. The foreign policy of the United States covers so much history and so many events that it seems capable of sustaining many interpretations, even contradictory ones, at the same time. Scholars are drawn to the study of foreign policy in efforts to develop powerful and satisfying accounts of the forces that shape policy. Yet very little agreement can be found over what those forces are and how they operate. The student of foreign policy is left with an array of historical cases and lots of theories. What is to be done?

Confronted with this predicament, happily, we can make some headway. We can begin by clarifying what exactly these theories seek to explain. A more precise understanding of the claims that a theoretical approach makes allows us to judge its plausibility; we put ourselves in a position to accept or reject the claims in the light of the historical evidence. This volume is organized so as to allow this process of clarification to take place. We are confronted with important and divergent approaches to American foreign policy. Presented with a sort of theoretical menu, we can see what each has to offer. What specifically is each theoretical approach attempting to explain? What are the forces and mechanisms at work? What explicit or implicit models of individual and state action are embedded within each approach? How generalizable are the claims? What unacknowledged normative claims linger below the surface concerning how American foreign policy is best conducted?

Coming to grips with the range of explanations for American foreign policy still leaves us with an overabundance of theory, but we can make headway here as well. In some cases we are confronted with competing explanations for policy—different theories that claim to explain the same events. In circumstances such as these we need to know how to evaluate the alternatives; we need standards of judgment as we sort through the theoretical options. Which types of theories provide the most powerful and robust explanations?

In other cases we are confronted with theories that are lodged at different levels of explanation. The theories are trained on different aspects of foreign policy

1

and are not in direct competition. Here we need to know how to provide layered analysis and to judge which levels are most enduring and fundamental. In both these cases we need a sort of methodology of choice, or a theory of theories, that provides guidance in how to deploy our analysis.

In this introduction I discuss each of these tasks—the clarification of theories and the methodology of choice. We begin this exercise with a sober appreciation of the problems of finding definitive answers to our questions. We must be willing to manage the ambiguity that is inherent in attempting to understand a seemingly unmanageable array of history that we loosely group together as American foreign policy. But the exercise is essential. Precisely because everybody has an opinion on foreign policy, we need to probe more deeply the theoretical assumptions that lie beneath the surface. At the very least we will come to a better understanding of the largely implicit theoretical commitments we often make in the heat of political debate. But we just might advance even further and cut through the welter of opinion to stake out a more systematic and reasoned set of views on American foreign policy. The absence of a systematic and reasoned set of views on foreign policy is often the first criticism we level at our political leaders. We should demand no less of ourselves.

VARIETIES OF THEORY AND LEVELS OF ANALYSIS

Part of the problem in clarifying and comparing alternative explanations of American foreign policy is that these explanations do not always seek to explain the same events. Foreign policy can be found, among other places, in the decisions of a president or secretary of state, in the policies of a government, or in the broad patterns of the nation's history. In explaining the American intervention in Vietnam, are we interested in understanding President Johnson's fateful 1965 decision to send combat troops to South Vietnam or in the larger sequence of American policy and the doctrine of containment that stretched over five administrations? Are we interested in explaining specific decisions of a single individual, or sequences of decisions that stretch over many years, or the policy outcomes of entire government bodies, such as Congress or the executive branch? The types of policy outcomes or decisions that we seek to explain may well influence what theoretical bodies of literature we want to draw on. At the same time what appear to be contradictory theoretical claims by different scholars may actually simply arise from differences in their choice of subject matter.

Levels of Analysis

In clarifying the range of foreign policy outcomes and the range of theoretical explanations, many scholars have invoked the notion of levels of analysis. Kenneth Waltz, concerning himself with international politics and not foreign policy as such, has specified three "images" of international politics: the individual, the state, and the state system.[1] Each image captures a different level of causation in international relations. The first image is the individual; as a source of behavior in international politics, it brings with it the idiosyncratic features and beliefs that constitute all individuals. How do you explain why a nation goes to war? You look at the ambitions and personalities of its leaders. The second image focuses on the characteristics of the nation-state, its culture, society, and political institutions. How do you explain why a nation goes to war? You look at the forces that grow out of its democratic or authoritarian or socialist institutions. The third image is the international system. At this systemic level the concern is with the enduring patterns and structures of power within the state system. How do you explain why a nation goes to war? You look at the competitive nature of the state system and the changing balance of power. Waltz argues that this level is the most powerful as a guide to understanding international politics. The systemic level identifies the forces within which individuals and states operate; it generates constraints and imperatives by which all individuals and states, regardless of their uniquenesses, must abide.

In another classic statement of the problem, J. David Singer also distinguishes levels of analysis. In assessing the levels' descriptive, explanatory, and predictive capabilities, Singer finds that the international system level is the most comprehensive and most capable of predictive generalizations. Yet in moving to a systemic model, such theory loses the richness and specificity of analysis on the national level. At the international level states take on a certain sameness as the analysis deemphasizes national autonomy and independence of choices.[2] In the end Singer argues for a balance of systemic and national-level analysis; an exclusive preoccupation with one or the other risks an exaggeration of either similarities or differences in states.

In a further refinement Robert Jervis distinguishes among four levels of analysis: the level of decision making; the level of bureaucracy; the nature of the state and the workings of domestic politics; and the international environment.[3] Apart from the decision-making level, which delineates the realm of choice for the actor, the other levels locate features of the actor's setting. Analysis at each of these levels makes a claim: that if we know enough about the setting in which foreign policy is made—bureaucratic, national or international—we can explain and predict the actor's behavior. Yet the emphasis on one of these variables seems to diminish the importance of the others. The importance of the international setting as a force that shapes foreign policy, for example, suggests an image of foreign policy officials relatively unconstrained by their own bureaucracy or domestic political system. Likewise, if bureaucracy plays a serious role in shaping policy, this has implications for the claims we might make about the role of political parties or public opinion. Specifying levels of analysis immediately reveals the theoretical tensions.

There is no uniform method for the classification of types of theories or variables. The organization of this book goes further than do the authors just discussed in distinguishing between types of variables or levels of analysis. Several of the sections, such as those concerning economic and cultural determinants of foreign policy, fall rather easily into Waltz's second image or Jervis's national level of analysis. The categorization of variables into levels of analysis is at least initially simply a matter of theoretical housekeeping. For our purposes the levels-of-analysis exercise organizes into manageable parts the various elements of social reality that bear on the making of foreign policy.

International and Domestic Structures

Running through the discussion of levels of analysis is the issue of the primacy of one level over the others. In this there is some controversy. Kenneth Waltz, as we have noted, gives pride of place to forces that operate at the international level. An anarchic state system and a prevailing distribution of power are unrelenting forces that operate on states. To begin one's analysis with more particularistic national or individual variables is to risk missing common international forces that impose their constraints on many states. Political culture or public opinion, for example, may influence foreign policy in specific cases and at the margin, but it is the basic structure of the international system that sets the terms of the conduct of foreign policy over the long run. J. David Singer is not as insistent on leaving explanations at the international level. Theorists of foreign policy are in effect caught between Scilla and Charybdis; a proper theoretical understanding of foreign policy must avoid the dangers that emerge when we move too far in either a national or systemic direction.

There is reason to be skeptical of the strongest claims of systemic analysis that the structure of the international system *determines* foreign policy; and indeed most of the controversy is really over how theoretically privileged this level of analysis should be. Most scholars who stress the importance of systemic forces argue that it sets constraints on foreign policy rather than shapes policy in any more direct sense; it is a necessary but not sufficient component of our analysis. Waltz's theory of international politics is just that: a theory that seeks to explain recurring patterns of behavior within the international system. As Waltz notes, to explain how any single nation-state will respond to the constraints imposed by the international structure requires a theory of foreign policy.[4] The international system influences but does not determine foreign policy.

Yet even if the international system (characterized by its competitive nature and prevailing distribution of power) manifests imperatives and constraints, it is still necessary to understand how and to what extent those imperatives and constraints operate. How does a state (or individuals within it) perceive and act on forces generated within a competitive state system? The international system may well create incentives for political leaders to protect their national autonomy and security, but many foreign policy outcomes are consistent with this demand. Statesmen may be pressed to attend to the nation's survival and well-being, but the international setting does not provide unambiguous clues about how best to do so. In the same way, the specification of international constraints may leave a wide range of options open to state officials. Constraints may be more or less confining, and so we need to know under what conditions they are more and under what conditions they are less confining. A focus on constraints tells us what is not possible. If constraints are very tight, we may have most of the story. If they are loose, we are left with little guidance concerning what is still possible.[5]

If the international setting does not provide enough explanatory power, we might want to turn to national-level variables. Here we are interested in such factors as the social and economic structure of the nation and the character of its domestic politics. The variety of domestic variables that may impinge on foreign policy is huge, and many of them are organized in the sections of this book. Some theories argue for the importance of the nation's culture, its economic and class structure, or its ruling political institutions. Some make strong claims that a particular variable determines foreign policy in conjunction with other variables. When we move to this level of analysis, the types of variables that may impinge on foreign policy proliferate.

In each case we are confronted with the same issues as those that arose in our discussion of systemic theory. Each approach makes a claim about the constraints and imperatives that are imposed by a particular set of characteristics in the decision maker's domestic setting. States with the same critical domestic feature should pursue similar sorts of foreign policy when they are in similar sorts of international situations (and also act similarly when confronted with significantly different situations); states that differ in this critical domestic feature should also differ in their foreign policy, even if they are confronted with similar sorts of international situations.[6] It is here that national-level theories of foreign policy are put to the test. Revisionist historians argue that the Cold War had its roots in the expansive behavior of American capitalist society. Critics of this position argue that United States policy toward the Soviet Union was motivated by geopolitical circumstances that would have been felt and acted on by American political leaders regardless of the nation's internal economic or political characteristics. History makes it very difficult to settle this controversy, but the theoretical issues at stake are clear.

Theories of foreign policy that stress the importance of domestic setting make the implicit claim that if different leaders were present in the same domestic circumstances, they would make the same choices. The stronger the claim made about the role of domestic setting, the less it is necessary to know about the activities and beliefs of the actual individuals who make decisions. But again we are confronted with theoretical challenges. Unless one takes an extreme position, the theory characterizes the domestic sources of foreign policy as constraints and imperatives that more or less shape policy. In what way do political leaders feel the pressures and constraints of culture or class or political institutions? What are the mechanisms? How do they operate? Under what conditions can they be ignored or transformed? If a particular type of domestic structure, such as class structure, is only loosely constraining, we may need to consider several sets of structures and entertain the possibility that they interact with one another. Bureaucratic politics may be magnified by the play of societal pressures, or it may insulate political leaders from the larger society. Political culture and ideals may manifest themselves most profoundly in the institutions of government that in turn help to influence the course of foreign policy.

Choice and Decision Making

When we have exhausted the explanatory power of a state's domestic and international setting, we are left with the decision makers themselves. The theories we have discussed to this point are *structural* theories. That is, they are theories that make predictions about foreign policy outcomes without reference to the cognition and actions of the actors themselves. According to these theories, setting, of whatever type, shapes policy. In their strongest form structural theories that stress domestic and international setting leave little or no room for individual beliefs, perceptions, or choices. Individuals are theoretically fungible. Substitute one individual for another, and if the setting remains the same, so too does foreign policy.

If structural theories do not satisfactorily explain foreign policy, we can turn to *decision-making* explanations of policy. Here we are interested in theories that explain policy in terms of the reasons, beliefs, and processes by which individuals make choices. Domestic and international structures may constrain and propel foreign policy, but when they leave room for meaningful choice, we need theories of individual and group decision making.[7]

The autonomy of the decision-making level remains a matter of some controversy. This issue is implicit when students of American foreign policy debate various historical "what-ifs." If Franklin Roosevelt had lived, would he have been able to prevent or moderate postwar hostilities between the United States and the Soviet Union beyond the talents of an inexperienced Harry Truman? If John F. Kennedy had not been killed in Dallas, would the tragedy of Vietnam have been avoided? Alternatively, in both these cases were the evolving geopolitical circumstances or shifting international currents leading these presidents in the same direction as their successors? In the most important episodes of postwar American foreign policy, when policy was made that lasted a generation, did individuals make a difference or were they swept up in larger historical forces? These are questions about the role of the individual in history. They are questions as stimulating as they are frustrating, and we cannot provide definitive answers to them. Nonetheless, if we are prepared to grant our foreign policy leaders a realm of choice, we must equip ourselves with a means to understand their decisions.

Several literatures probe the workings of foreign policy decision making. One group of theories focuses on the manner in which government bureaucracy shapes the content of policy. The claims of this type of explanation are fourfold: the de facto power to make foreign policy is divided across the executive establishment; the various "players" in the decision-making process have different goals and interests, largely determined by their bureaucratic position ("Where a person stands depends on when he sits"); decision making is a process of bargaining and compromise; and consequently, policy is a "resultant"—it is the product of a political rather than an analytical process. The seminal statement of this approach is provided by Graham Allison, and it is included in this volume along with major statements of critique.

The implication of this body of theory, if it is to be truly taken seriously, is that policy emerges not in response to the external setting of the actors charged with making decisions but rather from within the organizations of the state itself. It is the bureaucratic interests of government officials and the distribution of power within the state that determine the substantive content of policy. If, however, those interests and configurations of power are only a reflection of larger social interests and powers, the bureaucratic approach to explanation is substantially reduced in theoretical importance. We may want to know about the details of decision making within the "black box" of government, but that process is trivial as a guide to the forces that shape policy. Alternatively, bureaucratic politics and organizational process may be decisive sources of policy in the foreign policy backwaters—in areas of least significance. We must be prepared to differentiate policies as we search for explanations.

The decision-making level has also been approached by other scholars who focus on the beliefs and cognition of top leaders. As is the case with the bureaucratic politics approach, the attention to beliefs and perceptions assumes a realm of choice in policy making. The importance of cognitive variables may emerge in several situations. We may want to focus on this aspect of decision making if there are cases in which consistent differences exist between decision makers' perceptions and reality. These may be cases of major foreign policy blunders, when officials misjudge their position or that of their adversary. Such cases may provide evidence of the role of domestic constraints or pressures, but it is equally plausible that the officials were conducting policy with an inappropriate set of beliefs. Alternatively, we may want to probe the role of perceptions and beliefs when officials placed in the same situation behave differently. In these cases officials may bring to office very different sets of beliefs about the world.[8] These types of beliefs and cognitive frameworks are explored in Part Seven of this book.

Provided with these various levels of analysis and theoretical approaches, we can explore their utility in the study of foreign policy. We can begin to appreciate the various levels of social structure and decision making that may bear on policy. At the same time it is easy to see that we are supplied with an overabundance of theory. We need further guidance in making theoretical choices. It is not enough simply to pick some theoretical approach and run with it. We need guidance in how to proceed when different approaches seem to provide equally plausible explanations—to better understand when a particular level of analysis or type of variable is most suitable in rendering an account of foreign policy. We turn to these issues now.

THE PROBLEM OF THE OVERSUPPLY OF THEORY

Of the various approaches to foreign policy in this volume, each promises to explain some aspects of American foreign policy, and at each level there is seemingly great promise. The international system can be brought to bear in explaining almost all foreign policy. Internationally generated pressures of various sorts find their way into all facets of policy making. Foreign policy also elicits strong views from many segments of society, and some types of foreign policy serve to advantage and disadvantage various societal groups. Thus, even if direct pressure by these groups is not apparent, an underlying set of societal interests may still account for patterns of outcomes. Finally, political leaders and the bureaucracy have a hand in shaping foreign policy simply by virtue of their location and formal powers. Indeed, to no one's surprise, these officials find it easy to rationalize their actions in terms of national or "state" interests. It is clear that we are left not with an absence of adequate explanations of foreign policy but with an oversupply. As James Kurth puts the issue, "[t]he problem with questions about the making of military policy, and also about the making of foreign policy, is not that there are no answers but that there are too many answers."[9] How are we to proceed?

It may not be possible to settle these theoretical controversies—to decide which theory or level of analysis is most important. But we can put ourselves in a situation to judge the merits of various approaches to foreign policy. When we are confronted with competing and seemingly coequal explanations of foreign policy, we can turn to three methods by which to adjudicate the claims: empirical, aesthetic, and analytical.

The most obvious attempt to solve the problem of overdetermination is to turn the problem into an *empirical* problem. If we are confronted, for example, with a structural account and a decision-making account of an episode in American foreign policy, we may want to investigate the recollections of the government officials themselves to see what they perceived to be their realm of choice. Stanley Hoffmann provides a structural account of American policy in the early postwar period: "When the nature of Soviet power and policy and the crumbling of British strength became obvious, the United States simply had to fill the vacuum. President Truman's freedom of choice was strictly limited; it concerned the moment and the manner in which America's taking up the challenge would be demonstrated. Even in this respect the margin of choice was narrowed by the development of the crisis in Greece in 1947 . . . Rarely has freedom been more clearly the recognition of necessity, and statesmanship the imaginative exploitation of necessity."[10] This systemic argument about the forces that drove American policy (and the various bureaucratic, economic, and cultural accounts that compete against it) can be clarified by investigating the range of options that officials themselves entertained.

There are inherent limits, however, to empirical solutions to theoretical problems. Government officials may seek to rationalize their decisions by arguing that the imperatives of geopolitics left them no choice; or they may take credit for making a choice where none really existed. Even more problematic, the theories themselves point to different types of evidence, each with its own biases. In explaining why President Kennedy chose a policy of blockade during the Cuban missile crisis, we can find evidence to support a variety of explanations. We could point to the president's individual characteristics, to political pressures of the upcoming midterm election in 1962, or to the international balance of power. There is evidence that would seem to suit each type of explanation. Adjudication of the claims of various theories by strict reference to the historical "facts" runs into the same problem we have with the theories themselves: there is an overabundance, not a paucity, of empirical evidence. Empirical investigations may give us some help, but they do not resolve the problems of the oversupply of theory.

A second approach to the problem of competing explanations could be called the *aesthetic* solution. Competing theories are judged in terms of basic standards of theoretical rigor. These standards, as Harry Eckstein argues, include regularity (does a theory involve claims to "rulefulness" with statements of causation and probability?); reliability and validity (does the theory provide a set of conditions that if repeated would produce the same outcome?); foreknowledge (does the theory provide statements of anticipated outcomes in areas currently unknown?); and parsimony (how wide a range and number of phenomena can the theory order and how simple are the theoretical constructs it uses to do so?)[11]

From the standpoint of these elements of rigor, the theories in this volume present different strengths and weaknesses. Systemic theory, with its attention to international structural variables, is attractive for its parsimony. If we want to explain general characteristics of American foreign policy over long stretches of time, this is a good place to begin. Yet international-level theory, as we have already noted, posits constraints and imperatives on actors; it does not provide the basis for predicting specific outcomes. Systemic theory may still provide the most powerful explanation of foreign policy in some circumstances, yet its parsimony is often purchased at the price of less specificity in the outcomes it can explain. Other structural theories that specify the setting within which actors make decisions also suffer from problems of this sort. Theories that rely on political culture or ideology, although less parsimonious than systemic theory, also tend to have a huge variety of outcomes that are consistent with their predictions. Theories that are lodged at the decision-making level rely on variables that tend to come and go with the individuals themselves; patterns and regularities in foreign policy are tied closely to sets of intervening conditions. At the same time, decision-making theories may be able to capture more of the richness and critical detail of foreign policy.

It is clear that no one theory or set of variables can be the most important in all situations. Consequently, our efforts are probably not best served by seeking to find one approach that triumphs over the rest. The importance of a set of variables varies with the cases we are seeking to understand. This leads to a final method for dealing with the problem of the oversupply of theory—what we can call the *analytical* approach. Here the efforts are not to choose between the contending explanations as such, but to draw on each in various ways. This can be done in two ways. One approach is eclectic. In this we simply pick and choose from the various approaches in fashioning plausible accounts of American foreign policy. This approach appears reasonable at first glance, particularly because the types of policies we might wish to explain vary so enormously. Nonetheless, this ad hoc approach has flaws, as James Kurth criticizes: "It is intellectually unsatisfying and even self-abnegating. Further, it suffers from what might be called the $nth+1$ problem. Given n theories, the simply eclectic will accept them all and equally, for he has no standards with which to discriminate among them. But suppose someone offers another explanation, the $nth+1$ theory. The simply eclectic must accept this theory too. And the same is true for the $nth+2$, $nth+3$ . . . "[12]

The analytical solution, however, does not need to be eclectic. Rather than simply picking and choosing elements of the various approaches, this approach can involve the development of more overarching propositions that bring the various theories together in comprehensive ways. In effect what this final approach attempts to do is to develop "metatheory" that incorporates the several types of variables into larger-scale frameworks. An exercise of this sort is all the more useful when we note that many of the theories are not strictly speaking alternative and coequal. The explanatory usefulness of a variable, as we have argued, may depend on what level of generality we wish to locate our analysis. The international system may influence the general contours of American foreign policy, but domestic and decision-making variables are necessary to explain more specific aspects. Or it may be, as Robert Jervis argues, that the importance of variables at each level may vary with the stages of decision: "domestic politics may dictate that a given event be made the occasion for a change in policy; bargaining within the bureaucracy may explain what options are presented to the national leaders; the decision maker's predisposition could account for the choice that was made; and the interests and routines of the bureaucracies could explain the way the decision was implemented."[13]

Another way to make sense of the multitude of variables and levels is to pose their significance as conditional propositions. Thus, we can argue that systemic-level variables are most important during times of international crisis. It is at these moments that government officials are most attentive to the constraints and opportunities of the international system and most willing to ignore domestic political pressures. In the absence of a foreign policy crisis, domestic politics or the working of bureaucracy are more likely to come into play. One can also develop contingent propositions that relate variables to different types of foreign policy issues. Foreign economic policy may be subject to greater domestic pressures than military policy.[14] Doubtless there are many other ways to develop contingent propositions of this sort that link sets of variables with divergent aspects of American foreign policy. In the end we are still left with an overabundance of theory, but we now have methods with which to cope with the many possibilities.

CONCLUSION

The choices we make about how to probe the workings of American foreign policy carry with them normative implications. This is not evident at first glance. Discussions of theory, and even more so "metatheory," seem to be far removed from our own views about the conduct of foreign policy. Yet the link exists. In his essay in Part One, James Kurth observes that the conclusions we draw on the theory of foreign policy tell us, when we turn to policy advocacy, what needs to be reformed. If we conclude that high levels of military spending and an expansionary foreign policy are rooted in the very nature of the American capitalist system, as Marxists and others have argued, the agenda for change is profound indeed. If such policies are propelled by more transient sets of institutions or ruling coalitions, reform would lead in a different direction. Our theories give us guidance when we want to talk about improving American foreign policy.

Those who argue that the international system is an overpowering force in shaping foreign policy are faced with their own moral questions. If foreign policy officials are the faithful stewards of the balance of power, who is to be judged accountable? Robert Jervis poses this issue:

> When all people would respond the same way to a given situation, it is hard to praise or blame the decision maker. Thus, those accused of war crimes will argue that their behavior did not differ from others who found themselves in the same circumstance. And the prosecution will charge, as it did against Tojo and his colleagues, that "These defendants were not automatons; they were not replaceable cogs in a machine. . . . It was theirs to choose whether their nation would lead an honored life . . . or . . . would

become a symbol of evil throughout the world. They made their choice. For this choice they must bear the guilt."[15]

Our theories tell us who should be held accountable in the conduct of foreign policy. Is the president in control or is he the hostage of a massive federal bureaucracy? Do our democratic institutions shape foreign policy or is it guided by the hidden hand of class interests?

We may have to live with the fact that our answers to these questions are not definitive. The drawing of satisfying theoretical conclusions about the sources and purposes of American foreign policy is a complicated affair; we are left with a certain amount of theoretical ambiguity. We can remember Albert Einstein's advice that "if you wish to describe truth, leave elegance to the tailor." At the very least we can begin by being more theoretically self-conscious about our arguments and opinions. This book seeks to array the relevant literatures so as to allow such a process to go forward.

NOTES

1. Kenneth N. Waltz, *Man, the State, and War* (New York: Columbia University Press, 1959).
2. J. David Singer, "The Level-of-Analysis Problem in International Relations," in Klaus Knorr and Sidney Verba, eds., *The International System: Theoretical Essays* (Princeton: Princeton University Press, 1961).
3. Robert Jervis, *Perception and Misperception in International Politics* (Princeton: Princeton University Press, 1976), Chapter 1.
4. Kenneth N. Waltz, *Theory of International Politics* (Reading, Mass.: Addison-Wesley, 1979). Chapter 6, "Anarchic Orders and Balances of Power," reprinted in this book as Chapter 3.
5. For a very insightful discussion of the nature of constraints and determinants see Arthur A. Stein, "Structure, Purpose, Process, and Analysis of Foreign Policy: The Growth of Soviet Power and the Role of Ideology," in Roman Kolkowicz, ed., *The Roots of Soviet Power: Domestic Determinants of Foreign and Defense Policy* (Boulder: Westview Press, 1989).
6. See Jervis, *Perception and Misperception in International Politics*, p. 22.
7. See Stein, "Structure, Purpose, Process, and the Analysis of Foreign Policy."
8. Jervis, *Perception and Misperception in International Politics*, p. 29.
9. James R. Kurth, "A Widening Gyre: The Logic of American Weapons Procurement," *Public Policy* XIX (Summer 1971).
10. Stanley Hoffmann, "Restraints and Choices in American Foreign Policy," in Stanley Hoffmann, *The State of War: Essays on the Theory and Practice of International Politics* (Praeger Publishers, 1965).
11. Harry Eckstein, "Case Study and Theory in Political Science," in Nelson Polsby and Fred Greenstein, eds., *Handbook of Political Science* (Reading, Mass.: Addison-Wesley, 1975), vol. 2, p. 88. See also Alexander George, "Case Studies and Theory Development," in Paul Lauren, ed., *Diplomacy: New Approaches in Theory, History, and Policy* (New York: Free Press, 1979), pp. 43–68; and Alexander George and Tim McKeown, "Case Studies and Theories of Organizational Decision Making," in Robert Coulan and Richard Smith, eds., *Advances in Information Processing in Organizations* (Greenwich, CT: JAI Press, 1985), pp. 43–68. For a critique of the case study method,

see Olav Njolstad, "Learning from History? Case Studies and the Limits of Theory Building," in Njolstad, ed., *Arms Races: Technological and Political Dynamics* (Beverly Hills, CA: Sage, 1990), pp. 220–46. For discussion of the scientific method as it relates to the study of Soviet foreign policy, see Jack Synder, "Richness and Rigor, and Relevance in the Study of Soviet Foreign Policy," *International Security,* vol. 9, no. 3 (Winter 1984/85).

12. James R. Kurth, "United States Policies and Latin American Politics: Competing Theories and Comparative Analyses," unpublished paper, 1972.

13. Jervis, *Perception and Misperception in International Politics,* p. 17.

14. See Barry B. Hughes, *The Domestic Context of American Foreign Policy* (San Francisco: W.H. Freeman and Company, 1978), Chapter 7.

15. Jervis, *Perception and Misperception in International Politics,* pp. 15–16.

❧ PART ONE ❧

The Problem
of Explanation

The following two essays examine the general analytical problems of explaining foreign policy. The problem of explanation is not that there are no answers but that there are too many answers. The ability to arrive at determinate causal explanations of foreign policy is elusive. The authors argue, nonetheless, that progress can be made. They argue that it is important to tackle particular foreign policy puzzles—why the United States intervened abroad militarily or worked to create a new international institution, for example—armed with multiple explanatory lenses. Explaining American foreign policy involves a battle of explanations. The first step in the process is to clarify the various models or lenses which are relevant to a particular foreign policy episode. Explanations themselves often involve not proving one model or lens right and the others wrong—but showing how various models or lenses reveal different aspects of the puzzle.

Ole Holsti is interested in facilitating exchange between diplomatic historians and political scientists, which he does by offering a map of the various schools of thought in the professional study of international relations and foreign policy. Holsti's survey begins by examining theories of the international system: classical realism and its modern variations, global society and complex interdependence, and Marxism. Holsti moves on to examine various models of foreign policy decision making: bureaucratic politics, group dynamics, and individual decision making. Holsti argues that systemic and decision-making approaches each have advantages and limitations, and a satisfying explanation may need to work within both traditions. At the same time, it is important to clearly specify the outcome that one wants to explain; this also determines which model is most useful.

W. Michael Reisman is concerned with a more narrow question: how to make sense of the complex, ambivalent, and shifting relationship that the United States has had over the last century with multilateral institutions. He identifies four roles that the United States fulfills when it supports or resists involvement in international institutions. Each role reflects a different impulse or motivation behind American policy—visionary ideals, power politics, institutional routines, and domestic pressure politics. Reisman shows us how a proper understanding of the American encounter with global institutions requires a variety of analytical models.

ﻌﯩ

Models of International Relations and Foreign Policy

Ole R. Holsti

Universities and professional associations usually are organized in ways that tend to separate scholars in adjoining disciplines and perhaps even to promote stereotypes of each other and their scholarly endeavors. The seemingly natural areas of scholarly convergence between diplomatic historians and political scientists who focus on international relations have been underexploited, but there are also a few welcome signs that this may be changing. These include recent essays suggesting ways in which the two disciplines can contribute to each other; a number of prize-winning dissertations, later turned into books, by political scientists during the past decade that effectively combine political science theories and historical research and materials; collaborative efforts among scholars in the two disciplines; and the appearance of such interdisciplinary journals as *International Security* that provide an outlet for historians and political scientists with common interests.[1]

This essay is an effort to contribute further to an exchange of ideas between the two disciplines by describing some of the theories, approaches, and "models" that political scientists have used in their research on international relations during recent decades. A brief essay cannot do justice to the entire range of models that may be found in the current literature, if only because the period has witnessed a proliferation of approaches. But perhaps the models described here, when combined with citations to some representative works, will provide diplomatic historians with a useful, if sketchy, road map toward some of the more prominent landmarks in a neighboring discipline.

Because "classical realism" is the most venerable and persisting model of international relations, it provides a good starting point and baseline for comparison with competing models. Robert Gilpin may have been engaging in hyperbole when he questioned whether our understanding of international relations has advanced significantly since Thucydides, but one must acknowledge that the latter's analysis of the Peloponnesian War includes concepts that are not foreign to contemporary students of balance-of-power politics.[2]

Following a discussion of classical realism, an examination of "modern realism" will identify the continuities and differences between the two approaches. The essay then turns to several models that challenge one or more core premises of both classical and modern realism. The first two challengers focus on the sys-

Ole R. Holsti, "Models of International Relations and Foreign Policy," *Diplomatic History, 13, 1* (Winter 1989), pp. 15–43. Reprinted by permission of Blackwell Publishing.

tem level: Global-Society/Complex-Interdependence models and Marxist/World-System/Dependency models. Subsequent sections discuss several "decision-making" models, all of which share a skepticism about the adequacy of theories that focus on the structure of the international system while neglecting political processes within units that comprise the system.

Three limitations should be stated at the outset. Each of the three systemic and three decision-making approaches described below is a composite of several models; limitations of space have made it necessary to focus on the common denominators rather than on subtle differences among them. This discussion will also avoid purely methodological issues and debates; for example, what Stanley Hoffmann calls "the battle of the literates versus the numerates."[3] Finally, efforts of some political scientists to develop "formal" or mathematical approaches to international relations are neglected here; such abstract, often ahistorical models are likely to be of limited interest to historians.[4] With these caveats, let me turn now to classical realism, the first of the systemic models to be discussed in this essay.

There have always been Americans, such as Alexander Hamilton, who viewed international relations from a realist perspective, but its contemporary intellectual roots are largely European. Three important figures of the interwar period probably had the greatest impact on American scholarship: the historian E. H. Carr, the geographer Nicholas Spykman, and the political theorist Hans J. Morgenthau. Other Europeans who have contributed significantly to realist thought include John Herz, Hedley Bull, Raymond Aron, and Martin Wight, while notable Americans of this school include scholars Arnold Wolfers and Norman Graebner, as well as diplomat George F. Kennan, journalist Walter Lippmann, and theologian Reinhold Niebuhr.[5]

Although realists do not constitute a homogeneous school—any more than do any of the others discussed in this essay—most of them share at least five core premises about international relations. To begin with, they view as central questions the causes of war and the conditions of peace. They also regard the structure of the international system as a necessary if not always sufficient explanation for many aspects of international relations. According to classical realists, "structural anarchy," or the absence of a central authority to settle disputes, is the essential feature of the contemporary system, and it gives rise to the "security dilemma": in a self-help system one nation's search for security often leaves its current and potential adversaries insecure, any nation that strives for absolute security leaves all others in the system absolutely insecure, and it can provide a powerful incentive for arms races and other types of hostile interactions. Consequently, the question of *relative* capabilities is a crucial factor. Efforts to deal with this central element of the international system constitute the driving force behind the relations of units within the system; those that fail to cope will not survive. Thus, unlike "idealists" or "liberal internationalists," classical realists view conflict as a natural state of affairs rather than a consequence that can be attributed to historical circumstances, evil leaders, flawed sociopolitical systems, or inadequate international understanding and education.[6]

A third premise that unites classical realists is their focus on geographically based groups as the central actors in the international system. During other periods the major entities may have been city states or empires, but at least since the Treaties of Westphalia (1648), states have been the dominant units. Classical realists also agree that state behavior is rational. The assumption behind this fourth premise is that states are guided by the logic of the "national interest," usually defined in terms of survival, security, power, and relative capabilities. To Morgenthau, for example, "rational foreign policy minimizes risks and maximizes benefits." Although the national interest may vary according to specific circumstances, the similarity of motives among nations permits the analyst to reconstruct the logic of policymakers in their pursuit of national interests—what Morgenthau called the "rational hypothesis"—and to avoid the fallacies of "concern with motives and concern with ideological preferences."[7]

Finally, the nation-state can also be conceptualized as a *unitary* actor. Because the central problems for states are starkly defined by the nature of the international system, their actions are primarily a response to external rather than domestic political forces. At best, the latter provide very weak explanations for external policy. According to Stephen Krasner, for example, the state "can be treated as an autonomous actor pursuing goals associated with power and the general interest of the society."[8] However, classical realists sometimes use domestic politics as a residual category to explain deviations from rational policies.

Realism has been the dominant model of international relations during at least the past five decades, perhaps in part because it seemed to provide a useful framework for understanding World War II and the Cold War. Nevertheless, the classical versions articulated by Morgenthau and others have received a good deal of critical scrutiny. The critics have included scholars who accept the basic premises of realism but who found that in at least four important respects these theories lacked sufficient precision and rigor.

Classical realism usually has been grounded in a pessimistic theory of human nature, either a theological version (e.g., St. Augustine and Reinhold Niebuhr), or a secular one (e.g., Machiavelli, Hobbes, and Morgenthau). Egoism and self-interested behavior are not limited to a few evil or misguided leaders, as the idealists would have it, but are basic to *homo politicus* and thus are at the core of a realist theory. But according to its critics, because human nature, if it means anything, is a constant rather than a variable, it is an unsatisfactory explanation for the full range of international relations. If human nature explains war and conflict, what accounts for peace and cooperation? In order to avoid this problem, most modern realists have turned their attention from human nature to the structure of the international system to explain state behavior.

In addition, critics have noted a lack of precision and even contradictions in the way classical realists use such concepts as "power," "national interest," and "balance of power."[9] They also see possible contradictions between the central descriptive and prescriptive elements of classical realism. On the one hand, nations and their leaders "think and act in terms of interests defined as power," but, on the other, statesmen are urged to exercise prudence and self-restraint, as well as to recognize the legitimate national interests of other nations.[10] Power plays a central role in classical realism, but the correlation between the relative power balance and political outcomes is often less than compelling, suggesting the need to enrich analyses with other variables. Moreover, the distinction between "power as capabilities" and "useable options" is especially important in the nuclear age.

While classical realists have typically looked to history and political science for insights and evidence, the search for greater precision has led many modern realists to look elsewhere for appropriate models, analogies, metaphors, and insights. The discipline of choice is often economics, from which modern realists have borrowed a number of tools and concepts, including rational choice, expected utility, theories of firms and markets, bargaining theory, and game theory. Contrary to the assertion of some critics, however, modern realists *share* rather than reject the core premises of their classical predecessors.[11]

The quest for precision has yielded a rich harvest of theories and models, and a somewhat less bountiful crop of supporting empirical applications. Drawing in part on game theory, Morton Kaplan described several types of international systems—for example, balance-of-power, loose bipolar, tight bipolar, universal, hierarchical, and a unit-veto system in which any action requires the unanimous approval of all its members. He then outlined the essential rules that constitute these systems. For example, the rules for a balance-of-power system are: "(1) increase capabilities, but negotiate rather than fight; (2) fight rather than fail to increase capabilities; (3) stop fighting rather than eliminate an essential actor; (4) oppose any coalition or single actor that tends to assume a position of predominance within the system; (5) constrain actors who subscribe to supranational organizational principles; and (6) permit defeated or constrained essential actors to re-enter the system."[12] Richard Rosecrance, J. David Singer, Karl Deutsch, Bruce Russett, and many others, although not necessarily realists, also have developed models which seek to understand international relations by virtue of system-level explanations. Andrew M. Scott's survey of the literature, which yielded a catalogue of propositions about the international system, also illustrates the quest for greater precision in systemic models.[13]

Kenneth Waltz's *Theory of International Politics*, the most prominent effort to develop a rigorous and parsimonious model of "modern" or "structural" realism, has tended to define the terms of a vigorous debate during the past decade. It follows and builds upon another enormously influential book in which Waltz developed the Rousseauian position that a theory of war must include the system level (what he called the "third image") and not just first (theories of human nature) or second (state attributes) images. Why war? Because there is nothing in the system to prevent it.[14]

Theory of International Relations is grounded in analogies from microeconomics; international politics and foreign policy are analogous to markets and firms. Oligopoly theory is used to illuminate the dynamics of interdependent choice in a self-help anarchical system. Waltz explicitly limits his attention to a structural theory of international systems, eschewing the task of linking it to a theory of foreign policy. Indeed, he doubts that the two can be joined in a single theory and he is highly critical of many system-level analysts, including Morton Kaplan, Stanley Hoffmann, Richard Rosecrance, Karl Deutsch and J. David Singer, and others, charging them with various errors, including "reductionism"; that is, defining the system in terms of the attributes or interactions of the units.

In order to avoid reductionism and to gain rigor and parsimony, Waltz erects his theory on the foundations of three core propositions that define the structure of the international system. The first concentrates on the principles by which the system is ordered. The contemporary system is anarchic and decentralized rather than hierarchical; although they differ in many respects, each unit is formally equal.[15] A second defining proposition is the character of the units. An anarchic system is composed of similar sovereign units and therefore the functions that they perform are also similar rather than different; for example, all have the task of providing for their own security. In contrast, a hierarchical system would be characterized by some type of division of labor, as is the case in domestic politics. Finally, there is a distribution of capabilities among units in the system. Although capabilities are a unit-level attribute, the distribution of capabilities is a system-level concept.[16]

A change in any of these elements constitutes a change in system structure. The first element of structure as defined by Waltz is a quasi-constant because the ordering principle rarely changes, and the second element drops out of the analysis because the functions of units are similar as long as the system remains anarchic. Thus, the last of the three attributes, the distribution of capabilities, plays the central role in Waltz's model.

Waltz uses his theory to deduce the central characteristics of international relations. These include some non-obvious propositions about the contemporary international system. For example, with respect to system stability (defined as maintenance of its anarchic character and no consequential variation in the number of major actors) he concludes that: because the present bipolar system reduces uncertainty, it is more stable than alternative structures; interdependence has declined rather than increased during the twentieth century, a tendency that has actually contributed to stability; and the proliferation of nuclear weapons may contribute to rather than erode system stability.[17]

Unlike some system-level models, Waltz's effort to bring rigor and parsimony to realism has stimulated a good deal of further research, but it has not escaped controversy and criticism.[18] Leaving aside highly charged polemics—for example, that Waltz and his supporters are guilty of engaging in a "totalitarian project of global proportions"—most of the vigorous debate has centered on four alleged deficiencies relating to interests and preferences, system change, misallocation of variables between the system and unit levels, and an inability to explain outcomes.[19]

Specifically, a spare structural approach suffers from an inability to identify completely the nature and sources of interests and preferences because these are unlikely to derive solely from the structure of the system. Ideology or domestic considerations may often be at least as important. Consequently, the model is also unable to specify adequately how interests and preferences may change. The three defining characteristics of system structure are too general, moreover, and thus they are not sufficiently sensitive to specify the sources and dynamics of system change. The critics buttress their claim that the model is too static by pointing to Waltz's assertion that there has only been a single structural change in the international system during the past three centuries.

Another drawback is the restrictive definition of system properties, which leads Waltz to misplace, and therefore neglect, elements of international relations that properly belong at the system level. Critics have focused on his treatment of the destructiveness of nuclear weapons and interdependence. Waltz labels these as unit-level properties, whereas some of his critics assert that they are in fact attributes of the system.

Finally, the distribution of capabilities explains outcomes in international affairs only in the most general way, falling short of answering the questions that are of central interest to many analysts. For example, the distribution of power at the end of World War II would have enabled one to predict the rivalry that emerged between the United States and the Soviet Union, but it would have been inadequate for explaining the pattern of relations between these two nations—the Cold War rather than withdrawal into isolationism by either or both, a division of the world into spheres of influence, or World War III.[20] In order to do so, it is necessary to explore political processes *within* states—at minimum within the United States and the USSR—as well as *between* them.

Robert Gilpin shares with Waltz the core assumptions of modern realism, but his study of *War and Change in World Politics* also attempts to cope with some of the criticism leveled at Waltz's theory by focusing on the dynamics of system change. Drawing upon both economic and sociological theory, his model is based on five core propositions. The first is that the international system is stable—in a state equilibrium—if no state believes that it is profitable to attempt to change it. Second, a state will attempt to change the status quo of the international system if the expected benefits outweigh the costs; that is, if there is an expected net gain for the revisionist state. Related to this is the proposition that a state will seek change through territorial, political, and economic expansion until the marginal costs of further change equal or exceed the marginal benefits. Moreover, when an equilibrium between the costs and benefits of further change and expansion is reached, the economic costs of maintaining the status quo (expenditures for military forces, support for allies, etc.) tend to rise faster than the resources needed to do so. An equilibrium exists when no powerful state believes that a change in the system would yield additional net benefits. Finally, if the resulting disequilibrium between the existing governance of the international system and the redistribution of power is not resolved, the system will be changed and a new equilibrium reflecting the distribution of relative capabilities will be established.[21]

Unlike Waltz, Gilpin includes state-level processes in order to explain change. Differential economic growth rates among nations—a structural-systemic level variable—play a vital role in his explanation for the rise and decline of great powers, but his model also includes propositions about the law of diminishing returns on investments, the impact of affluence on martial spirits and on the ratio of consumption to investment, and structural change in the economy.[22] Table 2.1 summarizes some key elements of realism. It also contrasts them to two other system-level models of international relations—the Global-Society/Complex-Interdependence and the Marxist/World-System/Dependency models, to which we now turn our attention.

Just as there are variants of realism, there are several Global Society/Complex-Interdependence (GS/CI) models, but this discussion focuses on two common denominators; they all challenge the first and third core propositions of realism identified earlier, asserting that inordinate attention to the war/peace issue and the nation-state renders it an increasingly anachronistic model of global relations.[23] The agenda of critical problems confronting states has been vastly expanded during the twentieth century. Attention to the issues of war and peace is by no means misdirected, according to proponents of a GS/CI perspective, but

Table 2.1 THREE MODELS OF THE INTERNATIONAL SYSTEM

	Realism	Global society	Marxism
Type of model	Classical: descriptive and normative Modern: deductive	Descriptive and normative	Descriptive and normative
Central problems	Causes of war Conditions of peace	Broad agenda of social, economic, and environmental issues arising from gap between demands and resources	Inequality of exploitation Uneven development
Conception of current international system	Structural anarchy	Global society Complex interdependence (structure varies by issue-area)	World capitalist system
Key actors	Geographically based units (tribes, city-states, nation-states, etc.)	Highly permeable nation-states *plus* a broad range of onstate actors, including IOs, IGOs, NGOs, and individuals	Classes and their agents
Central motivations	National interest Security Power	Human needs and wants	Class interests
Loyalties	To geographically based groups (from tribes to nation-states)	Loyalties to nation-state declining To emerging global values and institutions that transcend those of the nation-state and/or to sub-national groups	To class values and interests that transcend those of the nation-state
Central processes	Search for security and survival	Aggregate effects of decisions by national and nonnational actors How units (not limited to nation-states) cope with a growing agenda of threats and opportunities arising from human wants	Modes of production and exchange International division of labor in a world capitalist system
Likelihood of system transformation	Low (basic structural element of system have revealed an ability to persist despite many other kinds of changes)	High in the direction of the model (owing to the rapid pace of technological change, etc.)	High in the direction of the model (owing to inherent contradiction within the world capitalist system)
Sources of theory, insights, and evidence	Politics History Economics (especially "modern" realists)	Broad range of social sciences Natural and technological sciences	Marxist-Leninist theory (several variants)

concerns for welfare, modernization, the environment, and the like are today no less potent sources of motivation and action. The diffusion of knowledge and technology, combined with the globalization of communications, has vastly increased popular expectations. The resulting demands have outstripped resources and the ability of existing institutions—notably the sovereign nation-state—to cope effectively with them. Interdependence arises from an inability of even the most powerful states to cope, or to do so unilaterally or at acceptable levels of cost and risk, with issues ranging from trade to AIDS, and immigration to environmental threats.

Paralleling the widening agenda of critical issues is the expansion of actors whose behavior can have a significant impact beyond national boundaries; indeed, the cumulative effects of their actions can have profound consequences for the international system. Thus, although nation-states continue to be important international actors, they possess a declining ability to control their own destinies. The aggregate effect of actions by multitudes of non-state actors can have potent effects that transcend political boundaries. These may include such powerful or highly visible non-state organizations as Exxon, the Organization of Petroleum Exporting Countries, or the Palestine Liberation Organization. On the other hand, the cumulative effects of decisions by less powerful or less visible actors may also have profound international consequences. For example, decisions by thousands of individuals, mutual funds, banks, pension funds, and other financial institutions to sell securities on 19 October 1987 not only resulted in an unprecedented "crash" on Wall Street, but also within hours its consequences were felt throughout the entire global financial system. Governments might take such actions as loosening credit or even closing exchanges, but they were largely unable to contain the effects of the panic.

The widening agenda of critical issues, most of which lack a purely national solution, has also led to creation of new actors that transcend political boundaries; for example, international organizations, transnational organizations, nongovernment organizations, multinational corporations, and the like. Thus, not only does an exclusive focus on the war/peace issue fail to capture the complexities of contemporary international life but it also blinds the analyst to the institutions, processes, and norms that permit cooperation and significantly mitigate some features of an anarchic system. In short, according to GS/CI perspectives, an adequate understanding of the emergent global system must recognize that no single model is likely to be sufficient for all issues, and that if it restricts attention to the manner in which states deal with traditional security concerns, it is more likely to obfuscate than clarify the realities of contemporary world affairs.

The GS/CI models have several important virtues. They recognize that international behavior and outcomes arise from a multiplicity of motives, not merely security, at least if security is defined solely in military or strategic terms. They also alert us to the fact that important international processes and conditions originate not only in the actions of nation-states but also in the aggregated behavior of other actors. These models not only enable the analyst to deal with a broader agenda of critical issues but, more importantly, they force one to contemplate a much richer menu of demands, processes, and outcomes than would be derived from power-centered realist models. Stated differently, GS/CI models are more sensitive to the possibility that politics of trade, currency, immigration, health, the environment, and the like may significantly and systematically differ from those typically associated with security issues.

On the other hand, some GS/CI analysts underestimate the potency of nationalism and the durability of the nation-state. Two decades ago one of them wrote that "the nation is declining in its importance as a political unit to which allegiances are attached."[24] Objectively, nationalism may be an anachronism but, for better or worse, powerful loyalties are still attached to nation-states. The suggestion that, because even some well-established nations have experienced independence movements among ethnic, cultural, or religious minorities, the sovereign territorial state may be in decline is not wholly persuasive. Indeed, that evidence perhaps points to precisely the opposite conclusion: In virtually every region of the world there are groups which seek to create or restore geographically based entities in which its members may enjoy the status and privileges associated with sovereign territorial statehood. Evidence from Poland to Palestine, Spain to Sri Lanka, Estonia to Eritrea, Armenia to Afghanistan, and elsewhere seems to indicate that obituaries for nationalism may be somewhat premature.

The notion that such powerful non-national actors as major multinational corporations (MNC) will soon transcend the nation-state seems equally premature. International drug rings do appear capable of dominating such states as Colombia and Panama. However, the pattern of outcomes in confrontations between MNCs and states, including cases involving major expropriations of corporate properties, indicate that even relatively weak nations are not always the hapless pawns of the MNCs. Case studies by Joseph Grieco and Gary Gereffi, among others, indicate that MNC-state relations yield a wide variety of outcomes.[25]

Underlying the GS/CI critique of realist models is the view that the latter are too wedded to the past and are thus incapable of dealing adequately with change. At least for the present, however, even if global dynamics arise from multiple sources (including non-state actors), the actions of nation-states and their agents would appear to remain the major sources of change in the international system. However, the last group of systemic models to be considered, the Marxist/World-System/Dependency (M/WS/D) models, downplays the role of the nation-state even further.

As in other parts of this essay, many of the distinctions among M/WS/D models are lost by treating them together and by focusing on their common features, but in the brief description possible here only common denominators will be presented. These models challenge both the war/peace and state-centered features of realism, but they do so in ways that differ sharply from challenges of GS/CI models.[26] Rather than focusing on war and peace, these models direct attention to quite different issues, including uneven development, poverty, and exploitation within and between nations. These conditions, arising from the dynamics of the modes of production and exchange, are basic and they must be incorporated into any analysis of intra- and inter-nation conflict.

At a superficial level, according to adherents of these models, what exists today may be described as an international system—a system of nation-states. More fundamentally, however, the key groups within and between nations are classes and their agents: As Immanuel Wallerstein put it, "in the nineteenth and twentieth centuries there has been only one world system in existence, the world capitalist world-economy."[27] The "world capitalist system" is characterized by a highly unequal division of labor between the periphery and core. Those at the periphery are essentially the drawers of water and the hewers of wood, whereas the latter appropriate the surplus of the entire world economy. This critical feature of the world system not only gives rise to and perpetuates a widening rather than narrowing gap between the wealthy core and poor periphery but also to a dependency relationship from which the latter are unable to break loose. Moreover, the class structure within the core, characterized by a growing gap between capital and labor, is faithfully reproduced in the periphery so that elites there share with their counterparts in the core an interest in perpetuating the system. Thus, in contrast to realist theories, M/WS/D models encompass and integrate theories of both the global and domestic arenas.

M/WS/D models have been subjected to trenchant critiques.[28] The state, nationalism, security dilemmas, and related concerns essentially drop out of these analyses; they are at the theoretical periphery rather than at the core: "Capitalism was from the beginning an affair of the world-economy," Wallerstein asserts, "not of nation-states."[29] A virtue of many M/WS/D models is that they take a long historical perspective on world affairs rather than merely focusing on contemporary issues. However, by neglecting nation-states and the dynamics arising from their efforts to deal with security in an anarchical system—or at best relegating these actors and motivations to a minor role—M/WS/D models lose much of their appeal. Models of world affairs during the past few centuries that fail to give the nation-state a central role seem as deficient as analyses of *Hamlet* that neglect the central character and his motivations.

Second, the concept of "world capitalist system" is central to these models, but its relevance for the late twentieth century can be questioned. Whether this term accurately describes the world of the 1880s could be debated, but its declining analytical utility or even descriptive accuracy for international affairs of the 1980s seems clear. Thus, one can question Wallerstein's assertion that "there are today no socialist systems in the world economy any more than there are feudal systems because there is only *one world system*. It is a world-economy and it is *by definition capitalist* in form."[30] Where within a system so defined do we locate the USSR or Eastern Europe? This area includes enough "rich" industrial nations that it hardly seems to belong in the periphery. Yet to place these states in the core of a "world capitalist system" would require terminological and conceptual gymnastics of a high order. Does it increase our analytical capabilities to describe the USSR and East European countries as "state capitalists?" Where do we locate China in this conception of the system? How do we explain dynamics within the "periphery," or the differences between rapid-growth Asian nations such as South Korea, Taiwan, or Singapore, and their slow-growth neighbors in Bangladesh, North Korea, and the Philippines? The inclusion of a third structural position—the "semi-periphery"—does not wholly answer these questions.

Third, M/WS/D models have considerable difficulty in explaining relations between noncapitalist nations—for example, between the USSR and its East European neighbors or China—much less outright conflict between them.

Indeed, advocates of these models usually have restricted their attention to West-South relations, eschewing analyses of East-East or East-South relations. Does one gain greater and more general analytical power by using the lenses and language of Marxism or of realism to describe relations between dominant and lesser nations; for example, the USSR and Eastern Europe, the USSR and India or other Third World nations, China and Vietnam, India and Sri Lanka, or Vietnam and Kampuchea? Are these relationships better described and understood in terms of such M/WS/D categories as "class" or such realist ones as "relative capabilities?"

Finally, the earlier observations about the persistence of nationalism as an element of international relations seem equally appropriate here. Perhaps national loyalties can be dismissed as prime examples of "false consciousness," but even in areas that have experienced almost two generations of one-party Communist rule, as in Poland, evidence that feelings of solidarity with workers in the Soviet Union or other nations have replaced nationalist sentiments among Polish workers is in short supply.

Many advocates of realism recognize that it cannot offer fine-grained analyses of foreign policy behavior and, as noted earlier, Waltz denies that it is desirable or even possible to combine theories of international relations and foreign policy. Decision-making models challenge the premises that it is fruitful to conceptualize the nation as a unitary rational actor whose behavior can adequately be explained by reference to the system structure—the second, fourth, and fifth realist propositions identified earlier—because individuals, groups, and organizations acting in the name of the state are also sensitive to pressures and constraints other than international ones, including elite maintenance, electoral politics, public opinion, pressure group activities, ideological preferences, and bureaucratic politics. Such core concepts as "the national interest" are not defined solely by the international system, much less by its structure alone, but they are also likely to reflect elements within the domestic political arena. Thus, rather than assuming with the realists that the state can be conceptualized as a "black box"—that the domestic political processes are both hard to comprehend and quite unnecessary for explaining its external behavior—decision-making analysts believe one must indeed take these internal processes into account, with special attention directed at decision-makers and their "definitions of the situation."[31] To reconstruct how nations deal with each other, it is necessary to view the situation through the eyes of those who act in the name of the nation-state: decision makers, and the group and bureaucratic-organizational contexts within which they act. Table 2.2 provides an overview of three major types of decision-making models that form the subject for the remainder of this essay, beginning with bureaucratic-organizational models.[32]

Traditional models of complex organizations and bureaucracy emphasized the positive contributions to be expected from a division of labor, hierarchy, and centralization, coupled with expertise, rationality, and obedience. Such models assumed that clear boundaries should be maintained between politics and decision making, on the one hand, and administration and implementation on the other. Following pioneering works by Chester I. Barnard, Herbert Simon, James G. March and Simon, and others, more recent theories depict organizations quite differently.[33] The central premise is that decision making in bureaucratic

Table 2.2 THREE MODELS OF DECISION MAKING

	Bureaucratic politics	Group dynamics	Individual decision making
Conceptualization of decision making	Decision making as the result of bargaining within bureaucratic organizations	Decision making as the product of group interaction	Decision making as the result of individual choice
Premises	Central organizational values are imperfectly internalized	Most decisions are made by small elite groups	Importance of subjective appraisal (definition of the situation) and cognitive processes (information processing, etc.)
	Organizational behavior is political behavior	Group is different than the sum of its members	
	Structure and SOPs affect substance and quality of decisions	Group dynamics affect substance and quality of decisions	
Constraints on rational decision making	Imperfect information, resulting from: centralization, hierarchy, and specialization	Groups may be more effective for some tasks, less for others	Cognitive limits on rationality
	Organizational inertia	Pressures for conformity	Information processing distorted by cognitive consistency dynamics (unmotivated biases)
	Conflict between individual and organizational utilities	Risk-taking propensity of groups (controversial)	Systematic and motivated biases in causal analysis
	Bureaucratic politics and bargaining dominate decision making and implementation of decisions	Quality of leadership	Individual differences in abilities related to decision making (e.g., problem-solving ability, tolerance of ambiguity, defensiveness and anxiety, information seeking, etc.)
		"Groupthink"	
Sources of theory, insights, and evidence	Organization theory	Social psychology	Cognitive dissonance
	Sociology of bureaucracies	Sociology of small groups	Cognitive psychology
	Bureaucratic politics		Dynamic psychology

organizations is not constrained only by the legal and formal norms that are intended to enhance the rational and eliminate the capricious aspects of bureaucratic behavior. Rather, all (or most) complex organizations are seen as generating serious "information pathologies."[34] There is an *emphasis* upon rather than a denial of the political character of bureaucracies, as well as on other "informal" aspects of organizational behavior. Complex organizations are composed of individuals and units with conflicting perceptions, values, and interests that may arise from parochial self-interest ("what is best for my bureau is also best for my career"), and also from different perceptions of issues arising ineluctably from a division of labor ("where you stand depends on where you sit"). Organizational norms and memories, prior policy commitments, normal organizational inertia routines, and standard operating procedures may shape and perhaps distort the structuring of problems, channeling of information, use of expertise, and implementation of executive decisions. The consequences of bureaucratic politics within the executive branch or within the government as a whole may significantly constrain the manner in which issues are defined, the range of options that may be considered, and the manner in which executive decisions are implemented by subordinates. Consequently, organizational decision making is essentially political in character, dominated by bargaining for resources, roles and missions, and by compromise rather than analysis.[35]

Perhaps owing to the dominant position of the realist perspective, most students of foreign policy have only recently incorporated bureaucratic-organizational models and insights into their analyses. An ample literature of case studies on budgeting, weapons acquisitions, military doctrine, and similar situations confirms that foreign and defense policy bureaucracies rarely conform to the Weberian "ideal type" of rational organization.[36] Some analysts assert that crises may provide the motivation and means for reducing some of the non-rational aspects of bureaucratic behavior: crises are likely to push decisions to the top of the organization where a higher quality of intelligence is available; information is more likely to enter the top of the hierarchy directly, reducing the distorting effects of information processing through several levels of the organization; and broader, less parochial values may be invoked. Short decision time in crises reduces the opportunities for decision making by bargaining, logrolling, incrementalism, lowest-common-denominator values, "muddling through," and the like.[37]

However, even studies of international crises from a bureaucratic-organizational perspective are not uniformly sanguine about decision making in such circumstances. Graham T. Allison's analysis of the Cuban missile crisis identified several critical bureaucratic malfunctions concerning dispersal of American aircraft in Florida, the location of the naval blockade, and grounding of weather reconnaissance flights from Alaska that might stray over the Soviet Union. Richard Neustadt's study of two crises involving the United States and Great Britain revealed significant misperceptions of each other's interests and policy processes. And an examination of three American nuclear alerts found substantial gaps in understanding and communication between policymakers and the military leaders who were responsible for implementing the alerts.[38]

Critics of some organizational-bureaucratic models and the studies employing them have directed their attention to several points.[39] They point out, for instance, that the emphasis on bureaucratic bargaining fails to differentiate adequately between the positions of the participants. In the American system, the president is not just another player in a complex bureaucratic game. Not only must he ultimately decide but he also selects who the other players will be, a process that may be crucial in shaping the ultimate decisions. If General Matthew Ridgway and Attorney General Robert Kennedy played key roles in the American decisions not to intervene in Indochina in 1954 or not to bomb Cuba in 1962, it was because Presidents Eisenhower and Kennedy chose to accept their advice rather than that of other officials. Also, the conception of bureaucratic bargaining tends to emphasize its non-rational elements to the exclusion of genuine intellectual differences that may be rooted in broader concerns—including disagreements on what national interests, if any, are at stake in a situation—rather than narrow parochial interests. Indeed, properly managed, decision processes that promote and legitimize "multiple advocacy" among officials may facilitate high-quality decisions.[40]

These models may be especially useful for understanding the slippage between executive decisions and foreign policy actions that may arise during implementation, but they may be less valuable for explaining the decisions themselves. Allison's study of the Cuban missile crisis does not indicate an especially strong correlation between bureaucratic roles and evaluations of the situation or policy recommendations, as predicted by his "Model III" (bureaucratic politics), and recently published transcripts of deliberations during the crisis do not offer more supporting evidence for that model.[41] On the other hand, Allison does present some compelling evidence concerning policy implementation that casts considerable doubt on the adequacy of "Model I" (the traditional realist conception of the unitary rational actor).

Another decision-making model used by some political scientists supplements bureaucratic-organizational models by narrowing the field of view to top policymakers. This approach lends itself well to investigations of foreign policy decisions, which are usually made in a small-group context. Some analysts have drawn upon sociology and social psychology to assess the impact of various types of group dynamics on decision making.[42] Underlying these models are the premises that the group is not merely the sum of its members (thus decisions emerging from the group are likely to be different than what a simple aggregation of individual preference and abilities might suggest), and that group dynamics, the interactions among its members, can have a significant impact on the substance and quality of decisions.

Groups often perform better than individuals in coping with complex tasks owing to diverse perspectives and talents, an effective division of labor, and high-quality debates centering on evaluations of the situation and policy recommendations for dealing with it. Groups may also provide decision makers with emotional and other types of support that may facilitate coping with complex problems. On the other hand, they may exert pressures for conformity to group norms, thereby inhibiting the search for information and policy options or cutting it off prematurely, ruling out the legitimacy of some options, curtailing independent evaluation, and suppressing some forms of intragroup conflict that might serve to clarify goals, values, and options. Classic experiments by the psychologist Solomon Asch revealed the extent to which group members will suppress their beliefs and judgments when faced with a majority adhering to the contrary view, even a counterfactual one.[43]

Drawing upon a series of historical case studies, social psychologist Irving L. Janis has identified a different variant of group dynamics, which he labels "groupthink" to distinguish it from the more familiar type of conformity pressure on "deviant" members of the group.[44] Janis challenges the conventional wisdom that strong cohesion among the members of a group invariably enhances performance. Under certain conditions, strong cohesion can markedly degrade the group's performance in decision making. Thus, the members of a cohesive group may, as a means of dealing with the stresses of having to cope with consequential problems and in order to bolster self-esteem, increase the frequency and intensity of face-to-face interaction. This results in a greater identification with the group and less competition within it. The group dynamics of what Janis calls "concurrence seeking" may displace or erode reality testing and sound information processing and judgment. As a consequence, groups may be afflicted by unwarranted feelings of optimism and invulnerability, stereotyped images of adversaries, and inattention to warnings. Janis's analyses of both "successful" (the Marshall Plan, the Cuban missile crisis) and "unsuccessful" (Munich Conference of 1938, Pearl Harbor, the Bay of Pigs invasion) cases indicate that "groupthink" or other decision-making pathologies are not inevitable, and he develops some guidelines for avoiding them.[45]

Still other decision-making analysts focus on the individual. Many approaches to the policymaker emphasize the gap between the demands of the classical model of rational decision making and the substantial body of theory and evidence about various constraints that come into play in even relatively simple choice situations.[46] The more recent perspectives, drawing upon cognitive psychology, go well beyond some of the earlier formulations that drew upon psychodynamic theories to identify various types of psychopathologies among political leaders: paranoia, authoritarianism, the displacement of private motives on public objects, etc.[47] These more recent efforts to include information-processing behavior of the individual decision maker in foreign policy analyses have been directed at the cognitive and motivational constraints that, in varying degrees, affect the decision-making performance of "normal" rather than pathological subjects. Thus, attention is directed to all leaders, not merely those, such as Hitler or Stalin, who display evidence of clinical abnormalities.

The major challenges to the classical model have focused in various ways on limited human capabilities for performing the tasks required by objectively rational decision making. The cognitive constraints on rationality include limits on the individual's capacity to receive, process, and assimilate information about the situation; an inability to identify the entire set of policy alternatives; fragmentary knowledge about the consequences of each option; and an inability to order preferences on a single utility scale.[48] These have given rise to several competing conceptions of the decision maker and his or her strategies for dealing with complexity, uncertainty, incomplete or contradictory information, and, paradoxically, information overload. They variously characterize the decision maker as a problem solver, naive or intuitive scientist, cognitive balancer, dissonance avoider, information seeker, cybernetic information processor, and reluctant decision maker.

Three of these conceptions seem especially relevant for foreign policy analysis. The first views the decision maker as a "bounded rationalist" who seeks satisfactory rather than optimal solutions. As Herbert Simon has put it, "the capacity of the human mind for formulating and solving complex problems is very small compared with the size of the problem whose solution is required for objectively rational behavior in the real world—or even a reasonable approximation of such objective rationality."[49] Moreover, it is not practical for the decision maker to seek optimal choices; for example, because of the costs of searching for information. Related to this is the more recent concept of the individual as a "cognitive miser," one who seeks to simplify complex problems and to find shortcuts to problem solving and decision making.

Another approach is to look at the decision maker as an "error prone intuitive scientist" who is likely to commit a broad range of inferential mistakes. Thus, rather than emphasizing the limits on search, information processing, and the like, this conception views the decision maker as the victim of flawed heuristics or decision rules who uses data poorly. There are tendencies to underuse rate data in making judgments, believe in the "law of small numbers," underuse diagnostic information, overweight low probabilities and underweight high ones, and violate other requirements of consistency and coherence. These deviations from classical decision theory are traced to the psychological principles that govern perceptions of problems and evaluations of options.[50]

The final perspective I will mention emphasizes the forces that dominate the policymaker, forces that will not or cannot be controlled.[51] Decision makers are not merely rational calculators; important decisions generate conflict, and a reluctance to make irrevocable choices often results in behavior that reduces the quality of decisions. These models direct the analyst's attention to policymakers' belief systems, images of relevant actors, perceptions, information-processing strategies, heuristics, certain personality traits (ability to tolerate ambiguity, cognitive complexity, etc.), and their impact on decision-making performance.

Despite this diversity of perspectives and the difficulty of choosing between cognitive and motivational models, there has been some convergence on several types of constraints that may affect decision processes.[52] One involves the consequences of efforts to achieve cognitive consistency on perceptions and information processing. Several kinds of systematic bias have been identified in both experimental and historical studies. Policymakers have a propensity to assimilate and interpret information in ways that conform to rather than challenge existing beliefs, preferences, hopes, and expectations. Frequently they deny the need to confront tradeoffs between values by persuading themselves that an option will satisfy all of them. And, finally, they indulge in rationalizations to bolster the selected option while denigrating those that were not selected.

An extensive literature on styles of attribution has revealed several types of systematic bias in causal analysis. Perhaps the most important for foreign policy analysis is the basic attribution error—a tendency to explain the adversary's behavior in terms of his characteristics (for example, inherent aggressiveness or hostility) rather than in terms of the context or situation, while attributing one's own behavior to the latter (for example, legitimate security needs arising from a dangerous and uncertain environment) rather than to the former. A somewhat related type of double standard has been noted by George Kennan: "Now is it our view that we should take account only of their [Soviet] capabilities, disregarding their intentions, but we should expect them to take account only for our supposed intentions, disregarding our capabilities?"[53]

Analysts also have illustrated the important effect on decisions of policymakers' assumptions about order and predictability in the environment. Whereas a policymaker may have an acute appreciation of the disorderly environment in which he or she operates (arising, for example, from domestic political processes), there is a tendency to assume that others, especially adversaries, are free of such constraints. Graham T. Allison, Robert Jervis, and others have demonstrated that decision makers tend to believe that the realist "unitary rational actor" is the appropriate representation of the opponent's decision processes and, thus, whatever happens is the direct result of deliberate choices. For example, the hypothesis that the Soviet destruction of KAL flight 007 may have resulted from intelligence failures or bureaucratic foulups, rather than from a calculated decision to murder civilian passengers, was either not given serious consideration or it was suppressed for strategic reasons.[54]

Drawing upon a very substantial experimental literature, several models linking crisis-induced stress to decision processes have been developed and used in foreign policy studies.[55] Irving L. Janis and Leon Mann have developed a more general conflict-theory model which conceives of man as a "reluctant decisionmaker" and focuses upon "when, how and why psychological stress generated by decisional conflict imposes limitations on the rationality of a person's decisions."[56] One may employ five strategies for coping with a situation requiring a decision: unconflicted adherence to existing policy, unconflicted change, defensive avoidance, hypervigilance, and vigilant decision making. The first four strategies are likely to yield low-quality decisions owing to an incomplete search for information, appraisal of the situation and options, and contingency planning, whereas the vigilant decision making characterized by a more adequate performance of vital tasks is more likely to result in a high-quality choice. The factors that will affect the employment of decision styles are information about risks, expectations of finding a better option, and time for adequate search and deliberation.

A final approach we should consider attempts to show the impact of personal traits on decision making. There is no shortage of typologies that are intended to link leadership traits to decision-making behavior, but systematic research demonstrating such links is in much shorter supply. Still, some efforts have borne fruit. Margaret G. Hermann has developed a scheme for analyzing leaders' public statements of unquestioned authorship for eight variables: nationalism, belief in one's ability to control the environment, need for power, need for affiliation, ability to differentiate environments, distrust of others, self-confidence, and task emphasis. The scheme has been tested with impressive results on a broad range of contemporary leaders.[57] Alexander L. George has reformulated Nathan Leites's concept of "operational code" into five philosophical and five instrumental beliefs that are intended to describe politically relevant core beliefs, stimulating a number of empirical studies and, more recently, further significant conceptual revisions.[58] Finally, several psychologists have developed and tested the concept of "integrative complexity," defined as the ability to make subtle distinction along multiple dimensions, flexibility, and the integration of large amounts of diverse information to make coherent judgments.[59] A standard content-analysis technique has been used for research on documentary materials generated by top decision makers in a wide range of international crises, including World War I, Cuba (1962), Morocco (1911), Berlin (1948–49 and 1961), Korea, and the Middle East wars of 1948, 1956, 1967, and 1973.[60]

Decision-making approaches clearly permit the analyst to overcome many limitations of the systemic models described earlier, but not without costs. The three decision-making models described here impose increasingly heavy data burdens on the analyst. Moreover, there is a danger that adding levels of analysis may result in an undisciplined proliferation of categories and variables with at least two adverse consequences: it may become increasingly difficult to determine which are more or less important; and ad hoc explanations for individual cases erode the possibilities for broader generalizations across cases. However, several well-designed, multicase, decision-making studies indicate that these and other traps are not unavoidable.[61]

The study of international relations and foreign policy has always been a somewhat eclectic undertaking, with extensive borrowing from disciplines other than political science and history.[62] At the most general level, the primary differences today tend to be between two broad approaches. Analysts of the first school focus on the structure of the international system, often borrowing from economics for models, analogies, insights, and metaphors, with an emphasis on *rational preferences and strategy* and how these tend to be shaped and constrained by the structure of the international system. Decision-making analysts, meanwhile, display a concern for domestic political processes and tend to borrow from social psychology and psychology in order to understand better the *limits and barriers* to information processing and rational choice.

At the risk of ending on a platitude, it seems clear that for many purposes both approaches are necessary and neither is sufficient. Neglect of the system structure and its constraints may result in analyses that depict policymakers as relatively free agents with an almost unrestricted menu of choices, limited only by the scope of their ambitions and the resources at their disposal. At worst, this type of analysis can degenerate into Manichean explanations that depict foreign policies of the "bad guys" as the external manifestation of inherently flawed leaders or domestic structures, whereas the "good guys" only react from necessity. Radical right explanations of the Cold War often depict Soviet foreign policies as driven by inherently aggressive totalitarian communism and the United States as its blameless victim; radical left explanations tend to be structurally similar, with the roles of aggressor and victim reversed.[63]

Conversely, neglect of foreign policy decision making not only leaves one unable to explain the dynamics of international relations, but many important aspects of a nation's external behavior will be inexplicable. Advocates of the realist model have often argued its superiority for understanding the "high" politics of deterrence, containment, alliances, crises, and wars, if not necessarily for "low" politics. But there are several rejoinders to this line of reasoning. First, the low politics of trade, currencies, and other issues that are almost always highly sensitive to domestic pressures are becoming an increasingly important element of international relations. Second, the growing literature on the putative domain *par excellence* of realism, including deterrence, crises, and wars, raises substantial doubts about the universal validity of the realist model even for these issues.[64] Finally, exclusive reliance on realist models and their assumptions of rationality may lead to unwarranted complacency about dangers in the international system. Nuclear weapons and other features of the system have no doubt contributed to the "long peace" between major powers.[65] At the same time, however, a narrow focus on power balances, "correlations of forces," and other features of the international system will result in neglect of dangers—for example, the command, communication, control, intelligence problem or inadequate information processing—that can only be identified and analyzed by a decision-making perspective.[66]

At a very general level, this conclusion parallels that drawn three decades ago by the foremost contemporary proponent of modern realism: the "third image" (system structure) is necessary for understanding the context of international behavior, whereas the first and second images (decision makers and domestic political processes) are needed to understand dynamics within the system.[67] But to acknowledge the existence of various levels of analysis is not enough. *What* the investigator wants to explain and the *level of specificity and comprehensiveness* to be sought should determine which level(s) of analysis are relevant and necessary. In this connection, it is essential to distinguish two different dependent variables: foreign policy decisions by states, on the one hand, and the outcomes of policy and interactions between two or more states, on the other. If the goal is to understand the former—foreign policy decisions—Harold and Margaret Sprout's notion of "psychological milieu" is relevant and sufficient; that is, the objective structural variables influence the decisions via the decision maker's perception and evaluation of those "outside" variables.[68] However, if the goal is to explain outcomes, the "psychological milieu" is quite inadequate; the objective factors, if misperceived or misjudged by the decision maker, will influence the outcome. Political scientists studying international relations are increasingly disciplining their use of multiple levels of analysis in studying outcomes that cannot be adequately explained via only a single level of analysis.[69]

Which of these models and approaches are likely to be of interest and utility to the diplomatic historian? Clearly there is no one answer; political scientists are unable to agree on a single multilevel approach to international relations and foreign policy; thus they are hardly in a position to offer a single recommendation to historians. In the absence of the often-sought but always-elusive unified theory of human behavior that could provide a model for all seasons and all reasons, one must ask at least one further question: A model for what purpose? For example, in some circumstances, such as research on major international crises, it may be important to obtain systematic evidence on the beliefs and other intellectual baggage that key policymakers bring to their deliberations. Some of the approaches described above should prove very helpful in this respect. Conversely, there are many other research problems for which the historian would quite properly decide that this type of analysis requires far more effort than could possibly be justified by the benefits to be gained.

Of the systemic approaches described here, little needs to be said about classical realism because its main features, as well as its strengths and weaknesses, are familiar to most diplomatic historians. Those who focus on security issues can hardly neglect its central premises and concepts. On the other hand, modern or structural realism of the Waltz variety is likely to have rather limited appeal to historians, especially if they take seriously his doubts about being able to incorporate foreign policy into it. It may perhaps serve to raise consciousness about the importance of the systemic context within which international relations take place, but that may not be a major gain—after all, such concepts as "balance of power" have long been a standard part of the diplomatic historian's vocabulary. Gilpin's richer approach, which employs both system- and state-level variables to explain international dynamics, may well have greater appeal. It has already been noted that there are some interesting parallels between Gilpin's *War and Change in World Politics* and Paul Kennedy's recent *The Rise and Fall of the Great Powers.*

The Global-Society/Complex-Interdependence models will be helpful to historians with an interest in evolution of the international system and with the growing disjuncture between demands on states and their ability to meet them—the "sovereignty gap." One need not be very venturesome to predict that this gap will grow rather than narrow in the future. Historians of all kinds of international and transnational organizations are also likely to find useful concepts and insights in these models.

It is much less clear that the Marxist/World-System/Dependency models will provide useful new insights to historians. They will no doubt continue to be employed, but for reasons other than demonstrated empirical utility. If one has difficulty in accepting certain assumptions as *true by definition*—for example, that there has been and is today a single "world capitalist system"—then the kinds of analyses that follow are likely to seem seriously flawed. Most diplomatic historians also would have difficulty in accepting models that relegate the state to a secondary role. Until proponents of these models demonstrate a greater willingness to test them against a broader range of cases, including East-South and East-East relations, their applicability would appear to be limited at best. Finally, whereas proponents of GS/CI models can point with considerable justification to current events and trends that would appear to make them more rather than less relevant in the future, supporters of the M/WS/D models have a much more difficult task in this respect.

Although the three decision-making models sometimes include jargon that may be jarring to the historian, many of the underlying concepts are familiar. Much of diplomatic history has traditionally focused on the decisions, actions, and interactions of national leaders who operate in group contexts, such as cabinets or ad hoc advisory groups, and who draw upon the resources of such bureaucracies as foreign and defense ministries or the armed forces. The three types of models described above typically draw heavily upon psychology, social psychology, organizational theory, and other social sciences; thus for the historian they open some important windows to highly relevant developments in these fields. For example, theories and concepts of "information processing" by individuals, groups, and organizations should prove very useful to diplomatic historians.

Decision-making models may also appeal to diplomatic historians for another important reason. Political scientists who are accustomed to working with fairly accessible information such as figures on gross national products, defense budgets, battle casualties, alliance commitments, United Nations votes, trade and investments, and the like, often feel that the data requirements of decision-making models are excessive. This is precisely the area in which the historian has a decided comparative advantage, for the relevant data are usually to be found in the paper trails—more recently, also in the electronic trails—left by policymakers, and they are most likely to be unearthed by archival research. Thus, perhaps the appropriate point on which to conclude this essay is to reverse the question posed earlier: Ask not only what can the political scientist contribute to the diplomatic historian but ask also what can the diplomatic historian contribute to the political scientist. At the very least political scientists could learn a great deal about the validity of their own models if historians would use them and offer critical assessments of their strengths and limitations.

NOTES

1. See, for example, John Lewis Gaddis, "Expanding the Data Base: Historians, Political Scientists, and the Enrichment of Security Studies," *International Security* 12 (Summer 1987): 3–21; John English, "The Second Time Around: Political Scientists Writing History," *Canadian Historical Review* 57 (March 1986): 1–16; Jack S. Levy, "Domestic Politics and War," *Journal of Interdisciplinary History* 18 (Spring 1988): 653–73; Joseph S. Nye, Jr., "International Security Studies," in *American Defense Annual,* 1988–1989, ed. Joseph Kruzel (Lexington, MA, 1988), 231–43; Deborah Larson, *Origins of Containment: A Psychological Explanation* (Princeton, 1985); Timothy Lomperis, *The War Everyone Lost–And Won: America's Intervention in Viet Nam's Twin Struggles* (Washington, 1987); Barry Posen, *The Sources of Military Doctrine: France, Britain, and Germany between the World Wars* (Ithaca, 1984); Paul Gordon Lauren, ed., *Diplomacy: New Approaches to History, Theory, and Policy* (New York, 1979); and Richard R. Neustadt and Ernest R. May, *Thinking in Time: The Use of History for Decision-Makers* (New York, 1986). Many other examples could be cited.
2. Robert Gilpin, *Change and War in World Politics* (Cambridge, England, 1981).
3. Stanley Hoffmann, "An American Social Science: International Relations," *Daedalus* 106 (Summer 1977): 54.
4. The British meteorologist Lewis Fry Richardson is generally regarded as the pioneer of mathematical approaches to international relations. See his *Statistics of Deadly Quarrels* (Pittsburgh, 1960); and his *Arms and Insecurity: A Mathematical Study of the Causes and Origins of War* (Chicago, 1960). These are summarized for nonmathematicians in Anatol Rapport, "L. F. Richardson's Mathematical Theory of War," *Journal of Conflict Resolution* 1 (September 1957): 249–99. For a more recent effort see Bruce Bueno de Mesquita, *The War Trap* (New Haven, 1981); and idem, "The War Trap

Revisited: A Revised Expected Utility Model," *American Political Science Review* 79 (March 1985): 156–77.

5. Among the works that best represent their realist perspectives are E. H. Carr, *Twenty Years' Crisis* (London, 1939); Nicholas Spykman, *America's Strategy in World Politics: The United States and Balance of Power* (New York, 1942); Hans J. Morgenthau, *Politics among Nations: The Struggle for Power and Peace,* 5th ed. (New York, 1973); John Herz, *International Politics in the Atomic Age* (New York, 1959); Hedley Bull, *The Anarchical Society: A Study of Order in World Politics* (London, 1977); Raymond Aron, *Peace and War* (Garden City, NY, 1966); Martin Wight, "The Balance of Power and International Order," in *The Bases of International Order: Essays in Honor of C. A. W. Manning,* ed. Alan James (London, 1973); Arnold Wolfers, *Discord and Collaboration* (Baltimore, 1962); Norman A. Graebner, *America as a World Power: A Realist Appraisal from Wilson to Reagan* (Wilmington, DE, 1984); George F. Kennan, *American Diplomacy, 1900–1950* (Chicago, 1951); Walter Lippmann, *U.S. Foreign Policy: Shield of the Republic* (Boston, 1943); and Reinhold Niebuhr, *The Children of Light and the Children of Darkness* (New York, 1945).

6. For useful comparisons of realism and liberalism see Joseph Grieco, "Anarchy and the Limits of Cooperation: A Realist Critique of the Newest Liberal Institutionalism," *International Organization* 42 (Summer 1988): 485–507; and Joseph S. Nye, Jr., "Neorealism and Neoliberalism," *World Politics* 40 (January 1988): 235–51.

7. Morgenthau, *Politics,* 7, 5.

8. Stephen D. Krasner, *Defending the National Interest: Raw Materials Investment and U.S. Foreign Policy* (Princeton, 1978), 33. Krasner's study compares realist, interest-group liberal, and Marxist theories.

9. Inis L. Claude, *Power and International Relations* (New York, 1962); James S. Rosenau, "National Interest," *International Encyclopedia of the Social Sciences,* vol. 11 (New York, 1968), 34–40; Alexander L. George and Robert Keohane, "The Concept of National Interests: Uses and Limitations," in *Presidential Decision-Making in Foreign Policy: The Effective Use of Information and Advice,* ed. Alexander George (Boulder, 1980); Ernst B. Haas, "The Balance of Power: Prescription, Concept, or Propaganda?" *World Politics* 5 (July 1953): 442–77; Dina A. Zinnes, "An Analytical Study of the Balance of Power," *Journal of Peace Research* 4, no. 3 (1967): 270–88.

10. Morgenthau, *Politics,* 5.

11. Richard K. Ashley, "The Poverty of Neorealism," *International Organization* 38 (Spring 1984): 225–86.

12. Morton Kaplan, *System and Process in International Politics* (New York, 1957).

13. Richard Rosecrance, *Action and Reaction in International Politics* (Boston, 1963); idem, "Bipolarity, Multipolarity, and the Future," *Journal of Conflict Resolution* 10 (September 1966): 314–27; Kenneth Waltz, "The Stability of a Bipolar World," *Daedalus* 93 (Summer 1964): 881–909; J. David Singer, "Inter-Nation Influence: A Formal Model," *American Political Science Review* 57 (June 1963): 420–30; Bruce M. Russett, "Toward a Model of Competitive International Politics," *Journal of Politics* 25 (May 1963): 226–47; Karl W. Deutsch and J. David Singer, "Multipolar Power Systems and International Stability," *World Politics* 16 (April 1964): 390–406; Andrew Scott, *The Functioning of the International Political System* (New York, 1967).

14. Kenneth Waltz, *Theory of International Politics* (Reading, MA, 1979); idem, *Man, the State, and War* (New York, 1959).

15. Because Waltz strives for a universal theory that is not limited to any era, he uses the term "unit" to refer to the constituent members of the system. In the contemporary

system these are states, but in order to reflect Waltz's intent more faithfully, the term "unit" is used here.

16. Waltz, *Theory*, 82–101.

17. Waltz, "The Myth of National Interdependence," in *The International Corporation,* ed. Charles P. Kindleberger (Cambridge, MA, 1970); Waltz, "The Spread of Nuclear Weapons: More May Be Better," *Adelphi Papers,* no. 171 (1981).

18. Joseph M. Grieco, *Cooperation Among Nations: Europe, America, and Non-Tariff Barriers to Trade* (Ithaca: Cornell University Press, 1990); Stephen M. Walt, *The Origin of Alliances* (Ithaca, 1987). The best single source for the various dimensions of the debate is Robert Keohane, ed., *Neorealism and Its Critics* (New York, 1986).

19. Ashley, "Poverty," 228.

20. I am grateful to Alexander George for this example.

21. Gilpin, *War and Change,* 10–11.

22. *Ibid.,* Chap. 4. Gilpin's thesis appears similar in a number of respects to Paul Kennedy, *The Rise and Fall of the Great Powers: Economic Change and Military Conflict from 1500 to 2000* (New York, 1987).

23. Robert Keohane and Joseph S. Nye, Jr., *Power and Interdependence: World Politics in Transition* (Boston, 1977); Edward Morse, *Modernization and the Transformation of International Relations* (New York, 1967); James N. Rosenau, *The Study of Global Interdependence* (London, 1980); Richard Mansbach and John Vasquez, *In Search of Theory: A New Paradigm for Global Politics* (New York, 1981); Andrew M. Scott, *The Dynamics of Interdependence* (Chapel Hill, 1982); James N. Rosenau, *Turbulence in World Politics: A Theory of Change and Continuity* (Princeton: Princeton University Press, 1990).

24. Rosenau, "National Interest," 39. A more recent statement of this view may be found in Richard Rosecrance, *The Rise of the Trading State* (New York, 1986). See also John H. Herz, "The Rise and Demise of the Territorial State," *World Politics* 9 (July 1957): 473–93; and his reconsideration in "The Territorial State Revisited: Reflections on the Future of the Nation-State," *Polity* 1 (Fall 1968): 12–34.

25. Joseph Grieco, *Between Dependence and Autonomy: India's Experience with the International Computer Industry* (Berkeley, 1984); Gary Gereffi, *The Pharmaceutical Industry and Dependency in the Third World* (Princeton, 1983).

26. John Galtung, "A Structural Theory of Imperialism," *Journal of Peace Research* 8, no. 2 (1971): 81–117; James Cockroft, André Gunder Frank, and Dale L. Johnson, *Dependence and Under-Development* (New York, 1972); Immanuel Wallerstein, *The Modern World-System* (New York, 1974); idem, "The Rise and Future Demise of the World Capitalist System: Concepts for Comparative Analysis," *Comparative Studies in Society and History* 16 (September 1974): 387–415; Christopher Chase-Dunn, "Comparative Research on World System Characteristics," *International Studies Quarterly* 23 (December 1979): 601–23; idem, "Interstate System and Capitalist World Economy: One Logic or Two?" *ibid.* 25 (March 1981): 19–42; J. Kubalkova and A. A. Cruickshank, *Marxism and International Relations* (Oxford, 1985). Debates among advocates of these models are illustrated in Robert A. Denemark and Kenneth O. Thomas, "The Brenner-Wallerstein Debates," *International Studies Quarterly* 32 (March 1988): 47–66.

27. Wallerstein, "Rise and Future Demise," 390.

28. Tony Smith, "The Underdevelopment of Development Literature: The Case of Dependency Theory," *World Politics* 31 (January 1979): 247–88; Aristide R. Zolberg, "Origins of the Modern World System," *ibid.* 33 (January 1981): 253–81.

29. Wallerstein, "Rise and Future Demise," 401.

30. *Ibid.*, 412 (emphasis added).

31. Richard C. Snyder, H. W. Bruck, and Burton Sapin, eds., *Foreign Policy Decision-Making* (New York, 1962).

32. There are also models that link types of polities with foreign policy. Two of the more prominent twentieth-century versions—the Leninist and Wilsonian—have been effectively criticized by Waltz in *Man, the State, and War.* Although space limitations preclude a discussion here, for some recent and interesting research along these lines see, among others, Rudolph J. Rummel, "Libertarianism and International Violence," *Journal of Conflict Resolution* 27 (March 1983): 27–71; Michael Doyle, "Liberalism and World Politics," *American Political Science Review* 80 (December 1986): 1151–70; and Doyle, "Kant, Liberal Legacies, and Foreign Affairs," *Philosophy and Public Affairs* 12 (Winter 1983): 205–35.

33. Chester Barnard, *Functions of the Executive* (Cambridge, MA, 1938); Herbert Simon, *Administrative Behavior: A Study of Decision-Making Processes in Administrative Organization* (New York, 1957); James G. March and Herbert Simon, *Organizations* (New York, 1958).

34. Harold Wilensky, *Organizational Intelligence: Knowledge and Policy in Government and Industry* (New York, 1967).

35. Henry A. Kissinger, "Domestic Structure and Foreign Policy," *Daedalus* 95 (Spring 1966): 503–29; Graham T. Allison, *Essence of Decision: Explaining the Cuban Missile Crisis* (Boston, 1971); Graham T. Allison and Morton Halperin, "Bureaucratic Politics: A Paradigm and Some Policy Implications," *World Politics* 24 (Supplement 1972): 40–79; Morton Halperin, *Bureaucratic Politics and Foreign Policy* (Washington, 1974).

36. The literature is huge. See, for example, Samuel R. Williamson, Jr., *The Politics of Grand Strategy: Britain and France Prepare for War, 1904–1914* (Cambridge, MA, 1969); Paul Gordon Lauren, *Diplomats and Bureaucrats: The First Institutional Responses to Twentieth-Century Diplomacy in France and Germany* (Stanford, 1975); and Posen, *Sources of Military Doctrine.*

37. Wilensky, *Organizational Intelligence;* Theodore J. Lowi, *The End of Liberalism: Ideology, Policy, and the Crisis of Public Authority* (New York, 1969); Sidney Verba, "Assumptions of Rationality and Non-Rationality in Models of the International System," *World Politics* 14 (October 1961): 93–117.

38. Charles F. Hermann, "Some Consequences of Crises which Limit the Viability of Organizations," *Administrative Science Quarterly* 8 (June 1963): 61–82; Allison, *Essence;* Richard Neustadt, *Alliance Politics* (New York, 1970); Scott Sagan, "Nuclear Alerts and Crisis Management," *International Security* 9 (Spring 1985): 99–139.

39. Robert Rothstein, *Planning, Prediction, and Policy-Making in Foreign Affairs: Theory and Practice* (Boston, 1972); Stephen D. Krasner, "Are Bureaucracies Important? (Or Allison Wonderland)" *Foreign Policy* 7 (Summer 1972): 159–70; Robert J. Art, "Bureaucratic Politics and American Foreign Policy: A Critique," *Policy Sciences* 4 (December 1973): 467–90; Desmond J. Ball, "The Blind Men and the Elephant: A Critique of Bureaucratic Politics Theory," *Australian Outlook* 28 (April 1974): 71–92; Amos Perlmutter, "Presidential Political Center and Foreign Policy: A Critique of the Revisionist and Bureaucratic-Political Orientations," *World Politics* 27 (October 1974): 87–106.

40. Alexander L. George, "The Case for Multiple Advocacy in Making Foreign Policy," *American Political Science Review* 66 (September 1972): 751–85, 791–95.

41. David A. Welch and James G. Blight, "The Eleventh Hour of the Cuban Missile Crisis: An Introduction to the ExComm Transcripts," *International Security* 12 (Winter

1987/88): 5–29; McGeorge Bundy and James G. Blight, "October 27, 1962: Transcripts of the Meetings of the ExComm," *ibid.*, 30–92.

42. Joseph de Rivera, *The Psychological Dimension of Foreign Policy* (Columbus, OH, 1968); Glenn D. Paige, *The Korean Decision, June 24–30, 1950* (New York, 1968); Irving L. Janis, *Victims of Groupthink: A Psychological Study of Foreign Policy Decisions and Fiascos* (Boston, 1972); idem, *Groupthink: Psychological Studies of Policy Decisions and Fiascos* (Boston, 1982); Margaret G. Hermann, Charles F. Hermann, and Joe D. Hagan, "How Decision Units Shape Foreign Policy Behavior," in *New Directions in the Study of Foreign Policy,* ed. Charles F. Hermann, Charles W. Kegley, and James N. Rosenau (London, 1987); Charles F. Hermann and Margaret Hermann, "Who Makes Foreign Policy Decisions and How: An Initial Test of a Model" (Paper presented at the annual meeting of the American Political Science Association, Chicago, 1987); Philip D. Stewart, Margaret G. Hermann, and Charles F. Hermann, "The Politburo and Foreign Policy: Toward a Model of Soviet Decision Making" (Paper presented at the annual meeting of the International Society of Political Psychology, Amsterdam, 1986).

43. Leon Festinger, "A Theory of Social Comparison Processes," and Solomon Asch, "Opinions and Social Pressure," in *Small Groups: Studies in Social Interaction,* ed. A. Paul Hare, Edgar F. Borgatta, and Robert F. Bales (New York, 1965); Asch, "Effects of Group Pressures upon Modification and Distortion of Judgment," in *Group Dynamics: Research and Theory,* ed. Dorwin Cartwright and A. Zander (Evanston, IL, 1953).

44. Janis, *Victims;* idem, *Groupthink.* See also Philip Tetlock, "Identifying Victims of Groupthink from Public Statements of Decision Makers," *Journal of Personality and Social Psychology* 37 (August 1979): 1314–24; and the critique in Lloyd Etheredge, *Can Governments Learn? American Foreign Policy and Central American Revolutions* (New York, 1985), 112–14.

45. Janis, *Groupthink,* 260–76.

46. For a review of the vast literature see Robert Abelson and A. Levi, "Decision Making and Decision Theory," in *Handbook of Social Psychology,* 3d ed., vol. 1, ed. Gardner Lindzey and Elliot Aronson (New York, 1985). The relevance of psychological models and evidence for international relations is most fully discussed in Robert Jervis, *Perception and Misperception in International Politics* (Princeton, 1976); John Steinbruner, *The Cybernetic Theory of Decision: New Dimensions of Political Analysis* (Princeton, 1974); and Robert Axelrod, ed., *The Structure of Decision: The Cognitive Maps of Political Elites* (Princeton, 1976).

47. See, for example, Harold Lasswell, *Psychopathology and Politics* (Chicago, 1931).

48. March and Simon, *Organizations,* 113.

49. Simon, *Administrative Behavior,* 198.

50. Amos Tversky and Daniel Kahneman, "The Framing of Decisions and the Psychology of Choice," *Science* 211 (30 January 1981): 453–58; Kahneman and Tversky, "On the Psychology of Prediction," *Psychological Review* 80 (July 1973): 237–51; Kahneman, Paul Slovic, and Tversky, *Judgment under Uncertainty: Heuristics and Biases* (Cambridge, England, 1982).

51. Irving L. Janis and Leon Mann, *Decision Making: A Psychological Analysis of Conflict, Choice, and Commitment* (New York, 1977); Miriam Steiner, "The Search for Order in a Disorderly World: Worldviews and Prescriptive Decision Paradigms," *International Organization* 37 (Summer 1983): 373–414; Richard Ned Lebow, *Between Peace and War* (Baltimore, 1981).

52. Donald Kinder and J. R. Weiss, "In Lieu of Rationality: Psychological Perspectives on Foreign Policy," *Journal of Conflict Resolution* 22 (December 1978): 707–35; Ole R. Holsti, "Foreign Policy Formation Viewed Cognitively," in Axelrod, *Structure of Decision.*

53. George F. Kennan, *The Cloud of Danger: Current Realities of American Foreign Policy* (Boston, 1978), 87–88.

54. Allison, *Essence;* Jervis, *Perception;* Seymour M. Hersh, *The Target Is Destroyed: What Really Happened to Flight 007 and What America Knew about It* (New York, 1986).

55. Charles F. Hermann, International Crises: Insights from Behavioral Research (New York, 1972); Margaret G. Hermann and Charles F. Hermann, "Maintaining the Quality of Decision-Making in Foreign Policy Crises," in Report of the Commission on the Organization of the Government for the Conduct of Foreign Policy, vol. 2 (Washington, 1975); Margaret G. Hermann, "Indicators of Stress in Policy-Makers during Foreign Policy Crises," *Political Psychology* 1 (March 1979): 27–46; Ole R. Holsti, *Crisis, Escalation, War* (Montreal, 1972); Ole R. Holsti and Alexander L. George, "The Effects of Stress on the Performance of Foreign Policy-Makers," *Political Science Annual,* vol. 6 (Indianapolis, 1975); Lebow, *Between Peace and War.*

56. Janis and Mann, *Decision Making,* 3.

57. Margaret G. Hermann, "Explaining Foreign Policy Behavior Using Personal Characteristics of Political Leaders," *International Studies Quarterly* 24 (March 1980): 7–46; idem, "Personality and Foreign Policy Decision Making," in *Perceptions, Beliefs, and Foreign Policy Decision Making,* ed. Donald Sylvan and Steve Chan (New York, 1984).

58. Nathan Leites, *The Operational Code of the Politburo* (New York, 1951); Alexander L. George, "The 'Operational Code': A Neglected Approach to the Study of Political Leaders and Decision-Making," *International Studies Quarterly* 13 (June 1969): 190–222; Stephen G. Walker, "The Interface between Beliefs and Behavior: Henry Kissinger's Operational Code and the Vietnam War," *Journal of Conflict Resolution* 21 (March 1977): 129–68; idem, "The Motivational Foundations of Political Belief Systems: A Re-Analysis of the Operational Code Construct," *International Studies Quarterly* 27 (June 1983): 179–202; idem, "Parts and Wholes: American Foreign Policy Makers as 'Structured' Individuals" (Paper presented at the annual meeting of the International Society of Political Psychology, Secaucus, New Jersey, 1988).

59. Integrative simplicity, on the other hand, is characterized by simple responses, gross distinctions, rigidity, and restricted information usage.

60. Peter Suedfeld and Philip Tetlock, "Integrative Complexity of Communications in International Crises," *Journal of Conflict Resolution* 21 (March 1977): 169–86; Suedfeld, Tetlock, and C. Romirez, "War, Peace, and Integrative Complexity: UN Speeches on the Middle East Problem, 1947–1976," *ibid.* (September 1977): 427–42; Theodore D. Raphael, "Integrative Complexity Theory and Forecasting International Crises: Berlin 1946–1962," *ibid.* 26 (September 1982): 423–50; Tetlock, "Integrative Complexity of American and Soviet Foreign Policy Rhetoric: A Time Series Analysis," *Journal of Personality and Social Psychology* 49 (December 1985): 1565–85.

61. Alexander L. George and Richard Smoke, *Deterrence in American Foreign Policy: Theory and Practice* (New York, 1974); Smoke, *Escalation* (Cambridge, MA, 1977); Glenn H. Snyder and Paul Diesing, *Conflict among Nations: Bargaining, Decision Making, and System Structure in International Crises* (Princeton, 1977); Michael Brecher and Barbara Geist, *Decisions in Crisis: Israel, 1967 and 1973* (Berkeley, 1980); Lebow, *Between Peace and War.* Useful discussions on conducting theoretically relevant case studies may be found in Harry Eckstein, "Case Study and Theory in Political Science," in *Handbook of Political Science,* ed. Fred I. Greenstein and Nelson W. Polsby (Reading, MA, 1975), 7: 79–138; and Alexander L. George, "Case Studies and Theory Development: The Method of Structured, Focused Comparison," in *Diplomacy: New Approaches in History, Theory, and Policy,* ed. Paul Gordon Lauren (New York, 1979), 43–68.

62. The classic overview of the field and the disciplines that have contributed to it is Quincy Wright, *The Study of International Relations* (New York, 1955).

63. Ole R. Holsti, "The Study of International Politics Makes Strange Bedfellows: Theories of the Radical Right and the Radical Left," *American Political Science Review* 68 (March 1974): 217–42.

64. In addition to the literature on war, crises, and deterrence already cited see Richard Betts, *Nuclear Blackmail and Nuclear Balance* (Washington, 1987); Robert Jervis, Richard Ned Lebow, and Janice G. Stein, *Psychology and Deterrence* (Baltimore, 1985); Lebow, *Nuclear Crisis Management: A Dangerous Illusion* (Ithaca, 1987); and Ole R. Holsti, "Crisis Decision-Making," and Jack S. Levy, "The Causes of War: A Review of Theories and Evidence," in *Behavior, Society, and Nuclear War*, vol. 1, ed. Philip E. Tetlock et al. (New York, 1989).

65. John Lewis Gaddis, "The Long Peace: Elements of Stability in the Postwar International System," *International Security* 10 (Spring 1986): 99–142.

66. Paul Bracken, *Command and Control of Nuclear Forces* (New Haven, 1983); Bruce Blair, *Strategic Command and Control: Redefining the Nuclear Threat* (Washington, 1985); John D. Steinbruner, "Nuclear Decapitation," *Foreign Policy* 45 (Winter 1981–82): 16–28; Sagan, "Nuclear Alerts"; Alexander L. George, *Presidential Decision-Making in Foreign Policy: The Effective Use of Information and Advice* (Boulder, 1980).

67. Waltz, *Man, the State, and War*, 238.

68. Harold and Margaret Sprout, "Environmental Factors in the Study of International Politics," *Journal of Conflict Resolution* 1 (December 1957): 309–28.

69. See, for example, David B. Yoffie, *Power and Protectionism: Strategies of the Newly Industrializing Countries* (New York, 1983); John Odell, *U.S. International Monetary Policy: Markets, Power, and Ideas as Sources of Change* (Princeton, 1982); Jack Snyder, *The Ideology of the Offensive: Military Decision Making and the Disaster of 1914* (Ithaca, 1984); Vinod K. Aggarwal, *Liberal Protectionism: The International Politics of Organized Textile Trade* (Berkeley, 1985); Larson, *Origins of Containment;* Posen, *Sources of Military Doctrine;* and Walt, *Alliances.*

࿥

The United States and International Institutions

W. Michael Reisman

Each state that elects to participate in a multilateral institution realises a different constellation of costs and benefits, but some denominators are common. Each state sacrifices a measure of (often theoretical) freedom of action in the area of regulation, in return for a package of benefits that is expected to include compa-

W. Michael Reisman is McDougal Professor of Law, Yale Law School. *Survival 41–4*, Winter 1999–2000, pp. 62–80. © The International Institute for Strategic Studies. Reprinted by permission of Oxford University Press.

rable restraints on the actions of others. Each expects to gain an amplification of national power in the pursuit of specific objectives when the multilateral institution which it joins becomes the vehicle for action that might otherwise have been undertaken (if at all) unilaterally.

For small and very small states, multilateral institutions may become the major avenues for diplomacy, far outstripping bilateral relations and offering the most prized diplomatic posts. The small states' votes in these institutions may become their most formidable and possibly their only base of power, and their representatives may acquire a degree of influence far beyond what they might expect as ambassadors in a bilateral relationship. The larger the state and the greater its power, the more will bilateral diplomacy be preferred over multilateral, and the more measured will be the attitude towards multilateral institutions. But no state can afford to be oblivious to multilateral institutions: world-wide communications and the movement of persons, goods and services have created interdependencies, to the point where the apparatus of even the most effective states can no longer adequately and economically achieve their objectives without the authority and material support available only through external alignments.

In this, as in other areas of international life, the United States is like other states and yet is also quite different from them. Although it is the most powerful state in the international arena, the US has helped to conceive, and today participates in, a wide variety of multilateral institutions, each of which is marked by some sort of formal, rule-based decision-making process that, in many ways, proves more constricting for American action than would the unilateral exercise of its power. The US espouses multilateralism as a virtue. Like every other state, it also seeks to use multilateral institutions as instruments for achieving its own policies.

In apparent contrast to other members, the US is able, by virtue of its power—at least in the short run—to suspend or to modify institutional rules in particular cases, absorb whatever political and diplomatic costs ensue, and accomplish its objectives unilaterally. When this happens, other member-states often attribute cynicism and hypocrisy to American declarations of support for multilateral diplomacy and international law, and assume America's avowed support for multilateralism to be no more than a fig leaf for opportunism.

This conclusion simplifies a much more complex relationship that, on the one hand, puts the US among the most avid supporters of multilateral institutions, and yet, in different circumstances, pits it against the members and administration of some of those same institutions. The relationship is most dramatic with the UN, but applies in varying degree to every institution to which the US is party. In some ways, US behaviour with respect to the international institutions in which it participates is indistinguishable from the foreign-policy techniques of other states or state groupings.[1] In other critical ways, the modes in which the US relates to multilateral institutions and to endeavours within areas of their formal competence are both more complex and more distinctive than would first appear, and are driven by factors different from those frequently assumed by many commentators. America's complex relations with multilateral international institutions is best understood in terms of four international political roles which it continuously and simultaneously plays (and in some instances is called upon to play) in contemporary world politics:

- *A prophetic and reformist role.* For more than a century, the US has seen its destiny as linked to the reform of international politics, an impulse that arises from many strands in American political and civic culture. This sense of mission has led it to conceive and support the establishment of international institutions endowed with formal decision-making procedures, in which, as in its domestic experience, law and legal symbols figure prominently.

- *An infra-organisational role.* Within the organisational politics of each institution, the US sometimes—but less often than its power would allow—operates in ways characteristic of all states in multilateral institutions. Yet US behaviour is magnified by virtue of its preponderant power, and is aggravated by the apparent inconsistency of actions taken in pursuit of specific interests with its prophetic and reformist role.

- *A custodial role.* The United States functions as the ultimate custodian of international order, the actor of last resort in matters of fundamental importance to contemporary international politics. The custodial role may involve usurping ordinary decision-making procedures in order to vouchsafe the fundamental goals of the larger system which the institution is supposed to serve. The custodial role sometimes requires the US to resist organic institutional developments which it may have initiated or previously supported, even though they are natural outgrowths of its reformist role, or to act extra-legally or supra-legally with respect to those same institutions when an urgent issue of minimum world public order is at stake. The custodial role may generate acute connects with other members of the institution, especially when military action is required and when the coalition leader is constrained to favour its own view of efficiency or institutional amelioration over prescribed coalition procedures, a choice which brings stress to the coalition. In a government marked by rule of law, the custodial role may also exacerbate tensions between internal governmental participants, for whom rule-of-law is their core ideology, and those charged with external responsibilities.

- *A domestic-pressure reactive role.* The foreign-policy establishment of the United States, itself a complex organism that incorporates government officials and private persons, frequently identifies what many of its members consider to be a national interest. But as a complex constitutional system and a robustly effective democracy, the US acting externally must respond to the demands—whether intermittent or persistent—of internal constituencies, which are sometimes generated, refracted, or amplified by the mass media. The transfer of foreign-affairs power from a specialist professional class to a much wider slice of the community is characteristic of modern democracies, but is particularly advanced in the US. The dynamic that operates here sometimes moves what the specialists would characterise as a micro-issue or marginal issue to centre stage, and often 'localises'—in this context a preferable term to its pejorative counterpart 'parochialises'—perspective and evaluation, at least from the alternative perspective of the foreign-policy specialist.

Each of these roles has its own internal dynamic. Some are uniquely American and deeply rooted in the US national experience or derive from its power; others are shared, in varying degree, by different states. But in the case of the US, their effects on the institution concerned are greatly magnified by its predominant power in contemporary world politics. On occasion all four roles are performed harmoniously, such as during the 1991 Gulf War. But the intersection of these roles in particular cases may lead to inconsistent and sometimes conflicting US behaviour. Such situations can cause the United States to conduct its international institutional diplomacy less efficiently and more abrasively than intended, to the point where the inherent dynamics of some of the roles may undermine the performance of others and generate periodic crises in relations with multilateral institutions and in the institutions themselves.

THE U.S. AS REFORMER

Since the late nineteenth century, the focus of US foreign policy and, as a critical part of it, discussions among intellectuals, church groups, and popular movements, has shifted from the choice of a role *within* an existing system to a role of innovative architect and redesigner *of* that system, engaged in increasingly ambitious projects to change radically the structure of and, as a result, behaviour within that system. The creation of the Permanent Court of Arbitration, the precursor of the Permanent and now International Court of Justice, was largely an American initiative at the 1899 Hague Peace Conference (which had actually been convened by the Tsar in the hope of securing an interim arms control agreement that would retard the development of comparative German and Austro-Hungarian advantages).[2] The notion that an international court could transform the historically violent and destructive methods of conflict resolution into orderly judicial procedures had deep roots in the 'Peace Movement', a popular, religious-based mass movement in the United States that took shape in the nineteenth century. The League of Nations, as a mechanism for and guarantor of collective security, was, of course, President Woodrow Wilson's pet project. (US membership in the League was blocked in the Senate, largely because of the ailing Wilson's mishandling of the matter rather than because of an essential antipathy to an active foreign policy.) The International Labor Organization was largely an American invention. The basic ideas for the United Nations, the World Bank and many of the specialised agencies were also largely conceived and pushed by the US during the Second World War.

Thus, one of the distinctive characteristics of US participation in international politics for the past century has been the desire to engage in major international social engineering, expecting that, if properly done, initiatives involving the design and creation of new institutions would transform the essential nature and procedures of those politics. It is fair to call this energetic bully-pulpitism a 'prophetic role' in the non-religious sense in which the Oxford English Dictionary uses the term: 'the accredited spokesman, proclaimer, or preacher of some principle, cause or movement'. The particular content of the policies for restructuring international politics has varied from period to period, but the common objective has been to change world politics so that they take on the character of what Americans believe their own politics to be. The symbol of law is extremely important. Law is to play as large a role in international politics as Americans believe it plays in their own domestic processes, and judicial institutions (that is to say, institutions *applying law* as opposed to third-party procedures which simply resolve disputes) are deemed central. Over time, the deep belief that the savagery of international and domestic politics can be tamed and transformed has prevailed, along with the belief that these can be significantly improved by new patterns of institutional collaboration, and that it is wholly appropriate for the US to take the lead, indeed to press vigorously for those changes if necessary.

This is not a narrow or arcané litist interest, protectively couched in inaccessible specialist jargon. Analysis of public opinion over time demonstrates consistent strong popular support for such international programmes. Nor has it been merely a popular amusement for the rank-and-file. For most of the twentieth century, the United States has probably been the only country in the world in which significant numbers of serious and accomplished businessmen, clergy, politicians and diplomats—the sort of people who consider their time very 'valuable'—have met publicly and privately over extended periods of time to collaborate in the production of plans for new institutional arrangements to effect the transformation of the world or particular regions. This practice was conducted with great seriousness during the Second World War and has been pursued continuously since then.[3] And not for modest projects: the targets have included matters as varied as the restructuring of the global economy, the control of the diffusion of the most destructive weapons, the redesign of the UN, the reorganisation of the world health system, 'nation-building' within particular states or, most ambitiously, the international human-rights programme, which in essence seeks to change the technique of governance everywhere so that it comports with what is taken to be a Western ideal.

Dramatic US behaviour that is interpreted as 'anti-institutional' or 'organisation-bashing' should be viewed in terms of this prophetic and reformist role. When the US withdraws from an international institution—for example, the International Labor Organization—or when it withholds funds from an institution—for example, the UN—it does not signal a fit of pique nor a withdrawal into isolationism. On the contrary, in the US view it is corrective, contingent behaviour designed to secure precise adjustments which the institution in question must undertake as the condition for US re-entry or repayment.[4] Part of the angry reaction that these acts precipitate among other members has less to do with the gravamen—the particular pathology in the organisation concerned—and more to do with the fact that, precisely because its power and wealth are necessary for the institution's optimal operation, the US can arrogate to itself the right to demand corrections in such a fashion. The angry reaction may make the reform initiative less effective or more costly than would a suave diplomatic approach, but because both action and reaction here are driven by their own forces, the collision between them seems inevitable.

Some observers would say that, whether consciously or not, the policies which the US pursues in these macro-social reform initiatives are designed to enhance and sustain American power and interests. Although avowedly altruistic behaviour usually has a core of self-interest, claims that the US, in its reformist role, is exclusively pursuing its own self-interest are grotesquely exaggerated. While the values espoused are—not surprisingly—essentially American and hence congenial to Americans (and indeed to many others), quite a few of the policies and institutional arrangements that have been pursued—for example, free trade—are, if the theory is correct, supposed to 'level the playing field', something one would not expect a superpower to seek. Others—for example, democracy and human rights—give no real gains to US power, limit the ambit of operation of some executive agencies, put the US on the defensive when it finds itself constrained to support, to paraphrase Franklin D. Roosevelt, one of 'our SOBs', and often vex relations with governments that are important and sometimes vital to American foreign relations. Demands for the achievement everywhere of multi-cultural and nonracial societies, values that are central to the American political experiment, promise no particular gains for the US, and often embroil it in conflicts in which 'national interests', as foreign-policy specialists might define them, are not really engaged and in which prospects for meaningful achievement of goals are slim.

Prior to the Second World War, these kinds of American initiatives were viewed by many as romantic, quixotic, idealistic, irritating or ridiculous. Since that war, and certainly since the end of the Cold War, they are also viewed as policies to be reckoned with, precisely because the United States, unlike other states that intermittently seek the bully pulpit for prophetic and reformist purposes, is the major international actor, and disposes of the power and money to press these programmes vigorously.

THE INFRA-ORGANISATIONAL FACTOR

The prophet who envisions a new religion, institution, or organisation and who is concerned about his historical image would do well to time the moment of its creation with his own bodily ascent to heaven. If he does not, his prophetic mantle will become more and more tattered as he tries to participate in his creation and is sucked ever deeper into the gritty quotidian politics inherent in every working institution. This virtual iron law of status decay is particularly painful when the founder-prophet is a state and the institution concerned is a multilateral intergovernmental one. And it is uniquely problematic for the US.

In international institutions—the constant celebration of the supposedly preeminent authority of the institution notwithstanding—the actual assignment of each state's representative is to pursue that state's particular objectives and to reinforce the powers of the international institution only insofar as it contributes to that end. From the standpoint of government officials charged with the conduct of their country's external affairs, a multilateral institution is an instrument of policy to be wielded, like other instruments, in the pursuit of national interest. The personnel of governments who decide on and implement national policies within and through the international institutions identify with their states; though some may harbour secret loyalties to more inclusive identities, their public commitments, supported by oath and often reinforced by promises of material and symbolic rewards and threats of severe criminal sanctions, continue to be to their own states. Within the state, there may be official programmes— in schools, churches and the media—extolling this multilateral institution or that, but primary loyalty to the state continues to be demanded and policed.

Thus, rhetoric notwithstanding, national officials are not romantic about international institutions. They better than anyone know that the institutions are created by the agreements of individuals who occupy high positions in governments; that the highest-level personnel in the institutions are selected by high government representatives and, in effect, often serve at their pleasure; that the national personnel who create and maintain multilateral institutions select the managerial level of multilateral institutions and, as in most selection processes, seek to replicate their own values as best they can; that the monetary resources of such institutions depend upon continuing contributions by governments; and that the capacities of these institutions to engage in coercive action—the *ultima ratio* of politics—depend upon provision of the necessary resources by governments.

Understood in this context, the extent to which the US defers to and defends established institutional and bureaucratic decision procedures and does not use its power to influence decisions that would favour its or its nationals' interests is remarkable. Nonetheless, a significant amount of day-to-day American behaviour *within* a multilateral organisation is likely to be driven by the same sorts of interests that motivate other member-states—that is, after all, one of the functions of diplomacy in these institutions. But while observers and commentators may be understanding about the vigorous insistence on the satisfaction of minimum security or economic concerns voiced by, let us say, Ireland, Israel, Italy or some other smaller state, and view it as perfectly normal (indeed as normative international institutional behaviour), they are prone to be very critical when the US insists on positions within an organisation that accommodate its own interests. Partly because of its self-assumed prophetic role, the US is held to a higher standard.

As in all law, legal arrangements are created within political processes, and necessarily incorporate the values and demands of the most politically relevant actors. It should come as no surprise, therefore, that in their constitutions and prescribed procedures, international institutions reflect the relative power positions of the states that formed them. Politics is, at its most elemental, the pursuit of values by means of power, and those who have more power are hardly likely to create institutions that minimise that power and discriminate against their own values. But the constitution of each organisation must still incorporate divergent interests, so the life of every political institution is marked by a constant testing and stressing of legal and other power arrangements, by those who feel themselves prejudiced by them, in search of changes they believe will benefit them.

Once a decision procedure has been established within an institution, the US, like every other state, does defend its rights under it. All members of these institutions struggle to hold on to the power they have, or to acquire more: in a power arena, power is the coin of exchange and actors quite naturally seek to preserve or expand their 'monetary reserves'. Multilateral international institutions, despite their legal character, continue to be arenas of the larger power process. In the UN, where organisational power is essentially assigned to a Security Council in which five states have permanent membership with a veto right over decisions they oppose, there is a constant struggle between small and mid-sized powers, on the one hand, who seek to change the charter system, and the permanent members who seek to preserve their status and 'acquired rights', on the other. While the struggle often pits emotive symbols such as 'democracy' and 'equality' against equally emotive symbols such as 'fidelity to law', it is essentially a struggle for power. The same state that insists on 'democracy' in this context is likely to insist on its 'sovereign rights' *vis-à-vis* a smaller state in another, and to resist indignantly as an unlawful interference in its domestic jurisdiction any examination of the absence of democracy in its internal processes. The technique of international institutional diplomacy is to clothe frequent claims of special interest in the signs and symbols of common interest. Happily, the very multiplicity of actors with diverse interests acts, in the aggregate, as some restraint on the pursuit of special interest, while the constant reiteration by all of the symbols of common interest helps to reinforce the authority that undergirds the institution.

Once an institution is established, however, its internal power process may become quite different from the surrounding power arena. Institutions acquire lives of their own, they engage employees who devote their lives to them, and they generate affirmative attitudes and even loyalties in different sectors within and outside, not least in parts of the media, the neural system of modem mass society. And although every organisation is created by and reflects a political power process, once an organisation is established, the formulation of its procedures in the language of the law brings the lawyers into play, inevitably introducing a complex calculus of legal values that henceforth influences how it will operate. Elements such as these are, in their own way, bases of power which introduce new factors into the international power process.

Consider the UN Charter, which has created organs besides the Security Council. In many of them, power is distributed quite differently than it is in the Security Council, whose permanent members have most of the population, wealth and power of the world community and which, as a result, more accurately mirrors the composition and dynamics of 'the real world'. From time to time, these other organs may be mobilised by coalitions of smaller opposing states attempting to change the allocation of power within the institution. When this happens, the more powerful and organisationally endowed states react in ways that preserve their power. Take the International Court of justice, the UN's principal judicial organ. It has a broadly defined competence.[5] None of its 15 members, a collegium which is always likely to include the nominees of the permanent members of the Security Council, has a veto. So one can envision initiatives to change the UN structure, that would surely be vetoed in the Security Council, producing a different and veto-proof outcome in the Court.[6] Although implementation of a judgement of the Court will ultimately depend on the discretion of the Security Council, the mere authority of a judgement or opinion as to what the law is may have a significant political valence in some contexts.[7]

When the International Court sought to go beyond its conventional ambit and to condemn the US for its activities in support of one side in the Nicaraguan civil war,[8] the US withdrew its declaration of jurisdiction to the optional clause of the

Court's statute.[9] But this particular response was not unique to the United States. A decade earlier, the Court, on the basis of only arguable jurisdiction, had subjected France's nuclear-weapons testing programme to its review,[10] whereupon France withdrew its declaration of jurisdiction.[11]

As a major architect of the UN Charter and a permanent member of the Security Council, one would expect the United States to behave conservatively when initiatives to reduce its power are pressed in the United Nations. But on occasion the US has sought to expand the power of the General Assembly, at the expense of the Security Council, precisely because it wished to use the authority of a multilateral institution rather than 'go it alone'. After the eruption of the 1950–53 Korean War, for example, the US conceived the so-called 'Uniting For Peace' Resolution.[12] This resolution purported to authorise the General Assembly to exercise some of the powers of the Security Council with regard to peace and security when the Council was blocked. The theme was the 'democratisation' of the UN. At the time the US was confident that it would always be able to marshal a majority in the Assembly. Fifteen years later, at the end of the Six Day War when the Soviet Union indicated that it planned to convene the Assembly under 'Uniting for Peace', the United States resisted in the name of fidelity to the Charter. Thereafter, with the rise of an independent Non-Aligned Movement in the Assembly, both the US and the Soviet Union became adherents to the principle of fidelity to the text of the Charter. In the run-up to the March–June 1999 military action in Kosovo, when the US unsuccessfully explored the possibility of a Security Council authorisation, it probably could have marshalled a majority in the Assembly under the 'Uniting For Peace' resolution. Presumably, it eschewed this option because of the precedential implications of a constitutional change, enhancing the power of the Assembly *vis-à-vis* the Council, that would have persisted long after that event.

The infra-organisational role of the US often generates tension with its own closest and most powerful allies. This occurs not because these allies do not understand the multiple roles the US plays, but because, in pursuing their own policies, they find in the conflicts of the various American roles opportunities to enhance their own positions. The two democratic permanent members of the Security Council that often cooperate with the US in the performance of custodial functions compete nonetheless for power and the manifold advantages it offers. Sometimes they take advantage of unpopular positions that the American perception of its roles and responsibilities forces it to defend. The 1998 diplomatic conference in Rome that produced a statute for an International Criminal Court (ICC) provides an interesting example. France, like the US, did not initially support the ICC, for parallel and in some cases converging reasons. But when it became apparent in Rome that there would be a statute, France effected a dramatic *volte face*, and announced its support for the project. In the tumultuous moments of the final vote, the French ambassador stood and clapped enthusiastically, as the American delegation sat in gloom.

The custodial role of the US is perceived as conflicting with the ICC as it was structured by the Rome Conference, because it may obstruct or raise the cost of the performance of certain critical custodial functions. Yet, without the active support of the US, it is difficult to see how the Criminal Court can achieve its objectives. That does not mean that its existence and operation, however ineffective in terms of its manifest goals, will not affect the international political process. Once the ICC seemed inevitable, a major power like France could calculate that while the operation of the new court would complicate the discharge of American functions, it could also provide new opportunities to France for competition with the US. As a party to the statute of the ICC, France could participate in the selection of the judges and critical staff of the Court and, even more important, play a major parliamentary-diplomatic role in the Assembly of States, the ultimate control mechanism of the ICC. Since one of the latent functions of the ICC is to reduce the power of the Security Council, France can thus benefit from the existence of the Criminal Court at the expense of the US, serving as the indispensable link between Council and Court, while remaining confident that, when circumstances require it, the United States will still function as the custodian of world order.

THE U.S. AS CUSTODIAN

As the strongest power in the world community, the US is called upon to play an additional and unique role: that of the ultimate custodian of the fundamental goals of the multilateral institutions that it has helped to establish, when these institutions prove unable to act. And they often prove unable to act, because one of the sad facts of international life is that multilateral institutions have certain inherent defects that arise from the very nature of international politics. International institutions are created by the states that elect to participate in them for the purpose of achieving their common and particular objectives. The institutions testify, by their very existence, to a shared perception of certain common interests, sufficient at least to create them, and they may have great appeal for sectors or strata of the rank-and-file if they promise to enhance values which they seek. But no matter how romanticised the institutions may be, any honest appraisal should locate them clearly in the reality of an international politics still dominated by actors operating largely from national perspectives. Those actors create institutions that require their agreement for decision and action, but they are subsequently unlikely to agree on many of the most fundamental issues that call for decision.

The most avid proponents of multilateralism tend to believe that international institutional paralysis results from transient factors: the Cold War, the North-South division, the Palestine problem and so on. Solve the relevant transient problem and the institutions will be able to function as planned. But when the transient problem is resolved or recedes because it has ceased to be important, the institutions still suffer paralysis at the moment they are most needed. The reason is as apparent as the seating system in any international institution: despite a certain homogenisation of global culture, the elites (and many of the rank-and-file) of these states continue to operate with identifications, demands and matter-of-fact assumptions about past and future that are significantly different from those held by their counterparts in other states. They perceive events and value outcomes differently. In the aggregate, they have different interests and those differences become painfully apparent when multilateral institutions have to make fundamental decisions about world order. As currently structured, the institutions often prove unable to act, whether because of a veto right or a requirement of consensus. But a change of procedure will not resolve the problem, for the obstacles to action are reflections of the international political process itself. So the alternatives for a state that is able to act unilaterally are to do nothing, because unilateral action would be 'against the law', or to act alone, if necessary, to preserve the system in ways that might be deemed inconsistent with the law. For the US, for all the centrality of law to its national experience, the answer has been as simple as it is ineluctable, whether domestically or internationally. In Justice Oliver Wendell Holmes' pithy apophthegm, 'a constitution is not a suicide pact'.

The word 'custodian' is used advisedly, because the emphasis here is on a role that requires the incumbent to act in the best interests of those in its custody—as the custodian sees it. In this respect, the term is different from 'leadership', which American politicians frequently use to describe the national role, as well as from 'hegemony', which is used just as frequently by critics of the US role. Nor is the term synonymous with 'the world's policeman', a controversial term in US domestic politics, for it implies that, like the domestic 'cop on the beat' American military power will be deployed for each and every infraction—from border wars to *coups d'etat* to human-rights violations—when the UN is unable or unwilling to repair them. These and similar events may have great political or moral importance, but the custodian of the system is concerned with threats to the system as such, not infractions within it.

The US is acutely aware of its status in world politics, and its officials perforce plan for contingencies in which it will be called upon to act as custodian. But in moments of crisis, the initial invocation of the custodial role is likely to come from other beleaguered or otherwise involved states, who urgently remind the US of its 'responsibilities'. American reactions to many of these calls may appear inconsistent, and the internal debate within the US about the appropriate response may suggest deep internal divisions about custodianship. In fact, the United States has been rather consistent in fulfilling the custodial role, but the divergence between insiders and outsiders with regards to its 'when, why and how' underlines another aggravating factor in the performance of this role: it is the custodian who ultimately decides when, why, and how to act.

The custodial role conflicts with the formally prescribed procedures of multilateral institutions in a number of ways. The custodian guarantees the ultimate goals of the system, but without explicit authority and outside the processes or procedures that have been established within each institution for making decisions. If they were followed in these instances, there would be no decision. In the UN, the ultimate goal is the maintenance of minimum world order, a concept that originally meant the protection of the territory of states from aggression, but has now been extended to include the policing of selected activities within states if their foreseeable consequences threaten minimum world order. In the economic agencies, the ultimate goal is the maintenance of the international economic and financial infrastructure that undergirds the science-based and technological civilisation of key parts of the world. This goal may require the salvaging of distressed national economies or their 'restructuring', usually in ways that are costly and painful in the domestic politics of those undergoing the transformation.

In circumstances where the ultimate goals are gravely at issue, but the processes and procedures of the institutions that have been established to secure them are unlikely to produce the decisions that are called for, the custodian, frequently with the support of other significant actors, may have to act outside the established legal framework of the institution in order to secure the international goals at stake. This supra-legal or extra-legal action is justified as 'lawful' rather than 'legal'—that is to say, in conformity with the ultimate goals of the system or institution in question, if not with the procedures that have been prescribed to achieve them. Sometimes these actions can still be 'legalised' by adroit manipulation of key elastic terms in the constitutive instruments of the institution. For example, unilateral action inconsistent with the authority assigned to the Security Council to respond to acts of aggression, breaches of the peace and threats to the peace may be 'legalised' by an expansive reading of the 'inherent right of self-defence' in another article of the Charter. Despite the fact that the UN Charter reserves the powers to maintain minimum order to the Security Council, where action otherwise supported by a majority could still be vetoed by a Permanent Member, the 'Uniting for Peace' resolution purported to self-authorise the General Assembly to exercise its newly discovered 'secondary competence'.

In the performance of custodial functions, there are real advantages to conducting operations through a multilateral institution. It is clear that US policymakers prefer that route, when it is possible, for reasons of both efficiency and ideology. It is in this context that one must understand the affirmation of a conditional commitment by the Clinton administration (and, indeed, preceding administrations): 'multilateral when we can, unilateral when we must'. Unfortunately, it is not always possible to do things through multilateral institutions. To wield the not-inconsiderable authority available in Chapter VII of the UN Charter, the United States must win the acquiescence, within the Security Council, of two other advanced industrial democracies, one unstable government in an uncertain transition, and one unapologetic dictatorship, any one of whom may veto Council action, or impose unacceptable costs or conditions, as its price for consent. To go to the General Assembly under 'Uniting for Peace' may afford authority for a particular action, but reduces, precedentially, the exclusive power of the Security Council, in which the US enjoys a veto. That would conflict with the infra-organisational role considered above and could, moreover, compromise future custodial operations. Hence, in the Kosovo action, President Bill Clinton repeatedly stated that the United States and NATO were operating on behalf of 'the world-community'. As an empirical matter, they probably were. Yet the alliance did not go to the basic institution of the world community to receive an explicit authorisation.

The perceptions that are a critical part of the custodial role are frequently different from those of other friendly members of the institutions concerned. In the Siberian-pipeline controversy of the 1980s, the US, as ultimate guarantor of security in Europe *vis-à-vis* the Soviet Union, tried to exercise a custodial role with respect to an incipient arrangement that it felt would increase Western Europe's dependence and vulnerability to Soviet economic pressure.[13] The European governments felt that the matter was simply one of economic utility. To Europeans, American behaviour, including its insistence on the stringent application of its import-export controls, represented a violation of the norms and ethics of multilateral trade institutions, driven by crude and imperfectly concealed self-interest. From the American perspective, its own actions were driven by the imperatives of custodianship of the security of the free world, which it had preserved twice before in the century, at the cost of considerable blood and treasure, a responsibility which it hoped to avert a third time by prudently restraining the formation of economic dependencies on the adversary.

During the Cold War, a similar dynamic operated within the Coordinating Committee on Multilateral Export Controls (COCOM) with regard to sales of dual-use materials to explicit or latent adversaries. The United States, as the ultimate custodian of security, was more likely to view the sales in terms of urgent security, of which it was the guarantor, while its allies and partners in COCOM would incline to view them as simply economic.[14] For example, since the US submarine leg of the nuclear triad was the ultimate deterrent to nuclear war, the sale by a Japanese company to the Soviet Union of technology that permitted Soviet submarines to substantially reduce the radial area of their noise—and hence the ability of the US navy to locate them—was viewed gravely by the US Department of Defense; some circles in other parts of the alliance considered this a hysterical overreaction. Currently, the tension between custodial responsibilities and economic interests of other friendly states continues with respect to nuclear proliferation and the spread of missile technology.

The custodial role may lead to actions that are apparently incompatible with the prophetic role, in immediate cases as well as prospectively. In an immediate case, such as the 1990 Iraqi invasion of Kuwait, the US made it clear that it would expel Iraq, acting unilaterally if necessary, should the Security Council fail to provide authorisation. In the 1999 Kosovo crisis, the US, through NATO, acted without explicit Security Council authorisation. Given the distribution of power in the larger arena, a decision by the United States to proceed puts pressure on recalcitrant members of the institution to go along by bartering the institutional authority which they can dispense; thus they may retain some influence over actions that will, in any case, inevitably follow. Yet even when other members of the institution concerned get on board, it is clear that exercise of the custodial role is still challenging the institutional procedures that the US itself had worked to establish, and committed itself to follow, and is leaving in its wake a residuum of resentment.

In some circumstances, evolutions within institutions the US has helped to establish have required it to adjust its relationship in order to protect its custodial role. Thus, after the jurisdictional decision by the International Court of Justice in the Nicaragua case, the US denounced its optional declaration to the jurisdiction of the Court. The action caused real anguish in many quarters of the Executive Branch where there had been a strong commitment and prior leadership with respect to the expansion of international adjudication as a mode of international dispute resolution. Yet it was plain that new alignments within the

Court on critical substantive matters, coupled with a new approach to jurisdiction, made American subjection to the Court's appraisal at the initiative of virtually any member of the UN incompatible with the future performance of its custodial responsibilities.

Because the executive agencies of the US are acutely aware of the custodial role they may be called upon to perform, their personnel look at incipient changes in multilateral institutions in terms of the impact on custodial performance in a variety of future scenarios. This sometimes results in national positions that are inconsistent with developments within those institutions, as well as with prior positions taken by the US. Thus the 1997 Land Mines Convention was opposed by elements within the Executive Branch of the US who believed that such weapons were indispensable to the performance of certain international security functions that would remain a US responsibility for several decades. The International Criminal Court was initially espoused by the US and supported with funds and personnel—indeed more than by any other state—in its early incarnation as the Former Yugoslav and Rwanda Tribunals, and in the draft proposed by the International Law Commission. Washington ultimately opposed the court, however, because the instrument that emerged from the 1998 Rome Conference was viewed as likely to obstruct the custodial role the US could expect to be called upon to perform militarily.

The custodial role would be more compatible with the prophetic and reformist role if the institutional modalities the US helped put into place were not so legalistic. But precisely because the emphasis on law is so strong in the reformist role of the US, immediate or prospective custodial actions are often viewed by many, within the US as well as beyond, not simply as violations of the legal procedures of the institutions, but as violations of the prophetic role itself.

THE INFLUENCE OF DOMESTIC PRESSURE

In international political and legal analysis, states are frequently regarded as monads. But, obviously, internal political dynamics play a considerable role in determining external political behaviour. Even in democracies, the internal factor may vary according to the constitutional structure: in the Westminster model, for example, the Executive can wield considerably more foreign-affairs power than can its counterpart in a republican, constitutional model, such as that found in the US. A unitary as opposed to federal system minimises the internal diffusion of power.

The internal politics of the United States are a critical and insufficiently appreciated dimension of American relations to multilateral institutions, with a profound influence on the content of decisions and their modes of implementation. The US is a robust, federated democracy, whose constitutional structure, unlike the Westminster model, distributes competence among three branches. These three branches check and balance each other in different ways in virtually all areas, including foreign affairs. In a federal system, state law and administration is often the direct target of international-treaty activity. As a practical political matter, the US federal government may find that its room for international manoeuvre is quite limited in many negotiations by values and policies of state and local officials.

The political-party system in the US makes the legislative branch particularly diverse in its foreign-policy conceptions. The now golden age of a 'bipartisan' foreign policy did not depend upon consensus, but upon political parties with sufficient internal discipline to enable party leaders to enforce a position, once adopted, on all the members. That discipline derived, in no small part, from the party leaders' capacity to grant or withhold funds for local elections. That discipline is gone, and with it the relatively easy possibility of a president striking a foreign-policy deal with the congressional leadership of the opposition party, knowing that Congress will then implement it. Moreover, the proliferation of mass media now greatly enhances the capacity of each member of Congress to address the public directly. The competitive structure of the media means that more dramatic and simple presentations are often more likely to gain attention. While many in the US lament an apparent nadir of civility in federal politics, the problems that relate to foreign policy are structural and are likely to persist, even if civility returns.

The representative character of the American system means that relatively small pressure groups that focus on a single issue—whether they are a small industry, a region or an ethnic or religious group whose members happen to be distributed strategically in electoral districts—may amplify their power and sometimes have a significant influence on the formation of policy. If they are unsuccessful in one branch, there is always another. Nor can internal bureaucratic politics be ignored: in some cases, the policies espoused by these groups may be resisted by groups, within the Executive, that have a different view of a particular national interest. With all these internal forces operating, the notion of an objectively verifiable 'national interest' is difficult to apply to US politics. American scholars use the term 'foreign-policy process' in order to describe more accurately the way American external policy is formed. It is important to bear this in mind if one is to understand why, for example, the US is on the one hand a critical supporter of UNICEF, a highly respected multilateral institution dedicated to the protection of children, and yet is often a fierce opponent of dissemination of birth-control information and technology, a policy with some obvious connections to the achievement of UNICEF's mission. (No one who wishes to understand American political behaviour should underestimate the passions engaged in the controversy over legalised abortion.) Or why the US can so anger or confound its friends in multilateral institutions on matters concerning Cuba, Israel or, for that matter, China.

The impact of the internal constitutional factor on American participation in institutions created to prescribe and apply human-rights norms is particularly ironic. Human rights have been a critical part of the vision and politics of America and of its international prophetic and reformist role; moreover, the US has been a central, indispensable initiator and sustainer of many of the international supervisory mechanisms of the modern programmes for the international protection of human rights. Yet it is not a party to the American Convention on Human Rights, despite the fact that it has been the major financial supporter of the Commission and Court, the oversight mechanisms of this regional human-rights system. And while it was the primary mover of the Universal Declaration of Human Rights, it only became party to the Covenant on Civil and Political Rights in 1992, and then quickly became embroiled in controversy with its oversight body. Some incline to personalise this conflict and to blame particular senators or representatives, but the problem is not personalities. Even though the US generally meets or exceeds the international standard and has effective internal mechanisms for correcting abuses, there seems to be a unique lack of fit between the way the US is structured and the international human-rights institutions.

When domestic politics within a large state create stresses in the relations with the international multilateral institutions in which it participates, there is a tendency to see the domestic influences as some sort of moral failure, especially if one assumes that multilateral institutions are essentially 'progressive' while states are always regressive atavisms. That assumption should be examined carefully. For all the mutations it has undergone, the state as an institution has been a remarkably efficient response to individual need for security. There always have been and still are cogent reasons why people organise themselves in exclusive rather than ever-more inclusive groups.

The reasons why people tend to respect and value their own communities are greatly reinforced in democracies, especially with respect to decisions about war and peace. The moral premise of democracy is that those who are affected by decisions should participate in making them. The political and possibly empirical premise of democracy is that people, with their mix of abilities, education and experience, will more often decide what is best for them than will aristocrats, autocrats, *soi disant* philosopher kings and sundry pundits, and armchair strategists. There may have been a time in the past when these premises did not apply with full force to foreign affairs, and they may not apply to the application of certain military technologies such as naval movements or electronic interventions or covert operations. But with a more efficient democracy, and a vigilant media which legitimises itself by 'exposing' such actions, politicians in the great modern democracies must increasingly accept the fact that they are bound in a sometimes unstated but nonetheless clearly understood compact with their constituents. This compact holds that leaders will not engage the people in conflicts that threaten significant consumption of blood and treasure unless a compelling case can be made that urgent national interests need to be protected, and no less costly method is feasible. A case for elective military action can still be successfully made, but it will depend on a fragile quotient of the modalities and the costs likely to be incurred.

In democratic societies, multilateral institutions may provoke complex and inconsistent reactions in many sectors of the public. The *raison d'etre* of the state is to provide security and the conditions for welfare, while remaining responsive to individual demands. Paradoxically, the more that multilateral international institutions attract loyalty and operate effectively, the more they are likely to generate anxieties and deep and contradictory reactions in both the leadership and rank-and-file of precisely those states that are perceived as democratic and effective—a reaction demonstrated by the often ambivalent popular responses to the evolving European Union.[15] These feelings are likely to be further aggravated by the perception of loss of power which membership in each institution engenders: citizens in stronger states will always feel that they have not received a measure commensurate with the responsibility and the costs that their states' power in the larger arena actually imposes on them; citizens of weaker states, insisting on the international norm of the 'equality of states', will always bemoan the asymmetrical distribution of power in the institution concerned.[16]

CONCLUSION

Sophisticated observers appreciate that the foreign policy of the government of every state is subject to conflicting forces and pressures. The United States is exceptional, not so much in the diversity of forces that operate on it in the formation of its international policy, as in the four roles it plays, each of which is magnified by its relative size and power. Tensions between the prophetic reformist, infra-organisational and custodial roles are all rendered more acute by the political uncertainties endemic to a large, federated democracy. The formation of foreign policy is therefore influenced by the comparative intensities of internal demands, and shifts in those demands are bound to aggravate other members of the institutions and organisations in which the US participates. The lack of congruence between the aspirations and powers of comprehensive security organisations such as the UN means that the US will feel compelled and will be called upon to act as custodian in exigent circumstances, and the four roles it plays mean that it will sometimes perform the custodial role in ways that displease some other states and actors in the international political system. There may be spikes of greater tension—as occurred after the passage of the General Assembly's 'Zionism is racism' resolution—or periods of greater harmony—as occurred after the Gulf War—but the essential pattern of the relationship will persist.[17]

Because making real decisions ineluctably indulges some and deprives others, it is inevitable that some actors in the international political process will resent the US—with varying degrees of intensity. That commonplace aside, many students of foreign affairs believe that the United States sometimes underuses multilateral institutions and needlessly aggravates its partners—in the issue of its unpaid UN dues, for example. They may be right, but it should be clear from the analysis of the four roles that reactions of other states to these aggravations are a relatively small part of the anger and tension that often attends—and will continue to attend—American relations with multilateral international institutions. More members of Congress—and the Executive—may become more sensitive to the feelings of other states, may better appreciate that multilateral institutions are useful tools of policy, may pay dues on time and appreciate that even a larger share of them is a pittance for the infra-institutional influence they bring. But the tensions between the US and other members of international institutions are systemic and, in that respect, tragic. Considering the way world politics now work, there appears to be no escape from them.

One can imagine alternative futures in which the international political predominance of the US is neutralised. Such a future could result, for example, from a more tightly organised Europe with a coherent foreign policy and an adequately funded effective military instrument to implement it, if need be; or by alignments of Russia and China that challenge the US. If these developments were to occur, they could change American relationships to multilateral institutions. It is doubtful, however, that either of these hypothetical futures promises a better system of international order for the people of the world than the fragile and imperfect one we now have. In any case, such projections seem idle, for the more probable future is one in which the United States continues to be paramount and, because of its character and the multiplicity of its roles, continues to stir controversy in its complex relationships with international institutions.

ACKNOWLEDGEMENTS

Mahnoush Arsanjani, Allan Gerson and Andrew Willard read drafts of this paper and made valuable criticisms and comments.

NOTES

1. To cite one example, the EU has its problems with the Appellate Body of the World Trade Organization (WTO), just as Japan and the US have theirs; if one substitutes 'animal hormones' for 'alcohol' or 'bananas', the attacks on the WTO are equivalent in terms of intensity of vitriol and apparent disregard for the viability and future of the institution.
2. See Geoffrey Best, 'Peace Conferences and The Century of Total War. The 1899 Hague Conference and What Came After', *International Affairs*, vol. 75 (1999) pp. 619, 622.
3. See, for example, Dorothy B. Robins, *Experiment in Democracy: The Story of U.S. Citizen Organizations in Forging the Charter of the United Nations* (New York: Parkside Press, 1971); on the role of private groups in pressing for human rights instruments, see Michael Reisman, 'Private International Declaration Initiatives', in *La Déclaration universelle des droits de l'homme 1948–49* (Paris: La Documentation Française, 1998), pp. 79–116.
4. Paradoxically, when the United States suspends payment of its dues, it often continues to make large voluntary contributions to programmes conducted by the institutions in question.
5. Article 36(1) of the Statute of the International Court of Justice provides that the 'jurisdiction of the Court comprises all cases which the parties refer to it and all matters specially provided for in the Charter of the United Nations or in treaties of convention in force'.
6. For an examination of this, see Michael Reisman, 'The Constitutional Crisis in the United Nations', *American Journal of International Law*, vol. 87 (1993), p. 83.
7. UN Charter Article 94(2).
8. *Military and Paramilitary Activities in and against Nicaragua (Nicaragua v. U.S.), Jurisdiction and Admissibility*, 1984 ICJ Reports, p. 392 (Judgement of November 26).
9. In a letter dated 4 October 1985, the US notified the Secretary General of the United Nations that it was terminating its declaration of jurisdiction, effective six months from 7 October 1985. For text and details, see *American Journal of International Law*, vol. 80 (1986), pp. 163–65.
10. *Nuclear Tests Case (Australia v. France), Request for the Indication of Interim Measures*, 1973 ICJ Reports, p. 99.

11. Letter of 2 January 1974, terminating the French declaration of acceptance of compulsory jurisdiction of 16 May 1966: 562 United Nations Treaty Series, No. 8196.
12. GA Resolution 377 (V), UN GAOR, 5th Session, Supp. No. 20 at 10, UN Doc. A/1775 (1950); repr. in 1950 UN Year Book, p. 193.
13. See Patrick J. DeSouza, 'The Soviet Gas Pipeline Incident: Extension of Collective Security Responsibilities to Peacetime Commercial Trade', in Michael Reisman and Andrew Willard, *International Incidents: The Law that Counts in World Politics* (Princeton, NJ: Princeton University Press, 1988), pp. 85–114.
14. See the examination of US export-control regimes from this perspective in Michael Reisman and William Araiza, 'National Reports: United States of America', in Karl M. Meesen, (ed.) *International Law of Export Control, Jurisdictional Issues* (London: Graham & Trotman, 1992), p. 163.
15. Robert A. Dahl, *Democracy and its Critics* (New Haven and London: Yale University Press, 1989) p. 319.
16. United Nations Charter Article 2(1).
17. GA Resolution 3379, 30 UNGAOR Supp. (No. 34) at 83–84, UN Doc. A/10034 (1975); repealed by GA Resolution 46/86 UNGAOR 46th Sess. 74th plen. mtg. at 1, UN Doc A/Res/46/86 (1992).

✌ PART TWO ✌

International Sources of Foreign Policy

Pride of place is often given to systemic explanations of foreign policy. It is here that the structural forces of the international system shape and constrain the choices of foreign policy officials. What are the characteristics of the international system, and how does the international system actually influence foreign policy? Scholars continue to debate these questions. The most consistent advocates of systemic explanations are realist scholars who focus on the enduring competitive nature of international politics.

Kenneth Waltz produces one of the most influential realist analyses of international politics. In this chapter from his influential book, *Theory of International Politics*, Waltz details the essential organizational characteristics of the international system, organizational characteristics he calls anarchy. Waltz insists on fundamental distinctions between the organizing principles of domestic politics and those of international politics. Domestic politics is the realm of specialization and hierarchy. International politics takes place in a self-help system with inherent limits on the level of integration and specialization. With the anarchic nature of the international system properly understood, Waltz is able to describe recurrent types of strategies that states pursue to safeguard their security. In particular, states act to promote or ensure a balance of power. Waltz does not present a theory of foreign policy; rather, he argues that the anarchic system and the distribution of power produce a certain sameness in the behavior of states. The international system does not directly shape the foreign policy of states, but it does present powerful constraints and imperatives in terms of which states are likely to abide.

Melvyn Leffler is a diplomatic historian who is interested in discovering the fundamental strategic and economic factors that shaped the American concept of national security after World War II. In effect, this essay probes the actual experience of government officials who sought to interpret and respond to the emerging postwar international structure. Leffler finds American defense planners and other officials preoccupied with preserving the geopolitical balance of power in Europe and Asia, but the perceived threat to that balance came less from Soviet military capability as from the communist exploitation of widespread social and economic disarray and turmoil. The essay reveals the bureaucratic and intellectual complexities that confronted postwar planners as they attempted to create and implement an American concept of national security.

Ikenberry explores the actual way in which the United States, as a newly hegemonic post-World War II country, attempted to use its power to build a postwar order. A conventional view of American foreign policy after the war holds that the United States used its power relatively easily to build its desired postwar economic and security order. Ikenberry argues that America's weaker partners—particularly Britain—were able to shape and influence the postwar settlement more than the conventional view appreciates. In the words of the article: "the United States got less than it wanted and more than it bargained for in the construction of postwar order." The postwar world economy reflected European ideas about the management of an open system of capitalism, and the Europeans effectively drew a reluctant United States into an ongoing security commitment. The United States was hegemonic and used its unprecedented power to organize a cooperative and institutionalized postwar order—but it was an order where bargaining, ideas, and political leverage created by the emerging Cold War mattered a great deal.

Anarchic Orders
and Balances of Power

Kenneth Waltz

I

1. Violence at Home and Abroad

The state among states, it is often said, conducts its affairs in the brooding shadow of violence. Because some states may at any time use force, all states must be prepared to do so—or live at the mercy of their militarily more vigorous neighbors. Among states the state of nature is a state of war. This is meant not in the sense that war constantly occurs but in the sense that with each state deciding for itself whether or not to use force, war may at any time break out. Whether in the family, the community, or the world at large, contact without at least occasional conflict is inconceivable; and the hope that in the absence of an agent to manage or to manipulate conflicting parties the use of force will always be avoided cannot be realistically entertained. Among men as among states, anarchy, or the absence of government, is associated with the occurrence of violence.

The threat of violence and the recurrent use of force are said to distinguish international from national affairs. But in the history of the world surely most rulers have had to bear in mind that their subjects might use force to resist or overthrow them. If the absence of government is associated with the threat of violence, so also is its presence. A haphazard list of national tragedies illustrates the point all too well. The most destructive wars of the hundred years following the defeat of Napoleon took place not among states but *within* them. Estimates of deaths in China's Taiping Rebellion, which began in 1851 and lasted thirteen years, range as high as twenty million. In the American Civil War some six hundred thousand people lost their lives. In more recent history, forced collectivization and Stalin's purges eliminated five million Russians, and Hitler exterminated six million Jews. In some Latin American countries coups d'état and rebellions have been normal features of national life. Between 1948 and 1957, for example, two hundred thousand Colombians were killed in civil strife. In the middle 1970s most inhabitants of Idi Amin's Uganda must have felt the lives becoming nasty, brutish, and short, quite as in Thomas Hobbes's state of nature. If such cases constitute aberrations, they are uncomfortably common ones. We easily lose sight of the fact that struggles to achieve and maintain power, to establish order, and to contrive a kind of justice within states may be bloodier than wars among them.

If anarchy is identified with chaos, destruction, and death, then the distinction between anarchy and government does not tell us much. Which is more precarious: the life of a state among states, or of a government in relation to its subjects? The answer varies with time and place. Among some states at some times, the actual or expected occurrence of violence is low. Within some states at some times, the actual or expected occurrence of violence is high. The use of force or the constant fear of its use are not sufficient grounds for distinguishing international from domestic affairs. If the possible and the actual use of force mark both national and international orders, then no durable distinction between the two realms can be drawn in terms of the use or the nonuse of force. No human order is proof against violence.

To discover qualitative differences between internal and external affairs one must look for a criterion other than the occurrence of violence. The distinction between international and national realms of politics is not found in the use or the nonuse of force but in their different structures. But if the dangers of being violently attacked are greater, say, in taking an evening stroll through downtown Detroit than they are in picnicking along the French and German border, what practical difference does the difference of structure make? Nationally as internationally, contact generates conflict and at times issues in violence. The difference between national and international politics lies not in the use of force but in the different modes of organization for doing something about it. A government, ruling by some standard of legitimacy, arrogates to itself the right to use force—that is, to apply a variety of sanctions to control the use of force by its subjects. If some use private force, others may appeal to the government. A government has no monopoly on the use of force, as is all too evident. An effective government, however, has a monopoly on the *legitimate* use of force, and legitimate here means that public agents are organized to prevent and to counter the private use of force. Citizens need not prepare to defend themselves. Public agencies do that. A national system is not one of self-help. The international system is.

2. Interdependence and Integration

The political significance of interdependence varies depending on whether a realm is organized, with relations of authority specified and established, or remains formally unorganized. Insofar as a realm is formally organized, its units are free to specialize, to pursue their own interests without concern for developing the means of maintaining their identity and preserving their security in the presence of others. They are free to specialize because they have no reason to fear the increased interdependence that goes with specialization. If those who specialize most benefit most, then competition in specialization ensues. Goods are manufactured, grain is produced, law and order are maintained, commerce is conducted, and financial services are provided by people who ever more narrowly specialize. In simple economic terms the cobbler depends on the tailor for his pants and the tailor on the cobbler for his shoes, and each would be ill-clad without the services of the other. In simple political terms Kansas depends on Washington for protection and regulation and Washington depends on Kansas for beef and wheat. In saying that in such situations interdependence is close, one need not maintain that the one part could not learn to live without the other. One need only say that the cost of breaking the interdependent relation would be high. Persons and institutions depend heavily on one another because of the different tasks they perform and the different goods they produce and exchange. The parts of a polity bind themselves together by their differences.[1]

Differences between national and international structures are reflected in the ways the units of each system define their ends and develop the means for reaching them. In anarchic realms like units coact. In hierarchic realms unlike units interact. In an anarchic realm, the units are functionally similar and tend to remain so. Like units work to maintain a measure of independence and may even strive for autarchy. In a hierarchic realm the units are differentiated and they tend to increase the extent of their specialization. Differentiated units become closely interdependent, the more closely so as their specialization proceeds. Because of the difference of structure, interdependence within and interdependence among nations are two distinct concepts. So as to follow the logicians' admonition to keep a single meaning for a given term throughout one's discourse, I shall use *integration* to describe the condition within nations and *interdependence* to describe the condition among them.

Although states are like units functionally, they differ vastly in their capabilities. Out of such differences something of a division of labor develops. The division of labor across nations, however, is slight in comparison with the highly articulated division of labor within them. Integration draws the parts of a nation closely together. Interdependence among nations leaves them loosely connected. Although the integration of nations is often talked about, it seldom takes place.

Nations could mutually enrich themselves by further dividing not just the labor that goes into the production of goods but also some of the other tasks they perform, such as political management and military defense. Why does their integration not take place? The structure of international politics limits the cooperation of states in two ways.

In a self-help system each of the units spends a portion of its effort, not in forwarding its own good, but in providing the means of protecting itself against others. Specialization in a system of divided labor works to everyone's advantage, though not equally so. Inequality in the expected distribution of the increased product works strongly against extension of the division of labor internationally. When faced with the possibility of cooperating for mutual gain, states that feel insecure must ask how the gain will be divided. They are compelled to ask not "Will both of us gain?" but "Who will gain more?" If an expected gain is to be divided, say, in the ratio of two to one, one state may use its disproportionate gain to implement a policy intended to damage or destroy the other. Even the prospect of large absolute gains for both parties does not elicit their cooperation so long as each fears how the other will use its increased capabilities. Notice that the impediments to collaboration may not lie in the character and the immediate intention of either party. Instead, the condition of insecurity—at the least the uncertainty of each about the other's future intentions and actions—works against their cooperation.

In any self-help system, units worry about their survival, and the worry conditions their behavior. Oligopolistic markets limit the cooperation of firms in much the way that international political structures limit the cooperation of states. Within rules laid down by governments, whether firms survive and prosper depends on their own efforts. Firms need not protect themselves physically against assaults from other firms. They are free to concentrate on their economic interests. As economic entities, however, they live in a self-help world. All want to increase profits. If they run undue risks in the effort to do so, they must expect to suffer the consequences. As William Fellner[2] says, it is "impossible to maximize joint gains without the collusive handling of all relevant variables." And this can be accomplished only by "complete disarmament of the firms in relation to each other." But firms cannot sensibly disarm even to increase their profits. This statement qualifies rather than contradicts the assumption that firms aim at maximum profits. To maximize profits tomorrow as well as today, firms first have to survive. Pooling all resources implies, again as Fellner puts it, "discounting the future possibilities of all participating firms." But the future cannot be discounted. The relative strength of firms changes over time in ways that cannot be foreseen. Firms are constrained to strike a compromise between maximizing their profits and minimizing the danger of their own demise. Each of two firms may be better off if one of them accepts compensation from the other in return for withdrawing from some part of the market. But a firm that accepts smaller markets in exchange for larger profits will be gravely disadvantaged if, for example, a price war should break out as part of a renewed struggle for markets. If possible, one must resist accepting smaller markets in return for larger profits. "It is," Fellner insists, "not advisable to disarm in relation to one's rivals." Why not? Because "the potentiality of renewed warfare always exists." Fellner's reasoning is much like the reasoning that led Lenin to believe that capitalist countries would never be able to cooperate for their mutual enrichment in one vast imperialist enterprise. Like nations, oligopolistic firms must be more concerned with relative strength than with absolute advantage.

A state worries about a division of possible gains that may favor others more than itself. That is the first way in which the structure of international politics limits the cooperation of states. A state also worries lest it become dependent on others through cooperative endeavors and exchanges of goods and services. That is the second way in which the structure of international politics limits the cooperation of states. The more a state specializes, the more it relies on others to supply the materials and goods that it is not producing. The larger a state's imports and exports, the more it depends on others. The world's well-being would be increased if an ever more elaborate division of labor were developed, but states would thereby place themselves in situations of ever closer interdependence. Some states may not resist that. For small and ill-endowed states the costs of doing so are excessively high. But states that can resist becoming ever more enmeshed with others ordinarily do so in either or both of two ways. States that are heavily dependent or closely interdependent worry about securing that which they depend on. The high interdependence of states means that the states in question experience or are subject to the common vulnerability that high interdependence entails. Like other organizations, states seek to control what they depend on or to lessen the extent of their dependency. This simple thought explains quite a bit of the behavior of states: their imperial thrusts to widen the scope of their control and their autarchic strivings toward greater self-sufficiency.

Structures encourage certain behaviors and penalize those who do not respond to the encouragement. Nationally, many lament the extreme development of the division of labor, a development that results in the allocation of ever narrower tasks to individuals. And yet specialization proceeds, and its extent is a measure of the development of societies. In a formally organized realm a premium is put on each unit's being able to specialize in order to increase its value to others in a system of divided labor. The domestic imperative is "specialize!" Internationally, many lament the resources states spend unproductively for their own defense and the opportunities they miss to enhance the welfare of their people through cooperation with other states. And yet the ways of states change little. In an unorganized realm each unit's incentive is to put itself in a position to be able to take care of itself, since no one else can be counted on to do so. The international imperative is "take care of yourself!" Some leaders of nations may understand that the well-being of all of them would increase through their participation in a fuller division of labor. But to act on the idea would be to act on a domestic imperative, an imperative that does not run internationally. What one might want to do in the absence of structural constraints is different from what one is encouraged to do in their presence. States do not willingly place themselves in situations of increased dependence. In a self-help system considerations of security subordinate economic gain to political interest.

What each state does for itself is much like what all of the others are doing. They are denied the advantages that a full division of labor, political as well as economic, would provide. Defense spending, moreover, is unproductive for all and unavoidable for most. Rather than increased well-being, their reward is in the maintenance of their autonomy. States compete, but not by contributing their individual efforts to the joint production of goods for their mutual benefit. Here is a second big difference between international-political and economic systems.

3. Structures and Strategies

That motives and outcomes may well be disjoined should now be easily seen. Structures cause actions to have consequences they were not intended to have. Surely most of the actors will notice that, and at least some of them will be able to figure out why. They may develop a pretty good sense of just how structures work their effects. Will they not then be able to achieve their original ends by appropriately adjusting their strategies? Unfortunately, they often cannot. To show why this is so I shall give only a few examples; once the point is made, the reader will easily think of others.

If shortage of a commodity is expected, all are collectively better off if they buy less of it in order to moderate price increases and to distribute shortages equitably. But because some will be better off if they lay in extra supplies quickly, all have a strong incentive to do so. If one expects others to make a run on a bank, one's prudent course is to run faster than they do even while knowing that if few others run, the bank will remain solvent, and if many run, it will fail. In such cases pursuit of individual interest produces collective results that nobody wants, yet individuals by behaving differently will hurt themselves without altering outcomes. These two much-used examples establish the main point. Some courses of action I cannot sensibly follow unless you do too, and you and I cannot sensibly follow them unless we are pretty sure that many others will as well. Let us go more deeply into the problem by considering two further examples in some detail.

Each of many persons may choose to drive a private car rather than take a train. Cars offer flexibility in scheduling and in choice of destination; yet at times, in bad weather for example, railway passenger service is a much-wanted convenience. Each of many persons may shop in supermarkets rather than at corner grocery stores. The stocks of supermarkets are larger, and their prices lower; yet at times the corner grocery store, offering, say, credit and delivery service, is a much-wanted convenience. The result of most people usually driving their own cars and shopping at supermarkets is to reduce passenger service and to decrease the number of corner grocery stores. These results may not be what most people want. They may be willing to pay to prevent services from disappearing. And yet individuals can do nothing to affect the outcomes. Increased patronage *would* do it, but not increased patronage by me and the few others I might persuade to follow my example.

We may well notice that our behavior produces unwanted outcomes, but we are also likely to see that such instances as these are examples of what Alfred E. Kahn describes as large changes that are brought about by the accumulation of small decisions. In such situations people are victims of the "tyranny of small decisions," a phrase suggesting that "if one hundred consumers choose option x, and this causes the market to make decision X (where X equals 100 x), it is not necessarily true that those same consumers would have voted for that outcome if that large decision had ever been presented for their explicit consideration."[3] If the market does not present the large question for decision, then individuals are doomed to making decisions that are sensible within their narrow contexts even though they know all the while that in making such decisions they are bringing about a result that most of them do not want. Either that or they organize to overcome some of the effects of the market by changing its structure—for example by bringing consumer units roughly up to the size of the units that are making producers' decisions. This nicely makes the point: So long as one leaves the structure unaffected, it is not possible for changes in the intentions and the actions of particular actors to produce desirable outcomes or to avoid undesirable ones. Structures may be changed, as just mentioned, by changing the distribution of capabilities across units. Structures may also be changed by imposing requirements where previously people had to decide for themselves. If some merchants sell on Sunday, others may have to do so in order to remain competitive even though most prefer a six-day week. Most are able to do as they please only if all are required to keep comparable hours. The only remedies for strong structural effects are structural changes.

Structural constraints cannot be wished away, although many fail to understand this. In every age and place the units of self-help systems—nations, corporations, or whatever—are told that the greater good, along with their own, requires them to act for the sake of the system and not for their own narrowly defined advantage. In the 1950s, as fear of the world's destruction in nuclear war grew, some concluded that the alternative to world destruction was world disarmament. In the 1970s, with the rapid growth of population, poverty, and pollution, some concluded, as one political scientist put it, that "states must meet the needs of the political ecosystem in its global dimensions or court annihilation."[4] The international interest must be served; and if that means anything at all, it means that national interests are subordinate to it. The problems are found at the global level. Solutions to the problems continue to depend on national policies. What are the conditions that would make nations more or less willing to obey the injunctions that are so often laid on them? How can they resolve the tension between pursuing their own interests and acting for the sake of the system? No one has shown how that can be done, although many wring their hands and plead for rational behavior. The very problem, however, is that rational behavior, given structural constraints, does not lead to the wanted results. With each country constrained to take care of itself, no one can take care of the system.

A strong sense of peril and doom may lead to a clear definition of ends that must be achieved. Their achievement is not thereby made possible. The possibility of effective action depends on the ability to provide necessary means. It depends even more so on the existence of conditions that permit nations and other organizations to follow appropriate policies and strategies. World-shaking problems cry for global solutions, but there is no global agency to provide them. Necessities do not create possibilities. Wishing that final causes were efficient ones does not make them so.

Great tasks can be accomplished only by agents of great capability. That is why states, and especially the major ones, are called on to do what is necessary for the world's survival. But states have to do whatever they think necessary for their own preservation, since no one can be relied on to do it for them. Why the advice to place the international interest above national interests is meaningless can be explained precisely in terms of the distinction between micro and macro theories. Among economists the distinction is well understood. Among political scientists it is not. As I have explained, a microeconomic theory is a theory of the market built up from assumptions about the behavior of individuals. The theory shows how the actions and interactions of the units form and affect the market and how the market in turn affects them. A macro theory is a theory about the national economy built on supply, income, and demand as systemwide aggregates. The theory shows how these and other aggregates are interconnected and indicates how changes in one or some of them affect others and the performance of the economy. In economics, both micro and macro theories deal with large realms. The difference between them is found not in the size of the objects of study, but in the way the objects of study are approached and the theory to explain them is constructed. A macro theory of international politics would show how the international system is moved by systemwide aggregates. One can imagine what some of them might be—amount of world GNP, amount of world imports and exports, of deaths in war, of everybody's defense spending, and of migration, for example. The theory would look something like a macroeconomic theory in the style of John Maynard Keynes, although it is hard to see how the international aggregates would make much sense and how changes in one or some of them would produce changes in others. I am not saying that such a theory cannot be constructed, but only that I cannot see how to do it in any way that might be useful. The decisive point, anyway, is that a macro theory of international politics would lack the practical implications of macroeconomic theory. National governments can manipulate systemwide economic variables. No agencies with comparable capabilities exist internationally. Who would act on the possibilities of adjustment that a macro theory of international politics might reveal? Even were such a theory available, we would still be stuck with nations as the only agents capable of acting to solve global problems. We would still have to revert to a micropolitical approach in order to examine the conditions that make benign and effective action by states separately and collectively more or less likely.

Some have hoped that changes in the awareness and purpose, in the organization and ideology, of states would change the quality of international life. Over the centuries states have changed in many ways, but the quality of international life has remained much the same. States may seek reasonable and worthy ends, but they cannot figure out how to reach them. The problem is not in their stupidity or ill will, although one does not want to claim that those qualities are lacking. The depth of the difficulty is not understood until one realizes that intelligence and goodwill cannot discover and act on adequate programs. Early in this century Winston Churchill observed that the British-German naval race promised disaster *and* that Britain had no realistic choice other than to run it. States facing global problems are like individual consumers trapped by the "tyranny of small decisions." States, like consumers, can get out of the trap only by changing the structure of their field of activity. The message bears repeating: The only remedy for a strong structural effect is a structural change.

4. The Virtues of Anarchy

To achieve their objectives and maintain their security, units in a condition of anarchy—be they people, corporations, states, or whatever—must rely on the means they can generate and the arrangements they can make for themselves. Self-help is necessarily the principle of action in an anarchic order. A self-help situation is one of high risk—of bankruptcy in the economic realm and of war in a world of free states. It is also one in which organizational costs are low. Within an economy or within an international order, risks may be avoided or lessened by moving from a situation of coordinate action to one of super- and subordination, that is, by erecting agencies with effective authority and extending a system of rules. Government emerges where the functions of regulation and management themselves become distinct and specialized tasks. The costs of maintaining a hierarchic order are frequently ignored by those who deplore its absence. Organizations have at least two aims: to get something done and to maintain themselves as organizations. Many of their activities are directed toward the second purpose. The leaders of organizations, and political leaders preeminently, are not masters of the matters their organizations deal with. They have become leaders not by being experts on one thing or another but by excelling in the organizational arts—in maintaining control of a group's members, in eliciting predictable and satisfactory efforts from them, in holding a group together. In making political decisions the first and most important concern is not to achieve the aims the members of an organization may have but to secure the continuity and health of the organization itself.[5]

Along with the advantages of hierarchic orders go the costs. In hierarchic orders, moreover, the means of control become an object of struggle. Substantive issues become entwined with efforts to influence or control the controllers. The hierarchic ordering of politics adds one to the already numerous objects of struggle, and the object added is at a new order of magnitude.

If the risks of war are unbearably high, can they be reduced by organizing to manage the affairs of nations? At a minimum management requires controlling the military forces that are at the disposal of states. Within nations, organizations have to work to maintain themselves. As organizations, nations, in working to maintain themselves, sometimes have to use force against dissident elements and areas. As hierarchical systems, governments nationally or globally are disrupted by the defection of major parts. In a society of states with little coherence, attempts at world government would founder on the inability of an emerging central authority to mobilize the resources needed to create and maintain the unity of the system by regulating and managing its parts. The prospect of world government would be an invitation to prepare for world civil war. This calls to mind Milovan Djilas's reminiscence of World War II.[6] According to him, he and many Russian soldiers in their wartime discussions came to believe that human struggles would acquire their ultimate bitterness if all men were subject to the same social system, "for the system would be untenable as such and various sects would undertake the reckless destruction of the human race for the sake of its greater 'happiness.'"[7] States cannot entrust managerial powers to a central agency unless that agency is able to protect its client states. The more powerful the clients and the more the power of each of them appears as a threat to the others, the greater the power lodged in the center must be. The greater the power of the center, the stronger the incentive for states to engage in a struggle to control it.

States, like people, are insecure in proportion to the extent of their freedom. If freedom is wanted, insecurity must be accepted. Organizations that establish relations of authority and control may increase security as they decrease freedom. If might does not make right, whether among people or states, then some institution or agency has intervened to lift them out of nature's realm. The more influential the agency, the stronger the desire to control it becomes. In contrast, units in an anarchic order act for their own sakes and not for the sake of preserving an organization and furthering their fortunes within it. Force is used for one's own interest. In the absence of organization, people or states are free to leave one another alone. Even when they do not do so, they are better able, in the absence of the politics of the organization, to concentrate on the politics of the problem and to aim for a minimum agreement that will permit their separate existence rather than a maximum agreement for the sake of maintaining unity. If might decides, then bloody struggles over right can more easily be avoided.

Nationally, the force of a government is exercised in the name of right and justice. Internationally, the force of a state is employed for the sake of its own protection and advantage. Rebels challenge a government's claim to authority; they question the rightfulness of its rule. Wars among states cannot settle questions of authority and right; they can only determine the allocation of gains and losses among contenders and settle for a time the question of who is the stronger. Nationally, relations of authority are established. Internationally, only relations of strength result. Nationally, private force used against a government threatens the political system. Force used by a state—a public body—is, from the international perspective, the private use of force; but there is no government to overthrow and no governmental apparatus to capture. Short of a drive toward world hegemony, the private use of force does not threaten the system of international politics, only some of its members. War pits some states against others in a struggle among similarly constituted entities. The power of the strong may deter the weak from asserting their claims, not because the weak recognize a kind of rightfulness of rule on the part of the strong, but simply because it is not sensible to tangle with them. Conversely, the weak may enjoy considerable freedom of action if they are so far removed in their capabilities from the strong that the latter are not much bothered by their actions or much concerned by marginal increases in their capabilities.

National politics is the realm of authority, of administration, and of law. International politics is the realm of power, of struggle, and of accommodation. The international realm is preeminently a political one. The national realm is variously described as being hierarchic, vertical, centralized, heterogeneous, directed, and contrived; the international realm, as being anarchic, horizontal, decentralized, homogeneous, undirected, and mutually adaptive. The more centralized the order, the nearer to the top the locus of decisions ascends. Internationally, decisions are made at the bottom level, there being scarcely any other. In the vertical-horizontal dichotomy, international structures assume the prone position. Adjustments are made internationally, but they are made without a formal or authoritative adjuster. Adjustment and accommodation proceed by mutual adaptation. Action and reaction, and reaction to the reaction, proceed by a piecemeal process. The parties feel each other out, so to speak, and define a situation simultaneously with its development. Among coordinate units adjustment is achieved and accommodations arrived at by the exchange of "considerations," in a condition, as Chester Barnard put it, "in which the duty of command and the desire to obey are essentially absent."[8] Where the contest is over considerations, the parties seek to maintain or improve their positions by maneuvering, by bargaining, or by fighting. The manner and intensity of the competition are determined by the desires and the abilities of parties that are at once separate and interacting.

Whether or not by force, each state plots the course it thinks will best serve its interests. If force is used by one state or its use is expected, the recourse of other states is to use force or be prepared to use it singly or in combination. No appeal can be made to a higher entity clothed with the authority and equipped with the ability to act on its own initiative. Under such conditions the possibility that force will be used by one or another of the parties looms always as a threat in the background. In politics force is said to be the ultima ratio. In international politics force serves not only as the ultima ratio but indeed as the first and constant one. To limit force to being the ultima ratio of politics implies, in the words of Ortega y Gasset, "the previous submission of force to methods of reason."[9] The constant possibility that force will be used limits manipulations, moderates demands, and serves as an incentive for the settlement of disputes. One who knows that pressing too hard may lead to war has strong reason to consider whether possible gains are worth the risks entailed. The threat of force internationally is comparable to the role of the strike in labor and management bargaining. "The few strikes that take place are in a sense," as Livernash has said, "the cost of the strike option which produces settlements in the large mass of negotiations."[10] Even if workers seldom strike, their doing so is always a possibility. The possibility of industrial disputes leading to long and costly strikes encourages labor and management to face difficult issues, to try to understand each other's problems, and to work hard to find accommodations. The possibility that conflicts among nations may lead to long and costly wars has similarly sobering effects.

5. Anarchy and Hierarchy

I have described anarchies and hierarchies as though every political order were of one type or the other. Many, and I suppose most, political scientists who write of structures allow for a greater and sometimes for a bewildering variety of types. Anarchy is seen as one end of a continuum whose other end is marked by the presence of a legitimate and competent government. International politics is then described as being flecked with particles of government and alloyed with elements of community—supranational organizations whether universal or regional, alliances, multinational corporations, networks of trade, and whatnot. International political systems are thought of as being more or less anarchic.

Those who view the world as a modified anarchy do so, it seems, for two reasons. First, anarchy is taken to mean not just the absence of government but also the presence of disorder and chaos. Since world politics, although not reliably peaceful, falls short of unrelieved chaos, students are inclined to see a lessening of anarchy in each outbreak of peace. Since world politics, although not formally organized, is not entirely without institutions and orderly procedures, students are inclined to see a lessening of anarchy when alliances form, when transactions across national borders increase, and when international agencies multiply. Such views confuse structure with process, and I have drawn attention to that error often enough.

Second, the two simple categories of anarchy and hierarchy do not seem to accommodate the infinite social variety our senses record. Why insist on reducing the types of structure to two instead of allowing for a greater variety? Anarchies are ordered by the juxtaposition of similar units, but those similar units are not identical. Some specialization by function develops among them. Hierarchies are ordered by the social division of labor among units specializing in different tasks, but the resemblance of units does not vanish. Much duplication of effort continues. All societies are organized segmentally or hierarchically in greater or lesser degree. Why not, then, define additional social types according to the mixture of organizing principles they embody? One might conceive some societies approaching the purely anarchic, of others approaching purely hierarchic, and of still others reflecting specified mixes of the two organizational types. In anarchies the exact likeness of units and the determination of relations by capability alone would describe a realm wholly of politics and power with none of the interaction of units guided by administration and conditioned by authority. In hierarchies the complete differentiation of parts and the full specification of their functions would produce a realm wholly of authority and administration with none of the interaction of parts affected by politics and power. Although such pure orders do not exist, to distinguish realms by their organizing principles is nevertheless proper and important.

Increasing the number of categories would bring the classification of societies closer to reality. But that would be to move away from a theory claiming explanatory power to a less theoretical system promising greater descriptive accuracy. One who wishes to explain rather than to describe should resist moving in that direction if resistance is reasonable. Is it? What does one gain by insisting on two types when admitting three or four would still be to simplify boldly? One gains clarity and economy of concepts. A new concept should be introduced only to cover matters that existing concepts do not reach. If some societies are neither anarchic nor hierarchic, if their structures are defined by some third ordering principle, then we would have to define a third system. All societies are mixed. Elements in them represent both of the ordering principles. That does not mean that some societies are ordered according to a third principle. Usually one can easily identify the principle by which a society is ordered. The appearance of anarchic sectors within hierarchies does not alter and should not obscure the ordering principle of the larger system, for those sectors are anarchic only within limits. The attributes and behavior of the units populating those sectors within the larger system differ, moreover, from what they would be and how they would behave outside of it. Firms in oligopolistic markets again are perfect examples of this. They struggle against one another, but because they need not prepare to defend themselves physically, they can afford to specialize and to participate more fully in the division of economic labor than states can. Nor do the states that populate an anarchic world find it impossible to work with one another, to make agreements limiting their arms, and to cooperate in establishing organizations. Hierarchic elements within international structures limit and restrain the exercise of sovereignty but only in ways strongly conditioned by the anarchy of the larger system. The anarchy of that order strongly affects the likelihood of cooperation, the extent of arms agreements, and the jurisdiction of international organizations.

But what about borderline cases, societies that are neither clearly anarchic nor clearly hierarchic? Do they not represent a third type? To say that there are borderline cases is not to say that at the border a third type of system appears. All categories have borders, and if we have any categories at all, we have borderline cases. Clarity of concepts does not eliminate difficulties of classification. Was China from the 1920s to the 1940s a hierarchic or an anarchic realm? Nominally a nation, China looked more like a number of separate states existing alongside one another. Mao Tse-tung in 1930, like Bolshevik leaders earlier, thought that striking a revolutionary spark would "start a prairie fire." Revolutionary flames would spread across China, if not throughout the world. Because the interdependence of China's provinces, like the interdependence of nations, was insufficiently close, the flames failed to spread. So nearly autonomous were China's provinces that the effects of war in one part of the country were only weakly registered in other parts. Battles in the Hunan hills, far from sparking a national revolution, were hardly noticed in neighboring provinces. The interaction of largely self-sufficient provinces was slight and sporadic. Dependent neither on one another economically nor on the nation's center politically, they were not subject to the close interdependence characteristic of organized and integrated polities.

As a practical matter observers may disagree in their answers to such questions as just when did China break down into anarchy, or whether the countries of western Europe are slowly becoming one state or stubbornly remaining nine. The point of theoretical importance is that our expectations about the fate of those areas differ widely depending on which answer to the structural question becomes the right one. Structures defined according to two distinct ordering principles help to explain important aspects of social and political behavior. That is shown in various ways in the following pages. This section has explained why two and only two types of structure are needed to cover societies of all sorts.

II

How can a theory of international politics be constructed? Just as any theory must be. First, one must conceive of international politics as a bounded realm or domain; second, one must discover some lawlike regularities within it; and third,

one must develop a way of explaining the observed regularities. . . . Political structures account for some recurrent aspects of the behavior of states and for certain
repeated and enduring patterns. Wherever agents and agencies are coupled by
force and competition rather than by authority and law, we expect to find such
behaviors and outcomes. They are closely identified with the approach to politics
suggested by the rubric realpolitik. The elements of realpolitik, exhaustively listed,
are these: the ruler's, and later the state's, interest provides the spring of action;
the necessities of policy arise from the unregulated competition of states; calculation based on these necessities can discover the policies that will best serve a
state's interests; success is the ultimate test of policy, and success is defined as preserving and strengthening the state. Ever since Machiavelli, interest and necessity—and raison d'état, the phrase that comprehends them—have remained the
key concepts of realpolitik. From Machiavelli through Meinecke and Morgenthau
the elements of the approach and the reasoning remain constant. Machiavelli
stands so clearly as the exponent of realpolitik that one easily slips into thinking
that he developed the closely associated idea of balance of power as well.
Although he did not, his conviction that politics can be explained in its own terms
established the ground on which balance-of-power theory can be built.

Realpolitik indicates the methods by which foreign policy is conducted and
provides a rationale for them. Structural constraints explain why the methods are
repeatedly used despite differences in the persons and states who use them.
Balance-of-power theory purports to explain the result that such methods produce. Rather, that is what the theory should do. If there is any distinctively political theory of international politics, balance-of-power theory is it. And yet one
cannot find a statement of the theory that is generally accepted. Carefully survey-
ing the copious balance-of-power literature, Ernst Haas discovered eight distinct
meanings of the term, and Martin Wight found nine. Hans Morgenthau, in his
profound historical and analytic treatment of the subject, makes use of four different definitions.[11] Balance of power is seen by some as being akin to a law of
nature; by others, as simply an outrage. Some view it as a guide to statesmen; others as a cloak that disguises their imperialist policies. Some believe that a balance
of power is the best guarantee of the security of states and the peace of the world;
others, that it has ruined states by causing most of the wars they have fought.

To believe that one can cut through such confusion may seem quixotic. I shall
nevertheless try. It will help to hark back to several basic propositions about theory. (1) A theory contains at least one theoretical assumption. Such assumptions
are not factual. One therefore cannot legitimately ask if they are true, but only if
they are useful. (2) Theories must be evaluated in terms of what they claim to
explain. Balance-of-power theory claims to explain the results of states' actions
under given conditions, and those results may not be foreshadowed in any of the
actors' motives or be contained as objectives in their policies. (3) Theory, as a general explanatory system, cannot account for particularities.

Most of the confusions in balance-of-power theory, and criticisms of it,
derive from misunderstanding these three points. A balance-of-power theory,
properly stated, begins with assumptions about states: They are unitary actors

who at a minimum seek their own preservation and at a maximum drive for universal domination. States, or those who act for them, try in more or less sensible ways to use the means available in order to achieve the ends in view. Those means fall into two categories: internal efforts (moves to increase economic capability, to increase military strength, to develop clever strategies) and external efforts (moves to strengthen and enlarge one's own alliance or to weaken and shrink an opposing one). The external game of alignment and realignment requires three or more players, and it is usually said that balance-of-power systems require at least that number. The statement is false, for in a two-power system the politics of balance continue, but the way to compensate for an incipient external disequilibrium is primarily by intensifying one's internal efforts. To the assumptions of the theory we then add the condition for its operation: that two or more states coexist in a self-help system, one with no superior agent to come to the aid of states that may be weakening or to deny to any of them the use of whatever instruments they think will serve their purposes. The theory, then, is built up from the assumed motivations of states and the actions that correspond to them. It describes the constraints that arise from the system that those actions produce, and it indicates the expected outcome: namely, the formation of balances of power. Balance-of-power theory is micro theory precisely in the economist's sense. The system, like a market in economics, is made by the actions and interactions of its units, and the theory is based on assumptions about their behavior.

A self-help system is one in which those who do not help themselves or who do so less effectively than others will fail to prosper, will lay themselves open to dangers, will suffer. Fear of such unwanted consequences stimulates states to behave in ways that tend toward the creation of balances of power. Notice that the theory requires no assumptions of rationality or of constancy of will on the part of all of the actors. The theory says simply that if some do relatively well, others will emulate them or fall by the wayside. Obviously, the system won't work if all states lose interest in preserving themselves. It will, however, continue to work if some states do while others do not choose to lose their political identities, say, through amalgamation. Nor need it be assumed that all of the competing states are striving relentlessly to increase their power. The possibility that force may be used by some states to weaken or destroy others does, however, make it difficult for them to break out of the competitive system.

The meaning and importance of the theory are made clear by examining prevalent misconceptions of it. Recall our first proposition about theory. A theory contains assumptions that are theoretical, not factual. One of the most common misunderstandings of balance-of-power theory centers on this point. The theory is criticized because its assumptions are erroneous. The following statement can stand for a host of others:

> If nations were in fact unchanging units with no permanent ties to each other, and if all were motivated primarily by a drive to maximize their power, except for a single balancer whose aim was to prevent any nation from achieving preponderant power, a balance of power might in fact result. But we have seen that these assumptions are

not correct, and since the assumptions of the theory are wrong, the conclusions are also in error.[12]

The author's incidental error is that he has compounded a sentence some parts of which are loosely stated assumptions of the theory and other parts not. His basic error lies in misunderstanding what an assumption is. From previous discussion we know that assumptions are neither true nor false and that they are essential for the construction of theory. We can freely admit that states are in fact not unitary purposive actors. States pursue many goals, which are often vaguely formulated and inconsistent. They fluctuate with the changing currents of domestic politics, are prey to the vagaries of a shifting cast of political leaders, and are influenced by the outcomes of bureaucratic struggles. But all of this has always been known, and it tells us nothing about the merits of balance-of-power theory.

A further confusion relates to our second proposition about theory. Balance-of-power theory claims to explain a result (the recurrent formation of balances of power) which may not accord with the intentions of any of the units whose actions combine to produce that result. To contrive and maintain a balance may be the aim of one or more states, but then again it may not be. According to the theory, balances of power tend to form whether some or all states consciously aim to establish and maintain a balance, or whether some or all states aim for universal domination. Yet many, and perhaps most, statements of balance-of-power theory attribute the maintenance of a balance to the separate states as a motive. David Hume, in his classic essay "Of the Balance of Power," offers "the maxim of preserving the balance of power" as a constant rule of prudent politics.[13] So it may be, but it has proved to be an unfortunately short step from the belief that a high regard for preserving a balance is at the heart of wise statesmanship to the belief that states must follow the maxim if a balance of power is to be maintained. This is apparent in the first of Morgenthau's four definitions of the term: namely, "a policy aimed at a certain state of affairs." The reasoning then easily becomes tautological. If a balance of power is to be maintained, the policies of states must aim to uphold it. If a balance of power is in fact maintained, we can conclude that their aim was accurate. If a balance of power is not produced, we can say that the theory's assumption is erroneous. Finally, and this completes the drift toward the reification of a concept, if the purpose of states is to uphold a balance, the purpose of the balance is "to maintain the stability of the system without destroying the multiplicity of the elements composing it." Reification has obviously occurred where one reads, for example, of the balance operating "successfully" and of the difficulty that nations have in applying it.

Reification is often merely the loose use of language or the employment of metaphor to make one's prose more pleasing. In this case, however, the theory has been drastically distorted, and not only by introducing the notion that if a balance is to be formed, somebody must want it and must work for it. The further distortion of the theory arises when rules are derived from the results of states' actions and then illogically prescribed to the actors as duties. A possible effect is turned into a necessary cause in the form of a stipulated rule. Thus, it is said, "the balance of power" can "impose its restraints upon the power aspirations of nations" only if they first "restrain themselves by accepting the system of the balance of power as the common framework of their endeavors." Only if states recognize "the same rules of the game" and play "for the same limited stakes" can the balance of power fulfill "its functions for international stability and national independence."[14]

The closely related errors that fall under our second proposition about theory are, as we have seen, twin traits of the field of international politics: namely, to assume a necessary correspondence of motive and result and to infer rules for the actors from the observed results of their action. . . . In a purely competitive economy, everyone's striving to make a profit drives the profit rate downward. Let the competition continue long enough under static conditions, and everyone's profit will be zero. To infer from that result that everyone, or anyone, is seeking to minimize profit, and that the competitors must adopt that goal as a rule in order for the system to work, would be absurd. And yet in international politics one frequently finds that rules inferred from the results of the interactions of states are prescribed to the actors and are said to be a condition of the system's maintenance. Such errors, often made, are also often pointed out, though seemingly to no avail. S. F. Nadel has put the matter simply: "an orderliness abstracted from behaviour cannot guide behaviour."[15]

Analytic reasoning applied where a systems approach is needed leads to the laying down of all sorts of conditions as prerequisites to balances of power forming and tending toward equilibrium and as general preconditions of world stability and peace. Some require that the number of great powers exceed two; others that a major power be willing to play the role of balancer. Some require that military technology not change radically or rapidly; others that the major states abide by arbitrarily specified rules. But balances of power form in the absence of the "necessary" conditions, and since 1945 the world has been stable, and the world of major powers remarkably peaceful, even though international conditions have not conformed to theorists' stipulations. Balance-of-power politics prevail wherever two and only two requirements are met: that the order be anarchic and that it be populated by units wishing to survive.

For those who believe that if a result is to be produced, someone or everyone must want it and must work for it, it follows that explanation turns ultimately on what the separate states are like. If that is true, then theories at the national level or lower will sufficiently explain international politics. If, for example, the equilibrium of a balance is maintained through states abiding by rules, then one needs an explanation of how agreement on the rules is achieved and maintained. One does not need a balance-of-power theory, for balances would result from a certain kind of behavior explained perhaps by a theory about national psychology or bureaucratic politics. A balance-of-power theory could not be constructed because it would have nothing to explain. If the good or bad motives of states result in their maintaining balances or disrupting them, then the notion of a balance of power becomes merely a framework organizing one's account of what happened, and that is indeed its customary use. A construction that starts out to be a theory ends up as a set of categories. Categories then multiply rapidly to cover events that the embryo theory had not contemplated. The quest for explanatory power turns into a search for descriptive adequacy.

Finally, and related to our third proposition about theory in general, balance-of-power theory is often criticized because it does not explain the particular policies of states. True, the theory does not tell us why state X made a certain move last Tuesday. To expect it to do so would be like expecting the theory of universal gravitation to explain the wayward path of a falling leaf. A theory at one level of generality cannot answer questions about matters at a different level of generality. Failure to notice this is one error on which the criticism rests. Another is to mistake a theory of international politics for a theory of foreign policy. Confusion about the explanatory claims made by a properly stated balance-of-power theory is rooted in the uncertainty of the distinction drawn between national and international politics or in the denials that the distinction should be made. For those who deny the distinction, for those who devise explanations that are entirely in terms of interacting units, explanations of international politics *are* explanations of foreign policy, and explanations of foreign policy *are* explanations of international politics. Others mix their explanatory claims and confuse the problem of understanding international politics with the problem of understanding foreign policy. Morgenthau, for example, believes that problems of predicting foreign policy and of developing theories about it make international-political theories difficult, if not impossible, to contrive.[16] But the difficulties of explaining foreign policy work against contriving theories of international politics only if the latter reduces to the former. Graham Allison betrays a similar confusion. His three "models" purport to offer alternative approaches to the study of international politics. Only model I, however, is an approach to the study of international politics. Models II and III are approaches to the study of foreign policy. Offering the bureaucratic-politics approach as an alternative to the state-as-an-actor approach is like saying that a theory of the firm is an alternative to a theory of the market, a mistake no competent economist would make.[17] If Morgenthau and Allison were economists and their thinking continued to follow the same pattern, they would have to argue that the uncertainties of corporate policy work against the development of market theory. They have confused and merged two quite different matters.

Any theory covers some matters and leaves other matters aside. Balance-of-power theory is a theory about the results produced by the uncoordinated actions of states. The theory makes assumptions about the interests and motives of states, rather than explaining them. What it does explain are the constraints that confine all states. The clear perception of constraints provides many clues to the expected reactions of states, but by itself the theory cannot explain those reactions. They depend not only on international constraints but also on the characteristics of states. How will a particular state react? To answer that question we need not only a theory of the market, so to speak, but also a theory about the firms that compose it. What will a state have to react to? Balance-of-power theory can give general and useful answers to that question. The theory explains why a certain similarity of behavior is expected from similarly situated states. The expected behavior is similar, not identical. To explain the expected differences in national responses, a theory would have to show how the different internal structures of states affect their external policies and actions. A theory of foreign policy would not predict the detailed content of policy but instead would lead to different expectations about the tendencies and styles of different countries' policies.

Because the national and the international levels are linked, theories of both types, if they are any good, tell us some things, but not the same things, about behavior and outcomes at both levels. . . .

III

. . . Before subjecting a theory to tests, one asks whether the theory is internally consistent and whether it tells us some things of interest that we would not know in its absence. That the theory meets those requirements does not mean that it can survive tests. Many people prefer tests that, if flunked, falsify a theory. Some people, following Karl Popper,[18] insist that theories are tested only by attempting to falsify them. Confirmations do not count because among other reasons confirming cases may be offered as proof, while consciously or not, cases likely to confound the theory are avoided. This difficulty, I suggest later, is lessened by choosing hard cases—situations, for example, in which parties have strong reasons to behave contrary to the predictions of one's theory. Confirmations are also rejected because numerous tests that appear to confirm a theory are negated by one falsifying instance. . . . However, [there is] the possibility of devising tests that confirm. If a theory depicts a domain and displays its organization and the connections among its parts, then we can compare features of the observed domain with the picture the theory has limned.[19] We can ask whether expected behaviors and outcomes are repeatedly found where the conditions contemplated by the theory obtain.

Structural theories, moreover, gain plausibility if similarities of behavior are observed across realms that are different in substance but similar in structure, and if differences of behavior are observed where realms are similar in substance but different in structure. This special advantage is won: International-political theory gains credibility from the confirmation of certain theories in economics, sociology, anthropology, and other such nonpolitical fields.

Testing theories, of course, always means inferring expectations, or hypotheses, from them and testing those expectations. Testing theories is a difficult and subtle task, made so by the interdependence of fact and theory, by the elusive relation between reality and theory as an instrument for its apprehension. Questions of truth and falsity are somehow involved, but so are questions of usefulness and uselessness. In the end one sticks with the theory that reveals most, even if its validity is suspect. I shall say more about the acceptance and rejection of theories elsewhere. Here I say only enough to make the relevance of a few examples of theory testing clear. Others can then easily be thought of. . . .

Tests are easy to think up, once one has a theory to test, but they are hard to carry through. Given the difficulty of testing any theory and the added difficulty of testing theories in such nonexperimental fields as international politics, we should exploit all of the ways of testing I have mentioned—by trying to falsify, by devising hard confirmatory tests, by comparing features of the real and the theoretical worlds, by comparing behaviors in realms of similar and of different structure. Any good theory raises many expectations. Multiplying hypotheses and varying tests are all the more important because the results of testing theories are necessarily problematic. That a single hypothesis appears to hold true may not be very impressive. A theory becomes plausible if many hypotheses inferred from it are successfully subjected to tests.

Knowing a little bit more about testing, we can now ask whether expectations drawn from our theory can survive subjection to tests. What will some of the expectations be? Two that are closely related arise in the above discussion. According to the theory, balances of power recurrently form, and states tend to emulate the successful policies of others. Can these expectations be subjected to tests? In principle the answer is yes. Within a given arena and over a number of years, we should find the military power of weaker and smaller states or groupings of states growing more rapidly, or shrinking more slowly, than that of stronger and larger ones. And we should find widespread imitation among competing states. In practice to check such expectations against historical observations is difficult.

Two problems are paramount. First, though balance-of-power theory offers some predictions, the predictions are indeterminate. Because only a loosely defined and inconstant condition of balance is predicted, it is difficult to say that any given distribution of power falsifies the theory. The theory, moreover, does not lead one to expect that emulation among states will proceed to the point where competitors become identical. What will be imitated, and how quickly and closely? Because the theory does not give precise answers, falsification again is difficult. Second, although states may be disposed to react to international constraints and incentives in accordance with the theory's expectations, the policies and actions of states are also shaped by their internal conditions. The failure of balances to form, and the failure of some states to conform to the successful practices of other states, can too easily be explained away by pointing to effects produced by forces that lie outside of the theory's purview.

In the absence of theoretical refinements that fix expectations with certainty and in detail, what can we do? As I have just suggested . . . we should make tests ever more difficult. If we observe outcomes that the theory leads us to expect even though strong forces work against them, the theory will begin to command belief. To confirm the theory one should not look mainly to the eighteenth-century heyday of the balance of power when great powers in convenient numbers interacted and were presumably able to adjust to a shifting distribution of power by changing partners with a grace made possible by the absence of ideological and other cleavages. Instead one should seek confirmation through observation of difficult cases. One should, for example, look for instances of states allying in accordance with the expectations the theory gives rise to even though they have strong reasons not to cooperate with one another. The alliance of France and Russia, made formal in 1894, is one such instance. . . . One should, for example, look for instances of states making internal efforts to strengthen themselves, however distasteful or difficult such efforts might be. The United States and the Soviet Union following World War II provide such instances: the United States by rearming despite having demonstrated a strong wish not to by dismantling the most powerful military machine the world had ever known; the Soviet Union by maintaining about three million men under arms while striving to acquire a costly new military technology despite the terrible destruction she had suffered in war.

These examples tend to confirm the theory. We find states forming balances of power whether or not they wish to. They also show the difficulties of testing. Germany and Austria-Hungary formed their Dual Alliance in 1879. Since detailed inferences cannot be drawn from the theory, we cannot say just when other states are expected to counter this move. France and Russia waited until 1894. Does this show the theory false by suggesting that states may or may not be brought into balance? We should neither quickly conclude that it does nor lightly chalk the delayed response off to "friction." Instead, we should examine diplomacy and policy in the fifteen-year interval to see whether the theory serves to explain and broadly predict the actions and reactions of states and to see whether the delay is out of accord with the theory. Careful judgment is needed. For this historians' accounts serve better than the historical summary I might provide.

The theory leads us to expect states to behave in ways that result in balances forming. To infer that expectation from the theory is not impressive if balancing is a universal pattern of political behavior, as is sometimes claimed. It is not. Whether political actors balance each other or climb on the bandwagon depends on the system's structure. Political parties, when choosing their presidential candidates, dramatically illustrate both points. When nomination time approaches and no one is established as the party's strong favorite, a number of would-be leaders contend. Some of them form coalitions to check the progress of others. The maneuvering and balancing of would-be leaders when the party lacks one is like the external behavior of states. But this is the pattern only during the leaderless period. As soon as someone looks like the winner, nearly all jump on the bandwagon rather than continuing to build coalitions intended to prevent anyone from winning the prize of power. Bandwagoning, not balancing, becomes the characteristic behavior.

Bandwagoning and balancing behavior are in sharp contrast. Internally, losing candidates throw in their lots with the winner. Everyone wants someone to win; the members of a party want a leader established even while they disagree on who it should be. In a competition for the position of leader, bandwagoning is sensible behavior where gains are possible even for the losers and where losing does not place their security in jeopardy. Externally, states work harder to increase their own strength, or they combine with others if they are falling behind. In a competition for the position of leader, balancing is sensible behavior where the victory of one coalition over another leaves weaker members of the winning coalition at the mercy of the stronger ones. Nobody wants anyone else to win; none of the great powers wants one of their number to emerge as the leader.

If two coalitions form and one of them weakens, perhaps because of the political disorder of a member, we expect the extent of the other coalition's military preparation to slacken or its unity to lessen. The classic example of the latter effect is the breaking apart of a war-winning coalition in or just after the moment of victory. We do not expect the strong to combine with the strong in order to increase the extent of their power over others, but rather to square off and look for allies who might help them. In anarchy security is the highest end. Only if survival is assured can states safely seek such other goals as tranquility, profit, and power. Because power is a means and not an end, states prefer to join the weaker of two coalitions. They cannot let power, a possibly useful means, become the end they pursue. The goal the system encourages them to seek is security. Increased power may or may not serve that end. Given two coalitions, for example, the greater success of one in drawing members to it may tempt the other to risk preventive war, hoping for victory through surprise before disparities widen. If states wished to maximize power, they would join the stronger side, and we would see not balances forming but a world hegemony forged. This does not happen because balancing, not bandwagoning, is the behavior induced by the system. The first concern of states is not to maximize power but to maintain their positions in the system.

Secondary states, if they are free to choose, flock to the weaker side; for it is the stronger side that threatens them. On the weaker side they are both more appreciated and safer, provided, of course, that the coalition they join achieves enough defensive or deterrent strength to dissuade adversaries from attacking. Thus Thucydides records that in the Peloponnesian War the lesser city states of Greece cast the stronger Athens as the tyrant and the weaker Sparta as their liberator.[20] According to Werner Jaeger, Thucydides thought this "perfectly natural in the circumstances," but saw "that the parts of tyrant and liberator did not correspond with any permanent moral quality in these states but were simply masks which would one day be interchanged to the astonishment of the beholder when the balance of power was altered."[21] This shows a nice sense of how the placement of states affects their behavior and even colors their characters. It also supports the proposition that states balance power rather than maximize it. States can seldom afford to make maximizing power their goal. International politics is too serious a business for that.

The theory depicts international politics as a competitive realm. Do states develop the characteristics that competitors are expected to display? The question poses another test for the theory. The fate of each state depends on its responses to what other states do. The possibility that conflict will be conducted by force leads to competition in the arts and the instruments of force. Competition produces a tendency toward the sameness of the competitors. Thus Bismarck's startling victories over Austria in 1866 and over France in 1870 quickly led the major continental powers (and Japan) to imitate the Prussian military staff system, and the failure of Britain and the United States to follow the pattern simply indicated that they were outside the immediate arena of competition. Contending states imitate the military innovations contrived by the country of greatest capability and ingenuity. And so the weapons of major contenders, and even their strategies, begin to look much the same all over the world. Thus at the turn of the century Admiral Alfred von Tirpitz argued successfully for building a battleship fleet on the grounds that Germany could challenge Britain at sea only with a naval doctrine and weapons similar to hers.[22]

The effects of competition are not confined narrowly to the military realm. Socialization to the system should also occur. Does it? Again, because we can almost always find confirming examples if we look hard, we try to find cases that are unlikely to lend credence to the theory. One should look for instances of states conforming to common international practices even though for internal reasons they would prefer not to. The behavior of the Soviet Union in its early years is one such instance. The Bolsheviks in the early years of their power preached international revolution and flouted the conventions of diplomacy. They were saying, in effect, "we will not be socialized to this system." The attitude was well expressed by Trotsky, who, when asked what he would do as foreign minister, replied, "I will issue some revolutionary proclamations to the peoples and then close up the joint."[23] In a competitive arena, however, one party may need the assistance of others. Refusal to play the political game may risk one's own destruction. The pressures of competition were rapidly felt and reflected in the Soviet Union's diplomacy. Thus Lenin, sending foreign minister Chicherin to the Genoa Conference of 1922, bade him farewell with this caution: "Avoid big words."[24] Chicherin, who personified the carefully tailored traditional diplomat rather than the simply uniformed revolutionary, was to refrain from inflammatory rhetoric for the sake of working deals. These he successfully completed with that other pariah power and ideological enemy, Germany.

The close juxtaposition of states promotes their sameness through the disadvantages that arise from a failure to conform to successful practices. It is this sameness, an effect of the system, that is so often attributed to the acceptance of so-called rules of state behavior. Chiliastic rulers occasionally come to power. In power, most of them quickly change their ways. They can refuse to do so and yet hope to survive only if they rule countries little affected by the competition of states. The socialization of nonconformist states proceeds at a pace that is set by the extent of their involvement in the system. And that is another testable statement.

The theory leads to many expectations about behaviors and outcomes. From the theory one predicts that states will engage in balancing behavior whether or not balanced power is the end of their acts. From the theory one predicts a strong tendency toward balance in the system. The expectation is not that a balance, once achieved, will be maintained, but that a balance, once disrupted, will be restored in one way or another. Balances of power recurrently form. Since the theory depicts international politics as a competitive system, one predicts more specifically that states will display characteristics common to competitors: namely, that they will imitate each other and become socialized to their system. . . .

NOTES

1. E. Durkheim, *The Division of Labor in Society* (New York: Free Press, 1964).
2. W. Fellner, *Competition among the Few* (New York: Knopf), pp. 35, 132, 177, 199, 217–18.
3. A. Kahn, "The tyranny of small decisions: market failures, imperfections, and the limits of econometrics." In Bruce M. Russett (ed.), *Economic Theories of International Relations* (Chicago: Markham, 1968), p. 523.
4. R. W. Sterling, *Macropolitics: International Relations in a Global Society* (New York: Knopf), p. 336.
5. P. Diesing, *Reason in Society* (Urbana: University of Illinois Press, 1962), pp. 198–204. A. Downs, *Inside Bureaucracy* (Boston: Little, Brown, 1967), pp. 262–70.
6. M. Djilas, *Conversations with Stalin* (New York: Harcourt, Brace and World, 1962), p. 50.

7. C. Barnard, "On planning for world government," in Barnard (ed.), *Organization and Management* (Cambridge: Harvard University Press, 1948), pp. 148–52. M. Polanyi, "The growth of thought in society," *Economica,* vol. 8, 1941, pp. 428–56.

8. C. Barnard, "On planning for world government," in Barnard (ed.), *Organization and Management* (Cambridge: Harvard University Press, 1948), pp. 150–51.

9. Quoted in C. Johnson, *Revolutionary Change* (Boston: Little, Brown, 1966), p. 13.

10. E. R. Livernash, "The relation of power to the structure and process of collective bargaining," in Bruce M. Russett (ed.), *Economic Theories of International Politics* (Chicago: Markham, 1968), p. 430.

11. E. Haas, "The balance of power: prescription, concept, or propaganda?" *World Politics,* vol. 5, 1953. M. Wight, "The balance of power," in H. Butterfield and Martin Wight (eds.), *Diplomatic Investigations: Essays in the Theory of International Politics* (London: Allen and Unwin, 1966). H. Morgenthau, *Politics Among Nations,* 5th ed. (New York: Knopf, 1953).

12. A. F. K. Organski, *World Politics,* 2nd ed. (New York: Knopf, 1968), p. 292.

13. D. Hume, "Of the balance of power," in Charles W. Hendel (ed.), *David Hume's Political Essays* (Indianapolis: Bobbs-Merrill, 1953), pp. 142–44.

14. H. Morgenthau, *Politics Among Nations,* 5th ed. (New York: Knopf, 1973), pp. 167–74, 202–207, 219–20.

15. S. F. Nadel, *The Theory of Social Structure* (Glencoe, Ill.: Free Press, 1957), p. 148. E. Durkheim, *The Division of Labor in Society* (New York: Free Press, 1964), pp. 386, 418. M. Shubik, *Strategy and Market Structure* (New York: Wiley, 1959), pp. 11, 32.

16. H. Morgenthau, *Truth and Power* (New York: Praeger, 1970), pp. 253–58.

17. G. T. Allison, *Essence of Decision* (Boston: Little, Brown, 1971), and Morton Halperin, "Bureaucratic politics: a paradigm and some policy implications," *World Politics,* vol. 24, 1972.

18. K. Popper, *The Logic of Scientific Discovery* (New York: Basic Books, 1959), Chapter 1.

19. E. E. Harris, *Hypothesis and Perception* (London: Allen and Unwin, 1970).

20. Thucydides, *History of the Peloponnesian War* (New York: Modern Library, Random House, 1951), Book 5, Chapter 17.

21. W. Jaeger, *Paideia: The Ideals of Greek Culture,* vol. 1 (New York: Oxford University Press), 1939.

22. R. J. Art, "The influence of foreign policy on seapower: new weapons and Weltpolitik in Wilhelminian Germany," *Sage Professional Paper in International Studies,* vol. 2. (Beverly Hills: Sage Publications, 1973), p. 16.

23. T. H. Von Laue, "Soviet Diplomacy: G. V. Chicherin, People's Commissar for Foreign Affairs 1918–1930." In Gordon A. Craig and Felix Gilbert (eds.), *The Diplomats, 1919–1939,* vol. 1 (New York: Atheneum, 1963), p. 235.

24. B. Moore, Jr., *Soviet Politics: The Dilemma of Power* (Cambridge: Harvard University Press, 1950), p. 204.

ॐ

The American Conception
of National Security
and the Beginnings of
the Cold War, 1945–1948*

Melvyn P. Leffler

In an interview with Henry Kissinger in 1978 on "The Lessons of the Past," Walter Laqueur observed that during World War II "few if any people thought . . . of the structure of peace that would follow the war except perhaps in the most general terms of friendship, mutual trust, and the other noble sentiments mentioned in wartime programmatic speeches about the United Nations and related topics." Kissinger concurred, noting that no statesman, except perhaps Winston Churchill, "gave any attention to what would happen after the war." Americans, Kissinger stressed, "were determined that we were going to base the postwar period on good faith and getting along with everybody."[1]

That two such astute and knowledgeable observers of international politics were so uninformed about American planning at the end of the Second World War is testimony to the enduring mythology of American idealism and innocence in the world of Realpolitik. It also reflects the state of scholarship on the interrelated areas of strategy, economy, and diplomacy. Despite the publication of several excellent overviews of the origins of the Cold War, despite the outpouring of incisive monographs on American foreign policy in many areas of the world, and despite some first-rate studies on the evolution of strategic thinking and the defense establishment, no comprehensive account yet exists of how American defense officials defined national security interests in the aftermath of World War II. Until recently, the absence of such a study was understandable, for scholars had limited access to records pertaining to national security, strategic thinking, and war planning. But in recent years documents relating to the early years of the Cold War have been declassified in massive numbers.

This documentation now makes it possible to analyze in greater depth the perceptions, apprehensions, and objectives of those defense officials most concerned

---

*The extensive footnotes of the original article have been heavily redacted in this reprint. Interested readers should consult the original publication for the excellent detailed literature review and original research that Professor Leffler provides there.

Melvyn P. Leffler, "The American Conception of National Security and the Beginnings of the Cold War, 1945–48," *American Historical Review*, Vol. 89, no. 2 (April 1984) pp. 346–381. © 1984 American Historical Association. Reprinted by permission.

with defining and defending the nation's security and strategic interests.[2] This essay seeks neither to explain the process of decision making on any particular issue nor to dissect the domestic political considerations and fiscal constraints that narrowed the options available to policy makers. Furthermore, it does not pretend to discern the motivations and objectives of the Soviet Union. Rather, the goal here is to elucidate the fundamental strategic and economic considerations that shaped the definition of American national security interests in the postwar world. Several of these considerations—especially as they related to overseas bases, air transit rights, and a strategic sphere of influence in Latin America—initially were the logical result of technological developments and geostrategic experiences rather than directly related to postwar Soviet behavior. But American defense officials also considered the preservation of a favorable balance of power in Eurasia as fundamental to U.S. national security. This objective impelled defense analysts and intelligence officers to appraise and reappraise the intentions and capabilities of the Soviet Union. Rather modest estimates of the Soviets' ability to wage war against the United States generated the widespread assumption that the Soviets would refrain from military aggression and seek to avoid war. Nevertheless, American defense officials remained greatly preoccupied with the geopolitical balance of power in Europe and Asia, because that balance seemed endangered by communist exploitation of postwar economic dislocation and social and political unrest. Indeed, American assessments of the Soviet threat were less a consequence of expanding Soviet military capabilities and of Soviet diplomatic demands than a result of growing apprehension about the vulnerability of American strategic and economic interests in a world of unprecedented turmoil and upheaval. Viewed from this perspective, the Cold War assumed many of its most enduring characteristics during 1947–48, when American officials sought to cope with an array of challenges by implementing their own concepts of national security.

AMERICAN OFFICIALS FIRST BEGAN to think seriously about the nation's postwar security during 1943–44. Military planners devised elaborate plans for an overseas base system. Many of these plans explicitly contemplated the breakdown of the wartime coalition. But, even when strategic planners postulated good postwar relations among the Allies, their plans called for an extensive system of bases. These bases were defined as the nation's strategic frontier. Beyond this frontier the United States would be able to use force to counter any threats or frustrate any overt acts of aggression. Within the strategic frontier, American military predominance had to remain inviolate. Although plans for an overseas base system went through many revisions, they always presupposed American hegemony over the Atlantic and Pacific oceans. These plans received President Franklin D. Roosevelt's endorsement in early 1944. After his death, army and navy planners presented their views to President Harry S. Truman, and Army Chief of Staff George C. Marshall discussed them extensively with Secretary of State James C. Byrnes.

Two strategic considerations influenced the development of an overseas base system. The first was the need for defense in depth. Since attacks against the United States could only emanate from Europe and Asia, the Joint Chiefs of Staff concluded as early as November 1943 that the United States must encircle the

Western Hemisphere with a defensive ring of outlying bases. In the Pacific this ring had to include the Aleutians, the Philippines, Okinawa, and the former Japanese mandates. Recognizing the magnitude of this strategic frontier, Admiral William E. Leahy, chief of staff to the president, explained to Truman that the joint chiefs were not thinking of the immediate future when, admittedly, no prospective naval power could challenge American predominance in the Pacific. Instead, they were contemplating the long term, when the United States might require wartime access to the resources of southeast Asia as well as "a firm line of communications from the West Coast to the Asiatic mainland, plus denial of this line in time of war to any potential enemy."[3] In the Atlantic, strategic planners maintained that their minimum requirements included a West African zone, with primary bases in the Azores or Canary Islands. Leahy went even further, insisting on primary bases in West Africa itself—for example, at Dakar or Casablanca. The object of these defensive bases was to enable the United States to possess complete control of the Atlantic and Pacific oceans and keep hostile powers far from American territory.[4]

Defense in depth was especially important in light of the Pearl Harbor experience, the advance of technology, and the development of the atomic bomb. According to the Joint Chiefs of Staff, "Experience in the recent war demonstrated conclusively that the defense of a nation, if it is to be effective, must begin beyond its frontiers. The advent of the atomic bomb reemphasizes this requirement. The farther away from our own vital areas we can hold our enemy through the possession of advanced bases . . . , the greater are our chances of surviving successfully an attack by atomic weapons and of destroying the enemy which employs them against us." Believing that atomic weapons would increase the incentive to aggression by enhancing the advantage of surprise, military planners never ceased to extol the utility of forward bases from which American aircraft could seek to intercept attacks against the United States.[5]

The second strategic consideration that influenced the plan for a comprehensive overseas base system was the need to project American power quickly and effectively against any potential adversary. In conducting an overall examination of requirements for base rights in September 1945, the Joint War Plans Committee stressed that World War II demonstrated the futility of a strategy of static defense. The United States had to be able to take "timely" offensive action against the adversary's capacity and will to wage war. New weapons demanded that advance bases be established in "areas well removed from the United States, so as to project our operations, with new weapons or otherwise, nearer the enemy." Scientists, like Vannevar Bush, argued that, "regardless of the potentialities of these new weapons [atomic energy and guided missiles], they should not influence the number, location, or extent of strategic bases now considered essential." The basic strategic concept underlying all American war plans called for an air offensive against a prospective enemy from overseas bases. Delays in the development of the B-36, the first intercontinental bomber, only accentuated the need for these bases.

In October 1945 the civilian leaders of the War and Navy departments carefully reviewed the emerging strategic concepts and base requirements of the military planners. Secretary of the Navy James Forrestal and Secretary of War Robert P. Patterson discussed them with Admiral Leahy, the Joint Chiefs of Staff, and Secretary of State Byrnes. The civilian secretaries fully endorsed the concept of a far-flung system of bases in the Atlantic and Pacific oceans that would enhance the offensive capabilities of the United States. Having expended so much blood and effort capturing Japanese-held islands, defense officials, like Forrestal, naturally wished to devise a base system in the Pacific to facilitate the projection of American influence and power. The Philippines were the key to southeast Asia, Okinawa to the Yellow Sea, the Sea of Japan, and the industrial heartland of northeast Asia. From these bases on America's "strategic frontier," the United States could preserve its access to vital raw materials in Asia, deny these resources to a prospective enemy, help preserve peace and stability in troubled areas, safeguard critical sea lanes, and, if necessary, conduct an air offensive against the industrial infrastructure of any Asiatic power, including the Soviet Union.

Control of the Atlantic and Pacific oceans through overseas bases was considered indispensable to the nation's security regardless of what might happen to the wartime coalition. So was control over polar air routes. Admiral Leahy criticized a Joint Strategic Survey Committee report of early 1943 that omitted Iceland and Greenland as primary base requirements. When General S. D. Embick, the senior member of that committee, continued to question the desirability of a base in Iceland, lest it antagonize the Russians, he was overruled by Assistant Secretary of War John McCloy. McCloy charged that Embick had "a rather restricted concept of what is necessary for national defense." The first postwar base system approved by both the Joint Chiefs of Staff and the civilian secretaries in October 1945 included Iceland as a primary base area. The Joint War Plans Committee explained that American bases must control the air in the Arctic, prevent the establishment of enemy military facilities there, and support America's own striking forces. Once Soviet-American relations began to deteriorate, Greenland also was designated as a primary base for American heavy bombers and fighters because of its close proximity to the industrial heartland of the potential enemy. As the United States sought rights for bases along the Polar route in 1946 and 1947, moreover, American defense officials also hoped to thwart Soviet efforts to acquire similar rights at Spitzbergen and Bear Island.

In the immediate postwar years American ambitions for an elaborate base system encountered many problems. Budgetary constraints compelled military planners to drop plans for many secondary and subsidiary bases, particularly in the South Pacific and Caribbean. These sacrifices merely increased the importance of those bases that lay closer to a potential adversary. By early 1948, the joint chiefs were willing to forego base rights in such places as Surinam, Curacoa-Aruba, Cayenne, Nounea, and Vivi-Levu if "joint" or "participating" rights could be acquired or preserved in Karachi, Tripoli, Algiers, Casablanca, Dharan, and Monrovia. Budgetary constraints, then, limited the depth of the base system but not the breadth of American ambitions. Furthermore, the governments of Panama, Iceland, Denmark, Portugal, France, and Saudi Arabia often rejected or abolished the exclusive rights the United States wanted and sometimes limited the number of American personnel on such bases. Washington, therefore, negotiated a variety of arrangements to meet the objections of host governments. By early 1948, for example, the base in Iceland was operated by a civilian company under contract to the United States Air Force; in the Azores, the base was manned by a detachment of Portuguese military personnel operating under the Portuguese flag, but an air force detachment serviced the American aircraft using the base. In Port Lyautey, the base was under the command of the French navy, but under a secret agreement an American naval team took care of American aircraft on the base. In Saudi Arabia, the Dharan air strip was cared for by 300 U.S. personnel and was capable of handling B–29s. Because these arrangements were not altogether satisfactory, in mid–1948 Secretary of Defense Forrestal and Secretary of the Army Kenneth Royall advocated using American economic and military assistance as levers to acquire more permanent and comprehensive base rights, particularly in Greenland and North Africa.

Less well known than the American effort to establish a base system, but integral to the policymakers' conception of national security, was the attempt to secure military air transit and landing rights. Military planners wanted such rights at critical locations not only in the Western Hemisphere but also in North Africa, the Middle East, India, and southeast Asia. To this end they delineated a route from Casablanca through Algiers, Tripoli, Cairo, Dharan, Karachi, Delhi, Calcutta, Rangoon, Bangkok, and Saigon to Manila. In closing out the African–Middle East theater at the conclusion of the war, General H. W. Aurand, under explicit instructions from the secretary of war, made preparations for permanent rights at seven airfields in North Africa and Saudi Arabia. According to a study by the Joint Chiefs of Staff, "Military air transit rights for the United States along the North African–Indian route were most desirable in order to provide access to and familiarity with bases from which offensive and defensive action might be conducted in the event of a major war, and to provide an alternate route to China and to United States Far Eastern bases." In other words, such rights would permit the rapid augmentation of American bases in wartime as well as the rapid movement of American air units from the eastern to the western flank of the U.S. base system. In order to maintain these airfields in a state of readiness, the United States would have to rely on private airlines, which had to be persuaded to locate their operations in areas designated essential to military air transit rights. In this way, airports "in being" outside the formal American base system would be available for military operations in times of crisis and war. Assistant Secretary McCloy informed the State Department at the beginning of 1945 that a "strong United States air transport system, international in scope and readily adapted to military use, is vital to our air power and future national security." Even earlier, the joint chiefs had agreed not to include South American air bases in their strategic plans so long as it was understood that commercial fields in that region would be developed with a view to subsequent military use.[6]

In Latin America, American requirements for effective national security went far beyond air transit rights. In a report written in January 1945 at Assistant Secretary McCloy's behest, the War Department urged American collaboration with Latin American armed forces to insure the defense of the Panama Canal and the Western Hemisphere. Six areas within Latin America were considered of special significance either for strategic reasons or for their raw materials: the Panama Canal and approaches within one thousand miles; the Straits of Magellan; northeast Brazil; Mexico; the river Plate estuary and approaches within five hundred miles; and Mollendo, Peru-Antofagusta, and Chile. These areas were so "important," Secretary of War Patterson explained to Secretary of State Marshall in early 1947, "that the threat of attack on any of them would force the United States to come to their defense, even though it were not certain that attack on the United States itself would follow." The resources of these areas were essential to the United States, because "it is imperative that our war potential be enhanced . . . during any national emergency."[7]

While paying lip service to the United Nations and worrying about the impact of regional agreements in the Western Hemisphere on Soviet actions and American influence in Europe, the Joint Chiefs of Staff insisted that in practice non-American forces had to be kept out of the Western Hemisphere and the Monroe Doctrine had to be kept inviolate. "The Western Hemisphere is a distinct military entity, the integrity of which is a fundamental postulate of our security in the event of another world war."[8] Developments in aviation, rockets, guided missiles, and atomic energy had made "the solidarity of the Hemisphere and its united support of the principles of the Monroe Doctrine" more important than before. Patterson told Marshall that effective implementation of the Monroe Doctrine now meant "that we not only refuse to tolerate foreign colonization, control, or the extension of a foreign political system to our hemisphere, but we take alarm from the appearance on the continent of foreign ideologies, commercial exploitation, cartel arrangements, or other symptoms of increased non-hemispheric influence. . . . The basic consideration has always been an overriding apprehension lest a base be established in this area by a potentially hostile foreign power." The United States, Patterson insisted, must have "a stable, secure, and friendly flank to the South, not confused by enemy penetration, political, economic, or military."[9]

The need to predominate throughout the Western Hemisphere was not a result of deteriorating Soviet-American relations but a natural evolution of the Monroe Doctrine, accentuated by Axis aggression and new technological imperatives.[10] Patterson, Forrestal, and Army Chief of Staff Dwight D. Eisenhower initially were impelled less by reports of Soviet espionage, propaganda, and infiltration in Latin America than by accounts of British efforts to sell cruisers and aircraft to Chile and Ecuador; Swedish sales of anti-aircraft artillery to Argentina; and French offers to build cruisers and destroyers for both Argentina and Brazil. To foreclose all foreign influence and to insure United States strategic hegemony, military officers and the civilian secretaries of the War and Navy departments argued for an extensive system of United States bases, expansion of commercial airline facilities throughout Latin America, negotiation of a regional defense pact, curtailment of all foreign military aid and foreign military sales, training of Latin American military officers in the United States, outfitting of Latin American armies with U.S. military equipment, and implementation of a comprehensive military assistance program.[11]

The military assistance program, as embodied in the Inter-American Military Cooperation Act, generated the most interagency discord. Latin American experts in the State Department maintained that military assistance would stimulate regional conflicts, dissipate Latin American financial resources, and divert attention from economic and social issues. Before leaving office, Byrnes forcefully presented the State Department position to Forrestal and Patterson. Instead of dwelling on the consequences of military assistance for Latin America, Byrnes maintained that such a program would be too costly for the United States, would focus attention on a region where American interests were relatively unchallenged, and would undermine more important American initiatives elsewhere on the globe. "Greece and Turkey are our outposts," he declared.[12]

The secretary of state clearly did not think that Congress would authorize funds for Latin America as well as for Greece and Turkey. Although Truman favored military assistance to Latin America, competing demands for American resources in 1947 and 1948 forced both military planners and U.S. senators to give priority to Western Europe and the Near East. In June 1948 the Inter-American Military Cooperation Act died in the Senate. But this signified no diminution in American national security imperatives; indeed, it underscored Byrnes's statement of December 1946 that the "outposts" of the nation's security lay in the heart of Eurasia.[13]

FROM THE CLOSING DAYS OF WORLD WAR II, American defense officials believed that they could not allow any prospective adversary to control the Eurasian land mass. This was the lesson taught by two world wars. Strategic thinkers and military analysts insisted that any power or powers attempting to dominate Eurasia must be regarded as potentially hostile to the United States. Their acute awareness of the importance of Eurasia made Marshall, Thomas Handy, George A. Lincoln, and other officers wary of the expansion of Soviet influence there. Cognizant of the growth in Soviet strength, General John Deane, head of the United States military mission in Moscow, urged a tougher stand against Soviet demands even before World War II had ended. While acknowledging that the increase in Soviet power stemmed primarily from the defeat of Germany and Japan, postwar assessments of the Joint Chiefs of Staff emphasized the importance of deterring further Soviet aggrandizement in Eurasia. Concern over the consequences of Russian domination of Eurasia helps explain why in July 1945 the joint chiefs decided to oppose a Soviet request for bases in the Dardanelles; why during March and April 1946 they supported a firm stand against Russia in Iran, Turkey, and Tripolitania; and why in the summer of 1946 Clark Clifford and George Elsey, two White House aides, argued that Soviet incorporation of any parts of Western Europe, the Middle East, China, or Japan into a communist orbit was incompatible with American national security.

Yet defense officials were not eager to sever the wartime coalition. In early 1944 Admiral Leahy noted the "phenomenal development" of Soviet power but still hoped for Soviet-American cooperation. When members of the Joint Postwar Committee met with their colleagues on the Joint Planning Staff in April 1945, Major General G. V. Strong argued against using U.S. installations in Alaska for staging expeditionary forces, lest such a move exacerbate Russo-American relations. A few months later Eisenhower, Lincoln, and other officers advised against creating a central economic authority for Western Europe that might appear to be an anti-Soviet bloc.[14] The American objective, after all, was to avoid Soviet hegemony over Eurasia. By aggravating Soviet fears, the United States might foster what it wished to avoid. American self-restraint, however, might be reciprocated by the Soviets, providing time for Western Europe to recover and for the British to reassert some influence on the Continent.[15] Therefore, many defense officials in 1945 hoped to avoid an open rift with the Soviet Union. But at the same time they were determined to prevent the Eurasian land mass from falling under Soviet and communist influence.

Studies by the Joint Chiefs of Staff stressed that, if Eurasia came under Soviet domination, either through military conquest or political and economic "assimilation," America's only potential adversary would fall heir to enormous natural resources, industrial potential, and manpower. By the autumn of 1945, military planners already were worrying that Soviet control over much of Eastern Europe and its raw materials would abet Russia's economic recovery, enhance its war-making capacity, and deny important foodstuffs, oil, and minerals to Western Europe. By the early months of 1946, Secretary Patterson and his subordinates in the War Department believed that Soviet control of the Ruhr-Rhineland industrial complex would constitute an extreme threat. Even more dangerous was the prospect of Soviet predominance over the rest of Western Europe, especially France. Strategically, this would undermine the impact of any prospective American naval blockade and would allow Soviet military planners to achieve defense in depth. The latter possibility had enormous military significance, because American war plans relied so heavily on air power and strategic bombing, the efficacy of which might be reduced substantially if the Soviets acquired outlying bases in Western Europe and the Middle East or if they "neutralized" bases in Great Britain.[16]

Economic considerations also made defense officials determined to retain American access to Eurasia as well as to deny Soviet predominance over it. Stimson, Patterson, McCloy, and Assistant Secretary Howard C. Peterson agreed with Forrestal that long-term American prosperity required open markets, unhindered access to raw materials, and the rehabilitation of much—if not all—of Eurasia along liberal capitalist lines. In late 1944 and 1945, Stimson protested the prospective industrial emasculation of Germany, lest it undermine American economic well being, set back recovery throughout Europe, and unleash forces of anarchy and revolution. Stimson and his subordinates in the Operations Division of the army also worried that the spread of Soviet power in northeast Asia would constrain the functioning of the free enterprise system and jeopardize American economic interests. A report prepared by the staff of the Moscow embassy and revised in mid-1946 by Ambassador (and former General) Walter Bedell Smith emphasized that "Soviet power is by nature so jealous that it has already operated to segregate from world economy almost all of the areas in which it has been established." While Forrestal and the navy sought to contain Soviet influence in the Near East and to retain American access to Middle East oil, Patterson and the War Department focused on preventing famine in occupied areas, forestalling communist revolution, circumscribing Soviet influence, resuscitating trade, and preserving traditional American markets especially in Western Europe. But American economic interests in Eurasia were not limited to Western Europe, Germany, and the Middle East. Military planners and intelligence officers in both the army and navy expressed considerable interest in the raw materials of southeast Asia, and, as already shown, one of the purposes of the bases they wanted was to maintain access to those resources and deny them to a prospective enemy.[17]

While civilian officials and military strategists feared the loss of Eurasia, they did not expect the Soviet Union to attempt its military conquest. In the early Cold War years, there was nearly universal agreement that the Soviets, while eager to expand their influence, desired to avoid a military engagement. In October 1945, for example, the Joint Intelligence Staff predicted that the Soviet Union would seek to avoid war for five to ten years. In April 1946, while Soviet troops still remained in Iran, General Lincoln, the army's principal war planner, concurred with Byrnes's view that the Soviets did not want war. In May, when there was deep concern about a possible communist uprising in France, military intelligence doubted the Kremlin would instigate a coup, lest it ignite a full scale war. At a high-level meeting at the White House in June, Eisenhower stated that he did not think the Soviets wanted war; only Forrestal dissented. In August, when the Soviet note to Turkey on the Dardanelles provoked consternation in American policy-making circles, General Hoyt Vandenberg, director of central intelligence, informed President Truman that there were no signs of unusual Soviet troop movements or supply build-ups. In March 1947, while the Truman Doctrine was being discussed in Congress, the director of army intelligence maintained that the factors operating to discourage Soviet aggression continued to be decisive. In September 1947, the CIA concluded that the Soviets would not seek to conquer Western Europe for several reasons: they would recognize their inability to control hostile populations; they would fear triggering a war with the United States that could not be won; and they would prefer to gain hegemony by political and economic means. In October 1947, the Joint Intelligence Staff maintained that for three years at least the Soviet Union would take no action that would precipitate a military conflict.

Even the ominous developments during the first half of 1948 did not alter these assessments. Despite his alarmist cable of March 5, designed to galvanize congressional support for increased defense expenditures, General Lucius Clay, the American military governor in Germany, did not believe war imminent. A few days later, the CIA concluded that the communist takeover in Czechoslovakia would not increase Soviet capabilities significantly and reflected no alteration in Soviet tactics. On March 16, the CIA reported to the president, "The weight of logic, as well as evidence, also leads to the conclusion that the Soviets will not resort to military force within the next sixty days." While this assessment was far from reassuring, army and navy intelligence experts concurred that the Soviets still wanted to avoid war; the question was whether war would erupt as a result of "miscalculation" by either the United States or Russia. After talking to Foreign Minister V. M. Molotov in June, Ambassador Smith concluded that Soviet leaders would not resort to active hostilities. During the Berlin blockade, army intelligence reported few signs of Soviet preparations for war; naval intelligence maintained that the Soviets desired to avoid war yet consolidate their position in East Germany. In October 1948, the Military Intelligence Division of the army endorsed a British appraisal that "all the evidence available indicates that the

Soviet Union is not preparing to go to war in the near future." In December Acting Secretary of State Robert Lovett summed up the longstanding American perspective when he emphasized that he saw "no evidence that Soviet intentions run toward launching a sudden military attack on the western nations at this time. It would not be in character with the tradition or mentality of the Soviet leaders to resort to such a measure unless they felt themselves either politically extremely weak, or militarily extremely strong."

Although American defense officials recognized that the Soviets had substantial military assets, they remained confident that the Soviet Union did not feel extremely strong. Military analysts studying Russian capabilities noted that the Soviets were rapidly mechanizing infantry units and enhancing their firepower and mobility. It was estimated during the winter of 1946–47 that the Soviets could mobilize six million troops in thirty days and twelve million in six months, providing sufficient manpower to overrun all important parts of Eurasia. The Soviets were also believed to be utilizing German scientists and German technological know-how to improve their submarine force, develop rockets and missiles, and acquire knowledge about the atomic bomb. During 1947 and 1948, it was reported as well that the Soviets were making rapid progress in the development of high performance jet fighters and already possessed several hundred intermediate range bombers comparable to the American B-29.

Even so, American military analysts were most impressed with Soviet weaknesses and vulnerabilities. The Soviets had no long-range strategic air force, no atomic bomb, and meager air defenses. Moreover, the Soviet navy was considered ineffective except for its submarine forces. The Joint Logistic Plans Committee and the Military Intelligence Division of the War Department estimated that the Soviet Union would require approximately fifteen years to overcome wartime losses in manpower and industry, ten years to redress the shortage of technicians, five to ten years to develop a strategic air force, fifteen to twenty-five years to construct a modern navy, ten years to refurbish military transport, ten years (or less) to quell resistance in occupied areas, fifteen to twenty years to establish a military infrastructure in the Far East, three to ten years to acquire the atomic bomb, and an unspecified number of years to remove the vulnerability of the Soviet rail-net and petroleum industry to long-range bombing.[18] For several years at least, the Soviet capability for sustained attack against North America would be very limited. In January 1946 the Joint Intelligence Staff concluded that "the offensive capabilities of the United States are manifestly superior to those of the U.S.S.R. and any war between the U.S. and the U.S.S.R. would be far more costly to the Soviet Union than to the United States."[19]

Key American officials like Lovett, Clifford, Eisenhower, Bedell Smith and Budget Director James Webb were cognizant of prevailing Soviet weaknesses and potential American strength. Despite Soviet superiority in manpower, General Eisenhower and Admiral Forrest E. Sherman doubted that Russia could mount a surprise attack, and General Lincoln, Admiral Cato Glover, and Secretaries Patterson and Forrestal believed that Soviet forces would encounter acute logistical problems in trying to overrun Eurasia—especially in the Near East, Spain, and Italy. Even Forrestal doubted reports of accelerating Soviet air capabilities.

American experts believed that most Soviet planes were obsolescent, that the Soviets had insufficient airfields and aviation gas to use their new planes, and that these planes had serious problems in their instrumentation and construction.

In general, improvements in specific areas of the Soviet military establishment did not mean that overall Soviet capabilities were improving at an alarming rate. In July 1947, the Military Intelligence Division concluded, "While there has been a slight overall improvement in the Soviet war potential, Soviet strength for total war is not sufficiently great to make a military attack against the United States anything but a most hazardous gamble." This view prevailed in 1946 and 1947, even though the American nuclear arsenal was extremely small and the American strategic bombing force of limited size. In the spring of 1948 the Joint Intelligence Committee at the American embassy in Moscow explained why the United States ultimately would emerge victorious should a war erupt in the immediate future. The Soviets could not win because of their "inability to carry the war to U.S. territory. After the occupation of Europe, the U.S.S.R. would be forced to assume the defensive and await attacks by U.S. forces which should succeed primarily because of the ability of the U.S. to outproduce the U.S.S.R. in materials of war."[20]

Awareness of Soviet economic shortcomings played a key role in the American interpretation of Soviet capabilities. Intelligence reports predicted that Soviet leaders would invest a disproportionate share of Russian resources in capital goods industries. But, even if such Herculean efforts enjoyed some success, the Soviets still would not reach the pre–World War II levels of the United States within fifteen to twenty years. Technologically, the Soviets were behind in the critical areas of aircraft manufacturing, electronics, and oil refining. And, despite Russia's concerted attempts to catch up and to surpass the United States, American intelligence experts soon started reporting that Soviet reconstruction was lagging behind Soviet ambitions, especially in the electronics, transportation, aircraft, construction machinery, nonferrous metals, and shipping industries. Accordingly, throughout the years 1945–48 American military analysts and intelligence experts believed that Soviet transportation bottlenecks, industrial shortcomings, technological backwardness, and agricultural problems would discourage military adventurism.

IF AMERICAN DEFENSE OFFICIALS DID NOT EXPECT a Soviet military attack, why, then, were they so fearful of losing control of Eurasia? The answer rests less in American assessments of Soviet military capabilities and short-term military intentions than in appraisals of economic and political conditions throughout Europe and Asia. Army officials in particular, because of their occupation roles in Germany, Japan, Austria, and Korea, were aware of the postwar plight of these areas. Key military men—Generals Clay, Douglas MacArthur, John Hilldring, and Oliver P. Echols and Colonel Charles H. Bonesteel—became alarmed by the prospects of famine, disease, anarchy, and revolution. They recognized that communist parties could exploit the distress and that the Russians could capitalize upon it to spread Soviet influence. As early as June 1945, Rear Admiral Ellery Stone, the American commissioner in Italy, wrote that wartime devastation had created fertile soil for the growth of communism in Italy and the enlargement of the Soviet sphere. MacArthur also feared that, if the Japanese economy remained emasculated and reforms were not undertaken, communism would spread. Clay, too, was acutely aware that German communists were depicting themselves and their beliefs as their country's only hope of salvation. In the spring of 1946 military planners, working on contingency plans for the emergency withdrawal of American troops from Germany, should war with Russia unexpectedly occur, also took note of the economic turmoil and political instability in neighboring countries, especially France. Sensitivity to the geopolitical dimensions of the socioeconomic crisis of the postwar era impelled Chief of Staff Eisenhower to give high priority in the army budget to assistance for occupied areas.

Civilian officials in the War, Navy, and State departments shared these concerns. In the autumn of 1945, McCloy warned Patterson that the stakes in Germany were immense and economic recovery had to be expedited. During the first half of 1946 Secretary Patterson and Assistant Secretary Peterson continually pressed the State Department to tackle the problems beleaguering occupation authorities in Germany and pleaded for State Department support and assistance in getting the Truman administration to provide additional relief to the devastated areas of Europe. On Peterson's urging, Acheson wrote Truman in April 1946, "We have now reached the most critical period of the world food crisis. We must either immediately greatly increase the exports of grain from the United States or expect general disorder and political upheaval to develop in [most of Eurasia]."[21] Forrestal had already pressed for a reassessment of occupation policies in Germany and Japan. In May, Clay suspended reparation payments in order to effect an accord on German economic unity. In June, Patterson began to support the merger of the American and British zones. The man most responsible for this latter undertaking was William Draper, Forrestal's former partner in Dillon, Read, and Co., and Clay's chief economic assistant. Draper firmly believed that "economic collapse in either [France or Germany] with probable political break-down and rise of communism would seriously threaten American objectives in Europe and in the world."[22]

American defense officials, military analysts, and intelligence officers were extremely sensitive to the political ferment, social turmoil, and economic upheaval throughout postwar Europe and Asia. In their initial postwar studies, the Joint Chiefs of Staff carefully noted the multiplicity of problems that could breed conflict and provide opportunities for Soviet expansion. In the spring of 1946 army planners, including General Lincoln, were keenly aware that conflict was most likely to arise from local disputes (for example, in Venezia-Giulia) or from indigenous unrest (for example, in France), perhaps even against the will of Moscow. A key War Department document submitted to the State-War-Navy Coordinating Committee in April 1946 skirted the issue of Soviet military capabilities and argued that the Soviet Union's strength emanated from totalitarian control over its satellites, from local communist parties, and from worldwide chaotic political and economic conditions. In October 1946 the Joint Planning Staff stressed that for the next ten years the major factor influencing world political developments would be the East-West ideological conflict taking place in an impoverished and strife-torn Europe and a vacuum of indigenous power in Asia. "The greatest danger to the security of the United States," the CIA concluded in mid-1947, "is the possibility of economic collapse in Western Europe and the consequent accession to power of Communist elements."[23]

In brief, during 1946 and 1947, defense officials witnessed a dramatic unravelling of the geopolitical foundations and socioeconomic structure of international affairs. Britain's economic weakness and withdrawal from the eastern Mediterranean, India's independence movement, civil war in China, nationalist insurgencies in Indo-China and the Dutch East Indies, Zionist claims to Palestine and Arab resentment, German and Japanese economic paralysis, communist inroads in France and Italy—all were ominous developments. Defense officials recognized that the Soviet Union had not created these circumstances but believed that Soviet leaders would exploit them. Should communists take power, even without direct Russian intervention, the Soviet Union, it was assumed, would gain predominant control of the resources of these areas because of the postulated subservience of communist parties everywhere to the Kremlin. Should nationalist uprisings persist, communists seize power in underdeveloped countries, and Arabs revolt against American support of a Jewish state, the petroleum and raw materials of critical areas might be denied the West. The imminent possibility existed that, even without Soviet military aggression, the resources of Eurasia could fall under Russian control. With these resources, the Soviet Union would be able to overcome its chronic economic weaknesses, achieve defense in depth, and challenge American power—perhaps even by military force.

IN THIS FRIGHTENING POSTWAR ENVIRONMENT American assessments of Soviet long-term intentions were transformed. When World War II ended, military planners initially looked upon Soviet aims in foreign affairs as arising from the Kremlin's view of power politics, Soviet strategic imperatives, historical Russian ambitions, and Soviet reactions to moves by the United States and Great Britain. American intelligence analysts and strategic planners most frequently discussed Soviet actions in Eastern Europe, the Balkans, the Near East, and Manchuria as efforts to establish an effective security system. Despite enormous Soviet gains during the war, many assessments noted that, in fact, the Soviets had not yet achieved a safe security zone, especially on their southern periphery. While Forrestal, Deane, and most of the planners in the army's Operations Division possessed a skeptical, perhaps even sinister, view of Soviet intentions, the still prevailing outlook at the end of 1945 was to dismiss the role of ideology in Soviet foreign policy yet emphasize Soviet distrust of foreigners; to stress Soviet expansionism but acknowledge the possibility of accommodation; to abhor Soviet domination of Eastern Europe but discuss Soviet policies elsewhere in terms of power and influence; and to dwell upon the Soviet preoccupation with security yet acknowledge doubt about ultimate Soviet intentions.

This orientation changed rapidly during 1946. In January, the Joint War Plans Committee observed that "the long-term objective [of the Soviet Union] is deemed to be establishment of predominant influence over the Eurasian land mass and the strategic approaches thereto." Reports of the new military attaché . . . in Moscow went further, claiming that "the ultimate aim of Soviet foreign policy seems to be the dominance of Soviet influence throughout the world" and "the final aim . . . is the destruction of the capitalist system." Soon thereafter, Kennan's "long telegram" was widely distributed among defense officials, on whom it had considerable impact. Particularly suggestive was his view that Soviet leaders needed the theme of capitalist encirclement to justify their autocratic rule. Also influential were Kennan's convictions that the Soviet leaders aimed to shatter the international authority of the United States and were beyond reason and conciliation.

During the spring and summer of 1946, defense officials found these notions persuasive as an interpretation of Soviet intentions because of the volatile international situation, the revival of ideological fervor within the Soviet Union, and the domestic political atmosphere and legislative constraints in the United States. President Truman wished to stop "babying the Soviets," and his predilection for a tougher posture probably led his subordinates to be less inclined to give the Soviets the benefit of any doubt when assessing Russian intentions.[24] Forrestal believed the Soviet communist threat had become more serious than the Nazi challenge of the 1930s; General John E. Hull, director of the Operations Division, asserted that the Soviets were "constitutionally incapable of being conciliated"; and Clark Clifford and George Elsey considered Soviet fears "absurd." A key subcommittee of the State-War-Navy Coordinating Committee declared that Soviet suspicions were "not susceptible of removal," and in July 1946 the Joint Chiefs of Staff declared the Soviet objective to be "world domination." By late 1946 it was commonplace for intelligence reports and military assessments to state, without any real analysis, that the "ultimate aim of Soviet foreign policy is Russian domination of a communist world."[25] There was, of course, plentiful evidence for this appraisal of Soviet ambitions—the Soviet consolidation of a sphere of influence in Eastern Europe; the incendiary situation in Venezia Giulia; Soviet violation of the agreement to withdraw troops from Iran; Soviet relinquishment of Japanese arms to the Chinese communists; the Soviet mode of extracting reparations from the Russian zone in Germany; Soviet diplomatic overtures for bases in the Dardanelles, Tripolitania, and the Dodecanese; Soviet requests for a role in the occupation of Japan; and the Kremlin's renewed emphasis on Marxist-Leninist doctrine, the vulnerability of capitalist economies, and the inevitability of conflict.

Yet these assessments did not seriously grapple with contradictory evidence. While emphasizing Soviet military capabilities, strategic ambitions, and diplomatic intransigence, reports like the Clifford-Elsey memorandum of September 1946 and the Joint Chiefs of Staff report 1696 (upon which the Clifford-Elsey memorandum heavily relied) disregarded numerous signs of Soviet weakness, moderation, and circumspection. During 1946 and 1947 intelligence analysts described the withdrawal of Russian troops from northern Norway, Manchuria, Bornholm, and Iran (from the latter under pressure, of course). Numerous intelligence sources reported the reduction of Russian troops in Eastern Europe and the extensive demobilization going on within the Soviet Union. In October 1947 the Joint Intelligence Committee forecast a Soviet army troop strength during 1948 and 1949 of less than two million men. Soviet military expenditures appeared to moderate. Other reports dealt with the inadequacies of Soviet transportation and bridging equipment for the conduct of offensive operations in Eastern Europe. And, as already noted, assessments of the Soviet economy revealed persistent problems likely to restrict Soviet adventurism.

Experience suggested that the Soviet Union was by no means uniformly hostile or unwilling to negotiate with the United States. In April 1946, a few days after a State-War-Navy subcommittee issued an alarming political estimate of Soviet policy (for use in American military estimates), Ambassador Smith reminded the State Department that the Soviet press was not unalterably critical of the United States, that the Russians had withdrawn from Bornholm, that Stalin had given a moderate speech on the United Nations, and that Soviet demobilization continued apace. The next month General Lincoln, who had accompanied Byrnes to Paris for the meeting of the council of foreign ministers, acknowledged that the Soviets had been willing to make numerous concessions regarding Tripolitania, the Dodecanese, and Italian reparations. In the spring of 1946, General Echols, General Clay, and Secretary Patterson again maintained that the French constituted the major impediment to an agreement on united control of Germany. At the same time the Soviets ceased pressing for territorial adjustments with Turkey. After the diplomatic exchanges over the Dardanelles in the late summer of 1946 the Soviets did not again ask for either a revision of the Montreux Convention or the acquisition of bases in the Dardanelles. In early 1947 central intelligence delineated more than a half-dozen instances of Soviet moderation or concessions. In April the Military Intelligence Division noted that the Soviets had limited their involvement in the Middle East, diminished their ideological rhetoric, and given only moderate support to Chinese communists. In the months preceding the Truman Doctrine, Soviet behavior—as noted by American military officials and intelligence analysts—hardly justified the inflammatory rhetoric Acheson and Truman used to secure congressional support for aid to Greece and Turkey. Perhaps this is why General Marshall, as secretary of state, refrained from such language himself and preferred to focus on the socioeconomic aspects of the unfolding crisis.

In their overall assessments of Soviet long-term intentions, however, military planners dismissed all evidence of Soviet moderation, circumspection, and restraint. In fact, as 1946 progressed, these planners seemed to spend less time analyzing Soviet intentions and more time estimating Soviet capabilities.[26] Having accepted the notion that the two powers were locked in an ideological struggle of indefinite duration and conscious of the rapid demobilization of American forces and the constraints on American defense expenditures, they no longer explored ways of accommodating a potential adversary's legitimate strategic requirements or pondered how American initiatives might influence the Soviet Union's definition of its objectives.[27] Information not confirming prevailing assumptions either was ignored in overall assessments of Soviet intentions or was used to illustrate that the Soviets were shifting tactics but not altering objectives. Reflective of the emerging mentality was a report from the Joint Chiefs of Staff to the president in July 1946 that deleted sections from previous studies that had outlined Soviet weaknesses. A memorandum sent by Secretary Patterson to the president at the same time was designed by General Lauris Norstad, director of the War Department's Plans and Operations Division, to answer questions about relations with the Soviet Union "without ambiguity." Truman, Clark Clifford observed many years later, liked things in black and white.

DURING 1946 AND EARLY 1947, the conjunction of Soviet ideological fervor and socioeconomic turmoil throughout Eurasia contributed to the growth of a myopic view of Soviet long-term policy objectives and to enormous apprehension lest the Soviet Union gain control of all the resources of Eurasia, thereby endangering the national security of the United States. American assessments of Soviet short-term military intentions had not altered; Soviet military capabilities had not significantly increased, and Soviet foreign policy positions had not greatly shifted. But defense officials were acutely aware of America's own rapidly diminishing capabilities, of Britain's declining military strength, of the appeal of communist doctrine to most of the underdeveloped world, and of the opportunities open to communist parties throughout most of Eurasia as a result of prevailing socioeconomic conditions. War Department papers, studies of the joint chiefs, and intelligence analyses repeatedly described the restiveness of colonial peoples that had sapped British and French strength, the opportunities for communist parties in France, Italy, and even Spain to capitalize upon indigenous conditions, and the ability of the Chinese communists to defeat the nationalists and make the resources and manpower of Manchuria and North China available to the Soviet Union. In this turbulent international arena, the survival of liberal ideals and capitalist institutions was anything but assured. "We could point to the economic benefits of Capitalism," commented one important War Department paper in April 1946, "but these benefits are concentrated rather than widespread, and, at present, are genuinely suspect throughout Europe and in many other parts of the world."[28]

In this environment, there was indeed no room for ambiguity or compromise. Action was imperative—action aimed at safeguarding those areas of Eurasia not already within the Soviet sphere. Even before Kennan's "long telegram" arrived in Washington the joint chiefs adopted the position that "collaboration with the Soviet Union should stop short not only of compromise of principle but also of expansion of Russian influence in Europe and in the Far East."[29] During the spring and summer of 1946, General Lincoln and Admiral Richard L. Conolly, commander of American naval forces in the eastern Atlantic and Mediterranean, worked tirelessly to stiffen Byrnes's views, avert American diplomatic concessions, and put the squeeze on the Russians.[30] "The United States," army planners explained, "must be able to prevent, by force if necessary, Russian domination of either Europe or Asia to the extent that the resources of either continent could be mobilized against the United States." Which countries in Eurasia were worth fighting over remained unclear during 1946. But army and navy officials as well as the joint chiefs advocated a far-reaching program of foreign economic assistance coupled with the refurbishment of American military forces.[31]

During late 1946 and early 1947, the Truman administration assumed the initiative by creating German Bizonia, providing military assistance to Greece and Turkey, allocating massive economic aid to Western Europe, and reassessing economic policy toward Japan. These initiatives were aimed primarily at tackling the internal sources of unrest upon which communist parties capitalized and at rehabilitating the industrial heartlands of Eurasia. American defense officials supported these actions and acquiesced in the decision to give priority to economic aid rather than rearmament. Service officers working on foreign assistance programs of the

State-War-Navy Coordinating Committee supported economic aid, showed sensitivity to the socioeconomic sources of unrest, and recognized that economic aid was likely to be the most efficacious means of preserving a favorable balance of power in Eurasia. Because they judged American military power to be superior and war to be unlikely, Forrestal, Lovett, and Webb insisted that military spending not interfere with the implementation of the Marshall Plan, rehabilitation of Germany, and revival of Japan. "In the necessarily delicate apportioning of our available resources," wrote Assistant Secretary of War Peterson, "the time element permits present emphasis on strengthening the economic and social dikes against Soviet communism rather than upon preparing for a possibly eventual, but not yet inevitable, war."[32]

Yet if war should unexpectedly occur, the United States had to have the capability to inflict incalculable damage upon the Soviet Union. Accordingly, Truman shelved (after some serious consideration) proposals for international control of atomic energy. The Baruch Plan, as it evolved in the spring and summer of 1946, was heavily influenced by defense officials and service officers who wished to avoid any significant compromise with the Soviet Union. They sought to perpetuate America's nuclear monopoly as long as possible in order to counterbalance Soviet conventional strength, deter Soviet adventurism, and bolster American negotiating leverage. When negotiations at the United Nations for international control of atomic energy languished for lack of agreement on its implementation, the way was clear for the Truman administration gradually to adopt a strategy based on air power and atomic weapons. This strategy was initially designed to destroy the adversary's will and capability to wage war by annihilating Russian industrial, petroleum, and urban centers. After completing their study of the 1946 Bikini atomic tests, the Joint Chiefs of Staff in July 1947 called for an enlargement of the nuclear arsenal. While Truman and Forrestal insisted on limiting military expenditures, government officials moved vigorously to solve problems in the production of plutonium, to improve nuclear cores and assembly devices, and to increase the number of aircraft capable of delivering atomic bombs. After much initial postwar disorganization, the General Advisory Committee to the Atomic Energy Commission could finally report to the president at the end of 1947 that "great progress" had been made in the atomic program. From June 30, 1947, to June 30, 1948, the number of bombs in the stockpile increased from thirteen to fifty. Although at the time of the Berlin crisis the United States was not prepared to launch a strategic air offensive against the Soviet Union, substantial progress had been made in the development of the nation's air-atomic capabilities. By the end of 1948, the United States had at least eighteen nuclear-capable B-50s, four B-36s, and almost three times as many nuclear-capable B-29s as had been available at the end of 1947.

During late 1947 and early 1948, the administration also responded to pleas of the Joint Chiefs of Staff to augment the overseas base system and to acquire bases in closer proximity to the Soviet Union. Negotiations were conducted with the British to gain access to bases in the Middle East and an agreement was concluded for the acquisition of air facilities in Libya. Admiral Conolly made a secret deal with the French to secure air and communication rights and to stockpile oil, aviation gas, and ammunition in North Africa. Plans also were discussed for post-occupation bases in Japan, and considerable progress was made in refurbishing and constructing airfields in Turkey. During 1948 the Turks also received one hundred eighty F-47 fighter-bombers, thirty B-26 bombers, and eighty-one C-47 cargo planes. The F-47s and B-26s, capable of reaching the vital Ploesti and Baku oil fields, were more likely to be used to slow down a Soviet advance through Turkey or Iran, thereby affording time to activate a strategic air offensive from prospective bases in the Cairo-Suez area.

Despite these developments, the joint chiefs and military planners grew increasingly uneasy with the budgetary constraints under which they operated. They realized that American initiatives, however necessary, placed the Soviet Union on the defensive, created an incendiary situation, and made war more likely—though still improbable. In July 1947, intelligence analysts in the War Department maintained that the Truman Doctrine and the Marshall Plan had resulted in a more aggressive Soviet attitude toward the United States and had intensified tensions. "These tensions have caused a sharper line of demarcation between West and East tending to magnify the significance of conflicting points of view, and reducing the possibility of agreement on any point." Intelligence officers understood that the Soviets would perceive American efforts to build strategic highways, construct airfields, and transfer fighter bombers to Turkey as a threat to Soviet security and to the oilfields in the Caucuses. The latter, noted the director of naval intelligence, "lie within easy air striking range of countries on her southern flank, and the Soviet leaders will be particularly sensitive to any political threat from this area, however remote." Intelligence analysts also recognized that the Soviets would view the Marshall Plan as a threat to Soviet control in Eastern Europe as well as a death-knell to communist attempts to capture power peacefully in Western Europe. And defense officials were well aware that the Soviets would react angrily to plans for currency reform in German Trizonia and to preparations for a West German republic. "The whole Berlin crisis," army planners informed Eisenhower, "has arisen as a result of . . . actions on the part of the Western Powers." In sum, the Soviet clampdown in Eastern Europe and the attempt to blockade Berlin did not come as shocks to defense officials, who anticipated hostile and defensive Soviet reactions to American initiatives.

The real consternation of the Joint Chiefs of Staff and other high-ranking civilian and military officials in the defense agencies stemmed from their growing conviction that the United States was undertaking actions and assuming commitments that now required greater military capabilities. Recognizing that American initiatives, aimed at safeguarding Eurasia from further communist inroads, might be perceived as endangering Soviet interests, it was all the more important to be ready for any eventuality. Indeed, to the extent that anxieties about the prospects of war escalated in March and April 1948, these fears did not stem from estimates that the Soviets were planning further aggressive action after the communist seizure of power in Czechoslovakia but from apprehensions that ongoing American initiatives might provoke an attack. On March 14 General S. J. Chamberlin, director of army intelligence, warned the chief of staff that "actions taken by this country in opposition to the spread of Communism . . . may decide the question of the outbreak of war and of its timing." The critical question explicitly faced by the intelligence agencies and by the highest policy makers was whether passage of the Selective Service Act, or of universal military training, or of additional appropriations for the air force, or of a military assistance program to Western European countries, or of a resolution endorsing American support for West European Union would trigger a Soviet attack. Chamberlin judged, for example, that the Soviets would not go to war just to make Europe communist but would resort to war if they felt threatened. The great imponderable, of course, was what, in the Soviet view, would constitute a security threat justifying war.

Recognizing the need to move ahead with planned initiatives but fearing Soviet countermeasures, the newly formed staff of the National Security Council undertook its first comprehensive assessment of American foreign policy. During March 1948, after consulting with representatives of the army, navy, air force, State Department, CIA, and National Security Resources Board, the National Security Council staff produced NSC 7, "The Position of the United States with Respect to Soviet-Dominated World Communism." This study began with the commonplace assumption that the communist goal was "world conquest." The study then went on to express the omnipresent theme behind all conceptions of American national security in the immediate postwar years. "Between the United States and the USSR there are in Europe and Asia areas of great potential power which if added to the existing strength of the Soviet world would enable the latter to become so superior in manpower, resources, and territory that the prospect for the survival of the United States as a free nation would be slight." Accordingly, the study called, first, for the strengthening of the military potential of the United States and, second, for the arming of the non-Soviet world, particularly Western Europe. Although this staff study was never formally approved, the national security bureaucracy worked during the spring and summer of 1948 for West European unity, military assistance to friendly nations, currency reform in Trizonia, revitalization of the Ruhr, and the founding of the Federal Republic of Germany.

The priority accorded to Western Europe did not mean that officials ignored the rest of Eurasia. Indeed, the sustained economic rejuvenation of Western Europe made access to Middle Eastern oil more important than ever. Marshall, Lovett, Forrestal, and other defense officials, including the joint chiefs, feared that American support of Israel might jeopardize relations with Arab nations and drive them into the hands of the Soviet Union. Although Truman accepted the partition of Palestine and recognized Israel, the United States maintained an embargo on arms shipments and sought to avoid too close an identification with the Zionist state lest the flow of oil to the West be jeopardized. At the same time, the Truman administration moved swiftly in June 1948 to resuscitate the Japanese economy. Additional funds were requested from Congress to procure imports of raw materials for Japanese industry so that Japanese exports might also be increased. Shortly thereafter, Draper, Tracy S. Voorhees, and other army officials came to believe that a rehabilitated Japan would need the markets and raw materials of Southeast Asia. They undertook a comprehensive examination of the efficacy and utility of a Marshall Plan for Asia. Integrating Japan and Southeast Asia into a viable regional economy, invulnerable to communist subversion and firmly ensconced in the Western community, assumed growing significance, especially in view of the prospect of a communist triumph in China. But communist victories in China did not dissuade policymakers from supporting, for strategic as well as domestic political considerations, the appropriation of hundreds of millions of dollars in additional aid to the Chinese nationalists in the spring of 1948. And the American commitment to preserve the integrity of South Korea actually increased, despite the planned withdrawal of occupation forces.

The problem with all of these undertakings, however, was that they cost large sums, expanded the nation's formal and informal commitments, and necessitated larger military capabilities. Yet on March 24, 1948, just as NSC 7 was being finished, Truman's Council of Economic Advisors warned that accelerating expenditures might compel the president "to set aside free market practices—and substitute a rather comprehensive set of controls." Truman was appalled by this possibility and carefully limited the sums allocated for a build-up of American forces. Key advisers, like Webb, Marshall, Lovett, and Clifford, supported this approach because they perceived too much fat in the military budget, expected the Soviets to rely on political tactics rather than military aggression, postulated latent U.S. military superiority over the Soviet Union, and assumed that the atomic bomb constituted a decisive, if perhaps short-term, trump card. For many American policy makers, moreover, the Iranian crisis of 1946, the Greek civil war, and the ongoing Berlin airlift seemed to demonstrate that Russia would back down when confronted with American determination, even if the United States did not have superior forces-in-being.

As secretary of defense, however, Forrestal was beleaguered by pressures emanating from the armed services for a build-up of American military forces and by his own apprehensions over prospective Soviet actions. He anguished over the excruciatingly difficult choices that had to be made between the imperatives of foreign economic aid, overseas military assistance, domestic rearmament, and fiscal orthodoxy. In May, June, and July 1948, he and his assistants carefully pondered intelligence reports on Soviet intentions and requested a special State Department study on how to plan American defense expenditures in view of prospective Soviet policies. He also studied carefully the conclusions of an exhaustive study of the navy's contribution to national security undertaken by the General Board of the navy under the direct supervision of Captain Arleigh Burke. Still not satisfied, Forrestal asked the president to permit the National Security Council to conduct another comprehensive examination of American policy objectives. Forrestal clearly hoped that this reassessment would show that a larger proportion of resources should be allocated to the military establishment.

The Policy Planning Staff of the Department of State prepared the initial study that Forrestal requested and Truman authorized. Extensively redrafted it reappeared in November 1948 as NSC 20/4 and was adopted as the definitive statement of American foreign policy. Significantly, this paper reiterated the longstanding estimate that the Soviet Union was not likely to resort to war to achieve its objectives. But war could erupt as a result of "Soviet miscalculation of the determination of the United States to use all the means at its command to safeguard its security, through Soviet misinterpretation of our intentions, and through

U.S. miscalculation of Soviet reactions to measures which we might take." Immediately following this appraisal of the prospects of war, the National Security Council restated its conception of American national security: "Soviet domination of the potential power of Eurasia, whether achieved by armed aggression or by political and subversive means, would be strategically and politically unacceptable to the United States."[33]

Yet NSC 20/4 did not call for a larger military budget. With no expectation that war was imminent, the report emphasized the importance of safeguarding the domestic economy and left unresolved the extent to which resources should be devoted to military preparations. NSC 20/4 also stressed "that Soviet political war-fare might seriously weaken the relative position of the United States, enhance Soviet strength and either lead to our ultimate defeat short of war, or force us into war under dangerously unfavorable conditions." Accordingly, the National Security Council vaguely but stridently propounded the importance of reducing Soviet power and influence on the periphery of the Russian homeland and of strengthening the pro-American orientation of non-Soviet nations.[34]

Language of this sort, which did not define clear priorities and which projected American interests almost everywhere on the globe, exasperated the joint chiefs and other military officers. They, too, believed that the United States should resist communist aggression everywhere, "an overall commitment which in itself is all-inclusive." But to undertake this goal in a responsible and effective fashion it was necessary "to bring our military strength to a level commensurate with the distinct possibility of global warfare." The Joint Chiefs of Staff still did not think the Soviets wanted war. But, given the long-term intentions attributed to the Soviet Union and given America's own aims, the chances for war, though still small, were growing.

Particularly worrisome were studies during 1948 suggesting that, should war occur, the United States would have difficulty implementing basic strategic under-takings. Although the armed services fought bitterly over the division of funds, they concurred fully on one subject—the $15 billion ceiling on military spending set by Truman was inadequate. In November 1948, military planners argued that the $14.4 billion budget would jeopardize American military operations by con-stricting the speed and magnitude of the strategic air offensive, curtailing conven-tional bombing operations against the Soviet Union, reducing America's ability to provide naval assistance to Mediterranean allies, undermining the nation's ability to control Middle East oil at the onset of a conflict, and weakening initial overall offensive capabilities. On November 9, the joint chiefs informed the secretary of defense that the existing budget for fiscal 1950 was "insufficient to implement national policy in any probable war situation that can be foreseen."

From the viewpoint of the national military establishment, the deficiency of forces-in-being was just one of several problems. Forrestal told Marshall that he was more concerned about the absence of sufficient strength to support interna-tional negotiations than he was about the availability of forces to combat overt acts of aggression, which were unlikely in any case. During 1948, the joint chiefs also grew increasingly agitated over the widening gap between American commit-ments and interests on the one hand and American military capabilities on the other. In November, the Joint Chiefs of Staff submitted to the National Security Council a comprehensive list of the formal and informal commitments that already had been incurred by the United States government. According to the joint chiefs, "current United States commitments involving the use or distinctly possible use of armed forces are very greatly in excess of our present ability to fulfill them either promptly or effectively." Limited capabilities meant that the use of American forces in any specific situation—for example, in Greece, Berlin, or Palestine— threatened to emasculate the nation's ability to respond elsewhere.[35]

HAVING CONCEIVED OF AMERICAN NATIONAL SECURITY in terms of Western control and of American access to the resources of Eurasia outside the Soviet sphere, American defense officials now considered it imperative to develop American military capabilities to meet a host of contingencies that might emanate from further Soviet encroachments or from indigenous communist unrest. Such contingencies were sure to arise because American strategy depended so heavily on the rebuilding of Germany and Japan, Russia's traditional enemies, as well as on air power, atomic weapons, and bases on the Soviet periphery. Such contingencies also were predictable because American strategy depended so heavily on the restoration of stability in Eurasia, a situation increasingly unlikely in an era of nationalist turmoil, social unrest, and rising economic expectations. Although the desire of the national military establishment for large increments in defense expenditures did not prevail in the tight budgetary environment and presidential election year of 1948, the mode of thinking about national security that subsequently accelerated the arms race and precipitated military interventionism in Asia was already widespread among defense officials.

Indeed, the dynamics of the Cold War after 1948 are easier to comprehend when one grasps the breadth of the American conception of national security that had emerged between 1945 and 1948. This conception included a strategic sphere of influence within the Western Hemisphere, domination of the Atlantic and Pacific oceans, an extensive system of outlying bases to enlarge the strategic frontier and project American power, an even more extensive system of transit rights to facilitate the conversion of commercial air bases to military use, access to the resources and markets of most of Eurasia, denial of those resources to a prospective enemy, and the maintenance of nuclear superiority. Not every one of these ingredients, it must be emphasized, was considered vital. Hence, American officials could acquiesce, however grudgingly, to a Soviet sphere in Eastern Europe and could avoid direct intervention in China. But cumulative challenges to these concepts of national security were certain to provoke a firm American response. This occurred initially in 1947–48 when decisions were made in favor of the Truman Doctrine, Marshall Plan, military assistance, Atlantic alliance, and German and Japanese rehabilitation. Soon thereafter, the "loss" of China, the Soviet detonation of an atomic bomb, and the North Korean attack on South Korea intensified the perception of threat to prevailing concepts of national security. The Truman administration responded with military assistance to southeast Asia, a decision to build the hydrogen bomb, direct military intervention in Korea, a commitment to station troops permanently in Europe, expansion of the American alliance system, and a massive rearmament program in the United States. Postulating a long-term Soviet intention to gain world domination, the American conception of national security, based on geopolitical and economic imperatives, could not allow for additional losses in Eurasia, could not risk a challenge to its nuclear supremacy, and could not permit any infringement on its ability to defend in depth or to project American force from areas in close proximity to the Soviet homeland.

To say this is neither to exculpate the Soviet government for its inhumane treatment of its own citizens nor to suggest that Soviet foreign policy was idle or benign. Indeed, Soviet behavior in Eastern Europe was often deplorable; the Soviets sought opportunities in the Dardanelles, northern Iran, and Manchuria; the Soviets hoped to orient Germany and Austria toward the East; and the Soviets sometimes endeavored to use communist parties to expand Soviet influence in areas beyond the periphery of Russian military power. But, then again, the Soviet Union had lost twenty million dead during the war, had experienced the destruction of seventeen hundred towns, thirty-one thousand factories, and one hundred thousand collective farms, and had witnessed the devastation of the rural economy with the Nazi slaughter of twenty million hogs and seventeen million head of cattle. What is remarkable is that after 1946 these monumental losses received so little attention when American defense analysts studied the motives and intentions of Soviet policy; indeed, defense officials did little to analyze the threat perceived by the Soviets. Yet these same officials had absolutely no doubt that the wartime experiences and sacrifices of the United States, though much less devastating than those of Soviet Russia, demonstrated the need for and entitled the United States to oversee the resuscitation of the industrial heartlands of Germany and Japan, establish a viable balance of power in Eurasia, and militarily dominate the Eurasian rimlands, thereby safeguarding American access to raw materials and control over all sea and air approaches to North America.

To suggest a double standard is important only insofar as it raises fundamental questions about the conceptualization and implementation of American national security policy. If Soviet policy was aggressive, bellicose, and ideological, perhaps America's reliance on overseas bases, air power, atomic weapons, military alliances, and the rehabilitation of Germany and Japan was the best course to follow, even if the effect may have been to exacerbate Soviet anxieties and suspicions. But even when one attributes the worst intentions to the Soviet Union, one might still ask whether American presuppositions and apprehensions about the benefits that would accrue to the Soviet Union as a result of Communist (and even revolutionary nationalist) gains anywhere in Eurasia tended to simplify international realities, magnify the breadth of American interests, engender commitments beyond American capabilities, and dissipate the nation's strength and credibility. And, perhaps even more importantly, if Soviet foreign policies tended to be opportunist, reactive, nationalistic, and contradictory, as some recent writers have claimed and as some contemporary analysts suggested, then one might also wonder whether America's own conception of national security tended, perhaps unintentionally, to engender anxieties and to provoke countermeasures from a proud, suspicious, insecure, and cruel government that was at the same time legitimately apprehensive about the long-term implications arising from the rehabilitation of traditional enemies and the development of foreign bases on the periphery of the Soviet homeland. To raise such issues anew seems essential if we are to unravel the complex origins of the Cold War.

NOTES

1. Kissinger, *For the Record: Selected Statements, 1977–1980* (Boston, 1980), 123–24.
2. I use the term "defense officials" broadly in this essay to include civilian appointees and military officers in the departments of the Army, Navy, and Air Force, in the office of the secretary of defense, in the armed services, in the intelligence agencies, and on the staff of the National Security Council. While purposefully avoiding a systematic analysis of career diplomats in the Department of State, who have received much attention elsewhere, the conclusions I draw here are based on a consideration of the views of high-ranking officials in the State Department, including James F. Byrnes, Dean Acheson, George C. Marshall, and Robert Lovett.
3. For Leahy's explanation, see JCS, "Strategic Areas and Trusteeships in the Pacific," October 10, 18, 1946, RG 218, ser. CCS 360 (12-9-42), JCS 1619/15, 19; JCS, "United States Military Requirements for Air Bases," November 2, 1943; JCS, "Overall Examination of United States Requirements for Military Bases and Base Rights," October 25, 1945, *ibid.,* JCS 570/40.
4. JCS, "United States Military Requirements for Air Bases," November 2, 1943; JCS, Minutes of the 71st meeting, March 30, 1943, RG 218, ser. CCS 360 (12-9-42); Leahy, Memorandum for the President, November 15, 1943, *ibid.;* Nimitz, Memorandum, October 16, 1946, *ibid.,* JCS 1619/16; and Joint Planning Staff [hereafter, JPS], "Basis for the Formulation of a Post-War Military Policy," August 20, 1945, RG 218, ser. CCS 381 (5-13-45), JPS 633/6.
5. JCS, "Statement of Effect of Atomic Weapons on National Security and Military Organization," March 29, 1946, RG 165, ser. ABC 471.6 Atom (8–17–45), JCS 477/10. Also see JCS, "Guidance as to the Military Implications of a United Nations Commission on Atomic Energy," January 12, 1946, *ibid.,* JCS 1567/26; and JCS, "Over-All Effect of Atomic Bomb on Warfare and Military Organization," October 30, 1945, *ibid.,* JCS 1477/1.
6. JPS, "Over-All Examination of Requirements for Transit Air Bases . . . ," January 20, 1946, RG 218, ser. CCS 360 (10-9-42), JPS 781/1; and McCloy, Memorandum to the Department of State, January 31, 1945, RG 165, OPD 336 (top secret). Also see JPS, "Over-All Examination of Requirements for Transit Air Bases," January 8, 1946; and, for the joint chiefs' view on South American air fields, see JCS, Minutes of the 69th meeting, March 23, 1943, RG 218, CCS 360 (12-9-42).
7. P&O, "The Strategic Importance of Inter-American Military Cooperation" [January 20, 1947], RG 319, 092 (top secret). Also see H. A. Craig, "Summary," January 5, 1945, RG 107, Records of the Assistant Secretary of War for Air, Establishment of Air Fields and Air Bases, box 216 (Latin America); and War Department, "Comprehensive Statement" [January 1945], *ibid.*
8. JCS, "Foreign Policy of the United States," February 10, 1946, RG 218, ser. CCS 092 United States (12-21-45), JCS 1592/2; and JCS to the Secretary of the Navy and Secretary of War, September 19, 1945, *ibid.,* ser. CCS 092 (9-10-45), JCS 1507/2. For JCS views on the Western Hemisphere, also see JCS to the Secretary of the Navy and

Secretary of War, February 11, 1945, *ibid.*, ser. CCS 092 (1-18-45); JCS, "International Organization for the Enforcement of World Peace and Security," April 14, 1945, *ibid.*, ser. CCS 092 (4-14-45), JCS 1311; and JCS, "Guidance as to Command and Control of the Armed Forces to be Placed at the Disposal of the Security Council of the United Nations," May 26, 1946, *ibid.*, JCS 1670/5.

9. For Patterson's views, see P&O, "Strategic Importance of Inter-American Military Cooperation" [January 20, 1947]; and Patterson to Byrnes, December 18, 1946, RG 107, RPPP, safe file, box 3.

10. This evaluation accords with the views of Chester J. Pach, Jr.; see his "The Containment of United States Military Aid to Latin America, 1944–1949," *Diplomatic History,* 6 (1982):232–34.

11. See, for example, Craig, "Summary," January 5, 1945; JPS, "Military Arrangements Deriving from the Act of Chapultepec Pertaining to Bases," January 14, 1946, RG 218, ser. CCS 092 (9-10-45), JPS 761/3; Patterson to Byrnes, December 18, 1946; and P&O, "Strategic Importance of Inter-American Military Cooperation" [January 20, 1947].

12. Minutes of the meeting of the Secretaries of State, War, and the Navy, December 18, 1946, April 23, May 1, 1947, RG 107, RPPP, safe file, box 3; and M. B. Ridgway, Memorandum for the Assistant Secretary of War, February 1947, *ibid.*, HCPP, 092 (classified).

13. Pach, "Military Aid to Latin America," 235–43.

14. Leahy, excerpt from letter, May 16, 1944, RG 59, lot 54D394 (Records of the Office of European Affairs), box 17. For Strong's opinion, see JPS, Minutes of the 199th meeting, April 25, 1945, RG 218, ser. CCS 334 (3-28-45); and, for the views of Eisenhower and Lincoln, see Lincoln, Memorandum for Hull, June 24, 1945, USMA, GLP, War Dept. files; and Leahy, Memorandum for the President [late June 1945], *ibid.*

15. For the emphasis on expediting recovery in Western Europe, see, for example, McCloy, Memorandum for Matthew J. Connelly, April 26, 1945, HTL, HSTP, PSF, box 178; and, for the role of Britain, see, for example, Joint Intelligence Staff [hereafter, JIS], "British Capabilities and Intentions," December 5, 1945, RG 218, ser. CCS 000.1 Great Britain (5-10-45), JIS 161/4.

16. See, for example, JIS, "Military Capabilities of Great Britain and France," November 13, 1945, RG 218, ser. CCS 000.1 Great Britain (5-10-45), JIS 211/1; JIS, "Areas Vital to Soviet War Effort," February 12, 1946, *ibid.*, ser. CCS 092 (3-27-45), JIS 226/2; and JIS, "Supplemental Information Relative to Northern and Western Europe," April 18, 1947, *ibid.*, JIS 275/1.

17. Strategy Section, OPD, "Post-War Base Requirements in the Philippines," April 23, 1945; JCS, "Strategic Areas and Trusteeships in the Pacific," October 18, 1946; MID, "Positive U.S. Action Required to Restore Normal Conditions in Southeast Asia," July 3, 1947, RG 319, P&O, 092 (top secret); and Lauris Norstad to the Director of Intelligence, July 10, 1947, *ibid.*

18. JLPC, "Russian Capabilities," November 15, 1945; and MID, "Intelligence Estimate of the World Situation for the Next Five Years," August 21, 1946, RG 319, P&O, 350.05 (top secret). For a contemporary analysis of the Soviet transport network, also see Paul Wohl, "Transport in the Development of Soviet Policy," *Foreign Affairs,* 24 (1946): 466–83.

19. JIS, "Soviet Post-War Military Policies and Capabilities," January 15, 1946, RG 218, ser. CCS 092 USSR (3-27-45), JIS 80/24; MID. "Ability of Potential Enemies to Attack the Continental United States," August 8, 1946; and P&O, "Estimate of the Situation Pertaining to the Northeast Approaches to the United States," August 12, 1946, RG 319, P&O, 381 (top secret).

20. MID, "Estimate of the Possibility of War between the United States and the USSR Today from a Comparison with the Situation as It Existed in September 1946," July 21, 1947, RG 319, P&O, 350.05 (top secret); and JIC, Moscow Embassy, "Soviet Intentions," April 1, 1948.

21. Acheson to Truman, April 30, 1946, RG 107, HCPP, general subject file, box 1. Also see McCloy to Patterson, November 24, 1945, *ibid.*, RPPP, safe file, box 4. For pressure on the State Department, see Patterson to Byrnes, December 10, 1945, RG 165, Civil Affairs Division [hereafter, CAD], ser. 014 Germany; Patterson to Byrnes, February 25, 1946; OPD and CAD, "Analysis of Certain Political Problems Confronting Military Occupation Authorities in Germany," April 10, 1946, RG 107, HCPP, 091 Germany (classified); and "Combined Food Board" file, spring 1946, *ibid.*, HCPP, general subject file, box 1.

22. William Draper, Memorandum [early 1947], RG 107, HCPP, 091 Germany (classified); and Forrestal to Acheson, January 14, 1946, ML, JFP, box 68. For Clay's initiative, see Smith, *Papers of General Lucius D. Clay*, 1:203–04, 213–14, 218–23; John F. Gimbel, *The American Occupation of Germany: Politics and the Military, 1945–1949* (Stanford, 1968), 35–91; John H. Backer, *The Decision to Divide Germany: American Foreign Policy in Transition* (Durham, N.C., 1978), 137–48; and Bruce Kuklick, *American Policy and the Division of Germany: The Clash with Russia over Reparations* (Ithaca, N.Y., 1972), 205–35. For Patterson's concerns and his support of Bizonia, see Patterson to Byrnes, June 11, 1946, RG 107, HCPP, 091 Germany (classified); Patterson to Truman, November 20, 1946, *ibid.*, RPPP, safe file, box 4; Minutes of the War Council meeting, December 5, 1946, *ibid.*, box 7; and Patterson to Palmer Hoyt, December 27, 1946, *ibid.*, box 4. For the merger of the zones, also see *FRUS, 1946*, 5:579–659; Smith, *Papers of General Lucius D. Clay*, 1:245, 248–49; and, for Draper's importance, also see Carolyn Eisenberg, "U.S. Social Policy in Post-War Germany: The Conservative Restoration," paper delivered at the Seventy-Fourth Annual Meeting of the Organization of American Historians, held in April 1981, in Detroit.

23. CIA, "Review of the World Situation as It Relates to the Security of the United States," September 26, 1947. Also see, for example, JCS, "Strategic Concept and Plan for the Employment of United States Armed Forces," Appendix A, September 19, 1945; JPS, Minutes of the 249th and 250th meetings; Lincoln to Wood, May 22, 1946, RG 165, ser. ABC 381 (9-1-45); [Giffin (?)] "U.S. Policy with Respect to Russia" [early April 1946], *ibid.*, ser. ABC 336 (8-22-43); JPS, "Estimate of Probable Developments in the World Political Situation up to 1956," October 31, 1946, RG 218, ser. CCS 092 (10-9-46), JPS 814/1; MID, "World Political Developments Affecting the Security of the United States during the Next Ten Years," April 14, 1947, RG 319, P&O, 350.05 (top secret).

24. Robert L. Messer, *The End of an Alliance: James F. Byrnes, Roosevelt, Truman, and the Origins of the Cold War* (Chapel Hill, N.C., 1982), 152–94, and "Paths Not Taken," 297–319.

25. Forrestal to Clarence Dillon, April 11, 1946, ML, JFP, box 11; Hull to Theater Commanders, March 21, 1946, RG 165, ser. ABC 336 (8-22-43); for the Clifford-Elsey viewpoint, see Krock, *Memoirs: Sixty Years on the Firing Line*, 428; and SWNCC, "Resume of Soviet Capabilities and Possible Intentions," August 29, 1946, NHC, SPD, ser. 5, box 106, A8. For the SWNCC estimate, see JCS, "Political Estimate of Soviet Policy for Use in Connection with Military Studies," April 5, 1946, RG 218, ser. CCS 092 USSR (3-27-45), JCS 1641/4; and JCS "Presidential Request for Certain Facts and Information Regarding the Soviet Union," July 25, 1946. Some of the most thoughtful studies on Soviet intentions, like that of the Joint Intelligence Staff in early

January 1946 (JIS 80/20), were withdrawn from consideration. See the evolution of studies and reports in RG 218, ser. CCS 092 USSR (3-27-45), sects. 5–7.

26. Both the quantity and the quality of JCS studies on Soviet intentions seem to have declined during 1946. In "Military Position of the United States in Light of Russian Policy" (January 8, 1946), strategic planners of the Joint War Plans Committee maintained that it was more important to focus on Soviet capabilities than on Soviet intentions. During a key discussion at the White House, Admiral Leahy also was eager to dismiss abstract evaluations of Russian psychology and to focus on Russian capabilities; S. W. D., Memorandum for the Record, June 12, 1946. My assessment of the quality of JCS studies is based primarily on my analysis of the materials in RG 218, ser. CCS 092 USSR (3-27-45); ser. CCS 381 USSR (3-2-46); RG 319, P&O, 350.05 (top secret); and NHC, SPD, central files, 1946–48, A8.

27. During 1946 it became a fundamental tenet of American policy makers that Soviet policy objectives were a function of developments within the Soviet Union and not related to American actions. See, for example, Kennan's "long telegram," in *FRUS, 1946*, 4:696–709; JCS, "Political Estimate of Soviet Policy," April 5, 1946; JCS, "Presidential Request," July 25, 1946; and the Clifford/Elsey memorandum, in Krock, *Memoirs*, esp. 427–36.

28. [Giffin] "U.S. Policy with Respect to Russia" [early April 1946]. Also see Giffin, Draft of Proposed Comments for Assistant Secretary of War on "Foreign Policy," [early February 1946]; MID. "Intelligence Estimate," June 25, 1946; JPS, "Estimate of Probable Developments in the World Political Situation," October 31, 1946, RG 218, ser. CCS 092 (10-9-46), JPS 814/1; Special Ad Hoc Committee of SWNCC, "Study on U.S. Assistance to France," April 9, 1947, RG 165, ser. ABC 400.336 France (3-20-47); MID, "World Political Developments," April 14, 1947; JWPC, "The Soviet Threat against the Iberian Peninsula and the Means Required to Meet It," May 8, 1947, RG 218, ser. CCS 381 USSR (3-2-46), JWPC 465/1; and CIA. "Review of the World Situation," September 26, 1947.

29. JCS, "Foreign Policy of the United States," February 10, 1946.

30. Lincoln to Hull [April 1946], RG 59, Office of European Affairs, box 17; Lincoln, Memorandum for the Record, April 16, 1946; Lincoln to Hull, April 16, 1946, RG 165, ser. ABC 092 USSR (11-15-44); Lincoln to Cohen, June 22, 1946, *ibid.,* ABC 381 (9-1-45); Richard L. Conolly, oral history (Columbia, 1960), 293–304; Lincoln, Memorandum for Chief of Staff, May 20, 1946; and Lincoln, Memorandum for Norstad, July 23, 1946, USMA, GLP, War Department files.

31. Giffin, "Draft of Proposed Comments" [early February 1946]. Also see, for example, JCS, "Foreign Policy of the United States," February 10, 1946; [Giffin] "U.S. Policy with Respect to Russia" [early April 1946]; JCS, "Political Estimate of Soviet Policy," April 5, 1946; and Sherman, Memorandum for Forrestal, March 17, 1946, ML, JFP, box 24.

32. Peterson, as quoted in Chief of Staff, Memorandum [July 1947], RG 165, ser. ABC 471.6 Atom (8-17-45). Also see, for example, Lovett diaries, December 16, 1947, January 5, 15, 1948; Baruch to Forrestal, February 7, 1948, ML, JFP, box 78; Forrestal to Baruch, February 10, 1948, *ibid.;* and Excerpt of Phone Conversation between Forrestal and C. E. Wilson, April 2, 1948, *ibid.,* box 48.

33. NCS 20/1 and 20/4 may be found in Gaddis and Etzold, *Containment,* 173–211 (the quotations appear on page 208). Also see *FRUS, 1948,* 1:589–93, 599–601, 609–11, 615–24, 662–69.

34. Gaddis and Etzold, *Containment,* 209–10.

35. For the position of the JCS, see NSC 35, "Existing International Commitments," November 17, 1948, *FRUS, 1948,* 1:656–62. For Forrestal's view, see *ibid.,* 644–46.

For background, see William A. Knowlton, Memorandum for the Chief of Staff, October 21, 1948, RG 319, P&O, 092 (top secret); for the reference to Greece, see JCS, "The Position of the United States with Respect to Greece," April 13, 1948, RG 218, ser. CCS 092 Greece (12-30-47), JCS 1826/8.

Rethinking the Origins of American Hegemony

G. John Ikenberry

In recent years no topic has occupied the attention of scholars of international relations more than that of American hegemonic decline. The erosion of American economic, political, and military power is unmistakable. The historically unprecedented resources and capabilities that stood behind United States early postwar diplomacy, and that led Henry Luce in the 1940s to herald an "American century," have given way to an equally remarkable and rapid redistribution of international power and wealth. In the guise of theories of "hegemonic stability," scholars have been debating the extent of hegemonic decline and its consequences.[1]

Although scholars of international political economy have analyzed the consequences of American hegemonic decline, less effort has been directed at examining the earlier period of hegemonic ascendancy. Theorists of hegemonic power and decline pass rather quickly over the early postwar period. In rather superficial fashion, it is assumed that the United States used its power to organize the operation of the non-Communist international system—to "make and enforce the rules for the world political economy" as one scholar put it.[2] While the rest of the industrialized world lay in economic and political ruin, American resources and capabilities were at their peak. Out of these historical circumstances, the conventional view suggests, the United States got its way and created a postwar order of its choosing.

This conventional view, wielded by those scholars more interested in hegemonic decline, requires closer attention; and so it is useful to reexamine the origins and character of American power in the early postwar era. The questions are several: How was U.S. hegemonic power used after World War II in constructing the postwar world order? How successful was the United States in creating a postwar order of its choosing? What did the United States want and what did it get in

G. John Ikenberry is assistant professor of politics and international affairs at Princeton University. He is the author of *Reasons of State: Oil Politics and the Capacities of American Government*, coauthor of *The State* (with John A. Hall), and coeditor of *The State and American Foreign Economic Policy*. *Political Science Quarterly*, Volume 104, Number 3, 1989. Reprinted by permission.

the early postwar years? Most importantly, what does a hegemonic state, such as the United States, do when it is being hegemonic?

The answers to these questions require us to rethink the nature of American hegemonic power. I argue that the United States got both less than it wanted and more than it bargained for in the early postwar period. In terms of the ideals and plans it originally articulated, the United States got much less than it wanted; in terms of direct involvement in leading the postwar western system, it got much more involved than it wanted. The United States was clearly hegemonic and used its economic and military position to construct a postwar order. But that order was not really of its own making. There was less exercise of coercion than is commonly assumed in the literature on hegemonic power, and where it was used, it was less successful than often thought.

I want to make three general points. First, the early efforts by the United States to build a postwar liberal multilateral system largely failed. Those efforts, in part attractive to the United States because they did not require a direct political or military presence in Europe, failed because of the rise of the East-West struggle and the underestimated problems of postwar economic and political reconstruction in Europe. Second, at each step along the way, the United States sought to minimize its direct (that is, formal, hierarchical) role in Europe. It was the European governments that sought to elicit and influence the projection of U.S. power into Europe—and they did so primarily for security and resource reasons. In short, U.S. hegemony in Europe was largely an empire by invitation. Third, while European nations sought to promote U.S. involvement in Europe, they also acted to rework the liberal, multilateral ideas that initially propelled the United States during and after World War II. In effect, the European nations successfully modified liberal multilateralism into a welfare state liberalism (or embedded liberalism). The United States tried to use its power to create a system that would allow it to stay out of Europe—a sort of self-regulating and automatic international political economy. This failed, and the United States was drawn into a more direct role in Europe, defending a system that the Europeans themselves effectively redefined.

This article traces the evolution of U.S. policy as it reveals the mechanisms and limits of hegemonic power. U.S. policy traveled through different phases: the one world ideals of liberal multilateralism (1941–1947); the shift to a two worlds concept and the attempt to build a United Europe (1947–1950); and the subsequent emergence of an ongoing and direct American political and security presence in Europe—an empire by invitation. A close historical reading of policy change suggests the need to rethink the nature and limits of U.S. hegemonic power.

THEORIES OF HEGEMONIC POWER

The central claim of hegemonic stability theory is that a single Great Power is necessary to create and sustain order and openness in the international political economy. Accordingly, *Pax Britannica* and *Pax Americana* both represent historical eras when a hegemonic power held sway and used its dominant position to ensure an orderly and peaceful international system. Reflecting this position, Robert Gilpin argues that "Great Britain and the United States created and enforced the rules of a liberal international economic order."[3] Likewise, as the power of these hegemonic nations declines, so also does the openness and stability of the international economic system. The decline of Britain's nineteenth-century order foreshadowed the decline of America's postwar system. In each era it was the dominant role of the hegemonic nation that ensured order and liberal relations among nations.

This thesis draws powerful conceptual links between the rise and decline of nations and the structure of international relations. Scholarly interest in this type of argument was stimulated by the writings of Charles Kindleberger and Robert Gilpin. In a study of the sources of the Great Depression, Kindleberger argued that the stability of the pre-World War I international political economy rested on the leadership of Britain.[4] This leadership role involved the provision of a variety of collective goods, in particular the willingness of Britain to extend credit abroad and to maintain open markets at home. In the midst of falling commodity prices beginning in 1927 and the emerging shortage of international credit, the United States failed to act in a counter-cyclical manner to reverse the flow of funds and raised protectionist barriers. The collapse of the system in the interwar period was due to the absence of a hegemonic leader able and willing to maintain open markets for surplus goods and capable of maintaining the flow of capital. Kindleberger argues that the return to mercantilist relations in the interwar period was largely due to the inability of a weakened Britain to continue to play this leadership role and the unwillingness of the United States to take up these international responsibilities.

Similarly, Robert Gilpin developed a theory of global leadership emphasizing the active role of the hegemonic nation in creating and sustaining international economic and political order.[5] The rise of a hegemonic nation, Gilpin argues, "resolves the question of which state will govern the system, as well as what ideas and values will predominate, thereby determining the ethos of succeeding ages."[6] In this formulation, the hegemonic nation dominates the creation of the rules and institutions that govern international relations in a particular age. Gilpin's argument was that Britain undermined its own economic base of hegemonic power by investing heavily in overseas production at the expense of its own economy.[7] In the twentieth century, moreover, the United States was in danger of repeating the cycle of hegemonic decline and instability.[8]

In these studies and in the literature on hegemonic stability that they continue to inspire, attempts are made to find systematic links between the prevailing distribution of power (that is, military capabilities, control over trade, capital, and raw materials) and the organization of international political and economic processes. In doing so these theories share several assumptions. First, they tend to conceive of power in traditional resource terms. Reflecting this position, Robert Keohane defines hegemony as "preponderance of material resources."[9] Thus, the constitutive elements of hegemonic power, as it relates to the world political economy, include control over raw materials, markets, and capital as well as competitive advantages in highly valued goods. Second, according to this perspective, these material resources provide the means for the hegemon to "make and enforce the rules for the world political economy."[10] Power is exercised by the hegemon primarily through the use of coercion, inducements, or sanctions. In effect, power is manifest as arm twisting.

While sharing these basic assumptions, scholars working in this tradition disagree over the manner in which hegemonic power is exercised.[11] Some writers, such as Kindleberger, see that power as basically benign, centering around the provision of public goods and leadership.[12] The image of the hegemon in this formulation is that of an enlightened leader, submerging narrow and short-term national interests to the preservation of a well-ordered and mutually beneficial international system. Others stress the importance of self-regarding actions by the hegemon directed at the creation and enforcement of the essential rules of the system.[13] Here the image is of a much more coercive hegemon, structuring the system to strengthen its own international economic position.

The debate within this literature tends to focus on the implications of the loss of American hegemonic power. The questions at this level are two-fold. One concerns the manner and extent to which the loss of hegemonic power has impacts on international regimes. The debate here is about how autonomous and powerful regimes may be as an independent force for order and openness, even with the declining hegemon playing a less constructive role.[14] A second debate asks the prior question of the extent to which the United States has in fact lost its hegemonic capabilities.[15]

This literature provides fertile ground for research on American power in the postwar period by drawing bold lines between the rise and decline of nations and the international political economy. Its power is in its simplicity, and the images it presents are evocative. Nonetheless, it suffers from at least two problems—one theoretical and the other historical. Theoretically, the literature suffers from the absence of a clear theoretical understanding of the manner in which hegemonic power is manifest as it promotes international order and openness. The mechanisms and the texture of hegemonic power has not been captured in the literature. Susan Strange notes that "we have not clearly understood the alternative ways hegemons exercise power and the alternative uses to which their power may be put."[16] What factors determine when and how the rich and militarily strong nations are able to convert their power into hegemonic domination? Through what mechanisms and processes does power manifest itself? Why do some states come to accept, even invite, the rule of the hegemon, while others resist? And how do the goals of the hegemon change in the process of building international order? These questions remain unanswered because the focus of hegemonic stability theory remains fixed on the material resources of power and fails to explore the larger dimensions of power.

The second problem is historical. As noted above, the literature on hegemonic stability passes very briefly over the early phases of the cycle of rise and decline. In particular, it is assumed that the rules and institutions that emerged in the early postwar period are essentially the creations of the United States. The unprecedented position of the United States gave it a unique historical license to create international order on its own terms, or so it is thought. We are left only to trace the course of that power and analyze the fate of the rules and institutions it fathered. This image is a distortion: it is, to borrow Dean Acheson's memorable phrase, a view that is "clearer than the truth." And it serves to mislead the subsequent inquiry into the processes of hegemonic decline. If the capabilities of the United States in the early postwar period were less overpowering than commonly assumed, and if that power was exercised in less direct ways, this is important for the way we are to judge the current period of decline.

The Limits of American Postwar Power

Viewed in terms of material capabilities, the United States did occupy an over-whelmingly powerful position at the close of the war. The disparity in resources and capabilities was huge, not only in general aggregate economic and military terms, but also in the wide assortment of resources the United States had at its disposal. As early as 1900 the United States was already the world's largest industrial producer; on the eve of World War I the United States had twice the share of world industrial production as Britain and Germany, its nearest industrial rivals. This trend toward economic dominance was rendered more pronounced by the war itself, which destroyed the industrial base of the European economies and further expanded the American counterpart.[17]

The unprecedented nature of the American position is reflected in comparisons with British economic strength in the nineteenth century. While the British in 1870, at the zenith of their power, possessed 32 percent of the global distribution of industrial production, the United States held 48 percent of the global share in 1948. The scope of British and American power, in their respective eras, is often found to be similar; yet in terms of the preponderance of material resources, American power was much greater.

As the hegemonic account of the early postwar period suggests, the United States did employ its resources to help shape the global political and economic order. American oil reserves were used in the 1950s and 1960s to make up for global short-falls triggered by a series of crises and embargoes in the Middle East. Lend-lease arrangements and loans were used to influence British commercial policy immediately after the war. Foreign aid was used to influence European monetary policy in the 1950s.[18] An entire range of postwar rulemaking and institution-building exercises were influenced and supported by the American resort to inducements and coercion, all backed by U.S. resource capabilities.

Closer historical scrutiny of the period suggests that the absence of success by the United States in implementing its liberal designs for order was more pervasive than the hegemonic account allows. American officials consistently were forced to modify their plans for a liberal, multilateral order; and they often found themselves at a loss in attempting to draw others into such a system. In the various commercial negotiations after the war, the United States was unable or unwilling to pursue consistent liberal policies. The most ambitious efforts at trade liberalization, embodied in the International Trade Organization proposal, were blocked by the United States Congress.[19] The General Agreement on Tariffs and Trade (GATT) that did survive was less extensive, contained escape clauses and exemptions, and left agriculture trade outside the multilateral framework. In areas such as maritime rights and shipping, as Susan Strange notes, the United States also pursued less than liberal policies.[20] Moreover, despite the unprecedented power position of the United States, holding the dollars and relief funds desperately needed in Britain and on the continent, American officials were less than successful in persuading Europe to embrace U.S. policies. In a recent study, Michael Mastanduno finds that the United States was surprisingly ineffective in convincing Europe to adopt its hardline East-West trade strategies.[21] Moreover, the U.S. was unable to push the European governments toward full-scale economic integration, despite its continued efforts and the massive aid of the Marshall Plan.

FROM LIBERAL MULTILATERALISM TO A UNITED EUROPE

The unprecedented opportunity for the United States to construct a postwar international order congenial with its interests and ideals was not wasted. The order that took shape in the late 1940s, however, was not what wartime planners had envisaged or sought to implement during and immediately after the war. The one world of American wartime planning gave way to efforts to build Europe into an independent center of global power; these revised plans, signaled by the Marshall Plan, in turn gave way to a bipolar system and the active courtship by Europe of American hegemonic leadership.

The chief focus of wartime planners was the construction of a postwar economy based on liberal, multilateral designs. The primacy of economic planning reflected both principle and prudence. It was part of the liberal faith that if the economic foundation were properly laid, the politics would follow. "If goods can't cross borders, soldiers will" was the slogan of the time, capturing the liberal faith.

The absence of postwar political and military planning also followed from more explicit wartime constraints. Franklin D. Roosevelt's vision of Great Power postwar cooperation held sway, an approach difficult to break with as long as the war persisted. Well into 1947 the idea that postwar order would be one world, with collective security and a liberal international economy, continued to drive policy in the Roosevelt and Truman administrations.

Domestic considerations, moreover, made a large-scale peacetime military commitment to Europe and a spheres-of-influence policy difficult to sustain.[22] A liberal, multilateral system would allow the United States to project its own ideals onto a world where depression and war had clearly demonstrated the bankruptcy of European ideas of spheres of influence and economic nationalism. If the United States could no longer isolate itself from the affairs of Europe, it would need to alter the terms of international politics. Only on this basis would congressional and public opinion allow the United States to play an internationalist role. A liberal, multilateral system, once established, would be self-regulating and would not require direct American involvement in Europe. For an American public eager to see its troops return home, ideals and prudence reinforced the initial American designs for postwar order.

The Failure of Liberal Multilateralism

The tenets of liberal multilateralism were several: trade and financial relations are best built around multilateral rather than bilateral or other partial arrangements; commercial relations are to be conducted primarily by private actors in markets; and states are to become involved in setting the domestic and international institutional framework for trade and financial relations, both participating in liberalizing international negotiations and facilitating domestic adjustment to international economic change.[23]

American officials involved in economic planning in the Departments of State and Treasury were strikingly in accord on the need for the creation of international institutions to support liberal, multilateral economic relations. All were influenced by the failures after World War I: the lack of preparation, the failure of American participation in the League of Nations, the inadequacy of attention to economic problems.[24] "The postwar planners were united in their determination to break with the legacy of economic nationalism. . . . They recognized that the United States, despite its comparative self-sufficiency, had a very great stake in the economic well-being of the rest of the world, not only because it needed foreign markets for the produce of its factories and farms, but because it needed a healthy environment on which to base its efforts at world peace."[25]

Most of the American wartime efforts to insure a liberal, multilateral system were directed at Britain. British economic planners were generally sympathetic to American liberal, multilateral ideas; but outside of the government, political groups and individuals were profoundly divided. On the Left, free markets were associated with unemployment and social injustice. Segments of British industry feared competition with American industry. On the Right, liberal multilateralism was a threat to the Imperial Preference system (providing privileged trade relations among commonwealth nations) and the remains of the British Empire.[26] In various ways these groups favored national, bilateral, or regional economic relations.

Directed primarily at dismantling British Imperial Preferences, American officials resorted to several bargaining tools and advantages. In 1941 Lend-Lease negotiations, the United States sought to tie aid to the removal of discriminatory British trade practices.[27] Compromises were achieved, and the British were able to resist a firm commitment to multilateral principles.[28]

The most far-reaching discussions between the United States and Britain over the principles and mechanisms of postwar economic order were agreed upon at the 1944 Bretton Woods conference in New Hampshire.[29] In these monetary negotiations, the British-American differences were considerable in regard to the provision for liquidity and the allocation of responsibility for adjustment between creditor and debtor countries. The British emphasized the primacy of national control over fiscal and monetary policy, the importance of biasing the arrangements toward economic expansion, and the need for a large international reserve and relatively easy terms of access to adjustment funds.

In the compromise agreement that created the charters of the International Monetary Fund and the International Bank for Reconstruction and Development (World Bank), major differences of perception remained between the British and

Americans. In the American Senate debate, administration officials gave the impression that the institutional foundations had been laid for a liberal, multilateral system. Further funds would not be necessary for British economic reconstruction, and a British commitment to nondiscrimination had been achieved. The British, for their part, understood that the United States had committed itself to helping Britain in what would be a lengthy economic transition period, and that the American government would make the sacrifices necessary to insure postwar economic expansion.[30]

At the same time that British-American negotiations dealt with monetary arrangements, the framework for international trade was also debated. In 1945 a set of proposals were worked out between the two countries on commercial policy. British reluctance to endorse the full array of American proposals for nondiscriminatory trade and multilateral tariff reductions were similar to those in the monetary area. The British were not prepared to eliminate the Imperial Preference arrangements. Concerns about employment and economic stability made the British cautious of a full-blown, liberal trading system.[31]

Further efforts by the United States to use its economic preeminence to alter British commercial and monetary practices came during consideration of the British loan in 1945–1946. The core of this effort was to gain a British pledge to lift discriminatory controls earlier than mandated by the Bretton Woods agreement. Negotiations over the British loan provided the most coercive use of American power for liberal, multilateral purposes during this period. Reflecting the attitude of Congress on this issue, a congressional report argued that "the advantages afforded by the United States loans and other settlements are our best bargaining asset in securing political and economic concessions in the interest of world stability."[32] The British found little room to reject the conditions of the loan.[33]

Under the terms of the Anglo-American Financial Agreement, the British were obliged to make sterling externally convertible. Yet this action led in only six weeks to a massive drain on British reserves, forcing the suspension of convertibility. Despite its commanding bargaining position, the United States was unable to bring Britain into a multilateral order. Moreover, the chief political strength of the British (and the Europeans generally) in resisting American designs was their economic weakness. The early move toward multilateralism would not be possible.

Throughout the 1944–1947 period, the United States attempted to build a framework for international economic relations with the reconstruction of multilateral trade as its centerpiece. This objective largely failed. The most basic obstacle in the way of American policy was the economic and political dislocation of the war itself. The American proposals required, as Richard Gardner maintains, a reasonable state of economic and political equilibrium. "The multilateral system could not be achieved unless individual nations were in approximate balance with the world as a whole. Unfortunately the post-war planners did not foresee the full extent of the measures necessary to achieve such balances after the destruction and dislocation of the Second World War. . . . The institutions they built for the achievement of multilateralism were not designed to withstand the unfavorable pressures of the post-war transition period."[34] The objectives of the hegemonic power were not in balance with the power and influence at its disposal.

Moreover, in the rush to international economic rulemaking, important differences were masked concerning the proper role of governments in promoting full employment, price stability, and social welfare. These differences would reappear as the transition period of reconstruction and alliance building ended in the late 1940s.

Finally, there was the problem of the emergence of U.S.-Soviet hostilities. Ernst H. Van Der Beugel notes: "The political hopes of the United States were shattered by the nature of Soviet policy. The total ruin of Europe destroyed the hope of economic stability.[35] Taken together, the early efforts to usher in a period of liberal multilateralism were thwarted by the same forces that destroyed the wartime vision of one world. American officials were determined not to repeat the errors of World War I, but the plans themselves would need revision. In the end, as Richard Gardner notes, the assumptions of an early return to political and economic equilibrium were unfounded.[36] In political terms, the postwar world was moving toward two worlds, not one. In economic terms, the Europeans suffered from a severe dollar shortage, importing as much as seven times the value of goods they were exporting to the United States.

The Marshall Plan and a European Third Force

As the difficulties of implementing the liberal, multilateral proposals became evident, American policy began to involve efforts to bolster the political and economic foundations of Europe—to create in effect a third force. Burton Berry, a career Foreign Service officer, noted in July 1947 that it was time to "drop the pretense of one world."[37] The need to search for a new approach to Europe was underscored by State Department official Charles Bohlen:

> The United States is confronted with a condition in the world which is at direct variance with the assumptions upon which, during and directly after the war, major United States policies were predicated. Instead of unity among the great powers—both political and economic—after the war, there is complete disunity between the Soviet Union and the satellites on one side and the rest of the world on the other. There are, in short, two worlds instead of one. Faced with this disagreeable fact, however much we may deplore it, the United States in the interest of its own well-being and security and those of the free non-Soviet world must reexamine its major policy objectives.[38]

American officials were forced to attend to the balance of power in Europe. Accordingly, the new policy emphasis—embodied in the proposals for a European Recovery Program (what became known as the Marshall Plan)—was to establish a strong and economically integrated Europe.[39] Importantly, the policy shift was not to a sphere-of-influence approach with a direct and ongoing American military and political presence in Europe. Rather, the aim was to build Europe into an *independent center* of military and economic power, a third force.

This new policy was advanced by several groups within the State Department.[40] The new emphasis on building centers of power in Europe was a view

George Kennan had already held, and it was articulated with some vigor by Kennan's Policy Planning staff, newly organized in May 1947. "It should be a cardinal point of our policy," Kennan argued in October 1947, "to see to it that other elements of independent power are developed on the Eurasian land mass as rapidly as possible in order to take off our shoulders some of the burden of 'bi-polarity.' "[41]

Kennan's Policy Planning staff presented its first recommendations to Secretary of State George Marshall on 23 May 1947. Their emphasis was not on the direct threat of Soviet activities in Western Europe, but on the war-ravaged economic, political, and social institutions of Europe that made communist inroads possible. An American effort to aid Europe "should be directed not to combatting communism as such, but to the restoration of the economic health and vigor of European society."[42] In a later memorandum the Policy Planning staff argued that the program should take the form of a multilateral clearing system to lead to the reduction of tariffs and trade barriers and eventually to take the form of a European Customs Union.[43] Moreover, the Policy Planning staff argued that the initiative and responsibility for the program should come from the Europeans themselves. This group clearly envisaged a united and economically integrated Europe standing on its own apart from both the Soviet sphere and the United States.[44] "By insisting on a joint approach," Kennan later wrote, "we hoped to force the Europeans to think like Europeans, and not like nationalists, in this approach to the economic problems of the continent."[45]

Another group of State Department officials working on European recovery prepared a memorandum of major importance in May 1947 that outlined objectives of American foreign aid.[46] The chief objective of U.S. policy, they argued, should be to strengthen the political and economic countries of Europe and by so doing create the conditions in Europe to induce the Soviets to negotiate with the West rather than continue a policy of unilateral expansion. The objective was to foster a strong and economically integrated Europe. Moreover, the memorandum argued that U.S. policy should be directed at increasing the western orientation of European leaders. In France, Italy, and Germany, in particular, policy should be directed at preventing leaders from drifting to the extreme Left or Right. A European recovery program, these officials argued, would need to stress political and ideological as well as economic objectives. In summarizing the document, Beugel notes that in meeting these objectives a "purely economic program would be insufficient. Non-communist Europe should also be provided with possible goals to help fill the present ideological and moral vacuum. The only possible ideological content of such a program was European unity."[47] The idea of a united Europe was to provide the ideological bulwark for European political and economic reconstruction.

Other State Department voices echoed the call for a shift in policy. Under Secretary of State William Clayton returned from Europe on 19 May alarmed by the economic distress of Europe. In a memorandum to Acheson and Marshall, Clayton argued that the United States had underestimated the destruction of Europe's economy and stressed the need for immediate and large-scale action.[48] On 8 May Under Secretary Acheson took the occasion of a public speech to outline the imperatives of European recovery and foreshadowed the Marshall Plan.[49]

The public turning point in U.S. policy came on 5 June 1947 with Marshall's speech at Harvard University. The American government was now ready to play a much more direct and systematic role in European reconstruction. Yet State Department officials, in a theme echoed throughout this period, were insistent that European leaders themselves take responsibility for organizing the program. At a State Department meeting on 29 May 1947, for example, Kennan "pointed out the necessity of European acknowledgement of responsibility and parentage in the plan to prevent the certain attempts of powerful elements to place the entire burden on the United States and to discredit it and us by blaming the United States for all failures." Similarly, Bohlen noted that the United States had to balance the "danger of appearing to force 'the American way' on Europe and the danger of failure if the major responsibility is left to Europe." The United States would need to make it clear to the Europeans, Bohlen argued, that "the only politically feasible basis on which the United States would be willing to make the aid available is substantial evidence of a developing overall plan for economic cooperation by the Europeans themselves, perhaps an economic federation to be worked out over 3 or 4 years."[50]

A policy of fostering European independence rather than a spheres-of-influence policy had both practical and ideological considerations. Within the Truman administration some officials stressed the policy's importance in strengthening European democracies against communist subversion. Others focused on its usefulness in rebuilding Franco-German relations. Still others found the policy important in promoting expanded production and stability of the European economy.

There were also domestic political reasons for administration support for a united Europe. Congress and American public opinion were in 1947 still wary of permanent political and military commitments to Europe. Such domestic considerations are evident in discussions by Truman administration officials as they prepared to sell the Marshall Plan aid program to Congress. In the foreign assistance legislation that funded the European Recovery Program, Congress made greater European unification a condition for aid.[51]

The idea of a united Europe also fit well with American ideals. "The vague uneasiness and even irritation about the fragmentation of the old world and the genuine desire to transplant the American image to the shattered European countries were translated into a plan and subsequent action." Moreover, State Department officials felt that by encouraging independence and self-determination in Europe, the emergence of democratic institutions would be more likely to succeed. John Gaddis summarizes this notion: "the view in Washington persisted throughout the late 1940s that the viability of political systems depended in large part upon their autonomy, even spontaneity. For this reason, Americans were willing to tolerate a surprising amount of diversity within the anti-Soviet coalition."[52]

The European Recovery Program put the economic and political reconstruction of Europe into a security framework. It was at this juncture that Kennan's ideas most resonated with official U.S. policy. The crisis of Europe, according to these officials, was not due to the pressure of communist activities. Policy Planning and the others believed that "the present crisis resulted in large part from the disruptive effects of the war on the economic, political and social structure of Europe."[53]

European responses to American efforts to assist in economic and political reconstruction were initially quite enthusiastic. British Foreign Minister Ernest Bevin, listening to Marshall's speech on the BBC, accepted the offer of assistance immediately; and he quickly traveled to Paris to begin consultations with the French. The new attitude toward European unity was later reaffirmed by Bevin on 22 January 1948. Announcing that "the time had arrived for a new consolidation of Western Europe, Bevin argued for European civilization." United States officials welcomed Bevin's speech as a signal of European initiative.[54]

The major product of the early negotiations among European officials was the Organization for European Economic Cooperation (OEEC), which came into being on 5 June 1948. At each step along the way, the United States used its economic strength, primarily in the form of dollar aid, to promote European unity, while at the same time attempting to remain outside the negotiations. In addition to organizations devoted to the administration of U.S. aid, monetary and trade liberalization agreements were also forged.

Yet the building of a third force, the central objective of American policy between 1947 and 1950, fell short of American hopes. Disagreements between the British and the French over the extensiveness of supranational political authority and economic integration left the early proposals for unity unfulfilled. W.W. Rostow notes: "[B]ecause the British opposed it, because the economic requirements of unity did not converge with requirements for prompt recovery, and because the United States was unclear as to how its influence should be applied—the Marshall Plan did not succeed in moving Western Europe radically towards unity."[55]

In late 1949 a tone of urgency was heard in State Department discussions of European integration. In a memorandum written by Secretary of State Acheson, shifts in administration thinking were evident. With British reluctance to lead a movement toward European integration, Acheson noted that "[t]he key to progress towards integration is in French hands." Moreover, Acheson was willing to settle for integration on the continent itself and introduced the possibility of American participation in the Organization of European Economic Cooperation. Yet on these revised terms the United States continued to push for integration that would involve "some merger of sovereignty."[56]

The United States wanted to encourage an independent Europe—a third force and not to establish an American sphere of influence. Yet the Europeans could not agree among themselves to organize such a center of global power; the United States, despite its hegemonic power, could not see to its implementation. Just as in the earlier phase, when the goal of U.S. policy was that of global, liberal multilateralism, severe limits of U.S. power were experienced. Beugel makes this point:

> In dealing with sovereign states, even if these states are impoverished and politically and economically impotent, as was the case in Europe during the first years of the Marshall Plan, there is a limit beyond which even a country of the unique power of the United States cannot go in imposing far-reaching measures such as those leading to European integration.[57]

The irony is that while the United States was unwilling and probably unable to use more direct coercive power to encourage European unity, European resistance was not to the use of American power but to the ends toward which it was to be put. The United States wanted to avoid a direct, ongoing security commitment to Western Europe and the emergence of a sphere of influence that such a policy would entail. Yet as East-West tensions increased and as British and continental governments frustrated plans for a geopolitical third force, a new phase of American policy unfolded. Europe actively courted the extension of American power and, in the guise of NATO, a subordinate position in an American sphere of influence.

THE "PULL" OF EUROPE: EMPIRE BY INVITATION

In 1947 and the following years, the United States appeared to hold the military and economic power needed to shape the terms of European reconstruction. With a monopoly on the atomic bomb, a massive (although demobilizing) standing army, and an industrial economy enlarged by the war, the United States appeared to have all the elements of hegemonic power. Moreover, the United States had what Europeans needed most: American dollars. "More and more as week succeeds week," the Economist noted in May 1947, "the whole of European life is being overshadowed by the great dollar shortage. The margin between recovery and collapse throughout Western Europe is dependent at this moment upon massive imports from the U.S."[58]

It is all the more striking, therefore, how successful the European governments were at blunting and redirecting American policy toward Europe. This resistance by Europe to the construction of a third force had several sources and differed from country to country. Each sought to use American hegemonic power for its own rational purposes. At the same time, the same considerations that led to the rejection of a full-blown united Europe prompted these same governments to encourage a direct American political and security presence in Europe.

The British were the most resistant to a united Europe. Britain initially reacted positively to the larger political objectives of Marshall Plan aid. A secret Cabinet session in March 1948 concluded that Britain "should use United States aid to gain time, but our ultimate aim should be to attain a position in which the countries of western Europe could be independent both of the United States and of the Soviet Union."[59] Yet as a practical matter, the British resisted significant steps in that direction. In a meeting of American ambassadors in Europe in October 1949, David Bruce argued: "We have been too tender with Britain since the war: she has been the constant stumbling block in the economic organization of Europe. . . ."[60]

The British were eager to maintain their special relationship with the United States, but feared it would be undermined by the emergence of a confederation with European countries. Moreover, the political and economic burdens of sustaining a European center of power would only further strain the British Commonwealth system. As with several of the other European countries, the British also feared the eventual dominance of Germany or even Russia in a unified Europe. These considerations implied the need for more, not less, American involvement in postwar Europe, particularly in the form of the NATO security relationship. As David Calleo has recently noted: "NATO seemed an ideal solution. With American commanders and forces taking primary responsibility for European ground defense, no question would remain about America's willingness to come to Europe's aid. Britain could reserve for itself those military and naval commands needed to retain control over its own national defense."[61] Indeed, in 1952 the British sought to reduce the role of the OEEC and transfer its functions to NATO—an attempt to build the Atlantic relationship at the expense of European unity.[62]

British officials were more concerned with preventing a return by the United States to an isolationist position than with an overbearing American hegemonic presence in Europe. "The fear was not of American expansionism," Gaddis notes, "but of American isolationism, and much time was spent considering how such expansionist tendencies could be reinforced."[63] It is no surprise, therefore, that in encouraging the United States to lead a security protectorate of Europe, the British began to stress the seriousness of the Soviet threat in Europe. In January 1948, British Foreign Minister Ernest Bevin warned Washington of "the further encroachment of the Soviet tide" and the need to "reinforce the physical barriers which still guard Western civilization."[64]

The French also sought to put American resources to their own national purposes and encourage an Atlantic security relationship. To be sure, France was more sympathetic to American ideas of European integration. Integration was useful in fostering French-dominated coalitions of governments in Western Europe. A political and economic union would also allow France to have some influence over the reemergence of the German economy as well as tie Germany to a larger regional framework.[65] At the same time, however, the French also had an interest in encouraging a larger American security relationship with Europe. NATO, even more than a European community, would serve to contain Germany and the Soviets. Moreover, as with Britain, an American presence would free French resources, otherwise tied up in European defense, for purposes of preserving the remains of its colonial empire.[66]

Germany also supported American leadership of NATO. For West Germany's Chancellor Konrad Adenauer, the Atlantic security relationship was a means of rebuilding German sovereignty and equality on the continent. Germany had less room for maneuver than Britain or France, but participation in regional integration and NATO served the goals of political and economic reconstruction.[67]

In late 1947, efforts intensified by Europeans to draw the United States into a security relationship. British Foreign Minister Bevin outlined his ideas on military cooperation to Secretary of State Marshall on 15 December 1947. A regional European organization centered around Britain, France, and the Benelux countries would be linked to the other Western European countries and to the United States. Marshall signaled his interest in the plan but later indicated that the United States could not presently make any commitments.[68] Other European officials, such as Belgian Prime Minister (and Foreign Minister) Paul-Henri Spaak, were also calling for American military cooperation.[69]

Bevin's urgings were given prominence in his 22 January 1948 speech in the House of Commons. Later Bevin argued that European defense efforts would not be possible without American assistance. "The treaties that are being proposed cannot be fully effective nor be relied upon when a crisis arises unless there is assurance of American support for the defense of Western Europe."[70]

The French also sought to draw the United States into playing a military role in Western Europe. Foreign Minister Georges Bidault called upon the United States "to strengthen in the political field, and as soon as possible in the military one, the collaboration between the old and the new worlds, both so jointly responsible for the preservation of the only valuable civilization."[71]

Some officials in the Truman administration, such as Director of the Office of European Affairs John D. Hickerson, were urging military cooperation with Western Europe.[72] Others, most notably George Kennan, resisted the idea of a military union, arguing that it would be destructive of the administration's goal of European unity.[73] The official position of the Truman administration during this period was ambiguous: it was sympathetic to European concerns but reluctant to make a commitment. After repeated British attempts to obtain an American pledge of support, Under Secretary Robert Lovett informed the British ambassador that the Europeans themselves must proceed with discussions on European military cooperation. Only afterward would the United States consider its relationship to these initiatives.[74] The British, undeterred, continued to insist on American participation in plans for Western European defense.

It was not until 12 March, after the coup in Czechoslovakia, which demonstrated the Soviet hold on East Europe, and the further deterioration of East-West relations, that the United States agreed to engage in joint talks with the West Europeans on an "Atlantic security system."[75] In the months that followed, American and European differences narrowed, largely with the United States coming to agree on an integrated security system with itself at the center.

Taken together, the United States and State Department officials such as George Kennan were much more eager to see an independent Europe than the Europeans themselves. In the end, the European governments were not willing to take the risks, expend the resources, or resolve the national differences that would necessarily be a part of an independent, third force. Political life within an American hegemonic system and a bipolar world was the more acceptable alternative.

Part of the reason for this "craving for dependence,"[76] as David Calleo has recently put it, is that the European nations, except perhaps for Germany, were able to develop the means for maneuver within that American hegemonic system. Such was the case for Britain, as it is noted by Charles Maier:

> Within the American "hegemony" Britain preserved as much of her Commonwealth position, her shielding of her balance of payments, as possible. She also played what might be termed the "Polybian" strategy, attempting to become the Greeks in America's Roman empire, wagering on the "special relationship" to prolong their influence and status.[77]

The more general point is that the European encouragement of an American presence in Europe served a variety of national needs. The room for maneuver within that hegemonic system ensured that those needs would at least in part be met. Moreover, to tie the United States to a formal security relationship with Europe would provide a much more effective basis for the Europeans to influence and shape the American exercise of hegemonic power than would be the case with a less encumbered America. Even as Britain and the continental governments invited America's political and military presence in Europe, it ensured that the international economic system that would attend that new relationship was sufficiently based on European terms.

FROM LIBERAL MULTILATERALISM TO "EMBEDDED LIBERALISM"

The United States failed in its initial attempt to bring liberal multilateralism to Europe. The coercive use of American hegemonic power, most explicitly evident in the British loan, was largely self-defeating. The Marshall Plan represented a shift in policy toward regional reconstruction and a politically independent and integrated Europe. The Europeans took the aid but declined the invitation to move toward a third force in a multipolar world. At the same time, as we have seen, the Europeans (with leadership from British Foreign Minister Bevin) actively sought to extend the American security presence to Western Europe.

The United States was prevailed upon to defend a grouping of western industrial democracies. But what kind of grouping? In late 1949 officials within the Truman administration were uncertain. "It is not yet clear," Acheson argued, "what is the most desirable ultimate pattern of deeper international association of the United States, British Commonwealth, and Europe, and I do not believe that anyone should blueprint a course far ahead with any great rigidity."[78] Nonetheless, even as American policy shifted, the Truman administration clung to a now more distant objective of liberal multilateralism. Liberal economic internationalism, although initially blocked by the imperatives of European reconstruction and the unfolding cold war, was not abandoned, at least in rhetoric. William Clayton noted this in a broadcast on 22 November 1947: "The Marshall Plan, or the European Recovery Program, has to do with the short-term emergency needs of one part of the world. The International Trade Organization has to do with long-range trade policies and trade of all the world. They are highly complementary and interrelated."[79]

This observation was more a hope than anything else. The Marshall Plan was not simply an interim step to place the European economies in a position to participate in a system based on earlier elaborated American plans for liberal multilateralism. Rather, the working out of these policy shifts served to alter the substantive character of those liberal, multilateral designs. This policy retreat and what it reveals about American hegemonic power is noted by Fred Hirsch and Michael Doyle:

The limited capacity of the United States to determine the international economic order actually in force, even at the peak of American military-economic predominance in the immediate aftermath of World War II, is a striking indication of the extent to which relationships between the United States and other major Western powers at this time fell short of unqualified American hegemony. For the striking fact is that the United States was not able to impose its preferred multilateral trading order on the major trading countries. It was able to set the frame for such an order, as embodied in the major provisions of the IMF [International Monetary Fund] and the proposed International Trade Organization (ITO). But these provisions themselves had to be considerably modified, as compared with the original United States proposals, to make them acceptable to other governments. The original United States conception was thus weakened substantially by the resulting allowance made for transitional provisions, for exceptions to nondiscrimination and absence of restrictions, and for the ultimate escape by countries from the discipline of the international system through exchange adjustment.[80]

Throughout the period, these concessions and compromises were indirect and were manifest as the United States sought to promote political stability and noncommunist regimes in Western Europe. The effort to encourage noncommunist alternatives in continental Europe was pursued from many quarters of the American government. At the State Department Charles Bohlen argued in 1946 that the United States should direct the Left in democratic directions. "It is definitely in the interest of the United States to see that the present left movement throughout the world, which we should recognize and even support, develops in the direction of democratic as against totalitarian systems."[81] Later, George Kennan argued that the Marshall Plan itself was the key to building the strength of anticommunist forces.[82] Where serious communist parties contended for power, such as in Italy and France, the United States was willing to come to the aid of all parties to their right, including socialists.

United States involvement in support of noncommunist forces in Italy during the crucial 1948 national elections reveals this strategy. An immediate aim during this period was the bolstering of the noncommunist Italian Socialists. The American ambassador, James Dunn, searched for ways to channel funds to strengthen the fragile political base of the Socialists as well as those to the right.[83] The attempt was made to prevent the Italian Socialist Party from joining the ranks of the communist-led electoral alliance. In the end, with massive American covert aid and threats of the cut-off of Marshall Plan assistance, the Christian Democrats won a commanding electoral victory and a majority in parliament.

The primacy of stability in Western Europe, built around noncommunist political parties, had larger ramifications for American foreign economic policy. Indirectly at least, this commitment meant that the United States would need to accommodate social democratic goals in the construction of international economic order. The successful political reconstruction of Europe meant not just a delay in the realization of liberal, multilateral goals, but their permanent alteration.

Although not framed as an explicit shift in international economic objectives, the United States did gradually move to accept a modified liberal, multilateral order. For the most part this took the form of exemptions and abridgements in trade and financial arrangements. Together, these compromises allowed a larger measure of national economic autonomy and a stronger role of the state in pursuing full employment and social welfare. The discipline of the international market would be softened by the welfare state. The differences between Britain and the United States over postwar economic arrangements were representative of the larger American-European split. At each turn during negotiations over monetary and trade rules and institutions, Britain sought arrangements that would be congenial with an expanded domestic state role in employment and social welfare.

Compromises between multilateralism in international economic relations and state intervention in the domestic economy and society are what John Ruggie has termed "embedded liberalism."[84] "The task of postwar institutional reconstruction," Ruggie argues, was to "devise a framework which would safeguard and even aid the quest for domestic stability without, at the same time, triggering the mutually destructive external consequences that had plagued the interwar period."[85] In other words, rules would be devised to allow for nondiscrimination in commercial and monetary relations, but also to facilitate the welfare state.

Ruggie argues that a loose consensus existed among the industrial democracies, even during the war, on the need to make compromises between postwar liberal multilateralism and domestic interventionism. This was the case, however, only at the most general level. The types of compromises were achieved in piecemeal fashion over the course of the entire 1940s. European countries gave ground on the American insistence that multilateralism be at the core of international economic arrangements. The United States came to accept the need to protect newly emerging Keynesian economic policies and the provisions of the welfare state. But these compromises were less explicit and negotiated than a product of the failure of such instruments of liberal multilateralism as the Anglo-American Financial Agreement and the International Trade Organization.

At each stage of negotiation the British sought to make American monetary and commercial proposals contingent on expanded production and employment. Behind Britain's conditional response to American initiatives were various factions on the Left and Right that opposed liberal multilateralism.[86] Uniting these groups was a skepticism of economic liberalism at home or abroad. A British newspaper of the day noted: "We must . . . reconcile ourselves once and for all to the view that the days of *laissez-faire* and the unlimited division of labor are over; that every country—including Great Britain—plans and organizes its production in the light of social and military needs, and that the regulation of this production by such 'trade barriers' as tariffs, quotas, and subsidies is a necessary and integral part of this policy."[87]

In British debates on the various trade and financial agreements, as Gardner notes, officials "devoted considerable efforts to showing that full employment and domestic planning would not be impeded by the multilateral arrangements."[88] In negotiations over the ITO these concerns were manifest in safeguards and escape clauses, in the removal of agriculture from the framework, and in transition periods to multilateralism. As one British official noted in discussions over trade arrangements, "There must be in the international settlement which we are now devising sufficient escape clauses, let-outs, special arrangements, call them what you will, which will enable those countries which are adopting internal measures for full employment to protect themselves. . . ."[89]

These efforts to protect domestic economic and social obligations of the state came primarily from Britain and the other European countries. The Europeans themselves were crucial in recasting the terms of liberal multilateralism—if only in resisting, modifying, and circumventing American proposals. In insisting on the primacy of domestic stability in the development of international economic rules and institutions, the Europeans (and most importantly the British) successfully recast the character of postwar economic order. The story of postwar international political economy is as much that of the triumph of the welfare state as of the halting and partial emergence of liberal multilateralism.

CONCLUSION

The structure of the early postwar system bears the profound marks of American ideas and the projection of its power; about this there is no dispute. The task here has been to reconsider the conventional understanding of that power and the fate of those ideas. American power was unprecedented, but it was not unalloyed. The United States was not able to implement the full range of its proposals for postwar order; but it did get drawn into a larger hegemonic role in Europe than it anticipated or wanted. In understanding this duality of the American postwar experience, we are better able to appreciate the substance, scope, and limits of American hegemonic power.

The failure of the first efforts at multilateralism and the failure of policies to promote European unity say a great deal about the character of American hegemonic power after the war. The direct use of American power to coerce European acceptance of liberal, multilateral designs (seen most clearly in the British loan episode) were singularly unsuccessful. Less direct methods of pursuing even a revised plan for European regional cooperation also fell short. The purpose of the Marshall Plan was to restore the political confidence of the Europeans. Yet as Gaddis notes, once this was the objective, it was the Europeans who could dictate what it would take to produce confidence.[90] In the end, this required a direct American military commitment.

The Europeans wanted a stronger and more formal hegemonic system than the United States was initially willing to provide. The initial one world plans of collective security and economic universalism would have been a very cost-effective form of *Pax Americana*. The obligations to Europe would have been minimal and they would have accorded with prevailing U.S. congressional and popular public opinion. The system, once constituted, was envisaged to be self-regulating. Given American economic size and competitiveness, this global open door would both serve its own interests and resonate with time-honored American liberal ideas of politics and economics. However, not only were the assumptions behind this vision of postwar order wrong, but the United States, despite its preponderance of economic and military resources, was unable to implement its essential parts.

The revised strategy of a European third force and the construction of a multipolar order was equally elusive. It again revealed the limits of American postwar power. These limits were recognized by many of the American officials themselves. In promoting the idea of a united Europe in the context of Marshall Plan aid, the Truman administration insisted that Europe itself take the initiative. More direct American pressure would have been self-defeating, but its absence also ensured that the Europeans could set the limits on cooperation and integration. It was the very weakness of the European economies and societies that prevented the United States from translating its array of power resources into bargaining assets. The United States could not push too hard. The Europeans, in turn, could set the terms upon which to pull the United States into economic and security relationships.

In the end the United States had to settle for a more traditional form of empire—a *Pax Americana* with formal commitments to Europe. The result was an institutional relationship that diverted American resources to Europe in the form of a security commitment, allowing the Europeans to employ their more scarce resources elsewhere and providing the ongoing institutional means for the Europeans to influence and render predictable American hegemonic power. In blunting and altering the substantive character of international economic relations to ensure the survival of budding welfare states, the Europeans succeeded in drawing the United States into protecting a system that they were able to effectively redefine. As students of empire have often noted, the flow of ideas and influence between empirical center and periphery works in both directions.[91] Unable to secure a less formal and more ambitious *Pax Americana,* the United States found itself experiencing the similar two-way flow of ideas and influence.

The sequence of shifts in American policy toward postwar order is often understood as a set of adjustments to the emergence of East-West hostilities. It was the rise of perceptions of threat from the Soviet Union that forced the compromises and that shifted the center of gravity from economic-centered postwar designs to security-centered designs. There are at least two problems with this understanding. First, this interpretation obscures the failures of American policy and the limited ability of the United States to exercise hegemonic power on its own terms. The focus on failure to implement policy in the first two phases of U.S. policy reveals these limits and the striking ability with which the Europeans could resist American initiatives from a position of weakness.

Second, perhaps more fateful for the way in which American policy unfolded after World War II was the utter collapse of Great Britain, not the rise of the Soviet Union. In a meeting of American ambassadors in Paris in the autumn of 1949, John J. McCloy, the high commissioner for Germany, argued that perhaps too much emphasis had been given to "the increase of Russian power in the world and too little thought to the enormously important factor that is the collapse of the British Empire."[92] Scholars may have suffered a similar problem. This decline of British power, recognized for decades, accelerated by the destruction of the war, and taking a dramatic turn in 1947, was crucial in weakening the overall political and economic position of Europe in the late 1940s. If the argument made above has merit, it was precisely the weakness of Britain and continental Europe that undermined the ability of the United Slates to successfully employ its hegemonic position after the war. Ironically, it might well be the case that less disparity in the relationship between Europe and the United States after the war could possibly have provided the basis for the realization of more of the American postwar agenda.*

* The author wishes to thank John Lewis Gaddis, Lloyd Gardner, and Klaus Knorr for helpful comments and suggestions. An earlier version of the paper was presented to a seminar on Postwar American Foreign Policy at Rutgers University. Research was supported by funds form the J. Howard Pew Freedom Trust and the Center of International Studies, Princeton University.

NOTES

1. Recent discussions of the implications of American decline include Robert Gilpin, "American Policy in the Post-Reagan Era," *Daedalus* 116 (Summer 1987): 33–67; and Paul Kennedy, *The Rise and Fall of the Great Powers* (New York: Random House, 1988); David P. Calleo, *Beyond American Hegemony: The Future of the Western Alliance* (New York: Basic Books, 1987).
2. Robert O. Keohane, *After Hegemony: Cooperation and Discord in the World Political Economy* (Princeton, N.J.: Princeton University Press, 1984), 37.
3. Robert Gilpin, *War and Change in World Politics* (New York: Cambridge University Press, 1981), 145.
4. Charles P. Kindleberger, *The World in Depression, 1929–39* (Berkeley: University of California Press, 1973).
5. Gilpin, *War and Change.* An earlier formulation of hegemonic power emphasizing similarities in the rise and decline of *Pax Britannica* and *Pax Americana* is in Gilpin, *U.S. Power and the Multinational Corporation* (New York: Basic Books, 1975).
6. Gilpin, *War and Change,* 203.
7. Gilpin, *U.S. Power and the Multinational Corporation.*
8. Gilpin notes: "Much as it happened in the latter part of the nineteenth century and the interwar period, the relative decline of the dominant economy and the emergence of new centers of economic power have led to increasing economic conflicts. During such periods of weak international leadership, international economic relations tend to be characterized by a reversion to mercantilism (economic nationalism), intense competition and bargaining among economic powers, and the fragmentation of the liberal interdependent world economy into exclusive blocs, rival nationalisms, and economic alliances." "Economic Interdependence and National Security in Historical Perspective" in Klaus Knorr and Frank N. Trager, eds., *Economic Issues and National Security* (Lawrence: Regents Press of Kansas, 1977), 61.
9. Keohane, *After Hegemony,* 32.
10. Ibid., 37.
11. Duncan Snidal makes a distinction between hegemony that is benign and exercised by persuasion, hegemony that is benign but exercised by coercion, and hegemony that is coercive and exploitive. Snidal, "Hegemonic Stability Theory Revisited," *International Organization* 39 (Autumn 1985). In another effort to distinguish between types of hegemonic power, Hirsch and Doyle note those of cooperative leadership, hegemonic regime, and imperialism. See Fred Hirsch and Michael Doyle, *Alternatives to Monetary Disorder* (New York: McGraw Hill, 1977), 27.

12. Kindleberger, *World in Depression;* see also Kindleberger, "Dominance and Leadership in the International Economy," *International Studies Quarterly* 25 (June 1981): 242–54.

13. Gilpin, *War and Change;* Stephen Krasner, "State Power and the Structure of International Trade," *World Politics* 28 (April 1976): 317–43.

14. For an overview of this literature see Stephan Haggard and Beth Simmons, "International Regimes," *International Organization* 41 (Summer 1987). Some scholars, employing a sociological perspective, focus on the role of regimes as institutions that inform the process by which nations define and pursue their interests. See Stephen Krasner, ed., *International Regimes* (Ithaca, N.Y.: Cornell University Press, 1983). Others have developed microeconomic models that relate the maintenance of regimes to strategic interactions of states. See Keohane, *After Hegemony.*

15. Bruce Russett, "The Mysterious Case of Vanishing Hegemony; or Is Mark Twain Really Dead?" *International Organization* 39 (Spring 1985); Susan Strange, "The Persistent Myth of Lost Hegemony," *International Organization* 41 (Autumn 1987).

16. Strange, "The Persistent Myth of Lost Hegemony," 555.

17. U.S. National output more than doubled in real terms during the war: American GNP rose from $91 billion in 1939 to $210 billion in 1945.

18. Krasner, "American Policy and Global Economic Stability" in William P. Avery and David P. Rapkin, eds., *America in a Changing World Political Economy* (New York: Longman, 1982), 32.

19. This does not in itself argue against the presence of the hegemonic power, but it does suggest the importance of congenial domestic coalitions to support its exercise.

20. Strange, "The Persistent Myth of Lost Hegemony," 560–561.

21. Michael Mastanduno, "Postwar East-West Trade Strategy," *International Organization* 42 (Winter 1987/88).

22. Franz Schurmann argues that the isolationist heritage made a postwar internationalist strategy difficult to sustain unless it was clothed in liberal ideals. The reluctance of portions of American public opinion to get involved in the atavistic power politics of Europe weighed heavily on foreign policy officials. Such involvement, it was argued, had a corrupting influence on the exceptionalism of American politics. Internationalism, consequently, would need to involve reforming and remaking European power politics in an American image–to export American exceptionalism. Schurmann, *The Logic of World Power* (New York: Pantheon, 1974).

23. American liberal multilateral ideas have long historical roots. They can be traced to John Hay's "Open Door" and to the third of Woodrow Wilson's Fourteen Points: "the removal, so far as possible, of all economic barriers." Richard N. Gardner's study remains the most comprehensive account of these ideas and their fate in postwar economic diplomacy. Gardner, *Sterling-Dollar Diplomacy: The Origins and the Prospects of Our International Economic Order* (New York: McGraw Hill, 1969).

24. Ibid., 4.

25. Ibid., 12.

26. Ibid., 31–35.

27. Article Seven to the Mutual Aid Agreement was the object of these negotiations.

28. Gardner, *Sterling-Dollar Diplomacy,* 68. On American wartime efforts to extract British concessions on the postwar trading system, see Lloyd C. Gardner, "Will Clayton, the British Loan, and the Political Economy of the Cold War" in Gardner, *Architects of Illusion: Men and Ideas in American Foreign Policy, 1941–1949* (Chicago: Quadrangel Books 1970), 113–38.

29. For systematic accounts of these monetary agreements, see Gardner, *Sterling-Dollar Diplomacy;* and Armand Van Dormael, *Bretton Woods: Birth of a Monetary System* (London: Macmillan, 1978).
30. For a summary of differences in American and British understandings of Bretton Woods, see Gardner, *Sterling-Dollar Diplomacy,* 143–44. See also Alfred E. Eckes, Jr., *A Search for Solvency: Bretton Woods and the International Monetary System, 1941–1971* (Austin: University of Texas Press, 1975); and Van Dormael, *Bretton Woods.*
31. Gardner, *Sterling-Dollar Diplomacy,* 158.
32. Quoted in ibid., 198.
33. See Robin Edmonds, *Setting the Mould: The United States and Britain 1945–1950* (New York: Norton, 1986), chap. 8.
34. Gardner, *Sterling-Dollar Diplomacy,* 382.
35. Ernst H. Van Der Beugel, *From Marshall Aid to Atlantic Partnership: European Integration as a Concern of American Foreign Policy* (Amsterdam: Elsevier Publishing Co., 1966), 19.
36. Gardner, *Sterling-Dollar Diplomacy,* 294.
37. Quoted in John Gaddis, "Spheres of Influence: The United States and Europe, 1945–1949" in Gaddis *The Long Peace* (New York: Oxford University Press, 1987), 57.
38. Bohlen memorandum, 30 August 1947, *Foreign Relations of the United State* [henceforth FRUS] 1947 (Washington, D.C.: U.S. Government Printing Office, 1973), vol. 1, 763–64.
39. On the role of Europe in American wartime planning and the "relative indifference of the administration to regionalist ideas," see Max Beloff, *The United States and the Unity of Europe* (Washington, D.C.: Brookings Institution, 1963), chap. 1.
40. See Buegel, *From Marshall Plan to Atlantic Partnership,* 41–45. For a fascinating account of the emerging policy views of State Department and other top government officials concerning the rebuilding of Europe, see Walter Isaacson and Evan Thomas, *The Wise Men: Six Friends and the World They Made* (New York: Simon and Schuster, 1987), 402–418.
41. Kennan to Cecil B. Lyon, 13 Octo/Æber 1947, Policy Planning Staff Records. Quoted in Gaddis, "Spheres of Influence," 58.
42. Kennan quotes the memorandum in his memoirs. George Kennan, *Memoirs: 1925–1950* (Boston: Little, Brown, 1967), 336.
43. Beugel, *From Marshall Plan to Atlantic Partnership,* 43.
44. Kennan, *Memoirs: 1925–1950,* 325–353; *FRUS, 1947,* III: 223–230.
45. Kennan, *Memoirs: 1925–1950,* 337.
46. The document was dated 12 June 1947, a week after Marshall's Harvard speech; but the main ideas were circulated earlier. This group, composed of H. van D. Cleveland, Ben T. Moore, and Charles Kindleberger, prepared the memorandum for a major State-War-Navy Coordinating Committee report. Parts of the document are reprinted in Charles P. Kindleberger, *Marshall Plan Days* (Boston: Allen & Unwin, 1987), 4–24. See also Michael Hogan, "European Integration and the Marshall Plan" in Stanley Hoffman and Charles Maire, eds., *The Marshall Plan: A Retrospective* (Boulder, Colo.: Westview Press, 1984), 4–5.
47. Beugel, *From Marshall Plan to Atlantic Partnership,* 45.
48. "The European Situation," Memorandum by the Under Secretary of State for Economic Affairs, *FRUS, 1947,* III: 230–232. Joseph Jones argues that this report had a decisive influence on Marshall's speech and may have prompted the speech itself. *The Fifteen Weeks* (New York: Viking Press, 1955), 203. Clayton's memo reportedly moved

Marshall to confirm his tentatively scheduled appointment to speak at Harvard's commencement exercises. The next day Marshall gave a copy of Clayton's memorandum and Kennan's Policy Planning paper to Bohlen and instructed him to write a speech that would invite Europe to request American aid.

49. Summarized by Beugel, *From Marshall Plan to Atlantic Partnership*, 47–49; see also Dean Acheson, *Present at the Creation* (New York: New American Library, 1966), 227–230.

50. "Summary of Discussion on Problems of Relief, Rehabilitation and Reconstruction of Europe," 29 May 1947, *FRUS, 1947*, III: 235.

51. Section 102(a) of the Economic Cooperation Act of 1948, as amended, stated that: "It is further declared to be the policy of the people of the US to encourage the unification of Europe. . . ."

52. Gaddis, "Spheres of Influence," 59. See also Michael J. Hogan, *The Marshall Plan: America, Britain, and the Reconstruction of Western European, 1947–1952* (New York: Cambridge University Press, 1987).

53. Beugel, *From Marshall Plan to Atlantic Partnership*, 42.

54. Ibid., 121–122.

55. W. W. Rostow, *The United States in the World Arena, an Essay in Recent History* (New York: Harper & Row, 1960), 216. See also Alan S. Milward, *The Reconstruction of Western Europe, 1945–51* (Berkeley: University of California Press, 1984).

56. "The Secretary of State to the Embassy in France," 19 October 1949, *FRUS, 1949*, IV: 469–472. In the subsequent meeting of American ambassadors in Paris, agreement was reached among them that European integration could not proceed without British participation.

57. Beugel, *From Marshall Plan to Atlantic Partnerships*, 220–21.

58. *The Economist*, 31 May 1947.

59. Quoted in Gaddis, "Sphere of Influence," 66.

60. "Summary Record of a Meeting of United States Ambassadors at Paris," 21–22 October 1949, *FRUS, 1949*, IV: 492.

61. David P. Calleo, *Beyond American Hegemony: The Future of the Western Alliance* (New York: Basic Books, 1988), 35.

62. Beloff, *The United States and the Unity of Europe*, 69.

63. John Lewis Gaddis, "The Emerging Post-Revisionist Synthesis on the Origins of the Cold War," *Diplomatic History* 7 (Summer 1983). This statement is based, at least in part, on newly opened records of the British Foreign Office.

64. "Summary of a Memorandum Representing Mr. Bevin's Views on the Formation of a Western Union," enclosed in Inverchapel to Marshall, 13 January 1948, *FRUS, 1948*, III: 4–6.

65. See Maier, "Supranational Concepts and National Continuity in the Framework of the Marshall Plan," 34.

66. Calleo, *Beyond American Hegemony*, 35. See also Michael M. Harrison, *The Reluctant Ally: France and Atlantic Security* (Baltimore: Johns Hopkins University Press, 1981).

67. Calleo, *Beyond American Hegemony*, 35.

68. Memorandum by the British Foreign Office, undated, *FRUS, 1947*, III: 818–819. See also Geir Lundestad, *America, Scandinavia, and the Cold War, 1945–1949* (New York: Columbia University Press, 1980), 171–72.

69. Lundestad, *America, Scandinavia, and the Cold War, 1945–1949*, 172.

70. *FRUS, 1948*, III: 14. In his memoirs, British Prime Minister C. R. Attlee referred to the "making of the Brussels treaty and the Atlantic Pact" as "the work of Bevin." Attlee, *As It Happened* (London: Heinemann, 1954), 171. See also Escott Reid, *Time of Fear and*

Hope: The Making of the North Atlantic Treaty, 1947–1949 (Toronto: McClelland and Steward, 1977).

71. Quoted in Lundestad, "Empire by Invitation? The United States and Western Europe, 1945–1952," *Journal of Peace Research* 23 (1986): 270.

72. Hickerson memorandum, *FRUS, 1948*, IIIL 6–7.

73. Kennan memorandum to Secretary of State, 20 January 1948, *FRUS, 1948*, III: 7–8. See also Kennan, *Memoirs: 1925–1950*, 397–406.

74. Lovett to Inverchapel, 2 February 1948, *FRUS, 1948, III:* 17–18.

75. Ibid., III: 48.

76. Calleo, *Beyond American Hegemony*, 35.

77. Maier, "Supranational Concepts and National Continuity in the Framework of the Marshall Plan," 34.

78. "The Secretary of State to the Embassy in France," 19 October 1949, *FRUS 1949*, IV: 469.

79. Quoted in Beloff, *The United States and the Unity of Europe*, 28.

80. Hirsch and Doyle, *Alternatives to Monetary Disorder*, 29.

81. Quoted in Gaddis, "Dividing Adversaries" in Gaddis, *The Long Peace*, 150.

82. Ibid., 154.

83. James Edward Miller, *The United States and Italy, 1940–1950: The Politics and Diplomacy of Stabilization* (Chapel Hill: University of North Carolina Press, 1986), 243–49.

84. John Gerard Ruggie, "International Regimes, Transactions, and Change: Embedded Liberalism in the Postwar Economic Order," *International Organization* 36 (Spring 1982): 379–415. See also Robert Keohane, "The World Political Economy and the Crisis of Embedded Liberalism" in John H. Goldthorpe, ed., *Order and Conflict in Contemporary Capitalism: Studies in the Political Economy of Western European Nations* (Oxford, Eng.: Clarendon Press, 1984), 15–38.

85. Ruggie, "International Regimes, Transactions, and Change," 393.

86. See Gardner, *Sterling-Dollar Diplomacy*, 30–35.

87. *The Times* (London), 11 January 1941. Quoted in Gardner, *Sterling-Dollar Diplomacy*, 31.

88. Gardner, *Sterling-Dollar Diplomacy*, 234.

89. Ibid., 277.

90. Gaddis, "Spheres of Influence," 62.

91. See Michael W. Doyle, *Empires* (Ithaca, N.Y.: Cornell University Press, 1986).

92. "Summary Record of a Meeting of United States Ambassadors at Paris," 21–22 October 1949, *FRUS, 1949*, IV: 485.

❧ PART THREE ❧

Capitalism, Class, and Foreign Policy

A merican foreign policy is conducted in the leading capitalist society. Accordingly, an important theoretical tradition has investigated the linkages between capitalism, economic interests, and foreign policy. The earliest scholarship in this area emerged in the years before and after World War I, when Marxist and other writers probed the economic and class determinants of European imperialism and war. In the United States the tradition was invigorated again during the Vietnam War as scholars provided radical critiques of American foreign policy. Some writers have focused on the underlying structures of capitalist society and the general pattern of imperialist foreign policy. Here the linkages between capitalism and policy are deep and structural: governmental officials, whether they know it or not, act to protect and advance the interest of capitalism as a whole. The limited range of foreign policy options are generated by the system itself. Others adopt a more narrow instrumental perspective, and focus on particular capitalist elites and particular policies. In this approach it is the capitalists themselves who act within the institutions of government to advance their own class interests.

Jeff Frieden, working primarily within the instrumentalist tradition, provides an interpretation of the historic shift during the interwar period in American foreign economic policy from nationalism to internationalism. After World War I, Frieden argues, many U.S. banks and corporations saw opportunities in overseas expansion and attempted to push American policy in an internationalist direction. Other U.S. corporations saw international competition as a threat and supported the prevailing isolationist stance of government. Throughout the 1920s and early 1930s the two coalitions struggled to dominate foreign economic policy, each attaching themselves to different parts of the governmental apparatus. The standoff ended with the triumph of the internationalist wing of American capitalism, a victory made possible by the crisis of the 1930s and the destruction of foreign economic competition following World War II. Historic shifts in American foreign policy make sense, Frieden argues, only when related to the underlying struggles among competing class factions.

Andrew Bacevich suggests that America's foreign policy establishment created and sustained, for over one hundred years and continuing, a strategy of openness described as "the removal of barriers to the movement of goods, capital, people, and ideas, thereby fostering an integrated international order conducive to American interests governed by American norms, regulated by American power, and, above all, satisfying the expectations of the American people for ever greater abundance." This strategy derives from two core beliefs. The first is that robust and continuing economic growth is an imperative, absolute, and unconditional. The second is that by itself the internal American market is insufficient to sustain the necessary level of economic growth. Over time, this strategy of openness has transcended economic desires and become inseparable from national security. Bacevich illustrates and justifies his argument with an in-depth analysis of the Clinton administration's foreign policy.

Robert Hunter Wade argues that the vast framework of international economic rules and rule-making organizations that underpin the American-led international order benefits the United States at the expense of others, serving to reinforce and strengthen American hegemony. This arrangement, often referred to as globalization, is justified by the claim that it is the natural expression of fairness and common sense. It is anything but. Wade supports his argument with an analysis of international financial architecture and international organizations. He concludes that globalization as we presently understand it is constructed to sustain a grossly unequal world; a redesign of the structural arrangements will be necessary to produce more equitable results.

Sectoral Conflict and U.S. Foreign Economic Policy, 1914–1940

Jeff Frieden

The period from 1914 to 1940 is one of the most crucial and enigmatic in modern world history and in the history of modern U.S. foreign policy. World War I catapulted the United States into international economic and political leadership, yet in the aftermath of the war, despite grandiose Wilsonian plans, the United States quickly lapsed into relative disregard for events abroad: it did not join the League of Nations, disavowed responsibility for European reconstruction, would not participate openly in many international economic conferences, and restored high levels of tariff protection for the domestic market. Only in the late 1930s and

Jeffry A. Frieden, "Sectoral Conflicts and U.S. Foreign Economic Policy:1914–1940,"*International Organization*, 42:1 (Winter, 1988), pp. 59–90. © 1988 by the World Peace Foundation and the Massachusetts Institute of Technology. Reprinted by permission of MIT Press Journals.

1940s, after twenty years of bitter battles over foreign policy, did the United States move to center stage of world politics and economics: it built the United Nations and a string of regional alliances, underwrote the rebuilding of Western Europe, almost single-handedly constructed a global monetary and financial system, and led the world in commercial liberalization.

This article examines the peculiar evolution of U.S. foreign economic policy in the interwar years and focuses on the role of domestic socioeconomic and political groups in determining foreign policy. The American interwar experience powerfully demonstrates that the country's international position and economic evolution do not sufficiently explain its foreign policy. Indeed, although the contours of the international system and the place of the United States in it changed dramatically during and after World War I, these changes had a very different impact on different sectors of American society. World War I dramatically strengthened the overseas economic interests of many major U.S. banks and corporations, who fought hard for more political involvement by the United States in world affairs. Yet domestically oriented economic groups remained extremely powerful within the United States and sought to maintain a relatively isolated America. Through the 1920s and early 1930s, the two broad coalitions battled to dominate foreign economic policy. The result was an uneasy stand-off in which the two camps entrenched themselves in different portions of the state apparatus, so that policy often ran on two tracks and was sometimes internally contradictory. Only the crisis of the 1930s and the eventual destruction of most of America's overseas competitors led to an "internationalist" victory that allowed for the construction of the American-led post–World War II international political economy.

THE PROBLEM

To virtually all observers then and since, at the end of World War I the United States seemed to dominate the international political economy. It had financed the victorious war effort and provided most of the war matériel that went into it; its industry was by far the world's largest and most productive. Despite its traditional economic insulation, the sheer size of the U.S. economy made the country the world's largest trading power. The center of world finance had shifted from London to New York. The United States clearly had the military, industrial, and financial capacity to impose its will on Europe. Yet after World War I the United States, in the current arcane iconography of the field, did not play the part of international economic hegemon, arbiter, and bank roller of the world economic order. The United States was capable of hegemonic action, and President Woodrow Wilson had hegemonic plans, but they were defeated. The problem was not in Europe, for although the British and French were stronger in 1919 than they would be in 1946, they could hardly have stood in the way of American hegemony. Indeed, European complaints about the United States after World War I were in much the opposite direction: the Europeans bitterly protested America's *refusal* to accept the responsibilities of leadership. The Europeans charged that the United States was stingy with its government finance, hostile in its trade policy, scandalous in its refusal to join the League of Nations, unwilling to get involved in overseeing and smoothing Europe's squabbles. The British and French tried for years to entice and cajole a reluctant America into leadership. America would not be budged, at least until 1940.

The world's most powerful nation pursued a contradictory and shifting set of foreign economic policies. The country both asserted and rejected world leadership, simultaneously initiated and blocked efforts at European stabilization, and began such major cooperative ventures as the League of Nations and the Dawes Plan only to limit its participation in these American initiatives in ultimately fatal ways. The analytical problem bedevils both economic determinists and political Realists. For those who believe in the primacy of international power politics, it is difficult to explain why a United States able to reconstruct the world political system was unwilling to do so. For those who look at economic affairs first and foremost, America's unchallenged position as the world's leading capital exporter should have accelerated the trend towards trade liberalization and international monetary leadership begun before World War I; instead, the pendulum swung back towards protectionism and little public U.S. government involvement in international monetary issues.

The relevant international relations literature, faced with such analytical anomalies, generally falls back on vague reference to domestic constraints in explaining U.S. foreign economic policy in the interwar period. Charles Kindleberger, whose comparison of the era with the Pax Britannica and Pax Americana is the foundation stone for most international relations thinking on the interwar years, cites E. H. Carr approvingly to the effect that "in 1918, world leadership was offered, by almost universal consent, to the United States . . . [and] was declined," and concludes that "the one country capable of leadership [i.e. the United States] was bemused by domestic concerns and stood aside."[1]

Seen from the perspective of American domestic politics, however, the problem is quite reversed. In the context of traditional American apathy or even hostility toward world affairs, the interwar years saw an amazing flurry of global activity by the country's political, economic, and cultural leaders. Against the backdrop of the long-standing indifference of most of the American political system to events abroad, the level of overseas involvement in the 1920s and 1930s appears both startling and unprecedented.[2]

The contradictory role of the United States in the interwar period can be traced to the extremely uneven distribution of international economic interests within American society. America's international economic position did change during and after World War I, yet overseas assets were accumulated by a very concentrated set of economic actors. This left most of the U.S. economy indifferent to foreign economic affairs, while some of the country's leading economic sectors were both deeply involved and deeply concerned with the international economy. American foreign policy was thus torn between insularity and internationalism; the segments of the foreign-policy bureaucracy that reflected internationally oriented interests tried to use American power to reorganize the world's political economy, while portions of the government tied to domestically oriented sectors insisted on limiting America's international role. The crisis of the 1930s dissolved many of the entrenched interests that had kept policy stalemated and allowed a new group of political leaders to reconstitute a more coherent set of policies.

This article builds on the work of historians investigating the interwar period[3] and on the contributions of other social scientists concerned with the relationship between the international and domestic political economies. The work of Charles Kindleberger and Peter Gourevitch, among many others, has shown the importance of sectoral economic interests in explaining domestic politics and foreign-policy making in advanced industrial societies. Both Gourevitch and Thomas Ferguson have used a sectoral approach to elucidate domestic and international events in the 1930s. The present article is thus an attempt to build on existing sectoral interpretations of modern political economies and an extension of the approach to problems in international relations.[4]

THE ARGUMENT SUMMARIZED

Between 1900 and 1920 the United States went from a position of relative international economic insignificance to one of predominance. A major international borrower and host of foreign direct investment before 1900, by 1920 the United States was the world's leading new lender and foreign direct investor. The development of American overseas investments was in itself unsurprising, and in this the United States simply repeated the experience of other developed countries. Yet the rapidity of the country's shift from a major capital importer and raw-materials exporter to the leading exporter of capital, largely because of the peculiarities of the international economy in the ten years after 1914, was quite extraordinary. Even as a few major American economic actors were catapulted into global economic leadership, most of the economy remained as inward-looking as ever. This division in American economic orientation was at the root of the foreign-policy problems of the 1920s and 1930s.

As American industry and finance matured and the country became richer in capital, many large American corporations and banks looked abroad for markets and investment opportunities. United States overseas investment thus grew gradually from the 1890s until the eve of World War I. As Table 7.1 indicates, American foreign direct investment was appreciable by 1900; it was concentrated in raw materials extraction and agriculture in the Caribbean basin. By 1912 foreign direct investment was quite substantial and overseas lending had become of some importance; the focus was still the Caribbean area.

The gradual expansion of American overseas investment, especially overseas lending, was given a tremendous shove by World War I. The war forced several belligerent countries to borrow heavily from the United States, and previous borrowers from European capital markets now turned to the United States to satisfy their needs for capital. As Table 7.1 shows, American holdings of foreign bonds soared from less than 5 percent of total American holdings of nongovernment bonds in 1912 to nearly 17 percent in 1922. Foreign direct investment also grew rapidly as European preoccupation with war and reconstruction cleared the way for many American corporations to expand further into the Third World and after the war ended in Europe itself. The 1920s saw a continuation of the wartime

Table 7.1   INDICATORS OF THE IMPORTANCE OF U.S. FOREIGN INVESTMENT, 1900–1939 (IN MILLIONS OF DOLLARS AND PERCENT)

	1900	1912	1922	1929	1933	1939
1. U.S. foreign direct investment	751	2,476	5,050	7,850	7,000[e]	6,750
2. Domestic corporate and agricultural wealth[a]	37,275	75,100	131,904	150,326	109,375	119,324
3. Row 1 as a percent of Row 2	2.0%	3.3%	3.8%	5.2%	6.4%	5.7%
4. U.S. foreign bondholdings[b]	159[d]	623	4,000	7,375	5,048[f]	2,600[g]
5. U.S. holdings of non-government bonds[c]	5,151	14,524	23,687	38,099	37,748	32,502
6. 4/5, percent	3.1%	4.3%	16.9%	19.4%	13.4%	8.0%

[a] Net reproducible tangible wealth of U.S. corporations and agriculture.

[b] Due to the different sources used, figures here conflict with those in Table 7.4; those of Table 7.4 are probably more reliable, but to ensure comparability Goldsmith's figures are used throughout the table.

[c] Excludes only holdings of securities issued by U.S. federal, state, or local governments.

[d] Includes stocks (for 1900 only).

[e] Author's estimates.

[f] Figures are for 1934, from Foreign Bondholders Protective Council, *Annual Report for 1934* (Washington, D.C.: FBPC, 1935), p. 224. This includes only bonds being serviced; a more reasonable measure would include the market value of bonds in default. If this averaged 30% of par value, figures for 1933–34 would be $5,954 million and 15.8% for rows 4 and 6, respectively.

[g] Figures for 1939 holdings of foreign bonds are from Goldsmith and are probably understated.

Source: Foreign investment: Raymond Goldsmith, *A Study of Saving in the United States,* vol. 1 (Princeton, N.J.: Princeton University Press, 1955), p. 1093.

Domestic data: Raymond Goldsmith, Robert Lipsey, and Morris Mendelson, *Studies in the National Balance Sheet of the United States,* vol. 2 (Princeton, N.J.: Princeton University Press, 1963), pp. 72–83.

increase in overseas American lending and investment. American overseas investment in industrial production—especially manufacturing and utilities—and petroleum grew particularly rapidly.

By 1929 American overseas private assets—direct and portfolio investments, along with other assorted long- and short-term assets—were $21 billion. Overseas investments in 1929 were equivalent to over one-fifth of the country's gross national product, a level that was reached again only in 1981.[5]

Although America's overseas investments were substantial by the 1920s, they were very unevenly distributed among important sectors of the U.S. economy. Tables 7.2 and 7.3 illustrate that while overseas investment was extremely important for the financial community and some industrial sectors, most other sectors' foreign assets were insignificant. American foreign investments in mining and petroleum were considerable, both absolutely and relative to capital invested in corresponding activities within the United States. Foreign investment was also of great relative importance to corporations in machinery and equipment (especially electrical appliances), motor vehicles, rubber products,

Table 7.2   FOREIGN DIRECT INVESTMENT AND BOOK VALUE OF FIXED CAPITAL OF SELECTED U.S. INDUSTRIES, 1929 (IN MILLIONS OF DOLLARS AND PERCENT)

Sector	A Foreign direct investment	B Book value of fixed capital	A/B in percent
Mining and petroleum[a,b]	$2,278	$12,886	17.7%
Public utilities, transport, and communications	1,625	41,728[c]	3.9%
Manufacturing	1,534	23,672	6.5%
Machinery and equipment	444	1,907	23.3%
Motor vehicles	184	1,232	14.9%
Rubber products	60	434	13.8%
Chemicals	130	1,497	8.7%
Foodstuffs	222	4,001	5.5%
Lumber and products	69	2,001	3.4%
Metals and products	150	4,788	3.1%
Textiles and products	71	2,932	2.4%
Stone, clay and glass products	23	1,451	1.6%
Leather and products	4	269	1.3%
Agriculture[d]	875	51,033	1.5%

[a] Figures for total manufacturing do not include petroleum refining, which is included under "Mining and petroleum."

[b] Figures for domestic mining and petroleum-invested capital are for the book value of capital including land but excluding working capital.

[c] Value of plant and equipment.

[d] Domestic invested capital is reproducible tangible assets of agricultural sector.

Source: Foreign direct investment: U.S. Department of Commerce, *American Direct Investments in Foreign Countries* (Washington, D.C.: GPO, 1930), pp. 29–36.

Domestic fixed capital: Daniel Creamer, Sergei Dobrovolsky, and Israel Borenstein, *Capital in Manufacturing and Mining* (Princeton, N.J.: Princeton University Press, 1960), pp. 248–51, 317–18; Melville J. Ulmer, *Capital in Transportation, Communications and Public Utilities* (Princeton, N.J.: Princeton University Press, 1960), pp. 235–37; Raymond Goldsmith, Robert Lipsey, and Morris Mendelson, *Studies in the National Balance Sheet of the United States* vol. 2 (Princeton, N.J.: Princeton University Press, 1963), pp. 78–79.

and chemicals. Yet these sectors, which accounted for well over half of all overseas investment in manufacturing, represented barely one-fifth of the country's manufacturing plant; far more American industries were quite uninvolved in overseas production.

Although only a few industries had major foreign operations, foreign lending was a favorite activity on Wall Street. As Table 7.3 shows, between 1919 and 1929 new foreign capital issues in New York averaged over a billion dollars a year, over one-sixth of all issues (excluding federal, state, and local securities); in a couple of years the proportion approached one-third. The United States was the world's principal long-term lender, and foreign lending was very important to American finance.

The reasons for the uneven pattern of overseas investment are fairly straight forward. It is not surprising that a capital-starved world would turn for loans to the capital-rich United States, especially to the Northeastern financial powerhouses.

Table 7.3   NEW CORPORATE AND FOREIGN CAPITAL ISSUES IN NEW YORK,
1919–1929 (IN MILLIONS OF DOLLARS AND PERCENT)

	A All corporate issues	B Foreign issues	B/A in percent
1919	$2,742	$771	28.1%
1920	2,967	603	20.3%
1921	2,391	692	28.9%
1922	2,775	863	31.1%
1923	2,853	498	17.5%
1924	3,831	1,217	31.8%
1925	6,219	1,316	21.2%
1926	8,628	1,288	14.9%
1927	9,936	1,577	15.9%
1928	9,894	1,489	15.0%
1929	11,604	706	6.1%
Total, 1919–1929	63,840	11,020	17.3%
Annual average, 1919–1929	5,804	1,002	17.3%

Source: United States Department of Commerce, *Handbook of American Underwriting of Foreign Securities* (Washington, D.C.: GPO, 1930), pp. 32–37.

Foreign direct investment, on the other hand, responded to more specific incentives. Tariff barriers, which proliferated after World War I, forced former or prospective exporters to locate production facilities in overseas markets; often the advantages of local production were great even in the absence of tariffs. Foreign direct investment was thus largely confined to firms with specific technological, managerial, or marketing advantages, such as motor vehicles, electric appliances and utilities, and petroleum, as well as in the extraction of resources available more readily abroad. There was little overseas investment by industries producing such relatively standardized goods as steel, clothing, and footwear; they generally had little exporting experience and few advantages over firms in their lines of business abroad. Thus the major money-center investment and commercial banks were highly international, as were the more technologically advanced manufacturing and extractive industries; traditional labor-intensive industries, which were by far the majority, were little involved in foreign investment.

American industrial export interests were similar to its foreign investments. The major industrial sectors with overseas investments were also the country's leading industrial exporters, as product-cycle theory would predict.[6] Refiners of copper and petroleum and producers of machinery and equipment, motor vehicles, chemicals, and processed food were all major exporters as well as major foreign investors. The only important exceptions to the general congruence of trade and asset diversification were the steel industry and some agricultural interests, especially in the South. Neither steel producers nor, of course, cotton and tobacco farmers had many overseas investments. To a large extent, then, the trade and foreign investment line-ups were complementary.[7]

Sectors with major overseas investment interests would be expected to have a different foreign economic and political outlook than sectors with little or no international production or sales. Internationally oriented banks and corporations would be generally favorable to freer trade, the former to allow debtors to earn foreign exchange and the latter both because intrafirm trade was important to them and because they tended to fear retaliation. Internationally oriented sectors could also be expected to support an extension of American diplomatic commitments abroad, both specifically to safeguard their investments and more generally to provide an international environment conducive to foreign economic growth. Those sectors that sold but did not invest abroad would be sympathetic to American attempts to stabilize foreign markets but might oppose international initiatives that reinforced competing producers overseas. Economic sectors with few foreign assets or sales could be anticipated to support protectionist policies in their industries because they were not importing from overseas subsidiaries, tended to be less competitive, and had few worries about retaliation. Such sectors would be unsupportive of major American international involvement that might strengthen real or potential competitors of U.S. industry.

Two broad blocs on foreign economic policy did indeed emerge after World War I, and their preferences were more or less as might have been predicted. One group of economic interests was "internationalist": it supported American entry into the League of Nations, U.S. financing of European reconstruction, commercial liberalization, and international monetary and financial cooperation. The other cluster of economic interests was the "isolationists": it opposed the league and American financing of Europe, called for renewed trade protection, and was indifferent or hostile to global financial and monetary accords.[8] The two sets of policy preferences were competing rather than complementary, and although there were some actors in a middle ground, the extreme unevenness of American overseas economic expansion meant that preferences tended to harden in their opposition.

The central dilemma of U.S. foreign economic policy for fifteen years after World War I was the great economic strength of two opposing sets of economic and political actors, neither of which was powerful enough to vanquish the other. Among the consequences of interest to the analyst of international relations is that the state *did not* undertake to impose a foreign policy derived from America's international position upon recalcitrant domestic actors; instead, the central state apparatus found itself torn between conflicting interests. The various economic interests entrenched themselves in the political arena and found allies within the government bureaucracy, so that domestic sociopolitical strife was carried out *within* the state apparatus. The Federal Reserve System and the State Department were dominated by economic internationalists, whether of the Wilsonian or Republican variants; the majority of the Congress and the powerful Commerce Department were more closely aligned with the economic nationalists who might support limited measures to encourage American exports but stopped there.

The result was a foreign policy that was eminently contradictory and volatile. The same administration encouraged foreign lending and trade protection against the goods of the borrowers, worked for international monetary cooperation and sought to sabotage it, struggled to reinforce European reconstruction and impeded it at crucial junctures. This was not due to policy stupidity but to the underlying differences in international outlook of powerful domestic socioeconomic groups. The period is thus a useful and illuminating illustration of the interaction of international and domestic sources of foreign policy.

Although it concentrates on the analytical issues of the 1920s and early 1930s, the article shows how after 1933 the world crisis served to thaw some of the policy paralysis that had characterized the postwar Republican administrations. The international and domestic crises both changed the relative strength of important social actors and allowed policy makers to reformulate their relationship to these social actors.

The remainder of this article analyzes the development of American foreign economic policy from 1914 to 1940 in the light of the preceding considerations. The analysis focuses on the interests and activities of America's international bankers. The nation's international financiers were both the most internationally oriented group of economic actors in the United States at the time (as they are today) and the most powerful and prominent members of the internationalist coalition. Their trajectory demonstrates the general lines of the approach taken here quite well, and also clarifies the role of the differentiated state apparatus in the evolution of U.S. foreign economic policy after World War I. The article does not present a complete account of the period in question—this would require a much more detailed discussion of, among other things, overseas events, America's economic nationalists, and institutional and bureaucratic developments—but it does discuss enough of the era to show how a fuller analysis could be developed.

THE EMERGENCE OF AMERICAN ECONOMIC INTERNATIONALISM, 1914–1933

For fifty years before World War I, the American political economy was oriented to the needs of domestic industry. The war accelerated a process already under way, the expansion of international investments by one segment of the U.S. business community. Along with this economic change came the development of a new set of political interests that challenged the previous pattern of foreign economic policy. In the fifteen years after World War I, the economic internationalists developed great, if quite private, influence over foreign policy but lost many public political battles. Until the Depression, American foreign economic policy was divided between measures to support "nationalist" industries and most of agriculture and those preferred by "internationalist" banks, industries, and some export agriculture.

From the Civil War until the early 1900s, however, the country's foreign economic policy was clearly designed to serve domestic industry, mostly home production for the home market and some exportation. The strategy adopted had a number of aims and evolved over time, as David Lake has demonstrated.[9] Raw materials available overseas needed to be developed and imported. Industrial goods, especially the products of basic industry, needed to find overseas markets.

American tariffs on raw materials might come down, but the American market was essentially closed to industrial goods.

In this picture America's embryonic international bankers played a subsidiary but important role. They financed overseas raw materials developments and facilitated the transport and sale of raw materials to American industry. They lent dollars to overseas consumers of America's basic industrial products—railways, railroad and subway cars, mining equipment, ships. And of course they financed much of the domestic expansion and merger activity of the industrial combines.

World War I was a turning point in the evolution of American international economic interests. During the war and the period immediately following it, New York became the world's center for long-term lending. American financial supremacy drew America's internationally oriented business people and politicians into world leadership during the war and in the postwar reconstruction of Europe, a role that was to be severely hampered by the strength of economic nationalists within the United States.

The outbreak of hostilities caused financial chaos on European money markets. Panic was only narrowly averted in New York, but by early 1915 the New York market had been stabilized and was the only fully functioning major capital market in the world. Originally the Wilson administration had indicated that it considered the extension of all but short-term loans to the warring powers by American financiers "inconsistent with the true spirit of neutrality." But as the fighting continued, the belligerents began to place major orders in the United States to supply their industries and compensate for their lagging agricultures. American munitions exports went from $40 million in 1914 to nearly $1.3 billion in 1916; all merchandise exports increased from $2.4 billion in 1914 to $5.5 billion in 1916, from about 6 percent to about 12 percent of gross national product. Because imports remained near prewar levels, between 1914 and 1917 the United States averaged an astounding annual trade surplus of $2.5 billion, more than five times the immediate prewar average.[10]

The Allies, who accounted for most of this export expansion (the Central Powers were effectively blockaded), financed some of their American purchases by selling back to United States investors about $2 billion in American securities between the beginning of the war and U.S. entry. This was insufficient, of course, and soon the Wilson administration reversed its earlier financial neutrality. In October 1915, J. P. Morgan and Co. underwrote a $500 million loan to the English and French governments. Because of the opposition of neutralists and anti-Russian, German-American, and Irish-American forces, Morgan was only able to secure the full amount with some difficulty.[11]

Despite widespread hostility to their efforts, the New York bankers continued to finance the Allies. In addition, their long-standing ties with the big industrial combines placed the bankers well to arrange for Allied purchases and shipping. Thus Morgan acted during the war as the purchasing agent in the United States for the British and French, and in the three-year period up to June 1917 these purchases amounted to over one-quarter of all American exports.[12]

The Allies' financial requirements increased as the war dragged on, as did American sympathy for the Allied cause. Morgan led a series of syndicates in a further $250 million loan to England in August 1916, another of $300 million in October 1916, a $250 million issue in January 1917; France floated a $100 million bond in March 1917. All told, between January 1915 and 5 April 1917 the Allies borrowed about $2.6 billion: Great Britain and France $2.11 billion, Canada and Australia $405 million, Russia and Italy $75 million.[13]

Upon American entry into the war, private lending to the belligerents essentially ceased. Instead, between May 1917 and April 1919 the U.S. government issued four Liberty Loans and one postwar Victory Loan and used the proceeds to lend the Allies $9.6 billion.[14] American banks also took the opportunity to establish or drastically expand their branches in France to service the hordes of arriving American troops.[15]

Private lending resumed almost as soon as wartime conditions ended, as Table 7.3 indicates. Especially after the 1924 Dawes Plan, which symbolized for many the economic stabilization of Europe, lending boomed. As can be seen in Table 7.4 in the early 1920s American lending also shifted away from the wartime allies and toward "non-traditional borrowers": Germany, Canada, Italy, smaller Western European countries, the more commercially important countries of South America, and the Dutch East Indies. United States banks also expanded their branch network overseas from 26 in 1914 to 154 in 1926. As we have mentioned, direct investment abroad by American corporations also rose very rapidly, from $2.7 billion in 1914 to $7.9 billion in 1929.

The rapid overseas expansion of United States businesses after 1914 led to the maturation of an outward-looking internationalist perspective, especially on the part of the international bankers. The leaders of American finance took a new, broader view of the world in which they had invested and decided that as Woodrow Wilson said in 1916, "We have got to finance the world in some important degree, and those who finance the world must understand it and rule it with their spirits and with their minds."[16]

Apart from the general expansion of their lending, the bankers' customers had changed. No longer were the loans going to specific raw-materials projects or railroad development. The new debtors of the 1920s were more advanced nations; many of them, like Germany, were major competitors of U.S. industry. Concern about American tariffs on manufactured goods was thus logical. The debtors were also usually governments, and the close ties the bankers were building with, for example, Central and Eastern European regimes made them especially interested in European economic reconstruction and political harmony. The major international bankers, then, wanted a more internationalist foreign policy for the United States, lower tariffs, and American aid for a European settlement.

The financiers acted on their beliefs, and the postwar period saw the construction of formal and informal institutions and networks that have ever since been at the center of the American foreign policy establishment. The Council on Foreign Relations was formed right after the war: John W. Davis, Morgan's chief counsel and later a Democratic candidate for president, was the council's first president; Alexander Hemphill, chairman of the Guaranty Trust Co., headed the

Table 7.4 AMERICAN PORTFOLIO OF FOREIGN SECURITIES, 1914–1935 (IN MILLIONS OF DOLLARS; EXCLUDES INTERGOVERNMENT WAR DEBTS)

	1914	1919	1924	1929	1935
Europe	196	1,491	1,946	3,473	2,586
Austria	1	0	27	72	57
Belgium	0	12	181	214	152
Czechoslovakia	—	0	32	32	30
Denmark	0	15	89	165	135
Finland	—	0	29	63	32
France	10	343	449	343	158
Germany	23	2	132	1,019	829
Great Britain	122	891	414	287	42
Hungary	—	0	9	63	57
Italy	0	38	41	365	271
Netherlands	0	0	99	62	132
Norway	3	5	97	185	151
Poland	0	0	30	132	97
Russia	29	127	104	104	104
Sweden	5	20	66	196	213
Switzerland	0	35	116	49	0
Yugoslavia	0	0	18	50	47
Other Europe*a*	3	3	13	72	79
Canada	179	729	1,551	2,003	1,965
South America	43	113	464	1,294	1,241
Argentina	26	58	188	370	344
Bolivia	8	10	38	62	59
Brazil	6	41	146	325	320
Chile	1	1	53	238	237
Colombia	0	1	15	167	146
Peru	2	0	9	77	74
Uruguay	0	2	15	45	51
Venezuela	0	0	0	10	10
Caribbean Region	310	305	390	430	434
Cuba	35	33	76	95	115
Dominican Republic	5	6	15	19	16
Haiti	0	0	17	15	10
Mexico	266	265	270	266	261
Central America	4	2	12	35	32
Asia	217	227	519	926	772
Australia	0	1	24	241	253
China	7	20	23	23	21
Dutch East Indies	0	0	150	175	25
Japan	184	166	234	387	384
Philippines	26	40	88	100	89
Other and international	0	0	0	18	29
Total	945	2,862	4,870	8,144	7,026

Source: Adapted from Cleona Lewis, *America's Stake in International Investments* (Washington, D.C.: Brookings Institution, 1938), pp. 654–55.

a In descending order of financial importance in 1929: Greece, Bulgaria, Rumania, Luxemburg, Ireland, Estonia, Danzig, and Lithuania.

council's finance committee. Thomas W. Lamont of J. P. Morgan and Co. played an active role in the council and brought the founding editor of the council's journal, *Foreign Affairs,* to the job (he was editor of Lamont's *New York Evening Post*). Otto Kahn and Paul Warburg of the investment bank Kuhn, Loeb were founding directors, as was Paul Cravath, the firm's lawyer. Norman H. Davis, another founding director, was a Wall Street banker who served as assistant secretary of the treasury and undersecretary of state under Wilson; he worked closely with Lamont and financier Bernard Baruch in defining the postwar economic settlement in Europe.[17]

The council was the most important such organization, but the internationalist segment of the American business community, headed by the international bankers, also worked with other similar groups. The Foreign Policy Association, the Carnegie Endowment for International Peace (founded 1908), the League of Nations Association, and many others brought scholars, bankers, journalists, politicians, and government officials together in the pursuit of internationalism. In addition to consultation, coordination, and research, the internationalist network aimed to convince average Americans, in the words of the chairman of the Foreign Policy Association, "that their stake in the restoration of normal economic conditions in Europe is in reality as direct and vital as that of the international banker."[18]

More direct was the initiation during World War I of a system of close cooperation between foreign-policy makers, especially those concerned with foreign economic policy, and America's international bankers. It was common for important figures in American international financial circles to serve on policy advisory bodies and sometimes to rotate through positions in government, usually at the State Department and the Federal Reserve Bank of New York. Indeed, during and after the war the State Department and the Federal Reserve Bank of New York established durable working relations with the New York bankers. On every significant foreign policy initiative of the 1920s—from the Versailles Treaty itself to war debts and reparations, to the tariff issue, to the Dawes and Young Plans, to the boom in foreign borrowing and the establishment of the Bank for International Settlements—the international bankers worked together with the like-minded internationalists of the State Department and the Federal Reserve Bank of New York in the evolution of policy.

The financial and other internationalists faced the opposition of extremely powerful forces of economic nationalism in the United States. Senior Morgan partner Thomas Lamont decried "the failure of the American people to understand that the United States of America held a new position in the world" and later reflected on the unfortunate fact that "America entered upon the new decade of the 1920s in full panoply of wealth and power, but possessing little ambition to realize her vast potentialities for strengthening the world in stability and peace."[19]

The stumbling block was the existence of a considerable anti-internationalist political bloc with support from business people who had little interest in foreign affairs, worried about foreign competition, and opposed the export of American capital. The Commerce Department of Herbert Hoover, the prime mover of U.S. economic policy in the 1920s, was closely linked and deeply committed to American domestic industry. In foreign economic affairs its principal concern was thus to promote industrial exports and primary imports, not overseas lending and manufacturing investment. America's domestic industrialists could, like Hoover, agree on some things with the bankers. They all favored expanding American exports, and some kinds of imports. Yet there was little sympathy in domestically oriented industry for freer trade insofar as it meant manufactured imports. Domestic industrialists were also unhappy with American bank loans to foreign competitors, and some of them were wary of capital exports in general. As Hoover put it, "a billion dollars spent upon American railways will give more employment to our people, more advance to our industry, more assistance to our farmers, than twice that sum expended outside the frontiers of the United States."[20]

The United States faced a bewildering array of foreign-policy problems in the 1920s, and in virtually every case the tension between internationalists and nationalists defined the discussion and outcome. There is no need to describe these debates at length, for there is an ample literature on them.[21] Three broad problems—European reconstruction, trade policy, and capital exports—were of special importance, and later I shall summarize the major issues involved in these debates and note the common pattern. In virtually every case internationalist financiers and their allies in the State Department and the Federal Reserve faced the opposition of nationalist forces in Congress and other segments of the executive. The internationalists were almost always defeated, forced to compromise, or forced to adopt some form of semiofficial arrangement that kept the process out of the public eye.

European Reconstruction and War Debts

The general desire of the United States international bankers was for the rapid reconstruction of Europe. Private funds might be used for this purpose, but the financial shakiness of the potential borrowers (especially in Central Europe) made U.S. government involvement preferable. Inasmuch as the debts owed the U.S. government by the Allies were an obstacle to European reconstruction, especially since they encouraged the French to demand larger reparations payments from the Germans, the American financiers favored partial or total cancellation of official war debts.[22] All of this required American leadership: the United States government should help the Europeans back onto the gold standard, arrange for a government-backed bankers' consortium to restore Europe's shattered currencies, regularize and encourage American private capital exports to Europe, force the Europeans to negotiate a reduction of Germany's reparations burden in return for war debts leniency, and combat economic nationalism on the Continent.

This leadership was not forthcoming. Talk of war debt cancellation was quashed by economic nationalists in the cabinet and in Congress, for whom war-debt forgiveness represented a levy on American taxpayers, who would be called upon to make up the Treasury's loss, in favor of the country's European competitors. Although some refunding and reduction did occur, the bankers were forced to retreat. Government-backed loans to the Europeans were also vetoed, as was any official American involvement in the reparations tangle. Only in monetary matters, where the bankers' house organ, the Federal Reserve Bank of New York, was given fairly free rein, was limited progress made.[23]

Opposition to the bankers' plans solidified under President Warren Harding in the early 1920s. Congress and much of the executive branch were intransigent on the war debts and reparations issues. Herbert Hoover's Commerce Department was not generally favorable to financial schemes that might strengthen overseas competitors of American industry or that might allow foreign raw materials producers to raise prices to American manufacturers.[24] Morgan partner Thomas Lamont bitterly blasted "ill-advised steps for the collection of that debt, every penny, principal and interest," while Lamont's *New York Evening Post* editorialized: "We cannot emphasize too often the mischief for the European situation to-day wrought by Herbert Hoover's assertion that 95 percent of America's claims on the continent are good."[25]

It was not for lack of trying that the bankers were unable to secure government involvement. Benjamin Strong at the Federal Reserve Bank of New York played a major role in European reconstruction planning and implementation. As he said when proposing central-bank cooperation for exchange stabilization to an October 1921 meeting of the Board of Governors of the Federal Reserve System, "whether we want to or not we are going to take some part in this situation abroad. We probably won't do it politically, but we have to do it financially and economically." The governors, far more sympathetic to the desperate straits of European finances than the administration, were strongly in favor, as Governor Norris of Philadelphia indicated:

> I think the three great opportunities that we have had to accomplish the stabilization of foreign exchange were, first, to go into the League of Nations; second, to make a readjustment of our tariff . . . and the third was to empower the Secretary of the Treasury to deal in an intelligent way with the refunding of foreign obligations. . . . But because we have lost those three it does not follow, of course, that we ought to throw aside and discard all others . . . [and] it seems to me that the proposition you have suggested is one that undoubtedly has merit and may reasonably be expected to accomplish some results.[26]

Yet a month later the executive branch refused to allow a central bank conference that Strong and Montagu Norman of the Bank of England had proposed. Strong wrote to Norman at the time, "between the lines I read that there would in fact be no objection if the matter were undertaken privately and without government support or responsibility." Thus when the League of Nations's Financial Committee was supervising an Austrian stabilization program in 1922–1923, the New York bankers were regularly consulted to ensure that the program would meet with the approval of U.S. financial markets—which it did when the U.S. portion of the stabilization loan was floated in June 1923.[27]

Nevertheless, for all intents and purposes the bankers' plans for an American-supervised economic settlement in Europe were foiled. As the Central European economies collapsed in 1923 and 1924, the administration attempted to balance the financiers' insistence on American involvement against equally insistent nationalist demands that the United States stay out of Europe. The State Department, anxious to use American influence and finance to stabilize Europe, began the process that would lead to the Dawes Plan in April 1924. The arrangement worked out was ingenious: negotiations were entrusted to an unofficial delegation of American business people, headed by internationally minded Chicago banker Charles G. Dawes and Owen D. Young, chairman of the board of General Electric. The prominent internationalist bankers and business people at the center of the negotiations consulted closely, if surreptitiously, with the State Department and the Federal Reserve Bank of New York.[28]

The Dawes Plan called for foreign supervision of German public finances, with reparations payments overseen by an American with discreet ties to Morgan's. The German currency was stabilized and investor confidence in Germany restored with a $200 million bond flotation, of which J. P. Morgan and Co. managed $110 million in New York.[29] All things considered, the plan was a reasonable compromise: it used American financial supremacy to settle (at least temporarily) a major European wrangle without committing the U.S. government directly. The only open government involvement was an encouragement to American investors to subscribe to the Dawes loan, and indeed Morgan received over a billion dollars in applications, ten times the amount of the loan. The settlement satisfied most internationalists and most nationalists in the United States temporarily, and even this was quite a feat.[30]

Free Trade and the Tariff

Fundamental domestic differences over U.S. trade policy were harder to paper over. Indeed, the future of America's traditional protectionism was perhaps the most contentious issue in American politics in the 1920s. During World War I, the administration had apparently committed itself to low and flexible tariffs, in line with the bankers' preferences. When the United States became a major lender, foreign borrowers had to be permitted freer access to the U.S. market or loans could not be serviced. Tariff barriers, argued the bankers, were a cause of useless trade rivalries and war. As Morgan partner Dwight Morrow put it, "leadership in world trade is not a thing to be sought by any nation to the exclusion of all others."[31]

But in Congress those American economic actors who demanded protection from foreign imports had the upper hand. In 1921 Congress passed a restrictive Emergency Tariff Act that was followed in 1922 by the Fordney-McCumber tariff.[32] This act had provisions that attempted to satisfy both protectionist industrialists and farmers, and less successfully, internationalist bankers, investors, and traders. The compromise was generally unsatisfactory to both factions, and controversy on the tariff raged throughout the 1920s. Few doubted that traditional American protectionism had returned, and the French Finance Ministry called Fordney-McCumber "the first heavy blow directed against any hope of effectively restoring a world trading system."[33]

Such financiers as Otto Kahn looked with dismay on the continued strength of protectionist sentiment:

> Having become a creditor nation, we have got now to fit ourselves into the role of a creditor nation. We shall have to make up our minds to be more hospitable to imports.

We shall have to outgrow gradually certain inherited and no longer applicable views and preconceptions and adapt our economic policies to the changed positions which have resulted from the late war.[34]

Supervision of Foreign Loans

In the early 1920s opposition to the export of American capital mounted. Domestic industrial interests were concerned that the loans were strengthening foreign competitors, especially in Germany, and reducing the capital available to domestic producers. They were also concerned that loans to raw-materials producers might be used to organize producers' cartels that would raise prices charged to U.S. industry. Hoover and Treasury Secretary Andrew Mellon thus wanted to make new loans contingent on the use of at least part of them for the purchase of American goods, or to a commitment by the borrowers to allow American suppliers to bid on ensuing contracts; they also opposed lending to nations disinclined to service their war debts to the U.S. government and lending that might reinforce the position of suppliers to or competitors with American industry. The bankers, of course, along with Benjamin Strong of the Federal Reserve Bank of New York, opposed any government controls; Secretary of State Charles E. Hughes leaned towards their position.

In 1921 President Harding, Hoover, Hughes, and Mellon met with the leading New York bankers and reached an agreement that the banks would notify the Department of State of all foreign loans and give the department the opportunity to object. Formalized in 1922, the policy was applied as sparingly as possible by a State Department that supported the bankers. Even so, in a number of instances Hoover was able to override the bankers; two prominent successes were blocked loans to a French—German potash cartel and to Brazilian coffee growers. The commerce secretary warned "the American banking community" that "the commissions which might be collected on floating such loans would be no compensation" for the "justifiable criticism . . . from the American potash and coffee consumers when [they] become aware that American capital was being placed at the disposal of these agencies through which prices were being held against our own people." Hoover also threatened to form a pool to break a British rubber cartel, complained about American lending to the German steel trust, and he and Mellon succeeded in stopping several loans for reasons related to war debts or other foreign policy objectives.[35]

Here, again, the conflict between the international interests of financiers and the national concerns of many American business people and politicians clashed. Once more, the outcome was indecisive; the State Department succeeded in blunting most of Hoover's attacks on foreign lending he regarded as excessive, yet pressure never let up.

The deadlock between internationalism and nationalism that formed in the early 1920s remained in place throughout the Coolidge and Hoover administrations. Foreign economic policy retained much of its ambiguity, with government departments and the international bankers cooperating and colliding, depending on the issue and the department involved. Internationalist bankers and business people complained bitterly of the Commerce Department's attempts to restrict their activities and to penalize their overseas clients. As Owen Young wrote to Hoover in 1926, "I am sincerely troubled by our national program, which is demanding amounts from our debtors up to the breaking point, and at the same time excluding their goods from our American markets, except for those few raw materials which we must have."[36]

Although a wide range of issues in American foreign economic policy remained unsolved, the financiers fought continually to implement some form of European economic reconstruction. After the Dawes Plan gave Germany, and by implication other Central European borrowers, the stamp of approval of international finance, loans to Europe exploded. Between 1925 and 1930 Americans lent a total of $5.3 billion to foreigners; $1.3 billion went to Canada, $1.6 billion to Latin America, and $305 million to Japan. Virtually all of the rest—$2.6 billion— went to Europe, as follows: Germany $1.2 billion (47 percent of the European total), Italy $345 million (13 percent), Eastern and Southeastern Europe $386 million (15 percent), and Scandinavia $385 million (15 percent); the remainder was scattered across a number of lesser borrowers.[37]

The United States had become the world's leading capital exporter, its bankers often acting as leaders in international financial consortia. By far the most important borrower was Germany; by 1929 American portfolio investment there had gone from nearly nothing to over a billion dollars (see Table 7.4). Germany and Central European prosperity, deemed essential to the political and economic stabilization of Europe, depended largely on injections of United States capital. Between 1925 and 1928 foreigners provided 39 percent of all long-term borrowing by the German public sector and 70 percent of all long-term private borrowing; half of the foreign lending was from America.[38]

Yet it was clear to the financiers that European economic expansion was precarious, and the fundamental division of American foreign economic policy made it more so. The bankers and their allies in the State Department and the Federal Reserve System did what they could to solidify their tenuous attempts at international economic leadership. The curious and often awkward modus vivendi that evolved was illustrated by the financial stabilization programs arranged in a series of European nations between late 1926 and late 1928. In Belgium, Poland, Italy, and Rumania, cooperative central-bank credits—generally put together by the Bank of England and the Federal Reserve Bank of New York—were extended in conjunction with longer-term private loans, of which American banks typically provided at least half. The private bankers were closely involved in the negotiations leading up to the stabilization agreements.[39]

In early 1929 the international bankers who had put together the Dawes Plan—including many who had participated in the financial stabilization programs of the late 1920s—came together again to attempt a further regularization of international financial matters. The United States was represented (unofficially, of course, as at the Dawes Conference) by Owen Young and J. P. Morgan; Thomas Lamont was Morgan's alternate. After dealing with German issues, the conference established the Bank for International Settlements (BIS) to accept continuing German reparations (renamed *annuities*) payments, and more broadly, to manage the international financial system. The BIS, which was the product of the

American financiers, was to promote financial stability and take finance out of the hands of unreliable politicians. Indeed, it was founded in such a way as to make congressional approval unnecessary and congressional oversight impossible.[40]

The BIS, however, was powerless to counter the effects of the Great Depression. In May 1931, the Kreditanstalt failure triggered panic throughout Central Europe. President Hoover recognized the inevitable and in late June 1931 declared a moratorium on the payment of war debts in an attempt to stave off, in Treasury Undersecretary Ogden Mills's words, "a major catastrophe of incalculable consequences to the credit structure of the world and to the economic future of all nations."[41] Nevertheless, in 1932 defaults began in Hungary, Greece, Bulgaria, Austria, Yugoslavia, Sweden, and Denmark; in 1933 Germany and Rumania joined the list. By the end of 1934 over 40 percent of American loans to Europe were in default.[42] In the interim, of course, the United States substantially raised tariffs, even though, as Morgan's Thomas Lamont recalled, "I almost went down on my knees to beg Herbert Hoover to veto the asinine Hawley-Smoot Tariff."[43]

The contradictory nature of American foreign economic policy in the 1920s was much noted by financiers and scholars at the time. On the one hand, there was a massive outflow of private capital to Europe, while on the other, European exports to the United States, necessary to debt service, were severely restricted. To top it off, the Harding-Coolidge-Hoover administrations insisted on considering the Allies' war debts to the U.S. government as binding commercial obligations, which further restricted Europe's capacity to service American commercial debts.[44] The reason for this vacillation was that two powerful sets of interests, economic nationalists and economic internationalists, were fighting for power within the United States, and the battle raged through the 1920s and into the 1930s.

The degree to which the contradictions of U.S. foreign economic policy were recognized by the general public is indicated in Franklin Delano Roosevelt's August 1932 campaign-speech explanation of American foreign lending in *Alice in Wonderful* style:

> A puzzled, somewhat skeptical Alice asked the Republican leadership some simple questions:
> "Will not the printing and selling of more stocks and bonds, the building of new plants, and the increase of efficiency produce more goods than we can buy?"
> "No," shouted Humpty Dumpty. "The more we produce the more we can buy."
> "What if we produce a surplus?"
> "Oh, we can sell it to foreign consumers."
> "How can the foreigners pay for it?"
> "Why, we will lend them money."
> "I see," said little Alice, "they will buy our surplus with our money. Of course these foreigners will pay us back by selling us their goods?"
> "Oh, not at all," said Humpty Dumpty. "We set up a high wall called the tariff."
> "And," said Alice at last, "how will the foreigners pay off these loans?"
> "That is easy," said Humpty Dumpty. "Did you ever hear of a moratorium?"
> And so, at last, my friends, we have reached the heart of the magic formula of 1928.[45]

From 1914 on, major overseas investors, led by the international banks, rapidly extended their influence abroad and at home. Yet the battle for control of the state was undecided; instead of a unitary foreign-policy making apparatus with a coherent strategy, the United States had a foreign economic policy in the 1920s and early 1930s that was dualistic and irrational, in the sense that its various parts were in direct conflict with one another.[46] The political ambiguity of American foreign policy left American financial and other internationalists alone with their grandiose plans in a devastated world, determined that they would not again be defeated by forces that did not share their world vision.

THE RISE OF AMERICAN ECONOMIC INTERNATIONALISM, 1933–1940

Just as the shock of World War I dramatically accelerated the extension of American international economic interests, the shock of the 1930s accelerated the demise of America's economic nationalists. During the first two Roosevelt administrations, economic internationalism gradually and haltingly came to dominate U.S. foreign policy, even as policy making became ever more protected from the economic nationalists who continued to dominate the legislature. Faced with international and domestic economic crises of unprecedented depth and scope, the Roosevelt administration, after a brief attempt to rebuild international economic cooperation, retreated into domestic New Deal reforms, then slowly reemerged in the mid- and late-1930s with a series of international economic initiatives that foreshadowed the postwar Bretton Woods system.

The Depression, indeed, had a devastating impact on the traditional economic and political base of the economic nationalists. Industrial production did not regain its 1929 peak until World War II, and in the interim few regarded industry as the dynamo it had been. Agriculture was even more devastated. The banking system, of course, was also hard-hit, but most of the failures were of smaller banks. The big internationally oriented banks remained active both at home and abroad, although their economic and political influence was reduced both by the Depression itself and by Depression-era banking reforms. Table 7.1 demonstrates the continuing importance of international economic interests. Foreign direct investment, as a percentage of total corporate and agricultural invested capital, climbed through the 1930s, largely due to domestic deflation. Foreign bondholdings, of course, dropped because of defaults; this certainly harmed the bondholders but had little effect on the big investment and commercial banks themselves. In any case, holdings of foreign bonds remained substantial, and international bankers continued to hope that pre-1930 levels of lending could be restored.

When Roosevelt took office in March 1933, he hoped to reconcile two major goals: to stabilize international economic relations and to resolve the country's pressing domestic economic problems. Britain had gone off the gold standard in 1931 to devalue the pound and improve Britain's trade position; it had also moved towards trade protection within the empire. By 1933 international monetary, financial, and trade relations were in shambles. At the same time the United States was in the midst of a serious banking crisis, and the agricultural depression that had begun in the late 1920s was deepening. Roosevelt made no secret of the fact that his first priority was domestic, not international, stability.

The administration went into the international economic conference, which began in London in June 1933, willing to discuss some form of monetary cooperation with the British and French but determined that these discussions should not interfere with domestic economic measures. As it turned out, the participants in the London conference were unable to reconcile national economic priorities with internationalism. Early in July Roosevelt effectively wrecked the conference and any hopes for international currency stabilization, saying that "what is to be the value of the dollar in terms of foreign currencies is and cannot be our immediate concern."[47]

With the collapse of international cooperative efforts Roosevelt turned his attention to the domestic economy. In October the U.S. began devaluing the dollar's gold value from $20.67 to $35 an ounce. Although the devaluation was not quite the success its proponents had expected, it did mark the administration's disenchantment with internationally negotiated attempts at stabilization.[48]

Many international bankers approved of Roosevelt's domestic banking decisions and of the dollar devaluation. Yet as 1933 wore on, they were alarmed by his more unorthodox positions. Hostility between the administration and the financiers continued despite the attempts of Roosevelt and some of the bankers to call a truce, and in late 1933 and 1934, a number of financiers and policy makers close to the financial community left the administration or denounced it.[49]

The first two years of the Roosevelt administration were in fact characterized by divisions within the administration and the banking community, as well as a great deal of policy experimentation. Within the administration a running battle was waged between Wilsonian Democrat Cordell Hull as secretary of state, Assistant Secretary Francis Sayre (an international lawyer and Wilson's son-in-law) and other free-trade internationalists on the one hand, and such economic nationalists as Presidential Foreign Trade Advisor and first President of the Export-Import Bank George Peek on the other.[50] To add to the confusion, Treasury Secretary Henry Morgenthau, Roosevelt's closest adviser on economic affairs, was both fascinated by and ignorant of international financial matters.

The nearly desperate economic crisis made the early Roosevelt administration willing to consider politically and ideologically unorthodox policies.[51] Indeed, much of the bankers' distrust of FDR in 1933–1934 stemmed from the belief that he was embracing the notion of national self-sufficiency—economic nationalism with feeling—that was becoming so popular at the time and was often laced with semifascist ideology. For his part, Roosevelt was seriously concerned with the Depression's effect on the nation's social fabric and was convinced that the British and French were insurmountable obstacles to a stabilization agreement that would allow for American economic recovery. Alarmed by the domestic political situation and thoroughly disenchanted with the British and French, Roosevelt enacted emergency measures to stabilize the system. Some financiers approved; most did not.

After the first frenzied phase of crisis management, however, the administration did indeed begin to move in a cautiously internationalist direction. In June 1934 Congress passed Hull's Reciprocal Trade Agreements Act, which was broadly understood as a move towards freer trade. By 1934, too, the value of the dollar had been essentially fixed at $35 an ounce, indicating a renewed commitment to currency stability. In spring 1935 Roosevelt began cooperating with the French (over British objections) to stabilize the franc and pushed for English, American, and French collaboration for exchange-rate stability.[52] In late 1935 George Peek resigned in disgust over Roosevelt's drift to internationalism.

The financiers responded optimistically, if cautiously, to the administration's international initiatives. Early in 1936 Leon Fraser of the First National Bank of New York expressed his general approval of administration policy and his wish that this policy might become wholehearted:

> . . . [A]fter a period of painful trial and harmful error, the authorities have seemingly reached three conclusions, each vital to monetary stabilization at home and abroad. First, they have in fact, but in silence, rejected the proposed elastic dollar and have relinked the dollar to gold instead of to some commodity index. Second, they have been, and are, practising the gold standard internationally, subject to certain qualifications deemed to be necessary because of the present chaos. Third, as the logical next step, they stand ready to participate with other countries in the restoration of foreign exchange stabilization . . . Excellent—but a more affirmative stand will become necessary, a more explicit recognition of the responsibility which the advocacy of stabilization implies, and some assurances of a readiness to discharge these responsibilities in order to maintain the reestablished order.[53]

The commitment Fraser sought was indeed forthcoming. Through the summer of 1936 the administration, the British, and the French moved slowly towards a "gentlemen's agreement" to restore their currencies' convertibility to gold and commit themselves to mutual consultations and intervention to avoid exchange-rate fluctuations. On 25 September 1936, the three governments agreed on a scheme embodying these commitments, with a dollar effectively linked to gold. The Tripartite Agreement—soon joined by Belgium, Switzerland, and the Netherlands—was a step towards rebuilding international economic cooperation. As one scholar has noted, "the Tripartite system may be seen as the beginning of an historical evolution that would issue after World War II in a global dollar standard."[54] For the first time the United States participated openly and prominently in leading the way towards international monetary cooperation, and the symbolic importance was more significant than any real accomplishments of the agreement.

By 1937, one prominent banker was able to name three developments that had given hope to those whose greatest fear was economic nationalism:

> First, the tripartite monetary agreement of last September was a challenge to the application of economic nationalism in monetary affairs. Second, our bilateral trade negotiations are a challenge to economic nationalism in trade affairs . . . Third, some progress is being made in the direction of the re-creation of a normal international capital market in the Western hemisphere by the recent and current negotiations with South America.[55]

Yet the developing internationalism was hardly the same as the bankers' gold-standard liberal orthodoxy. The new system compromised more with domestic countercyclical demand management and with the imperatives of the embryonic "welfare state."[56] Many of the financiers indeed realized that a return to the classical gold standard was unthinkable and with Leon Fraser in 1936 looked forward merely to "a union of what was best in the old gold standard, corrected on the basis of experience to date, and of what seems practicable in some of the doctrines of 'managed currencies'."[57] Yet during the late New Deal, the foreign exchange cooperation of the Trilateral Agreement, the tentative attempts at trade liberalization (by 1939 the reciprocal trade agreements covered 30 percent of American exports and 60 percent of imports[58]) and newfound moderation towards errant debtors all indicated a less ambiguous internationalist course than at any time since Wilson.

THE EPISODE CONSIDERED

Economic nationalism reigned supreme in the U.S. political economy from 1860 until World War I, while since World War II, economic internationalism has dominated; the period considered here marks the transition from a protected home market to full participation in and leadership of world investment and trade. As such, it is of great interest to those who would draw more general conclusions about the origins of state policy in the international arena. The era involved open conflict over the levers of foreign economic policy. In the midst of this conflict the state was unable to derive and implement a unitary foreign economic policy; faced with a fundamentally divided set of domestic economic interests in foreign economic policy, the state and its policies were also divided. Each grouping of economic interests concentrated its forces where it was strongest: economic internationalists built ties with the State Department and the Federal Reserve System, while economic nationalists concentrated their efforts on Congress and a congenial Commerce Department. As socioeconomic interests were split, so too were policy makers and foreign economic policy itself.

The Depression and eventually World War II weakened the economic nationalists and allowed the state to reshape both policies and policy networks. By the late 1930s, economic nationalists were isolated or ignored, and most relevant decisions were placed within the purview of relatively internationalist bureaucracies. As economic internationalism was consolidated, the foreign-policy bureaucracy came to reflect this tendency—even as, in pre-World War I days, the apparatus had been unshakably nationalist in economic affairs.

The evidence examined here provides little support for theories that regard nation-states as rational, unitary actors in the international system. The most serious challenge of the interwar period is to "statist" assertions that foreign-policy makers represent a national interest that they are able to define and defend.[59] By extension, interwar American foreign-policy making calls into question systemic-level approaches that attempt to derive national foreign policies solely from the position of the nation-state in the international structure.[60]

The national interest is not a blank slate upon which the international system writes at will; it is internally determined by the socioeconomic evolution of the nation in question. Some nations aim primarily to expand their primary exports, others to restrict manufactured imports, still others to protect their overseas investments. These goals are set by the constraints and opportunities that various domestic economic interests face in the world arena and by the underlying strength of the various socioeconomic groups. The ability to pursue these "national interests" successfully, and the best strategy to do so, may similarly be determined by international conditions, but the interests themselves are domestically derived and expressed within the domestic political economy. A nation dominated by agro-exporters may respond to a world depression with redoubled efforts to expand exports, while a nation dominated by domestically oriented industry may respond to the same events with a spurt of industrial protectionism.

Nonetheless, underlying socioeconomic interests are mediated through a set of political institutions that can alter their relative influence. Although the relative importance of American overseas investment to the U.S. economy was roughly equal in the 1920s and 1970s, the institutional setting in the first period was far less suited to the concerns of overseas investors than it was in the second period. By the same token, policy makers can at times take the initiative in reformulating the institutional setting and the policies it has produced, as the Roosevelt administration did in the 1930s.

Indeed, one of the questions this survey of interwar American policy raises is the role of major crises in precipitating changes in political institutions, and in policy makers' room to maneuver. The Depression and World War II removed many of the institutional, coalitional, and ideological ties that had bound policy makers in the 1920s. In the United States the result was the defeat of economic nationalism, but of course the crisis had very different effects elsewhere. It would be comforting to regard the victory of economic internationalism in the United States in the 1930s and 1940s as predetermined by the country's previous evolution and experiences, but this is far too facile a solution to a complex problem. A fuller explanation of the forces underlying American foreign-policy making in the 1930s and 1940s is clearly needed, and indeed it is the logical next step for the historians who have added so much to our understanding of the 1919–1933 period or for their followers.

More generally, the interwar period in American foreign economic policy is a fascinating and extreme case of a broader problem, the conflict between domestic and international interests in modern political economies. Virtually all nations have some economic actors for whom the international economy represents primarily opportunities and others for whom it is mostly threats. This tension is especially evident in major capital exporters, since the needs of holders of overseas assets may well conflict with the desires of domestic groups. The twentieth century is full of examples in which the international-domestic divide has been central to political developments in advanced industrial societies: Britain and Germany in the interwar years are perhaps the best-known examples.[61] The American interwar experience is thus an important example of conflict between internationally oriented and domestically based interests. The conditions under which such interaction leads to major sociopolitical clashes or is overcome, and under which the foreign-policy outcome is aggressively nationalistic or internationally cooperative, or some mix of the two, are obviously of great interest to analysts of international politics.

CONCLUSION

This essay has used the evolution of U.S. foreign economic policy from 1914 to 1940 as a benchmark against which to examine the role of international and domestic determinants in the making of foreign economic policy. We have argued that the foreign economic policy of the United States in the interwar period was the result of domestic political struggle between domestic economic actors with conflicting interests in the international economy, and thus different foreign economic policy preferences. After World War I many U.S. banks and corporations saw great opportunities for overseas expansion, and fought for U.S. foreign economic policy to be assertively "internationalist." Other U.S. corporations saw the world economy primarily as a competitive threat and fought for protection and "isolationism." The evolution of the international political and economic environment, the reaction of domestic actors to this evolution, and the unfolding of domestic political struggle combined to determine U.S. foreign economic policy. This essay's effort to specify the interplay of international and domestic forces in the making of foreign policy, raises real questions about approaches that ignore domestic determinants of foreign policy. Between 1914 and 1940 at least, the foreign economic policy of the United States simply cannot be understood without a careful analysis of conflict among the disparate socioeconomic and political forces at work inside the United States itself. Such domestic forces deserve careful, rigorous, and systematic study.

NOTES

1. Charles Kindleberger, *The World in Depression 1929–1939* (Berkeley: University of California Press, 1973), pp. 297–99. The Carr citation is from his *The Twenty Years Crisis, 1919–1930* (London: Macmillan, 1939), p. 234. A popular British satirical history of the 1930s, under the heading, "A Bad Thing," summarized the results of the Great War somewhat more succinctly: "America was thus clearly top nation, and History came to an end." Walter Sellar and Robert Yeatman, *1066 And All That* (New York: Dutton, 1931), p. 115.

2. Robert Dallek, *The American Style of Foreign Policy* (New York: Knopf, 1983) is a good survey of traditional American insularity.

3. The historical literature on the period is so enormous that it is feasible only to cite the most recent important additions. Two review essays and a forum are a good start: Kathleen Burk, "Economic Diplomacy Between the Wars," *Historical Journal* 24 (December 1981), pp. 1003–15; Jon Jacobson, "Is There a New International History of the 1920s?" *American Historical Review* 88 (June 1983), pp. 617–45; and Charles Maier, Stephen Schuker, and Charles Kindleberger, "The Two Postwar Eras and the Conditions for Stability in Twentieth-Century Western Europe," *American Historical Review* 86 (April 1981). Other important works include Denise Artaud, *La question des dettes interalliées et la reconstruction de l'Europe* (Paris: Champion, 1979); Frank Costigliola, *Awkward Dominion: American Political, Economic, and Cultural Relations with Europe 1919–1933* (Ithaca, N.Y.: Cornell University Press, 1984); Michael J. Hogan, *Informal Entente: The Private Structure of Cooperation in Anglo-American Economic Diplomacy, 1918–1928* (Columbia: University of Missouri Press, 1977); Melvyn Leffler, *The Elusive Quest: America's Pursuit of European Stability and French Security, 1919–1933* (Chapel Hill: University of North Carolina Press, 1979); William

McNeil, *American Money and the Weimar Republic* (New York: Columbia University Press, 1986); Stephen Shucker, *The End of French Predominance in Europe* (Chapel Hill: University of North Carolina Press, 1976); and Dan Silverman, *Reconstructing Europe after the Great War* (Cambridge: Harvard University Press, 1982). Many of the leading scholars in the field summarize their views in Gustav Schmidt, ed., *Konstellationen Internationaler Politik 1924–1932* (Bochum, W. Ger.: Studienverlag Dr. N. Brockmeyer, 1983).

4. Charles Kindleberger, "Group Behavior and International Trade," *Journal of Political Economy* 59 (February 1951), pp. 30–46; Peter Gourevitch, "International Trade, Domestic Coalitions, and Liberty: Comparative Responses to the Crisis of 1873–1896," *Journal of Interdisciplinary History* 8 (Autumn 1977), pp. 281–313; Peter Gourevitch, "Breaking with Orthodoxy: the Politics of Economic Policy Responses to the Depression of the 1930s," *International Organization* 38 (Winter 1984), pp. 95–129; Thomas Ferguson, "From Normalcy to New Deal: Industrial Structure, Party Competition, and American Public Policy in the Great Depression," *International Organization* 38 (Winter 1984), pp. 41–94.

5. For figures on U.S. foreign private assets see Raymond Goldsmith, *A Study of Savings in the United States,* vol. 1 (Princeton, N.J.: Princeton University Press, 1955), p. 1093.

6. The classical explanation of the process is Raymond Vernon, "International Investment and International Trade in the Product Cycle," *Quarterly Journal of Economics* 80 (May 1966), pp. 190–207.

7. On agricultural and industrial trade preferences in the 1920s, see Barry Eichengreen, "The Political Economy of the Smoot-Hawley Tariff," Discussion Paper No. 1244, Harvard Institute for Economic Research, May 1986.

8. Opposition to the league was indeed led by a prominent nationalist Massachusetts senator whose adamant insistence on protecting manufactured goods while allowing the free import of inputs was ably captured by "Mr. Dooley," who noted that "Hinnery Cabin Lodge pleaded f'r freedom f'r th' skins iv cows" in ways that "wud melt th' heart iv th' coldest mannyfacthrer iv button shoes." Cited in John A. Garraty, *Henry Cabot Lodge* (New York: Knopf, 1953), p. 268; the book contains ample, and somewhat weightier, evidence of Lodge's economic nationalism.

9. David Lake, "The State and American Trade Strategy in the Pre-Hegemonic Era," *International Organization* 42 (Winter 1988).

10. George Edwards, *The Evolution of Finance Capitalism* (London: Longmans, 1938), pp. 204–5, and U.S. Department of Commerce, *Historical Statistics of the United States* (Washington: GPO, 1960), pp. 139, 537. The definitive work on the period is Kathleen Burk, *Britain, America and the Sinews of War, 1914–1918* (Boston: Allen & Unwin, 1985). See also David Kennedy, *Over Here: The First World War and American Society* (New York: Oxford University Press, 1980); John T. Madden, Marcus Nadler, and Harry C. Sauvain, *America's Experience as a Creditor Nation* (New York: Prentice-Hall, 1937), pp. 44–46; Alexander Dana Noyes, *The War Period of American Finance* (New York: Putnam, 1926), pp. 113–18; William J. Schultz and M. R. Caine, *Financial Development of the United States* (New York: Prentice-Hall, 1937), 503–4.

11. Harold Nicolson, *Dwight Morrow* (New York: Macmillan, 1935), pp. 171–75.

12. Cleona Lewis, *America's Stake in International Investments* (Washington, D.C.: Brookings Institution, 1938), p. 352. See for a discussion of the experience Roberta A. Dayer, "Strange Bedfellows: J. P. Morgan and Co., Whitehall, and the Wilson Administration During World War I," *Business History* 18 (July 1976), pp. 127–51.

13. Lewis, *America's Stake,* p. 355; Nicolson, *Dwight Morrow,* pp. 177–82; Vincent P. Carosso, *Investment Banking in America: A History* (Cambridge, Mass.: Harvard

University Press, 1970), pp. 205–14. For a thoughtful survey of the political effects, see John Milton Cooper, Jr., "The Command of Gold Reversed: American Loans to Britain, 1915–1917," *Pacific Historical Review* 45 (May 1976), pp. 209–30.

14. This is Lewis's figure; *America's Stake*, p. 362. Others give different amounts. See for example Noyes, *The War Period*, pp. 162–93; Schultz and Caine, *Financial Development*, pp. 525, 533–42; Hiram Motherwell, *The Imperial Dollar* (New York: Brentano's, 1929), p. 85.

15. Charles Kindleberger, "Origins of United States Direct Investment in France," *Business History Review* 48 (Autumn 1974), p. 390.

16. Scott Nearing and Joseph Freeman, *Dollar Diplomacy* (New York: Huebsch, 1925), p. 273.

17. Lawrence H. Shoup and William Minter, *Imperial Brain Trust: The Council on Foreign Relations and United States Foreign Policy* (New York: Monthly Review, 1977), pp. 11–28.

18. Cited in Frank Costigliola, "United States–European Relations and the Effort to Shape American Public Opinion, 1921–1933," in Schmidt, ed., *Konstellationen Internationaler Politik*, p. 43. See also Costigliola, *Awkward Dominion*, pp. 56–75 and 140–66, and Robert A. Divine, *Second Chance: The Triumph of Internationalism in America During World War II* (New York: Atheneum, 1972), pp. 6–23.

19. Thomas W. Lamont, *Across World Frontiers* (New York: Harcourt, Brace, 1951), pp. 215, 217–18.

20. Jacob Viner, "Political Aspects of International Finance," *Journal of Business of the University of Chicago* 1 (April 1928), p. 146.

21. See, in addition to works cited above, Paul P. Abrahams, *The Foreign Expansion of American Finance and its Relationship to the Foreign Economic Policies of the United States, 1907–1921* (New York: Arno, 1976); Herbert Feis, *The Diplomacy of the Dollar: First Era 1919–1932* (Baltimore: Johns Hopkins University Press, 1950); Joan Hoff Wilson, *American Business and Foreign Policy, 1920–1933* (Lexington: University Press of Kentucky, 1971); Frank Costigliola, "The United States and the Reconstruction of Germany in the 1920s," *Business History Review* 50 (Winter 1976), pp. 477–502; and Frank Costigliola, "Anglo-American Financial Rivalry in the 1920s," *Journal of Economic History* 38 (December 1977), pp. 911–34. Because the issues are so widely treated, citations will only be given where necessary to confirm a specific fact, controversial interpretation, or direct quotation.

22. On these issues see the articles by Thomas Lamont, James Sheldon, and Arthur J. Rosenthal in *Annals of the American Academy of Political and Social Science* 88 (March 1920), pp. 114–38.

23. See especially Abrahams, *Foreign Expansion of American Finance;* and Costigliola, "Anglo-American Financial Rivalry," pp. 914–20. For an interesting view of one aspect of the war debts tangle, see Robert A. Dayer, "The British War Debts to the United States and the Anglo-Japanese Alliance, 1920–1923," *Pacific Historical Review* 45 (November 1976), pp. S69–95.

24. Joseph Brandes, *Herbert Hoover and Economic Diplomacy* (Pittsburgh: University of Pittsburgh Press, 1962), pp. 170–96; and Melvyn Leffler, "The Origins of Republican War Debt Policy, 1921–1923," *Journal of American History* 59 (December 1972), pp. 585–601.

25. Cited in Silverman, *Reconstructing Europe*, pp. 157 and 189.

26. Cited in U.S. Congress, House of Representatives, Committee on Banking and Currency, Subcommittee on Domestic Finance, *Federal Reserve Structure and the Development of Monetary Policy, 1915–1935: Staff Report* (Washington, D.C.: GPO, 1971), p. 62. I am grateful to Jane D'Arista for bringing these and other documents to my attention.

27. Hogan, *Informal Entente,* pp. 62–66.
28. See, for example, Stephen V. O. Clarke, *Central Bank Cooperation 1924–1931* (New York: Federal Reserve Bank of New York, 1967), pp. 46–57, and Charles G. Dawes, *A Journal of Reparations* (London: Macmillan, 1939), pp. 262–64, for evidence of just how central the bankers were.
29. The agent-general, S. Parker Gilbert, was a close associate of Morgan partner Russell Leffingwell. Costigliola, "The United States and the Reconstruction of Germany," pp. 485–94; Feis, *Diplomacy of the Dollar,* pp. 40–43; Leffler, *Elusive Quest,* pp. 90–112; Nearing and Freeman, *Dollar Diplomacy,* pp. 221–32; Nicolson, *Dwight Morrow,* pp. 272–78; Schuker, *French Predominance in Europe,* pp. 284–89.
30. For Lamont's optimism, see *Proceedings of the Academy of Political Science* 11 (January 1925), pp. 325–32.
31. Nicolson, *Dwight Morrow,* pp. 191–92.
32. Wilson, *American Business,* pp. 70–75.
33. Cited in Silverman, *Reconstructing Europe,* p. 239.
34. Mary Jane Maltz, *The Many Lives of Otto Kahn* (New York: Macmillan, 1963), pp. 204–5. For the similar views of Norman H. Davis, see *Proceedings of the Academy of Political Science* 12 (January 1928), pp. 867–74. See also Wilson, *American Business,* pp. 65–100.
35. Hoover is cited in Joseph Brandes, "Product Diplomacy: Herbert Hoover's Anti-Monopoly Campaign at Home and Abroad," in Ellis Hawley, ed., *Herbert Hoover as Secretary of Commerce* (Iowa City: University of Iowa Press, 1981), p. 193. See also H. B. Elliston, "State Department Supervision of Foreign Loans," in Charles P. Howland, ed., *Survey of American Foreign Relations 1928* (New Haven, Conn.: Yale University Press for the Council on Foreign Relations, 1928), pp. 183–201; John Foster Dulles, "Our Foreign Loan Policy," *Foreign Affairs* 5 (October 1926), pp. 33–48; Brandes, *Herbert Hoover,* pp. 151–96; Feis, *Diplomacy of the Dollar,* pp. 7–17; Leffler, *Elusive Quest,* pp. 58–64.
36. David Burner, *Herbert Hoover: A Public Life* (New York: Alfred A. Knopf, 1979), p. 186.
37. These are recalculated from Lewis, *America's Stake,* pp. 619–29; her aggregate figures are inexplicably inconsistent.
38. McNeil, *American Money,* p. 282.
39. See Richard H. Meyer, *Banker's Diplomacy* (New York: Columbia University Press, 1970).
40. Frank Costigliola, "The Other Side of Isolationism: The Establishment of the First World Bank, 1929–1930." *Journal of American History* 59 (December 1972), and Harold James, *The Reichsbank and Public Finance in Germany 1924–1933* (Frankfurt: Knapp, 1985), pp. 57–94. On BIS attempts at international financial cooperation from 1930 to 1931, see William A. Brown, Jr., *The International Gold Standard Reinterpreted, 1914–1934,* vol. 2 (New York: National Bureau of Economic Research, 1940), pp. 1035–47. For the views of New York bankers see the articles by Shepard Morgan of Chase and Jackson Reynolds of the First National Bank of New York in *Proceedings of the Academy of Political Science* 14 (January 1931), pp. 215–34, and Shepard Morgan, "Constructive Functions of the International Bank," *Foreign Affairs* 9 (July 1931), pp. 580–91. For an excellent overview of this period, see Clarke, *Central Bank Cooperation.*
41. Cited in Leffler, *Elusive Quest,* p. 238. On German-American financial relations after 1930, see Harold James, *The German Slump: Politics and Economics 1924–1936* (Oxford: Clarendon Press, 1986), pp. 398–413.
42. Lewis, *America's Stake,* pp. 400–1; Foreign Bondholders Protective Council, *Annual Report for 1934* (New York: FBPC, 1934), pp. 218–24.
43. Burner, *Herbert Hoover,* p. 298.

44. M. E. Falkus, "United States Economic Policy and the 'Dollar Gap' in the 1920s," *Economic History Review* 24 (November 1972), pp. 599–623, argues that America's enormous balance-of-trade surplus in the 1920s was due more to the structure and composition of U.S. industry and trade than to trade barriers. Whether this is true or not, the fact remains, as Falkus recognizes, that contemporaries on both sides of the tariff wall *perceived* U.S. tariffs to be of major significance in limiting European exports.

45. Feis, *Diplomacy of the Dollar,* p. 14.

46. These conclusions about American foreign policy in the 1920s differ a bit from those of some of the historians upon whose work my analysis is based. Leffler and Costigliola, especially, stress what they see as the unity of American policy, although both emphasize the importance of domestic constraints on this policy. In my view both scholars, despite their innovations, are too wedded to a modified Open-Door interpretation that overstates the unity and purposiveness of U.S. economic interests, and this methodological overlay colors their conclusions. I believe that the evidence, even as presented by them, warrants my analytical conclusions.

47. Stephen V. O. Clarke, *The Reconstruction of the International Monetary System: The Attempts of 1922 and 1933*, Princeton Studies in International Finance No. 33 (Princeton, N.J.: International Finance Section, Department of Economics, 1973), pp. 19–39; James R. Moore, "Sources of New Deal Economic Policy: The International Dimension," *Journal of American History* 61 (December 1974), pp. 728–44.

48. See especially John Morton Blum, *Roosevelt and Morgenthau* (Boston: Houghton Mifflin, 1970), pp. 45–53, and Ferguson, "Normalcy to New Deal," pp. 82–85. For a sympathetic European view of Roosevelt's policy, see Paul Einzig, *Bankers, Statesmen and Economists* (London: Macmillan, 1935), pp. 121–57.

49. See Blum, *Roosevelt and Morgenthau*, pp. 40–42, and for an interesting example Irving S. Mitchelman, "A Banker in the New Deal: James P. Warburg," *International Review of the History of Banking* 8 (1974), pp. 35–59. For an excellent survey of the period, see Albert Romasco, *The Politics of Recovery: Roosevelt's New Deal* (New York: Oxford University Press, 1983).

50. For details of the Hull-Peek controversy, see Frederick C. Adams, *Economic Diplomacy: The Export-Import Bank and American Foreign Policy 1934–1939* (Columbia: University of Missouri Press, 1976), pp. 81–93 and Robert Dallek, *Franklin D. Roosevelt and American Foreign Policy 1932–1945* (New York: Oxford University Press, 1979), pp. 84–85, 91–93.

51. For a discussion of the impact of crisis on ideologies and institutions, see Judith Goldstein, "Ideas, Institutions and American Trade Policy," *International Organization* 42 (Winter 1988).

52. Blum, *Roosevelt and Morgenthau*, pp. 64–67; Stephen V. O. Clarke, *Exchange Rate Stabilization in the Mid-1930s: Negotiating the Tripartite Agreement*, Princeton Studies in International Finance No. 41 (Princeton, N.J.: International Finance Section, Department of Economics, 1977), pp. 8–21.

53. *Proceedings of the Academy of Political Science* 17 (May 1936), p. 107.

54. Harold van B. Cleveland, "The International Monetary System in the Inter-War Period," in Benjamin Rowland, ed., *Balance of Power or Hegemony: The Interwar Monetary System* (New York: NYU Press, 1976), p. 51. For a lengthier explanation of the ways in which the Tripartite Agreement marked the turning point in the evolution of U.S. economic internationalism, see Charles Kindleberger, *The World in Depression 1929–1939* (Berkeley: University of California Press, 1973), pp. 257–61. See also Blum, *Roosevelt and Morgenthau*, pp. 76–88; and Clarke, *Exchange Rate Stabilization*, pp. 25–58.

55. Robert B. Warren, "The International Movement of Capital," *Proceedings of the Academy of Political Science* 17 (May 1937), p. 71.

56. John G. Ruggie, "International Regimes, Transactions, and Change: Embedded Liberalism in the Postwar Economic Order," *International Organization* 36 (Spring 1982), pp. 379–415, discusses the order that emerged.

57. *Proceedings of the Academy of Political Science* 17 (May 1936), p. 113.

58. Herbert Feis, *The Changing Pattern of International Economic Affairs* (New York: Harper, 1940), p. 95. Stephen Schuker has, in personal communication, insisted that it was not until 1942 or 1943 that Roosevelt moved away from extreme economic nationalism. He marshals important evidence and convincing arguments to this effect, but the account presented here reflects current scholarly consensus. If, as he has done in the past, Schuker can disprove the conventional wisdom, this analysis of U.S. foreign economic policy in the late 1930s would, of course, need to be revised in the light of new data.

59. See, for example, Stephen D. Krasner, *Defending the National Interest* (Princeton, N.J.: Princeton University Press, 1978).

60. As, for example, David A. Lake, "International Economic Structures and American Foreign Policy, 1887–1934," *World Politics* 35 (July 1983), pp. 517–43.

61. For a survey of each see Frank Longstreth, "The City, Industry and the State," in Colin Crouch, ed., *State and Economy in Contemporary Capitalism* (London: Croom Helm, 1979), and David Abraham, *The Collapse of the Weimar Republic* (Princeton, N.J.: Princeton University Press, 1981). On a related issue see Paul Kennedy, "Strategy *versus* Finance, in Twentieth-Century Britain," in his *Strategy and Diplomacy 1870–1945* (London: Allen & Unwin, 1983).

Strategy of Openness

Andrew J. Bacevich

> Fate has written our policy for us; the trade of the world must and shall be ours . . . And American law, American order, American civilization, and the American flag will plant themselves on shores hitherto bloody and benighted, but by those agencies of God henceforth to be made beautiful and bright.
>
> Albert Beveridge, April 1898

America's strategy of openness, in place for more than a century, derives from twin convictions widely held by member of the political elite and the foreign policy establishment. The first conviction is that robust and continuing economic growth is an imperative, absolute and unconditional. The aggregate wealth and sheer affluence of American society may be the greatest that the world has ever seen, but they do not suffice. In the aftermath of the Cold War, the famed slogan devised by James Carville during the 1992 Clinton-Gore campaign has enshrined itself as an inviolable rule of national politics: "It's the economy, stupid." According

Andrew Bacevich *American Empire: The Realities and Consequences of U.S. Diplomacy,*
Cambridge MA, Harvard University Press. pp. 79–116, Cambridge, Mass.: Harvard University Press,
copyright © 2002 by the President and Fellows of Harvard College.

to Carville's Law, officeholders who allow the economy to stagnate get sent packing. Those who can plausibly claim credit for fostering prosperity, whatever their other misdeeds or indiscretions, win forgiveness—and reelection.

But the imperative of economic growth is not simply a matter of electoral politics. It also grows out of far-reaching changes in the nation's culture.

During the half-century following World War II, the bonds of American civic identity noticeably frayed. In his detailed and persuasive assessment of American community, Robert Putnam described the broad trend toward civic disengagement and the mounting sense of social isolation, both accelerating as the "long civic generation" that fought World War II began passing from the scene.[1] As one consequence of the resulting "democratic malaise"—the term is Christopher Lasch's—the once robust plant of American citizenship withered.[2] Apart from a requirement to pay taxes, personal responsibilities demanded of the larger community during the 1990s were nil. Even in national elections, the majority of eligible voters could not motivate themselves to go to the polls.[3]

As for the ancient republican tradition that citizenship entailed a duty to contribute to the nation's defense, it got left behind on the near side of President Clinton's famous bridge to the twenty-first century. To the extent that some vestige of patriotism survived into the post–Cold War era, it did so as nostalgia, sentimentality, martial exhibitionism, and a readily exploitable source of entertainment. The moviegoers who thronged to *Saving Private Ryan* stood in awe of the "greatest generation," which had surmounted the Great Depression and won World War II. But they evinced little intention of modeling themselves after that generation and could not conceive of making comparable sacrifices on behalf of country.[4] The core values of the "bourgeois bohemians," constituting according to David Brooks the new establishment and defining the sensibility of the age, were individualism and freedom—chiefly their own personal freedom. Their missions were consumption and self-actualization. They exhibited little interest in enlisting in great crusades—especially if doing so threatened to crimp their lifestyle.[5]

In a society in which citizens were joined to one another by little except a fetish for shopping, professional sports, and celebrities along with a ravenous appetite for pop culture, prosperity became a precondition for preserving domestic harmony. Arguing on behalf of a populist vision of an engaged, independent, self-reliant citizenry, an acerbic critic like Lasch might rail against luxury as morally repugnant, insisting that "a democratic society cannot allow unlimited accumulation." But in reality the prospect of unlimited accumulation had long since become the lubricant that kept the system functioning. A booming economy alleviated, or at least kept at bay, social and political dysfunction. Any interruption in economic growth could induce friction, stoke discontent, and bring to the surface old resentments, confronting elected officials with problems for which they possessed no readily available solutions. Lasch may well have been correct in charging that "the reduction of the citizen to a consumer" produces a hollowed-out American democracy.[6] But by the 1990s no one knew how to undo the damage without risking a massive conflagration.

A second aspect of cultural change complicated the problem even further, namely, the growing confusion over whether and to what extent the United States qualified any longer as a "nation." Even before the Cold War had ended, in progressive quarters especially, a faint odor of disrepute had enveloped the very concept of nationhood. To the extent that nationalism implied a homogeneous outlook, values shared by the members of one group and distinguishing that group from all others, it was suspect. Among the enlightened, terms such as *nationalist* or *nationalistic* were understood as sinister code words suggesting suffocating conformity if not the threat of violence against those not qualifying for tribal membership or those violating its code.[7] By the end of the twentieth century, nationalism—still on display in places such as the former Yugoslavia and the Middle East—has become synonymous with bigotry and atavism.

Within recent memory, the proposition that the United States possessed its own distinctive national identity had been noncontroversial. That the project launched in 1776 had created a distinctively American "new man" was taken for granted. That as a result the United States differed from France or Japan as much as each differed from the other was all but self-evident. Indeed, documenting and celebrating those differences became a point of pride. Serious people—H. L. Mencken, Vernon L. Parrington, and, of course, the Beards—wrote thick, influential books limning the characteristics of "The American Language," exploring the "Main Currents of American Thought," and tracing "The Rise of American Civilization." Specialists surveyed the literature, art, music, and architecture produced on native grounds and saw there the outlines of a unique and vibrant American culture.[8]

The chief ornaments of that culture and their very distinctiveness offered cause for celebration: they testified to the peculiar genius of the American people. Indeed, a common American culture encompassed the character, ideals, and aspirations of all who lived in the United States, however, recent and whatever the circumstances of their arrival. At least so the mythology of the melting pot prevailing through the first half of the twentieth century asserted.

In the second half of that century, serious people devoted themselves to debunking that notion and to demolishing the mythology of a common culture. From its outset, the Cold War that began at mid-century was a conflict fought on two fronts at once: a political and military struggle abroad and a political and cultural struggle at home. By the end of the twentieth century it was apparent that the side that had won abroad had lost at home—and vice versa. In the external conflict, the forces of democratic capitalism, led by the United States, vanquished the forces of Marxism-Leninism, embodied by the Soviet Union. But in the internal conflict, the cultural left prevailed, not by destroying the right but by compromising it irredeemably. The counterculture of the 1960s had by the 1990s effectively become the dominant culture. As Eugene Genovese has explained, the débacle of 1989 may have "exposed the false premises on which the Left has proceeded, but it has done so at a time in which the Right is embracing many of those premises, notably, personal liberation and radical egalitarianism." Or, as Gertrude Himmelfarb, reflecting the chagrin of many Cold Warriors, has observed: "Having been spared the class revolution that Marx predicted, we have succumbed to the cultural revolution."[9]

That cultural revolution invalidated the old notion of the American melting pot and replaced it with the creed of America as multicultural mosaic. As Michael Lind rightly noted, multiculturalism became not simply a proposal or a possibility but "the de facto orthodoxy of the present American regime."[10] According to the terms of that orthodoxy, the United States was called upon to become a country embracing no particular culture but one in which all cultures, values, and beliefs might enjoy equal standing. (In this context, President Clinton professed to be troubled by the concept of "tolerance," since it seemed to imply "that there's a dominant culture putting up with a subordinate one.")[11] No longer was the basis of society the individual created in the image of God and possessed of inalienable rights. Rather it was the group, its identity and interests determined by considerations of race, class, ethnicity, gender, or sexual orientation.

In such a society anything smacking of enforced conformity was bad; "diversity" by definition was good. Indeed, diversity bestowed legitimacy. Thus, in the workplace, the media, the arts, the university, and throughout modern American politics, a commitment to "inclusiveness" became obligatory. Obeisance to diversity signaled that one acknowledged (and repudiated) the error of viewing Americans as a people deriving a common identity from heterosexual white Protestant males whose forebears had arrived from northern and western Europe. To embrace multiculturalism was to renounce the old habit of "privileging" White Anglo-Saxon Protestant conventions (and hypocrisies). By default, the preeminent American value became recognizing the equal legitimacy of all values, all artistic traditions, all moral codes, all religions, and all "lifestyles." When Vice President Al Gore translated the motto *E pluribus unum* as "out of one, many," he committed a famous gaffe.[12] But his faulty translation captured quite nicely the emerging zeitgeist.

The terms of that zeitgest complicated the crafting of U.S. foreign policy during the 1990s. In the midst of continuing cultural fragmentation, accurately discerning an overarching common interest became problematic. Mobilizing national power in pursuit of those interests posed a daunting challenge. The past practice of conceding such matters to the purview of the repressive "white patriarchy" whose authority cultural revolutionaries aimed to overthrow obviously would not do.

The notorious Whitney Museum Biennial of 1993 illustrated the point. To "absolve themselves" of cultural imperialism, visitors entering this exhibit of cutting-edge art were obliged to don buttons that read "I can't imagine wanting to be white."[13] But when it came to political, diplomatic, or military affairs, the traditional face of power *was* both white and male. A culture war seeking to discredit the white patriarchy found itself also compelled to discredit or transform the institutions that the patriarchy had created and over which it held sway.

The commissioning of female fighter pilots and black generals and the appointment of gay ambassadors and of Madeleine Albright and Colin Powell as successive secretaries of state were all touted as milestones in this effort to chip away at the dominance that straight white males enjoyed in the world of power. But however notable they may have been in a personal sense, these achievements were largely beside the point: in practice, the individuals involved proved to be far more likely to be transformed by their institutions than they were to become agents of fundamental institutional change.

Creating a policy elite that "looks like America" might appease some proponents of cultural change, but it would not remedy the underlying problem with which the culture war has confronted policymakers: in practice, the abandonment of a common culture points toward the loss of collective purpose, especially if pursuing that purpose might entail sacrifice or loss.

To the curators who mounted the Whitney Biennial, their exhibit was a bracing expression of a larger enterprise to challenge limits, celebrate the marginalized, and settle scores with groups and institutions that had been the source of repression. To its critics, the show offered irrefutable evidence that that project was giving rise to a vulgar debased, and narcissistic culture.[14] But the concern here is not with artistic merit. Rather, it is that in its disdain for national mythology, its rejection of the very concept of truth, and its embrace of "skeptical relativism," that project of which the Biennial is representative recasts America as an entity that no one in his right mind would view as worth dying for.[15]

In short, multiculturalism and value-free, nonjudgmental tolerance combined with an ever-widening definition of personal autonomy had produced indifference to the fate of the nation. In the wake of the cultural revolution, apart from providing an excuse for fireworks, quaint parades, and long holiday weekends, authentic patriotism had become absurd. By the 1990s Memorial Day was no more about revering those who had made the supreme sacrifice than Christmas was about recalling the birth of Jesus Christ. The common folk, bobbing along behind the tsunami of cultural change, may not have fully comprehended all that was transpiring. But the inhabitants of faculty clubs, board rooms, and editorial offices—that is, the privileged minority of citizens actually in the know—certainly did.[16]

For the would-be statesman, the implication were clear: an ever-expanding pie satisfying ever more expansive appetites was the only "crusade" likely to command widespread and durable popular enthusiasm. Political rhetoric might still swell with stirring Wilsonian allusions to democracy, peace, and freedom, but these amounted to little more than window dressing. They were not words entailing any obligation to act. Pressing for ever more material comforts and pleasures with ever fewer restraints on the sovereign self: this defined the closest thing to a national purpose. The condition might prove reversible, but by the 1990s at least the American people no longer held *in common* any higher purpose.

Old-line liberals and neoconservatives devoted to the spread of democracy worldwide or passionately committed to the protection of human rights and eager to expend serious national resources on behalf of those goals bridled at such an assertion. They insisted that American power had always served larger and grander purposes and that it must continue to do so. "Our mission is the advance of freedom." proclaimed Michael Ledeen, expressing sentiments common in this camp.[17]

In American political discourse today, such views are still accorded a place of honor, much as many a Bible remains prominently displayed even in households whose members have long since abandoned the church. The familiar language of idealism reassured Americans that they had not yet sold their souls. The homage regularly paid by senior officials to hallowed ideals was a way of asserting that self-interest alone did not explain U.S. policy and that in its willingness to take moral considerations into account the United States differed from every other great power in history. But homage should not be confused with influence. When it came to motivating the majority of Americans to throw their support behind a course of action, it was the rare policymaker who counted on Wilsonian ideals to carry the day.

In addition to ever-increasing prosperity as the surviving residue of national purpose, a second conviction underlay the strategy of openness. The nation's political leaders and their economic advisers concluded that by itself the internal American market was insufficient to sustain the necessary level of economic growth.

Reiterating views that Beard and Williams attributed to prior generations, U.S. officials in the 1990s—especially members of the Clinton administration—concluded that American prosperity was unsustainable absent access to an ever-expanding array of lucrative new outlets for trade and investment. According to Warren Christopher, "We've passed the point where we can sustain prosperity on sales just within the United States."[18] Given the limitations of the internal market, expansion abroad became essential. Speaking with characteristic directness, Samuel R. Berger said that "we have to continue to open markets" for one very obvious reason: "because that's where the customers are . . . We have a mature market—we have to expand, we have to grow." Madeleine Albright agreed: "our own prosperity depends on having partners that are open to our exports, investments, and ideas." Or, most succinctly, "Growth at home depends upon growth abroad." Those particular words are Bill Clinton's, but the sentiment is one that both Democrats and Republicans have endorsed: if the United States is to expand economically, it has no choice but to look abroad.[19]

That said, the strategy of openness is not merely an avaricious scheme for increasing market share, of interest chiefly to entrepreneurs, plutocrats, and their tribunes in the Department of Commerce or the Office of the United States Trade Representative. In the age of globalization, economic considerations have become inseparable from those of national security. "Trade," according to Lawrence H. Summers, secretary of the treasury in Clinton's second term, "is the pursuit of peace by other means."[20] Both peace and prosperity require order. Both demand adherence to particular norms: respect for private property, financial transparency, and some semblance of checks on corruption. In that sense the strategy of openness encompasses and integrates a wide range of interests, both tangible and intangible. It is not simply the business of agencies concerned with economic or commercial policy. Architects of the strategy are just as likely to work in the State Department and the Pentagon. Indeed, they are as likely to work in Congress as in the executive branch and in the private sector as in government.

Although the strategy of openness implies expansion, it does not qualify as "imperialistic," at least in the conventional sense of the term. It is, for example, strongly averse to acquiring territory or colonies. But the strategy does seek to consolidate and even enlarge a particular conception of global order. More specifically, it seeks to make permanent the favored position that the United States enjoys as victor in two world wars and the Cold War, the furtive hegemony to which most Americans purport to be oblivious, but that others recognize as the dominant reality of contemporary international politics.

Thus, rather than a departure from past practice, the strategy of openness marks the fulfillment of that practice. Despite claims of novelty by its proponents, especially in the Clinton era, it is as much concerned with completing a project long under way as it is with striking out in some altogether new direction. Long before the Cold War ended, John Lukács noted with remarkable acuity that "If we judge events by their consequences, the great world revolutionary was Wilson rather than Lenin."[21] The strategy of openness returns to the revolutionary project that President Woodrow Wilson outlined during and immediately after World War I: bringing the world as a whole into conformity with American principles and American policies.[22]

The prevailing conception of America's role in world affairs does not easily admit to that of an engine of revolution. During the turbulent half-century from 1940 to 1990, the orthodox narrative characterized U.S. policy as an effort to *thwart* revolution, whether from the extreme right or the extreme left. Others attempted to overturn the existing international order; responding reluctantly to their provocations, the United States acted to preserve that order. Thus, during World War II the United States led a great effort to turn back German and Japanese aggression and restore peace. At the outset of the Cold War it rallied others to contain Soviet efforts to export Marxism-Leninism and to prevent the outbreak of a third world war. Conveying the impression that America's strategic orientation was defensive, the orthodox narrative served a useful purpose, endowing contemporary history with a powerful moral logic. Nor was the narrative wrong. It was, however, incomplete and therefore misleading.

To characterize any strategy as either defensive or offensive is to misconstrue the competitive nature of politics. Any strategy worthy of the name aims to protect important interests. But it does much more. It also aims to advance important goals. It attempts to limit efforts by competitors to increase their power. It also attempts to acquire power. It seeks to gain advantages, not only over adversaries but also at the expense of nominal allies. All these points apply to U.S. foreign policy throughout several decades of Cold War. As Ronald Steel has observed, it becomes clear in retrospect that containment *and* expansion formed the "twin anchors" of U.S. policy: "containment of Soviet territorial temptations through military and economic power; expansion through alliances, bases, investments, and bribes."[23] Yet until 1989 the anchor of expansionism remained largely hidden from view, concealed by incessant warnings about the omnipresent danger of communist aggression and the insistence of American political leaders that the imperative of defending freedom in the face of that danger provided the justification for U.S. policy.

By the end of the 1980s, with the Soviet empire now in a state of advanced decay, the ostensible threat posed by communism had become downright implausible. Containment—and seemingly, therefore, U.S. strategy itself—had outlived its usefulness. By the early 1990s, the irrelevance of guarding against communist aggression suggested the emergence of a policy vacuum, setting off a heated competition to devise a new strategic paradigm. Throughout the first decade following the end of the Cold War, the quest for the one Big Idea (or sound bite) to supersede containment continued unabated.

From the outset, that quest has been a phony one, as much an exercise in political theater as a genuine search for policy. Though seldom acknowledged as such, an operative strategic paradigm exists and claims broad bipartisan support.

The Big Idea guiding U.S. strategy is openness: the removal of barriers to the movement of goods, capital, people, and ideas, thereby fostering an integrated international order conducive to American interests, governed by American norms, regulated by American power, and, above all, satisfying the expectations of the American people for ever-greater abundance. The open world that describes the ultimate aim of U.S. strategy revives an approach to policy identified years ago by Beard and Williams and once subsumed within containment.

The strategy of openness may not be able to resolve all the anomalies or untangle all the contradictions of American policy since the fall of the Berlin Wall. Alone, it cannot explain why the United States in 1992 made a grand gesture on behalf of starving Somalis and then in 1994 callously ignored Rwandans suffering a far worse fate. Absent a larger context, it cannot explain why the United States began the 1990s insisting that the Balkans were a European not an American problem and ended the decade by exaggerating the plight of Kosovar Albanians to create a pretext for launching a war against Yugoslavia. At the end of the day, no single factor can account for every detail of U.S. policy abroad, in all its fits and starts. Certainly, one should never discount the extent to which pandering to a particular domestic constituency, the jockeying of opposing political parties or of rival government bureaucracies, or the yearning of a lame-duck president to leave a "legacy" may explain a particular initiative. But in the long view, and to a greater extent than any other factor, the pursuit of openness defines the essential azimuth of the U.S. policy, a course set more than a century ago and followed ever since.

As his résumé attests, George Bush fashioned a career out of being a Cold Warrior, a career culminating in 1988 with his election as president. The abrupt end of the Cold War a year into his presidency caught Bush by surprise. Rummaging through his own personal experience and his understanding of U.S. history for an explanation of what would come next, the president came up with useful if familiar odds and ends: the importance of American leadership backed by military strength, the efficacy of market principles, the value of free trade, and, of course, the evils of isolationism. But Bush failed to mold these elements into a fully realized explanation of where history was headed now that communism had failed and the Soviet Union had ceased to be America's archenemy.

As a candidate for president, Bill Clinton liked to play up his own connection with and appreciation for the long struggle against communism. "I am literally a child of the Cold War," he proclaimed on the stump.[24] In reality, Clinton's immediate, personal engagement with the Cold War was negligible. During the watershed decade that began in the mid-1960s, he had not gone to Vietnam, where he might have risked being killed. Not had he taken the equally honorable path of actively resisting the war, which carried the risk of prison. Rather, Clinton artfully steered a course that enabled him to avoid military service while preserving his "viability" for a career in politics.[25]

In truth, the Cold War did not figure prominently in Clinton's worldview and possessed little relevance to his conception of politics. By 1992 this proved to be a real advantage. However dubious his credentials as a Cold Warrior, Clinton possessed one essential quality that George Bush lacked and that was more germane to the task at hand; he was a careful student of the forces transforming American society and the world at large.

In addition, of course, Clinton was a naturally gifted politician—glib, energetic, infinitely flexible in his principles, a man of outsized appetites for attention and power. Unencumbered by Cold War baggage and possessing a far surer grasp of how culture and technology were changing the United States, the nominally inexperienced Clinton arrived in the White House far better equipped than his predecessor to articulate a persuasive rationale for U.S. strategy. He scooped up Bush's odds and ends, appropriated a few ingredients picked up from the marketplace of fashionable ideas, and kneaded the result into something that—before his first term ended—he could proudly claim was very much his own creation. As an exercise in statesmanship, the result had more to do with style than with substance. Clinton imparted the appearance of freshness to notions that, coming from Bush, had seemed insipid or shopworn. But the accomplishment was a noteworthy one.

The process was by no means without misstep. Clinton and his lieutenants committed egregious errors in judgment—the most disastrous being the experiment with "nation-building" in Somalia that produced a war against Mohamed Farah Aidid and culminated by October 1993 in a costly defeat. They discarded ideas that either misfired or simply failed to catch fire—the ill-conceived concept of "assertive multilateralism" chief among them.[26] Over time the president's strategic vision both sharpened and became more expansive. But it ended up precisely where anyone familiar with the writings of Charles Beard and William Appleman Williams would have expected. In short, in his embrace of openness, Clinton did not invent something new to supplant a Cold War strategy that had outlived its usefulness; instead he renovated and revived a strategy that predated the Cold War by several decades.

Upon entering the White House, Clinton by all accounts was not especially well schooled in specific foreign policy issues.[27] But as a politician he had absorbed one great truth that had eluded George Bush, namely, that U.S. diplomacy is intimately and inextricably linked to domestic concerns. American statecraft is not, in the first instance, about "them"; it is about "us."

Indeed, Clinton fancied that he himself was the first to divine this truth, laying down the axiom early in his campaign for the presidency that "foreign and domestic policy are inseparable in today's world." Five years later, toward the end of his first term, Clinton still professed to be impressed by the significance of this discovery. "Something I need to take on even more," he told reporters, "is trying to figure out a way to make the American people believe . . . that there's no longer an easy dividing line between foreign policy and domestic policy, that the world we're living in doesn't permit that luxury any more."[28]

If Clinton had unearthed the taproot of U.S. policy, he was hardly the first to have done so. As early as 1935, Charles A. Beard had observed that for the United States "foreign policy and domestic policy are aspects of the same thing."[29] In 1957 William Appleman Williams endorsed that view, arguing that "domestic *and* foreign policy are two sides of the same coin."[30] Thus when candidate Clinton announced his discovery in 1991, it was not as original as he imagined it to be. But it was a crucial insight from which much else flowed.

Clinton defeated George Bush in 1992 by convincing a plurality of voting citizens that the country had stagnated economically and that Republicans were bereft of ideas about how to stimulate recovery. Once elected, Clinton vowed that he would "focus like a laser beam" on alleviating the nation's economic woes.[31]

That priority directly shaped the administration's initial diplomatic gambits. From the outset, foreign policy and economic policy became all but interchangeable. Secretary of State Warren Christopher bragged that the Clinton team had "placed economic policy at the heart of our foreign policy."[32] Indeed, in ticking off the administration's foreign policy priorities, Christopher ranked economic interests first. This was to be the administration's hallmark, setting its approach to diplomacy apart from its immediate predecessors'. To the extent that America's relations with the rest of the world could contribute to pulling the nation's economy out of the doldrums, they mattered. To the extent that a particular foreign policy issue did not promise near-term economic benefit, it was unlikely to attract more than lip service.[33]

This principle directly informed the administration's handling of those foreign policy issues—Bosnia and China—on which Clinton during the campaign had attacked George Bush. In both cases, candidate Clinton portrayed himself as someone who would put moral and humanitarian concerns first. Whereas Bush had resisted calls for the United States to intervene in the Balkans, Clinton insisted that he would act forcefully, using American air power if necessary to lift the siege of Sarajevo and put a stop to further ethnic cleansing.[34] While Bush in the aftermath of Tiananmen Square had labored to salvage relations with Beijing and in June 1992 renewed China's Most Favored Nation (MFN) trade status, Clinton ripped his opponent for "coddling dictators" and subordinating human rights and democratic values to trade.[35] This, Clinton vowed, he would never do.

Once in office, the new president jettisoned these views.

With regard to Bosnia, Clinton in the spring of 1993 flirted ever so briefly with an option known as "lift-and-strike." Acting in concert with its major European allies, the United States proposed to lift the arms embargo that had the practical effect of working to the disadvantage of the Bosnian Muslims, the principal victims of ethnic cleansing, and to the benefit of the Bosnian Serbs, the principal perpetrators. With the embargo removed, the Muslims could arm themselves and have at least a chance of putting up a meaningful defense. A more balanced military situation might eventually foster conditions conducive to a political settlement. At the same time, the United States and its allies would stand ready to launch air strikes to punish the Bosnian Serbs if they used the embargo's removal as a pretext for stepping up the level of violence. (Military involvement apart from air strikes was out of the question: the Pentagon adamantly opposed placing U.S.

troops on the ground, and Clinton was not inclined to challenge the military on that score.)

In May 1993 Clinton sent Secretary of State Warren Christopher on a mission to European capitols to brief allied leaders on the American plan. As Christopher admits in his memoir, his instructions were to take a "conciliatory approach" with the allies, commending "lift-and-strike" to their consideration and "asking for their support."[36] The administration was unwilling to contemplate unilateral U.S. action. Nor was it willing to ride roughshod over European sensibilities, especially given the presence on the ground in Bosnia of lightly armed (and hence vulnerable) peacekeepers from several European nations.

But the Europeans had no stomach for involving themselves in a shooting war. Given the administration's tepid enthusiasm for its own proposal, withholding support seemed unlikely to entail real penalties. So Great Britain, France, Germany, and Russia all joined in categorically rejecting Christopher's proposal. "Lift-and-strike" was dead on arrival.

Humiliated, the secretary of state abandoned his mission. By the time he arrived back in Washington, he found that his boss, too, had lost whatever limited appetite he might have had for involving himself in the Balkan imbroglio. Thus, as Christopher delicately phrased it, for the next two years the Clinton administration's efforts to resolve the Bosnian crisis "proceeded fitfully."[37] More accurately, Clinton bought into his predecessor's policy of inaction. With the administration focused on economic recovery at home, for the moment, at least, Bosnia did not qualify for serious attention.

Something of the same occurred regarding China. There, however, the additional influence of economic considerations made Clinton's turnabout seem more craven.

Clinton launched his China policy on an exalted note. In the United States, public discussion of U.S.-China relations centered on the question of trade. The annual renewal of China's MFN status provided an occasion for critics to vent their dissatisfaction with Beijing, especially on the matter of human rights. In May 1993 Clinton made it clear where he stood on this controversy when with considerable fanfare—Chinese dissidents attended the Oval Office ceremony—he issued an executive order that made the linkage between trade with China and human rights his administration's policy.

While extending China's trading privileges for another year, Clinton's executive order stipulated specific measures that Beijing needed to take to qualify for any subsequent extension. If a year hence Beijing failed to meet the standards that Washington had established—loosening emigration restrictions, curbing the use of prison labor, releasing dissidents, and permitting international radio and television broadcasts, for example—the United States would punish China by revoking its MFN status.[38]

Clinton's executive order enraged the government in Beijing, which refused to play along. Over the months that followed, China made no discernible effort to meet any of the standards that Clinton had set. As if to emphasize their defiance, when Secretary Christopher made his first official visit to Beijing in the spring of 1994, China's leaders made a point of launching a crackdown on pro-democracy dissidents. In meetings with the secretary of state, Premier Li Peng and Foreign Minister Qian Qichen laughed off his warning that China's behavior was placing MFN in jeopardy. They taunted Christopher—who had headed the panel formed to investigate the 1992 Los Angeles riot—by suggesting that the United States attend to its own human rights problems.[39]

At home Clinton's executive order also irked U.S. corporate executives whose firms had a growing stake in the China market. They, in turn, mobilized congressional support and dissenters within Clinton's own administration in a campaign to sever the link between commercial relations and human rights.[40]

Well before Clinton's June 1994 deadline, the failure of his get-tough policy had become evident. Whatever spotty improvements in China's human right record optimists might detect, even Warren Christopher had to admit that progress was "not nearly enough to meet the standards we had announced."[41]

Faced with the prospect of forfeiting $40 billion in trade annually—an amount that was increasing rapidly—while getting nothing in return, Clinton caved. On May 26, 1994, he renewed China's MFN status without qualification and announced that U.S. policy toward China would henceforth "take a new path." The essential element of that path, as Christopher explained in a speech the following day, was "a comprehensive U.S. strategy of engagement" aiming "to integrate China into the global community."[42] In plain language, the United States would henceforth downplay human rights and emphasize commercial interests. Like his predecessor, Clinton had found it expedient, for the moment at least, to cozy up to the dictators in Beijing.

No one possessed a clearer understanding of where this new path pointed than did Clinton's enterprising secretary of commerce, Ronald H. Brown. Hardly had the shift in policy been announced than Brown was organizing a major trade mission to China. With U.S. executives in two, the commerce secretary was soon off to Beijing, where he closed $5 billion in deals, thereby imparting substance to the concept of comprehensive engagement. Addressing a business audience in Beijing, Brown all but apologized for the temerity of his colleagues who had found fault with China's domestic policies. Declaring that "China's long history is deserving of respect and even deference that she has not always received," he emphasized that the United States was now sending "substantive signals that we regard China as a commercial ally and partner." "Once divided by ideology," he continued, eliminating in a phrase any differences between democratic capitalism and communism, "we are now drawn together by shared economic interests."[43]

In the eyes of his critics, Clinton's failure to make good on his campaign promises concerning Bosnia and China amounted to prima facie evidence that his administration was either weak, incompetent, or callow—or all three. It is more accurate to say that Clinton's turnabout on Bosnia and China manifested the shifting priorities of a team making the transition from campaigning to governing (while, inevitably, also continuing to campaign). As long as the U.S. economy was still limping along, ethnic cleansing in distant lands did not really matter. When faced with a choice between access to a market of particular promise and support for human rights, all other things being equal, human rights would have to give way. The inelegance with which the administration engineered these policy reversals may have caused it unnecessary embarrassment. But the outcome was in accord with a logic both hardheaded and realistic: foreign policy served domestic interests, and in 1993 the overriding domestic imperative was clearly to spur economic recovery.

In a negative sense, the foreign policy priorities of the new administration had required an abandonment of campaign commitments regarding Bosnia and China. In a positive sense, those priorities required a full-court press to gain greater access to foreign markets for American goods and capital. What Christopher referred to as "the new centrality of economic policy in our foreign policy" manifested itself as an all-out effort to remove obstacles to foreign trade and investment.[44] This the administration proceeded to pursue with a globe-straddling gusto reminiscent of jingoes like Albert Beveridge nearly a century before.

President Clinton himself offered a preview of the administration's intentions in a speech delivered at American University barely a month after he took office. Shamelessly comparing his purpose to that of John F. Kennedy, who in a notable 1963 appearance at the same podium had described the quest for world peace as the foremost challenge of his day, Clinton announced that the paramount challenge of *his* day was asserting mastery over the emerging global economy. According to the president, it no longer made sense to talk about a domestic policy or a domestic economy. The United States was "woven inextricably into the fabric of a global economy." he said. "Capital clearly has become global . . . Products have clearly become more global . . . Services have become global . . . Most important of all, information has become global and has become king of the global economy." The implications were clear: American enterprise needed to operate on a global scale or it would stagnate and fail. "The truth of our age is this and must be this," Clinton declared: "Open and competitive commerce will enrich us as a nation." As a result, it had become "time for us to make trade a priority element of American security." The president promised a comprehensive trade policy that would "open other nations' markets" and "establish clear and enforceable rules on which to expand trade." Openness would benefit the entire world, economically and politically, but it would benefit the United States most of all.[45]

This was not simply idle talk. In his remarks at American University, the president singled out the North American Free Trade Agreement (NAFTA) as an example of the policies that promised to ignite growth. Creating a common market encompassing Canada, Mexico, and the United States, NAFTA was actually the handiwork of the Bush administration. But Bush's clock ran out before he gained the congressional approval needed to put the agreement into effect. Securing that approval became in Clinton's first year in office a major foreign policy priority.

Doing so obliged Clinton to ignore a clamor of opposition from organized labor and environmentalists, prominent among the constituencies that had elected him. When in November 1993 the president, relying largely on Republican votes, secured the necessary implementing legislation, he was more than justified in claiming that he had won a significant victory. Henry Kissinger touted NAFTA as "the first and crucial step" in the creation of a new architecture for U.S. foreign policy.[46] Clinton made it the cornerstone of his strategy.

The fact that NAFTA subsequently failed the job-creating expectations of its supporters is to a large extent beside the point. NAFTA was important as both signal and precedent. It showed that an administration of so-called New Democrats was no less friendly to corporate interests than its Republican predecessors had been. Furthermore, passage of NAFTA marked just the beginning of a campaign to remove barriers to trade and investment. In support of the administration's effort to open up the world, U.S. trade negotiators trolled the world in search of deals. By 1996, proud references to having signed "200-plus" trade agreements became a staple of administration rhetoric.[47] (By 2000 the number had jumped to over 300.)[48] Clinton's trade policy focused particularly on improving U.S. access to especially promising "emerging markets"—Mexico, Brazil, Turkey, China, and South Africa, for example—projected to absorb within a decade $1.5 trillion in investments for airport expansion and telecommunications infrastructure alone.[49]

More important still was the creation of the World Trade Organization (WTO), promising worldwide reductions in trade barriers and guarantees of access and equitability. As with NAFTA, gaining congressional approval of the WTO found the White House making common cause with Republicans. But the role of the WTO's chief salesman was one in which Clinton enthusiastically cast himself. "It creates hundreds of thousands of high-paying American jobs," he proclaimed. "It slashes tariffs on manufactured and agricultural goods. It protects intellectual property. It's the largest international tax cut in history. Most importantly, this agreement requires all trading nations to play by the same rules. And since the United States has the most productive and competitive economy in the world, that is good news for our workers and our future." Removing barriers to trade and investment would benefit every participating economy, but the United States most of all. That became Clinton's constant refrain: "We are building prosperity at home by opening markets abroad."[50]

Not surprisingly, when the nation's economic performance improved dramatically, the administration was quick to credit its own policies at the chief cause. Americans found the claim to be at least plausible. In 1996 a country increasingly giddy with prosperity decisively elected Clinton to a second term. By 1998, with Clinton embroiled in sexual scandal, opinion surveys showed that the American public—whatever its reservations about the president's character—rated him the most successful foreign policy president of the entire postwar era.[51] But that success was measured almost entirely in economic terms. Beginning in 1998, a federal budget that had been in the red every year since 1969 was producing a substantial and growing surplus.[52] By the summer of 2000 the administration was claiming credit for having increased U.S. exports by 36 percent since the WTO's creation and for having created 22 million new jobs. The unemployment rate fell to 4.0 percent, the lowest the country had seen in three decades. During the Clinton presidency, average hourly earnings had jumped nearly 30 percent.[53] Politically, the administration's emphasis on economic expansionism abroad had been a thundering success.

But did NAFTA, the WTO, and a passel of bilateral trade agreements really constitute a genuine basis for grand strategy? Any serious strategy must necessarily satisfy political and security need as well as economic ones. Grand strategy implies a coherent vision for organizing and deploying power in pursuit of the state's larger purposes. In a democracy, it must give at least passing attention to moral considerations. Was not the Clinton administration—perpetrator of egregious flip-flops on Bosnia and China, suspected of being soft on defense and uncomfortable with the use of force—guilty of giving short shrift to noneconomic concerns in its headlong effort to restore a popular sense of well-being? Was the Clinton "strategy" not little more than a crass scheme to guarantee the president's reelection?

From the outset, senior administration officials invested considerable energy in attempting to show that such was not the case—that seizing a dominant position in the globalizing economy translated directly into political preeminence and offered the best guarantee of U.S. national security. Especially noteworthy in that regard was a much-publicized speech by Anthony Lake, the president's national security adviser, at Johns Hopkins University on September 21, 1993. If Clinton at American University had offered a blueprint for mastering the global economy, Lade at Johns Hopkins provided the most comprehensive explanation to date of how the administration's economic priorities formed one component of a subtle and sophisticated grand strategy.

The title of Lake's remarks conveyed his thesis: "From Containment to Enlargement."[54] Though couched in caveats and carefully avoiding the Wolfowitz Indiscretion, Lake's speech outlined a startlingly ambitious project. It was, in essence, a proclamation that the defensive phase of U.S. strategy, never intended to be more than temporary, had now officially ended. Changing circumstances dictated a more proactive, enterprising approach. Expressed in military terms, the United States in defeating communism had won a great battle. The moment was now at hand to exploit that success to achieve the final victory.

Lake began his presentation by identifying several large "facts" shaping the Clinton administration's worldview. First, freedom had prevailed. As a consequence, democracy and "market economics" (Lake resolutely avoided the term *capitalism*) were on the march. Second, the United States had emerged without question as the world's dominant power, economically and militarily and as the model of a "dynamic, multiethnic society." Third, the information revolution was accelerating the pace of global change. One notable result of that revolution was to create "new and diverse ways for us to exert our influence."

For the United States, these conditions were ripe with opportunity. The final triumph of democratic capitalism had become a reasonable prospect. Completing the process of aligning other nations with the United States ideologically—or, as Lake phrased it, securing the "enlargement of the world's community of free nations"—had become the proper goal of U.S. policy. Success would make for a world that was "more humane and peaceful." Not incidentally, it would also make the United States "more secure, prosperous, and influential." It would—although Lake did not state this outright—preserve and reinforce American preeminence.

On the one hand, the spread of democratic capitalism loomed as all but inevitable. On the other hand, the process was likely to be frustrated unless the United States exercised leadership commensurate with the position to which it had ascended. But leadership did not, in Lake's understanding, imply a futile and exhausting crusade in pursuit of grandiose ideals. The national security adviser emphasized that the fundamental purpose of pursuing a strategy of enlargement was to serve concrete U.S. interests. The Clinton administration was not proposing a full-throated Wilsonian revival.[55] The United States was not to become a global relief agency. Humanitarianism for its own sake would be the exception not the rule. Referring specifically to Somalia and Bosnia, Lake insisted that "they do not by themselves define our broader strategy in the world." Nor did enlargement imply that the administration was automatically reclassifying every non-democratic country as an enemy; Lake went out of his way to emphasize that the United States would "befriend and even defend non-democratic states" when doing so served American interests. A handful of holdouts—Lake called them "backlash" states—resisted the inevitable tide of history. As long as such nations remained recalcitrant—by way of example, Lake cited Iran and Iraq—it was incumbent upon the United States "to isolate them diplomatically, militarily, economically, and technologically." Sooner or later they would see the light—or be swept into the dustbin of history.

With regard to the feasibility of this scheme, Lake professed to be less concerned about any tricks the backlash states might have up their sleeves than about the capacity of the American people to see the project through. Raising the old hobgoblin of isolationism, he worried about the growing influence of "those in both parties who would have us retreat within the isolated shell we occupied in the 1920s and 1930s." He therefore enjoined internationalists of all stripes to set aside their differences over specifics policies long enough to thwart this internal threat to American engagement with the outside world.

Lake's was a masterly performance incorporating and updating a variety of familiar themes. But the speech was as instructive for what it left out as for what it included. For starters, it left little room for politics, at least as that term is conventionally understood. Implicit in Lake's strategy of enlargement was a conception of international politics that was nothing if not revolutionary. At the end of a century in which various causes, most of them bad, had inspired men to slaughter one another with unprecedented ferocity, Lake seemed to imply that there was really nothing left to fight about. History had decided the big questions. Given the necessary U.S. leadership, globalization would combine with the widening community of democratic capitalist nations so supersede power politics and create what Lake described as "virtuous circles of international economic action." Cooperative economic interaction was now replacing antagonistic political competition.

And should that cooperation on occasion break down, the United States would retain the prerogative of setting things right. Absent from Lake's presentation was any reference to two goals that had long been at the center of the liberal internationalist agenda: worldwide disarmament and the creation of an effective global collective security organization. Both had figured prominently among Wilson's famous Fourteen Points. Both had regularly received lip service from U.S. administrations ever since. Neither figured in Lake's strategy of enlargement. It was not difficult to see why: to pursue disarmament would forfeit the ultimate expression of American authority. Similarly, to revert to the original conception of the United Nations would necessarily diminish American freedom of action. Lake could not say so directly, but his strategy of enlargement required that the United States retain its position of unquestioned military superiority and its ability to act unilaterally. They were essential to expanding and perpetuating the Pax Americana, which was the strategy's unspoken purpose.

For all its brilliance, Lake's exposition of the Clinton administration's strategy of enlargement was incomplete. Apart from reciting a handful of clichés, he had not spelled out *how* the United States would bring others into conformity with the principles he described as "both American and universal." What was the operative mechanism? Nor had he provided a clear picture of precisely how the progressively enlarging community of democratic capitalist nations would function. How would it be organized and regulated?

In the months that followed. Lakes' colleagues—and the president himself—expanded on and embroidered the themes that he had enunciated (although the term *enlargement* was soon dropped). As the U.S. economic recovery took hold, those representations became more forceful and direct. Once Clinton won reelection in 1996 and replaced his national security team—the lawyerly Christopher, the unassuming Lake, and William Perry, the technocratic secretary of defense—administration officials became positively buoyant in expressing their conviction that they had crafted a strategy ideally suited to the age of globalization.

Senior administration officials returned time and again to the same point: the means to the end that Lake had described—the key to exploiting the potential of globalization, ensuring the spread of democratic capitalism, and perpetuating American dominance—was "openness."

The *New York Times* might characterize the program as "peace through trade," but it was much more than that.[56] The key opportunity created by the end of the Cold War, Christopher explained, was "to shape a more secure world of open societies and open markets."[57] Christopher's successor, Madeleine Albright, was even more emphatic: "the driving force behind economic growth," she declared, "is openness—open markets, open investment, open communications and open trade." Indeed, with openness, growth would cease. According to Albright, "the health of the global economy will depend on maintaining and expanding the commitment to open trade, open markets, and open books." Without openness, the revival of old conflicts became possible. Therefore, "across the globe," U.S. policy was "emphasizing the value of open markets, open investments, open communications and open trade."[58] The drive for openness, declared Samuel R. Berger, who had served as Lake's deputy and then succeeded him as national security adviser, was "the President's strategy for harnessing the forces of globalization for the benefit of the people of the United States and the world." By the end of his second term Clinton had made himself, in the words of an admiring editorial in the *Boston Globe*, "the pied piper of capitalism," traveling the world to extol the virtues of openness as the means to achieve global prosperity.[59]

But the creation of an open world was not in the first instance a program of global uplift. Globalization is not social work. The pursuit of openness is first of all about Americans' doing well; that an open world might also benefit others qualifies at best as incidental. An open global order in which American enterprise enjoys free rein and in which American values, tastes, and lifestyle enjoy pride of place is a world in which the United States remains preeminent. Clinton and his advisers understood this.

Pursuing the goal of openness in the 1990s did not oblige the United States to exert itself on all fronts with equal energy. Priorities were necessary. To maintain a semblance of balance between means and ends, the Clinton administration sought, as Lake himself indicated, to "focus our efforts where we have the most leverage." The idea was to attend first to regions "that affect our strategic interests."[60] In a rough if imprecise way, U.S. policy priorities in the first decade after the Cold War reflected this determination to match the level of commitment to the interests at stake and the prospects of achieving success.

Where significant interests coincided with substantial American leverage, the United States could be counted on to make a major effort. Europe offers a prime example. There the strategy of openness demanded that the United States promote continuing progress toward European integration and prevent any erosion in the credibility of Washington's claims that despite its location on the opposite side of the Atlantic Ocean the United States was Europe's leading power. The foremost Cold War–era expression of those claims—NATO—offered the most readily available vehicle for enhancing both the depth and breadth of European openness. But with the fall of the Berlin Wall and the collapse of communism, NATO had achieved the purpose for which it had been created: deterring or, if need be, defending against Soviet aggression. NATO's obsolescence prompted the United States to launch a major effort to "reinvent" the alliance—an effort that George Bush first conceived but that the Clinton administration adopted as its own. By 1997 that effort had produced a precedent-setting eastward expansion. NATO invited three former Warsaw Pact states—Poland, Hungary, and the Czech Republic—to join the alliance, with President Clinton vowing that "the first new members will not be the last."[61]

As if with a flick of the cartographer's pen, the cluster of nations that for decades had constituted "Eastern Europe"—and by implication had represented the antithesis of "Western Europe"—were redesignated. They now became "Central Europe," situated in the very heart of the continent, poised to be incorporated into "the West," in which it turned out they had always truly belonged. Short of Russia itself, there was to be no predetermined limit on how far NATO—and, by implication, American influence in Europe—might expand.

But NATO's reinvention implied more than simply adding new members. Having outlived its usefulness as a defensive alliance, NATO needed a new purpose, ideally one based on a broader definition of security and more proactive in its orientation. The problem to which a new NATO needed to respond, said Bill Clinton, was "creeping instability"—shadowy, hydra-headed, posing a threat as much political as military.[62] This problem obliged the alliance to develop new capabilities. In place of large, mechanized formations, long its mainstay, the alliance required smaller, lighter, more mobile units. Those units should be configured and trained for a wide variety of contingencies to include peacekeeping, peace enforcement, and humanitarian relief. Creeping instability also required that the alliance be willing to venture "out of area," exerting its influence beyond its territorial limits. But from an American perspective, all of this had to be accomplished in a way that preserved for the United States its leading role in the alliance. Thus, for example, American enthusiasm for reinventing NATO did not extend to such notions as appointing a European to the post of Supreme Allied Commander Europe (SACEUR). NATO's top-ranking military officer had always been and would remain a U.S. officer.

At the Washington Summit, convened in April 1999 on the fiftieth anniversary of NATO's founding, the alliance unveiled a "new strategic concept" responding to those requirements.[63] Whether coincidentally or not, as NATO's leaders convened their anniversary conclave the alliance itself was actively engaged in a major demonstration of the new concept—a war against Yugoslavia.

Operation Allied Force was actually NATO's second Balkan war of the 1990s. The first, Operation Deliberate Force, in August and September 1995, had been a brief bombing campaign—carried out largely by U.S. aircraft—directed against Bosnian Serb forces with the expressed intent of establishing some basis for a negotiated end to the Bosnian civil war. The same Bill Clinton who had flinched from using force in Bosnia in 1993 now embraced both an experiment in coercive diplomacy and the open-ended military occupation of Bosnia arranged during U.S.-sponsored peace talks in Dayton, Ohio. Clinton reversed course in 1995 not, as claimed, to put a stop to ethnic cleansing of in response to claims of conscience, but to preempt threats to the cohesion of NATO and the credibility of American power, each called into question by events in Bosnia.[64] In short, it was not Bosnia itself that counted, but Europe and U.S. leadership in Europe.

Much the same can be said with regard to the much larger military enterprise launched in connection with Kosovo in March 1999. Assertions that the United States and its allies acted in response to massive Serb repression of Kosovar Albanians simply cannot survive close scrutiny. Operation Allied Force was neither planned nor conducted to alleviate the plight of the Kosovars. When Slobodan Milošević used the start of the bombing as a pretext to intensify Serb persecution of the Kosovars, that point became abundantly clear: NATO persisted in a bombing campaign that neither stopped nor even retarded Serb efforts to empty the province of Muslims. To the extent that General Wesley Clark, the SACEUR, modified the script of his original campaign plan, he did so not by providing protection to the victims of Serb repression but by victimizing Serb civilians.[65]

Indeed, some members of the Clinton administration actively sought a showdown with Milošević: Secretary of State Madeleine Albright designed the so-called Rambouillet peace conference in February and March 1999 so as to ensure that the Yugoslav president would reject any negotiated settlement of the Kosovo issue.[66] Effective diplomacy would have precluded NATO action. But military action was what the United States wanted: a demonstration of what a new, more muscular alliance under U.S. direction could accomplish in thwarting "creeping instability." The intent of Operation Allied Force was to provide an object lesson to any European state fancying that it was exempt from the rules of the post–Cold War era. It was not Kosovo that counted, but affirming the dominant position of the United States in a Europe that was unified, integrated, and open. As Clinton himself explained on March 23, 1999, just before the start of the bombing campaign, "if we're going to have a strong economic relationship that includes our ability to sell around the world, Europe has got to be a key . . . That's what this Kosovo thing is all about."[67]

When it came to measuring the success of the strategy of openness in Europe, NATO's two Balkan military interventions—each resulting in a semipermanent U.S. troop commitment—signified little. Military intervention was simply part of the inevitable price of doing business. The essence of that strategy *was* business and American political clout. Viewed within the frame of reference of U.S. policymakers, other indicators counted for much more than peacekeeping missions in Bosnia and Kosovo as evidence of what openness had wrought in Europe. For these policymakers, the real payoff lay in the fact that U.S. investment in Europe increased sevenfold between 1994 and 1998 and that trade between the United States and the European Union also rose handsomely, to $450 billion per year.[68] There was also the knowledge, vividly demonstrated in the skies over Kosovo, that Europe in the first decade after the Cold War had become more not less dependent upon the United States for its security. As European nations after 1989 cut their defense budgets, they forfeited all but the most modest military capabilities; as NATO ventured out of area, U.S. domination of the alliance became all the greater—to American policymakers a welcome development.

Europe was by no means the only region where interests combined with leverage to create the conditions guaranteeing sustained U.S. attention. Japan and South Korea, Russia and China, the "emerging markets" of Latin America and Southeast Asia, and, of course, the North American continent: each in its own way offered fertile ground in which the United States could plant the seeds of greater openness. The specific approach—particularly the emphasis placed on the U.S. military power—varied from case, specific policies being tailored to local circumstances. But in each of these cases, U.S. policymakers nursed expectations that opening countries through trade, investment, and technology transfers would result in immediate benefits to the United States while in the longer term—thanks to globalization and the information revolution—fostering political liberalization. When it came to China, President Clinton even specified the threshold of interaction that would cause the dam to burst. "When over 100 million people in China can get on the Net," he announced in May 2000, "it will be impossible to maintain a closed political and economic system."[69]

In regions where U.S. interests were substantial but not matched by comparable leverage, policymakers opted for a less direct and more patient approach. American policy in the oil-rich Middle East illustrates the point. In 1991 Operation Desert Storm boosted the United States in the Persian Gulf to a position of unrivaled influence. But that influence rarely extended beyond matters related to military security. Any heavy-handed attempt to "break down barriers," especially in infringing upon culture and the political authority of entrenched elites, was too likely to backfire. The economic consequences of a bungled effort—

a possible cutoff in the flow of oil—were unacceptable. Thus Washington—prior to September 11, 2001, at least—concluded that opening the Arab world was something that could wait for another day. In the torrent of high-sounding rhetoric churned out by the White House and the State Department, "Arab democracy" was seldom mentioned.

Diffidence did not imply a hands-off approach. Instead, through arms sales, advisory programs, frequent exercises, military-to-military contacts, and the continuing presence of U.S. forces—signified most prominently by the enforcement of the no-fly zones over Iraq—the United States sought to preserve the favored position it had won by liberating Kuwait. After 1991, U.S. troops garrisoned the Persian Gulf not to pry the region open to American enterprise and American values but to prop up the status quo. But only temporarily: in due course, the opportunity to open the Arab world would present itself.[70] For if, as members of the American policy elite insisted with near unanimity, democracy, market principles, and globalization were indeed sweeping the world, then existing regimes in key states like Egypt and Saudi Arabia were living on borrowed time. When it became expedient to do so, senior U.S. officials could be expected to unveil all the truths that the White House and the State Department had for many years chosen to soft-pedal or ignore: that these regimes were deeply corrupt, denied civil liberties, engaged in wholesale violations of human rights, and resolutely opposed anything even remotely resembling popular rule. When they went, few members of the American foreign policy establishment would lament their demise. Virtually all would applaud the "opening" of the region to democratic capitalism that would presumably ensue. In the meantime, with the West as a whole maintaining its access to (relatively) cheap oil while the United States enjoyed the (sometimes lucrative) advantages that accrued from being chief guarantor of the developed world's energy lifeline, it was considered impolitic to speak openly of such things.[71]

Finally, where interests were slight, the United States seldom bothered even to make the effort to assert any substantial leverage. American policy toward Africa illustrates the point. Offering only the most modest near-term prospects for trade and investment, sub-Saharan Africa consistently ranks dead last in U.S. strategic priorities. The Bush's administration seemingly quixotic intervention in Somalia in 1992 suggested a departure from that pattern. But the Clinton administration, bruised by its defeat in Mogadishu the following year, soon turned its back on Africa. As evinced most vividly by the administration's studied inaction during the Rwandan genocide of 1994, the usual order of things had been restored.

In the wake of Rwanda, Africa qualified for presidential apologies and symbolic gestures but little effective action. In March 1998 Clinton made a highly publicized six-nation, eleven-day tour of the continent during which he expressed regret for "the sin of neglect and ignorance" that the United States had committed in its treatment of Africa, particularly during the Cold War. The president announced that it was "time for Americans to put a new Africa on our map" and for the United States to forge a new beginning in its relations with the peoples of that continent.[72]

The centerpiece of that new beginning, according to Susan E. Rice, assistant secretary of state for African affairs during the Clinton years, was a promise "to accelerate Africa's integration into the global economy." Expropriating the standard imagery of American economic expansionism, Rice portrayed Africa as the "last frontier for U.S. exporters and investors." The frontier that beckoned had in fact already been staked out by others. With the continent "still largely the province of our European and Asian competitors," taming it required that American business find ways to displace the competition, thereby gaining access to an indigenous population that commercial-minded U.S. officials referred to as "Africa's 700 million consumers." Increased U.S. economic penetration of Africa would benefit both Americans and Africans. For the United States, it meant the promise of jobs. For Africa, it meant development. "As economic growth spreads, as entrepreneurial talent is unleashed, and basic needs are satisfied," Rice promised, "democracy and respect for human rights will also lay down deep roots in Africa."[73]

In May 2000 the Clinton administration's Africa initiative assumed material form as the Africa Growth and Opportunity Act, designed to promote trade and investment. In President Clinton's view, this legislation cemented a "genuine partnership" between the United States and the nations of sub-Saharan Africa, "based on not what we can do for them, not what we can do about them, but on what we can do with them to build democracy together."[74] Taken at face value, such expansive language might suggest that in U.S. efforts to create an open, integrated world, Africa had achieved a standing comparable to that traditionally enjoyed by other parts of the world that commanded American attention.

Such was by no means the case. To be sure, the Africa Growth and Opportunity Act held out the prospect of Africa's someday taking its place in the global system that the United States aspires to organize. But with Africa currently accounting for a minuscule 1 percent of total U.S. trade, that moment is not now. The legislation was at best a promissory note, to be redeemed at Washington's convenience.[75] It did not imply any immediate commitment or obligation to eradicate the problems impeding African development. To put it bluntly, conditions that in the Balkans or the Persian Gulf the United States found intolerable were in Africa merely unfortunate.

Hence, when it came to specific cases, action did not match rhetoric. In domestic American politics, to find out who and what really counts, you follow the money. When it comes to U.S. strategy, the applicable rule is to follow the military. The presence of American troops and the willingness to employ U.S. military muscle offer the best measure of what policymakers actually value.

As a practical matter, even in the White House the old map of Africa remained in place—a map depicting a slough of ethnic violence, extreme poverty, and daunting social problems, all presided over by brutal and venal kleptocrats. Expectations that the continent might make significant progress toward peace and prosperity at any time in the foreseeable future were simply unrealistic. Actual U.S. policy reflected that sober assessment. Consider, for example, how the Clinton administration—ostensibly chastened by its moral failure in Rwanda and vowing never again to avert its gaze from massive suffering and injustice—responded to a large, yet not atypical, African catastrophe: the civil war in Sudan.

Sudan's internal crisis predated the end of the Cold War.[76] At the time of the president's heralded visit to Africa in 1998, the civil war was entering its sixteenth year. During that period, according to the State Department's own estimates, fighting between the secessionist South—mostly African and either Christian or animist—and the government-controlled North—mostly Arab and Muslim—had killed two million Sudanese and created another four million internal refugees. In its efforts to suppress the Sudan People's Liberation Movement, the Islamist government in Khartoum as a matter of policy engaged in widespread torture, routinely bombed civilian villages, forcibly conscripted children into the army, and coerced non-Muslims to convert to Islam. In the words of the State Department human rights report, Sudanese security forces "beat refugees, raped women, and reportedly harassed and detained persons on the basis of their religion."[77] Christians, in particular, were singled out for abuse, with government forces desecrating churches and destroying Christian schools. Slavery and other trafficking in human beings flourished. In the scale of humanitarian catastrophes, Sudan in the 1990s ranked as high as Somalia and Bosnia and well ahead of Panama, "Kurdistan," and Haiti, where conditions had compelled Presidents Bush and Clinton to intervene.

In the eyes of the Bush and Clinton administrations, Sudan never qualified for even remotely comparable attention. In Bush's foreign policy memoir the entire continent of Africa receives not a single mention. Before Clinton's Africa trip the U.S. response to the Sudanese civil war consisted of little more than conscience-salving gestures. State Department officials regularly condemned the behavior of the Sudanese government, affirmed U.S. support for international efforts to isolate Khartoum, and funneled money through the United Nations and other nongovernmental organizations to support Operation Lifeline Sudan, a program aimed at alleviating the suffering of the war's innocent victims. During the 1990s the United States contributed more than a billion dollars to that effort.[78] But U.S. support for Lifeline Sudan did nothing to address the cause of that suffering and may have actually prolonged the conflict. To draw an analogy with the 1940s, it was the moral equivalent of mailing relief supplies to those imprisoned in ghettos and concentration camps while refraining from entering the war against Germany.

To be sure, on November 4, 1997, President Clinton issued an executive order finding that the Sudanese government posed "an unusual and extraordinary threat to the national security and foreign policy of the United States." The president then proceeded to declare "a national emergency" to deal with that threat. But the sum total of the government's response to that emergency was to impose economic sanctions on Sudan.[79] Advertised as stringent and comprehensive, the sanctions did not live up to their billing. The fine print permitted most of the few existing American activities in Sudan to continue unimpeded. In a veiled reference to Sudan's oil reserves, the new policy even left the door open to continued commercial relations, promising that trade in a select "few cases" would be considered on "a case-by-case basis."[80] Although senior American officials insisted that it was U.S. policy "to isolate the Government of Sudan and to pressure it to change fundamentally its behavior," the pressure actually applied seldom rose above expressions of moral outrage.[81]

Only once in the 1990s—and then very briefly—did military power figure in the relationship between the United States and Sudan. On August 20, 1998, a handful of cruise missiles launched by U.S. Navy warships demolished the Al Shifa pharmaceutical factory in Khartoum. Yet this surprise American military action was completely unrelated to developments inside Sudan. Rather, the action came in response to the bombing earlier that month of U.S. diplomatic missions in Kenya and Tanzania that had left twelve Americans and several hundred Africans dead and many more injured. "Our target was terror," President Clinton told the American people in announcing the attack.[82]

In fact neither the Sudanese government nor the privately owned pharmaceutical factory was directly implicated in the embassy bombings. U.S. officials attributed responsibility for those attacks to the Islamic radical Osama bin Laden, thought to be hiding in Afghanistan. But Washington had long accused Sudan of offering safe haven to other terrorists (although in 1996 it had expelled bin Laden),[83] and U.S. intelligence agencies suspected that the Al Shifa plant was being used surreptitiously to produce Empta, a compound necessary for the production of nerve gas. The real purpose of leveling Al Shifa was less retaliatory than preemptive, the first shot in a campaign to deny would-be terrorists access to weapons of mass destruction.[84]

The fact that the Clinton administration chose Sudan as the place to make a statement about terrorism did not mean that it had reevaluated that nation's importance. On the contrary, no sooner did the United States complete its attack on Al Shifa than it forgot Sudan, once again averting its gaze from the ongoing civil war. But the story did not end there. Subsequent investigation by highly reputable American scientists provided compelling evidence that Al Shifa had never been used to produce Empta.[85] The factory had in fact been what it had appeared to be: a facility producing desperately needed pharmaceuticals for an impoverished Third World population. That the United States had used armed force not on behalf of the long-suffering Sudanese but to destroy the country's sole producer of pharmaceuticals said more about Africa's actual standing in American eyes than did the assurances of friendship and sympathy cascading out of the White House and the State Department.

Two years after President Clinton's trip to Africa, Richard Holbrooke, the U.S. permanent representative to the United Nations, was hard at work trying "to put to rest the canard that Africa doesn't matter."[86] But the canard keeps coming back. It does so not because U.S. policymakers are racists who value the lives of white Europeans above those of black Africans, but because Africa doesn't pay, at least not in comparison with other regions of the world. Even a major commitment to opening Africa would be unlikely to contribute much to U.S. economic well-being or American political clout—and such an effort would necessarily come at the expense of other areas possessing greater immediate promise. Viewed strictly in accordance with the logic of the strategy of openness—and despite earnest professions by U.S. officials to the contrary—American indifference to Africa makes sense.

In the global age, Bill Clinton liked to observe, "we can no longer choose not to know. We can only choose not to act, or to act."[87] As the Clinton era drew to a close, Assistant Secretary of State Susan Rice made a brief visit to Sudan. Having listened to the firsthand testimony of Sudanese just freed from bondage, she declared: "The U.S. will never tolerate slavery and will never rest until the suffering you and many others have experienced is ended." Rice than pledged $150,000 [*sic*] in U.S. aid to "provide southern Sudan with access to information technology" and departed.[88] When it came to Sudan—and much of the rest of sub-Saharan Africa—the United States, adhering to its strategic priorities, chose not to act.[89]

Perhaps confusing hope with reality, Madeleine Albright in 1998 proclaimed that the strategy of openness had succeeded: "what we've done is kind of opened the whole system up."[90] But to Albright and other architects of U.S. policy an open system did not imply one in which anarchy prevailed. The rewards of openness rightly belonged to the most innovative, energetic, and competitive, not to those most adept at deception and fraud. "Experience tells us," Albright explained, "that there will always be some who will seek to take advantage by denying access to our products, pirating our copyrighted goods, or underpricing us through sweatshop labor." According to the secretary of state, "maintaining the equity of the system" required continuous vigilance against such intolerable practices.[91]

In short, an open system still had to *be* a system. It required order, stability, predictability. As President Clinton remarked in the wake of the Asian economic collapse of 1998, "The global economy simply cannot live with the kinds of vast and systematic disruptions that have occurred over the past year."[92]

Even as it worked to open up the global system, the United States claimed for itself the prerogative of detailing the rules governing that system. Citing the United States as the model that others should emulate, the president instructed the annual meeting of the International Monetary Fund and the World Bank: "No nation can avoid the necessity of an open, transparent, properly regulated financial system; an honest, effective tax system; and laws that protect investment."[93] In ticking off the prerequisites for economic soundness, Clinton stressed that "this is not an American agenda. These are the imperatives of the global marketplace."[94] As always, American policies and principles were universal in application. The imperatives of the marketplace were just that: mandatory and inescapable. As the president explained to an audience of Russian students in 1998, "There is no way out of playing by the rules of the international economy if you wish to be a part of it."[95]

To the extent that these rules prevailed, globalization would foster what Albright termed a "process of constructive integration."[96] Out of that process a new international order would emerge. Consistent with the fashion of the 1990s, the preferred metaphor for describing that order was a web or network—fluid, without formal hierarchy, lacking a fixed structure, yet all the more supple and resilient as a result.

At the very center of that network, situated so as to play a commanding role, would be the United States. Describing her vision of the emerging global network,

Albright declared that "America's place is at the center of this system." The United States is the "dynamic hub of the global economy."[97] Clinton himself insisted that "We have to be at the center of every vital global network." Such a central position, according to the president, "dramatically increases our leverage to work with people for peace, for human rights and for stability."[98]

The smooth functioning of the global network would, in the eyes of American statesmen, serve the interests of all. It followed, therefore, that most states would willingly submit to its discipline. In the event that the occasional dissenter might flout the rules and pose a hazard to the system, the United States with the assistance of like-minded allies would mete out the appropriate punishment and bring that violator back into conformity with the prescribed norms.

According to Secretary Albright, "however one states it, at this stage the United States is kind of the organizing principal of the international system."[99] It is not a misreading of Albright's intent to amend her statement just slightly: she and other senior officials were convinced that having shouldered the responsibilities of the world's organizing principal, it was incumbent upon the United States to play that role in perpetuity.

Just as George H. W. Bush had warned against a rising tide of isolationism, just as Anthony Lake in sounding the trumpet for enlargement singled out would-be isolationists for censure, so, too, other representatives of the Clinton administration preemptively fastened to critics of its politics this most damning of labels. Characterizing the United States as "a large country that has traditionally looked inward," Secretary of the Treasury Lawrence H. Summers lamented the ostensible American tendency to oscillate disastrously "between isolationism and global engagement." According to Vice President Al Gore, those who opposed the drive for openness spoke with "the shrill voices of isolation." When it came to entertaining dissent, proponents of American indispensability during the 1990s—Republicans and Democrats alike—were an intolerant lot. To question the strategy of openness invited charges of provincialism, expediency, and a level of partisanship bordering on treason. "These new isolationists," Gore charged, "seek nothing less than to impede President Clinton's ability to defend American interests and values."[100]

"We want 'enlargement' of both our values and our Pizza Huts," Thomas Friedman has written. "We want the world to follow our lead and become democratic and capitalistic, with a Web site in every pot, a Pepsi on every lip, Microsoft Windows on every computer and with everyone, everywhere, pumping their own gas."[101] And, Friedman might have added, we want all of that on the cheap and with a clear conscience.

Across a century or more, an underlying consistency has informed the fundamentals of U.S. policy. Among other things, how the United States views itself in relation to the rest of the world has not changed. The end of the Cold War did not constitute a great discontinuity. The new era reputed to have commenced in 1989 does not necessarily differ as markedly from what had gone before as American policymakers profess to believe. It is all a matter of what story one wishes to tell.

For those who conceive of the twentieth century as an epic political and moral drama in which liberalism (or freedom or democracy) succeeded at staggering cost in beating back challengers from the totalitarian left and right, the century ended in 1989. For those who conceive of that century as the epic geopolitical drama in which the rising colossus of the New World eliminated or eclipsed all other competitors for global dominance, the events of 1989 are a mere historical blip, and the "American century" continues. The first narrative is true but retains little direct relevance for the world we now inhabit. The second narrative is also true— and it offers the additional advantage of possessing enormous relevance. It is all a matter of perspective.

Proclaiming to the United States Senate in January 1917 that American principles and policies were those of all mankind, Woodrow Wilson went on to propose that the nations of all world should "with one accord adopt the doctrine of President Monroe as the doctrine of the world." Universalizing this quintessentially American policy, he continued, meant that henceforth "no nation should seek to extend its polity over any other nation or people." The result of making the Monroe Doctrine the doctrine of all humankind would be "that every people should be left free to determine its own polity, its own way of development, unhindered, unthreatened, unafraid, the little along with the great and powerful."[102]

Who could doubt that in uttering these words, Wilson, a man of high ideals whose devotion to the cause of peace was unwavering, spoke with conviction and from the heart? But outside the Senate chamber, at least in some quarters, a different perspective prevailed. According to that perspective, even within the Western Hemisphere the impact of the Monroe Doctrine was other than benign. Even during Wilson's own presidency, it served not as a guarantee that all nations would be permitted to determine their destiny unhindered, unthreatened, and unafraid, but as a mechanism for ordering relations between the strong and the weak according to terms dictated by the strong. By the time of Wilson's presidency, the Monroe Doctrine had evolved into a rationale for U.S. military intervention and the expansion of American power. Eager to see democracy prevail in the Caribbean (and unwilling to tolerate anything that smacked of radicalism or instability), Wilson sent U.S. troops into Haiti in 1915. Just weeks before his January 1917 speech, U.S. troops occupied the Dominican Republic. In each instance, the American stay proved to be a protracted one; in neither country did democracy flower as a result. Confident that he could shape the course of the Mexican Revolution and eager to teach other to "elect good men," Wilson had also medled incessantly in Mexican internal affairs and dispatched military expeditions into Mexico in 1914 and 1916.[103] His quest to make the revolution more democratic and more humane failed utterly. Wilson succeeded only in poisoning U.S.-Mexican relations for decades to come. Yet in the president's own view, all these actions were well intentioned, and none was inconsistent with the doctrine of President Monroe.

In their urge to implement American principles and policies on a global scale, today's advocates of an open world are Wilson's heirs. Like Wilson, they categorically reject the notion that other might construe U.S. aspirations as imperialistic. They insist that the United States, uniquely among the great powers of history, employs its power to act on behalf of the common good. They profess to believe that the cause of openness is the cause of peace and development, democracy and human rights.

To compare the sincerity of those professions and Wilson's would be presumptuous. But it is neither presumptuous nor unfair to note the consequences that followed from Wilson's own convictions. It is precisely when those who tout American indispensability mean what they say that the danger of hubris looms large.

NOTES

1. Robert D. Putnam, *Bowling Alone* (New York, 2000), pp. 247–76.
2. Christopher Lasch, *The Revolt of the Elites and the Betrayal of Democracy* (New York, 1995), pp. 3–22.
3. In 1996, 49 percent of the voting-age population cast a ballot for president. From the beginning of World War II through the 1960s, the average turnout in presidential elections had been 59.1 percent; in the 1970s and 1980s it had averaged 53: U.S. Census Bureau, "Participation in elections for President and U.S. House of Representatives: 1932–1998," in *Statistical Abstract of the United States: 1999* (Washington, D.C., 1999), p. 301.
4. A nation of over 270 million today finds itself increasingly hard pressed to recruit the 200,000 qualified volunteers needed annually to sustain its military forces. For further discussion of this point, see Andrew J. Bacevich, "Losing Private Ryan," *National Review* 51 (August 9, 1999): 32–34.
5. David Brooks, *Bobos in Paradise: The New Upper Class and How They Got There* (New York, 2000).
6. Lasch, *Revolt of the Elites,* pp. 22, 82.
7. Michael Lind, *The Next American Nation* (New York, 1995), pp. 6–7.
8. For a comprehensive survey, see Michael Kammen, *Mystic Chords of Memory* (New York, 1991), pp. 299–527.
9. Eugene D. Genovese, *The Southern Tradition* (Cambridge, Mass., 1994), p. 38; Gertrude Himmelfarb, *One Nation, Two Cultures* (New York, 1999), p. 118.
10. Lind, *Next American Nation,* p. 97.
11. Bill Clinton, "A Foreign Policy for the Global Age," University of Nebraska at Kearney, December 8, 2000.
12. Al Gore, "Remarks by the Vice President in Foreign Policy Speech," Milwaukee, January 6, 1994.
13. Paul Richard, "Scrawling in the Margins: New York's Whitney Biennial Spits in the Face of Convention," *Washington Post,* March 4, 1993, p. C1. For another incisive critique of the 1993 Whitney Biennial, see Christopher Knight, "Crushed by Its Good Intentions," *Los Angeles Times,* March 10, 1993, p. F1.
14. The "works" on display at the Whitney Biennial included performance artists who would do a "native dance" or display their genitals, depending upon the amount of money offered, to make a political statement about the marginalization of Native Americans; large gnawed blocks of chocolate and lard intended to make a political statement about bulimia; numerous photographs of the nude male backside to make a political statement about homosexuality; an array of gilded gym shoes to make a political statement about the plight of young African-American men; and red telephones with instructions to dial 1-900-DESIRES providing the listener (for a fee) the opportunity to hear a woman discuss biracial sex.

15. The term *skeptical relativism* is that of Pope John Paul II, from his 1991 encyclical *Centesimus Annus.*

16. See, for example, the analysis of the United States Commission on National Security/21st Century, *New World Coming: American Security in the 21st Century* (Washington, D.C., 1999), p. 127, arguing that "multicultural fragmentation. . . . shifts in generational attitudes, [and] the decline in overt manifestations of national identification" are contributing to "a serious undermining of American identity and national will."

17. Michael Ledeen, *Freedom Betrayed: How America Led a Global Democratic Revolution, Won the Cold War, and Walked Away* (Washington, D.C., 1996), p. 147. In a similar vein, see Joshua Muravchik, *The Imperative of American Leadership: A Challenge to Neo-Isolationism* (Washington, D.C., 1996), pp. 1, 35, 173, 181.

18. Steven Erlanger and David E. Sanger, "On Global Stage, Clinton's Pragmatic Turn," *New York Times,* July 29, 1996, p. A16. Economists agreed. Jeffrey Garten, undersecretary of commerce for international trade from 1993 to 1995 before returning to academe as dean of the Yale School of Management, wrote in 1997 that absent increasing access to foreign markets, "The country can no longer generate enough growth, jobs, profits, and savings from domestic sources." Enough for what? Garten does not say. Jeffrey E. Garten, "Business and Foreign Policy," *Foreign Affairs* 76 (May/June 1997): 69.

19. Sandy Berger, "Press Briefing," Rio de Janeiro, October 15, 1997; Madeleine K. Albright, "Confirmation Hearing," Senate Foreign Relations Committee, January 8, 1997; Bill Clinton, "Remarks by the President to the Council on Foreign Relations," New York, September 14, 1998. This putative correlation between trade and economic growth was not merely the stuff of speeches. It was integral to official U.S. national security strategy. By 1998 published strategy would state categorically that "we must expand our international trade to sustain economic growth at home": William J. Clinton, *A National Security Strategy for a New Century* (Washington, D.C., 1998), p. 29.

20. Lawrence H. Summers, "Globalization That Works for People," Democratic Leadership Annual Conference, Washington, D.C., October 14, 1999, www.ustreas.gov/press/releases/ps154.htm.

21. John Lukacs, *The Passing of the Modern Age* (New York, 1970), p. 22.

22. For a superb essay describing the essential continuity of U.S. grand strategy in the twentieth century and the economic considerations shaping that strategy, see Benjamin C. Schwarz, "The Arcana of Empire and the Dilemma of American National Security," *Salmagundi* 101–102 (Winter–Spring 1994): 182–211.

23. Ronald Steel, *Temptations of a Superpower* (Cambridge, Mass., 1995), p. 22. For a similar argument that containment alone did not describe U.S. strategy during the Cold War, see William Kristol and Robert Kagan, "Introduction: National Interest and Global Responsibility," in *Present Dangers: Crisis and Opportunity in American Foreign and Defense Policy,* ed. Robert Kagan and William Kristol (San Francisco, 2000), p. 12.

24. Bill Clinton, "Remarks Prepared for Delivery," Foreign Policy Association, New York, April 1, 1992.

25. Clinton had explained his strategy in a letter to Colonel Eugene Holmes, director of the Reserve Officer Training Corps (ROTC) program at the University of Arkansas, in 1969. The complete text of the letter is available in "The 1992 Campaign: A letter by Clinton on his Draft Deferment," *New York Times,* February 13, 1992, p. A25.

26. R. Jeffrey Smith and Julia Preston, "U.S. Plans Wider Role in U.N. Peacekeeping," *Washington Post,* June 18, 1993, p. A1. Largely the handiwork of Madeleine Albright, then serving as U.S. ambassador to the United Nations, "assertive multilateralism" envisioned expanded American support to peacemaking missions with the United States

working through international organizations, especially a reformed and strengthened UN, rather than unilaterally. The concept emerged during the summer of 1993 and did not survive the collapse of peacemaking efforts in Somalia that fall. For a detailed explanation of the concept see Madeleine Albright, Testimony before the Terrorism, Narcotics, and Operations Subcommittee of the Senate Foreign Relations Committee, June 9, 1993, Federal News Service, accessed through LEXIS-NEXIS, August 28, 2000.

27. William G. Hyland, *Clinton's World: Remaking American Foreign Policy* (Westport Conn., 1999), p. 67.

28. Bill Clinton, "A New Covenant for American Security," Georgetown University, December 12, 1991; Clinton quoted in Steven Erlanger and David E. Sanger, "On Global State, Clinton's Pragmatic Turn," *New York Times,* July 29, 1996, p. A16.

29. Charles A. Beard, *The Open Door at Home* (New York, 1935), p. 301.

30. William Appleman Williams, "The Nature of Peace," *Monthly Review* 9 (July–August 1957: 112.

31. Thomas J. Friedman, "The Transition: Plans and Policies," *New York Times,* November 6, 1992, p. A1.

32. Warren Christopher, "Statement before the Senate Foreign Relations Committee," November 3, 1993.

33. There existed a handful of exceptions to this generalization, Russia and Israel being the foremost.

34. Richard C. Holbrooke, *To End a War* (New York, 1999), pp. 41–42.

35. CBS News Transcripts, "Campaign '92: Presidential Debate," October 11, 1992.

36. Christopher, *In the Stream of History,* p. 346.

37. Ibid., p. 347.

38. James Mann, *About Face* (New York, 1999), pp. 281–84.

39. Christopher, *In the Stream of History,* p. 154.

40. Mann, *About Fact,* pp. 285–88, 294–97.

41. Christopher, *In the Stream of History,* p. 153.

42. Ibid., p. 160.

43. David Holley, "In China, Brown Cites Success on Trade, Rights," *Los Angeles Times,* August 31, 1994, p. A1.

44. Christopher, "Statement before Senate Foreign Relations Committee," November 3, 1993.

45. Bill Clinton, "President Clinton's Speech at American University," February 26, 1993.

46. Henry Kissinger, "NAFTA Will Fuel Latin Revolution in Government, Commerce, *Houston Chronicle,* July 25, 1993, p. 5.

47. Bill Clinton, "Remarks by the President to the People of Detroit," October 22, 1996.

48. Bill Clinton, "Remarks by the President at Democratic Leadership Council Retreat," Franklin Delano Roosevelt Presidential Library, Hyde Park, N.Y., May 21, 2000.

49. Garten, "Business and Foreign Policy." p. 70. From 1993 through 1995, Garten served as undersecretary of commerce for international trade.

50. Bill Clinton, "Remarks by President Clinton, Sen. Dole, Sen. Moynihan, Sen. Packwood, and Ambassador Kantor," Washington, D.C., November 23, 1994; idem. "Remarks to the People of Detroit," October 22, 1996.

51. John E. Rielly, ed., *American Public Opinion and U.S. Foreign Policy 1999* (Chicago, 1999), p. 35.

52. Office of Management and Budget, http://w3access.gpo.gov/usbudget/fy2001, accessed August 22, 2000.

53. United States Trade Representative, "The WTO and U.S. Economic Growth," March 2, 2000, http://www.ustr.gov/new/wtofact2.html. Through 1999, U.S. exports in goods and services had jumped by over 50 percent during the Clinton era, from $617 billion to $956 billion. Imports had almost doubled, from $652 billion to $1.2 trillion. Data are from the International Trade Administration of the Department of Commerce, www.ita.doc.gov, assessed on August 22, 2000. Labor and wage statistics are from the Bureau of Labor Statistics, Department of Labor, http://stats.bls.gov/blshome.htm, accessed August 22, 2000.

54. Anthony Lake, "From Containment to Enlargement," Johns Hopkins University, September 21, 1993.

55. In a contemporaneous interview, Lake described his approach as "pragmatic neo-Wilsonianism"—in his mind, evidently, an important distinction; Thomas L. Friedman, "Clinton's Foreign Policy: Top Adviser Speaks Up," *New York Times,* October 31, 1993, p. 8.

56. "Clinton's Three Big Objectives Include Peace through Trade," *New York Times,* July 29, 1996, p. A17.

57. Warren Christopher, "Leadership for the Next American Century," John F. Kennedy School of Government, January 18, 1996.

58. Madeleine K. Albright, "International Economic Leadership: Keeping America on the Right Track for the 21st Century," Institute for International Economics, Washington, D.C., September 18, 1998; idem. "Address to the 10th Annual George C. Marshall Lecture," Vancouver, Wash., October 30, 1998; idem, "Address to the Milwaukee Business Community," October 2, 1998.

59. Berger, "Press Briefing," October 15, 1997; "A Pied Piper in Hanoi," *Boston Globe,* November 18, 2000, p. A16. The *Globe* editorial was written on the occasion of Clinton's end-of-term visit to Vietnam. It described the president's "bravura address" at Hanoi's National University as "irresistible" and concluded that if Vietnam's leaders would take his advice "to open the country to foreign capital and globalization," then Clinton, who had "already done his part for prosperity in America," would be remembered "as the president who did the most to undo communism in Vietnam."

60. Lake, "From Containment to Enlargement," September 21, 1993.

61. Bill Clinton, "Statement by the President on NATO Expansion," Washington, D.C., May 14, 1997.

62. Bill Clinton, "Remarks by the President at Intervention for the North Atlantic Council Summit," Brussels, January 10, 1994.

63. Office of the Press Secretary. The White House, "NATO Summit: The New Strategic Concept," April 24, 1999.

64. Steven L. Burg and Paul S. Shoup. *The War in Bosnia-Herzegovina* (Armonk, N.Y., 1999), pp. 384, 412.

65. Robert Fisk, "Was It Rescue or Revenge?" *The Independent* (London), June 21, 1999, p. 5.

66. Ivo H. Daalder and Michael E. O'Hanlon, *Winning Ugly: NATO's War to Save Kosovo* (Washington, D.C., 2000), p. 85.

67. Bill Clinton, "Remarks by the President to AFSCME Biennial Convention," Washington, D.C., March 23, 1999.

68. "Press Briefing by National Security Adviser Samuel Berger and National Economic Adviser Gene Sperling," Washington, D.C., May 25, 2000.

69. Bill Clinton, "Remarks by the President at the U.S. Coast Guard Academy's 119th Commencement," New London, Conn., May 17, 2000.

70. In the Maghreb, preliminary efforts to open the Arab world were already under way. In April 1999 the Clinton administration launched its "U.S.–North Africa Economic Partnership." According to Stuart Eizenstat, a senior Treasury Department official and point man for this policy, the aim was to prod Algeria, Tunisia, and Morocco "to open up their economies." The Eizenstat initiative sought "to provide the kind of investment climate through deregulation, through privatization, through transparent procurement rules, [and] through protecting intellectual property, that will enable us to encourage successfully U.S. companies to invest"; Stuart Eizenstat interview with Doris McMillon on Worldnet's "Dialogue," June 14, 1999.

71. As noted earlier, the strategy of openness cannot explain every facet of post–Cold War U.S. foreign policy. American support for Israel and the obsession of U.S. policymakers with the Middle East peace process provide two striking examples of commitments at best tangentially related to openness. The very genuine (but not necessarily irreversible) U.S. commitment to Israel is a reminder of the extent to which domestic politics, history, religious conviction, and a sense of moral obligation also affect policy. The never-ending maneuverings related to the peace process offer a reminder of how bureaucratic habit and the vanity of politicians yearning to win a Nobel Peace Prize can warp policy. That said, the assumptions underlying the peace process—that national identity is atavistic, that Arabs and Jews are basically alike, that the road to peace lies not through partition and separation but through reconciliation and integration—are all consistent with the American vision of an open world.

72. Bill Clinton, "Remarks by the President to the Community of Kisowera School," Mukono, Uganda, March 24, 1998; idem, "Remarks by the President to the People of Ghana," Accra, March 23, 1998.

73. Susan E. Rice, "Address before the Morehouse College Andrew Young Center for International Relations," Atlanta, March 25, 1999. See also idem, "U.S. and Africa in the 21st Century," World Affairs Council, Seattle, November 9, 1999.

74. Bill Clinton, "Remarks by the President at Bill Signing of Trade and Development Act of 2000," Washington, D.C., May 18, 2000.

75. In some respects, the level of U.S. engagement in Africa decreased in the 1990s. For example, the amount of aid provided to South Africa decreased from $210 million in 1994 to $47 million in 1999. Among the twenty-four most industrialized nations, by the end of the 1990s the United States ranked last in its economic aid to Africa; Kurt Shillinger, "Carter, Others say U.S. has faltered in Africa," *Boston Globe,* December 8, 1999. p. A2.

76. For a concise account of Sudan and its recent history, see Ann Mosely Lesch, *The Sudan—Contested National Identities* (Bloomington, Ind., 1998).

77. U.S. Department of State, Bureau of Democracy, Human Rights, and Labor, *1999 Country Reports on Human Rights Practices: Sudan* (Washington, D.C., February 25, 2000).

78. The figure on U.S. aid comes from Madeleine K. Albright, "Message from Secretary Albright to the Sudan Summit," Washington, D.C., November 9, 1999. A cynic might suggest that the chief objective of this aid effort is to purchase the acquiescence of humanitarian relief organizations in a policy otherwise characterized by inaction.

79. William J. Clinton, Executive Order pursuant to section 204(b) of the International Emergency Economic Powers Act, 50 U.S.C. 1703 (b), November 4, 1997.

80. Statement by the Press Secretary, The White House, "Sudan: Declaration of Emergency and Imposition of Sanctions," November 4, 1997.

81. Susan E. Rice, "Statement before the Subcommittees on Africa and on International Operations and Human Rights of the House International Relations Committee,"

Washington, D.C., July 29, 1998. See also Albright, "Message to the Sudan Summit," November 9, 1999.

82. Bill Clinton, "Address to the Nation by the President." Washington, D.C., August 20, 1998.

83. Kenneth R. McKune, "Sudan and Terrorism," Testimony before the Subcommittee on Africa, Senate Foreign Relations Committee, Washington, D.C., May 15, 1997. McKune was the State Department's acting coordinator for counterterrorism.

84. William S. Cohen, "We Are Ready to Act Again," *Washington Post,* August 23, 1998, p. C1.

85. James Risen and David Johnston, "Experts Find No Arms Chemicals at Bombed Sudan Plant, *New York Times,* February 9, 1999, p. A5.

86. Richard C. Holbrooke, "Statement during the Open Meeting on the Month of Africa," New York City, January 31, 2000.

87. William J. Clinton, "Opening Remarks at the National Summit on Africa," Washington Convention Center, Washington, D.C., February 17, 2000.

88. Andrew England, "U.S. Pledges to Ease Suffering in Sudan," *Boston Globe,* November 21, 2000, p. A8.

89. Explaining why the United States had limited itself to a largely consultative role in addressing the conflicts raging in Sudan, the Congo, Sierra Leone, Angola, and elsewhere. Samuel R. Berger explained that it was U.S. policy "to help Africans find African solutions to African conflicts." Such diffidence and self-restraint does not inhibit the U.S. from acting in regions such as Europe and the Persian Gulf, which command real strategic importance. Samuel R. Berger, "Remarks by Samuel R. Berger," Africare Dinner, Washington, D.C., September 27, 1999.

90. Madeleine K. Albright, "Remarks and Q & A Session," Howard University, April 14, 1998.

91. Albright, "Confirmation Hearing," Senate Foreign Relations Committee. January 8, 1997.

92. Bill Clinton, "Remarks by the President to Opening Ceremony of the 1998 International Monetary Fund/World Bank Annual Meeting," Washington, D.C., October 6, 1998.

93. Ibid.

94. Bill Clinton, "Remarks by the President to the Next Generation of Russian Leaders, Moscow University of International Relations," September 1, 1998.

95. Ibid.

96. Madeleine K. Albright, "Statement before the Senate Foreign Relations Committee," Washington, D.C., February 10, 1998.

97. Ibid.; Albright, "Confirmation Hearing," Senate Foreign Relations Committee, January 8, 1997.

98. Bill Clinton, "The State of the Union," *New York Times* (Internet edition), January 28, 2000; "Clinton's Three Big Objectives Include Peace through Trade," *New York Times,* July 29, 1996, p. A17. This article consists of excerpts from an interview with President Clinton conducted on July 8, 1996.

99. Albright, "Remarks and Q & A Session," Howard University, April 14, 1998.

100. Summers, "Globalization That Works for People"; Al Gore, "Remarks Prepared for Delivery by Vice President Al Gore, Kennan Institute/U.S.-Russia Business Council," Washington, D.C., October 19, 1995.

101. Thomas L. Friedman, "A Manifesto for the Fast World." *New York Times Magazine,* March 28, 1999, p. 43.

102. Woodrow Wilson, "An Address to the Senate," January 22, 1917, in *The Papers of Woodrow Wilson,* ed. Arthur S. Link et al., vol. 40 (Princeton, 1982), p. 539.

103. For a concise account of Wilson and Mexico, see Mark T. Gilderhus, *Diplomacy and Revolution: U.S.-Mexican Relations under Wilson and Carranza* (Tuscon, 1977).

✌⤳

The Invisible Hand
of the American Empire

Robert Hunter Wade

Before September 11, 2001, only critics linked the United States with empire. Since then many neoconservative commentators have talked with pride and promise of the "new American empire," "the new Rome," referring to the unipolar structure of the interstate system and America's dominant position of military and political power. But this empire has another face: the framework of international economic rules and rule-making organizations. With whatever degree of intentionality, today's international economic architecture ensures that the ordinary operation of world market forces—the process we call globalization—tends to shore up American power by yielding disproportionate economic benefits to Americans and conferring autonomy on U.S. economic policy-makers while curbing the autonomy of all others. It is legitimized by the widespread belief that markets are an expression of the deepest truths about human nature and that as a result they will ultimately be correct.[1] The economic benefits that accrue to the United States as the result of the normal working of market forces within this particular framework then provide the basis of American military supremacy, which helps to protect the framework.

To see this, try a thought experiment. Suppose you are an aspiring modern-day Roman emperor in a world of sovereign states, international markets, and capitalist economies. In order not to have to throw your military weight around more than occasionally, you need to act through hegemony rather that coercion and others must think that your predominance is the natural result of commonsensical institutional arrangements that are fair and just. If you—a unitary actor—could single-mindedly create an international framework of market rules to promote your interests, what kind of system would you create? After describing this imaginary system I will show how close it is to our current world system—surprisingly so, given that the United States is not at all a unitary actor.

ECONOMIC GOALS OF THE HEGEMON

As an aspiring hegemon, you need world economy arrangements that will yield you high economic growth, low inflation, low interest rates, high investment, high consumption, a high value of your currency (the dollar), and high prices of your

Robert Hunter Wade, "The Invisible Hand of the American Empire." *Ethics and International Affairs*, 17, no. 2 (Nov. 2003) pp. 77–88. Reprinted by permission of Carnegie Council on Ethics and International Affairs.

equities. Out of this prosperity you can finance a military many times bigger than anyone else's. You want to be able to ignore the resulting high current-account deficits, and let the rest of the world's savers finance them at very low interest rates (that is, at a very low financial cost to your economy). In this way your citizens do not have to cut their consumption to free resources for the military sector—they can have more guns *and* butter than anyone else.

You also want to be able to set key global market parameters in response to your own domestic conditions, especially the value of your currency. To sustain these parameters at your desired level, you need to be able to thwart resistance to your decisions from other major states and decisions in other states that are not to your liking—as, for example, decisions to revalue a currency.

You want the rest of the world—beyond the major states—to depend heavily for its prosperity on exporting to your market, and not to have a strong endogenous growth mechanism. In this way you can harness the rest of the world to your rhythms.

INTERNATIONAL FINANCIAL ARCHITECTURE

An international financial architecture that is conducive to your interests will have several features. First, there must be no constraint, such as a gold standard, on your ability to create your currency at will, so that you can finance large current-account deficits with the rest of the world simply by selling your government's debt securities.

Second, your currency must be the main international currency for foreign exchange reserves, international trade, and foreign exchange speculation. This ensures robust demand from the rest of the world to hold your assets, especially from the regions that are accruing the current-account surpluses that are the other side of your deficits. As a result, you can run your economy at a high growth rate with less fear of exchange rate volatility and macroeconomic instability than could other sovereign debtors, because when your currency falls relative to other currencies your debt service also falls—since your debt repayments are denominated in your own currency. This gives you more policy flexibility, especially freedom to run big deficits, than other debtors have. Most debtor nations are vulnerable to falls in the value of their currency, because their foreign debt burden goes up when the value of the currency falls; and they are therefore vulnerable to the demands of the creditors, who can influence the state of confidence in the foreign exchange markets and therefore the prospects of a fall in the debtor's currency. However, you, the emperor, want to arrange things so that you can borrow heavily from abroad—and sustain a large stock of debt held by foreigners—while escaping the usual drawbacks of being a debtor economy.

Third, your financial markets must be dominant in international finance. With the biggest, deepest financial markets and with world liquidity (specifically, foreign exchange reserves) being constantly pumped up by your deficit financing, you become the world's savings entrepôt. Your financial firms arrange the inflows of foreign funds needed to finance your deficits; and they also repackage these funds and invest them back in the rest of the world. Hence your financial benefit in boom times, and they benefit in crisis times in the rest of the world (provided the crisis is not bigger than regional) because they do the transactions of flight capital from the crisis region into your safe assets.

Fourth, there must be a single integrated private capital market worldwide, with no barriers to capital flows and no barriers to your financial services firms to enter and exit other countries' markets. Thus the principle of exit, or liquidity, becomes the basic principle of the international economic order, so as to give your asset holders maximum freedom to move in and out of markets anywhere in the world according to short-run profit considerations. It minimizes the extent to which other states can run their political economies on the principle of commitment or long-term obligations and the extent to which they can create an egalitarian capitalism under strict social controls. It supports your central international location.

DERIVED POWER

These four features of the international financial architecture give you powerful tools of *economic* statecraft relative to everyone else. You have more autonomy to affect the value of your currency in the foreign currency markets, compared to that of other states. In general you want the dollar to be highly valued. The high dollar makes your imports relatively cheap, which keeps domestic inflation down and consumption and investment up. At the same time the inflow of foreign funds needed to finance your deficits exerts downward pressure on your domestic interest rates, despite the high dollar. The lower interest rates also keep consumption and investment up. High investment (financed from the rest of the world's savings, since yours are low) keeps parts of your economy on the world frontier of innovation and productivity. The high dollar also helps your foreign mergers and acquisitions and your foreign military expenditures.

On the other hand, you also want the autonomy to make the dollar fall in order to deal with domestic problems, perhaps in order to boost exports, revive domestic industry, and shift growth and employment to your citizens at the expense of other countries.

When the main foreign exchange markets in the world are in your territory and your own nationals are playing the markets speculatively, a signal from your central bank that it is planning to change direction in exchange rate policy is instantly multiplied by your own nationals shorting the dollar. They are your policy multiplier. And when your currency accounts for the great majority of other countries' foreign exchange reserves the effect is amplified. You have the capacity to shift the dollar's value just by voicing an expectation.

Not only can you affect your own domestic conditions just by managing expectations, but you can also shift your parameters and the markets' expectations about conditions elsewhere so as to hurt the macroeconomic conditions of would-be rival states. Rival states may have to secure your cooperation in setting the value of some of their key parameters. For example, if they want to revive their economies from a downturn and lower their interest rates in order to depreciate their currency against yours, they need your cooperation not to lower your interest rates—more than you need their cooperation in the opposite case.

The main danger with this power is that it can over-perform and the dollar cannot simply fall, but crash. But you can rely on help from other central banks and finance ministries, since the last thing they want is an uncontrolled fall in the value of the main international currency.

The system puts poor countries in your power. It encourages them to borrow internationally, with the debt denominated in your currency and at variable interest rates linked to your interest rates. Hence your decisions about your currency, your interest rates, and your protection against imports from poor countries profoundly affect economic conditions in poor states—but not vice versa. In conditions of open capital markets, floating exchange rates, and debt incurred at variable interest rates, poor economies are likely to have more volatile growth, more financial crises, and hence higher demand for foreign exchange reserves of your assets (such as your treasury securities).

In fact, in several ways currency crises in poor countries help your economic growth, your economic preeminence, and your hegemony. They generate large inflows of funds into your financial markets even at low rates of interest. They also make the rest of the world more responsive to your signals about your intentions toward your currency and your interest rates. And they reduce the likelihood that over the long haul challengers to your dominance will arise from among the poor countries.

This economic system depends on a political system of sovereign states, not colonies, that can be made responsible for handling the crises it generates in particular territories. It is a postimperial empire. Only in cases of failing or rogue states that control vital resources do you intervene directly.

INTERNATIONAL ORGANIZATIONS

To supervise this international framework you need a flotilla of international organizations that look like cooperatives of member states and confer the legitimacy of multilateralism, but that you can control by setting the rules and blocking outcomes you don't like.

During crisis periods poor countries have to depend on bailouts from these organizations, and you can set the terms of the bailouts. You use the bailouts to "restructure" the crisis economies in such a way as to prioritize the repayment of your creditors and the advancement of your agenda of worldwide liberalization, privatization, and free capital mobility. The bailout conditionality may include cuts in the borrowing country's spending on health, education, and infrastructure in order to free up resources for debt servicing; a domestic recession for the same reason; a currency devaluation to generate more exports; elimination of capital controls, and cuts in tariff and nontariff barriers. Replicated across multiple crises these conditionalities generate intense competition among exporters from poor countries, which gives you an inflow of imports at constantly decreasing prices relative to the price of your exports, keeping your inflation down and your living standards up, while poor countries' terms of trade and living standards fall.

The bailout mechanism through international organizations has another useful function—it lets you shift the risks of debt default away from your private banks to the member states of the international organizations. In the face of a possible debt default to your banks you order one or more international organizations to lend heavily to the indebted countries, on the understanding that the countries will use the money to repay your banks. Your banks take the private profits, and you help them to spread the losses onto the rest of the world.

Likewise you use international organizations to confer the legitimacy of multilateralism—"the wish of the world community"—on your stringent rules of copyright and patent protection. Copyright and patents are one area where you would not preach the doctrine of liberalization, but rather stress the imperative of protection—since your artists and innovators are the predominant holders of copyright and patents. Therefore, you get the international organizations to embrace rules that set a long minimum period for patents and maximize the range of things over which private patent rights can be granted (for example, naturally occurring microorganisms, biological processes, and "community knowledge," including knowledge of traditional healers). Your firms must be able to patent *anything* they wish and then securely enjoy the rents for at least twenty years.

You also use international organizations to secure agreements that make it illegal for other countries to treat your firms operating in their territory differently from the way they treat their own firms. Measures to place your firms' foreign subsidiaries under various sorts of performance requirements—for local content, exports, joint venturing, technology transfer—are not allowed, because they might limit your firms' freedom of action. Your aim is to facilitate your firms' shifting of lower value-added operations to lower-wage countries while holding the higher value-added operations (innovation, marketing, and distribution) in your territory.

You also support agreements for reduced trade barriers, and you sponsor multilateral negotiations to do so in "development rounds." However, you craft the agreements so that you can maintain your barriers against other countries' exports in sectors important for your voters and financial backers—now described not as protection but as measures to protect your health, safety, the environment, and national security. Further, you maintain with any necessary rhetorical justification an escalation of obstacles to trade, such that the higher the value added the higher the obstacles—and therefore the higher the probability that profit-seeking firms will maintain the high value-added operations in your territory.

You combine pressures to expand the scope of the private sector in poor economies (partly via bailout requirements for cuts in public spending on social sectors) with international agreements on free trade in services, so that your private firms can take the world as their oyster for providing education, health, pension, and other services.

Finally, you advance your agenda by having multiple negotiating forums so that you can "forum shop." If you are forced by rules of multilateralism to give up more than you want to in one forum, you switch to another forum in which you have more power. Or you take agreements reached in a multilateral forum (on patents, for example) and then "turbo-charge" the agreements in bilateral or regional negotiations. You say to particular countries or blocs of countries, "You agreed to this and this in the multilateral agreement; but if you want to enjoy continued low tariff access to our market, without risk of us raising tariffs on your exports, you'd better agree to even more."

FOREIGN POLICY

Your foreign policy seeks to befriend the upper classes elsewhere and make sure they have good material reasons for supporting the framework. It seeks to render it unlikely that elites and masses should ever unite in nativistic reactions to your dominance or demand "nationalistic" development policies that nurture competitors to your industries. Your foreign policy need to include a strategic immigration policy that attracts the best brains in the rest of the world to your universities, firms, and research institutes. You want to have media, business schools, universities, think tanks, and management consultants that are independent enough to provide feedback on how to keep the system and your dominant position in it from falling into crisis.

Your foreign policy also calls for a very large military, so as to be able to back your hegemony with coercion. The world financial architecture allows you to fund overwhelming military strength "on the cheap." You can then shape the geopolitical security of all other states more than they can shape yours. You can control the sources and supply routes of the world's vital energy resources. You can "cash in" your military dominance in return for support for the various policies and agreements that boost your economic power.

THE BOTTOM LINE

This international economic architecture allows your people to consume far more than they produce; it allows your firms and your capital to enter and exit other markets quickly, maximizing short-run returns; it locks in net flows of technology rents from the rest of the world for decades ahead and thereby boosts incentives for your firms to innovate; and through market forces seemingly free of political power it reinforces your geopolitical dominance over other states. All the better if your social scientists explain to the public that a structureless and agentless process of globalization—the relentless technological change that shrinks time and distance—is behind all this, causing all states, including your own, to lose power vis-à-vis markets. You do not want others to think that globalization within the framework you have constructed raises your ability to have both a large military and prosperous civilian sector while diminishing everyone else's.

REAL-WORLD QUALIFICATIONS

A Machiavellian account of the U.S. role in the world economy since the end of the Bretton Woods fixed exchange rate regime around 1970? Certainly. To bring it closer to the real world we need to bring in a number of qualifications.

In reality the United States is far from being a unitary actor in pursuit of a grand design. Its central bank, the Federal Reserve, is independent of its finance ministry, the U.S. Treasury. Its policies are much affected by private-sector pressures, organized by economic sector and geographical region. Its trade protection, for example, is partly about chasing votes. The system was not the creation of the United States alone, either: Europe and Japan have joined in, though quite often in the face of force majeure. In the real world high U.S. living standards—and the ability to have more guns and butter than anyone else—depend not only on the ability to sustain large current-account deficits and earn large profits in finance. They also depend on a high rate of innovation in goods and services, which is only partially explained by the financial and selective immigration factors considered here.

In the real world the United States's ability to run large current-account deficits and maintain a large stock of dollar financial assets in foreign hands in a double-edged sword. It does give the United States an almost free lunch by allowing it to attract the necessary financing even while paying low interest rates. However, this "hegemonic debtor's gain" can turn into a "normal debtor's curse" if—as at present—the U.S. domestic and external debt rises to the point where the United States has to plead with other countries to revalue their currencies and to go on holding dollar assets in the face of higher returns elsewhere and opportunities to diversify into an alternative international currency, such as the euro. A loss of foreign cooperation might lead to sudden falls in the value of the dollar, and even though this would not carry the normal debtor's curse of raising the burden of debt servicing it could still inflict costs on the U.S. economy. These costs could be serious. given that foreign official holdings of Treasury securities now amount to about one-third of the total Treasury-issued debt.

To some extent this curbs U.S. autonomy, and specifically the country's monetary power vis-à-vis creditor governments. But only to some extent, since creditor governments barely attempt to coordinate their monetary decisions among themselves in order to counter the influence from the large U.S. economy. And it is striking how the East Asian countries—by far the world's biggest surplus countries—continue to hold mostly dollars, even though it is a certain bet that the dollar will fall over the next several years. They do so for two main reasons. First, they wish to maintain their currency at a relatively low value against the dollar as a way to maintain export competitiveness and keep up domestic employment. The by-product of this export-led growth strategy is the holding of a large stock of dollar reserves. Second, because they still trade mostly with the United States rather than the European Union, they do not want the disruptions caused by diversifying out of dollars and making the value of the dollar more volatile. They see the likely commercial losses as bigger than the likely financial losses of holding mainly dollars.

My imaginary account also ignores the evolution of the system. The system is less engineered "by design" than it implies. For example, the deep U.S. bond markets were initiated by the heavy debt financing of the two world wars. Unintendedly, the U.S. attempts in the 1960s to regulate interest rates led to the development of an offshore and unregulated financial market for dollars, which in turn generated pressures to liberalize capital markets worldwide. On the other hand, the explosive growth in the world bond market since the 1980s has clearly been by design. In order to fund massive budget deficits policy-makers sought to stimulate a bond market by tax cuts for the rich and the virtual elimination of taxes on capital gains.

Prior to the 1970s the United States dominated through production, not financial services, and therefore faced recurrent crises of excess capacity or over-accumulation of capital. It responded with varying combinations of New Deal–type investments in infrastructure, education, and social spending, Marshall Plan–type investments abroad, privatization drives, and war—all ways to absorb the excess domestic capacity, create new consumers abroad, or destroy capacity abroad. Since the 1970s the American system has developed a complementary line of response, domination through finance, as a way of expanding the play of the liquidity principle on behalf of U.S. holders of financial assets—making them mobile enough to save themselves from the periodic crises of excess capacity in the United States and elsewhere. My thought experiment emphasizes how a modern-day emperor would seek to cement this kind of domination through finance.

Again, one should distinguish between the faults of a very unequal, unipolar structure of wealth and power and the faults of the state that occupies the top position. One can be critical of the U.S. role while still recognizing that—if the unipolar structure is taken as given—the world is probably better off with the United States as the top dog than any of the likely alternatives. Certainly, when American has used its clout to "think for the world," the engineering of its dominance has at times been for the general good.

REAL-WORLD LIKENESSES

However, it is also true that the United States has often used its clout solely in the interests of its richest citizens and most powerful corporations, and this latter tendency has been dominant lately. In particular, the U.S. inaction on climate change; its protection of the agriculture, steel, apparel, and footwear sectors; its privileging of the interests of U.S. oil corporations; its willingness to invade Iraq partly to make sure that Russian, French, and Chinese companies do not get a lock on Iraq's enormous oil reserves (the second biggest proven in the world); and its insistence that Iraq oil reverts to being priced and paid for in U.S. dollars after Saddam Hussein's regime began to insist on euros and other oil exporters (Iran, Venezuela, Russia) began to show signs of making the same switch.[2]

My account of what the emperor wants with regard to patents and copyright corresponds closely to what the United States has obtained in the World Trade Organization's (WTO) Trade-Related Aspects of Intellectual Property Rights agreement—and when the subsequent Doha ministerial meeting clarified the interpretation in a way favorable to the developing countries, the United States and other rich countries shifted forums to bilateral and regional trade agreements and to the World Intellectual Property Organization to implement more demanding intellectual property standards. With regard to unrestricted foreign direct investment, my account corresponds closely to the WTO's Trade-Related Investment Measures. And the WTO's General Agreement on Trade in Services is facilitating a global market in private health care, welfare, pensions, education, and the like, in which U.S. firms tend to have an advantage. This may well undermine political support for universal access to social services in developing countries and facilitate upper-class citizens' "exit" from their nations as fate-sharing communities—making any kind of nationalistic or regional challenge to the current world rules less likely.[3]

The United States has steered the World Bank—through congressional conditions on the replenishment of the funds of the Bank's soft-loan facility, the International Development Association—to launch its biggest refocusing in a decade: a "private-sector development" agenda devoted to accelerating the private (and NGO) provision of basic services on a commercial basis. Yet the Bank has made no evaluation of its earlier, highly controversial efforts to support private participation in social sectors. Its new emphasis on private sector–led development, especially in the social sectors, is largely due to intense pressure from the United States.

The United States has encouraged developing countries to promote "external integration" into the world economy but not to promote, via industrial policies, "internal integration" between industrial, rural and urban, consumption and investment sectors; yet the twin-track approach of export orientation and import replacement is vital for stable growth that is not a hostage to export markets. Indeed the United States has been leading the drive, via the WTO agreements and via bilateral or regional free trade agreements and investment treaties, to coerce or induce other countries to abandon industrial policies that promote upgrading and diversification of their industries and services. At the same time the United States itself has for decades mounted a large-scale industrial policy that nurtures high-tech industries (including computers, advanced sensor devices, stealth materials, aircraft) with massive amounts of public finance and public authority. Much of it is flatly inconsistent with WTO agreements but protected from sanction by the rhetorical shield of "defense policy."

The United States's single most important thrust since the 1970s has been for open capital accounts and freedom of entry and exit for financial service firms. The institution of these rules is causing a parametric shift in the whole world economy, resulting in the loss of ability of all states to resist other parts of the U.S. agenda. The removal of restrictions on capital mobility, far from being a neutral policy, makes the adoption of an egalitarian capitalism under tight social regulation much more difficult, by weakening the means by which a national government could implement such a collective choice. This understanding is implied in the statement by the U.S. deputy treasury secretary, Lawrence Summers: "At Treasury, our most crucial international priority remains the creation of a well funded, truly global capital market."[4] The International Monetary Fund (IMF), too, pushed by the U.K. Treasury with the support of the U.S. Treasury, got its board of governors to endorse a plan to amend the articles of agreement for only the fourth time in its history, in 1997, to add "the promotion of capital flows" to the goals of the organization and add "the capital account" to its jurisdiction.

The IMF, urged on by the U.S. Treasury, went so far as to twist the arm of Ethiopia, one of the poorest countries in the world, to open its capital account in 1996–97. When the government refused (advised by the World Bank's chief economist, Joseph Stiglitz) the Fund made Ethiopia ineligible for the low-interest loans through the Extended Structural Adjustment Program, even though the government had already met virtually all other of the Fund's conditions. With that Ethiopia also lost its access to several other sources of cheap funds, including the World Bank, the European Union, and bilateral lenders—the eligibility for which is conditional on eligibility for the Fund's program.[5]

The drive to lock in a world commitment to open capital accounts stalled in the wake of the East Asian crisis of 1997–98. But by 1999 the IMF managing director, Michel Camdessus, was already saying, "I believe it is now time for momentum to be re-established. . . . Full liberalization of capital movement should be promoted in a prudent and well-sequenced fashion."[6] In 2003 U.S. treasury undersecretary John Taylor testified that the U.S. government believes the ability to transfer capital "freely into and out of a country without delay and at a market rate of exchange" is a "fundamental right," and that no country should ever impose restrictions on capital flows in times of financial crisis. The U.S. government, he said, is insisting in its free trade agreements and bilateral investment treaties that its counterpart governments agree never to place restrictions on capital flows, with provision for U.S. investors to claim for compensation if they do.[7]

These statements reflect not so much a failure to learn as "unlearning." The present push for free capital mobility repeats the faults of the 1920s. Then the U.S. and the U.K. governments and bankers concerted their demands for a new financial architecture based on balanced budgets, independent central banks, restoration of the gold standard, and free capital movements. They pushed this agenda through bilateral dealings with the war-devastated countries of Europe and through the Financial Committee of the League of Nations. The policies helped to usher in a spectacular financial boom that ended in economic collapse. Nevertheless, four years into the Great Depression, the World Economic Conference of 1933, led by the United States and the United Kingdom, continued to make the same four demands, with special emphasis on independent central banks and abolition of capital controls. It was only with the 1944 Bretton Woods agreement, which left the option of capital controls to the discretion of individual states provided that the controls were not intended to restrict trade, that this lesson was learned. John Maynard Keynes considered this to be perhaps the most important part of the agreement. "What used to be heresay is now endorsed as orthodox," he wrote. "Our right to control the domestic capital market is secured on firmer foundations than ever before, and is formally accepted as a proper part of agreed international arrangements."[8] Keynes of course had in mind the United Kingdom's precarious position as a massive wartime borrower facing the prospect of postwar insolvency if capital could leave the country unrestricted. But he also considered that world economic stability required that capital controls be an acceptable weapon of national economic management.

FROM UNIPOLAR TO MULTIPOLAR GLOBALIZATION

The current talk about "globalization" presents it as a general shrinkage of time and distance and widening of opportunities for all, with a corresponding erosion of the power of states to oppress their populations. Joseph Nye suggests that, although the world is very much "unipolar" on the chessboard of classic interstate military issues, it is "multipolar," or one of "balance of power," on the chessboard of interstate economic issues and "chaotically organized among state and non-state actors" on the third chessboard of transnational economic issues. "It makes no sense at all to call this [the second and third chessboards] a unipolar world or an American empire," he says.[9]

It is true that Europe and East Asia are not as passive as my empire picture suggests. For example, of the three-quarters of total world foreign currency reserves that are held in U.S. dollars, well over half are held by East Asian governments.[10] As noted, this reflects not only their large current-account surpluses but also a policy strategy to preserve export competitiveness by maintaining a relatively low value of their currencies vis-à-vis the dollar. Now the imbalances are so large that if the U.S. authorities want to make the dollar fall in value gradually rather than precipitously, they do need to secure the cooperation of East Asian governments—and others—to go on buying U.S. liabilities, and revalue, or in the case of China, further open its domestic market. Nevertheless, the bigger story is that economic globalization is being channeled by rules of the international economic regime, in the making of which the United States has exercised by far the dominant voice. Rules such as those for patents and copyright—which far from shrinking time and distance actually slow the diffusion of technology to the rest of the world and boost technology rents flowing to, disproportionately, Americans. And rules such as those that result in the U.S. dollar being the main international currency, the United States having the biggest financial sector, and free capital mobility worldwide. Globalization so constructed frees the U.S. government of constraints in key areas of economic policy while putting other states under tighter constraints.

This is the paradox of economic globalization—it look like "powerless" expansion of markets but it works to enhance the ability of the United States to harness the rest of the world and fortify its empire-like power.[11] And since it is occurring in a world of "sovereign" states its costs can be made the responsibility of each state to handle, not that of the prime beneficiary.

It is true and important that a lot of people in the world, especially in East Asia, are a lot better off than they were twenty years ago, and that this improvement would not have been possible had they not had access to rich country markets and rich country technology. To this extent the U.S.-directed globalization has worked. On the other hand, average living standards have risen hardly at all in Latin America, Africa, the non-oil-producing Middle East, and much of South Asia since 1980. World income inequality has probably widened.[12] The surge of jobs in apparel in China and Mexico during the 1990s—thanks to exports to North America—went with a fall in real wages and a sharp deterioration in working conditions (measured by what one report describes as the "startlingly high" incidence of violence and severed limbs and fingers in factories owned by Taiwanese, Korean, and Hong Kong intermediaries).[13]

Slow economic growth and vast income disparities, when seen as blocked opportunities, breed cohorts of partly educated young people who grow up in anger and despair. Some try by legal or illegal means to migrate to the West; some join militant ethnic or religious movements directed at each other and their own rulers; but not the idea has spread among a few vengeful fundamentalists that Western countries should be attacked directly. The United States and its allies can stamp out specific groups by force and bribery. But in the longer run, the structural arrangements that replicate a grossly unequal world have to be redesigned, in a way as significant as the redesign at the Bretton Woods conference was toward the end of the Second World War, so that globalization working within the new framework produces more equitable results.

The world would benefit from a less unipolar structure. A little competition between core states of the world economy for support from developing countries might lead to more commitment in the core states to creating dynamic capitalisms in developing countries, as was the case in geopolitically sensitive countries during the first decades of the Cold War.[14] To counterbalance American power, Europe, whether as a federation or as a "Europe of nations," has to create arrangements that permit a common foreign policy. This implies, among other things, that expansion to the East should be slowed down or two-tracked, because the entry of many new states seeing America as their protector against the overbearing leading states of the European Union will make it next to impossible for it to agree on any common foreign policy that runs counter to U.S. wishes. And in the longer term we have to look to growing cooperation between Europe and an East Asian bloc led by China, the third major growth pole in the world economy. Political leaders in both places should be making this a long-term project of high priority.

NOTES

1. This is Joshua Cooper Ramo's statement of the core economic value of Alan Greenspan, chairman of the U.S. Federal Reserve, in "The Three Marketeers," *Time*, February 15, 1999, pp. 34–42. For an astonishing illustration of this belief in action, see John Poindexter's scheme to create a futures market in political events such as terrorist attacks, assassinations, and coups. Carl Hulse, "Pentagon Prepares a Futures Market on Terror Attacks," *New York Times*, July 29, 2003, p. A1.

2. David Gisslequist, *Oil Prices and Trade Deficits: U.S. Conflicts with Japan and West Germany* (New York: Praeger, 1979), argues that the United States ensured the primary role for the dollar by getting OPEC to agree to accept payments for oil in dollars.

3. Robert Hunter Wade, "What Strategies Are Viable for Developing Countries Today? The WTO and the Shrinking of 'Development Space,'" *Review of International Political Economy* 10, no. 4 (2003), forthcoming. For the crucial role of counterfeiting in East Asia's development, see Robert Hunter Wade, *Governing the Market* (Princeton: Princeton University Press, 2003 [1990]), pp. 268, 294.

4. Lawrence Summers, "America's Role in Global Economic Integration" (speech given at the Brookings conference, "Integrating National Economies: The Next Step," Washington, D.C., January 9, 1996); available at www.ustreas.gov/press/releases/pr9701091.htm.

5. For the rest of the story, see Robert Hunter Wade, "Capital and Revenge: the IMF and Ethiopia," *Challenge* (September/October 2001), pp. 67–75.

6. Michel Camdessus, "Governments and Economic Development in a Globalized World" (speech given at 32nd International General Meeting of Pacific Basin Economic Council, Hong Kong, May 17, 1999); available at www.imf.org/external/np/ speeches/1999/051799.htm. The IMF has softened its insistence on capital-account liberalization since Camdessus left in 2000. A recent paper co-authored by IMF chief economist Kenneth Rogoff admits, "it is difficult to establish a robust casual relationship between the degree of financial integration and output growth performance . . . there is evidence that some countries may have experienced greater consumption volatility [hence welfare volatility] as a result [of financial integration]." Eswar Prasad, Kenneth Rogoff, Shang-Jin Wei, and M. Ayhan Kose, "Effects of Financial Globalization on Developing Countries: Some Empirical Evidence," IMF, March 17, 2003, p. 6; available at www.imf.org/external/np/res/docs/2003/031703.htm.

7. John Taylor, Under Secretary of the Treasury, testimony before the Subcommittee on Domestic and International Monetary Policy, Trade and Technology Committee on Financial Services, U.S. House of Representatives, April 1, 2003; available at www .ustreas.gov/press/releases/js149.htm.

8. Quoted in Louis Pauly, *Who Elected the Bankers?* (Ithaca: Cornell University Press, 1997), p. 94.

9. Joseph S. Nye, Jr., "A whole new ball game," *Financial Times*, December 28/29, 2002, p. 1.

10. Martin Wolf, "Asia is footing the bill for American guns and butter," *Financial Times*, February 19, 2003, p. 17.

11. See Peter Gowan, "Explaining the American Boom: The Roles of 'Globalisation' and United States Global Power," *New Political Economy* 6, no. 3 (2001), pp. 359–74; Peter Gowan, *The Global Gamble: Washington's Faustian Bid for World Dominance* (New York: Verso, 1999); and Richard Duncan, *The Dollar Crisis: Causes, Consequences, Cures* (Singapore: Wiley, 2003).

12. Robert Hunter Wade, "Is Globalization Reducing Poverty and Inequality?" *World Development*, forthcoming.

13. Robert Ross and Anita Chan, "From North-South to South-South: The True Face of Global Competition," *Foreign Affairs* (September/October 2002), pp. 8–13.

14. Robert Hunter Wade, "Creating Capitalisms: Introduction to the 2003 Printing," in *Governing the Market*.

✥ PART FOUR ✥

National Values, Democratic Institutions, and Foreign Policy

A distinctive set of values imbues American political culture and gives shape to its political institutions. These values and institutions in turn leave their mark on American foreign policy. In different ways the essays in this section attempt to give meaning to this set of relationships. Samuel Huntington provides the most encompassing examination. Arguing that there is an uneasy relationship between American values and American political institutions, Huntington contends that this gap in normative orientation and practice presents a dynamic of change that can be felt in foreign policy. The pull of American values is manifest in two ways: in attitudes about the institutions that make American foreign policy and in attitudes about changing the institutions and policies of other societies to conform with American values. Huntington argues that in both these areas American history is marked by efforts to close the gap between values of institutions, but that these efforts always embody tensions. The promotion of American liberty abroad often carries with it the need to expand the powers of American government, which in turn conflicts with domestic values of liberty. These tensions present an inevitable promise of disharmony.

Michael Mastanduno examines the old orthodoxy that democracies such as America are decidedly inferior in the conduct of foreign policy. Do democratic institutions inhibit coherent and effective foreign policy by being more responsive to interest groups than to the imperatives of international politics? Mastanduno finds the American experience to be decidedly mixed and concludes that there are as many advantages and virtues to decentralized and pluralistic institutions in the conduct of foreign policy as there are dangers and liabilities. The old conventional wisdom needs to be rethought.

G. John Ikenberry argues that the United States has pioneered what he calls a "liberal grand strategy." The most celebrated American grand strategy emerged during the Cold War, aimed at balancing against and containing Soviet power. But in the shadows of the Cold War the United States pursued a strategy of building liberal democratic order among the advanced industrial countries. The establishment

213

of a wide array of postwar international institutions, the promotion of free trade, and the encouragement of democracy were all part of this liberal grand design. This liberal grand strategy has struggled to emerge as the dominant impulse of American foreign policy after the Cold War.

Robert Keohane uses sovereignty as a conceptual lens to understand the problems facing the European-U.S. relationship and to identify opportunities for more troubled societies and regions. He identifies two types of sovereignty. The first, external sovereignty, implies supremacy over one's territory and external independence from outside authorities. The second, pooled sovereignty, provides for a sharing of sovereignty with other states and international organizations, limiting the prerogatives and powers of the state. Interestingly, as the European Union has moved away from classic conceptions of external sovereignty towards pooled and limited sovereignty, the United States has moved in the opposite direction. The result has been divergent visions of international order.

American Ideals Versus American Institutions

Samuel P. Huntington

Throughout the history of the United States a broad consensus has existed among the American people in support of liberal, democratic, individualistic, and egalitarian values. These political values and ideals constitute what Gunnar Myrdal termed "the American Creed," and they have provided the core of American national identity since the eighteenth century. Also throughout American history, political institutions have reflected these values but have always fallen short of realizing them in a satisfactory manner. A gap has always existed between the ideals in which Americans believed and the institutions that embodied their practice. This gap between ideals and institutional practice has generated continuing disharmony between the normative and existential dimensions of American politics. Being human, Americans have never been able to live up to their ideals; being Americans, they have also been unable to abandon them. They have instead existed in a state of national cognitive dissonance, which they have attempted to relieve through various combinations of moralism, cynicism, complacency, and hypocrisy. The "burr under the saddle," as Robert Penn Warren called it, and the efforts to remove that burr have been central features of American politics,

Samuel P. Huntington, "American Ideals Versus American Institutions," *Political Science Quarterly*, Vol. 97, No. 1 (Spring 1982). Reprinted with permission.

defining its dynamics and shape, since at least the eighteenth century and perhaps before. The question now is: Will the gap between ideals and institutional practices and the responses to it continue to play the same role in American politics in the future that they have in the past? Or are there changes taking place or likely to take place in American political ideals, political institutions, and the relation between them that will make their future significantly different from their past?

Three possibilities exist. The relation between ideals and institutions, first, could continue essentially unchanged; second, it could be altered by developments within American society; or third, it could be altered by developments outside American society and by American involvements abroad. Developments within American society or changes in the international environment could alter the relation between American political ideals and institutions in four ways: the content of the ideals could change; the scope of agreement on the ideals could change; the nature of American political institutions could more closely approximate American ideals, thereby reducing the gap between them; or American political institutions could be significantly altered in an illiberal, undemocratic, anti-individualistic direction; or some combination of these developments could take place.

HISTORY VERSUS PROGRESS?

At various periods in their history Americans have attempted to eliminate or reduce the gap between ideals and institutions by moralistic efforts to reform their institutions and practices so as to make them conform to the ideals of the American Creed. These periods include the Revolutionary years of the 1760s and 1770s, the Jacksonian surge of reforms in the 1820s and 1830s, the Progressive era from the 1890s to 1914, and the latest resurgence of moralistic reform in the 1960s and early 1970s. These four periods have much in common, and almost always the proponents of reform have failed to realize their goals completely. The relative success of reform, however, has varied significantly: in particular the goals of reform have tended to be more widely achieved in the early periods than in the later ones. In the earlier periods the affirmation of the goals of liberty, equality, democracy, and popular sovereignty was directed at the destruction or modification of traditional political and economic institutions; in the later periods, it was directed at the elimination or modification of modern political and economic institutions that had emerged in the course of historical development. In the earlier periods, in short, history and progress (in the sense of realizing American ideals) went hand in hand; in the later periods the achievement of American ideals involved more the restoration of the past than the realization of the future, and progress and history worked increasingly at cross purposes.

The revolutionaries of the 1770s were the first to articulate the American Creed on a national basis and were generally successful in effecting major changes in American institutions: the overthrow of British imperial power, the end of monarchy, the widespread acceptance of government based on popular consent, the extension of the suffrage, an end to what remained of feudal practices and privileges, and the substitution of a politics of opinion for a politics of status. In part the articulation of their goals was conservative; the rights asserted were justified by reference to common law and the rights of Englishmen. But the formulation and public proclamation of those rights was also a revolutionary event in terms of political theory and political debate.

In the Jacksonian years the American ideology was still new, fresh, and directed toward the elimination of the political restrictions on democracy, the broadening of popular participation in government, the abolition of status and the weakening of specialization—that is, of both ascriptive and achievement norms—in the public service, and the destruction of the Bank of the United States and other manifestations of the "money power," so as to open wide the doors of economic opportunity. "Originally a fight against political privilege, the Jacksonian movement . . . broadened into a fight against economic privilege, rallying to its support a host of 'rural capitalists and village entrepreneurs.'"[1] Except for the role of blacks and women in American society, the Jacksonian reforms did complete the virtual elimination of traditional institutions and practices, either inherited from a colonial past or concocted by the Federalist commercial oligarchy, which deviated from liberal-democratic values. All this was progressive in the broad sense, but it too carried with it elements of conservatism. The paradox of the Jacksonians was that even as they cleared away obstacles to the development of laissez-faire capitalism, they also looked back politically to ideals of rural republican simplicity.[2] Restoration, not revolution, was their message.

The institutional changes of the Jacksonian years did not, of course, bring political reality fully into accord with Jacksonian principle. Neither property nor power was equally distributed. In the major cities a small number of very wealthy people, most of whom had inherited their position, controlled large amounts of property.[3] As is generally the case, however, income was much more equally distributed than wealth, and both wealth and income were far more evenly distributed in the rural areas, where 90 percent of the population lived, than in the urban areas. In addition there were high levels of social and political equality, which never failed to impress European visitors, whether critical or sympathetic. All in all, money, status, and power were probably more equally distributed among white males in Jacksonian America than at any other time before or since. The other central values of the American Creed—liberty, individualism, democracy—were in many respects even more markedly embodied in American institutions at that time.

For these reasons, Gordon Wood argued, the Jacksonian generation "has often seemed to be the most 'American' of all generations." This "Middle Period" in American history has been appropriately labeled because

> many of the developments of the first two centuries of our history seem to be anticipations of this period, while many of the subsequent developments taking us to the present seem to be recessions from it. In the traditional sense of what it has meant to be distinctly American, this Middle Period of 1820–1860 marks the apogee in the overall trajectory of American history. Americans in that era of individualism, institutional weakness, and boundlessness experienced "freedom" as they rarely have since; power, whether expressed economically, socially, or politically, was as fragmented and diffused as at any time in our history.[4]

After the democratization of government and before the development of industry, the Middle Period is the time when the United States could least well be characterized as a disharmonic society. It was a period when Americans themselves believed that they had "fulfilled the main principles of liberty" and hence were exempt from "further epochal change."[5] All that was needed was to remain true to the achievements of the past.

In the Middle Period, in short, American dream and American reality came close to joining hands even though they were shortly to be parted. The gap between American ideals and institutions was clearly present in Jacksonian America but outside the South probably less so than at any other time in American history. The inequality of social hierarchy and political aristocracy had faded; the inequality of industrial wealth and organizational hierarchy had yet to emerge. Primogeniture was gone; universal (white male) suffrage had arrived; the Standard Oil trust was still in the future.

In the Middle Period and the years following, the only major institutional legacy that was grossly contradictory to the American Creed was slavery and the heritage of slavery, the remnants of which were still being removed a hundred years after the Civil War. With respect to the role of blacks, the creed played a continuingly progressive role, furnishing the basis for challenging the patterns of racial discrimination and segregation that ran so blatantly against the proposition that all men are created equal. Hence, in analyzing the American dilemma in the 1930s, Gunnar Myrdal could take an essentially optimistic attitude toward its eventual resolution. He could see hope in America because his attention was focused on the one area of inequality in American life that was clearly an anachronistic holdover from the past.

More generally, the Middle Period marked a turning point in the nature of progress in America. Prior to that time "progress" in terms of the realization of American ideals of liberty and equality did not conflict with "historical development" in terms of the improvement of economic well-being and security. After the Middle Period, however, progress and history began to diverge. Progress in terms of the "realization of the democratic ideal," in Herbert Croly's phrase, often ran counter to historical trends toward large-scale organization, hierarchy, specialization, and inequality in power and wealth that seemed essential to material improvement. Political progress involves a return to first principles; politically Americans move forward by looking backward, reconsecrating themselves to the ideals of the past as guidelines for the future. Historical development involves pragmatic responses to the increasing scale and complexity of society and economy and demands increasing interaction, both cooperative and competitive, with other societies.

This distinctive character of the Middle Period and its inappropriateness as a foretaste of things to come are well reflected in the observations of the most celebrated foreign observer of the Jacksonian scene. Tocqueville was in a sense half right and half wrong in the two overarching empirical propositions (one static, one dynamic) that he advanced about equality in America. The most distinctive aspect of American society, he argued, is "the general equality of condition among the people." This "is the fundamental fact from which all others seem to be derived and the central point at which all my observations constantly terminated." Second, the tendency toward equality in American and European society constitutes an "irresistible revolution"; the "gradual development of the principle of equality" is a "providential fact"; it is "lasting, it constantly eludes all human interference, and all events as well as all men contribute to its progress."[6] Like other European observers before and since, Tocqueville tended to confuse the values and ideals of Americans with social and political reality. His descriptive hypothesis, nonetheless, still rings true. By and large American society of the Middle Period was characterized by a widespread equality of condition, particularly in comparison to conditions in Europe. Tocqueville's historical projection, in contrast, clearly does not hold up in terms of the distribution of wealth and only in limited respects in terms of the distribution of political power.

In attempting to sum up the diversity and yet common purpose of the Jacksonian age, Joseph L. Blau employs a striking metaphor: "As one drives out of any large city on a major highway, he is bound to see a large signpost, with arrows pointing him to many possible destinations. These arrows have but one thing in common; all alike point away from the city he has just left. Let this stand as a symbol of Jacksonians. Though they pointed to many different possible American futures, all alike pointed away from an America of privilege and monopoly."[7] The Jacksonians were, however, more accurate in pointing to where America should go in terms of its democratic values and ideals than they were in pointing to the actual direction of economic and political development. Industrialization following the Civil War brought into existence new inequalities in wealth, more blatant corruptions of the political process, and new forms of "privilege and monopoly" undreamed of in the Jacksonian years. This divorce of history from progress had two consequences for the reaffirmation of American political values in the Progressive period.

First, during both the revolutionary and Jacksonian years, the articulation of American political ideals was couched to some degree in conservative and backward-looking terms, as a reaffirmation of rights that had previously existed and as an effort to reorder political life in terms of principles whose legitimacy had been previously established. During the Progressive era the backward-looking characteristics of the ideals and vision that were invoked stood out much more sharply. As Richard Hofstadter suggested, the Founding Fathers "dreamed of and planned for a long-term future," the Middle Period generations were absorbed with the present, and the Progressives consciously and explicitly looked to the past: "Beginning with the time of [William Jennings] Bryan, the dominant American ideal has been steadily fixed on bygone institutions and conditions. In early twentieth-century progressivism this backward-looking vision reached the dimension of a major paradox. Such heroes of the progressive revival as Bryan, [Robert M.] La Follette, and [Woodrow] Wilson proclaimed that they were trying to undo the mischief of the past forty years and re-create the old nation of limited and decentralized power, genuine competition, democratic opportunity, and enterprise."[8] The Progressives were reaffirming the old ideals in opposition to large-scale new organizations—economic and political—which were organizing and giving shape to the twentieth century. This was most manifest in William Jennings Bryan, who was, as Croly said, basically "a Democrat of the Middle Period." Bryan, according to Walter Lippmann, "thought he was fighting the plutocracy" but in actuality "was fighting something much deeper than that; he was fighting the larger scale of human life." Bryan was thus a "genuine conservative" who stood for "the popular tradition of America," whereas his enemies were trying to destroy that tradition.[9] But he was also a radical attempting to apply and to realize the ideals of the American Revolution. Bryan was, in fact, just as radical as William Lloyd Garrison, but Garrison was moving with history and Bryan against it. In a similar vein Woodrow Wilson also reacted to the growth of large-scale economic organization with the call to "restore" American politics to their former pristine, individualistic strength and vigor. To achieve this goal Wilson was willing to employ governmental power, thereby, as Lippmann pointed out, creating the inner contradiction that was at the heart of the Progressive outlook. Among the Progressives Theodore Roosevelt was most explicit in arguing that large-scale economic organizations had to be accepted; nonetheless he too held to much of the older ideal; his argument was couched in pragmatic rather than ideological terms: "This is the age of combination, and any effort to prevent all combination will be not only useless, but in the end vicious, because of the contempt for the law which the failure to enforce law inevitably produces."[10]

Second, the reaffirmation of American ideals at the turn of the century could not be as effective as the Revolutionary and Jacksonian affirmations in realizing those ideals in practice. At the extreme Bryan became the Don Quixote of American politics, battling for a vision of American society that could never be realized again. In the Revolutionary and Jacksonian periods the institutional reforms had been substantial and effective. In the Progressive period both economic and political reforms could at best be described as only partly successful. The antitrust laws and other efforts to curb the power of big business made a difference in the development of American business—as any comparison with Europe will demonstrate—but they clearly did not stop or reverse the tendencies toward combination and oligopoly. In the political sphere the introduction of primaries did not bring an end to political machines and bossism, and according to some may even have strengthened them. In Congress the attack on "Czar" Joseph Cannon established the dominance of the seniority system; paternalistic autocracy in effect gave way to gerontocratic oligarchy. The efforts to make government more responsible encouraged the growth of presidential power. That institutional changes were made is indisputable, but so is the fact that by and large they were substantially less successful than the changes of the Revolutionary and Jacksonian years in realizing the hopes and goals of their proponents.

The passion of the 1960s and 1970s was in some respects ideologically purer than the theories of the Progressives. Perhaps for this reason it was also somewhat more effective in eroding political authority. Yet outside of race relations its more specific reforms were little more successful than those of the Progressives. Economic power was assaulted but remained concentrated. Presidential authority was weakened but rebounded. The military and intelligence agencies declined in money, matériel, and morale in the 1970s but were reestablishing themselves on all three fronts by the early 1980s. It seemed likely that the institutional structure and the distribution of power in American society and politics in 1985 would not differ greatly from what they had been in 1960. With the important exception of race relations the gap between ideals and institutions of the early 1980s duplicated that of the early 1960s.

This changing record of success from one creedal passion period to the next reflected the changing nature of reform. In the earlier periods reform generally involved the dismantling of social, political, and economic institutions responsible for the ideals-versus-institutions gap. The disharmony of American politics was thought to be—and in considerable measure was—man-made. Remove the artificial restraints, and society and politics would naturally move in the direction in which they morally should move. In later creedal passion periods, beginning with the Progressive era, this assumption of *natural* congruence of ideal and reality was displaced by the idea of *contrived* congruence. Consciously designed governmental policy and action was necessary to reduce the gap. In the post-World War II period, for instance, "for the first time in American history, equality became a major object of governmental policy."[11] The Progressives created antitrust offices and regulatory commissions to combat monopoly power and promote competition. The reformers of the 1960s brought into existence an "imperial judiciary" in order to eliminate racial segregation and inequalities. To a much greater degree than in the earlier periods, in order to realize American values the reformers of the later periods had to create institutional mechanisms that threatened those values.

In a broader context the actual course of institutional development is the product of the complex interaction of social, political, economic, and ideological forces. In the United States any centralization of power produced by the expansion of governmental bureaucracy is mitigated by pluralistic forces that disperse power among bureaucratic agencies, congressional committees, and interest groups and that undermine efforts to subordinate lower-ranking executive officials to higher-ranking ones. Yet an increasingly sophisticated economy and active involvement in world affairs seem likely to create stronger needs for hierarchy, bureaucracy, centralization of power, expertise, big government specifically, and big organizations generally. In some way or another society will respond to these needs while still attempting to realize the values of the American Creed to which they are so contradictory. If history is against progress, for how long will progress resist history?

Acute tension between the requisites of development and the norms of ideology played a central role in the evolution of the People's Republic of China during its first quarter-century. China can avoid this conflict for as long as its leaders agree on the priority of development over revolution. In the United States, in contrast, no group of leaders can suppress by fiat the liberal values that have defined the nation's identity. The conflict between developmental need and ideological norm that characterized Mao's China in the 1960s and 1970s is likely to be duplicated in the American future unless other forces change, dilute, or eliminate the central ideals of the American Creed.

What is the probability of this happening? Do such forces exist? Several possibilities suggest themselves. First, the core values of the creed are products of the seventeenth and eighteenth centuries. Their roots lie in the English and American revolutionary experiences, in seventeenth-century Protestant moralism and eighteenth-century liberal rationalism. The historical dynamism and appeal of these ideals could naturally begin to fade after two centuries, particularly as those ideals come to be seen as increasingly irrelevant in a complex modern economy and a threatening international environment. In addition, to the extent that those ideals derive from Protestant sources, they must also be weakened by trends toward secularism that exist even in the United States. Each of the four creedal passion periods was preceded or accompanied by a religious "great awakening." These movements of religious reform and revival, however, have successively played less central roles in American society, that of the 1950s being very marginal in its impact compared to that of the 1740s. As religious passion weakens, how likely is the United States to sustain a firm commitment to its traditional values? Would an America without its Protestant core still be America?

Second, the social, economic, and cultural changes associated with the transition from industrial to postindustrial society could also give rise to new political values that would displace the traditional liberal values associated with bourgeois society and the rise of industrialism. In the 1960s and 1970s in both Europe and America social scientists found evidence of the increasing prevalence of "postbourgeois" or "postmaterialist" values, particularly among younger cohorts. In a somewhat similar vein George Lodge foresaw the displacement of Lockean individualistic ideology in the United States by a "communitarian" ideology, resembling in many aspects the traditional Japanese collectivist approach.[12]

Third, as Hofstadter and others argued, the early twentieth-century immigration of Orthodox, Catholics, and Jews from central, eastern, and southern Europe introduced a different "ethic" into American cities. In the late twentieth century the United States experienced its third major wave of postindependence immigration, composed largely of Puerto Ricans, Mexicans, Cubans, and others from Latin America and the Caribbean. Like their predecessors, the more recent immigrants could well introduce into American society political and social values markedly in contrast with those of Lockean liberalism. In these circumstances the consensus on this type of liberalism could very likely be either disrupted or diluted.

Fourth, the historical function of the creed in defining national identity could conceivably become less significant, and widespread belief in that creed could consequently become less essential to the continued existence of the United States as a nation. Having been in existence as a functioning national society and political entity for over two hundred years, the United States may have less need of these ideals to define its national identity in the future. History, tradition, custom, culture, and a sense of shared experience such as other major nations have developed over the centuries could also come to define American identity, and the role of abstract ideals and values might be reduced. The *ideational* basis of national identity would be replaced by an *organic* one. "American exceptionalism" would wither. The United States would cease to be "a nation with the soul of a church" and would become a nation with the soul of a nation.

Some or all of these four factors could alter American political values so as to reduce the gap between these values and the reality of American institutional practice. Yet the likelihood of this occurring does not seem very high. Despite their seventeenth- and eighteenth-century origins American values and ideals have demonstrated tremendous persistence and resiliency in the twentieth century. Defined vaguely and abstractly, these ideals have been relatively easily adapted to the needs of successive generations. The constant social change in the United States indeed underlies their permanence. Rising social, economic, and ethnic groups need to reinvoke and to reinvigorate those values in order to promote their own access to the rewards of American society. The shift in emphasis among values manifested by younger cohorts in the 1960s and 1970s does not necessarily mean the end of the traditional pattern. In many respects the articulation of these values was, as it had been in the past, a protest against the perceived emergence of new centers of power. The yearning for "belonging and intellectual and esthetic self-fulfillment" found to exist among the younger cohorts of the 1960s and 1970s[13] could in fact be interpreted as "a romantic, Luddite reaction against the bureaucratic and technological tendencies of postindustrialism." This confrontation between ideology and institutions easily fits into the well-established American pattern. Indeed, insofar as "the postindustrial society is more highly educated and more participatory than American society in the past and insofar as American political institutions will be more bureaucratic and hierarchical than before, the conflict between ideology and institutions could be more intense than it has ever been."[14]

Similarly, the broader and longer-term impact of the Latin immigration of the 1950s, 1960s, and 1970s could reinforce the central role of the American Creed both as a way of legitimizing claims to political, economic, and social equality and also as the indispensable element in defining national identity. The children and grandchildren of the European immigrants of the early twentieth century in due course became ardent adherents to traditional American middle-class values. In addition, the more culturally pluralistic the nation becomes, particularly if cultural pluralism encompasses linguistic pluralism, the more essential the political values of the creed become in defining what it is that Americans have in common. At some point traditional American ideals—liberty, equality, individualism, democracy—may lose their appeal and join the ideas of racial inequality, the divine right of kings, and the dictatorship of the proletariat on the ideological scrap heap of history. There is, however, little to suggest that this will be a twentieth-century happening.

If the gap between ideals and institutions remains a central feature of American politics, the question then becomes: What changes, if any, may occur in the traditional pattern of responses to this gap? Three broad possibilities exist. First, the previous pattern of response could continue. If the periodicity of the past prevails, a major sustained creedal passion period will occur in the second and third decades of the twenty-first century. In the interim moralism, cynicism, complacency, and hypocrisy will all be invoked by different Americans in different ways in their efforts to live with the gap. The tensions resulting from the gap will remain and perhaps increase in intensity, but their consequences will not be significantly more serious than they have been in the past. Second, the cycle of response could stabilize to a greater degree than it has in the past. Americans could acquire a greater understanding of their case of cognitive dissonance and through this understanding come to live with their dilemma on somewhat easier terms than they have in the past, in due course evolving a more complex but also more coherent and constant response to this problem. Third, the oscillations among the responses could intensify in such a way as to threaten to destroy both ideals and institutions.

In terms of the future stability of the American political system, the first possibility may be the most likely and the second the most hopeful, but the third is clearly the most dangerous. Let us focus on the third.

Lacking any concept of the state, lacking for most of its history both the centralized authority and the bureaucratic apparatus of the European state, the American polity has historically been a weak polity. It was designed to be so, and traditional inheritance and social environment combined for years to support the framers' intentions. In the twentieth century foreign threats and domestic economic and social needs have generated pressures to develop stronger, more authoritative decision-making and decision-implementing institutions. Yet the continued presence of deeply felt moralistic sentiments among major groups in American society could continue to ensure weak and divided government, devoid of authority and unable to deal satisfactorily with the economic, social, and foreign challenges confronting the nation. Intensification of this conflict between history and progress could give rise to increasing frustration and increasingly violent oscillations between moralism and cynicism. American moralism ensures that government will never be truly efficacious; the realities of power ensure that government will never be truly democratic.

This situation could lead to a two-phase dialectic involving intensified efforts to reform government followed by intensified frustration when those efforts produce not progress in a liberal-democratic direction but obstacles to meeting perceived functional needs. The weakening of government in an effort to reform it could lead eventually to strong demands for the replacement of the weakened and ineffective institutions by more authoritarian structures more effectively designed to meet historical needs. Given the perversity of reform, moralistic extremism in the pursuit of liberal democracy could generate a strong tide toward authoritarian efficiency. "The truth is that," as Plato observed, "in the constitution of society . . . any excess brings about an equally violent reaction. So the only outcome of too much freedom is likely to be excessive subjection in the state or in the individual; which means that the culmination of liberty in democracy is precisely what prepares the way for the cruelest extreme of servitude under a despot."[15]

American political ideals are a useful instrument not only for those who wish to improve American political institutions but also for those who wish to destroy them. Liberal reformers, because they believe in the ideals, attempt to change institutions to approximate those ideals more closely. The enemies of liberalism, because they oppose both liberal ideals and liberal institutions, attempt to use the former to undermine the latter. For them the gap between ideals and institutions is a made-to-order opportunity. The effectiveness of liberal-democratic institutions can be discredited by highlighting their shortcomings compared to the ideals on which they are supposedly modeled. This is a common response of foreigners critical of the American polity, but this approach is not limited to liberalism's foreign enemies. The leading theorists of the American Southern Enlightenment, for instance, took great delight in describing the inequality and repression of the Northern "wage slave" system not because they believed in equality and liberty for all workers but because they wished to discredit the economy that was threatening the future of slavery in the South. "Their obvious purpose [was] to belabor the North rather than to redeem it."[16]

Those who have battered liberal institutions with the stick of liberal ideals have, however, more often been on the left than on the right. There is a reason for this, which is well illustrated by the attitudes of conservatives, liberals, and revolutionaries toward political equality. Traditional conservatives oppose equality. They may perceive American political institutions as embodying more equality than they think desirable. In this case they normally opt out of American society in favor of either internal or external emigration. Traditional conservatives may also perceive and take comfort in the realities of power and inequality that exist in the United States behind the facade and rhetoric of equality. Liberal defenders of American institutions embrace the hypocritical response: they believe that inequality does not exist and that it should not exist. Both the perceptive conservatives and the liberal hypocrites are thus in some sense standpatters, satisfied with the status quo, but only because they have very different perceptions of what that status quo is and very different views about whether equality is good or bad. The ability of traditional conservatives and liberal hypocrites to cooperate in defense of the status quo is hence very limited: neither will buy the others' arguments. In addition, articulate traditional conservatives have been few and far between on the American political landscape, in large part because their values are so contrary to those of the American Creed (see Table 9.1).

On the other side of the political spectrum a very different situation exists. Like hypocritical liberals, moralist liberals believe that inequality is bad. Unlike the hypocrites, however, they perceive that inequality exists in American institutions and hence vigorously devote themselves to reform in an effort to eliminate it. To their left, however, the Marxist revolutionaries have views and beliefs that on the surface at least, coincide with those of moralistic liberals. Marxist revolutionaries hold inequality to be bad, see it as pervasive in existing institutions, and attack it and the institutions vigorously. At a deeper and more philosophical level Marxist revolutionaries may believe in the necessity of the violent overthrow of the

Table 9.1 POLITICAL BELIEFS AND POLITICAL EQUALITY

	Traditional conservative	Liberal		Marxist revolutionary
		Hypocrite	Moralist	
Perception of political equality	Does not exist	Does exist	Does not exist	Does not exist
Judgment on political equality	Bad	Good	Good	Good
		Standpatters		Radicals

capitalist order, the dictatorship of the proletariat, and a disciplined Leninist party as the revolutionary vanguard. If they blatantly articulate these beliefs, they are relegated to the outermost fringes of American politics and foreswear any meaningful ideological or political influence. It is, moreover, in the best Leninist tradition to see reform as the potential catalyst of revolution.[17] Consequently, major incentives exist for Marxist revolutionaries to emphasize not what divides them from the liberal consensus but what unites them with liberal reformers, that is, their perception of inequality and their belief in equality. With this common commitment to reform, liberal moralists and Marxist revolutionaries can cooperate in their attack on existing institutions, even though in the long run one group wants to make them work better and the other wants to overthrow them.

The role of Marxism in the consensus of society of America thus differs significantly from its role in the ideologically pluralistic societies of Western Europe. There the differences between liberal and Marxist goals and appeals are sharply delineated, the two philosophies are embraced by different constituencies and parties, and the conflict between them is unceasing. In the United States the prevalence of liberalism means a consensus on the standards by which the institutions of society should be judged, and Marxism has no choice but to employ those standards in its own cause. Philosophical differences are blurred as reform liberalism and revolutionary Marxism blend into a nondescript but politically relevant radicalism that serves the immediate interests of both. This convergence, moreover, exists at the individual as well as the societal level: particular individuals bring together in their own minds elements of both liberal reformism and revolutionary Marxism. American radicals easily perceive the gap between American ideals and American institutions; they do not easily perceive the conflict between reform liberalism and revolutionary Marxism. With shared immediate goals, these two sets of philosophically distinct ideas often coexist in the same mind.

This common ground of liberal reformer and revolutionary Marxist in favor of radical change contrasts with the distance between the liberal hypocrite and the traditional conservative. The hypocrite can defend American institutions only by claiming they are something that they are not. The conservative can defend them only by articulating values that most Americans abhor. The Marxist subscribes to the liberal consensus in order to subvert liberal institutions; the conservative rejects the liberal consensus in order to defend those institutions. The combined effect of both is to strengthen the attack on the established order. For paradoxically, the conservative who defends American institutions with conservative arguments (that they are good because they institutionalize political inequality) weakens those institutions at least as much as the radical who attacks them for the same reason. The net impact of the difficulties and divisions among the standpatters and the converging unity of the liberal and Marxist radicals is to enhance the threat to American political institutions posed by those political ideas whose continued vitality is indispensable to their survival.

Two things are thus clear. American political institutions are more open, liberal, and democratic than those of any other major society now or in the past. If Americans ever abandon or destroy these institutions, they are likely to do so in the name of their liberal-democratic ideals. Inoculated against the appeal of foreign ideas, America has only to fear its own.

AMERICA VERSUS THE WORLD?

The gap between ideals and institutions poses two significant issues with respect to the relations between the United States and the rest of the world. First, what are the implications of the gap for American institutions and processes concerned with foreign relations and national security? To what extent should those institutions and processes conform to American liberal, individualistic, democratic values? Second, what are the implications of the gap for American policy toward other societies? To what extent should the United States attempt to make the institutions and policies of other societies conform to American values? For much of its history when it was relatively isolated from the rest of the world, as it was between 1815 and 1914, the United States did not have to grapple seriously with these problems. In the mid-twentieth century, however, the United States became deeply, complexly, and seemingly inextricably involved with the other countries of the world. That involvement brought to the fore and gave new significance and urgency to these two long-standing and closely related issues. These issues are closely related because efforts to reduce the ideal-versus-institutions gap in the institutions and processes of American foreign relations reduce the ability of the United States to exercise power in international affairs, including its ability to reduce that gap between American values and foreign institutions and policies. Conversely, efforts to encourage foreign institutions and practices to conform to American ideals require the expansion of American power and thus make it more difficult for American institutions and policies to conform to those ideals.

Foreign-Policy Institutions

The relation of its institutions and processes concerned with foreign relations to the ideals and values of its political ideology is a more serious problem for the United States than for most other societies. The differences between the United States and Western Europe in this respect are particularly marked. First, the ideological pluralism of Western European societies does not provide a single set of political principles by which to judge foreign-policy institutions and practices. Those, as well as other institutions and practices, benefit in terms of legitimacy as a result of varied strands of conservative, liberal, Christian Democratic, and Marxist political thought that have existed in Western European societies. Second and more important, in most European societies at least an embryonic national community and in large measure a national state existed before the emergence of ideologies. So also did the need to conduct foreign relations and to protect the security of the national community and the state. National security bureaucracies, military forces, foreign offices, intelligence services, internal security, and police systems were all in existence when ideologies emerged in the eighteenth and nineteenth centuries. Although the ideologies undoubtedly had some implications for and posed some demands on these institutions, their proponents tended to recognize the prior claims of these institutions reflecting the needs of the national community in a world of competing national communities. European democratic regimes thus accept a security apparatus that exists in large part outside the normal process of democratic politics and that represents and defends the continuing interests of the community and the state irrespective of the ideologies that may from one time to another dominate its politics.

In Europe, ideology—or rather ideologies—thus followed upon and developed within the context of an existing national community and state. In America ideology in the form of the principles of the American Creed existed before the formation of a national community and political system. These principles defined the identity of the community when there were no institutions for dealing with the other countries of the world. It was assumed that the foreign-policy institutions, like other political institutions, would reflect the basic values of the preexisting and overwhelmingly preponderant ideology. Yet precisely these institutions—foreign and intelligence services, military and police forces—have functional imperatives that conflict most sharply and dramatically with the liberal-democratic values of the American Creed. The essence of the creed is opposition to power and to concentrated authority. This leads to efforts to minimize the resources of power (such as arms), to restrict the effectiveness of specialized bureaucratic hierarchies, and to limit the authority of the executive in the conduct of foreign policy. This conflict manifests itself dramatically in the perennial issue concerning the role of standing armies and professional military forces in a liberal society. For much of its history the United States was able to avoid the full implications of this conflict because its geographic position permitted it to follow a policy of extirpation—that is, almost abolishing military forces and relegating those that did exist to the distant social and geographic extremities of society.[18] Similarly, the United States did not seem to need and did not have an intelligence service, a professional foreign service, or a national police force.

In the twentieth century the impossibility of sustained isolation led the United States to develop all these institutions. Much more so than those in Western Europe, however, these institutions have coexisted in uneasy and fundamentally incompatible ways with the values of the prevailing ideology. This incompatibility became acute after World War II, when the country's global role and responsibilities made it necessary for the government to develop and to maintain such institutions on a large scale and to accord them a central role in its foreign policy. During the 1950s and early 1960s Americans tended to be blissfully complacent and to ignore the broad gap between ideals and institutions that this created in the foreign-policy and defense sectors of their national life. At the same time, various theories—such as Kennan's ideal of the detached professional diplomat and Huntington's concept of "objective civilian control"—were developed to justify the insulation of these institutions from the political demands of a liberal society.[19] In the end, however, the liberal imperatives could not be avoided, and the late 1960s and 1970s saw overwhelming political pressure to make foreign-policy and security institutions conform to the requirements of the liberal ideology. In a powerful outburst of creedal passion, Americans embarked on crusades against the CIA and FBI, defense spending, the use of military force abroad, the military-industrial complex, and the imperial presidency (to use Arthur Schlesinger, Jr.'s phrase), attempting to expose, weaken, dismantle, or abolish the institutions that protected their liberal society against foreign threats. They reacted with outraged moralistic self-criticism to their government engaging in the type of activities—

deception, violence, abuse of individual rights—to protect their society that other countries accept as a matter of course.

This penchant of Americans for challenging and undermining the authority of their political institutions, including those concerned with the foreign relations and security of the country, produces mixed and confused reactions on the part of Europeans and other non-Americans. Their initial reaction to a Pentagon Papers case, Watergate, or investigation of the CIA is often one of surprise, amazement, bewilderment. "What are you Americans up to and why are you doing this to yourselves?" A second reaction, which often follows the first, is grudging admiration for a society that takes its principles so seriously and has such effective procedures for attempting to realize them. This is often accompanied by somewhat envious and wistful comments on the contrast between this situation and the paramountcy of state authority in their own country. Finally, a third reaction often follows, expressing deep concern about the impact that the creedal upheaval will have on the ability of the United States to conduct its foreign policy and to protect its friends and allies.

This last concern over whether its liberal values will permit the United States to maintain the material resources, governmental institutions, and political will to defend its interests in the world becomes more relevant not just as a result of the inextricable involvement of the United States in world affairs but also because of the changes in the countries with which the United States will be primarily involved. During the first part of the twentieth century American external relations were largely focused on Western Europe, where in most countries significant political groups held political values similar to American values. Even more important, lodged deeply in the consciousness of Western European statesmen and intellectuals was the thought, impregnated there by Tocqueville if by no one else, that American political values in some measure embodied the wave of the future, that what America believed in would at some point be what the entire civilized world would believe in. This sympathy, partial or latent as it may have been, nonetheless gave the United States a diplomatic resource of some significance. European societies might resent American moral or moralistic loftiness, but both they and the Americans knew that the moral values set forth by the United States (sincerely or hypocritically) would have a resonance in their own societies and could at times be linked up with internal social and political movements that would be impossible for them to ignore.

In the mid-twentieth century the widespread belief in democratic values among younger Germans and to a lesser degree among younger Japanese provided some support for the convergence thesis. At a more general level, however, the sense that America was the future of Europe weakened considerably. More important, in the late twentieth century the countries with which the United States was having increasing interactions, both competitive and cooperative, were the Soviet Union, China, and Japan. The partial sense of identification and of future convergence that existed between the United States and Europe are absent in American relations with these three countries. Like the United States, these countries have a substantial degree of consensus or homogeneity in social and political values and ideology. The content of each country's consensus, however, differs significantly from that of the United States. In all three societies the stress in one form or another is on the pervasiveness of inequality in human relationships, the "sanctity of authority,"[20] the subordination of the individual to the group and the state, the dubious legitimacy of dissent or challenges to the powers that be. Japan, to be sure, developed a working democracy after World War II, but its long-standing values stressing hierarchy, vertical ranking, and submissiveness leave some degree of disharmony that has resemblances to but is just the reverse of what prevails in American society. The dominant ideas in all three countries stand in dramatic contrast to American ideas of openness, liberalism, equality, individual rights, and freedom to dissent. In the Soviet Union, China, and Japan the prevailing political values and social norms reinforce the authority of the central political institutions of society and enhance the ability of these nations to compete with other societies. In the United States the prevailing norms, insofar as Americans take them seriously, undermine and weaken the power and authority of government and detract, at times seriously, from its ability to compete internationally. In the small world of the West Americans were beguiling cousins; in the larger world that includes the East Americans often seem naïve strangers. Given the disharmonic element in the American political system—the continuing challenge, latent or overt, that lies in the American mind to the authority of American government—how well will the United States be able to conduct its affairs in this league of powers to whose historical traditions basic American values are almost entirely alien?

Foreign-Policy Goals

In the eyes of most Americans not only should their foreign-policy institutions be structured and function so as to reflect liberal values, but American foreign policy should also be substantively directed to the promotion of those values in the external environment. This gives a distinctive cast to the American role in the world. In a famous phrase Viscount Palmerston once said that Britain did not have permanent friends or enemies, it only had permanent interests. Like Britain and other countries, the United States also has interests, defined in terms of power, wealth, and security, some of which are sufficiently enduring as to be thought of as permanent. As a founded society, however, the United States also has distinctive political principles and values that define its national identity. These principles provide a second set of goals and a second set of standards—in addition to those of national interest—by which to shape the goals and judge the success of American foreign policy.

This heritage, this transposition of the ideals-versus-institutions gap into foreign policy, again distinguishes the United States from other societies. Western European states clearly do not reject the relevance of morality and political ideology to the conduct of foreign policy. They do, however, see the goal of foreign policy as the advancement of the major and continuing security and economic interests of their state. Political principles provide limits and parameters to foreign policy but not to its goals. As a result European public debate over morality versus power in foreign policy has except in rare instances not played the role that it has in the United States. That issue does come up with the foreign policy of

Communist states and has been discussed at length, in terms of the conflict of ideology and national interest, in analyses of Soviet foreign policy. The conflict has been less significant there than in the United States for three reasons. First, an authoritarian political system precludes public discussion of the issue. Since the 1920s debate of Trotsky versus Stalin over permanent revolution there has been no overt domestic criticism concerning whether Soviet foreign policy is at one time either too power-oriented or at another time too ideologically oriented. Second, Marxist-Leninist ideology distinguishes between basic doctrine on the one hand and strategy and tactics on the other. The former does not change; the latter is adapted to specific historical circumstances. The twists and turns in the party line can always be justified as ideologically necessary at that particular point in time to achieve the long-run goals of communism, even though those shifts may in fact be motivated primarily by national interests. American political values, in contrast, are usually thought of as universally valid, and pragmatism is seen not as a means of implementing these values in particular circumstances but rather as a means of abandoning them. Third, Soviet leaders and the leaders of other Communist states that pursue their own foreign policies can and do, when they wish, simply ignore ideology when they desire to pursue particular national interest goals.

For most Americans, however, foreign-policy goals should reflect not only the security interests of the nation and the economic interests of key groups within the nation but also the political values and principles that define American identity. If these values do define foreign-policy goals, then that policy is morally justified, the opponents of that policy at home and abroad are morally illegitimate, and all efforts must be directed toward overcoming the opponents and achieving the goals. The prevailing American approach to foreign policy thus has been not that of Stephen Decatur ("Our country, right or wrong!") but that of Carl Schurz ("Our country, right or wrong! When right, to be kept right; when wrong, to be put right!"). To Americans, achieving this convergence between self-interest and morality has appeared as no easy task. Hence the recurring tendencies in American history, either to retreat to minimum relations with the rest of the world and thus avoid the problem of reconciling the pursuit of self-interest with the adherence to principle in a corrupt and hostile environment, or the opposite solution, to set forth on a crusade to purify the world, to bring it into accordance with American principles and in the process to expand American power and thus protect the national interest.

This practice of judging the behavior of one's country and one's government by external standards of right and wrong has been responsible for the often substantial opposition to the wars in which the United States has engaged. The United States will only respond with unanimity to a war in which both national security and political principle are clearly at stake. In the two hundred years after the Revolution, only one war, World War II, met this criterion, and this was the only war to which there was no significant domestic opposition articulated in terms of the extent to which the goals of the war and the way in which it was conducted deviated from the basic principles of the American Creed. In this sense World War II was for the United States the "perfect war"; every other war has been an imperfect war in that certain elements of the American public have objected to it because it did not seem to accord with American principles. As strange as it may seem to people of other societies, Americans have had no trouble conceiving of their government waging an un-American war.

The extent to which the American liberal creed prevails over power considerations can lead to hypocritical and rather absolutist positions on policy. As Seymour Martin Lipset pointed out, if wars should only be fought for moral purposes, then the opponents against which they are fought must be morally evil and hence total war must be waged against them and unconditional surrender exacted from them. If a war is not morally legitimate, then the leaders conducting it must be morally evil and opposition to it in virtually any form is not only morally justified but morally obligatory. It is no coincidence that the country that has most tended to think of wars as crusades is also the country with the strongest record of conscientious objection to war.[21]

The effort to use American foreign policy to promote American values abroad raises a central issue. There is a clear difference between political action to make American political practices conform to American political values and political action to make *foreign* political practices conform to American values. Americans can legitimately attempt to reduce the gap between American institutions and American values, but can they legitimately attempt to reduce the gap between other people's institutions and American values? The answer is not self-evident.

The argument for a negative response to this question can be made on at least four grounds. First, it is morally wrong for the United States to attempt to shape the institutions of other societies. Those institutions should reflect the values and behavior of the people in those societies. To intrude from outside is either imperialism or colonialism, each of which also violates American values. Second, it is difficult practically and in most cases impossible for the United States to influence significantly the institutional development of other societies. The task is simply beyond American knowledge, skill, and resources. To attempt to do so will often be counterproductive. Third, any effort to shape the domestic institutions of other societies needlessly irritates and antagonizes other governments and hence will complicate and often endanger the achievement of other more important foreign-policy goals, particularly in the areas of national security and economic well-being. Fourth, to influence the political development of other societies would require an enormous expansion of the military power and economic resources of the American government. This in turn would pose dangers to the operation of democratic government within the United States.

A yes answer to this question can, on the other hand, also be justified on four grounds. First, if other people's institutions pose direct threats to the viability of American institutions and values in the United States, an American effort to change those institutions would be justifiable in terms of self-defense. Whether or not foreign institutions do pose such a direct threat in any given circumstance is, however, not easily determined. Even in the case of Nazi Germany in 1940 there were widely differing opinions in the United States. After World War II opinion was also divided on whether Soviet institutions, as distinct from Soviet policies, threatened the United States.

Second, the direct-threat argument can be generalized to the proposition that authoritarian regimes in any form and on any continent pose a potential threat to the viability of liberal institutions and values in the United States. A liberal-democratic system, it can be argued, can only be secure in a world system of similarly constituted states. In the past this argument did not play a central role because of the extent to which the United States was geographically isolated from differently constituted states. The world is, however, becoming smaller. Given the increasing interactions among societies and the emergence of transnational institutions operating in many societies, the pressures toward convergence among political systems are likely to become more intense. Interdependence may be incompatible with coexistence. In this case the world, like the United States in the nineteenth century or Western Europe in the twentieth century, will not be able to exist half-slave and half-free. Hence the survival of democratic institutions and values at home will depend upon their adoption abroad.

Third, American efforts to make other people's institutions conform to American values would be justified to the extent that the other people supported those values. Such support has historically been much more prevalent in Western Europe and Latin America than it has in Asia and Africa, but some support undoubtedly exists in almost every society for liberty, equality, democracy, and the rights of the individual. Americans could well feel justified in supporting and helping those individuals, groups, and institutions in other societies who share their belief in these values. At the same time it would also be appropriate for them to be aware that those values could be realized in other societies through institutions significantly different from those that exist in the United States.

Fourth, American efforts to make other people's institutions conform to American values could be justified on the grounds that those values are universally valid and universally applicable, whether or not most people in other societies believe in them. For Americans not to believe in the universal validity of American values could indeed lead to a moral relativism: liberty and democracy are not inherently better than any other political values; they just happen to be those that for historical and cultural reasons prevail in the United States. This relativistic position runs counter to the strong elements of moral absolutism and messianism that are part of American history and culture, and hence the argument for moral relativism may not wash in the United States for relativistic reasons. In addition the argument can be made that some element of belief in the universal validity of a set of political ideals is necessary to arouse the energy, support, and passion to defend those ideals and the institutions modeled on them in American society.

Historically Americans have generally believed in the universal validity of their values. At the end of World War II, when Americans forced Germany and Japan to be free, they did not stop to ask if liberty and democracy were what the German and Japanese people wanted. Americans implicitly assumed that their values were valid and applicable and that they would at the very least be morally negligent if they did not insist that Germany and Japan adopt political institutions reflecting those values. Belief in the universal validity of those values obviously reinforces and reflects those hypocritical elements of the American tradition that stress the United States's role as a redeemer nation and lead it to attempt to impose its values and often its institutions on other societies. These tendencies may, however, be constrained by a recognition that although American values may be universally valid, they need not be universally and totally applicable at all times and in all places.

Americans expect their institutions and policies that are devoted to external relations to reflect liberal standards and principles. So also in large measure do non-Americans. Both American citizens and others hold the United States to standards that they do not generally apply to other countries. People expect France, for instance, to pursue its national self-interests—economic, military, and political— with cold disregard for ideologies and values. But their expectations with respect to the United States are very different: people accept with a shrug actions on the part of France that would generate surprise, consternation, and outrage if perpetrated by the United States. "Europe accepts the idea that America is a country with a difference, from whom it is reasonable to demand an exceptionally altruistic standard of behaviour; it feels perfectly justified in pouring obloquy on shortcomings from this ideal; and also, perhaps inevitably, it seems to enjoy every example of a fall from grace which contemporary America provides."[22]

This double standard is implicit acknowledgment of the seriousness with which Americans attempt to translate their principles into practice. It also provides a ready weapon to foreign critics of the United States, just as it does to domestic ones. For much of its history, racial injustice, economic inequality, and political and religious intolerance were familiar elements in the American landscape, and the contrast between them and the articulated ideals of the American Creed furnished abundant ammunition to generations of European critics. "Anti-Americanism is in this form a protest, not against Americanism, but against its apparent failure."[23] This may be true on the surface. But it is also possible that failure—that is, the persistence of the ideals-versus-institutions gap in American institutions and policies—furnishes the excuse and the opportunity for hostile foreign protest and that the true target of the protest is Americanism itself.

POWER AND LIBERTY: THE MYTH OF AMERICAN REPRESSION

The pattern of American involvement in world affairs has often been interpreted as the outcome of these conflicting pulls of national interest and power on the one hand and political morality and principles on the other. Various scholars have phrased the dichotomy in various ways: self-interest versus ideals, power versus morality, realism versus utopianism, pragmatism versus principle, historical realism versus rationalist idealism, Washington versus Wilson.[24] Almost all, however, have assumed the dichotomy to be real and have traced the relative importance over the years of national interest and morality in shaping American foreign policy. It is, for instance, argued that during the Federalist years realism or power considerations were generally preponderant, whereas during the first four decades of the twentieth century moral considerations and principles came to be uppermost in the minds of American policy makers. After World War II a significant group of writers and thinkers on foreign policy—including Reinhold Niebuhr,

George Kennan, Hans Morgenthau, Walter Lippmann, and Robert Osgood—expounded a "new realism" and criticized the moralistic, legalistic, "utopian" Wilsonian approaches, which they claimed had previously prevailed in the conduct of American foreign relations. The new realism reached its apotheosis in the central role played by the balance of power in the theory and practice of Henry Kissinger. A nation's foreign policy, he said, "should be directed toward affecting the foreign policy" of other societies; it should not be "the principal goal of American foreign policy to transform the domestic structures of societies with which we deal."[25]

In the 1970s, however, the new realism of the 1950s and 1960s was challenged by a "new moralism." The pendulum that had swung in one direction after World War II swung far over to the other side. This shift was one of the most significant consequences of American involvement in Vietnam, Watergate, and the democratic surge and creedal passion of the 1960s. It represented the displacement onto the external world of the moralism that had been earlier directed inward against American institutions. It thus represented the first signs of a return to the hypocritical response to the gap between American values and American institutions. The new moralism manifested itself first in congressional action, with the addition to the foreign assistance act of Title IX in 1966 and human rights conditions in the early 1970s. In 1976 Jimmy Carter vigorously criticized President Ford for believing "that there is little room for morality in foreign affairs, and that we must put self-interest above principle."[26] As president, Carter moved human rights to a central position in American foreign relations.

The lines between the moralists and the realists were thus clearly drawn, but on one point they were agreed: they both believed that the conflict between morality and self-interest, or ideals and realism, was a real one. In some respects it was. In other respects, particularly when it was formulated in terms of a conflict between liberty and power, it was not. As so defined, the dichotomy was false. It did not reflect an accurate understanding of the real choices confronting American policy makers in dealing with the external world. It derived rather from the transposition of the assumptions of the antipower ethic to American relations with the rest of the world. From the earliest years of their society Americans have perceived a conflict between imperatives of governmental power and the liberty and rights of the individual. Because power and liberty are antithetical at home, they are also assumed to be antithetical abroad. Hence the pursuit of power by the American government abroad must threaten liberty abroad even as a similar pursuit of power at home would threaten liberty there. The contradiction in American society between American power and American liberty at home is projected into a contradiction between American power and foreign liberty abroad.

During the 1960s and 1970s this belief led many intellectuals to propagate what can perhaps best be termed the myth of American repression—that is, the view that American involvement in the politics of other societies is almost invariably hostile to liberty and supportive of repression in those societies. The United States, as Hans Morgenthau put it, is "repression's friend": "With unfailing consistency, we have since the end of the Second World War intervened on behalf of conservative and fascist repression against revolution and radical reform. In an age when societies are in a revolutionary or prerevolutionary stage, we have become the foremost counterrevolutionary status quo power on earth. Such a policy can only lead to moral and political disaster."[27] This statement, like the arguments generally of those intellectuals supporting the myth of American repression, suffers from two basic deficiencies.

First, it confuses support for the left with opposition to repression. In this respect, it represents another manifestation of the extent to which similarity in immediate objectives can blur the line between liberals and revolutionaries. Yet those who support "revolution and radical reform" in other countries seldom have any greater concern for liberty and human dignity than those who support "conservative and fascist repression." In fact, if it is a choice between rightist and Communist dictatorships, there are at least three good reasons in terms of liberty to prefer the former to the latter. First, the suppression of liberty in right-wing authoritarian regimes is almost always less pervasive than it is in left-wing totalitarian ones. In the 1960s and 1970s, for instance, infringements of human rights in South Korea received extensive coverage in the American media, in part because there were in South Korea journalists, church groups, intellectuals, and opposition political leaders who could call attention to those infringements. The absence of comparable reports about the infringements of human rights in North Korea was evidence not of the absence of repression in that country but of its totality. Right-wing dictatorships moreover are, the record shows, less permanent than left-wing dictatorships; Portugal, Spain, and Greece are but three examples of right-wing dictatorships that were replaced by democratic regimes. As of 1980, however, no Communist system had been replaced by a democratic regime. Third, as a result of the global competition between the United States and the Soviet Union, right-wing regimes are normally more susceptible to American and other Western influence than left-wing dictatorships, and such influence is overwhelmingly on the side of liberty.

This last point leads to the other central fallacy of the myth of American repression as elaborated by Morgenthau and others. Their picture of the world of the 1960s and 1970s was dominated by the image of an America that was overwhelmingly powerful and overwhelmingly repressive. In effect they held an updated belief in the "illusion of American omnipotence" that attributed the evil in other societies to the machinations of the Pentagon, the CIA, and American business. Their image of America was, however, defective in both dimensions. During the 1960s and 1970s American power relative to that of other governments and societies declined significantly. By the mid-1970s the ability of the United States to influence what was going on in other societies was but a pale shadow of what it had been a quarter-century earlier. When it had an effect, however, the overall effect of American power on other societies was to further liberty, pluralism, and democracy. The conflict between American power and American principles virtually disappears when it is applied to the American impact on other societies. In that case, the very factors that give rise to the consciousness of a gap between ideal and reality also limit in practice the extent of that gap. The United States is in practice the freest, most liberal, most democratic country in the world, with far better institutionalized protections for the rights of its citizens than any other society. As a consequence, any increase in the power or influence of the United States in world affairs generally results—not inevitably, but far more often than not—in the promotion of liberty and human rights in the world. The expansion of American power is not synonymous with the expansion of liberty, but a significant correlation exists between the rise and fall of American power in the world and the rise and fall of liberty and democracy in the world.

The single biggest extension of democratic liberties in the history of the world came at the end of World War II, when stable democratic regimes were inaugurated in defeated Axis countries: Germany, Japan, Italy, and, as a former part of Germany, Austria. In the early 1980s these countries had a population of over two hundred million and included the third and fourth largest economies in the world. The imposition of democracy on these countries was almost entirely the work of the United States. In Germany and Japan in particular the United States government played a major role in designing democratic institutions. As a result of American determination and power the former Axis countries were "forced to be free."[28] Conversely, the modest steps taken toward democracy and liberty in Poland, Czechoslovakia, and Hungary were quickly reversed and Stalinist repression instituted once it became clear that the United States was not able to project its power into Eastern Europe. If World War II had ended in something less than total victory, or if the United States had played a less significant role in bringing about the victory (as was indeed the case east of the Elbe), these transitions to democracy in central Europe and eastern Asia would not have occurred. But—with the partial exception of South Korea—where American armies marched, democracy followed in their train.

The stability of democracy in these countries during the quarter-century after World War II reflected in large part the extent to which the institutions and practices imposed by the United States found a favorable social and political climate in which to take root. The continued American political, economic, and military presence in Western Europe and eastern Asia was, however, also indispensable to this democratic success. At any time after World War II the withdrawal of American military guarantees and military forces from these areas would have had a most unsettling and perhaps devastating effect on the future of democracy in central Europe and Japan.

In the early years of the cold war, American influence was employed to ensure the continuation of democratic government in Italy and to promote free elections in Greece. In both cases, the United States had twin interests in the domestic politics of these countries: to create a system of stable democratic government and to ensure the exclusion of Communist parties from power. Since in both cases the Communist parties did not have the support of anything remotely resembling a majority of the population, the problem of what to do if a party committed to abolishing democracy gains power through democratic means was happily avoided. With American support, democracy survived in Italy and was sustained for a time in Greece. In addition, the American victory in World War II provided the stimulus in Turkey for one of the rarest events in political history: the peaceful self-transformation of an authoritarian one-party system into a democratic competitive party system.

In Latin America, the rise and fall of democratic regimes also coincided with the rise and fall of American influence. In the second and third decades of this century, American intervention in Nicaragua, Haiti, and the Dominican Republic produced the freest elections and the most open political competition in the history of those countries. In these countries, as in others in Central America and the Caribbean, American influence in support of free elections was usually exerted in response to the protests of opposition groups against the repressive actions of their own governments and as a result of American fears that revolution or civil war would occur if significant political and social forces were denied equal opportunity to participate in the political process. The American aim, as Theodore Wright made clear in his comprehensive study, was to "promote political stability by supporting free elections" rather than by strengthening military dictatorships. In its interventions in eight Caribbean and Central American countries between 1900 and 1933 the United States acted on the assumption that "the only way both to prevent revolutions and to determine whether they are justified if they do break out is to guarantee free elections."[29] In Cuba the effect of the Platt Amendment and American interventions was "to pluralize the Cuban political system" by fostering "the rise and entrenchment of opposition groups" and by multiplying "the sources of political power so that no single group, not even the government, could impose its will on society or the economy for very long. . . . The spirit and practices of liberalism—competitive and unregulated political, economic, religious, and social life—overwhelmed a pluralized Cuba."[30] The interventions by United States Marines in Haiti, Nicaragua, the Dominican Republic, and elsewhere in these years often bore striking resemblances to the interventions by federal marshals in the conduct of elections in the American South in the 1960s: registering voters, protecting against electoral violence, ensuring a free vote and an honest count.

Direct intervention by the American government in Central America and the Caribbean came to at least a temporary end in the early 1930s. Without exception the result was a shift in the direction of more dictatorial regimes. It had taken American power to impose even the most modest aspects of democracy in these societies. When American intervention ended, democracy ended. For the Caribbean and Central America, the era of the Good Neighbor was also the era of the bad tyrant. The efforts of the United States to be the former give a variety of unsavory local characters—Trujillo, Somoza, Batista—the opportunity to be the latter.

In the years after World War II, American attention and activity were primarily directed toward Europe and Asia. Latin America was by and large neglected. This situation began to change toward the later 1950s, and it dramatically shifted after Castro's seizure of power in Cuba. In the early 1960s Latin America became the focus of large-scale economic aid programs, military training and assistance programs, propaganda efforts, and repeated attention by the president and other high-level American officials. Under the Alliance for Progress, American power was to be used to promote and sustain democratic government and greater social equity in the rest of the Western Hemisphere. This high point in the exercise of United States power in Latin America coincided with the high point of democracy in Latin America. This period witnessed the Twilight of the

Tyrants: it was the age in which at one point all but one of the ten South American countries (Paraguay) had some semblance of democratic government.[31]

Obviously the greater prevalence of democratic regimes during these years was not exclusively a product of United States policy and power. Yet the latter certainly played a role. The democratic governments that had emerged in Colombia and Venezuela in the late 1950s were carefully nurtured with money and praise. Strenuous efforts were made to head off the attempts of both left-wing guerrillas and right-wing military officers to overthrow Betancourt in Venezuela and to ensure the orderly transition to an elected successor for the first time in the history of that country. After thirty years in which "the U.S. government was less interested and involved in Dominican affairs" than at any other time in history— a period coinciding with Trujillo's domination of the Dominican Republic— American opposition to that dictator slowly mounted in the late 1950s. After his assassination in 1961 "the United States engaged in the most massive intervention in the internal affairs of a Latin American state since the inauguration of the Good Neighbor Policy."[32] The United States prevented a return to power by Trujillo's family members, launched programs to promote economic and social welfare, and acted to ensure democratic liberties and competitive elections. The latter, held in December 1962, resulted in the election of Juan Bosch as president. When the military moved against Bosch the following year, American officials first tried to head off the coup and then, after its success, attempted to induce the junta to return quickly to constitutional procedures. But by that point American "leverage and influence [with the new government] were severely limited," and the only concession the United States was able to exact in return for recognition was a promise to hold elections in 1965.[33]

Following the military coup in Peru in July 1962, the United States was able to use its power more effectively to bring about a return to democratic government. The American ambassador was recalled; diplomatic relations were suspended; and $81 million in aid was canceled. Nine other Latin American countries were induced to break relations with the military junta—an achievement that could only have occurred at a time when the United States seemed to be poised on the brink of dispensing billions of dollars of largesse about the continent.[34] The result was that new elections were held the following year, and Belaunde was freely chosen president. Six years later, however, when Belaunde was overthrown by a coup, the United States was in no position to reverse the coup or even to prevent the military government that came to power from nationalizing major property holdings of American nationals. The power and the will that had been there in the early 1960s had evaporated by the late 1960s, and with it the possibility of holding Peru to a democratic path. Through a somewhat more complex process, a decline in the American role also helped produce similar results in Chile. In the 1964 Chilean elections, the United States exerted all the influence it could on behalf of Eduardo Frei and made a significant and possibly decisive contribution to his defeat of Salvador Allende. In the 1970 election, the American government did not make any comparable effort to defeat Allende, who won the popular election by a narrow margin. At that point, the United States tried to induce the Chilean Congress to refuse to confirm his victory and to promote a military coup to prevent him from taking office. Both these efforts violated the norms of Chilean politics and American morality, and both were unsuccessful. If on the other hand the United States had been as active in the popular election of 1970 as it had been in that of 1964, the destruction of Chilean democracy in 1973 might have been avoided.

All in all the decline in the role of the United States in Latin America in the late 1960s and early 1970s coincided with the spread of authoritarian regimes in that area. With this decline went a decline in the standards of democratic morality and human rights that the United States could attempt to apply to the governments of the region. In the early 1960s in Latin America (as in the 1910s and 1920s in the Caribbean and Central America), the goal of the United States was democratic competition and free elections. By the mid-1970s that goal had been lowered from the fostering of democratic government to attempting to induce authoritarian governments not to infringe too blatantly on the rights of their citizens.

A similar relationship between American power and democratic government prevailed in Asia. There too the peak of American power was reached in the early and mid-1960s, and there too the decline in this power was followed by a decline in democracy and liberty. American influence had been most pervasive in the Philippines, which for a quarter-century after World War II had the most open, democratic system (apart from Japan) in east and southeast Asia. After the admittedly fraudulent election of 1949 and in the face of the rising threat to the Philippine government posed by the Huk insurgency, American military and economic assistance was greatly increased. Direct American intervention in Philippine politics then played a decisive role not only in promoting Ramon Magsaysay into the presidency but also in assuring that the 1951 congressional elections and 1953 presidential election were open elections "free from fraud and intimidation."[35] In the next three elections the Philippines met the sternest test of democracy: incumbent presidents were defeated for reelection. In subsequent years, however, the American presence and influence in the Philippines declined, and with it one support for Philippine democracy. When President Marcos instituted his martial law regime in 1972, American influence in southeast Asia was clearly on the wane, and the United States held few effective levers with which to affect the course of Philippine politics. In perhaps even more direct fashion, the high point of democracy and political liberty in Vietnam also coincided with the high point of American influence there. The only free national election in the history of that country took place in 1967, when the American military intervention was at its peak. In Vietnam, as in Latin America, American intervention had a pluralizing effect on politics, limiting the government and encouraging and strengthening its political opposition. The defeat of the United States in Vietnam and the exclusion of American power from Indochina were followed in three countries by the imposition of regimes of almost total repression.

The American relationship with South Korea took a similar course. In the late 1940s, under the sponsorship of the United States, U.N.-observed elections inaugurated the government of the Republic of Korea and brought Syngman Rhee to power. During the Korean War (1950–1953) and then in the mid-1950s, when American economic assistance was at its peak, a moderately democratic system was maintained, despite the fact that South Korea was almost literally in a state of siege. In 1956 Rhee won reelection by only a close margin and the opposition party won the vice-presidency and swept the urban centers.

In the late 1950s, however, as American economic assistance to Korea declined, the Rhee regime swung in an increasingly authoritarian direction. The 1960 vice-presidential election was blatantly fraudulent; students and others protested vigorously; and as the army sat on the sidelines, Rhee was forced out of power. A democratic regime under the leadership of John M. Chang came into office but found it difficult to exercise authority and to maintain order. In May 1961 this regime was overthrown by a military coup despite the strong endorsement of the Chang government by the American embassy and military command. During the next two years, the United States exerted sustained pressure on the military government to hold elections and return power to a civilian regime. A bitter struggle took place within the military over this issue; in the end President Park Chung Hee, with American backing and support, overcame the opposition within the military junta, and reasonably open elections were held in October 1963, in which Park was elected president with a 43 percent plurality of the vote. In the struggle with the hard-line groups in the military, one reporter observed, "the prestige and word of the United States have been put to a grinding test"; by insisting on the holding of elections, however, the United States "emerged from this stage of the crisis with a sort of stunned respect from South Koreans for its determination— from those who eagerly backed United States pressures on the military regime and even from officers who were vehemently opposed to it."[36] Thirteen years later, however, the United States was no longer in a position to have the same impact on Korean politics. "You can't talk pure Jefferson to these guys," one American official said. "You've got to have a threat of some kind or they won't listen. . . . There aren't many levers left to pull around here. We just try to keep the civil rights issue before the eyes of Korean authorities on all levels and hope it has some effect."[37] By 1980 American power in Korea had been reduced to the point where there was no question, as there was in 1961 and 1962, of pressuring a new military leadership to hold prompt and fair elections. The issue was simply whether the United States had enough influence to induce the Korean government not to execute Korea's leading opposition political figure, Kim Dae Jung, and even with respect to that, one Korean official observed, "the United States has no leverage."[38] Over the years, as American influence in Korea went down, repression in Korea went up.

The positive impact of American power on liberty in other societies is in part the result of the conscious choices by presidents such as Kennedy and Carter to give high priority to the promotion of democracy and human rights. Even without such conscious choice, however, the presence or exercise of American power in a foreign area usually has a similar thrust. The new moralists of the 1970s maintained that the United States has "no alternative" but to act in terms of the moral and political values that define the essence of its being. The new moralists clearly intended this claim to have at least a normative meaning. But in fact it also describes a historical necessity. Despite the reluctance or inability of those imbued with the myth of American repression to recognize it, the impact of the United States on the world has in large part been what the new moralists say it has to be. The nature of the United States has left it little or no choice but to stand out among nations as the proponent of liberty and democracy. Clearly, the impact of no other country in world affairs has been as heavily weighted in favor of liberty and democracy as has that of the United States.

Power tends to corrupt, and absolute power corrupts absolutely. American power is no exception; clearly it has been used for good purposes and bad in terms of liberty, democracy, and human rights. But also in terms of these values, American power is far less likely to be misused or corrupted than the power of any other major government. This is so for two reasons. First, because American leaders and decision makers are inevitably the products of their culture, they are themselves generally committed to liberal and democratic values. This does not mean that some leaders may not at times take actions that run counter to those values. Obviously this happens: sensibilities are dulled; perceived security needs may dictate other actions; expediency prevails; the immediate end justifies setting aside the larger purpose. But American policy makers are more likely than those of any other country to be sensitive to these trade-offs and to be more reluctant to sacrifice liberal-democratic values. Second, the institutional pluralism and dispersion of power in the American political system impose constraints—unmatched in any other society—on the ability of officials to abuse power and also to ensure that those transgressions that do occur will almost inevitably become public knowledge. The American press is extraordinarily free, strong, and vigorous in its exposure of bad policies and corrupt officials. The American Congress has powers of investigation, legislation, and financial control unequaled by any other national legislature. The ability of American officials to violate the values of their society is therefore highly limited, and the extent to which the press is filled with accounts of how officials have violated those values is evidence not that such behavior is more widespread than it is in other societies but that it is less tolerated than in other societies. The belief that the United States can do no wrong in terms of the values of liberty and democracy is clearly as erroneous abroad as it is at home. But so, alas, is the belief—far more prevalent in American intellectual circles in the 1970s—that the United States could never do right in terms of those values. American power is far more likely to be used to support those values than to counter them, and it is far more likely to be employed on behalf of those values than is the power of any other major country.

The point is often made that there is a direct relation between the health of liberty in the United States and the health of liberty in other societies. Disease in one is likely to infect the other. Thus, on the one hand, Richard Ullman argued that "the quality of political life in the United States is indeed affected by the quality of political life in other societies. The extinction of political liberties in Chile, or their extension in Portugal or Czechoslovakia, has a subtle but nonetheless important effect on political liberties within the United States." Conversely, he also goes on to say, "just as the level of political freedom in other societies affects our own society, so the quality of our own political life has an important impact abroad."[39] This particular point is often elaborated into what is sometimes referred to as the clean hands doctrine—that the United States cannot effectively promote liberty in other countries so long as there are significant violations of liberty within its borders. Let the United States rely on the power of example and "first put our house in order," as Hoffmann phrased it. "Like charity, well-ordered crusades begin at home."[40]

Both these arguments—that of the corrupting environment and that of the shining example—are partial truths. By any observable measure the state of liberty in countries like Chile or Czechoslovakia has in itself no impact on the state of liberty in the United States. Similarly, foreigners usually recognize what Americans tend to forget—that the United States is the most open, free, and democratic society in the world. Hence any particular improvement in the state of liberty in the United States is unlikely to be seen as having much relevance to their societies. Yet these arguments do have an element of truth in them when one additional variable is added to the equation. This element is power.

The impact that the state of liberty in other societies has on liberty in the United States depends upon the power of those other societies and their ability to exercise that power with respect to the United States. What happens in Chile or even Czechoslovakia does not affect the state of liberty in the United States because those are small, weak, and distant countries. But the disappearance of liberty in Britain or France or Japan would have consequences for the health of liberty in the United States, because they are large and important countries intimately involved with the United States. Conversely, the impact of the state of liberty in the United States on other societies depends not upon changes in American liberty (which foreigners will inevitably view as marginal) but rather upon the power and immediacy of the United States to the country in question. The power of example works only when it is an example of power. If the United States plays a strong, confident, preeminent role on the world stage, other nations will be impressed by its power and will attempt to emulate its liberty in the belief that liberty may be the source of power. This point was made quite persuasively in 1946 by Turkey's future premier, Adnan Menderes, in explaining why his country had to shift to democracy:

> The difficulties encountered during the war years uncovered and showed the weak points created by the one-party system in the structure of the country. The hope in the miracles of [the] one-party system vanished, as the one-party system countries were defeated everywhere. Thus, the one-party mentality was destroyed in the turmoil of blood and fire of the second World War. No country can remain unaffected by the great international events and the contemporary dominating ideological currents. This influence was felt in our country too.[41]

In short, no one copies a loser.

The future of liberty in the world is thus intimately linked to the future of American power. Yet the double thrust of the new moralism was paradoxically to advocate the expansion of global liberty and simultaneously to effect a reduction in American power. The relative decline in American power in the 1970s has many sources. One of them assuredly was the democratic surge (of which the new moralism was one element) in the United States in the 1960s and early 1970s. The strong recommitment to democratic, liberal, and populist values that occurred during these years eventually generated efforts to limit, constrain, and reduce American military, political, and economic power abroad. The intense and sustained attacks by the media, by intellectuals, and by congressmen on the military establishment, intelligence agencies, diplomatic officials, and political leadership of the United States inevitably had that effect. The decline in American power abroad weakened the support for liberty and democracy abroad. American democracy and foreign democracy may be inversely related. Due to the mediating effects of power their relationship appears to be just the opposite of that hypothesized by Ullman.

The promotion of liberty abroad thus requires the expansion of American power; the operation of liberty at home involves the limitation of American power. The need in attempting to achieve democratic goals both abroad and at home is to recognize the existence of this contradiction and to assess the trade-offs between these two goals. There is, for instance, an inherent contradiction between welcoming the end of American hegemony in the Western Hemisphere and at the same time deploring the intensification of repression in Latin America. It is also paradoxical that in the 1970s those congressmen who were most insistent on the need to promote human rights abroad were often most active in reducing the American power that could help achieve that result. In key votes in the Ninety-fourth Congress, for instance, 132 congressmen consistently voted in favor of human rights amendments to foreign aid legislation. Seventy-eight of those 132 representatives also consistently voted against a larger military establishment, and another 28 consistent supporters of human rights split their votes on the military establishment. Only 26 of the 132 congressmen consistently voted in favor of both human rights and the military power whose development could help make those rights a reality.

The new realism of the 1940s and 1950s coincided with the expansion of American power in the world and the resulting expansion of American-sponsored liberty and democracy in the world. The new moralism of the 1970s coincided with the relative decline in American power and the concomitant erosion of liberty and democracy around the globe. By limiting American power the new moralism promoted that decline. In some measure, too, the new moralism was a consequence of the decline. The new moralism's concern with human rights throughout the world clearly reflected the erosion in global liberty and democratic values. Paradoxically, the United States thus became more preoccupied with ways of defending human rights as its power to defend human rights diminished. Enactment of Title IX to the foreign assistance act in 1966, a major congressional effort to promote democratic values abroad, came at the mid-point in the steady decline in American foreign economic assistance. Similarly, the various restrictions that Congress wrote into the foreign assistance acts in the 1970s coincided with the general replacement of military aid by military sales. When American power was clearly predominant, such legislative provisions and caveats were superfluous: no Harkin Amendment was necessary to convey the message of the superiority of liberty. The message was there for all to see in the troop deployments, carrier task forces, foreign-aid missions, and intelligence operatives. When these faded from the scene, in order to promote liberty and human rights Congress found it necessary to write more and more explicit conditions and requirements into legislation. These legislative provisions were in effect an effort to compensate for the decline of American power. In terms of narrowing the ideals-versus-institutions gap abroad, they were no substitute for the presence of American power.

Contrary to the views of both "realists" and "moralists," the contradiction arising from America's role in the world is not primarily that of power and self-interest versus liberty and morality in American foreign policy. It is rather the contradiction between enhancing liberty at home by curbing the power of the American government and enhancing liberty abroad by expanding that power.

THE PROMISE OF DISAPPOINTMENT

The term *American exceptionalism* has been used to refer to a variety of characteristics that have historically distinguished the United States from European societies—characteristics such as its relative lack of economic suffering, social conflict, political trauma, and military defeat. "The standing armies, the monarchies, the aristocracies, the huge debts, the crushing taxation, the old inveterate abuses, which flourish in Europe," William Clarke argued in 1881, "can take no root in the New World. The continent of America is consecrated to simple humanity, and its institutions exist for the progress and happiness of the whole people." Yet, as Henry Fairlie pointed out in 1975, "there now *are* standing armies of America; there now *is* something that, from time to time, looks very like a monarchy; there now *is* a permitted degree of inherited wealth that is creating some of the elements of an aristocracy; there now *is* taxation that is crushing."[42] In the same year Daniel Bell came to a similar conclusion by a different path. The "end of American exceptionalism," he argued, is to be seen in "the end of empire, the weakening of power, the loss of faith in the nation's future. . . . Internal tensions have multiplied and there are deep structural crises, political and cultural, that may prove more intractable to solution than the domestic economic problems."[43]

In the late twentieth century, the United States surely seemed to confront many evils and problems that were common to other societies but that it had previously avoided. These developments, however, affected only the incidental elements of American exceptionalism, those of power, wealth, and security. They did not change American political values and they only intensified the gap between political ideals and political institutions that is crucial to American national identity. They thus did not affect the historically most exceptional aspect of the United States, an aspect eloquently summed up and defended by a Yugoslav dissident.

> The United States is not a state like France, China, England, etc., and it would be a great tragedy if someday the United States became such a state. What is the difference? First of all, the United States is not a national state, but a multinational state. Second, the United States was founded by people who valued individual freedom more highly than their own country.
>
> And so the United States is primarily a state of freedom. And this is what is most important. Whole peoples from other countries can say, Our homeland is Germany, Russia, or whatever; only Americans can say, My homeland is freedom.[44]

Americans have said this throughout their history and have lived throughout their history in the inescapable presence of liberal ideals, semiliberal institutions, and the gap between the two. The United States has no meaning, no identity, no political culture or even history apart from its ideals of liberty and democracy and the continuing efforts of Americans to realize those ideals. Every society has its own distinctive form of tension that characterizes its existence as a society. The tension between liberal ideal and institutional reality is America's distinguishing cleavage. It defines both the agony and the promise of American politics. If that tension disappears, the United States of America as we have known it will no longer exist.

The continued existence of the United States means that Americans will continue to suffer from cognitive dissonance. They will continue to attempt to come to terms with that dissonance through some combination of moralism, cynicism, complacency, and hypocrisy. The greatest danger to the gap between ideals and institutions would come when any substantial portion of the American population carried to an extreme any one of these responses. An excess of moralism, hypocrisy, cynicism, or complacency could destroy the American system. A totally complacent toleration of the ideals-versus-institutions gap could lead to the corruption and decay of American liberal-democratic institutions. Uncritical hypocrisy, blind to the existence of the gap and fervent in its commitment to American principles, could lead to imperialistic expansion, ending in either military or political disaster abroad or the undermining of democracy at home. Cynical acceptance of the gap could lead to a gradual abandonment of American ideals and their replacement either by a Thrasymachusian might-makes-right morality or by some other set of political beliefs. Finally, intense moralism could lead Americans to destroy the freest institutions on earth because they believed they deserved something better.

To maintain their ideals and institutions, Americans have no recourse but to temper and balance their responses to the gap between the two. The threats to the future of the American condition can be reduced to the extent that Americans:

- continue to believe in their liberal, democratic, and individualistic ideals and also recognize the extent to which their institutions and behavior fall short of these ideals;
- feel guilty about the existence of the gap but take comfort from the fact that American political institutions are more liberal and democratic than those of any other human society past or present;
- attempt to reduce the gap between institutions and ideals but accept the fact that the imperfections of human nature mean the gap can never be eliminated;
- believe in the universal validity of American ideals but also understand their limited applicability to other societies;
- support the maintenance of American power necessary to protect and promote liberal ideals and institutions in the world arena, but recognize the dangers such power could pose to liberal ideals and institutions at home.

Critics say that America is a lie because its reality falls so far short of its ideals. They are wrong. America is not a lie; it is a disappointment. But it can be a disappointment only because it is also a hope.

NOTES

1. Richard Hofstadter, *The American Political Tradition* (New York: Alfred A. Knopf, 1951), pp. 65–66.
2. Marvin Meyers, *The Jacksonian Persuasion: Politics and Belief* (Stanford, Calif.: Stanford University Press, 1957), p. 8.
3. See Edward Pessen, "The Egalitarian Myth and the American Social Reality: Wealth, Mobility, and Equality in the 'Era of the Common Man,'" *American Historical Review* 76 (October 1971): 989–1034, and idem, *Riches, Class, and Power before the Civil War* (Lexington, Mass.: D. C. Heath, 1973). For critical discussions of Pessen's evidence and argument see Whitman Ridgway, "Measuring Wealth and Power in Ante-Bellum America: A Review Essay," *Historical Methods Newsletter* 8 (March 1975): 74–78, and Robert E. Gallman, "Professor Pessen on the 'Egalitarian Myth,'" *Social Science History* 2 (Winter 1978): 194–207. For Pessen's response, see his "On a Recent Cliometric Attempt to Resurrect the Myth of Antebellum Egalitarianism," *Social Science History* 3 (Winter 1979): 208–27.
4. Gordon S. Wood, *History Book Club Review* (June 1975): 16–17, commenting on Rush Welter's, *The Mind of America: 1820–1860* (New York: Columbia University Press, 1975).
5. Welter, *The Mind of America: 1820–1860*, pp. 7–10.
6. Alexis de Tocqueville, *Democracy in America*, 2 vols., ed. Phillips Bradley (New York: Vintage Books, 1954), 1:6–17.
7. Joseph L. Blau, ed., *Social Theories of Jacksonian Democracy* (New York: Liberal Arts Press, 1954), pp. xxvii–xxviii.
8. Hofstadter, *American Political Tradition*, p. vi.
9. Herbert Croly, *The Promise of American Life* (New York: Macmillan, 1909), p. 156; and Walter Lippmann, *Drift and Mastery* (Englewood Cliffs, N.J.: Prentice-Hall, 1961), pp. 81–82.
10. Hofstadter, *American Political Tradition*, p. 223.
11. J. R. Pole, *The Pursuit of Equality in American History* (Berkeley: University of California Press, 1978), p. 326.
12. See Ronald Inglehart, *The Silent Revolution: Changing Values and Political Styles among Western Publics* (Princeton, N.J.: Princeton University Press, 1977), and George C. Lodge, *The New American Ideology* (New York: Alfred A. Knopf, 1975).
13. Ronald Inglehart, "The Silent Revolution in Europe: Intergenerational Change in Post-Industrial Societies," *American Political Science Review* 65 (December 1971): 991–1017.
14. Samuel P. Huntington, "Postindustrial Politics: How Benign Will It Be?" *Comparative Politics* 6 (January 1974): 188–89.
15. Plato, *The Republic*, trans. Francis MacDonald Cornford (New York: Oxford University Press, 1945), p. 290.
16. Louis Hartz, *The Liberal Tradition in America* (New York: Harcourt, Brace, 1955), p. 181.
17. Samuel P. Huntington, *Political Order in Changing Societies* (New Haven, Conn.: Yale University Press, 1968), pp. 362–69.
18. See Samuel P. Huntington, *The Soldier and the State: The Theory and Politics of Civil-Military Relations* (Cambridge: Harvard University Press, 1957), esp. pp. 143–57.
19. George F. Kennan, *American Diplomacy 1900–1950* (Chicago, Ill.: University of Chicago Press, 1951), pp. 93–94; and Huntington, *The Soldier and the State*, pp. 80–97.
20. Lucian W. Pye, *The Spirit of Chinese Politics* (Cambridge, Mass.: MIT Press, 1968), p. 91.

21. Seymour Martin Lipset, "The Banality of Revolt," *Saturday Review*, 18 July 1970, p. 26.

22. Peregrine Worsthorne, "America—Conscience or Shield?" *Encounter*, no. 14 (November 1954): 15.

23. Henry Fairlie, "Anti-Americanism at Home and Abroad," *Commentary* 60 (December 1975): 35.

24. See for example Hans J. Morgenthau, *In Defense of the National Interest* (New York: Alfred A. Knopf, 1951), and idem, "Another 'Great Debate': The National Interest of the United States," *American Political Science Review* 46 (December 1952): 961–88; Reinhold Niebuhr, *Christian Realism and Political Problems* (New York: Charles Scribner's Sons, 1953), and idem, *The Irony of American History* (New York: Charles Scribner's Sons, 1952); Kennan, *American Diplomacy 1900–1950*: Robert E. Osgood, *Ideals and Self-Interest in America's Foreign Relations* (Chicago, Ill.: University of Chicago Press, 1953); and Richard H. Ullman, "Washington versus Wilson," *Foreign Policy*, no. 21 (Winter 1975–76): 97–124.

25. Henry A. Kissinger, quoted in Raymond Gastil, "Affirming American Ideals in Foreign Policy," *Freedom at Issue*, no. 38 (November–December 1976):12.

26. Jimmy Carter, address, B'nai B'rith convention, Washington, D.C., 8 September 1976.

27. Hans J. Morgenthau, "Repression's Friend," *New York Times*, 10 October 1974.

28. See John D. Montgomery, *Forced To Be Free: The Artificial Revolution in Germany and Japan* (Chicago, Ill.: University of Chicago Press, 1957).

29. Theodore P. Wright, *American Support of Free Elections Abroad* (Washington, D.C.: Public Affairs Press, 1964), pp. 137–38.

30. Jorge I. Dominguez, *Cuba: Order and Revolution* (Cambridge: Harvard University Press, 1978), p. 13.

31. See Tad Szulc, *The Twilight of the Tyrants* (New York: Henry Holt, 1959).

32. Jerome Slater, *Intervention and Negotiation* (New York: Harper & Row, 1970), p. 7.

33. Abraham F. Lowenthal, *The Dominican Intervention* (Cambridge: Harvard University Press, 1972), p. 16.

34. Jerome Levinson and Juan de Onis, *The Alliance that Lost Its Way* (Chicago, Ill.: Quadrangle Books, 1970), pp. 81–82.

35. H. Bradford Westerfield, *The Instruments of America's Foreign Policy* (New York: Thomas Y. Crowell, 1963), p. 416.

36. A. M. Rosenthal, *New York Times*, 8 April 1963.

37. Quoted by Andrew H. Malcolm, *New York Times*, 11 June 1976.

38. *The Economist*, 30 August 1980, pp. 27–28.

39. Ullman, "Washington versus Wilson," pp. 117, 123.

40. Stanley Hoffmann, "No Choice, No Illusions," *Foreign Policy*, no. 25 (Winter 1976–77): 127.

41. Adnan Menderes, *Cumhuriyef*, 18 July 1946, quoted in Kemal H. Karpat, *Turkey's Politics* (Princeton, N.J.: Princeton University Press, 1959), p. 140, n. 10.

42. Fairlie, "Anti-Americanism at Home and Abroad," p. 34, quoting William Clarke, 1881.

43. Daniel Bell, "The End of American Exceptionalism," in *The American Commonwealth 1976*, eds. Nathan Glazer and Irving Kristol (New York: Basic Books, 1976), p. 197.

44. Mihajlo Mihajlov, "Prospects for the Post-Tito Era," *New America* 17 (January 1980): 7.

ॐ

The United States Political System and International Leadership: A "Decidedly Inferior" Form of Government?

Michael Mastanduno

INTRODUCTION: THE DEMOCRATIC DILEMMA

The framers of the U.S. Constitution created, by conscious design, a constrained government. They were more concerned to avoid the abuse of political power than to create circumstances under which it could be easily exercised. Thus, instead of concentrating power they sought to disperse it, and created the familiar system of "checks and balances" to assure that no part of government accumulated enough influence to threaten the integrity of democracy.

Foreign policy did not constitute an exception to this principle, and the framers assured that the Executive and Congress shared power and decision-making authority. Indeed, in enumerating the powers of each branch they were arguably more generous to the legislature than to the president. On the crucial issue of war-making authority, for example, the president was named Commander-in-Chief, but Congress was given the authority to raise and support an army, provide and maintain a navy, and most importantly, to commit the nation to armed struggle by declaring war. The president, with the advice and consent of the Senate, was granted appointment and treaty-making powers. However, the all-important power to collect taxes and appropriate funds was given to the Congress, as was the equally crucial authority to regulate the commerce of the United States with other countries.

The design of a constrained government and the sharing of foreign policy authority created a dilemma, the core of which remains with the United States to this day. On the one hand, the dispersal of political power has the *internal advantage* of helping to promote and protect American democracy. On the other hand, the dispersal of power has an *external disadvantage*, in that it poses a potential constraint on the ability of the United States to conduct effective foreign policy.[1]

Michael Mastanduno, "The United States Political System and International Leadership: A 'Decidedly Inferior' Form of Government?" Paper prepared for background and discussion at the Dartmouth College-International House of Japan Conference. "The United States and Japan on the Eve of the 21st Century: Prospects for Joint Leadership," held at Dartmouth College, June 27–29, 1994. Reprinted with permission.

To survive or flourish in an international system characterized by anarchy, or the lack of a central governing authority, often requires speed, secrecy, and decisiveness in foreign policy decision-making. Governments must be able to seize opportunities, respond to threats and challenges, and make and honor commitments. They must pursue a set of core objectives with consistency, and at the same time manage conflicts among these objectives, make tactical compromises where necessary, and adjust to changing international circumstances. These qualities are more likely to be maximized in more centralized, rather than decentralized, political systems. Alexis de Tocqueville, in his classic appraisal of the United States, recognized this dilemma in concluding that "especially in their conduct of foreign relations, democracies appear to me decidedly inferior to other governments." They "obey impulse rather than prudence," have a propensity to "abandon a mature design for the gratification of a momentary passion," and in general are deficient in the qualities demanded by effective foreign policy.[2]

America's early statesmen were similarly cognizant of the so-called democratic dilemma, and they found a way to resolve it in the *substance* of U.S. foreign policy. By adopting an isolationist foreign policy, they reasoned, the internal benefits of democratic governance would be preserved while the external disadvantages would be minimized. If decentralized, deliberative government handicapped the United States in the age-old game of European power politics, the United States could choose not to play. Geography facilitated and reinforced this choice, since the Atlantic ocean provided a physical barrier that could not be overcome easily by the technologies of the day. The classic statement of the new nation's strategy was articulated by Washington in his Farewell Address, as he admonished his fellow citizens to "steer clear of permanent alliances" and counseled that "[t]he great rule of conduct for us in regard to foreign nations is . . . to have with them as little *political* connection as possible."[3]

The isolationist solution to the democratic dilemma was feasible for over one hundred years, but by the early part of the twentieth century, as U.S. economic power and political influence increased rapidly, strains were apparent. A return to isolationism following U.S. involvement in World War I resulted in an unmitigated disaster for world politics and the global economy. U.S. officials drew the appropriate lessons, and following World War II they abandoned isolationism and sought to exercise international leadership.[4] In the postwar era, U.S. officials were forced to confront directly the dilemma that had been so deftly avoided in earlier times.

DOMESTIC CONSTRAINTS AND U.S. LEADERSHIP

The view that the U.S. political system is "decidedly inferior," or a significant constraint on the ability of the United States to lead internationally approaches conventional wisdom among students and practitioners of U.S. foreign policy. George Kennan once made an unflattering comparison between the foreign policy of American democracy and the behavior of a dinosaur with a huge body and pin-sized brain: the beast is slow to rouse, but when it finally recognizes threats to its interests, it flails about indiscriminately, wrecking its native habitat while attempting to destroy its adversary.[5] Theodore Lowi has claimed that America's decentralized decision-making system creates incentives for leaders to adopt foreign policy strategies that compromise effectiveness, such as the inflation of foreign policy threats and the "overselling" of foreign policy opportunities. He argues that the domestic political system is an "anachronism in foreign affairs," and that it is "the system itself that has so often made our international relations so inimical to our own best interests."[6] In the context of international political economy, Stephen Krasner has popularized the conception of the United States as a "weak state" whose domestic institutions placed it at a considerable disadvantage in the conduct of commercial diplomacy—a disadvantage only offset by the fact that the United States has been extraordinarily powerful internationally.[7] In a 1984 book entitled *Our Own Worst Enemy*, I. M. Destler, Leslie Gelb, and (current Clinton National Security Advisor) Anthony Lake contended that "not only our government but our whole society has been undergoing a systemic breakdown when attempting to foster a coherent, consistent approach to the world."[8] More recently, the distinguished columnist David Broder, reflecting on the first year experience of the Clinton administration, argued that the "decayed condition of our vital institutions" has "damaged the capacity of our system to develop and sustain coherent policy."[9]

Why?

What is it about the U.S. political system that so handicaps foreign policy and international leadership? The answer is found in an analysis of the relationship between Executive and Congress: of the institutions of and relationships within the Executive: and of the role played by interest groups and the media in the foreign policy process.

Executive vs. Congress

The power-sharing arrangements stipulated by the U.S. Constitution invite the president and Congress to conduct an ongoing struggle over the control of foreign policy. For the first two decades after World War II, however, that struggle was held in abeyance. The two branches worked out an arrangement in which Congress delegated authority and deferred politically to the Executive, on the grounds that only the presidency possessed the institutional resources, intelligence capability, and decision-making qualities—speed, steadiness, resolve, and flexibility—required to conduct the cold war effectively and lead a global coalition in the struggle against the Soviet Union and communism. The eagerness of Congress to defer might also be attributed to its desire to atone for its contributions to the foreign policy disasters of the interwar period, such as the Smoot-Hawley tariff and the failure of the Versailles Treaty and the League of Nations. In any event, Congress took a secondary and in some cases peripheral role as presidents confronted the Soviet Union in a series of cold war crises, intervened covertly and overtly in the third world, and enmeshed the United States in an array of entangling alliances around the globe. In commercial policy, Congress delegated tariff-cutting authority to the president and passed export control legislation enabling him to restrict trade to any destination for reasons of national security or foreign policy. The great symbol of congressional acquiescence was the Tonkin Gulf Resolution of 1964, which President Johnson took as a green light to expand dramatically America's role in the Vietnam war.

The Vietnam experience shattered this interbranch arrangement and renewed the foreign policy struggle. Out of that debacle emerged the "new" Congress of the 1970s, 1980s, and 1990s—a Congress that was more assertive politically, less inclined to defer to an "imperial" presidency that had squandered U.S. international leadership, and in possession of greater resources and expertise in foreign affairs. Members of Congress have sought to reclaim or expand their authority over the direct use of force, covert intervention, weapons sales, intelligence oversight, trade policy, economic and security assistance, and numerous other aspects of the substance and process of foreign policy. They have increased the size of their personal and committee staffs and have strengthened the capacity of and their reliance upon collective resources such as the General Accounting Office, Congressional Budget Office, and Office of Technology Assessment. Members of Congress are now less reliant on the Executive for sources of foreign policy information and expertise, and possess the administrative resources to facilitate involvement—and potentially to contest the Executive—across a range of foreign policy issues.

Unfortunately, the new Congress has become less coherent institutionally as it has become more assertive. Reforms undertaken in the aftermath of Watergate and Vietnam created greater decentralization, with less emphasis on seniority and with the erosion of committee discipline. As a result, there are now 535 would-be secretaries of state (or commerce, or defense), each with more resources and political influence at his or her disposal. At the same time, these representatives remain beholden to their local constituencies and retain their tendency to approach foreign affairs from a more parochial, as opposed to national, perspective. In short, the Executive shares power with a Congress whose individual members demand and play a greater role in foreign policy, but without necessarily coordinating their initiatives or framing them in terms of a consistent national strategy. As a former member of the Senate, John Tower, has noted, "Five hundred and thirty-five Congressmen with different philosophies, regional interests, and objectives in mind cannot forge a unified foreign policy that reflects the interests of the United States as a whole."[10]

There are numerous examples of the Executive and newly-assertive Congress working at cross-purposes, to the detriment of coherent foreign policy and effective international leadership. With the passage of the Jackson-Vanik Amendment to the Trade Act of 1974, Congress made its mark on foreign policy by linking most-favored-nation (MFN) status to the human rights practices of communist countries. Unfortunately, the Nixon administration had already completed a trade agreement with the Soviet Union and committed itself to granting MFN without any explicit human rights conditions attached. The Amendment made the United States appear unreliable, and helped to destroy the detente strategy of Nixon and Kissinger.[11] Congress and the Executive clashed later in the decade over the SALT II Treaty, and once again the United States came across as an unreliable negotiating partner.

During the 1980s, the Reagan administration and Congress could not agree on the utility or desirability of aiding the Nicaraguan contras. The result was incoherent policy and the sending of mixed signals to allies and adversaries. The administration's foreign policy was ultimately driven into crisis as executive officials sought in frustration and poor judgment to evade congressional prohibitions through extra-legal means. In trade policy, the exposure of members of Congress to protectionist interests and their tendency to blame foreigners for the U.S. trade deficit led to initiatives—most notably the Super 301 provision of the Omnibus Trade and Competitiveness Act of 1988—that significantly complicated the task of the Executive as it attempted to move forward multilateral negotiations to liberalize international trade.[12]

Relations Within the Executive

One important reason the Executive is presumed to enjoy a "comparative advantage" over the Congress in the conduct of foreign policy is that the president has at his disposal an enormous bureaucratic machine to assist in the formulation and implementation of policy. The foreign policy bureaucracy was expanded greatly after World War II to provide the necessary resources and expertise to wage the cold war. State Department personnel multiplied in Washington and abroad, and the National Security Act of 1947 led to the development of parallel institutions— a permanent Department of Defense led by civilians, and a centralized intelligence establishment under the direction of the CIA.[13] In addition, postwar presidents could draw upon the foreign policy resources of the Commerce Department, the Treasury, the Department of Labor, the Office of the U.S. Trade Representative, and numerous other more specialized offices and agencies.

This very structure that provides advantages, however, also poses a potential constraint on foreign policy. Bureaucracies obviously are not passive instruments; they develop and defend their own institutional interests. Their interests come into conflict because they share jurisdiction over so many areas of U.S. foreign policy, and not surprisingly they compete with each other to control the agenda and the substance of policy. In the absence of central direction, the result is often stalemate or vacillation in foreign policy. The turbulent postwar history of U.S. export control policy, in which the Defense, Commerce, and State Departments have struggled over whether to liberalize or restrict trade in advanced technology often without clear guidance from the White House serves as an apt example.[14]

The president obviously needs to control and coordinate the various parts of the foreign policy bureaucracy, and in 1947 Congress provided the institutional means through the creation of the National Security Council (NSC). Eventually, this solution created new problems, as the staff of the NSC transcended its coordinating role and became yet another combatant in the inter-agency struggle to control foreign policy. This process began with President Kennedy, who desired an activist National Security Advisor to offset the inherent incrementalism of the State Department, and reached its zenith under President Nixon, whose National Security Advisor Henry Kissinger sought to neutralize the State Department and to run foreign policy directly from the White House with the assistance of a small staff.[15] The Nixon-Kissinger system produced significant accomplishments—the opening to China, detente with the Soviet Union, extrication from the Vietnam war—but also caused significant problems. Important issues were left unattended until they reached crisis proportions (e.g., international economic policy and the eventual "Nixon shocks" of August 1971), and the overall foreign policy was difficult to legitimate since much of it was conducted in behind-the-scenes negotiations by officials who were neither elected by the public nor accountable to members of Congress.[16]

The problem took a new form during the 1970s and 1980s, as secretaries of state and national security advisors battled to control U.S. foreign policy. During the Carter administration, Cyrus Vance and Zbigniew Brzezinski clashed over arms control, human rights, and policy towards Africa. Their debates were often public, exacerbating the incoherence and lack of direction in U.S. policy. During the Reagan administration, Alexander Haig and William Clark engaged in similar struggles over intervention in Lebanon and the U.S. response to energy trade between the Soviet Union and Western Europe. Although public conflict between the State Department and White House was more muted during Reagan's second term, the NSC staff contributed prominently to the turmoil in U.S. foreign policy created by the Iran-Contra initiatives. Congressional and other critics expressed concern that the NSC staff had moved beyond its traditional coordinating function and had usurped "operational control" of U.S. policy from other executive departments. In fact, the Reagan NSC was continuing, in more extreme fashion, the tradition of NSC control established during the Kennedy administration.[17]

The overall point should be clear. The Executive has been plagued to a significant degree by the same institutional weaknesses attributed to Congress—parochial interests, decentralization, and the lack of effective coordination. Even in the absence of congressional "interference," foreign policy by the Executive may tend to lack consistency or direction. With both branches engaged, the problems are multiplied.

The difficulties raised by the NSC in security policy are also found in foreign economic policy. There, too, interagency struggles are commonplace, usually involving the Departments of State, Treasury, Commerce, and Labor, the Council of Economic Advisors (CEA), the Office of Management and Budget, and several other agencies. The Office of the U.S. Trade Representative (USTR), lodged within the White House, takes on the job of coordinating agency positions and interests in trade policy. Like the NSC, however, USTR is a player as well as a coordinator, with its own set of institutional interests. USTR officials have clashed in recent years with their counterparts in Treasury over the Europe 1992 project, and with officials at the State Department, CEA, and OMB over U.S. trade policy toward Japan.

Two other issues that bear on the ability of the Executive to conduct effective foreign policy are worthy of note. First, although U.S. economic policy and security policy are each plagued by problems of coordination, the problems are far more profound when one considers the need for coordination *across* the two types of policies. As Destler has argued, the economic and security decision-making "complexes" within the executive are self-contained units and almost totally separate from each other in their day to day operations.[18] A President who focuses on one side of the foreign policy house may find it difficult to master or mobilize effectively the bureaucracy on the other side. Bill Clinton has devoted considerable energies to economic policy, and his foreign policy has been criticized as half-hearted, incoherent, and lacking in leadership.[19] In contrast, George Bush sought to master security policy, and often found himself handcuffed in economic policy—as demonstrated by this ill-fated trip to Japan in January 1992.

Issues that fall at the intersection of the two policy complexes are often handled poorly. The FSX dispute provides a clear example: the security complex (the State and Defense Departments) negotiated that agreement with Japan in isolation from the economic complex (the Commerce Department and USTR). The former believed the agreement was in the national security interest, while the latter saw it as violating the national economic interest. The resulting bureaucratic battle and decision to reconsider the agreement left America's most important Pacific ally to question the reliability and credibility of its alliance partner. In post-cold war foreign policy, as economic and security issues becoming increasingly intertwined and the United States grows more concerned about "economic security," the institutional divide between the two spheres of policy-making is likely to prove more troublesome. The latest institutional innovation—Clinton's creation of a National Economic Council to mirror the National Security Council and to coordinate economic policy—may reinforce rather than rectify the divide.

Second, the U.S. government has appropriately been called a "government of strangers."[20] The political appointments of each new administration reach far down into the executive bureaucracy. Although this has the advantage of enabling a new administration to put a distinctive stamp on policy, it leaves the United States with a deficit in experience and institutional memory, particularly in contrast to states characterized by "permanent government" such as Japan. Former U.S. negotiators often lament the disadvantage posed to U.S. commercial diplomacy by the fact that Japanese (and other negotiators) often have greater experience and knowledge of the United States than U.S. officials have of foreign countries.[21]

Interest Groups and the Media

Not only is the U.S. government fragmented and decentralized: it also affords ready access to private actors seeking to manipulate government policy to serve their particular interests. If, for government officials, the rule of bureaucratic politics is "where you stand depends on where you sit," the rule of interest group politics is "which way you lean depends on who is pushing you." A former U.S. Senator, Charles Mathias, noted recently in an assessment of U.S. Middle East policy that "as a result of the activities of the [Israeli] lobby, Congressional conviction has been measurably reinforced by the knowledge that political sanctions will be applied to any who fail to deliver."[22]

Interest groups hoping to influence U.S. foreign policy have a variety of channels through which to exert political pressure. They can "push" on members of the House and Senate, on the White House, and on the different agencies of the Executive. The decentralized structure also enables interest groups to play off one branch of government or agency against another, and thereby enhance their potential influence. This point has not been lost on U.S. firms seeking protection or market access abroad—the rule is if the State Department is unsympathetic, try Commerce or USTR; if the Executive as a whole is unresponsive, try the Congress, which may be able to solve your problem by itself, or at least can help to pressure the executive. In trade with Japan, the dogged determination of firms such as Motorola or Toys R Us to "work the system" has been rewarded by special negotiating efforts by U.S. government officials to achieve market access.

The U.S. government often responds more readily to principles that pragmatism, and thus the more powerful or skillful interest groups, can "capture" foreign policy by appealing to broad principles that transcend their narrow self-interest. During the cold war, firms frequently exploited the fear of communism to prod the government to use foreign policy to serve their corporate interests. The interventions in Guatemala in 1954 and Iran in 1953, in the interest of United Fruit and U.S. oil companies, respectively, serve as prominent examples.[23] Others have appealed more recently to "national security" or "fair trade" to bolster their case for protection or special treatment. The machine tool industry's efforts were rewarded by the Reagan administration's negotiation of a voluntary restraint agreement in 1986, and in that same year the semiconductor industry obtained a commitment to market access through the by now infamous U.S.-Japan Semiconductor Arrangement.

Interest groups do not always push in the same direction, and, since the government tends to be receptive, the result can be immobility or stalemate in foreign policy. Jeff Frieden has traced the ambivalence of the United States government toward international economic leadership during the interwar years to the conflict at the societal level between nationalist and internationalist coalitions.[24] Domestically-oriented industry and agriculture "captured" Congress and the Commerce Department, while internationally-oriented industry and finance held sway over the State and Treasury Departments. U.S. foreign policy, reflecting the industry group struggle, bounced back and forth incoherently between engagement and insularity. A similar problem appears to have plagued the Clinton administration's China policy prior to the May 1994 decision to delink trade and human rights. While Secretary of State Christopher lectured the Chinese on their human rights practices, high Commerce officials and large U.S. firms such as General Electric and AT&T conducted their own diplomacy to strengthen economic ties. Industry officials complained publicly that their economic interests were being jeopardized by the State Department, while State contended that its credibility and leverage as an enforcer of U.S. human rights principles had been undermined by the activities of Commerce and U.S. firms. The United States failed to speak with one voice, affording China the opportunity to exploit the divisions.[25]

It is important to note that access to the U.S. political system is readily available not only to domestic groups, but to *foreign* interest groups and governments as well. Foreign lobbying, of course, takes place in all countries and is a standard feature of international relations. The U.S. system is distinctive, however, in that it is especially accommodating to foreign influence. The same multiple channels of influence that are open to domestic groups are open to foreigners as well. And, since political appointments penetrate deeply into the government structure and high officials frequently stay in government for short periods of time and then return to lucrative careers in the private sector, there is a readily available stream of influential individuals for hire by foreign (as well as domestic) interests.

Over the past several years, as U.S.-Japanese economic frictions have intensified, Japanese lobbying efforts in the United States have become particularly contentious. Critics contend that Japanese firms and foundations have undertaken a systematic financial campaign to tip the U.S. political debate in a direction more sympathic to Japan's point of view, by generously endowing universities and think tanks, and by hiring influential former officials of the U.S. government.[26] There is ample evidence to support this view of a Japanese corporate effort: whether and to what extent that effort has been successful is less certain. Where Japanese firms have succeeded (e.g., in the Toshiba incident of 1987, or in keeping semiconductors off the Super 301 list in 1989), they have done so not by overturning a U.S. consensus on their own, but by throwing support behind one side or another in an on-going U.S. political debate either within the U.S. Executive or between the Executive and Congress.[27] This reinforces the main point—the decentralized and fragmented U.S. system allows ready access to powerful and skilled interest groups, whether they be domestic or foreign.

Like the role of Congress, the role of the *media* in foreign policy was affected profoundly by Vietnam and Watergate. Prior to those events, the media tended to act as a conduit for the executive's foreign policy by interpreting, amplifying, and often supporting official positions. After Vietnam, it became far more assertive and adversarial. Some argue that the media played a dominant role in the war itself, in that its critical stance helped to turn the U.S. public against the war effort.[28]

The new, more assertive media, like the new Congress, helps to preserve the integrity of American democracy. It provides a check on the imperial tendencies of the presidency by subjecting official policy to critical scrutiny and by assuring that voices other than that of the president and his inner circle are heard. Yet what is good for democracy may not necessarily be good for foreign policy. Although the media by itself hardly can be held responsible for incoherence in U.S. foreign policy, it clearly exacerbates any lack of coherence by consistently publicizing and dwelling on disputes among high officials and the contradictions and failures of administration policy. As David Broder has noted:

> Reporters are instinctively fight promoters. Consensus-building is not our forte—or our job. Carrying through policy requires sustained effort. The press in all its forms is episodic. We flit from topic to topic. We hate repetition. Our attitude toward institutions is cavalier.[29]

The media do not simply react to official initiatives, but increasingly have the power to help set the foreign policy agenda by shaping the public and official response to foreign events. Television has replaced print as the principal source of news information for Americans, and one consequence, in the words of Lloyd Cutler, is that foreign policy has been placed "on deadline."[30] Government officials react to the pressure of publicity, and the result is often hasty, ill-conceived policies that play to the immediate impulses of the public rather than to the long-term interests of the country. U.S. policy toward Somalia provides a striking example: the Bush administration's last minute decision to send the U.S. military on a humanitarian mission was driven in part by the strong public reaction to the images of starving children conveyed by evening news programs. Similarly, the

Clinton administration's subsequent and rather abrupt decision to abandon the military commitment was influenced by the visceral public reaction of outrage to the image of captured U.S. service personnel being dragged through the streets of Mogadishu. At the time, Secretary of State Christopher and other high officials cautioned against conducting "foreign policy by CNN," but that is precisely what the administration seemed to be doing.

LEADERSHIP IN SPITE OF DOMESTIC CONSTRAINTS?

The post-Vietnam Congress is assertive yet ineffective in foreign policy. The Executive has problems coordinating policy even within its own institutional setting, much less with the Congress. Domestic and foreign interest groups have easy access to government and can distort policy to suit their needs. The media prey on the incoherence of it all and distort policy further through their control of the information that reaches the public most quickly and directly.

This institutional landscape poses a forbidding constraint on the exercise of U.S. leadership. Or does it? In this section I argue, contrary to the conventional wisdom, that the extent to which the domestic political system frustrates or constrains U.S. leadership has been significantly exaggerated. First, the overall record of postwar U.S. foreign policy has been reasonably strong in terms of consistency, flexibility, and the ability to achieve major objectives.[31] Second, the record also indicates that the President has the means and capability to manage domestic constraints and minimize their detrimental impact on leadership. Third, the President can actually turn the domestic system into an asset, or source of strength, in the conduct of foreign policy and the exercise of leadership. A final point, made in a concluding section, is that power and purpose are at least as important as the structure of the domestic political system in determining the effectiveness of U.S. leadership.

The Postwar Record

"International leadership" was defined earlier as the ability to develop and sustain foreign policies that significantly affect the structure and substance of international relations and that contribute significantly to the solution of collective problems or the realization of collective opportunities. One way to approach the question of leadership capacity is to examine the performance record of the United States in the era in which it sought to exercise leadership. Notwithstanding the democratic dilemma and constraints of the domestic system, the postwar U.S. record is quite strong. U.S. officials managed to develop and pursue a set of policies that had a profound impact on the international system. They pursued these policies with consistency over an extended period of time and across administrations, and achieved a large measure of success. Moreover, U.S. policy has been flexible in adjusting to changes in the international environment, and in responding to crises that threaten core foreign policy objectives.

An obvious example of a foreign policy pursued with consistency and systemic effect was containment of the Soviet Union. From Kennan's long telegram in 1946 to the collapse of the Berlin Wall in 1989 (and the subsequent collapse of the Soviet Union itself), U.S. officials across nine administrations led the non-communist world in an effort to prevent the expansion of Soviet political and military influence. As Gaddis notes, different administrations may have pursued different "strategies" of containment.[32] Yet all agreed on the priority of the core objective of containment, irrespective of whether the party in power was Democratic or Republican, whether Congress was assertive or acquiescent, or whether the era was pre- or post-Vietnam. Deviations from containment were sometimes initiated but never pursued seriously as policy alternatives. In this category one might place the Eisenhower/Dulles exploration of rollback, the Carter administration's interest in shifting foreign policy from an "East-West" to a "North-South" emphasis, and the Reagan administration's half-hearted attempt at rollback symbolized by the Reagan Doctrine. The basic objective of containment remained intact and for the most part achieved success.

A corollary to containment was the formation and maintenance of a set of security alliances with non-Communist powers. Here, too, U.S. officials pursued a policy consistently over time that had a major impact on the international system. Notwithstanding discontent over burden-sharing, several major crises (e.g., Suez in 1956, the pipeline in 1982), and occasional domestic attempts to reconsider the core policy (e.g., the Mansfield Amendment), America's basic alliance commitments were not called into question, and in fact thus far have outlived the cold war.

Another core, postwar objective of the United States has been the creation and expansion of an open world economy and multilateral trading system. That objective has been pursued across administrations and has been institutionalized in international institutions such as the IMF and the GATT. The United States has remained the prime mover in the GATT as that institution first took on the tariff barriers that developed during the war and depression years, then attacked non-tariff barriers, and most recently has accepted the challenge of bringing excluded sectors and issues (e.g., agriculture, textiles, services) into the multilateral regime. As U.S. power has declined in relative terms, domestic pressure has built for protection and a reconsideration of the GATT commitment. U.S. officials have tried to resist the pressure, have not abandoned GATT, and instead have worked to strengthen its efficacy and credibility.

Other examples of core U.S. foreign policy objectives pursued with consistency and effectiveness might include the maintenance of a "zone of peace" that incorporated the aggressors of the last major war, and decolonization and the integration of less developed countries into the liberal world economy.[33] The main point should be clear—in terms of the main policies and objectives of postwar U.S. leadership, pursued over the long term, the domestic political system did *not* result in uncertainty, incoherence, or vacillation. Either the domestic constraints were modest, or executive officials apparently found ways to overcome them quite consistently.

The U.S. record also indicates a reasonable degree of *flexibility* in responding to structural changes in the global environment. The Nixon administration's opening to China, in the interest of exploiting the Sino-Soviet split, reversed decades of ideological hostility that was deeply embedded in public and elite sentiment. The opening was not a one-shot deal, as the commitment normalizing relations with China has been sustained through the Ford, Carter, Reagan, Bush, and Clinton administrations. Second, when faced during the early decades of the cold war with the choice between support for democracy or for anti-communist authoritarianism, U.S. officials consistently chose the latter. After Vietnam, U.S. officials began to rethink this approach, and gradually a "pro-democracy" emphasis came to replace uncritical support for right-wing dictators as a core foreign policy objective. The end of the cold war obviously has accelerated this development, but the initial thrust was quite apparent in both the Carter and Reagan administrations. In international monetary policy, the United States moved during the 1970s from supporting a fixed to a floating exchange rate system when it was clear (due in large part to America's own economic policies) that the fixed system was no longer viable. With the glaring exception of the first Reagan administration, U.S. officials have sought in the floating system to coordinate exchange rate and macroeconomic policies with other advanced industrial states in order to recapture the stability and predictability in international economic transactions achieved in the era of fixed rates.[34]

Finally, the democratic dilemma suggests that the nature of the domestic political system will make it difficult for the United States to respond with the necessary speed, secrecy, and decisiveness in times of foreign policy crisis. Again, the record suggests otherwise. Whether one considers threats to national security such as the Cuban Missile Crisis, threats to alliance stability such as the Suez crisis of 1956 or the 1973 Middle East war, or threats to international economic stability such as the Mexican debt crisis of 1982 or the extreme pressures for protection that accompanied record U.S. trade deficits during the mid-1980s, the domestic political system did not prevent U.S. officials from responding quickly and decisively to preserve core foreign policy objectives.

Managing Domestic Constraints

An important reason for the strength of the U.S. postwar record is that an administration with a clear sense of foreign policy purpose has the wherewithal to manage and deflect the potentially detrimental constraints of the domestic political system. Administration officials have at their disposal a variety of instruments and techniques. They can mobilize previously uninvolved domestic actors to support their preferred positions on a given issue. They can appeal to national security and exploit the "rally around the flag" effect as a way to centralize power and gain public support. They can enlist the support of international actors. They can bind the United States to pursue certain policies through international commitments, and then use the existence of those commitments to overcome domestic opposition to the policies. In short, administration officials can exploit their unique position at the intersection of the domestic system and the international system to further their objectives in each arena.[35] Several examples are useful to illustrate these points.

During the Korean war, the Truman and Eisenhower administrations had a severe disagreement with Congress over West European and Japanese trade with Communist countries.[36] Executive officials wanted to curtail that trade, yet recognized that it would be politically difficult and economically costly for

America's allies to sever it altogether. To demand and expect full compliance would likely do more damage to the alliance than to the Communist bloc, and thus executive officials were willing to compromise and tolerate some level of continued East-West trade. Congress was unwilling to compromise, believing that with U.S. soldiers dying in Korea it was incumbent upon America's allies, who were receiving U.S. financial assistance, to abandon their Eastern trade. To enforce this preference, members of Congress passed a controversial law (known as the Battle Act), which required America's allies to give up either their Eastern trade or their American economic and military aid.

Executive officials, caught between their domestic constraint and their interest in maintaining alliance cohesion, responded creatively. They lobbied for a loophole in the law that would allow exceptions to be made on national security grounds, and they negotiated a change in the alliance export control regime (CoCom) that enabled the allies to comply with the letter of the law without necessarily having to sever their trade completely. The Executive, not Congress, ultimately controlled negotiations with other non-communist states, and used that control to deflect congressional pressure and to achieve its objectives—to maintain as comprehensive an embargo as possible while preserving alliance cohesion.

A second example concerns the critical ability to commit the nation's armed forces to overseas conflict. After Vietnam, Congress sought to reassert its constitutional prerogative in this area with the passage of the War Powers Resolution in 1973. The Resolution helped to restore Congress' appropriate role, but also had the potential to frustrate the credibility and effectiveness of U.S. military statecraft. By imposing specific time limits on the deployment of U.S. troops and other requirements, the Resolution gives America's adversaries the opportunity to exploit divisions between the Executive and Congress when the former contemplates or threatens the use of force.[37]

Since 1973, Presidents have responded to these requirements in a way that allows Congress some role, but without compromising their ability to use force as necessary to further national or collective goals. As a matter of principle, no President has been willing to concede the constitutionality of the Resolution, but most have been willing to placate Congress by observing in practice at least some of its provisions some of the time. Presidents have been prepared to neglect the consultation or time limit provisions of the Resolution if they believed that to be necessary to protect national security or maintain diplomatic discretion. Even in the case where Congress played its most prominent role, the Persian Gulf conflict, the Bush administration devoted far more energy to gaining international support than to gaining congressional approval. The latter was sought and obtained very late in the process, after an international coalition had been mobilized and an ultimatum delivered to Saddam Hussein.

Third, throughout the postwar era successive administrations have had to defend the liberal trading order against interest groups and members of Congress more inclined toward economic nationalism and protectionism. Executive officials have relied upon delegations of authority from Congress to engage in international negotiations, have channeled demands for protection into the executive bureaucracy, and have cut special deals for interests (e.g., agriculture, textiles) too powerful politically to ignore.[38] Perhaps the most distinctive tactic adopted during the 1980s was the effort to "externalize" the demand for protection at home by focusing on market access abroad. This tactic was employed by the Reagan administration in 1985, as it mobilized export interests by initiating the Uruguay Round, utilizing Section 301 of U.S. trade law, and providing export subsidies in competition for agricultural markets.

The Bush administration similarly adopted a strategy for deflecting illiberal interests. By 1989, large and persistent bilateral trade deficits generated open hostility toward Japan and demands for "managed trade." The administration utilized Super 301, but more sparingly than Congress preferred. It compensated by working with Japan to launch the Structural Impediments Initiative, an ambitious attempt to get at the root causes of market access problems, and a plausible alternative to managed trade. In the face of intense congressional and industry scrutiny, the administration brought both Super 301 and SII negotiations to completion in the middle of 1990, deflecting congressional pressure and leaving Executive officials to focus full attention of their primary trade policy priority—the completion of the Uruguay Round and strengthening of GATT.

These examples suggest that even though Congress and interest groups play a prominent role, the result is not necessarily stalemate, ineffective policy, and the abdication of U.S. leadership. It may require time, effort, and the expense of political capital, but a determined President with a sense of foreign policy purpose can manage the constraints of the domestic political system.

The Domestic System as an Asset to Leadership

Foreign policy officials can do more than merely manage constraints or "limit the damage" of the domestic political system. That system itself can actually be an asset, which Presidents can use to further international leadership.

For example, the pressure exerted by Congress on the Executive can be transformed by the Executive into bargaining leverage. As Pastor has noted, "a president who is sensitive to the public mood that stimulates congressional concern can turn Congress into an incomparable bargaining asset in international negotiations."[39] Congressional pressure helps the Executive to negotiate more forcefully, by lending credibility to Executive demands while allowing Executive officials to appear moderate and reasonable. This dynamic is most readily apparent in trade policy, and is all-too-familiar to Japanese negotiators. U.S. negotiators hoping to open Japanese or other foreign markets have been able to claim, in effect, with a reasonable degree of plausibility, that "it's best for you to make a deal with us now, for if you wait, Congress will be far more unreasonable and harder on you than we are being." This tactic has also proven useful to presidents in other areas, such as the promotion of human rights.[40] The intense concern of Congress in this area and its willingness to tie U.S. economic and military assistance conditionally to the human rights record of foreign governments has given executive officials the potential to extract concessions in this area while still maintaining a focus on broader geopolitical and security concerns.

Presidents are also subject to the constraint of public opinion, but this, too, can actually be an asset to international leadership. The need for public support creates incentives for executive officials to develop policies that can command a public consensus—or that reflect one already in existence. Foreign policies and international commitments that reflect a public consensus are more likely to be sustained over the long run than are those which do not.

Until recently, the conventional view among political scientists and policy analysts was that on matters of foreign policy, public opinion tended to be impulsive, erratic, and ill-informed. Foreign policy required public consensus, but the public was moodish, unpredictable, and incapable of sound judgment—creating yet one more constraint on effective international leadership. Presidents, by implication, needed to "find a way around" public opinion. However, recent work by Shapiro and Page, among others, has challenged this view and developed what is, from the perspective of international leadership, a far more optimistic view of the public's role in and impact on foreign policy.[41] They find, tracing through decades of survey data, that public opinion on foreign policy issues is "coherent, consistent, and reflective of values that endure over long periods of time."[42] Public opinion is stable and constructive: it signals quite clearly the kind of policies and initiatives that are (or are not likely) to command enduring support. For example, a strong aversion to the direct use of military force—unless there is a clear threat to U.S. interests and no viable alternative—runs through decades of survey data, and was only reinforced by the Vietnam experience. On the other hand, since 1942 there has been high and stable support for an active U.S. role in world affairs, including support for the significant presence of U.S. troops in Europe and Asia. Surveys conducted through the 1970s and 1980s suggest some public sympathy for protectionism; yet, when questions were framed to emphasize reciprocity and the opportunities for U.S. exports, the postwar public consensus in favor of free trade resurfaced.

Although stable, public opinion is not immutable. Shapiro and Page find that public opinion "responds to new information and to objective changes in ways that are regular, predictable, and generally sensible."[43] The collective public is responsive to and can be educated by a President willing to devote the political energy and lay the groundwork for new or changed foreign policy priorities. The postwar shift in public opinion from isolationism to internationalism, and the more recent shift from viewing the Soviet Union as an "unfriendly enemy" to viewing Russia as a country worthy of economic assistance (despite the general and enduring aversion of the public to foreign aid) illustrate the point. The upshot of this revisionist view is that instead of something to be feared or evaded, the impact of public opinion on foreign policy should be welcomed and cultivated by executive officials.

Similarly, an administration with a sensitivity to public opinion can turn the media into an asset as well. One does not have to believe that U.S. public support for the Persian Gulf war was the result of a conspiracy between George Bush and the "punditocracy," to appreciate that the President did use the media effectively to convey his belief that Saddam Hussein represented a profound threat to U.S. interests and to the values of the international community.[44] Yet, administrations can miss opportunities as well. With regard to Japan, the Bush administration worked hard to defend liberal policies against economic nationalism, but did not always speak forcefully at the public level in favor of this preference. The rhetorical ground was left to the critics of administration policy, who were more inclined, for example, to depict Japanese foreign investment as part of a "Japanese invasion" than as an important contributor to the revitalization of the U.S. economy.

A crucial component of leadership is the ability to enter into and sustain international commitments. The United States has made a host of such commitments in the postwar era, and recently Peter Cowhey has argued that the structure of the U.S. political system actually helps U.S. officials to sustain them.[45] He finds that in systems where power is divided, once international commitments are made they are hard to reverse, since reversal requires the acquiescence of more than one center of power. Moreover, the fact that the U.S. system is open and transparent makes it easier for America's negotiating partners to monitor U.S. compliance with commitments. Since the willingness of other states to maintain commitments depends in part on their assessment of whether the United States will keep to the bargain, the transparency of the U.S. political system helps to increase the prospects for enduring international cooperation. Ironically, the "foreign penetration" of the U.S. political system, viewed by some as a weakness or threat, may actually enhance leadership by helping others to track U.S. adherence to international commitments.[46]

CONCLUSION: POWER, PURPOSE, AND LEADERSHIP

The postwar U.S. leadership record, the fact that administrations have techniques to manage domestic constraints, and the fact that the domestic system can actually be turned to international advantage all suggest that as the United States enters the post-cold war era, the foreign policy process need not be viewed as a serious impediment to the exercise of U.S. leadership. The domestic process, however, is only one possible determinant of international leadership. Two other important ones are international power and foreign policy purpose. Although widely debated of late, the United States retains sufficient international power to lead in a post-cold war world. Whether the United States also possesses the foreign policy purpose, however, is more uncertain.

Is the United States a great power in decline? If "power" is defined in terms of relative position over time, and operationalized as control over economic resources, the answer seems clear. The U.S. share of world trade, of financial reserves, and of global output of commodities such as steel and petroleum decreased sharply between 1950 and the 1980s. During the 1980s, the United States shifted from creditor to debtor status as its international financial position deteriorated sharply and rapidly. At the same time, it faced serious competition in world markets and a challenge to its pre-eminence in advanced technology from Japan.[47]

In absolute terms, however, the United States just as clearly remains a dominant power. Its economy remained the largest in terms of GNP, and its market is either the largest or second largest, depending on whether one aggregates the members of the European Union. U.S. productivity stagnated after 1973 but recently has rebounded, and although the United States does not lead in every sector, across manufacturing as a whole it retains its position as the most productive of the advanced industrial states.[48] Widespread concern during the mid-1980s that the United States was "de-industrializing" seems to have abated, and by the early 1990s attention was focused instead on the striking export performance of U.S. firms. A favorable exchange rate, generous amounts of foreign investment, and a concerted effort by U.S. firms to cut costs and improve quality all seemed to contribute to the renewed prowess of U.S. firms in international competition.[49]

Equally important, economic is not the sole form of international power. With the collapse of the Soviet Union, the United States is unambiguously the world's leading military power and is increasingly dominant in the production (and export) of sophisticated weaponry.[50] The United States also possesses the "soft" power resources of culture and ideology; as Russett and Nye argue, to the extent American values (e.g., anti-authoritarianism, liberal economies, individual rights) have become widespread, the United States has been able to retain control over international outcomes without having to exercise overt power over others.[51]

The point is not that United States enjoys complete mastery over international outcomes, or that it will always prevail in international disputes. It never enjoyed that degree of influence, even at the peak of its postwar power. Rather, the point is that despite its relative decline, the United States clearly retains sufficient power to contemplate seriously a leadership role internationally.

The United States may possess the power—does it also possess the foreign policy purpose? The cold war era was distinctive in that it witnessed the combination of U.S. power and purpose. The elements of U.S. foreign policy purpose are well-known: containment of the Soviet Union, permanent alliances with non-Communist states, a willingness to intervene using direct force if necessary to prevent Communist takeovers, and the pursuit of multilateralism in the international economy. With the end of the cold war, the U.S. purpose is no longer clear. There is no central enemy, and despite the best efforts of some officials, a collection of "nasty little states" such as Iraq and North Korea cannot substitute for the big nasty one. There is no consensus on when the United States should intervene, and for what reason. There is both support for, and suspicion of, joining with the United Nations in collective security efforts. The consensus in favor of economic liberalism and multilateralism has been challenged by advocates of industrial policy, managed trade, aggressive unilateralism, regionalism, and by those who view "geo-economic competition" as the principal source of great power rivalry in the years ahead.

The absence of foreign policy purpose is largely a function of the fact that the cold war ended rather abruptly and the adjustment to a new order is still taking place. Yet the problem has been exacerbated by the Clinton administration, which has been strikingly unsuccessful at providing purpose to U.S. policy. It has been noted often that President Clinton seems to wish for the world to stay still while he handles domestic problems, and that the world is clearly not cooperating. The *Economist* recently editorialized that Clinton's "undisguised disinterest in foreign policy, together with his administration's utter absence of a framework for thinking about America's place in the world, have convinced many of America's friends that their worst nightmare may be coming true: a one-superpower world in which the superpower does not have the faintest idea how to perform its central role of preserving peace through preserving the balance of power."[52]

In the absence of clear purpose, foreign policy tends to be reactive, episodic, and directionless. And this is precisely the context within which the potentially *negative* aspects of the U.S. political system weigh most heavily on foreign policy. When there is a lack of consensus at the top, bureaucratic battles within the executive develop and usually become public, as evidenced by the struggles between Brzezinski and Vance during the Carter years over how to deal with the Soviet Union. When the executive is perceived as weak or uncertain, Congress attempts to fill the void, even though it is institutionally incapable of doing so. When neither the executive nor Congress provide direction, the media and to some extent interest groups tend to fill the void, and the administration finds itself—as in recent policy toward Somalia, Bosnia, and NAFTA—catching up with and reacting to events rather than setting the foreign policy agenda, domestically and internationally.

In these circumstances, it is tempting to find fault with the process, and to retreat into the logic of the democratic dilemma. That, however, is to mistake the symptom for the cause. International leadership requires purpose, and when it exists, the system can be made to work.

NOTES

1. See, for example, John W. Spanier and Eric M. Uslaner, *American Foreign Policy Making and the Democratic Dilemmas* (New York: Macmillan Publishing Company, 6th ed., 1994), pp. 17–23.
2. Alexis De Tocqueville, *Democracy in America*, vol. I. trans. by Henry Reeve (Boston: John Allyn, 1882), pp. 299–300.
3. Washington is quoted in *ibid.*, pp. 296–97, emphasis in original.
4. By "international leadership" I mean the ability of a country to develop and sustain foreign policies that have a profound effect on the structure and substance of international relations. I would also include the ability to identify common problems and opportunities, and to take the initiative in mobilizing resources and coalitions to address them.
5. Kennan is quoted in Robert Pastor, "The President Versus Congress," in Robert J. Art and Seyom Brown, eds., *U.S. Foreign Policy: The Search for a New Role* (New York: Macmillan, 1993), p. 12. Pastor's essay is one of a small handful in the literature that challenges the conventional wisdom directly and effectively.
6. See Lowi, "Making Democracy Safe for the World: On Fighting the Next War," in G. John Ikenberry, ed., *American Foreign Policy: Theoretical Essays* (New York: HarperCollins, 1989), pp. 258–292, quotations at 288.
7. See Krasner, "United States Commercial and Monetary Policy: Unravelling the Paradox of External Strength and Internal Weakness," in Peter Katzenstein, ed., *Between Power and Plenty* (Madison: University of Wisconsin Press, 1978), pp. 51–88: *Defending the National Interest* (Princeton: Princeton University Press, 1978); and "Domestic Constraints on International Economic Leverage," in Klaus Knorr and Frank Trager, *Economic Issues and National Security* (Lawrence: University of Kansas Press, 1977), pp. 160–181.
8. Destler, Gelb, and Lake, *Our Own Worst Enemy: The Unmaking of American Foreign Policy* (New York: Simon and Schuster, 1984), p. 11.

9. Broder, "Can We Govern? Our Weakened Political System Sets Us Up For Failure," in *The Washington Post* (National Weekly Edition), January 31, 1994, p. 23.

10. Tower is quoted in James M. McCormick, *American Foreign Policy and Process,* 2nd ed. (Itasca, Illinois: F. E. Peacock Publishers, 1992), p. 341.

11. The Soviets abrogated the trade agreement after the Jackson-Vanik Amendment passed. See Paula Stern, *Water's Edge: Domestic Politics and the Making of Foreign Economic Policy* (Westport, Conn.: Greenwood Press, 1979).

12. Most of the world trading community viewed Super 301 as contrary to the spirit and possibly the letter of GATT, at a time when the United States was seeking to strengthen GATT and international adherence to it. See, for example, Jagdish Bhagwati, *Aggressive Unilateralism: America's 301 Trade Policy and the World Trading System* (Ann Arbor: University of Michigan Press, 1990).

13. See James A. Nathan and James K. Oliver, *Foreign Policy Making and the American Political System,* 2nd ed. (Boston: Little, Brown, 1987), pp. 24–25.

14. See Michael Mastanduno, *Economic Containment: CoCom and the Politics of East-West Trade* (Ithaca: Cornell University Press, 1992).

15. See Henry A. Kissinger, *White House Years* (Boston: Little, Brown, 1979).

16. Alexander L. George, "Domestic Constraints on Regime Change in U.S. Foreign Policy: The Need for Policy Legitimacy," in Ikenberry, ed., *American Foreign Policy,* pp. 583–608.

17. See John Canham-Clyne, "Business as Usual: Iran-Contra and the National Security State," in Eugene R. Wittkopf, ed., *The Domestic Sources of American Foreign Policy,* 2nd ed. (New York: St. Martin's, 1994), pp. 236–246, at 240–241.

18. I. M. Destler, "A Government Divided: The Security Complex and the Economic Complex," in David A. Deese, ed., *The New Politics of American Foreign Policy* (New York: St. Martin's, 1994), pp. 132–147.

19. For example, Dan Williams and Ann Devroy, "Buckling Under the Weight of the World: The White House Appears Weak and Wavering in Foreign Affairs," *Washington Post,* National Weekly Edition, May 2, 1994, p. 14.

20. Hugh Heclo, *A Government of Strangers* (Washington, D.C.: The Brookings Institution, 1976).

21. For example, Clyde V. Prestowitz, Jr., *Trading Places: How We Are Giving Our Future to Japan and How to Reclaim It,* 2nd ed. (New York: Basic Books, 1989).

22. See Mitchell G. Bard, "The Influence of Ethnic Interest Groups on American Middle East Policy," in Wittkopf, ed., *The Domestic Sources of American Foreign Policy,* pp. 79, 86.

23. See Krasner, *Defending the National Interest.*

24. Jeff Frieden, "Sectoral Conflict and U.S. Foreign Economic Policy, 1914–1940," in Ikenberry, ed., *American Foreign Policy,* pp. 133–161.

25. See Robert S. Greenberger, "Cacophony of Voices Drowns Out Message From U.S. to China," *Wall Street Journal,* March 22, 1994, p. A1.

26. The most prominent articulation of this argument is Pat Choate, *Agents of Influence: How Japanese Lobbyists in the United States Manipulate America's Political and Economic System* (New York: Knopf, 1990).

27. See John B. Judis, "The Japanese Megaphone: Foreign Influences on Foreign Policy-making," in Wittkopf, ed., *The Domestic Sources of American Foreign Policy,* p. 102.

28. See, for example, Spanier and Uslaner, *American Foreign Policy and the Democratic Dilemmas,* pp. 233–36.

29. Broder, "Can We Govern?," p. 23.

30. Lloyd Cutler, "Foreign Policy on Deadline." *Foreign Policy,* no. 56 (Fall 1984), pp. 113–128.

31. In his assessment of the interbranch relationship, Robert Pastor similarly argues that the U.S. performance record has been better than it is usually given credit for in terms of consistency and flexibility. See Pastor, "The President Versus Congress," pp. 16–22.
32. John Lewis Gaddis, *Strategies of Containment: A Critical Appraisal of Postwar American National Security Policy* (New York: Oxford University Press, 1982).
33. See Bruce Russett, "The Mysterious Case of Vanishing Hegemony; or, Is Mark Twain Really Dead?," *International Organization,* vol. 39, no. 2 (Spring 1985), pp. 207–231.
34. See John Odell, *U.S. International Monetary Policy* (Princeton: Princeton University Press, 1982), and Yoichi Funabashi, *From the Plaza to the Louvre* (Washington, D.C.: Institute for International Economics, 1989).
35. For an elaboration and illustration of these arguments, see John Ikenberry, David Lake, and Michael Mastanduno, eds., *The State and American Foreign Economic Policy* (Ithaca: Cornell University Press, 1988).
36. For full discussion, see Mastanduno, *Economic Containment*, Ch. 3.
37. A good discussion is McCormick, *American Foreign Policy and Process*, pp. 313–325.
38. See I. M. Destler, *U.S. Trade Politics: System Under Stress* (Washington, D.C.: Institute for International Economics, 1986).
39. Pastor, "The President versus Congress," p. 16.
40. *Ibid.*, p. 17.
41. See, for example, Robert Y. Shapiro and Benjamin J. Page, "Foreign Policy and Public Opinion," and Thomas W. Graham, "Public Opinion and U.S. Foreign Policy Decision-Making," in Deese, ed., *The New Politics of American Foreign Policy*, pp. 190–235. The shifting consensus in the literature is reviewed by Ole Holsti, "Public Opinion and Foreign Policy: Challenges to the Almond-Lippmann Consensus," *International Studies Quarterly*, vol. 36, no. 4 (December 1992), pp. 439–466.
42. Shapiro and Page, "Foreign Policy and Public Opinion," p. 217.
43. *Ibid.*, p. 226.
44. See Eric Alterman, "Operation Pundit Storm: The Media, Political Commentary, and Foreign Policy," in Wittkopf, *The Domestic Sources of American Foreign Policy*, pp. 120–131.
45. Peter Cowhey, "Domestic Institutions and the Credibility of International Commitments: Japan and the United States," *International Organization*, vol. 47, no. 2 (Spring 1993), pp. 299–326.
46. *Ibid.*, p. 314. Interestingly, Cowhey finds in comparative terms that the Japanese political system is less well-equipped for international leadership. The electoral system rewards private rather than public goods, reducing incentives for leaders to make international commitments; the parliamentary system makes it easier to reverse commitments; and the system is less transparent, making Japanese compliance with agreements harder to monitor.
47. The "declinist" argument has been made most forcefully by Robert Gilpin, *U.S. Power and the Multinational Corporation* (New York: Basic Books, 1975) and *The Political Economy of International Relations* (Princeton: Princeton University Press, 1987); Robert Keohane and Joseph Nye, *Power and Interdependence* (Boston: Little, Brown, 1977); and Paul Kennedy, *The Rise and Fall of the Great Powers* (New York: Random House, 1987).
48. A well-publicized report by McKinsey and Company in 1993 documented the overall superiority of the United States in manufacturing productivity relative to its primary competitors, Japan and Germany. See Sylvia Nasar, "The American Economy, Back on Top," *New York Times,* February 27, 1994, Sec. 3, pp. 1, 6, and "Why US is Indeed Productive," *New York Times,* October 22, 1993, p. D1.

49. See "Who's Sharper Now?," and "Ready to Take on the World," *The Economist*, January 15, 1994, pp. 15, 65–66.
50. Ethan Kapstein, "America's Arms-Trade Monopoly," *Foreign Affairs*, vol. 73, no. 3 (May/June 1994), pp. 13–19.
51. Russett, "The Mysterious Case of Vanishing Hegemony," pp. 228–230, and Joseph Nye, *Bound to Lead* (New York: Basic Books, 1990).
52. "Cornered by His Past," June 4, 1994, pp. 13–14.

America's Liberal Grand Strategy: Democracy and National Security in the Post–War Era

G. John Ikenberry

INTRODUCTION

It is thought by many that America's preoccupation with the promotion of democracy around the world is essentially an 'idealist' impulse rooted in the moralism and exceptionalism of the American political tradition. To the extent that this American preoccupation with democracy spills over into actual foreign policy, it is seen as the triumph of American ideas and ideology—often at the expense of the more sober pursuit of American national interests. At best, the American democratic impulse is a minor distraction, rhetorical window dressing fashioned to make foreign policy commitments more acceptable to the American public. At worst, it is a dangerous and overweening moralistic zeal, built around profound misconceptions about how international politics really operates, and fuelling periodic 'crusades' to remake the world—and, as Woodrow Wilson discovered after 1919, this democratic impulse can get the country in serious trouble.

This common view is wrong. The American promotion of democracy abroad in the broadest sense, particularly as it has been pursued after World War II, reflects a pragmatic, evolving, and sophisticated understanding of how to create a stable international political order and a congenial security environment: what might be called an American liberal grand strategy.[1] This orientation sees the

G. John Ikenberry, "America's Liberal Grand Strategy: Democracy and National Security in the Post–War Era," *American Democracy Promotion:Impulses, Strategies, and Impacts,* (New York: Oxford University Press, 2000). Reprinted with permission.

character of the domestic regimes of other states as hugely important for the attainment of American security and material interests. Put simply, the United States is better able to pursue its interests, reduce security threats in its environment, and foster a stable political order when other states—particularly the major great powers—are democracies rather than non-democracies. This view is not an idealist preoccupation but a distinctively American national security orientation that helps explain the American encouragement of democracy abroad as well as the wider imprint that the United States has left on the post-war world.

The argument of this chapter is three-fold. First, the American preoccupation with democracy promotion is part of a larger liberal view about the sources of a stable, legitimate, secure, and remunerative international order. This liberal orientation may be intellectually right or wrong, historically successful or unsuccessful, and in a given American foreign policy episode it may be a dominant or recessive characteristic. But it is a relatively coherent orientation rooted in the American political experience and an understanding of history, economics, and the sources of political stability. This American liberal grand strategy can be contrasted with more traditional grand strategies that grow out of the realist tradition and the foreign policy practices of balance of power, *Realpolitik,* and containment.

Second, this distinctively American liberal grand strategy is built around a wide-ranging set of claims and assumptions about how democratic politics, economic interdependence, international institutions, and political identity contribute independently and together to encourage stable and mutually acceptable political order. The richness and persistence of this American orientation is due in part to its manifold character; it is not just a single theoretical claim—for example, power transitions cause wars, democracies do not fight each other, stable order is built on a balance of power—but is a composite view built on a wide range of related claims about democracy, interests, learning, institutions, and economic change. Its richness and persistence is also due to the fact that various aspects of the liberal grand strategy are argued by different groups in the foreign policy community—this is what makes it a composite but also so stable. Some stressed democracy promotion, some stressed free trade and economic liberalization, and others stressed the construction of ambitious new international and regional economic and security institutions. But these separate emphases and agendas complemented each other—and together they came to constitute a liberal grand strategy.

Third, the dominance and appeal of this liberal grand strategy have survived the end of the cold war, even as most observers of American foreign policy do not fully recognize its character or accomplishments. It is an orientation that unites factions of the left and the right in American politics. Conservatives point to Ronald Reagan as the great cold war champion of the free world, democracy, and self-determination—ironically, Reagan is the great Wilsonian of our age. Liberals emphasize the role of human rights, multilateral institutions, and the progressive political effects of economic interdependence. For all the talk about drift and confusion in contemporary American foreign policy, the United States is seized by a robust and distinctive grand strategy.

I begin by sketching the basic debate about democracy promotion and American foreign policy, which took shape in the inter-war and post-war decades. Following this, I argue that the United States pursued two basic types of order-building strategies after World War II. One strategic orientation emerged really as a response to the rise of Soviet power and the cold war which culminated in the containment order. The other strategic orientation, which is more difficult to capture in a single set of policies, was aimed at restoring stable and open relations among the major democracies. It is this second order that bears the marks of America's liberal order-building designs. In the next section, I sketch the major claims that are brought together as liberal grand strategy and trace these claims to positions and groups within the foreign policy community. Finally, I reflect on the significance of this liberal democratic orientation for the current debate about American foreign policy.

LIBERALISM, REALISM, AND THE GREAT DEBATE

The idealist image of American liberal internationalists was fixed in the intellectual and popular imagination during the great world upheavals of the 1930s and 1940s. The seeming inability of the Wilsonian agenda to create order after 1919—the debacle of the League of Nations and the rise of German and Japanese revisionist power in the 1930s—discredited liberal internationalism and set the stage for the introduction of 'realist' thinking into American foreign policy. It was easy to argue that liberals had fundamentally misread the character of twentieth century world politics, putting the country at danger by substituting utopian thought and moral appeals for the more sober appreciation of material capabilities and power balancing. By the time the United States emerged as a hegemonic power after World War II, the great debate in American foreign policy was between an ascendant 'realism' and a beleaguered 'idealism'.

In one sense, the realist charge that liberals were sentimental idealists was justified. Woodrow Wilson embraced the liberal internationalist agenda as he sought to shape the post-war order, and in doing so he gave it a moralist cast. As Wilson himself put it, foreign policy must not be defined in 'terms of material interest', and should be 'more concerned about human rights than about property rights'. He brought to his political thinking and principles of political action deeply held religious and ethical beliefs that unified and defined his orientation toward the outside world. 'In the conduct of foreign affairs', Link notes, 'this idealism meant for him the subordination of immediate goals and material interests to superior ethical standards and the exaltation of moral and spiritual purposes'.[2]

Wilson's idealism had direct implications for his view about the goals of American foreign policy, including the centrality of democracy to the emerging international order. 'His belief in the inherent goodness of man, in progress as the law of organic life and the working out of the divine plan in history, and in democracy as the highest form of government led him straight to the conclusion that democracy must some day be the universal rule of political life.[3] When the United States was finally drawn into the European war, Wilson appropriated the ideas and proposals of the British and American peace movements, and, in competing with Lenin to define a new path away from the old and bloody power politics of Europe, gave liberal internationalism a moral, universal, and idealist face.[4]

It was against this backdrop—the seeming impotence of Wilsonian ideas in the face of the brutal aggression of the 1930s and 40s—that realism took root in America. The first stroke was E. H. Carr's *Twenty Years' Crisis,* which was, as Stanley Hoffmann notes, 'the work of a historian intent on deflating the pretences of Liberalism, and driven thereby to laying the foundations both of a discipline and of a normative approach, "realism," that was to have quite a future'.[5] The liberals, Carr claimed, were seized by utopian illusions that were dangerously revealed when military aggression of Germany and Japan made a mockery of the Versailles order. Liberal democracy did succeed during the nineteenth century within a few countries, Carr observes. 'But the view that nineteenth-century liberal democracy was based, not on a balance of forces peculiar to the economic development of the period and the countries concerned, but on certain *a priori* rational principles which had only to be applied in other contexts to produce similar results, was essentially utopian; and it was this view which, under Wilson's inspiration, dominated the world after the first world war.'[6] It was the triumph of this rationalist idealism in the 1919 settlement, so Carr argued, that set the stage for the violence and failures of the next two decades.

The second stroke was Hans Morgenthau, whose *Politics Among Nations* crystallized and brought to dominance the realist 'paradigm' for the study and conduct of foreign relations. This was a work that advanced a series of law-like precepts about international relations distilled from the nineteenth century and early twentieth century European diplomacy and balance of power politics. Like Carr, he too was intent on exposing the illusions of liberal idealism. Trained in international law and a refugee from Hitler's Germany, Morgenthau sought to disabuse Americans of their faith in law, morality, and mutual interest as foundations of world order. The remarkable and long-lived influence of Morgenthau's book, first published in 1948, was facilitated by emerging cold war hostilities, which only underscored the stark realities of *Realpolitik* and the balance of power.

But the ascent of realism was accomplished in part by the misrepresentation of liberal thinking about international relations. Pre-1914 writings by British and American liberals were actually quite materialist in their arguments about economics and politics. Apart from Wilson, the most famous early twentieth century liberal thinker who seemed to evince an idealist disregard for the realities of power politics was Norman Angell. His 1909 book *The Great Illusion,* which was first published at the author's expense as an obscure essay but eventually became a world-wide best-seller with over a million copies in print, has long been cited as arguing that the rise of economic interdependence between nations made war impossible.[7] But the book actually presented a more sophisticated argument about how interdependence altered the costs and benefits of territorial gains through war, and how in Europe the costs of disruption to trade and investment were greater than the fruits of territorial conquest. Angell sought to establish that: 'a nation's political and economic frontiers do not now necessarily coincide; that military power is socially and economically futile, and can have no relation to the prosperity of the people exercising it; that it is impossible for one nation to seize by force the wealth or trade of another; . . . that, in short, even when victorious, war can no longer achieve those aims for which peoples strive.'[8]

When critics of Angell argued that the 1912 Balkan War seemed to disprove his theories, Angell replied: 'War is not impossible . . . it is not the likelihood of war which is the illusion, but its benefits.'[9] As Miles Kahler notes, Angell's 'underlying argument was not idealist, it was materialist: The contemporary state system and its competitive nationalism was a poor fit with underlying economic reality'.[10] Angell and other liberals of that era were making arguments about the changing relationship between an increasingly interdependent world economy, a rising transnational society, and the military and political capacities of governments.

The liberal internationalists before and after World War I did not represent a coherent 'school' of thinking. The professionalization of the study of international relations had not yet taken off and liberal thinkers mingled with the League of Nations societies and peace movements. But rather than being unalloyed idealists, they were making arguments that were decidedly materialist and bear the marks of liberal thinking more generally: that modern industrialism and the expanding world economy were creating demands and incentives for new types of cooperative relations between states; that international institutions can and need to provide mechanisms for the governance of interstate relations; that free trade and open markets created opportunities for joint economic gains between countries; that new types of cosmopolitan identities and affiliations between societies were subversive of nationalism and facilitated international cooperation; and that democracy was a commanding force in history that had—or would—transform states and interstate relations.

Liberal thinking was cast in the shadows by the upheavals of world war and the cold war crisis. Not only was realist thinking seemingly more relevant in making sense of the realities of twentieth-century world politics, it was more coherent and straightforward as a doctrine that could inform American foreign policy. It was easy to conclude that the liberal doctrine—in the guise of Wilson's statecraft at Versailles—had been tried and failed. It was also easy to confuse Wilson's own idealism with the core of the tradition, and this confusion was quite useful to realists as they began the process of articulating realism within the academic and foreign policy community. A great and single statement of 'liberal theory' and its implications for American foreign policy was never produced in the inter-war or post-war decades. Liberal internationalism remained a collection of arguments, assumptions, and constructs that were never fully pulled together as a coherent theory or doctrine.

The failure of liberal internationalism was most evident in the mid-twentieth century professionalizing world of international relations and in the American foreign policy establishment. But in the shadows it retained a presence in the practical work of American officials as they sought to rebuild order after World War II—particularly in the work to reconstruct Europe and open the post-war world economy. Ideas were brought forward from the Wilsonian and League of Nations era, but the agenda of liberal internationalism became more complex and multifaceted. It became less centred on the creation of global institutions and universal principles. Lessons were learned from the earlier period, and the interwar problems of capitalism and the modern management of industrial societies infused the new post-war thinking. But liberal ideas and accomplishments remained obscured by the cold war.

THE LIBERAL POST-WAR SETTLEMENT

Even as liberal internationalism experienced a practical breakthrough after World War II, its agenda remained scattered and successes unheralded. In explaining this, it is useful to observe that American foreign policy after 1945 produced two post-war settlements. One was a reaction to deteriorating relations with the Soviet Union, and it culminated in the 'containment order'. It was a settlement based on the balance of power, nuclear deterrence, and political and ideological competition. The other settlement was a reaction to the economic rivalry and political turmoil of the 1930s and the resulting world war, and it culminated in a wide range of new institutions and relations among the Western industrial democracies—call it the 'liberal democratic order'. This settlement was built around economic openness, political reciprocity, and institutionalized management of an American-led liberal political order.[11]

The two settlements had distinct political visions and intellectual rationales, and at key moments the American president gave voice to each. On 12 March 1947, President Truman gave his celebrated speech before Congress announcing aid to Greece and Turkey, wrapping it in a new American commitment to support the cause of freedom around the world. The Truman Doctrine speech was a founding moment of the 'containment order'—rallying the American people to a new great struggle, this one against the perils of world domination by Soviet communism. A 'fateful hour' had arrived, Truman told the American people. The people of the world 'must choose between two alternative ways of life'. If the United States failed in its leadership, Truman declared, 'we may endanger the peace of the world'.[12]

It is forgotten, however, that six days before this historic declaration, Truman gave an equally sweeping speech at Baylor University. On this occasion, Truman spoke of the lessons the world must learn from the disasters of the 1930s. 'As each battle of the economic war of the thirties was fought, the inevitable tragic result became more and more apparent. From the tariff policy of Hawley and Smoot, the world went on to Ottawa and the system of imperial preferences, from Ottawa to the kind of elaborate and detailed restrictions adopted by Nazi Germany.' Truman reaffirmed American commitment to 'economic peace', which would involve tariff reductions and rules and institutions of trade and investment. In the settlement of economic differences, 'the interests of all will be considered, and a fair and just solution will be found'. Conflicts would be captured and domesticated in an iron cage of multilateral rules, standards, safeguards, and dispute resolution procedures. According to Truman, 'this is the way of a civilized community'.[13]

The 'containment order' is well known in the popular imagination. It is celebrated in our historical accounts of the early years after World War II, when intrepid American officials struggled to make sense of Soviet military power and geopolitical intentions. In these early years, a few 'wise men' fashioned a coherent and reasoned response to the global challenge of Soviet communism.[14] The doctrine of containment that emerged was the core concept that gave clarity and purpose to several decades of American foreign policy.[15] In the decades that followed, sprawling bureaucratic and military organizations were built on the containment orientation. The bipolar division of the world, nuclear weapons of growing size and sophistication, the ongoing clash of two expansive ideologies—all these circumstances gave life to and reinforced the centrality of the 'containment order'.

By comparison, the ideas and policies of the liberal democratic order were more diffuse and wide-ranging. It was less obvious that the liberal democratic agenda was a 'grand strategy' designed to advance American security interests. As a result, during the cold war it was inevitable that this agenda would be seen as secondary—a preoccupation of economists and American business. The policies and institutions that supported free trade and economic openness among the advanced industrial societies were quintessentially the stuff of 'low politics'. But this is an historical misconception. The liberal democratic agenda was built on a robust and sophisticated set of ideas about American security interests, the causes of war and depression, and the proper and desirable foundations of post-war political order. Indeed, although the 'containment order' overshadowed it, the ideas behind post-war liberal democratic order were more deeply rooted in the American experience and a thoroughgoing understanding of history, economics, and the sources of political order.

The most basic conviction behind the post-war liberal agenda was that the closed autarkic regions that had contributed to world depression and split the world into competing blocs before the war must be broken up and replaced by an open and non-discriminatory world economic system. Peace and security were impossible in a world of closed and exclusive economic regions. The challengers to liberal multilateralism occupied almost every corner of the advanced industrial world. Germany and Japan, of course, were the most overt and hostile challengers. Each had pursued a dangerous pathway into the modern industrial age that combined authoritarian capitalism with military dictatorship and coercive regional autarky. But the British Commonwealth and its imperial preference system was also a challenge to liberal multilateral order.[16] The hastily drafted Atlantic Charter was an American effort to insure that Britain signed on to its liberal democratic war aims.[17] The joint statement of principles affirmed free trade, equal access for countries to the raw materials of the world, and international collaboration in the economic field so as to advance labour standards, employment security, and social welfare. Roosevelt and Churchill were intent on telling the world that they had learned the lessons of the inter-war years—and those lessons were fundamentally about the proper organization of the Western world economy. It was not just America's enemies, but also its friends, that had to be reformed and integrated.

It was in this context that the post-1945 settlement within the advanced industrial world can be seen. It was a scattering of institutions and arrangements, reflecting the lessons of the 1930s and the new imperatives that emerged from a collapsed war-ravaged world and a newly powerful America. The cold war did overpower the thinking of American officials sooner or later, but the principles and practices of Western order came earlier and survived longer. They were principles and practices that emerged as officials grappled with real post-war problems—the liberal post-war agenda emerged as officials sought to stabilize, manage, integrate, organize, regulate, reciprocate, control, and achieve agreement. The specific ideas and operational visions can be identified more precisely and linked to the post-war transformation.

AMERICAN LIBERAL VISIONS AND STRATEGIES

America's liberal grand strategy is an amalgam of related but distinct claims about the sources of political order—and each has been pushed into the postwar foreign policy process by different groups and parts of the foreign policy establishment. Post-war presidents have stressed different aspects of this agenda, even though the various strategies complement and reinforce each other. Five strategies can be identified, each with its own theory and claims about international relations and each with its own distinctive impact on American foreign policy. In each instance these are liberal ideas that emerge from the American experience and its conceptions of the sources of desirable political order.

Democracy and Peace

Ideas about democratic peace, traced to Kant and developed recently by many analysts, hold that liberal constitutional democracies—or what Kant called 'republics'—tend to have peaceful relations with one another, because of both their internal structures and shared norms.[18] Some argue that the structures of democratic government limit and constrain the types of conflicts over which democratic leaders can mobilize society. Others stress the norms of peaceful resolution of conflict and the ways in which reciprocal democratic legitimacy places limits on the use of violence, while others emphasize the effect of democratic institutions on information and signalling in strategic interaction. Behind these institutional dynamics, others focus on the way in which democracies are built on shared social purposes and an underlying congruence of interests that limit the rise of conflicts worthy of war.[19]

American officials at various junctures have acted on this basic liberal view. Wilson, of course, placed the role of democracy at the centre of his optimism about the durability of a post-war peace. It was also his conception of the sources of war that led to his distinction between the German people and the German government: the former the legitimate source of authority and interest and the latter a dangerous militarist autocracy. The United States did not have a quarrel with the German people, but with their military dictators who had brought war to Europe. 'A steadfast concert of peace can never be maintained except by a partnership of democratic nations. No autocratic government could be trusted to keep faith within it or observe its covenants.'[20]

Wilson's claim was just the most emphatic version of a long tradition in American diplomacy arguing that the United States would be able to trust and get along better with democracies than non-democracies. The American decision to use its post-war occupation of Japan and Germany to attempt ambitious and unprecedented reforms of their states and societies was driven in large part by this belief in the security implications that would flow if Germany and Japan developed more democratic polities.[21] This impulse, of course, was not absolute, and cold war imperatives moderated the extent of actual democratic reform, particularly in Japan. But the argument that the world wars were caused fundamentally by the rise of illiberal, autocratic states and that American post-war security was dependent on the successful transition of these states to democracy was widespread and at the heart of American foreign policy. It was echoed recently by an American official who summarized the view:

> Our answer to the sceptics, the critics, and the self-styled realists is straightforward: look at history, and look at the world around us. Democracy contributes to safety and prosperity, both in national life and in international life—it's that simple. The ability of a people to hold their leaders accountable at the ballot box is good not just for a citizenry so enfranchised—it is also good for that country's neighbours, and therefore for the community of states.[22]

Beyond the democratic peace thesis, other arguments abound that link democracy and the rule of law to international agreement and the stable functioning of international institutions. One argument is that democracies are able to develop relations based on the rule of law rather than political expediency, and this facilitates stable and mutually beneficial dealings.[23] Another argument is that democracies are better able to cooperate in alliance organizations and establish binding institutional relations. The open and permeable character of democracies allows potential institutional partners to overcome uncertainties about domination or abandonment. This is true for three reasons. Democracies are more transparent than non-democracies, and this allows states to observe the domestic system of the other states, and therefore to have more confidence in promises and commitments. Democracies are also more open and accessible to the direct representations of other states, allowing potential partners to not just make agreements, but also to create a political process that allows them to actually influence policy in the other democracies. Finally, the multiple power centres of democracies make abrupt and untoward state actions more difficult—sharp change in policy requires more actors and institutions to sign up to it than in non-democracies.[24]

Overall, the liberal claim is that democracies are more capable of developing peaceful, continuous, rule-based, institutionalized, and legitimate relations among each other than is possible with or between non-democracies. This thesis was put forward by former National Security Council Director Anthony Lake in 1995 in explaining American foreign policy after World War II:

> We led the struggle for democracy because the larger the pool of democracies, the greater our own security and prosperity. Democracies, we know, are less likely to make war on us or on other nations. They tend not to abuse the rights of their people. They make for more reliable trading partners. And each new democracy is a potential ally in the struggle against the challenges of our time—containing ethnic and religious conflict; reducing the nuclear threat; combating terrorism and organized crime; overcoming environmental degradation.[25]

Free Trade, Economic Openness, and Democracy

Another liberal argument that found its way into American post-war policy stresses the importance of trade and economic openness in creating and reinforcing democracy. The claim is that open markets have a salutary impact on the political character of the regimes of other countries, dissolving autocratic and authoritarian structures and encouraging more pluralistic and accountable regimes. Because trade and economic openness have liberalizing political impacts, international order that is organized around free markets promotes and reinforces the types of states that are most inclined to pursue free markets. It is a self-reinforcing order.

Several different lines of argument are advanced. The most general argument is that trade has a positive impact on economic growth and this in turn encourages democratic institutions, and this in turn creates more stable and peaceful international relations. The logic is straightforward: FREE TRADE $\rightarrow$ PROSPERITY $\rightarrow$ DEMOCRACY $\rightarrow$ PEACE. The two claims that are introduced in this area are that trade promotes economic growth and that economic growth encourages democracy. The first of these arguments is an almost undisputed truth, at least among economists and theorists of economic growth. Economists understand why trade stimulates growth faster than within closed economies—factors of production are employed more efficiently, allowing the development and spread of technology and stimulating productivity gains. Opponents of free trade rarely dispute the growth effects of trade, but rather focus on its potentially adverse distributive, social, or national security implications.[26]

The argument that economic growth encourages democracies is more complicated and debated. But as two scholars recently summarize one version of the argument, 'it is only under conditions of prosperity and capitalism that elites can accept defeat peacefully at the polls, secure in the knowledge that they will have fair opportunities to regain political power, and opportunities for economic benefit when they are out of power'.[27] Moreover, there is strong empirical evidence to support the claim. Not all democracies are high-income and prosperous, but there is a strong correlation.[28]

The classic statement of the theory was advanced by Lipset in the 1950s, who attempted to explain why economic development had a positive effect on the likelihood of a country establishing and maintaining democracy. Two intervening factors were most important. First, economic development tends to produce increases in education, which in turn promotes a political culture and political attitudes that are conducive to democracy; and second, economic development tends to produce a social structure dominated by a rising middle class, which moderates class struggle and the appeal of anti-democratic parties and ideologies and increases the size of the population that supports democratic parties.[29] In this view, a rising middle class is the key to the rise and maintenance of democratic institutions, and this class increases in size and importance with economic growth and capitalist development.[30]

Subsequent debate on this argument has stressed complicating factors, particularly the role of income inequality, which some argue tends to counteract the positive influence of economic development on democracy. There also seem to be non-linear and threshold effects on the relationship: economic growth is most important at the lower and medium levels of development, and after some threshold the level of democracy tends to hold regardless of further economic development.[31]

This claim about the positive impact of trade on economic development and economic development on politics has had a long and well-established hold on official American foreign policy thinking. The American embrace of free trade and open markets gained its most secure foothold at the turn of the twentieth century with the articulation of the Open Door policy, driven most forcefully by American efforts to gain market access in Asia. Later, during the progressive era, arguments in favour of free trade moved beyond the simple struggle for markets or the restatement of Ricardo's classic claims. It was Wilson who claimed that free trade would have the added benefit of checking or undercutting domestic monopoly. Protectionism encouraged collusion and reinforced the dominance of big business, and this in turn distorted democratic politics.[32] This progressive era view was seen to hold outside the United States as well—free trade was a necessary condition for the spread of democracy abroad.

This liberal view makes an intensely materialist assumption: that economics shapes politics. Free trade and open markets strengthen society and create zones of autonomy that limit the reach of the state, empowering individuals and altering what they want and expect out of politics. This view lies at the core of American foreign policy efforts at 'engagement'—whether it is directed at South Africa, the Soviet Union, or China. Often unappreciated by the antidemocratic elites whose countries are engaged, trade and market openings are the sharp end of a liberalizing wedge that ultimately promotes economic development and democracy.

Free Trade, Economic Interdependence, and Peace

A related argument is that free trade and open markets promote not just economic advancement and democracy, but also encourage more intense and interdependent relations between states, which in turn foster mutual dependence and new vested interests that favour greater restraint and stability in international relations. This claim takes several forms. Some argue that trade makes states more prosperous, and therefore they are less likely to have grievances that lead to war. 'Prosperous neighbours are the best neighbours', remarked Roosevelt era Treasury official Harry Dexter White.[33] Others argue that trade creates more mutual dependencies, societies expand their mutual interests, and more stable relations result. Still others stress the transnational linkages that are fostered which help reshape political processes and identities. But the basic argument is clear: free and open trade breaks down the sources of antagonism and war.

These claims were advanced by American officials involved in the creation of an open trading system after World War II. The most forceful advocates of this position came from the Department of State and its Secretary, Cordell Hull. Throughout the Roosevelt presidency, Hull and other State Department officials consistently held the conviction that an open international trading system was central to American economic and security interests and was also fundamental to the maintenance of peace. Hull believed that bilateralism and the economic blocs of the 1930s, practised by Germany and Japan but also Britain, were the root cause of the instability of the period and the onset of war.[34] Charged with responsibility for commercial policy, the State Department championed tariff reduction agreements, most prominently in the 1934 Reciprocal Trade Agreement Act and the 1938 US-British trade agreement. Trade officials at the State Department saw liberal trade as a core American interest that reached back to the Open Door policy of the 1890s.[35] In the early years of World War II, this liberal economic vision dominated initial American thinking about the future world order and became the initial opening position as the United States engaged Britain over the post-war settlement. Emerging from the war with the largest and most competitive economic order would serve American interests. An open system was also seen as an essential element of a stable world political order; it would discourage ruinous economic competition and protectionism that was a source of depression and war. But just as importantly, this vision of openness—a sort of 'economic one-worldism'—would lead to an international order in which American 'hands on' management would be modest. The system would, in effect, govern itself.[36]

The connection between trade and the sources of order is made at several levels. There is an expectation that trade will create new forms of mutual dependence through the progressive evolution of specialization and functional differentiation of national economies. This process in turn creates a blurring of national economic borders and interests, which in turn debilitates he capacity of the state to determine and act upon narrow nationalist economic interests. The state's interests are broadened to include a stake in the stability and functioning of the larger international order. At the level of the state, the expansion of trade and investment creates new vested interests in economic openness and the political organization of international politics that is congenial with openness. For example, there is evidence that when firms invest overseas they not only develop an interest in international conditions that foster and protect those operations, but they also become a new voice back home in advocating the opening of the domestic market.[37]

More generally, when American foreign policy has sought to bring countries into the open trade order, they have had expectations that these involvements would have 'socializing' effects on these countries that would be conducive to the maintenance of order. Nowhere was this more explicit than in the Clinton administration's approach toward China. The administration argued that a 'China as a power that is stable, open, and non-aggressive, that embraces free markets, political pluralism, and the rule of law, that works with us to build a secure international order—that kind of China, rather than a China turned inward and confrontational, is deeply in the interests of the American people'. To move China in this direction, the administration embraced the dynamic vision of liberalism: that integration into the international economic order would promote reform at home, encourage the development of the rule of law, and socialize China into the prevailing order. This liberal vision was put directly by Clinton:

> China's economic growth has made it more and more dependent on the outside world for investment, markets, and energy. Last year it was the second recipient of foreign direct investment in the world.. These linkages bring with them powerful forces for change. Computers and the Internet, fax machines and photo-copiers, modems and

satellites all increase the exposure to people, ideas, and the world beyond China's borders. The effect is only just beginning to be felt.[38]

This is essentially the same argument made by Wilson, Roosevelt, Truman, and other American presidents. It now takes a more sweeping and vivid form because of recent developments: the dramatic collapse of the Soviet Union, the rapid rise of new technologies, and the continuing work of the relentless integrating forces of trade and investment. Free markets tend to force open societies, liberalize politics, and integrate and socialize countries.

Institutions and the Containment of Conflict

Another enduring and strongly held liberal view that is deeply entrenched in American foreign policy thinking is that institutions matter. The claim is that when states create and operate within international institutions, the scope and severity of their conflicts are reduced. The reasons involve a series of arguments about the relationship between states, interests, and the logic of dispute resolution. But fundamentally, when states agree to operate within international institutions (within a particular realm), they are in effect creating a political process that shapes, constrains, and channels state actions in desirable ways. Interstate institutions establish a political process that helps to contain conflict by creating mechanisms that can move the dispute toward some sort of mutually acceptable resolution.

At the heart of the American political tradition is the view that institutions can serve to overcome and integrate diverse and competing interests—state, section, ethnicity, class, and religion. American constitutionalism is infused with the belief that state power can be restrained and rights and protections of individuals insured through the many institutional devices and procedures that they specify. Separation of power, checks and balances, and other devices of the balanced constitution were advanced as ways to ensure limits on power. Theories of institutional balance, separation, oversight, and judicial review have an intellectual lineage that traces from Aristotle to Locke and Montesquieu. By specializing functional roles and dispersing political authority, the concentration of power and the possibility of tyranny is prevented.[39] In this way, institutional design can help define and ensure the durability of desirable political order.

It is this deeply held view that has made American officials so inclined to build and operate international institutions. Indeed, the historical record is striking. When the United States has had an opportunity to organize international relations—such as after the two world wars—it has been unusually eager to establish regimes and multilateral institutions.[40] After 1919 it was the League of Nations, and after 1945 it was a flood of institutions with different purposes, functions and scope. The American architects of post-war order are justly famous for their efforts to institutionalize just about everything: security, monetary relations, trade, development assistance, peacekeeping and dispute resolution.[41] When one compares and contrasts *Pax Britannica* and *Pax Americana,* one of the first things to note is that the American era was much more institutionalized.[42]

Of course, American interest in institutionalizing international relations is driven by a variety of factors. It mattered that the United States was in an unprecedented power position after the war. The sheer asymmetry of power relations between the United States and its potential post-war partners made institutions an attractive way to reassure Europe and Japan that it would neither dominate nor abandon them, and a functioning political process made possible by the wide array of institutions was useful in legitimizing America's post-war hegemony.[43] Likewise, the industrial great powers at mid-twentieth century passage were much more complex and interdependent than in the early nineteenth century—so there was just a lot more stuff to organize than before. The political calculus and social purpose of states had evolved, and this was reflected in the functional imperatives of the 1940s.[44]

But there are specific expectations that Americans had about how states operating within international institutions would dampen conflict and mitigate anarchy. Two types of general institutional 'effects' are most important: institutions constrain and socialize. Institutions constrain in that the rules and roles that institutions set out for states serve to create incentives and costs that channel states in particular directions. Violating the rules may create costs by provoking responses by others—such as sanctions and retaliation—or constraints may be manifest by creating 'sunk costs' that make it relatively more expensive to start from scratch and create a new institution. International institutions are not unlike domestic institutions; they create a 'political landscape' that provides advantages, constraints, obstacles, and opportunities for actors who inhabit them.[45] Properly engineered, they can bias state actions toward the desired rules and roles.

International institutions can also socialize states, which happens when they influence the way in which states think about their interests. In becoming socialized to accept certain ways of thinking, as Martha Finnemore argues, states 'internalize the roles and rules as scripts to which they conform, not out of conscious choice, but because they understand these behaviours to be appropriate'.[46] The underlying view is that the interests and preferences of states are not completely fixed, and that institutions could play a role in cultivating certain types of foreign and domestic policy orientations. States might initially agree to operate in an international institution because of the manipulation of incentives by the hegemon, but after a while through a complex process of socialization the rules and values of the institution would be embraced by the state as right and proper.[47]

American officials hoped that the post-war institutions would 'rub off' on the other states that agreed to join. In creating the United Nations, officials worked under the assumption that the establishment of mechanisms for dispute resolution would channel conflicts in non-violent directions.[48] In creating the GATT, officials also anticipated the economic conflicts that could be trapped and diffused in framework of rules, standards, and dispute resolution procedures. In establishing the Marshall Plan for aiding post-war Europe, American officials insisted that the Europeans create a joint institution that would force them to work together in allocating funds, and the hope was that a habit of cooperation would emerge.[49]

Both these ways in which institutions matter echo the American political tradition. The notion of institutional constraints is implicit in republican political theory, where the constitution, separation of powers, and the institutional layers and limits on authority create power distribution and checking mechanisms that inhibit the aggrandizement of power. The view that institutions can socialize is also an extension of the classical liberal view that the political system is not simply a mechanical process where preferences are aggregated, but it is a system where persuasion and justification matter as well.

Community and Identity

A final liberal claim is that a common identity among states facilitates the establishment of a peaceful and durable order. Values and a sense of community matter as sources of order—not just power and interests. Again, there are several layers of argument. One is that states with similar political values and social purposes will be more likely to understand each other, which facilitates cooperation. Another is that if the common values are liberal and democratic, substantive norms exist that specify expectations about how conflicts are to be resolved.

American foreign policy thinkers have been attracted to this liberal view, but the specific way they have sought to identify and develop common identity and community has varied. Wilson talked about a 'community of power' and associated common identity with democracy. This followed directly from his view that the world stood on the brink of a great democratic revolution, and so to build order around a universal democratic community was obvious. The problem was that the world did not culminate in democratic revolution after 1919; Russia, of course, moved in a different direction, but continental Europe also failed to develop democratic societies in the way Wilson expected. As a result, the universalism of the League of Nations was built on unfulfilled expectations.

This failure was a central lesson of the generation of American leaders who followed Wilson. The lesson was not that democracy was unrelated to American security and a durable post-war order, but that universalism was a bridge too far. Democracy was not as easily spread or deeply rooted as Wilson had assumed. Building order around like-mind democracies was still a desired goal of Roosevelt and Truman, but the realm of world politics that would be within this order and the way the order would be institutionalized differed after World War II.[50] The democratic community would exist primarily within the Atlantic world, and its institutional foundations would be more complex and layered.

This view was articulated by a variety of officials and activists in the 1940s who were primarily concerned with creating political order among the democracies of the North Atlantic region. The vision was of a community or union between the United States, Britain, and the wider Atlantic world. Ideas of an Atlantic union can be traced to the turn of the twentieth century and a few British and American statesmen and thinkers, such as John Hay, British Ambassador to Washington Lord Bryce, American Ambassador to London Walter Hines Page, Admiral Alfred T. Mahan, and Henry Adams. These writers and political figures all grasped the unusual character and significance of Anglo-American comity, and they embraced a vision of closer transatlantic ties.[51] These ideas were articulated and rearticulated over the following decades. During World War II, Walter Lippmann gave voice to this view, that the 'Atlantic Ocean is not the frontier between Europe and the Americas. It is the inland sea of a community of nations allied with one another by geography, history, and vital necessity'.[52]

Various experiences and interests fed into the Atlantic idea. One was strategic and articulated during and after the two world wars. Suspicious of Woodrow Wilson's League of Nations proposal, French Premier Georges Clemenceau proposed in 1919 an alliance between France, Britain, and the United States—an alliance only among what he called 'constitutional countries'.[53] The failure of the League of Nations reaffirmed in the minds of many Americans and Europeans the virtues of a less universal security community that encompassed the North Atlantic area.

Others focused on the protection of the shared democratic values that united the Atlantic world. These ideas were most famously expressed in Clarence Streit's 1939 book, *Union Now: The Proposal for Inter-democracy Federal Union.*[54] Concerned with the rise of fascism and militarism and the fragility of the Western democracies in the wake of a failed League of Nations, Streit proposed a federal union of the North Atlantic democracies.[55] In the years that followed, a fledgling Atlantic Union movement came to life. An Atlantic Union Committee was organized after the war and prominent Americans called for the creation of various sorts of Atlantic organizations and structures. American and European officials were willing to endorse principles of Atlantic community and unity—most explicitly in the 1941 Atlantic Charter—but they were less interested in supranational organization.

In more recent years, American officials have returned to this theme. In the aftermath of the cold war, the Bush administration was quick to remind its allies that they were more than a defensive alliance against communism—that the alliance was equally a positive embodiment of the values and community that they shared. In major speeches both President Bush and Secretary of State Baker talked about the Euro-Atlantic Community and the 'zone of democratic peace'. It had been relatively easy during the cold war to talk about the unity of the 'free world'. After 1991, this became more difficult and the older notions of democratic community were rediscovered. The Clinton administration also came to evoke similar sentiments about democratic community in making the case for NATO expansion.

There is an inherent ambiguity in specifying the precise character of democratic community, and this is reflected in foreign policy thinking. Some draw the borders of shared community rather narrowly. Samuel Huntington's famous argument about civilization, for example, has a rather limited notion of the West and shared community. It exists primarily in the Atlantic world. Others have more expansive notions. James Huntley has developed an elaborate set of criteria for determining the 'like-mindedness' of states, which in turn explains why 'some countries and their governments are more ready than others to engage in sophisticated forms of international cooperation'. These include a stable, experienced, and advanced democratic regime, advanced and knowledge-based modern economies and societies, and a substantial body of diplomats, civil servants, political leaders, and other elites who are oriented toward international cooperation.[56] In this view, democratic community is not absolute, but runs along a gradient, concentrated in a core of states and moving outward to less similar states.

THE COALITIONAL BASIS OF LIBERAL GRAND STRATEGY

These liberal claims and strategies are compatible, even synchronous, in some deep sense, and they have come together at various historical junctures, most fully after World War II. They have rarely been thought of or championed as a single package. But in the 1940s they came together. Today, with the end of the cold war, they are ideas and strategies that can be seen more clearly as a distinctive American grand strategy.

In the 1940s the various pieces came together. The free traders at the State Department had a clear line on the post-war order: it would be a free trade system. Others at the Treasury and New Dealers were eager to see international institutions established that would provide fixed mechanisms for the governance of the post-war economy. Other activists were focused on the United Nations and the creation of political governance institutions. Still others, such as George Kennan, were interested in rebuilding Europe as a stable counterweight to the Soviet Union.

In the background, other officials were focused on American geopolitical interests and the Eurasian rimlands. This is where American strategic thinkers began their debates in the 1930s, as they witnessed the collapse of the world economy and the emergence of German and Japanese regional blocs. The question these thinkers pondered was whether the United States could remain as a great industrial power within the confines of the western hemisphere. What were the minimum geographical requirements for the country's economic and military viability? For all practical purposes this question was answered by the time the United States entered the war. An American hemispheric bloc would not be sufficient; the United States must have security of markets and raw materials in Asia and Europe.[57] It must seek openness, access, and balance in Europe and Asia.

This view that America must have access to Asian and European markets and resources, and must therefore not let a prospective adversary control the Eurasian land mass, was also embraced by post-war defence planners. Defence officials also saw access to Asian and European raw materials, and the prevention of their control by a prospective enemy, as an American security interest. Leffler notes that 'Stimson, Patterson, McCloy, and Assistant Secretary Howard C. Peterson agreed with Forrestal that long-term American prosperity required open markets, unhindered access to raw materials, and the rehabilitation of much—if not all—of Eurasia along liberal capitalist lines'.[58] Some defence studies went further, and argued that post-war threats to Eurasian access and openness were more social and economic than military. It was economic turmoil and political upheaval that were the real threats to American security, as they invited the subversion of liberal democratic societies and Western oriented governments. Access to resources and markets, socioeconomic stability, political pluralism, and American security interests were all tied together.

The desirability of open markets, democratic states, and international institutions was something that liberal visionaries and hard-nosed geopolitical strategists could agree upon. Indeed, the durability of America's liberal grand strategy is partly due to the multiple agendas that are served in the process. This was true in 1945 as well as today. State Department officials advancing notions of an open world economy were reinforced by defence planners who linked American security interests to market and resource access to Asian and European regions. State Department planners, such as George Kennan, who were primarily concerned with rebuilding the economic and political infrastructure and wherewithal of western Europe made common cause with other officials who were concerned with encouraging the emergence of continental European governments committed to an open and integrated Western order. This convergence on liberal democratic order was facilitated by the reluctance of the Truman administration to pursue more far-reaching options, such as simple free trade or world government. An institutionalized and managed Western order that centred on openness and democracy was an appealing objective to some and an indispensable means to an end to others.

CONCLUSION

For those who thought cooperation among the advanced industrial democracies was primarily driven by cold war threats, the last few years must appear puzzling. Relations among the major Western countries have not deteriorated or broken down. What the cold war focus misses is an appreciation of the other and less heralded post-war American project: building a liberal democratic order within the West. The ideas, practices, lessons, and designs that American officials brought to bear on the problem of rebuilding order among the Western states was, taken together, a distinctively American grand strategy.

The robustness of the ideas behind Western liberal democratic order was partly a result of the manifold lessons and experiences that stimulated these ideas. It is sometimes argued that what differentiated the successful settlement after 1945 from the 'unsuccessful' settlement after 1919 is that it was based on more 'realist' understandings of power and order. Roosevelt, for example, was sensitive to considerations of power, and his notion of the 'Four Policemen' was a self-conscious effort to build a post-war settlement around a great-power collective security organization. But the actual post-war settlement reflected a more mixed set of lessons and calculations. 'Realist' lessons from the League of Nations debacle of the 1920s were combined with 'liberal' lessons from the regional imperialism and mercantilist conflict of the 1930s. The United States did show more willingness to use its military victory and occupation policy after 1945 to implement its post-war aims in Germany and Japan, but those aims were manifestly liberal in character.

It is commonly argued today that post-cold war American foreign policy has lost its way. The loss of containment as an organizing concept and grand strategy has left some bewildered. But if the other elements of American post-war grand strategy sketched in this paper are recognized, this perspective is less compelling. The United States has a deeper and more sophisticated set of policies and practices than a narrow focus on American cold war diplomacy would reveal. So to analysts who equate grand strategy with 'containment' and 'managing the balance of power', the liberal strategies of the United States will not be recognized, and these analysts will acknowledge the arrival of a new American grand strategy only when a new threat emerges that helps stimulate and organize balancing policies. But this is an intellectually and historically impoverished view, and it misses huge foreign policy opportunities in the meanwhile.

What is striking, in fact, and perhaps ironic, about American foreign policy after the cold war is how deeply bipartisan liberal internationalism is in foreign policy circles. Reagan and Bush pursued policies that reflected a strong commitment to the expansion of democracy, markets, and the rule of law. The Reagan administration's involvements in El Salvador, the Philippines, Chile, and elsewhere all reflected this orientation. Its shift from the Nixon-Kissinger 'permanent coexistence' approach to the Soviet Union toward a more active pursuit of a human rights and democracy promotion agenda also revealed this orientation. Following in line with a view articulated by Wilson, Roosevelt, Truman and others, the Reagan administration articulated the democratic peace argument—that the regime type of other states matters, and if they are democracies they will be less threatening to the United States. Jeane Kirkpatrick and other Kissinger-type realists were brought into the administration, but their view that democracy promotion was a counterproductive luxury did not dominate.

Today, a foreign policy agenda organized around business internationalism, multilateral economic and security organizations, and democratic community building is embraced by elites in both parties. It is a coalition not unlike the one that formed in the 1940s. Some elites embrace democracy, the rule of law, and human rights as an end in itself; others see its promotion as a way to expand and safeguard business and markets; and others see indirect payoffs for national security and alliance management. The Clinton administration's doctrine of 'enlargement' and its policy of engagement toward China were mere reflections of this long-standing liberal American orientation.[59] Many of the speeches that Clinton administration officials made on enlargement and engagement could just as easily have been generated by Reagan and Bush speech writers. There were differences of details, but the two major parties did not articulate two radically—or even moderately—different world-views.

Part of the reason for the stability of this general liberal strategic orientation is that the overall organizational character of the American system encourages it. International business is a coalition partner. Engagement of China, for example, was really the only option, given the huge stakes that American multinationals have in the Chinese and Asian markets. The United States also has a huge domestic constituency for democracy promotion and numerous non-government organizations keep the issue on the agenda. The groups and associations that have sought to build a more formal Atlantic community are also at work articulating notions of wider democratic community. Transnational groups that support the United Nations, the IMF and World Bank, and other major multilateral organizations also feed into the American foreign policy process. In other words, American foreign policy is only part of what generates and sustains the American liberal orientation. Democracies—particularly big and rich ones like the United States—seem to have an inherent sociability. Democracies are biased, structurally speaking, in favour of engagement, enlargement, interdependence, and institutionalization, and they are biased against containment, separation, balance, and exclusion. The United States is doomed to pursue a liberal grand strategy.

NOTES

1. The most sophisticated and systematic survey of American democracy promotion in this century is Tony Smith, *America's Mission: The United States and the Worldwide Struggle for Democracy in the Twentieth Century* (Princeton: Princeton University Press, 1994).
2. Arthur S. Link, *Wilson the Diplomatist* (New York: New Viewpoints, 1974), p. 13.

3. Link, *Wilson the Diplomatist*, p. 14.
4. See Thomas J. Knock, *To End All Wars: Woodrow Wilson and the Quest for a New World Order* (New York: Oxford University Press, 1992).
5. Stanley Hoffman, 'An American Social Science: International Relations', *Daedalus*, 106/3 (1977), p. 43.
6. E. H. Carr, *The Twenty Years' Crisis, 1919–1939*, 2nd edn (New York: Harper & Row, 1946), p. 27.
7. Norman Angell, *The Great Illusion: A Study of the Relation of Military Power to National Advantage* (New York and London: G. Putnam and Sons, 1910).
8. Angell, *The Great Illusion*, p. x.
9. Angell, *The Great Illusion*, pp. 386–7.
10. Miles Kahler, 'Inventing International Relations: International Relations Theory After 1945', in Michael Doyle and G. John Ikenberry (eds.), *New Thinking in International Relations Theory* (Boulder, CO: Westview Press, 1997), p. 23.
11. This section draws on G. John Ikenberry, 'The Myth of Post-Cold War Chaos,' *Foreign Affairs*, 75/3 (1996), pp. 79–91.
12. H. Truman, 'Address to Joint Session of Congress on Aid to Greece and Turkey', 12 March 1946. For historical accounts of this foreign policy turning point, see Dean G. Acheson, *Present at the Creation: My Years at the State Department* (New York: Norton, 1969); Howard Jones, 'A New Kind of War': America's Global Strategy and the Truman Doctrine in Greece* (New York: Oxford University Press, 1989). On whether the Truman Doctrine was a cold war watershed, see John Lewis Gaddis, 'Was the Truman Doctrine a Real Turning Point?', *Foreign Affairs*, 52 (1974), pp. 386–92.
13. H. Truman, 'Address on Foreign Economic Policy' (Baylor University: 6 March 1947).
14. For a popular account of the 'founding fathers' of the containment order, see Walter Isaacson and Evan Thomas, *The Wise Men: Six Friends and the World They Made* (New York: Simon and Schuster, 1986).
15. The seminal role of George Kennan as architect of containment policy is stressed in John Lewis Gaddis, *Strategies of Containment* (New York: Oxford University Press, 1984). More recently, Melvyn Leffler has argued that many American officials and experts from across the foreign and defence establishment independently began to embrace containment thinking. See *A Preponderance of Power* (Stanford: Stanford University Press, 1992). On Kennan's changing views of containment, see Kennan, *American Diplomacy, 1925–50* (Chicago: University of Chicago Press, 1951); *Memoirs, 1925–50* (Boston: Little, Brown and Co, 1967); and the interview with Kennan in 'X-Plus 25', *Foreign Policy*, 7 (1972), p. 353.
16. For arguments that the great mid-century struggle was between an open capitalist order and various regional autarkic challengers, see Bruce Cumings, 'Trilaterilism and the New World Order', *World Policy Journal*, 8/2 (1991), pp. 195–226; and Charles Maier, 'The Two Postwar Eras and the Conditions for Stability in Twentieth-Century Western Europe', in Charles Maier, *In Search of Stability: Explorations in Historical Political Economy*, part 1 (New York: Cambridge University Press, 1987); pp. 153–84. A similar sweeping historical argument, described as a struggle between 'liberal' and 'collectivist' alternatives, is made in Robert Skidelsky, *The World After Communism* (London: Macmillan, 1995).
17. Churchill insisted that the charter did not mandate the dismantlement of the British empire and its system of trade preferences, and only the last-minute sidestepping of this controversial issue ensured agreement. See Lloyd C. Gardner, 'The Atlantic Charter: Idea and Reality, 1942–1945', in Douglas Brinkley and David R. Facey-Crowther (eds), *The Atlantic Charter* (London: Macmillan, 1994), pp. 45–81.

18. See Michael Doyle, 'Kant, Liberal Legacies, and Foreign Affairs', *Philosophy and Public Affairs*, 12 (1983), pp. 205–35, 32–53; Michael Doyle, 'Liberalism and World Politics', *American Political Science Review*, 80/4 (1986), pp. 1151–69; Bruce Russett, *Grasping the Democratic Peace: Principles for a Post-Cold War World* (Princeton: Princeton University Press, 1993); James Lee Ray, *Democracy and International Conflict: An Evaluation of the Democratic Peace Proposition* (Columbia: University of South Carolina Press, 1995); William J. Dixon, 'Democracy and the Peaceful Settlement of International Conflict', *American Political Science Review*, 88/1 (1994), pp. 14–32.

19. Many of these arguments are brought together in Michael E. Brown, Sean Lynn-Jones, and Steven Miller (eds), *Debating the Democratic Peace* (Cambridge, MA: MIT Press, 1996).

20. Address to a Joint Session of Congress, 2 April 1917; in Arthur S. Link (ed.), *The Public Papers of Woodrow Wilson*, 41 (Princeton: Princeton University Press, 1983), pp. 519–27.

21. See Smith, *America's Mission*, Ch. 6.

22. 'Democracy and the International Interest', remarks by Deputy Secretary of State Strobe Talbott to the Denver Summit of the Eight Initiative on Democracy and Human Rights, 11 October 1997, p. 2. See also Strobe Talbott, 'Democracy and the National Interest', *Foreign Affairs*, 75/6 (1996), pp. 47–63.

23. See Anne-Marie Burley, 'Toward the Age of Liberal Nations', *Harvard International Law Journal*, 33/2 (1992), pp. 393–405; and 'Law Among Liberal States: Liberal Internationalism and the Act of State Doctrine', *Columbia Law Review*, 92/8 (1992), pp. 1907–96.

24. These arguments are developed in G. John Ikenberry, 'Liberal Hegemony: The Logic and Future of America's Postwar Order' (unpublished paper, 1997). See also Daniel Deudney and G. John Ikenberry, 'Liberal Competence: The Performance of Democracies in Great Power Balancing' (unpublished paper, 1994). For a good summary of this literature, see Kurt Taylor Gaubatz, 'Democratic States and Commitment in International Relations', *International Organization*, 50/1 (1997), pp. 109–39.

25. Anthony Lake, 'Remarks on the Occasion of the 10th Anniversary of the Center for Democracy' (Washington, DC: 26 September 1995).

26. See Douglas A. Irwin, *Against the Tide: An Intellectual History of Free Trade* (Princeton: Princeton University Press, 1996).

27. Thomas J. Volgy and John E. Schwarz, 'Free Trade, Economic Inequality and the Stability of Democracies in the Democratic Core of Peace', *European Journal of International Relations*, 3/2 (1997), p. 240.

28. See John B. Longregan and Keith Poole, 'Does High Income Promote Democracy?', *World Politics*, 49 (1996), pp. 1–30.

29. Seymour Martin Lipset, 'Some Social Requisites of Democracy: Economic Development and Political Legitimacy', *American Political Science Review*, 53 (1959), pp. 69–105.

30. The literature is summarized by Dietrich Rueschemeyer, Evelyne Huber Stephens, and John D. Stephens, *Capitalist Development and Democracy* (Chicago: University of Chicago Press, 1992). These authors modify the Lispet model, stressing the specific role of the urban working class.

31. See Edward N. Muller, 'Economic Determinants of Democracy', *American Sociological Review*, 60 (1995), pp. 966–82.

32. See Arthur S. Link, *Woodrow Wilson and the Progressive Era, 1910–1917* (New York: Harper and Row, 1954).

33. Alfred E. Eckes, Jr., *A Search for Solvency: Bretton Woods and the International Monetary System, 1944–71* (Austin: University of Texas Press, 1971), p. 52. This was a

reflection of the Cobdenite philosophy that trade protection and tariffs were linked to political conflict and, ultimately, war.

34. As Secretary Hull argued, 'unhampered trade dovetailed with peace; high tariffs, trade barriers, and unfair economic competition, with war'. Cordell Hull, *The Memoirs of Cordell Hull*, vol. 1 (New York: Macmillan, 1948), p. 81.

35. Herbert Feis, the State Department's economic adviser, noted the continuity of the department's position when he argued during the war that 'the extension of the Open Door remains a sound American aim'. See Herbert Feis, 'Economics and Peace', *Foreign Policy Reports*, 30 (April 1944), pp. 14–19. On the State Department's commitment to a post-war open trading system, see Lloyd Gardner, *Economic Aspects of New Deal Diplomacy* (Madison: University of Wisconsin Press, 1964); Richard Gardner, *Sterling-Dollar Diplomacy: The Origins and the Prospects of Our International Economic Order* (New York: McGraw Hill, 1969); and Alfred E. Eckes, Jr., *Opening America's market: U.S. Foreign Policy Since 1776* (Chapel Hill: The University of North Carolina Press, 1995), Ch. 5.

36. This argument is made in G. John Ikenberry, 'Rethinking the Origins of American Hegemony', *Political Science Quarterly*, 104 (1989), pp. 375–400.

37. Helen Milner and David B. Joffie, 'Between Free Trade and Protectionism: Strategic Trade Policy and a Theory of Corporate Trade Demands,' *International Organization*, 42/2 1989), pp. 239–72; Hidetaka Yoshimatsu, 'Economic Interdepedence and the making of Trade Policy: Industrial Demand for an Open Market in Japan', *The Pacific Review*, 11/1 (1998), pp. 28–50.

38. White House Press Release, 'Remarks by the President in Address on China and the National Interest' (24 October 1997).

39. See M. Richter, *The Political Theory of Montesquieu* (Cambridge: Cambridge University Press, 1977).

40. Of course, the Untied States has also been assiduous is ensuring that there are limits and escape clauses in the binding effects of institutions.

41. On the post-war surge in institution building, see Craig Murphy, *International Organization and Industrial Change* (New York: Oxford University Press, 1994).

42. For comparisons of American and British hegemony, see Robert Gilpin, *U.S. Power and the Multinational Corporation: The Political Economy of Foreign Direct Investment* (New York: Basic Books, 1975); and David Lake, 'British and American Hegemony Compared: Lessons for the Current Era of Decline', in Michael Fry (ed.), *History, the White House, and the Kremlin: Statesmen As Historians* (New York: Columbia University Press, 1991), pp. 106–22.

43. These arguments are made in G. John Ikenberry, *After Victory: Institutions, Strategic Restraint, and the Rebuilding of Order After Major Wars* (Princeton: Princeton University Press, 2000).

44. See John G. Ruggie, *Winning the Peace: America and World Order in the New Era* (New York: Columbia University Press, 1996).

45. For an overview of this perspective on institutions, see James G. March and Johan Olsen, 'The New Institutionalism: Organizational Factors in Political Life', *American Political Science Review*,78 (1984), pp. 734–49.

46. Martha Finnemore, *National Interests in International Society* (Ithaca: Cornell University Press, 1996), p. 29.

47. See G. John Ikenberry and Charles Kupchan, 'Socialization and Hegemonic Power', *International Organization*,43/3 (1990), pp. 283–315.

48. See Ruth B. Russell, *A History of The Untied Nations Charter: The Role of the United States, 1940–1945* (Washington, DC: The Brookings Institution, 1958).

49. See Ernst H. Van Der Beugel, *From Marshall Plan to Atlantic Partnership* (Amsterdam: Elsevier Publishing Co., 1966).
50. On the lessons drawn by order builders in 1945 from the failures of 1919, see David Fromkin, *In the Time of the Americans: The Generation that Changed America's Role in the World* (New York: Alfred Knopf, 1995).
51. See James Robert Huntley, *Uniting the Democracies: Institutions of the Emerging Atlantic-Pacific System* (New York: New York University Press, 1980), p. 4.
52. Walter Lippmann, *U.S. Foreign Policy: Shield of the Republic* (Boston: Little, Brown, 1943), p. 83.
53. The French proposal was to transform the League of Nations into a North Atlantic treaty organization—a union complete with an international army and a general staff. See Thomas J. Knock, *To End All Wars: Woodrow Wilson and the Quest for a New World Order* (New York: Oxford University Press, 1992), pp. 221–22.
54. Clarence Streit, *Union Now: The Proposal for Inter-democracy Federal Union* (New York: Harper and Brothers, 1939).
55. It would be a 'union of these few peoples in a great federal republic built on and for the thing they share most, their common democratic principle of government for the sake of individual freedom'. Streit, *Union Now*, p. 4.
56. James Robert Huntley, *Pax Democratica: A Strategy for the Twenty-first Century* (London: Macmillan, 1998), Appendix A.
57. The culmination of this debate and the most forceful statement of the new consensus was presented in Nicholas John Spykman's *America's Strategy in World Politics: The United States and the Balance of Power* (New York: Harcourt, Brace, 1942).
58. Melvin Leffler, 'The American Conception of National Security and the Beginnings of the Cold War, 1945–48', *American Historical Review*, 89/2 (1984), p. 358.
59. See Douglas Brinkley, 'Democratic Enlargement: The Clinton Doctrine', *Foreign Policy*, 106 (1997), pp. 111–27.

ᒫ

Ironies of Sovereignty: The European Union and the United States

Robert O. Keohane

From a scientific standpoint it is troubling that crucial concepts in international relations theory are subject to redefinition and reinterpretation as situations change. Concepts such as power, authority and commitment are altered as they

Robert O. Keohane, James B. Duke Professor of Political Science, Duke University. Paper prepared for the *Journal of Common Market Studies*, vol. 40, no. 4, pp. 743–765, 40th Anniversary Issue, November 2002. Reprinted by permission of Blackwell Publishing.

become objects of political struggle. The resulting reconceptualizations, however, offer interpretive opportunities to observers of world politics. By seeing how different societies view central concepts, we gain insight into their constructions of the world, and ultimately into their actions.

Sovereignty is such a concept. Since its invention in 16th century Europe, it has taken on a variety of denotations and connotations. The changing meanings of sovereignty enable it to be used as a conceptual lens, through which attitudes and policy preferences are refracted.

In this article I use sovereignty as a conceptual lens to understand how the different histories of Europe and the United States have affected present attitudes, and the language of policy that each side characteristically employs. Specifically, I put forward two conjectures based on observations of the different trajectories that the concept of sovereignty has taken in Europe and the United States over the past two centuries. Both conjectures rely on the observation that the countries of the European Union (EU) have embraced a notion of pooled sovereignty, whereas the United States has maintained a more classical conception of sovereignty. The first conjecture is that Europe's success could enable it to serve as a model, in some respects, for more troubled regions. The second is that different European and United State trajectories could also create more tension and conflict with the United States, thus undermining world order in the long run.

This paper argues that the concept of sovereignty—and divergences with respect to sovereignty between Europe and the United States—can help us understand both the opportunities for troubled societies and regions, and the problems facing the European-United States relationship.

The conception that a state must have control of its external policies and be free of external authority structures is an essentially European invention, dating from the 16th and 17th centuries. For over three hundred years such external sovereignty has been associated with political success. A major historic accomplishment of the European Union (EU) is that it has ended this association between sovereignty and success. The European Union has begun to institutionalize a conception of limited and pooled sovereignty, while at the same time successfully pursuing relatively autonomous policies, exercising influence in world politics, and maintaining very decent conditions of life for its citizens. Europe's emerging conception of pooled sovereignty affects all aspects of European life, from criminal justice to foreign policy.

The other side of the story may be equally historic, but more troubling. As the EU has moved away from the classical conception of external sovereignty, the United States has continued to embrace it, contributing to divergence in their policies, and to increasing discord in their relationships. I do not claim that their different notions of sovereignty are the principal *cause* of strains in the Euro-American relationship. However, they are good *indicators* of divergence.

Since Europe invented the concept of sovereignty, the post-1945 European move away from external sovereignty is ironic. Section I of this paper briefly surveys the history of the notion of sovereignty in Europe before the creation of the European Union, from Jean Bodin's explication of the concept in the late 16th century to the emergence of the European Community in the late 20th century.

The second irony in the sovereignty story is that the United States, from which the first republican critique of the concept of sovereignty emanated, has now become one of its staunchest defenders. Until the last quarter of the 18th century, external sovereignty was coupled with a unitary view of sovereignty: the concept that each state must have an institution that acts as a final and absolute authority. Before and during America's War of Independence, Great Britain sought to uphold this notion—that, in Dr. Samuel Johnson's words, "in sovereignty there are no gradations." But the colonists, fighting what they saw as arbitrary action by Parliament, developed a conception of sovereignty that allowed for its divisibility: what Madison called "the due partition of power between the general and local governments" (Bailyn 1967: 227–229). Such a conception of sovereignty was embedded in the American Constitution. The Constitution upholds the concept of external sovereignty but rejects the idea of unitary sovereignty. Even so, rejecting unitary sovereignty called external sovereignty into question. Indeed, it took a great civil war in the United States to resolve that issue in favor of external sovereignty. Since then, the United States has held onto its external sovereignty with considerable force, although it has occasionally made concessions in order to achieve cooperative outcomes that it valued. Section II of this paper sketches aspects of this story.

The ironic story of European sovereignty is a familiar one; but its positive implications for aspects of world order have not been fully appreciated. The separation of sovereignty from success creates an opening for innovative institutional thinking, free from the straightjacket of sovereignty. In particular, the fact that European states no longer cling to their external sovereignty provides an opportunity to design new institutional structures for troubled societies, whose state structures have failed to provide order and create the basis for economic growth. These structures may require the long-term involvement of external authority, violating fundamental principles of external sovereignty, in order to be viable. Section III makes the case that the concept of sovereignty *should* be altered fundamentally, to enable the problems of troubled societies to be resolved. Europe's experience provides a path toward such a resolution—a path that is not offered by external sovereignty, much less by its unitary version. A radical devaluation of sovereignty may be a necessary condition for political order in many troubled societies.

The final section of this paper sounds a warning that the divergence between European and American conceptions of sovereignty, outlined in Sections I and II, may signal a set of forces that threaten this productive partnership. While Europe has moved toward a conception of sovereignty as a resource to be used in international regimes, the United States has maintained much of the classical notion of sovereignty as a basis for autonomy and a barrier to unwanted movements across borders. These different conceptions partly reflect differences in geopolitical roles, and therefore interests. But they seem also to be results of very different societies, institutions, and national histories, and they may also have impacts of their own on definitions of roles, and on identities.

For allies who have been so successful together, Europeans and Americans do not seem to understand each other very well. Disagreements have long been common on economic and social issues, but issues involving military force have recently become particularly divisive. Americans tend to support Presidents who take bold military measures, whether successful or not, and they defer to the Pentagon on issues that might affect servicemen, such as the International Criminal Court (ICC). Conversely, proposals for military action divide Europeans, with their different histories of heroic defense of freedom, aggressive war, weakness and collapse, and neutrality. So it is quite natural for European politicians to stress foreign policy issues that reinforce common European values and that at the same time make Europeans feel good about themselves and the EU's role in the world. The attractive issues to emphasize are therefore those with high positive symbolic value, such as protection of the environment and human rights. Europe can do well by doing good, promoting values that serve as the moral equivalent of nationalism, reinforcing internal cohesion and a sense of European self-esteem. Europe has no Pentagon to stop it from ratifying a land-mines treaty or a treaty establishing the ICC.

The different approaches toward sovereignty of the European Union and the United States reflect, and perhaps affect, their relationship in the changed world after September 11. Although Europe's new conception of pooled and limited sovereignty may hold out promise for troubled societies, it seems to imply trouble for its relationship with the United States.

I. EUROPE: FROM EXTERNAL AND UNITARY TO POOLED SOVEREIGNTY

What I mean by "external sovereignty" is the doctrine that a state "is subject to no other state and has full and exclusive powers within its jurisdiction without prejudice to the limits set by applicable law" (Hoffman 1987: 172–73). That is, sovereignty means both internal supremacy over all other authorities within a given territory, and external independence of outside authorities (Bull 1977). What I mean by "unitary sovereignty" is the notion, enunciated by Jean Bodin in 1577, that the ultimate authority in the state must reside in one place: that by definition, sovereignty cannot be divided. This conception was original in Europe. The traditional Chinese tributary system provided a means of organizing international relations in East Asia, but "its 'ideal,' unlike the Western ideal, lacked the concept of sovereignty" (Oksenberg 2001: 91).

The concept of sovereignty emerged during a period of civil war, both in France and England. Acceptance of a unitary conception of sovereignty reinforced the power of the king. Indeed, long before the Treaty of Westphalia, sovereignty began "as a theory to justify the king being master in his new modem kingdom, absolute internally. Only subsequently was it turned outwards to become the justification of equality of such sovereigns in the international community, a theory of state-sovereignty" (Wight 1992: 2–3). The unitary conception of sovereignty was devised as an explicitly anti-democratic doctrine. Jean Bodin declared: "We see the principal point of sovereign majesty and absolute power to consist in giving laws to subjects in general, *without their consent*" (Keohane 1980: 71, translating Bodin 1577; emphasis added).

In general, the doctrines of external and unitary sovereignty prevailed in Europe throughout the nineteenth century. Even as countries such as Britain and France democratized, the unitary conception of sovereignty remained largely intact, although it was transferred away from the monarch. In England after 1688 sovereignty was said to reside in Parliament and in France after 1789 the notion of popular sovereignty came, despite various setbacks, to be widely accepted. Nevertheless, sovereignty was still seen as absolute and concentrated at a point. External sovereignty of course also persisted: the state remained supreme over a given territory and population and unconstrained except where it had consented to limitations.

Arbitrary and absolute sovereignty, however, was never feasible in practice, since the states of Europe had to conduct relations with one another. Even absolutist princes had to create some space within their own territories for the diplomats of their rivals. The result was a set of institutions involving diplomatic immunity and the creation of tiny islands of alien sovereignty—embassy compounds—within which foreign diplomats could operate freely, governed by their own laws and practices, including religious observance. In the early 17th century, says Garrett Mattingly, Hugo Grotius sought "by a slender line of logic to draw up Leviathan with a fish-hook," by accepting the concept of sovereignty and arguing that "on these terms it is to the interests of the State to accept the rule of law" (Mattingly 1955: 254–55).

The European conception of sovereignty between the 17th and 20th centuries was quite workable. It both legitimized the state and imposed limits, at least in principle, on its interference with other states. It enabled states to maintain the classic prerogatives of coining money and maintaining military force. The emphasis on the right of rulers to legal supremacy and independence implied limitations on the right of intervention, and therefore promoted order. Yet sovereignty also implied the ability to negotiate and ratify treaties, which could legally bind states: thus it did not prevent them from finding ways to cooperate, at least in specific and limited ways. For a state to bind its tariffs or agree to rules of navigation or to enter into an alliance is entirely consistent with external sovereignty.

What the conception of external sovereignty—which Stephen D. Krasner calls "Westphalian sovereignty"—did prevent, however, was the *delegation of powers* over the state to an external authority (Krasner 1999). That is, the classic conception of sovereignty prohibits governments from agreeing to rules defining a process, over which it does not have a veto, that can confer obligations not specifically provided for in the original agreement. When European countries began to establish multilateral institutions after World War I, their key commitments, such as that of Article 15 of the League of Nations Covenant, required unanimous agreement. Yet after World War II the unanimity rule was decisively broken in organizations such as the World Bank and International Monetary Fund, which have weighted voting, and in the United Nations for states that are not Permanent Members of the Security Council. The UN Charter impinges on the sovereignty of all such member states by requiring them, as a condition of membership, to accept commitments to support decisions of the Security Council, over which they do not exercise a veto.

States that are members of the European Union have broken sharply with the classical tradition of state sovereignty. Sovereignty is pooled, in the sense that in many areas, states' legal authority over internal and external affairs is transferred to the Community as a whole, authorizing action through procedures not involving state vetoes. Britain and France have not, however, given up their vetoes in the Security Council, so one cannot say that their attachment to pooled sovereignty is perfect. Even though each successive treaty expanding the EU's powers requires unanimous consent, law that is binding on the states of the Union can be made without such unanimous agreement. State sovereignty is also limited by supremacy and direct effect of European Union law (Weiler 1999).

Under conditions of extensive and intensive interdependence, formal sovereignty becomes less a territorially defined barrier than a bargaining resource. Indeed, Abram and Antonia Chayes have characterized "the new sovereignty" in terms of the ability to act within international regimes: "The only way most states can realize and express their sovereignty is through participation in the various regimes that regulate and order the international system" (Chayes and Chayes 1995: 27). As Anne-Marie Slaughter expresses the Chayes's point, a state's capacity to act effectively depends on its links with other states. In this view, "sovereignty is relational" (Slaughter 2001: 685). Sir Geoffrey Howe, the former British foreign secretary, put the point more pungently: "Sovereignty is not like virginity, which you either have or you don't. . . . It is a resource to be used, rather than a constraint that limits our capacity for action" (Howe 1990, cited in Grubb 1993).

It is important to note that although the states of Europe have exchanged classic for pooled sovereignty, the situation of the EU as a whole is more ambiguous. The EU does not make grand claims for sovereignty. However, on issues such as trade, the EU seeks vigorously to defend European interests and acts much like a sovereign state, wielding economic power to do so. Indeed, some American commentators have been uncomfortable with the EU's activism, and with the responsiveness to internal constituencies that its actions reflect (Van Oudenaren 2001). Their criticisms of Europe's "structural incoherence" are ironic, since they are so similar to traditional European criticisms of American trade policy, as being too responsive to special interests in the context of an institutionally fragmented political system.

High levels of interdependence give European states incentives to pool and limit their sovereignty in the interests of more sustained cooperation. Their ability to do so has steadily increased as the institutional capacity of the EU has grown. Indeed, mutual interference in one another's affairs is the rule, rather than the nominally prohibited exception (Cooper 1996; Sørensen 2001). Europe, the cradle of external and unitary sovereignty, now serves as the model of cooperative mutual interference.

II. UNITED STATES CONCEPTIONS OF SOVEREIGNTY: REVERSING THE EUROPEAN DIRECTION

The United States was born free of the unitary conception of sovereignty. Indeed, much of the colonial argument resisting the authority of Parliament and the King took the form of critiques of the unitary and absolutist conception of sovereignty then dominant in Europe (Bailyn 1967: 198–229). The Treaty of Peace that ended America's War of Independence was unusual, since the thirteen states were sovereign, not the confederation whose representatives negotiated the Treaty. "The

American party to the treaty was Congress, and Congress had only a limited power delegated by the thirteen sovereign states. It had no obligation to bind them, and not one of them incurred a single legal obligation under the Treaty of Paris" (Burt 1961: 97).

Such extreme decentralization was a source of weakness. Several southern states refused to agree to the safe return of Loyalists to their homes or to payment of debts to British merchants. "If we are to pay the debts due to British merchants," said one American, "what have we been fighting for all this while?" (Kaplan 1972: 154) The leader of the movement in Britain to restrict American trade, Lord Sheffield, declared in 1784 that "it will not be an easy matter to bring the American States to act as a nation, they are not to be feared by us. . . . No treaty can be made with the American States that can be binding on the whole of them" (Combs 1980: 8). Great Britain proceeded to refuse to comply with the provisions of the Treaty of Peace requiring it to evacuate several strategic forts on the United States-Canada frontier, from which it supported Indian tribes hostile to the United States.

America's lack of external sovereignty was a key reason for the Federalist movement to create a constitution. As Alexander Hamilton wrote in *Federalist* paper number 22:

> "No nation acquainted with the nature of our political association would be unwise enough to enter into stipulations with the United States, by which they conceded privileges of any importance to them, while they were apprised that the engagements on the part of the Union might at any point be violated by its members" (Hamilton et al. 1787–88/1961: 136).

Hamilton concluded that this experience showed "the necessity of laying the foundations of our national government deeper than in the mere sanction of delegated authority" (Hamilton et al. 1787–88/1961: 146). Indeed, the Constitution as ratified contains the famous Supremacy Clause, providing that the Constitution, laws of the United States, and treaties made under the authority of the United States, "shall be the supreme law of the land, and the judges in every state shall be bound thereby, anything in the Constitution or laws of any state to the contrary notwithstanding" (Article VI). The Supremacy Clause sought to establish the external sovereignty of the national government of the United States. Its effect was soon evident. In 1796 the Supreme Court ruled m *Ware v. Hyhon* that British debtors could receive judgments in courts throughout the country, although some state courts dragged their feet until well into the 19th century (Jensen 1950).

While the Federalists were busy establishing external sovereignty, they were equally intent on rejecting unitary sovereignty: the doctrine that there must be a single absolute authority in a polity, such as Parliament in Great Britain. On the contrary, the Constitution provided for a separation of powers among the legislative, executive and judicial branches, and sought to ensure the maintenance, in practice, of this "necessary partition of power among the several departments." To do so, Madison famously explained in *Federalist* paper number 51, "ambition must be made to counteract ambition" (Hamilton et al. 1787–88/1961: 347, 349).

In *Federalist* number 51 Madison also pointed out that the Constitution provided a "double security" against concentration of power, since authority is divided between state and national governments, as well as among the departments of the national government. Daniel Deudney has characterized the resulting system as "Philadelphian," as opposed to Westphalian, and has pointed out that the United States has often been regarded as "an alternative to the European Westphalian system rather than an oddly constituted state within it" (Deudney 1995: 193). This guarantee against tyranny, however, had been an impediment to a coherent foreign policy before 1789, and to some extent continued to hinder foreign policy-making until the Civil War. The "sovereignty" claimed by the states obstructed efforts by the national government to maintain its external sovereignty.

An example of such a contradiction between the early federal system and external sovereignty occurred over the issue of impressment. The United States complained, especially after 1803, that in the conduct of its naval war against France, Great Britain was seizing ("impressing") American seamen, on the grounds that they were actually British subjects who had deserted from the Royal Navy. In the summer of 1804, British warships, stationed right outside New York Harbor, forced dozens of American merchant ships each day to heave to and submit to search. Secretary of State James Madison declared in 1807 that to agree to British proposals permitting impressment "would necessarily surrender what they (the United States) deem an essential right of their flag, and of their sovereignty." Indeed, impressment became such a crucial issue that one historian concluded that "had there been no impressment problem, it seems likely that it would have been possible to work out some agreement between America and England" between 1803 and 1807 (Horsman 1962: 94). In the original instructions of the United States government for the peace negotiations, ending impressment was the only *sine qua non*, although this condition was later retracted.

During the Napoleonic wars, Great Britain would not relent on the impressment issue for fear of losing able-bodied seamen. Life in the Royal Navy was much harder and more perilous than life on American merchant ships. In 1818, however, negotiations on a number of Anglo-American issues resumed in time of peace, leading to a treaty that resolved a number of issues, including those involving fisheries and boundaries, between the United States and Great Britain. Impressment was on the original list of issues to be resolved in these negotiations, and Great Britain was conciliatory. It only demanded that the United States provide a definitive list of all naturalized seamen known to be in American service, in order to avoid its own subjects deserting in American ports, claiming American nationality, and going to sea again in American vessels. But the United States claimed that it could not provide such a list, for several reasons, which focused on state-federal relations and the Constitution. Prior to 1790 all aliens had been naturalized by state laws, although since 1790 the actual proceedings for naturalization, although governed by national laws, had taken place in state as well as federal courts. The state courts might refuse to provide the records that they held, even if asked by the national government; and the records, even if supplied, did not list occupation (Zimmerman 1925: 230; Berms 1949: 297–98). Hence, the United States feared, aliens naturalized prior to the treaty might be deprived both of citizenship and their right to pursue their chosen professions.

As a result of this impasse, the issue of impressment remained alive for several decades, although Great Britain never again enforced its supposed right. The key point of this story for our purposes is that the United States was unable to negotiate an agreement that would have safeguarded an aspect of its external sovereignty, because of a lack of full authority of national over state officials. Constitutional safeguards against unitary sovereignty undermined external sovereignty.

After the Civil War, the United States was able to reassert the sovereignty of the national government over that of the states. Especially important was the Fourteenth Amendment, which declares that "all persons born or naturalized in the United States, and subject to the jurisdiction thereof, are citizens of the United States." This provision for the first time decisively gave the national government authority over questions of citizenship. During the succeeding years, the United States became a great power, even an imperial power, exercising its sovereignty increasingly on a world stage.

Accompanying this reinforcement of external sovereignty was a partial move back toward a more unitary conception of sovereignty at home. The executive branch has gained further authority on issues of foreign affairs. In *United States v. Curtiss-Wright Export Corporation* (299 U.S. 304 [1936]), the Supreme Court ruled that in foreign affairs, the president had powers inherent in sovereignty and prior to the Constitution. These powers "accord to the president a degree of discretion and freedom from statutory restriction which would not be admissible were domestic affairs alone involved" (Koh 1990: 138, quoting Justice Sutherland's opinion). During the Cold War, and now again in the War on Terrorism, the powers of the Executive Branch have been extended. Congress has occasionally adopted measures such as the War Powers Resolution of 1973, designed to check this movement. The combination of loopholes in the law, presidential determination to maintain the foreign affairs powers of the presidency, and what Harold Koh calls "judicial tolerance," have combined, however, to render the War Powers Resolution ineffective. Indeed, the Court has continued to rely on *Curtiss-Wright* in a number of decisions upholding presidential power in foreign affairs (Koh 1990). In contrast to the 19th century, efforts to maintain external sovereignty in the 20th century have undermined constitutional safeguards against unitary sovereignty.

Since 1945, the United States has entered into an unprecedented number of international agreements, which undoubtedly limit its legal freedom of action. Many of the forces of interdependence and globalization that affect Europe have also exerted impacts on US behavior, generating unprecedented involvement of the United States, since World War II, in international cooperation (Keohane 1984, Keohane and Nye 2001). So the contrast between the United States and Europe should not be overdrawn.

Nevertheless, with few exceptions the United States has been much more reluctant than members of the European Union to limit its external sovereignty: that is, to agree to processes that could create binding legal commitments on the United States, not subject to a veto. When the NATO treaty was being negotiated in 1948, members of the Senate were insistent that the constitutional prerogatives of the Congress to declare war not be abridged. Hence Article 5 of the North Atlantic Treaty only commits the members, in the event of an armed attack on any of the parties in Europe or North America, to "assist the Party or Parties so attacked by taking forthwith, individually and in concert with other Parties, such action as it deems necessary, including the use of armed force, to restore and maintain the security of the North Atlantic area." An earlier phrase, "such military or other action as may be necessary," was altered on the grounds that it might imply automatic military action (Kaplan 1984, Kaplan 1994).

The United States continued to be cautious about accepting external authority structures after the Cold War. For example, in the negotiations of the late 1990s in Rome on a treaty establishing an International Criminal Court ICC, the United States unsuccessfully sought a veto by the Security Council over the exercise of jurisdiction over some types of cases by the ICC prosecutor. The United States also protested vehemently against the provision in the Rome treaty that would give the ICC jurisdiction over nationals of states not party to the treaty. The chief U.S. negotiator, David Scheffer, maintained that "a fundamental principle of international treaty law is that only states that are party to a treaty should be bound by its terms." In these and other ways, the United States sought "to preserve appropriate sovereign decision making in connection with obligations to cooperate with the court" (Scheffer 1999: 18; 15).

The most important exception to U.S. defense of external sovereignty is its agreement to the charter of the World Trade Organization in 1994. Unlike its predecessor, the GATT, WTO's dispute settlement provisions provide for binding settlement of disputes, without a state veto. Hence a panel, supported by the Appellate Body of the WTO, can legally interpret international law in a way that expands the obligations of members, without receiving their assent. However, unlike the rulings of the European Court of Justice, WTO rulings are not, in general, enforced by national courts. The WTO, therefore, cannot require a state to change its rules, but rather can only authorize states whose trading interests have been damaged by its actions, to retaliate.

Since 1787 Europe and the United States have changed places on the issue of sovereignty. European states led the way in the Rome negotiations, opposing United States' efforts to protect sovereign prerogatives. The United States, formerly critical of unitary sovereignty and unable in key respects to exercise external sovereignty early in its history, now is one of sovereignty's chief defenders.

This turnabout is surely due in substantial measure to the facts that Britain and France were world powers in 1787, whereas only the United States is genuinely a world power in 2002. Sovereignty is associated historically with the use of military force, and more robust forms of sovereignty come naturally to more powerful states. In his article explaining the U.S. position on the ICC, Ambassador Scheffer emphasized the unique geopolitical role of the United States:

> It is simply and logically untenable to expose the largest deployed military force in the world, stationed across the globe to help maintain international peace and security and to defend U.S. allies and friends, to the jurisdiction of a criminal court the U.S.

Government has not yet joined and whose authority over U.S. citizens the United States does not recognize. No other country, not even our closest military allies, has anywhere near as many troops and military assets deployed globally as does the United States (Scheffer 1999: 18).

Yet this essentially Realist explanation is not sufficient. Europe is more enmeshed than the United States in networks of interdependence, so European governments have more incentives to build institutions that cope with interdependence. These institutions, in turn, create further incentives to treat sovereignty as relational and pool it, rather than to treat it as an attribute of the state, to be hoarded. Furthermore, the different values and institutions of Europe and the United States also help to shape different views of sovereignty now, as they did at the Founding (Bukovansky 1997). A combination of different social identities, different levels of interdependence, and vastly contrasting geopolitical roles has created a sharp divergence between the views of sovereignty held by European governments and by the United States. I will speculate on some of the consequences of this divergence in Section IV below.

III.   IS THE EUROPEAN UNION A MODEL FOR TROUBLED SOCIETIES?

The European Union is a success; but is it a model? Could the European experience have a major impact on world order through the force of example? In the 1960s a considerable literature emerged discussing whether other areas of the world could imitate successful European efforts at economic and political integration. Unfortunately, however, the answer seemed to be a resounding "no." Experiments at political integration in the Americas and Africa have often failed, and have never even come close to the degree of institutionalization reached in Europe. Europe is not a model in the sense that its success can be replicated elsewhere.

But Europe could be a model in another way. Its movement away from classic conceptions of external sovereignty may create some space for institutional innovation elsewhere. The European Union demonstrates that success in the contemporary world can be achieved without state sovereignty. France, the Netherlands, and Spain are quite successful nation-states, although they no longer hold the traditional sovereign prerogatives of legal supremacy, coinage of money, and genuinely independent military forces able to wage war. After World War II, Germany regained its independence only as a "semi-sovereign state," in Peter Katzenstein's felicitous phrase (Katzenstein 1987). Its sovereignty was institutionally limited by the Paris Agreements of 1954, which prevented it from developing nuclear, biological or chemical weapons and assigned German forces to NATO's integrated command (Joffe 1987; Kugler 1993). Yet Germany is a respected, important country that plays an important role in Europe and in the world. It exercises what Chayes and Chayes refer to as "the new sovereignty," by operating effectively within international regimes. Engagement, as they argue, becomes a source of strength rather than an entanglement to be avoided.

The point is that accepting a matrix of norms, rules, practices and organizations is not necessarily a mark of weakness. On the contrary, doing so can be a sign of strength, self-confidence and sophistication about how to achieve security and welfare for one's citizens in a globalizing world.

The world today has many troubled societies, which are unable on their own to create order due to unfavorable social, political or economic circumstances. Countries from Afghanistan to Zimbabwe, and from Macedonia to Somalia, find themselves beset by civil strife. Often ethnic conflict aggravates the situation.

Troubled societies are often unable to create order without external assistance. They are often afflicted by conflict and abuses of human rights that drastically reduce levels of trust and willingness to compromise. Groups that seize sovereign power are likely to use it ruthlessly for the reasons Hobbes describes: fear of what others will do if they are given an opportunity. Even if new sovereign rulers were entirely benign and public-spirited, it would be difficult for them to make credible promises to act accordingly, especially since experiences such as that of Rwanda show that moderate leaders can sometimes quickly be eliminated by ruthless extremists. Unconditional sovereign independence creates "winner-take all" situations.

It might be possible to devise a domestic institutional formula that would assure responsible use of sovereignty by the government of a troubled society. Consociationalism, as defined by Arend Lijphart and discussed by David Wippman, is one possibility (Lijphart 1977; Wippmann 1998). Electoral institutions, as Donald Horowitz has argued, can be constructed to provide incentives to politicians to mobilize support across ethnic lines (Horowitz 1985). But institutional arrangements for consociationalism or to encourage cross-ethnic political mobilization have often broken down. As Wippman and Horowitz both admit, prospects for success of such domestic institutional solutions are mixed at best. Without trust, the parties cannot make enduring credible commitments.

Purely internal measures are consistent with classic external sovereignty; but they are unlikely to work in many troubled societies. To such societies, the European model can be useful as a strategy for order in two distinct ways. First, it shows that there are gradations in sovereignty: it is not a matter of "all or nothing." The current members of the European Union gradually accepted restraints on their external freedom of action, in return for the benefits of cooperation. By analogy, troubled societies could accept external constraints on their freedom of action, in return for credible institutions that protected life, liberty and property. Except for a small, self-serving elite, such institutions would be a good deal—as long as they themselves included guarantees against abuse by the powerful states that served as their sponsors. A requirement that the external authority only act by near-consensus decision making after laborious bureaucratic processes—for which the European Union is surely a model—would help make it more credible that outside assistance would not be abused in the interests of a particular state or small group of states. No assurances, of course, can be perfect; but if the alternative is unending chaos and civil violence, taking imperfect assurances from external institutions seems a good bet.

The second way in which the European Union can be a model for troubled societies is that it demonstrates that regaining sovereignty need not be one's long-term objective. The assumption has been generally made, since the delegitimation of colonialism, that any tutelary or trusteeship arrangements were only legitimate if they were presented as means toward achieving full sovereignty. But full sovereignty has been shown to be a disaster for the Cypruses, Somalias, and Afghanistans of the world. It was also a disaster for Germany, and the world, between 1933 and 1945. The European and American response was not to revive full German sovereignty as soon as possible, but quite the contrary: to constrain and limit it through international institutions constructed by, and responsible to, other great powers. The European experience suggests that the Afghans should not necessarily seek a sovereign Afghanistan to fight over among themselves. Instead, Afghans and their friends should try to design institutions for Afghanistan that would enable external authorities to maintain order, and reinforce the credibility of internal promises, while leading to substantial degrees of domestic sovereignty (Keohane 2003).

An obvious objection to this argument is that contemporary troubled societies will only learn to accept pooled sovereignty after they have gone through internecine warfare as severe as that experienced in Europe between the 16th and the 20th centuries. Fatalistically to accept this view, however, would be to render quixotic the study of history and politics and to nullify Santayana's famous epigram that "those who cannot remember the past are condemned to repeat it" (Andrews 1993: 409).

One need not place one's faith entirely in learning by the inhabitants of troubled society—admittedly a weak reed, since people seem to learn more from their own experiences than from those of others. People in western and central Europe, however, have learned from history, and they can not only seek to persuade their brethren to the southeast but use their power resources to make "offers that cannot be refused." In the Balkans the EU can make credible promises to provide substantial benefits to countries that respect human rights and international borders. Indeed, the prospect of eventual membership in the EU is a particularly effective inducement to democratic practices (Schimmelfennig 2001). Through institutions such as the Organization for Security and Cooperation in Europe (OSCE), Europeans may even be able to teach better practices, internally and externally, to the governments of the Balkan region (Ratner 2000). Those governments are hardly likely to accept such improved practices out of the goodness of their hearts, but the economic and political benefits that could come from being admitted into at least the penumbra of the European Union could, if handled well, provide incentives for improved behavior.

I conclude that Europe's successful experience with pooled sovereignty could have a significant impact on world order. Obviously, European institutional arrangements cannot be applied unchanged to societies such as Afghanistan and Somalia, and I am not suggesting that European practices can be easily adapted to troubled societies. As I have emphasized, forceful intervention as well as example may be required, if credible institutional arrangements are to be constructed. Nevertheless, the principle—that classical sovereignty is not a necessary attribute for successful societies in the modern world—is one that Europeans are well-equipped to endorse.

IV. THE EURO-AMERICAN SOVEREIGNTY DIVERGENCE AND WORLD ORDER

A premise of this article is that world order is enhanced by effective cooperation between Europe and the United States. If that cooperation were to suffer, world order would suffer as well. Unfortunately, the movement in Europe toward pooled sovereignty, and the resistance of the United States to a comparable movement, have created a divergence in conceptions of sovereignty between Europe and the United States, as sketched in Sections I and II.

If decisiveness is crucial, external sovereignty remains the primary political asset for the state. It needs to be able to act quickly, without warning, and in coordinated fashion—none of which is easy with allies. The war on terrorism proclaimed by the United States after September 11 naturally reinforces America's commitment to a modernist, classical conception of external sovereignty, linked traditionally to military power.

This effect, however, may be only part of the story. America's commitment to a modernist view of sovereignty is certainly not a product of September 11, since it predates the terrorist attacks. Indeed, this conception of sovereignty may have partly helped to shape the response of the United States to these events. At the very outset of the crisis, the attacks on New York and Washington were framed by the United States, and by most commentators in the United States, regardless of political affiliation, as acts requiring a combined military and political response. European commentators, on the other hand, seemed much more inclined to emphasize police work and the operation of criminal justice systems.

To some extent these different framings of the issues were surely due to the fact that the United States was the chief protagonist. The state that has been attacked, and that has soldiers at risk, seeks to use the most effective possible measures to defeat its opponents. Yet the different views of sovereignty characteristic of the United States and Europe may have also played a role. American commitment to modernist external sovereignty puts an emphasis on independence and effectiveness: state sovereignty in a bourgeois society is legitimated, above all, by demonstrations that the state is both necessary and effective in protecting residents of its territory from physical harm. Europe, by contrast, has adopted a conception of pooled sovereignty as a resource for cooperation, under conditions of minimal threats to physical security. Political leaders used to such practices find it difficult to adopt dramatically opposite modes of action when dealing with other parts of the world.

Conceptions of sovereignty are linked so closely to domestic structures that it is difficult to untangle the role of ideas from that of political organization and practice. Several decades ago, Kenneth N. Waltz (1967: 308) argued that domestic structure made the United States more effective than the United Kingdom in foreign policy. In a similar vein, Henry A. Kissinger contrasted a visionary foreign policy with one of bureaucratic management, lamenting that in the latter process "success consists of moving the administrative machinery to the point of decision, leaving relatively little energy for analyzing the decision's merits" (Kissinger 1969: 95).

Writing in the era of Anthony Eden, Harold Macmillan, and Harold Wilson, Waltz may have erred in attributing British indecisiveness to political structure. The United Kingdom certainly acted decisively in the Falklands War, in Iraq, and in response to the terrorist attacks of September 11. But the contrast that Waltz drew between the United States and the United Kingdom is surely applicable to the United States and the European Union. Tremendous energy is required in the EU to "move the administrative machinery to the point of decision," and a reactive, disjointed policy is the natural result. The pooling of sovereignty works well for the internal common market, which thrives on what Charles E. Lindblom (1965) once called "the science of muddling through." But it does not facilitate innovative and decisive strategic action outside of the EU's borders. Instead, the inevitable divergence of interests among Europe's states leads to a policy of quarrel and compromise, in which external policies emerge as a result more of internal politics than a coherent strategic design.

Such a pattern obviously characterizes the EU's relations with its aspiring members. Asymmetries of power, and the notable absence of alternatives for countries of central and eastern Europe, minimize the costs to the EU of its contorted decision-making process and grudging policies. Governments of the new members can be annoyed, but they have to accept the terms and processes laid down by the EU. On trade issues, contorted EU decision making can lead to stubborn persistence in retaining policies that are in conflict with World Trade Organization (WTO) rules, such as the European policy on bananas of the 1990s. External assertiveness is not precluded by internal incoherence, even if decisiveness and innovation may be strongly discouraged.

On military-political issues, Europe has been unable to act decisively. Dealing with devious enemies, such as Slobodan Milosevic in 1995, clearly requires more single-mindedness than the EU could muster. In this context, the European conception of pooled sovereignty fits comfortably with the reality that decisive action is structurally impossible, and with the diplomatic ideology that all issues are negotiable.

Different conceptions of sovereignty have implications for views of legitimacy. In normative political theory the concept of legitimacy refers to "a normative belief by an actor that a rule or institution ought to be obeyed" (Hurd 1999: 381). Since legitimacy refers to beliefs about obedience, it confers authority: institutions that have widespread legitimacy are authoritative. Authority implies power. Indeed, authority can be seen as socially legitimized power, which is much cheaper to exercise than illegitimate power, since the latter requires continual coercion and appeals to self-interest (Hurd 1999: 401).

Classical modernist conceptions of external sovereignty focus on the legitimacy of a government with its own citizens or subjects. To act decisively in foreign affairs requires voluntary support from the citizenry. Machiavelli famously advocated citizen rather than mercenary armies, not merely as a means of self-defense but also of aggrandizement (Machiavelli 1531/1962; Hulliung 1983). The Bush Administration has very effectively deployed the symbols of sovereignty to build popular support for its war on terrorism in the United States.

Conceptions of pooled sovereignty, on the contrary, emphasize the legitimacy of one's practices with one's partners. Leaders, and bureaucracies, need to act appropriately in light of prevailing expectations in the community of which one is a part. In its dealings with Brussels the United Kingdom has discovered the costs of incurring opprobrium from behaving in ways that are viewed by others as inappropriate. To do so can create severe diplomatic liabilities when one's bureaucrats and diplomats are seeking accommodations on a thousand small issues, not necessarily of principle but important to particular domestic constituencies. Pooled sovereignty therefore encourages the "rationalist and unheroic" arts of bureaucratic compromise (Schumpeter 1942: 137) rather than the heroic stance of the visionary national leader.

These different conceptions of sovereignty resonate with American and European publics. The United States public often holds sensible general sentiments about international cooperation, but it is insular and poorly informed about foreign policy (Nye 2002: 132–136). It is relatively easy for American leaders to persuade the public, in a crisis, to "rally around the flag," at least if the crisis is not an extended and painful one. President Bush has deployed a moralistic rhetoric of good and evil, quite consistent with America's conception of itself as a chosen nation, and has dismissed or ignored foreign criticism of U.S. policies. To Europeans, by contrast, Bush seems unwilling to engage in reasonable persuasion, which models of pooled sovereignty recommend and even glorify.

Since the "death of NATO" has been pronounced so many times before, one should be cautious. After the end of the Cold War, NATO dumbfounded those who thought it was obsolete by restructuring itself for new missions, as in the former Yugoslavia (Tuschoff 1999; Wallander 2000). Ties of interests and fundamental values are reinforced, in transatlantic relations, by common institutions. But it is important to note that the sources of the widening Euro-American breach do not simply lie in the different roles played by the United States and its allies in world politics, although those differences are important. The sources lie more deeply, in the nature of their domestic societies and their state structures, and in their very different conceptions of sovereignty. America's modernist conception of external sovereignty reinforces its leaders' tendencies to strike heroic poses, satisfy only domestic constituencies, and seek to act with decisive military force. Europe's conception of pooled sovereignty combines with its political structure and practices of bureaucratic accommodation to define its identity in world politics as that of creative negotiator and model for peaceful coexistence.

In the best of all worlds, these different orientations would be complementary, as in some ways, they were during the Cold War. The United States took the lead in military preparations and was more willing than Europe to confront the Soviet Union; European politicians were sometimes more subtle in working with the socialist countries to defuse tension, and in moderating American moralism. By analogy, in the war against terrorism we might expect a division of labor, in which the United States would act boldly and Europeans would be the chorus—sometimes applauding, sometimes complaining—to the American hero.

Yet during the Cold War the Soviets threatened Europe more directly than the United States; so European leaders had to defer, in the end, to the United States to avoid American disengagement. Now, Europeans might conclude that being tied to the American war-machine, and to America's support for Israel, simply made them targets for attack by Islamic fundamentalists and their supporters. And the United States might decide that deferring to European sensibilities was, on balance, a hindrance to effective warfare against implacable enemies. For different reasons, therefore, both sides might favor a parting of the ways.

The different conceptions of sovereignty held in Europe and America would not be the fundamental cause of such a rupture. Divergences in interests, values, and social structures would be more fundamental. But conceptions of sovereignty are a marker for more fundamental divergences—an indicator, like the "canary in the coal mine." These indicators should make us take more seriously the possibility that the EU and the United States would take fundamentally different paths.

CONCLUSION

European nation-states, which gave birth to the concept of external state sovereignty, have effectively renounced it. The United States, which rejected unitary sovereignty and had difficulty implementing external sovereignty, has now embraced the latter concept, albeit with some concessions to interdependence and globalization. Like speed skaters switching lanes in the middle of a race, the United States and Europe have reversed their positions on the question of sovereignty.

One result of Europe's conversion to a conception of limited and pooled sovereignty is unambiguously positive for world order. Europe can serve as a model for troubled societies, unable to create order on their own. The other result of Europe's movement toward pooled sovereignty, coupled with America's strong reluctance to do the same, is less benign: different conceptions of sovereignty could make it even more difficult for Europeans and Americans to understand one another. Differences in geopolitical roles and interests, societal values, and the role of state security institutions, all pull the United States and Europe apart. The language of sovereignty has long been the language of diplomacy; but in this sense, the United States and Europe now speak different languages.

From a normative standpoint, a divorce between America and Europe would likely be disastrous for order in world politics. Genuine progress on almost every issue facing the world today requires cooperation by liberal democracies, whose center of gravity remains in the Atlantic area. A transatlantic rupture would make it harder to engage in mutually beneficial cooperation on issues ranging from tax coordination to environmental protection to criminal justice.

Indeed, the need of both sides for each other—to foster prosperity, maintain the quality of the natural environment, and to prevent dangerous chaos in other areas of the world—is one source of reassurance that a European-American rupture will be prevented. Such a benign result, however, cannot be taken for granted. At this point in history it is the responsibility of intellectuals with a sense of history to emphasize the continuing gains from European-American cooperation, even as we analyze the sources of divergence and discord. Although we cannot determine whether a society speaks in the language of external or of pooled sovereignty, we can try at least to translate between them.

BIBLIOGRAPHY

Andrews, Robert. 1993. *The Columbia Dictionary of Quotations.* New York: Columbia University Press.

Bailyn, Bernard. 1967. *The Ideological Origins of the American Revolution.* Cambridge: the Belknap Press of Harvard University Press.

Bemis, Samuel Flagg. 1949. *John Quincy Adams and the Foundations of American Foreign Policy.* New York: Knopf.

Bodin, Jean. 1577. *Les Six livres de la republique.* Paris.

Bukovansky, Mlada. 1997. American identity and neutral rights from independence to the War of 1812. *International Organization,* vol. 51, no. 2 (spring): 209–243.

Bull, Hedley. 1977. *The Anarchical Society: A Study of Order in World Politics.* New York: Columbia University Press.

Burl, A. L. 1961. *The United States, Great Britain, and British North America: From the Revolution to the Establishment of Peace After the War of 1812.* New York: Russell & Russell.

Combs, Gerald A. 1970. *The Jay Treaty: Political Background of the Founding Fathers.* Berkeley: University of California Press.

Cooper, Robert. 1996. *The Post-Modern State and the World Order.* London: Demos.

Chayes, Abram and Antonia Handler Chayes. 1995. *The New Sovereignty: Compliance with International Regulatory Agreements.* Cambridge: Harvard University Press.

Deudney, Daniel. 1995. "The Philadelphian system: sovereignty, arms control and balance of power in the American states-union, circa 1787–1861. *International Organization,* vol. 49, no. 2 (spring): 191–228.

Grubb, Michael, et al. 1993. *The Earth Summit Agreements: A Guide and Assessment.* London: Royal Institute of International Affairs.

Hamilton, Alexander, John Jay and James Madison. 1787–88/1961. *The Federalist.* Ed. Jacob E. Cooke. Middletown: Wesleyan University Press.

Hoffmann, Stanley. 1987. *Janus and Minerva: Essays in the Theory and Practice of International Politics.* Boulder: Westview.

Holbrooke, Richard. 1998. *To End a War.* New York: Random House.

Horowitz, Donald. 1985. *Ethnic Groups in Conflict* (Berkeley and Los Angeles: University of California Press).

Horsman, Reginald. 1962. *The Causes of the War of 1812.* Philadelphia: University of Pennsylvania Press.

Howe, Geoffrey. 1990. "Britain's place in the world." *International Affairs,* vol. 66, no. 4 (October): 675–695.

Hulliung, Mark. 1983. *Citizen Machiavelli.* Princeton: Princeton University Press.

Hurd, Ian. 1999. Legitimacy and authority in international politics. *International Organization* 53–2 (spring): 379–408.

Jackson, John H. 1998. *The World Trade Organization: Constitution and Jurisprudence.* London: Royal Institute of International Affairs.

Jensen, Merrill. 1950. *The New Nation: A History of the United Stated During the Confederation, 1781–1789.* New York: Knopf.

Joffe, Joseph. 1987. *The Limited Partnership: Europe, the United States and the Burdens of Alliance.* Cambridge, MA: Ballinger Publishing.

Kaplan, Lawrence S. 1972. *Colonies Into Nation: American Diplomacy, 1763–1801*. New York: Macmillan.

Kaplan, Lawrence. 1984. *The United States and NATO: the Formative Years*. Lexington: University Press of Kentucky.

Kaplan, Lawrence. 1994. *NATO and the United States: the Enduring Alliance*. (New York: Twayne Publishers.

Katzenstein, Peter J. 1987. *Policy and Politics in West Germany: The Growth of a Semi-Sovereign State*. Philadelphia: Temple University Press.

Keohane, Nannerl O. 1980. *Philosophy and the State in France: the Renaissance to the Enlightenment*. Princeton: Princeton University Press.

Keohane, Robert O. 1984. *After Hegemony: Cooperation and Discord in the World Political Economy*. Princeton: Princeton University Press.

Keohane, Robert O. 2003. "Political Authority after Intervention: Gradations in Sovereignty." Forthcoming in J. L. Holzgrefe and Robert O. Keohane, eds., *Humanitarian Intervention: Principles, Institutions and Change*. Cambridge: Cambridge University Press.

Keohane, Robert O. and Joseph S. Nye, Jr. 2001. *Power and Interdependence*. New York: Addison-Wesley Longman, 3rd edition.

Kissinger, Henry A. 1969. *American Foreign Policy: Three Essays*. New York: Norton.

Koh, Harold Hongju. 1990. *The National Security Constitution: Sharing Power after the Iran-Contra Affair*. New Haven: Yale University Press.

Krasner, Stephen D. 1999. *Sovereignty: Organized Hypocrisy*. Princeton: Princeton University Press.

Kugler, Richard. 1993. *Commitment to Purpose: How Alliance Partnership Won the Cold War*. Santa Monica: RAND.

Lijphart, Arend. 1977. *Democracy in Plural Societies*. New Haven: Yale University Press.

Lindblom, Charles E. 1965. *The Intelligence of Democracy*. New York: Free Press.

Machiavelli, Niccolò, 1531/1962. *The Discourses*. In Max Lerner, ed., *The Prince and the Discourses*. New York: Modern Library.

Machiavelli, Niccolò. 1532/1962. In Max Lerner, ed., *The Prince and the Discourses*. New York: Modern Library.

Mathews, Jessica T. 2001. "Estranged Partners." *Foreign Policy*, November–December: 48–53.

Mattingly, Garrett. 1955. *Renaissance Diplomacy*. Baltimore: Penguin Books.

Nye, Joseph S., Jr. 2002. *The Paradox of American Power*. New York: Oxford University Press.

Oksenberg, Michel. 2001. "The issue of sovereignty in the Asian historical context." In Stephen D. Krasner, ed., *Problematic Sovereignty: Contested Rules and Political Possibilities*. New York: Columbia University Press.

Ratner, Steven. 2000. "Does international law matter in preventing ethnic conflict?" *New York University Journal of International Law and Politics*, vol. 32, no. 3: 591–724.

Scheffer, David J. 1999. "The United States and the International Criminal Court." *American Journal of International Law* 93–1 (January): 12–22.

Schimmelfennig, Frank. Liberal norms, rhetorical action and the enlargement of the EU. *International Organization*, vol. 55, no. 1 (winter): 47–80.

Schumpeter, Joseph A. 1942. *Capitalism, Socialism and Democracy*. New York: Harper and Row.

Silber, Laura and Allan Little. 1996. *Yugoslavia: Death of a Nation.* New York: Penguin Books.

Slaughter, Anne-Marrie. 2001. "In Memoriam: Abram Chayes." *Harvard Law Review,* vol. 114, no. 3 (January): 682–89.

Sørsenen, George. 2001. *Changes in Statehood: the Transformation of International Relations.* Hampshire and New York: Palgrave.

Tuschhoff, Christian. 1999. "Alliance cohesion and peaceful change in NATO." in Helga Haftendorn, Robert O. Keohane, and Celeste A. Wallander, eds., *Imperfect Unions: Security Institutions over Time and Space.* Oxford: Oxford University press.

Van Oudenaren, John. 2001. "E Pluribus Confusio: Living with the EU's Structural Incoherence." *The National Interest* (fall): 23–36.

Wallander, Celeste A. 2000. "NATO after the Cold War." *International Organization,* vol. 54, no. 2 (Autumn): 705–735.

Waltz, Kenneth N. 1967. *Foreign Policy and Democratic Politics: The American and British Experiences.* Boston: Little Brown.

Weiler, J. H. H. 1999. *The Constitution of Europe.* 1999. Cambridge: Cambridge University Press.

Wippman, David. 1998. "Practical and Legal Constraints on Internal Power Sharing." In David Wippman, ed., *International Law and Ethnic Conflict.* Ithaca: Cornell University Press.

Zimmerman, J. F. 1925. *Impressment of American Seamen.* New York: Columbia University Studies in History, Economics and Public Law.

⟿ PART FIVE ⟿

Public Opinion, Policy Legitimacy, and Sectional Conflict

These next four essays focus on the influence of the diffuse pressures of public opinion, reigning political images, and societal interests on American foreign policy. As such they share elements of several of the approaches in other sections. They share a general view that periods of American foreign policy are punctuated by crystallized sets of images and publicly held views about the proper direction of American foreign policy. Yet each provides a distinctive analytical cut into these domestic structures and processes.

Michael Roskin focuses on shifting generational views or paradigms of foreign policy. Each generation, Roskin argues, carries with it a set of strategic conventional wisdoms that are formed by a decisive historical event and that guide public orientations toward policy. The Pearl Harbor paradigm, according to Roskin, was interventionist. This view had many sources but took form in the traumatic events of Pearl Harbor and the Second World War. The paradigm reflected an imagery of the international system and a set of lessons to which American leaders must attend. Most important was the lesson that aggression must be met head on and not appeased. The imagery of Pearl Harbor took deep root and was not dislodged, Roskin argues, until the failures of Vietnam seemingly discredited its interventionist orientation. With Vietnam came a new set of lessons, wrapped in a paradigm of nonintervention. One is left to speculate about the mechanisms by which these changes occur and the lessons become entrenched.

Alexander L. George also focuses on diffuse sets of public views on foreign policy as powerful forces that set the terms of choice within government. George argues that government officials are not free to conduct foreign policy as they choose. Officials can sustain foreign policy only when it is developed within a consensus. Consequently, government officials build support for their policy. In analyzing the importance of domestic support George advances the notion of policy legitimacy, a measure of the degree to which the president has convinced Congress and the public of the soundness of his policy goals. The legitimation of policy, according to George, requires the president to persuade the public of the feasibility and desirability of that policy. These imperatives of domestic legitimacy set limits on what government officials can propose and sustain in the realm of foreign policy. In invoking the notion of legitimacy, therefore, George has focused on a particular mechanism in which a democratic society exerts an influence on the conduct of foreign policy.

In "Business Versus Public Influence in U.S. Foreign Policy" Lawrence R. Jacobs and Benjamin I. Page ask the critical question: who most influences U.S. foreign policy? It is epistemic communities of experts that possess the specialization to objectively analyze an increasingly complex global environment, organized pressure groups and, especially, businesses in order to advance their own narrow interests, or the mass public which exerts its power on politicians anxious to win their support? Jacobs and Page rely primarily upon multivariate regression analyses to test the independent variables. Their results indicate that business has a strong, consistent, and, at times, lopsided influence upon U.S. foreign policy and tend to confirm the theoretical expectations and case study research of the organized interest group literature in international relations. However, in keeping with calls for multi-causal research, these results also suggest that three of the most prominent lines of analysis of foreign policy—the interest group, epistemic community, and public opinion approaches—each have some merit.

Peter Trubowitz looks at the sources of political conflict in America foreign policy. Most analysts look to ideological or institutional cleavages at the national level as the most important sources of conflict over foreign policy. Taking a different approach, Trubowitz looks at geographically based sources of conflict. In an examination of Congressional voting on a variety of foreign policy issues, Trubowitz finds that sectional interests, particularly between the Northeast and South, featured prominently in Congressional debates during the Cold War. At their root, these conflicts were grounded in interregional struggles for political and economic advantage.

From Pearl Harbor to Vietnam: Shifting Generational Paradigms and Foreign Policy

Michael Roskin

United States foreign policy can be seen as a succession of strategic conventional wisdoms, or *paradigms*, on whether the country's defense should start on the near or far side of the oceans. An interventionist paradigm favors the latter, a noninter-

Michael Roskin, "From Pearl Harbor to Vietnam: Shifting Generational Paradigms and Foreign Policy." *Political Science Quarterly* 89 (Fall 1974): 563–588. Reprinted with permission.

ventionist paradigm, the former. This article argues that each elite American generation comes to favor one of these orientations by living through the catastrophe brought on by the application ad absurdum of the opposite paradigm at the hands of the previous elite generation. Thus the bearers of the "Pearl Harbor paradigm" (themselves reacting to the deficiencies of the interwar "isolationism") eventually drove interventionism into the ground in Vietnam, giving rise to a noninterventionist "Vietnam paradigm." These paradigms seem to shift at approximately generational intervals, possibly because it takes that long for the bearers of one orientation, formed by the dramatic experiences of their young adulthood, to come to power and eventually misapply the lessons of their youth.

Recently much foreign-policy discussion has focused on economic interpretation of United States actions, bureaucratic politics and malfunctions, and executive-legislative relations. While such approaches have made interesting contributions to the field, none have been able to gather together seemingly disparate elements of foreign policy into an overall view that explains this behavior over several decades. The reason is that these popular approaches consistently downplay or even ignore the key element to such an overall view: the strategic assumptions held by decision-making elites—that is, who defines what as strategic; why; and when.[1] In other words, these approaches failed to consider that in certain periods United States policy makers deem much of the globe to be worth fighting for, while at other times they regard most of the world with indifference.

THE CONCEPT OF *PARADIGM*

The concepts of *paradigm* and *paradigm shift* are borrowed from Thomas Kuhn, who used them to describe intellectual growth in the natural sciences. Kuhn called paradigms "universally recognized scientific achievements that for a time provide model problems and solutions to a community of practitioners."[2] A paradigm is the basic assumption of a field; acceptance of it is mandatory for practitioners (e.g., those who do not accept the conservation of energy are not physicists; those who do not accept the gas laws are not chemists). Practitioners, having accepted the paradigm, then typically engage in "normal science," that is, the interpretation and detailing of the basic paradigm, which itself is not open to question.[3]

The importance of Kuhn's framework for our purposes is that it is a dynamic view: the paradigms shift. When researchers, operating under their old paradigm, begin to notice that their empirical findings do not come out the way they are supposed to, disquiet enters into the profession. Anomalies or counter-instances crop up in the research and throw the old paradigm into doubt. Then an innovator looks at the data from another angle, reformulates the basic framework, and introduces a new paradigm. Significantly, these innovators tend to be younger men who, "being little committed by prior practice to the traditional rules of normal science, are particularly likely to see that those rules no longer define a playable game and to conceive another set that can replace them."[4] The new paradigm does not triumph immediately and automatically. Now there are two competing, antithetical paradigms; each demands its separate world view. The discussants "are bound partly to talk through each other" because they are looking at the same data from differing angles.[5] The new paradigm makes progress, however, because it claims it "can solve the problems that have led the old one to a crisis."[6] The new paradigm makes particular headway among younger workers. The old practitioners may be beyond conversion; they simply die out. This "paradigm shift" is what Kuhn calls a "scientific revolution," and these "revolutions close with a total victory for one of the two opposing camps."[7]

There is one more point we must include from Kuhn. Which paradigm, the old or the new, is the "truth"? The answer is neither. The new paradigm is at best merely a closer approximation to reality. It seems to explain the data better and offers better paths to future research; it is never the last word. Wide areas of uncertainty remain, especially during the changeover period, when the data can be interpreted ambiguously. It is impossible to say when—or even if—the holders of the old paradigm are completely wrong. The profession merely comes to turn its back on them, ignoring them, leaving them out in the cold.[8]

Kuhn has suggested a theory of the innovation and diffusion of knowledge applicable to all fields, including foreign policy. The crucial difference with foreign-policy paradigms is that they are far less *verifiable* than natural-science paradigms. Students of foreign policy have only the crudest sort of verification procedure: the perception that the old paradigm has given rise to a catastrophe. More subtle perceptions of marginal dysfunctionality tend to go unnoticed (by all but a handful of critics) until the general orientation produces an unmistakable disaster.

How, then, can we adapt the Kuhnian framework to the study of United States foreign policy? The community of practitioners is an elite of persons relevant to foreign policy—both in and out of government, the latter including such opinion leaders as professors and journalists—who structure the debate for wider audiences.[9] While the relationship between mass and elite opinion in foreign policy is well beyond our scope here, most scholarly opinion holds that the mass public has only low or intermittent interest in foreign affairs. One study, for example, found more "isolationism" as one moves down the educational ladder.[10] Foreign aid has never been popular with American voters; only elite opinion sustains it. When the elite ceases to define overseas situations as threats to United States security, the mass public soon loses interest. Major American participation abroad is sustainable only when the elite has been mobilized to support it. Lose this support, and America stays home.

The content of the foreign-policy paradigm varies in detail but is generally reducible to the question of whether overseas areas "matter" to United States security. That is, should the defense of America start on the far or near side of the ocean? The Yale scholar of geopolitics Nicholas Spykman recognized the question as "the oldest issue in American foreign policy" and posed it in 1942 as well as anyone has ever done: "Shall we protect our interests by defense on this side of the water or by active participation in the lands across the oceans?"[11] The former view constitutes what we shall call a "noninterventionist" paradigm; the latter is an "interventionist" paradigm. These antithetical views shift under the impact of catastrophes which seem to prove that the old paradigm was wrong and its adherents mistaken. At that point the previous outsiders (gadflies, radicals, revisionists, etc.)

find many of their views accepted as mainstream thinking; their critique becomes the new framework.

Our model resembles Kuhn's but with the important provision that neither old nor new foreign-policy paradigms have much intrinsic validity because neither can be objectively verified in an indeterminate world. Instead of verified, a new foreign-policy paradigm is merely internalized. Counterinstances are ignored; the range of conceivable strategic situations is narrowed to exclude possible alternate paradigms. It may be impossible to distinguish whether this process is emotional or rational, affective or cognitive. The acrimony accompanying foreign-policy paradigm shifts, however, suggests a strong emotional component. Chances are that a member of the American elite who as a young person witnessed the events leading up to Pearl Harbor has developed a very definite orientation to foreign policy, an interventionist one, the assumptions of which are not open for discussion. Similarly, by the early 1970s the interventionist views of Walt Rostow, Dean Rusk, and William Bundy produced mostly irritation (if not outright vituperation) on the part of younger foreign-policy thinkers.

It is here that we add the concept of generation to the Kuhnian model. Political scientists have not looked much at generations in their analyses. Some hold that to separate out a "political generation" is to reify an abstract and nebulous concept. People are born every day and constitute more of a continuum than a segment. The German sociologist Karl Mannheim agreed that generation is a reification, but no more so than the concept of social class, which is indispensable for much modern analysis.[12]

An elite generation freezes upon either an interventionist or noninterventionist paradigm usually after some foreign-policy catastrophe wrought by the application of the opposite paradigm. During a transition period the two paradigms clash. Because they are antithetical, compromise is impossible. The two generations with their different assumptions talk past each other. Eventually the new paradigm wins because it gains more younger adherents, while the advocates of the old paradigm retire and die off. The new paradigm triumphs not so much on an intellectual basis as on an actuarial one.

THE PEARL HARBOR PARADIGM

It may be profitable to look at the foreign-policy paradigm as having a natural life—a birth, a period of growth, and a death. The birth is characterized by a mounting criticism of the old paradigm and then by the conversion of a large portion of the elite to the new paradigm. An event "proves" the old paradigm wrong, as it did to Senator Arthur H. Vandenburg, a staunch isolationist whose turning to interventionism "took firm form on the afternoon of the Pearl Harbor attack. That day ended isolationism for any realist."[13] In honor of Vandenburg's conversion we can label this interventionist orientation the "Pearl Harbor paradigm."

Pearl Harbor, of course, was merely the culmination of an increasingly heated argument in the interwar period between the dominant noninterventionists and interventionist Cassandras. We could also call the latter view the Munich paradigm, the Ethiopian paradigm, or even the Manchurian paradigm.[14] But the Pearl Harbor attack clinched the interventionists' argument by demonstrating they were "right" in warning that an isolated America was impossible. The isolationists either shut up or quickly changed sides.[15] The handful of holdouts, such as those who charged Roosevelt with dragging the country into war, were by and large simply ignored.

The most clearly visible starting point for the rise of the Pearl Harbor paradigm was Secretary of State Stimson's 1932 "nonrecognition" of Japanese expansion into Manchuria. Thereafter concern slowly grew among the American elite that aggressive powers abroad could eventually threaten America. The growth of this concern among younger persons is important for two reasons: First, people who were in their twenties during the late 1930s were less committed to the then-prevailing noninterventionism of the older generation. Accordingly, more of the younger group were open to formulate a new paradigm—an interventionist one. Second, although some older elite members may have been similarly alarmed at overseas threats, it was mostly the younger generation that would staff foreign-policy positions in future decades.

By the time war broke out in Europe in 1939, elite opinion was starting to split. The formation of two committees expressed this division: the isolationist America First and the increasingly interventionist Committee to Defend America by Aiding the Allies. On December 7, 1941, the interventionists could (and did) say, "I told you so," and then enshrined their argument—permanently, they thought—as the basic assumption of American foreign policy: If we do not nip aggression in the bud, it will eventually grow and involve us. By not stopping aggressors immediately, you encouraged them. Apart from the moral issue of helping a victim of aggression, you are also setting up the first line of defense of your own country. Accordingly, altruism and self-interest merge.

The discredited "isolationists" could only meekly retort that in principle at least, the defense of the United States did not start on the other side of the globe, for that merely guarantees American participation in wars that were not intrinsically hers. The last gasps of the remaining noninterventionism came in the 1951 debate to limit troops in Europe and the 1954 Bricker amendment to restrict executive agreements. Occasional whiffs of preinterventionist views could be sensed in debates over foreign aid.

The interesting aspect of the Pearl Harbor paradigm, however, was its duration long past World War II. The interventionist orientation had been so deeply internalized in the struggle with the isolationists that it did not lapse with the Allied victory. By that time almost all sections of the globe now "mattered" to American security, particularly as a new hostile power—the Soviet Union—seemed bent on territorial and ideological aggrandizement. In the 1930s the fate of East Europe bothered Washington very little, but in the span of a decade East Europe became a matter of urgent American concern.[16] Not only had the Soviets inflicted brutal Hitlerlike dictatorships upon the nations of East Europe, it was taken for granted that they were preparing to do the same to West Europe and other areas. But this time America was smarter and stood prepared to stop aggression. In the span of one decade, 1945–1955, the United States committed itself to the defense of more than seventy nations.

A few quotes might suffice to demonstrate the persistence of the Pearl Harbor paradigm into the Vietnam era. Warning of a "new isolationism," Senator Thomas J. Dodd, in a 1965 floor speech, explained:

> The situation in Viet-Nam today bears many resemblances to the situation just before Munich. . . .
>
> In Viet-Nam today we are again dealing with a faraway land about which we know very little.
>
> In Viet-Nam today we are again confronted by an incorrigible aggressor, fanatically committed to the destruction of the free world, whose agreements are as worthless as Hitler's. . . .
>
> If we fail to draw the line in Viet-Nam, in short, we may find ourselves compelled to draw a defense line as far back as Seattle and Alaska, with Hawaii as a solitary out-post in mid-Pacific.[17]

Defense Secretary Robert McNamara, in commenting on Lin Piao's 1965 statement on the universal applicability of "people's war," said, "It is a program of aggression. It is a speech that ranks with Hitler's *Mein Kampf*."[18]

President Johnson too was immersed in the World War II imagery. In his 1965 Johns Hopkins speech he warned:

> The central lesson of our time is that the appetite of aggression is never satisfied. To withdraw from one battlefield means only to prepare for the next. We must say in Southeast Asia—as we did in Europe—in the words of the Bible: "Hitherto shalt thou come, but no further."[19]

In a 1966 speech to NATO parliamentarians, Senator Henry M. Jackson put it this way:

> Analogies with the past may be misleading and I would not argue that this is the 30's all over again. But looking back we think, as I am sure many of you do, that it is wise to stop aggression before the aggressor becomes strong and swollen with ambition from small successes. We think the world might have been spared enormous misfortunes if Japan had not been permitted to succeed in Manchuria, or Mussolini in Ethiopia, or Hitler in Czechoslovakia or in the Rhineland. And we think that our sacrifices in this dirty war in little Vietnam will make a dirtier and bigger war less likely.[20]

President Johnson said in a 1966 talk in New Hampshire:

> Few people realize that world peace has reached voting age. It has been twenty-one years since that day on the U.S.S. Missouri in Tokyo Bay when World War II came to an end. Perhaps it reflects poorly on our world that men must fight limited wars to keep from fighting larger wars; but that is the condition of the world. . . .
>
> We are following this policy in Vietnam because we know that the restrained use of power has for twenty-one years prevented the wholesale destruction the world faced in 1914 and again in 1939.[21]

The Pentagon Papers are replete with the World War II analogy. Among these, in a 1966 memo, Walt Rostow explained how his experience as an OSS major plotting German bomb targets taught him the importance of cutting the enemy's POL—petroleum, oil, and lubricants:

> With an understanding that simple analogies are dangerous, I nevertheless feel it is quite possible the military effects of a systematic and sustained bombing of POL in North Vietnam may be more prompt and direct than conventional intelligence analysis would suggest.[22]

Rostow seems to have retained a petroleum version of the Pearl Harbor paradigm and to have assumed that Hanoi had *Panzers* and a *Luftwaffe* that could be knocked out.

THE SPECIAL ROLE OF KENNEDY

One member of the foreign-policy elite deserves to be examined at greater length. John F. Kennedy not only internalized what we are calling the Pearl Harbor paradigm, he helped install it.[23] His 1940 best seller, *Why England Slept*, originally written [when] he was twenty-one to twenty-two, was his Harvard senior thesis. The book concerned not only Britain's interwar somnolence in the face of the German threat but posited America in the same position. Kennedy's position at that time, it is interesting to note, was in marked contrast to the isolationism of his father, who was then the United States ambassador to Britain.[24]

The *Why England Slept* of Kennedy's youth laid down a remarkably full-blown view of national security, one that Senator and later President Kennedy retained practically intact. The following were some of the important themes which first appeared in *Why England Slept* and then in his senatorial and presidential speeches:

1. Peace-loving democracy is weak in the face of expansionist totalitarianism.[25]
2. The democratic leader's role is to teach the population that isolated events form an overall pattern of aggression against them.[26]
3. Defense preparedness must be kept up, even if this means increasing defense expenditures.[27]
4. Reliance on a single-weapon defense system is dangerous; a country must have several good defense systems for flexibility.[28]
5. Civil defense measures must be instituted in advance to protect the population in case of war.[29]
6. The nation must be willing actually to go to war in the final crunch; bluffing will not suffice.[30]

In the case of Britain in the late 1930s, argued the young Kennedy, democracy simply did not take the Nazi menace seriously, and British leaders failed to point out the danger and build up defenses. British defense was overconcentrated on the fleet at the expense of the army and most importantly of the air force. Britain's civil defense was weak, particularly in antiaircraft batteries. And finally, British leaders had been so hesitant to actually apply force when needed that Hitler could not take them seriously.

Representative and later Senator Kennedy found these arguments highly applicable to the Eisenhower period, which he often compared to interwar Britain, as in this 1959 speech:

Twenty-three years ago, in a bitter debate in the House of Commons, Winston Churchill charged the British government with acute blindness to the menace of Nazi Germany, with gross negligence in the maintenance of the island's defenses, and with indifferent, indecisive leadership of British foreign policy and British public opinion. The preceding years of drift and impotency, he said, were "the years the locusts have eaten."

Since January 1953 this nation has passed through a similar period. . . . [31]

America in the 1950s, said Kennedy, refused to see the "global challenge" of Soviet penetration of the Third World. Eisenhower had let United States defense preparedness slide; a "missile gap" had appeared. America must spend more on defense: "Surely our nation's security overrides budgetary considerations. . . . Then why can we not realize that the coming years of the gap present us with a peril more deadly than any wartime danger we have ever known?"[32] The country relied on "massive retaliation" when it needed a flexible response of many options, including counterinsurgency. Kennedy accordingly opposed Republican cuts in our ground troops. And, in a 1959 interview, he emphasized that the United States must be willing to fight for Berlin:

> If we took the view which some Englishmen took, that Prague or the Sudentendeutsch were not worth a war in '38—if we took that view about Berlin, my judgment is that the West Berliners would pass into the communist orbit, and our position in West Germany and our relations with West Germany would receive a fatal blow. . . . They're fighting for New York and Paris when they struggle over Berlin.[33]

One might be tempted to dismiss Senator Kennedy's views as campaign rhetoric. But once in the presidency, Kennedy proceeded to implement them: bigger defense budgets, larger ground forces, "flexible response" (including counterinsurgency), civil defense (especially the 1961 fallout-shelter panic), and finally overt warfare in Southeast Asia. Throughout his presidency, Kennedy and his advisers stuck to the image of the Pearl Harbor paradigm. In his dramatic 1962 television address on the Soviet arms buildup in Cuba, Kennedy used his favorite analogy: "The 1930s taught us a clear lesson: aggressive conduct, if allowed to go unchecked and unchallenged, ultimately leads to war."[34] Vice-President Johnson, in a 1961 memo to Kennedy on Vietnam, wrote:

> The battle against Communism must be joined in South-east Asia with strength and determination to achieve success there—or the United States, inevitably, must surrender the Pacific and take up our defenses on our own shores.[35]

One wonders if Johnson or one of his assistants had read Spykman. Further perusal of the Pentagon Papers shows much the same evaluation of the alleged strategic importance of Vietnam; its fall was defined as a major setback to United States security.[36]

We do not here argue that Vietnam is important or unimportant to the defense of America. That is indeterminate, although within the last decade a considerable portion of elite opinion has switched from the former view to the latter. What interests us is the inability of Kennedy and his advisers to define Southeast Asia as anything but strategic.

Kennedy's age surely contributed to his highly interventionist orientation. He retained what we are calling the Pearl Harbor paradigm as a young man in his early twenties. Eisenhower, by way of contrast, was twenty-seven years older and witnessed the events that led up to American involvement in World War II as a man in his forties. It seems likely, then, that the impact of the events of the late 1930s and early 1940s was far stronger in forming Kennedy's foreign-policy orientation than Eisenhower's.

This perhaps partially explains why the Pearl Harbor paradigm eventually was applied to an extreme and why this process took about a generation. A generation of the United States elite experienced as relatively young people the momentous events leading up to Pearl Harbor. Kennedy was of this generation, which gradually surfaced into public life.[37] Each year there were more members of this generation in positions of foreign-policy leadership. The older generation retired and the proportion of this new generation increased. After about twenty years there were few members of the older generation left in the political machinery. By the time Kennedy assumed the presidency, there were few countervailing views to dilute and moderate a policy of thoroughgoing interventionism. In this sense, we can say that the Pearl Harbor paradigm "blossomed" under Kennedy, who applied it more completely than did Eisenhower.

But while Kennedy was applying the wisdom learned in his youth to its full extent—the Green Berets, the Peace Corps, the Agency for International Development, the Counterinsurgency Committee—the real world was going its own way, becoming less and less relevant to the mental constructs of American foreign-policy planners. We have then a "dysfunction" growing between policy and reality. On the one hand, we have a foreign orientation essentially frozen since the 1940s, and on the other hand, a world which defied pigeonholing into the compartments of the 1940s.

The most conspicuous indicator of this discrepancy was the persistent American inability to evaluate "communism" as no longer monolithic. Here, as with Kuhn's scientific paradigms, the data can be interpreted ambiguously in transitional periods. One side reads the data as still showing essentially a monolith, the other as a badly fractured movement. But at what point in time did it become unreasonable for United States foreign-policy planners to continue to hold the former view? Scholars had been emphasizing the Sino-Soviet split since the early 1960s,[38] but it was not until the early 1970s—after the trauma of Vietnam had set in—that reality was incorporated into policy. When communism became perceivable as nonmonolithic, under President Nixon, it perforce lost its most threatening attribute. Thus redefined, Indochina was no longer worth evaluating as a strategic prize, and American withdrawal became possible. The paradigm had shifted: Vietnam was no longer part of a gigantic pincer movement enveloping us.

After the Vietnam debacle was over, few voices could be heard advocating a return to "business as usual," that is, to continuing the interventionist paradigm. Nixon introduced a policy markedly different from that of his predecessors. It differed rhetorically in announcing to America's allies that they would have to bear primary responsibility for their defense,[39] and it differed physically in reducing United States ground forces to the point where few were available to send abroad.

(Total U.S. armed forces fell from 3.5 million in 1968 to 2.2 million in 1974; especially hard hit were the army and the marines, without whom there can be no overseas intervention.)

Just as Pearl Harbor brought with it a massive and general shift in the foreign-policy orientation of the United States elite, so did Vietnam. Pearl Harbor and Vietnam were the points in time at which critics could say, "I told you so," and win widespread if grudging agreement from the old guard. The Pearl Harbor paradigm, applied for three decades to a world from which it was increasingly alienated, eventually was "shipwrecked" on Vietnam.

THE VIETNAM PARADIGM

What follows? It is not difficult to discern an emerging noninterventionist orientation which can be termed the "Vietnam paradigm." Varying in emphasis and nuance, the bearers of the new view all urge *limitation* of American activity (above all, military activity) overseas, particularly in the Third World. John Kenneth Galbraith, for example, wants

> and even more positive commitment to coexistence with the Communist countries. It means a much more determined effort to get military competition with the Soviets under control. . . . It means abandoning the Sub-Imperial ambitions in the Third World and recognizing instead that there is little we can do to influence political development in this part of the world and less that we need to do.[40]

Arthur Schlesinger, Jr., believes the "lessons of Vietnam" show:

> *First, that everything in the world is not of equal importance to us.* Asia and Africa are of vital importance for Asians and Africans . . . but they are not so important for us. . . .
>
> *Second, that we cannot do everything in the world.* The universalism of the older generation was spacious in design and noble in intent. Its flaw was that it overcommitted our country—it overcommitted our policy, our resources, and our rhetoric. . . . [41]

The critics of only a few years ago might reflect with satisfaction on how much of their critique (not all, to be sure) has been absorbed by the Nixon doctrine.

A deluge of foreign-policy criticism has appeared in the last several years. If we were to boil down the new conventional wisdom and compare it with the old, it might look like this:[42]

Pearl Harbor Paradigm	Vietnam Paradigm
Communism is a monolithic threat.	Communism is a divided spastic.
If we don't intervene overseas, we may get dragged into a war.	If we do intervene overseas, we are sure to get into a war.
We must nip aggression in the bud.	We are not the world's policeman.
The dominoes are falling. Quick, let's do something!	The dominoes are falling. So what?
United States aid and technology will develop backward countries.	Backward countries will develop themselves or not at all.

The catastrophe that each generation experienced implanted viewpoints which, based on the importance for United States security accorded to overseas events, are flatly antithetical. Rational discussion between the two paradigms tends to be impossible, not for want of "facts" but for how they are structured. The structure, or paradigm, is imparted by a traumatic foreign-policy experience. Without such a trauma the inadequacies of the old paradigm might have gone unnoticed. Unfortunately, the indiscriminate application of one paradigm to increasingly changed circumstances tends to produce just that mishap. Given many interventions, it is likely that one will misfire. The adventures which do not misfire conspicuously—Lebanon, the Congo airlifts, Berlin, the Taiwan Straits, Santo Domingo—can be shrugged off or even used to justify continuing interventionism ("It worked there, didn't it?"). In this manner a foreign-policy paradigm actuates a built-in self-destruct mechanism: its eventual application *ad absurdum* by its elite generation.

THE FOREIGN-POLICY PARADIGMS OF YESTERYEAR

Is the above a comparison of just the two most recent epochs in United States diplomatic history, or might the approach be extended backward in time to validate the generational-paradigm approach as a more general tool of analysis? The author wishes to attempt the latter by dividing American foreign policy into periods on the basis of alternating interventionist and noninterventionist paradigms. To do this it is necessary to ask how the elite of a given period answered Spykman's old question of where the defense of America should start—on the near or far side of the oceans. If the answer is "far," then the lands across the seas "matter" to United States security. If the answer is "near," the lands across the seas "do not matter" so much to the security of the United States. In the former case, we have an interventionist period; in the latter, we have a noninterventionist period.

Let us examine United States diplomatic history, looking at periods first in reverse chronology and then by functional categories. As previously stated, the bearers of the Pearl Harbor paradigm were themselves reacting to what they believed were the gross deficiencies of the interwar "isolationism." The 1920 to 1940 period can be called the "Versailles paradigm"; its bearers were condemned as blind for failing to recognize the obvious threat from abroad in 1939–1941. Who were these people? Prominent among them were senators Borah, Hiram Johnson, Nye, and La Follette, the same "battalion of irreconcilables," who opposed the Versailles Treaty and League Covenant in 1919–1920.[43] For such persons World War II was a conflict the United States must and could—through rigorous application of the Neutrality Acts—avoid. Their great lesson was the aftermath of World War I, which, they believed, had achieved nothing: Europe stayed fractious, and even worse, refused to pay its war debts. American participation in that war had been a mistake. As with the Pearl Harbor paradigm, in their arguments self-interest and morality were intertwined. Versailles had been unfair to various nations (the demands of ethnic groups played a role here); the treaty enshrined the victors in positions of superiority; and the League of Nations's Covenant would then entangle America in the next European crisis. The depth of the interwar bitterness probably was not reached until the 1934–1936 Nye Committee hearings, which, in part, sought to blame munitions manufacturers for United States involvement. Out of the Nye hearings grew the Neutrality Acts of 1935–1937. Like the Pearl Harbor paradigm, the Versailles paradigm seems also to have reached full flowering shortly before its demise, exaggerating its increasing irrelevance to the world situation.

It took the critics of the Versailles paradigm at least half a decade to dislodge it. The "isolationists" fought the growing interventionism every inch of the way. Strong emotions came to the surface. "I could scarcely proceed further without losing my self-control," wrote Secretary of State Cordell Hull of a 1939 confrontation with Senator Borah in which the latter disparaged State Department cables on an impending war in Europe.[44] Other sources said that Hull actually wept at the meeting. It took the catastrophe at Pearl Harbor to squelch the obdurate bearers of the Versailles paradigm.

Was this Versailles paradigm a reaction to a previous orientation—an interventionist one? That there was a previous period, sometimes called imperialistic, from the 1890s extending into the next century cannot be doubted. The problem with labeling the period from 1898 (the Spanish-American War) through 1919 (the aftermath of World War I) an "imperial paradigm" is that the continuity of an interventionist policy between the two wars is not clear. With the Pearl Harbor paradigm we can show a consistent propensity for United States intervention over three decades, but with the 1898–1919 period we have interventions, mostly clustered at the beginning and end. In 1898 the United States occupied Cuba, Puerto Rico, the Philippines, Hawaii, and Wake (and part of Samoa in 1899). Then, mostly relating to World War I, the United States occupied or had troops in Mexico, the Virgin Islands, France, and Russia. In between there were only the relatively minor Caribbean occupations. Thus, if this was an imperial paradigm, it sagged in the middle. It may be further objected that two distinct lines of thought accompanied respectively the beginning and end of this period. The earlier thinking favored unilateral colony grabbing, in recognition of the fact that the great European powers were carving up the globe and leaving America without colonies or areas of influence. The later thinking, accompanying World War I, was much more internationalistic, stressing cooperation rather than unilateralism. Some figures, like Senator Albert J. Beveridge, were imperialists at the turn of the century and isolationists about World War I.[45]

The author agrees that such an imperial paradigm is not nearly so consistent as the later interventionist epoch, the Pearl Harbor paradigm. Nonetheless there is a good deal of unity in the three decades of the 1890s, 1900s, and 1910s, and the period generally was an interventionistic one. In the first place, it was a time of almost continual United States naval growth. Starting with Secretary of the Navy Benjamin Tracy's 1889 plans for a vast American fleet and pushed by Theodore Roosevelt (both as assistant secretary of the navy and as president), the U.S. Navy rose from sixth to fourth place in 1990, to third place in 1906, and to second place (to Britain) in 1907. The naval budget went from $21 million in 1885, to $31 million in 1891, to $79 million in 1902, to $104 million in 1906, and to $137 million in 1909. Wilson, although initially cutting the naval budget somewhat, ended up with a $2.2 billion one in 1919.[46] In respect to naval expenditures then, the imperial paradigm did not "sag in the middle."

Further, although some of the foreign-policy elite of this period moved from unilateral imperialism at the turn of the century to equally unilateral withdrawal from Europe's war, there was also a good deal of consistency in positing a need for a major United States role abroad. Woodrow Wilson, for example, after some uncertainty, endorsed both the war with Spain and the annexation of Hawaii and the Philippines. His motives, to be sure, differed from the imperialists; Wilson wanted to prepare Puerto Rico and the Philippines for self-government.[47] But we are less interested in motive than in general orientation, and in this Wilson was unmistakably an interventionist. Indeed, as president, Wilson "carried out more armed interventions in Latin America than any of his predecessors."[48] In 1898 the twenty-seven-year-old Cordell Hull even raised his own infantry company and went with his men as their captain to Cuba (although they requested the Philippines).[49] Liberalism by no means precludes interventionism, as Waltz has pointed out.[50]

We might even consider the imperial paradigm as a sort of training period for the senior staffers of the later Pearl Harbor paradigm: Congressman Hull as ardent Wilson supporter; Franklin D. Roosevelt as enthusiastic assistant secretary of the navy under Wilson; and Stimson as secretary of war under Taft. This helps explain why the Pearl Harbor period was not staffed exclusively by young converts to the growing interventionism of the late 1930s. There was on hand a much older age cohort who had internalized an interventionist framework some forty years earlier and who were eclipsed by the militant noninterventionism of the 1920s and 1930s. This group formed a countertrend subculture which sat out the interwar isolationism until called back into power for the higher positions during World War II. By the 1950s, however, they had mostly been replaced by the younger interventionists of the Kennedy generation.

Can we discern a period still further back out of which grew the imperial paradigm? The 1870s and 1880s are commonly considered the "nadir of diplomacy." The period was marked by massive indifference to overseas affairs, anglophobia (over Britain's aid to the Confederacy) preoccupation with filling out the presumably self-sufficient United States. We might therefore label this epoch the "Continental paradigm." As with later periods, a minority critique starts in the middle of it on the strategic assumptions of the established orientation. In this case there was a growing strategic insecurity and the efforts of navalists—of whom Admiral Mahan was not the first—to rebuild the decrepit United States Navy. The year 1889 was a turning point; the Harrison administration began to discard the passive, inert policies which had characterized the previous two decades and to start actively making policy for the first time since the Civil War.[51] One need only compare the relatively weak American reactions to the bloodshed of the Cuba uprising of 1868–1878 to the much firmer stand of the 1890s.

It is not necessary to go further back than this. Our principal analytical distinctions—a near or far defense, interventionism or noninterventionism, few or many troops overseas—do not readily apply to nineteenth-century America. The United States was too busy, in a Turnerian sense, with filling out its own frontiers.

Further, America had little to fear from Europe or Asia, especially with the British fleet ruling the waves.

COMPARING PARADIGMS

While this division of United States diplomatic history into periods is admittedly an artificial construct, we can compare the periods or the "paradigms" that accompany the periods. (This comparison is summarized in Table 13.1.) The concrete expression of an interventionist or noninterventionist view is the number of United States troops overseas. During the imperial and Pearl Harbor periods America had relatively many troops abroad, and they were abroad not merely because of World Wars I and II, respectively. Long before our entry into World War I, there were American soldiers in Cuba, the Philippines, and throughout the Caribbean, including Mexico. During the intervening Versailles period the troops came home not only from Europe but from the Caribbean as well. Only in Nicaragua and Haiti did United States occupation continue past the 1920s. The Philippines were lightly garrisoned and almost forgotten in the interwar period. During the Pearl Harbor period there were troops overseas not only during World War II but long after it. The United States foreign-policy elite during this time was disposed to consider an overseas defense as the only reasonable American strategy. With President Nixon, this strategy seems to be changing, and there are fewer troops overseas.

Much of United States foreign policy hinges on the relationship between the executive and the legislative branches of government. If the Congress follows the president's lead and delivers what he wants, the United States is then able to engage in interventionist moves. When the Congress, specifically the Senate, tires of such activity and starts resenting strong presidential leadership, the possibilities for intervention are reduced. We would therefore expect to find an assertive Congress during noninterventionist periods, particularly at the beginning of these periods. It is for this reason that we get dramatic showdowns between key senators and the president. Especially important is the Senate Foreign Relations Committee, whose chairmen appear "irascible and contentious" when they engage in limiting executive initiatives in foreign affairs. Ranting anglophobe Charles Sumner defeated President Grant's scheme to annex Santo Domingo in 1870. Henry Cabot Lodge (and William Borah) stopped America's entry into President Wilson's beloved League. J. William Fulbright (and Mike Mansfield) cut down President Nixon's foreign-aid program and tried to put the executive on a leash by means of the 1973 War Powers Bill.

There are also, to be sure, executive-legislative difficulties when the paradigm shifts the other way, from noninterventionist to interventionist, which are perhaps not quite as dramatic because in this case the congressional opponents are the "losers"(see below). From 1898 to 1900 there was the bitter but unsuccessful rear guard of those protesting the war with Spain and the Philippines annexation, such as George F. Hoar and George G. Vest in the Senate and Thomas B. Reed, Speaker of the House.[52] In 1939 to 1941 there was a similar rear guard (discussed earlier), of those demanding United States neutrality. One characteristic of a paradigm shift in either direction, then, is a serious fight between the White House

Table 1 PARADIGMS IN COMPARISON

	Continental 1870s, 1880s	Imperial 1890s–1910s	Versailles 1920s, 1930s	Pearl Harbor 1940s–1960s	Vietnam 1970s–?
General view of foreign areas	"Don't matter"	"Matters"	"Don't matter"	"Matters"	"Don't matter"
View of Europe	Indifference (Anglophobia)	Imitation (Anglophilia)	Irritation	Salvation	Irritation
Losers		Anti-imperialists	Wilsonian internationalists	Isolationists	Globalists
Troops overseas	Almost none	Caribbean, Philippines, China, West Europe, Russia, Mexico	Few in Caribbean, Philippines	Europe, Asia, Latin America, Africa	Decreasing
Congress	Obstructive	Cooperative	Obstructive	Cooperative	Obstructive
Funds for overseas	None	War loans	Begrudging of war debts, anticancellationists, Johnson Act	Marshall Plan, Point Four, AID, arms-sales credits	Begrudging of aid, balance of payments force cutback
Commitments	None	Open Door, Caribbean protectorates, Associated Power in World War I, Philippine defense	Continued Open Door, reduction of Caribbean protectorates	U.N., NATO, SEATO, (CENTO), Congressional resolutions on Formosa, Middle East, Cuba, Berlin, Vietnam	Senate res. 85, War Powers Bill, attempt to repeal resolutions

and Capitol Hill over who will have the upper hand in foreign policy. When the paradigm is established, conflict between the two branches subsides because there is relative consensus and the acquiescence of one branch to the other; a spirit of "cooperation" and "bipartisanship" then prevails.

The shift from one paradigm to another also involves a rather clearly identifiable group of "losers"—those whose orientation is repudiated. This is not a happy process and much rancor accompanies the displacement of the bearers of the old paradigm and their consignment to obscurity. The anti-imperialists of 1898–1900 sought to preserve a more limited, continental America. Their arguments—strategic, moral, constitutional, and economic—bear a striking resemblance to some of the arguments used to oppose the Vietnam war.[53] The anti-imperialists were condemned by the interventionists of their day; Theodore Roosevelt called them "simply unhung traitors." The losers of twenty years later, the Wilsonian internationalists, also did not go down without a vituperative fight. The isolationists were the clear and unhappy losers as the Pearl Harbor paradigm replaced the Versailles paradigm. One is not yet certain what to call the present crop of losers, but perhaps "globalists" is a label that will stick.[54] Those who defend the dying paradigm appear as obdurate fools who are unable to come to grips with the new realities and who must therefore be ignored. The losers, who stick with the old paradigm while the new one triumphs, gradually cease to be practitioners.

Another characteristic of noninterventionist periods is the begrudging to friends and allies of United States aid, which flowed rather freely during the preceding interventionist period. The failure of the European powers to pay their World War I debts created both a public and congressional furor in the 1920s and culminated in the 1934 Johnson Act prohibiting debtor nations from raising funds in the United States. The "anticancellationists" helped spread the feeling that America had been cheated by tricky and unreliable ex-partners. In the late 1960s a critique of United States foreign aid developed along similar lines: billions have been wasted; they'll never be repaid; we've been much too generous; the recipients are ungrateful; etc. The interesting point here is that the critique came not only from conservatives, but from liberals who previously spoke in favor of foreign aid.

Arms and munitions appear as a minor but interesting point in noninterventionist periods. Arms sales abroad are viewed with great suspicion, as a possible avenue by which the country could get dragged into foreign wars. The Nye Committee hearings and the ensuing Neutrality Acts in the 1930s were attempts to prevent a repetition of America's gradual entanglement in another European war. It can be argued that precisely such an entanglement was repeated under Roosevelt with "cash and carry," Lend Lease, and the destroyers-for-bases deal with Britain. It indeed led to de facto war in the North Atlantic between the United States and Germany months before Pearl Harbor. But, it is interesting to note, in the interventionist Pearl Harbor period there was practically no regret that the Neutrality Acts had thus been circumvented. The problem of arms sales again flared as the Pearl Harbor paradigm came under question. As a result of a 1967 Senate debate, arms sales by means of Export-Import Bank financing and

Pentagon loan guarantees were stopped. Nixon's program to supply military hardware instead of United States troops was severely trimmed in the Senate.

The movement away from interventionism seems also to include the congressional and popular scapegoating of manufacturers of munitions. While Senator Nye had his "merchants of death," Senator Proxmire has his "military-industrial complex." In both cases it was alleged that armaments programs take on a life of their own and weapons makers manipulate public spending to their own advantage. The Nye Committee even "began to attack the war-making potential of the executive branch of the government," records Wayne Cole, and "also began to see the president as part of the compound."[55]

In interventionist periods there is a willingness to enter into arrangements that pledge the country to military action overseas. Admittedly, this was slow in coming during World War I, which the United States entered belatedly and only as an "associate" of the Entente. During the Pearl Harbor period, however, the United States carpeted the globe with commitments.

Following these times of generous pledges have come periods of limiting or discarding commitments. In addition to the already-mentioned League rejection and the Neutrality Acts there was the interesting Ludlow Amendment (shelved in the House in 1937 by a vote of 209–188) to require a national referendum to declare war except for actual invasion. As the Vietnam paradigm took hold there was the National Commitments Resolution (without force of law) in 1969 expressing the sense of the Senate that America should fulfill no commitment without specific legislation. In 1973 a War Powers Bill to permit the president only ninety days to use troops abroad without additional legislation overrode Nixon's veto. Further conflict over commitments seemed inevitable as Senator Mansfield continued his efforts to prune United States forces in Europe.

On a more general level, in the noninterventionist periods there is a lessened interest in Europe and in the interventionist periods a heightened interest. During the Continental period there was aloof indifference to Europe buttressed by a sharp anglophobia in the wake of Britain's aid to the Confederacy. As American leaders adopted imperial views, there was an imitation of Europe (colony grabbing) and some cooperation, as in the Peking expedition in 1900. There was also a marked anglophilia starting in the Spanish-American War. After Versailles there was disgust at European greed and squabbling and regret that America had ever become involved in Europe's war. During the Pearl Harbor period there was the virtual United States occupation of West Europe and an almost crusading American involvement in European recovery, rearmament, and unification. By the early 1970s the devalued dollar and pressure to withdraw our forces marked the beginning of a diminished American role in Europe, a trend that was heightened in 1973 and 1974 by differing United States and European approaches to the Middle East and the petroleum shortage. Again the view surfaced that the Europeans were selfish and hopelessly fractious.

On a more general level still, in the noninterventionist periods the lands abroad "do not matter" much to the United States elite; in the interventionist periods foreign lands "matter" a great deal. (Professors in foreign-area and international studies, as well as of foreign languages, have recently noticed the former view among students.) We may also note that the last three periods each began with a catastrophe of overseas origin. Versailles appeared to demonstrate that American participation in a European war had been futile and a profound mistake. Pearl Harbor appeared to demonstrate that the interwar "isolationism" had been absurd and had led to a disaster. And Vietnam appeared to demonstrate that the long-standing interventionist policy had been "wrong" and had led to a disaster.

CYCLICAL THEORIES REVISITED

The approach to diplomatic history, of course, is not completely new or unique. Several writers have advanced views that United States foreign policy tends to swing like a pendulum (an image used by both President Nixon and Senator Fulbright) from extremes of overinvolvement to underinvolvement. Stanley Hoffmann, for example, discerned "the two *tempi* of America's foreign relations," alternating "from phases of withdrawal (or, when complete withdrawal is impossible, priority to domestic concerns) to phases of dynamic, almost messianic romping on the world stage."[56] Hans Morgenthau saw United States policy moving "back and forth between the extremes of an indiscriminate isolationism and an equally indiscriminate internationalism or globalism."[57]

Getting more specific, historian Dexter Perkins divided American foreign relations into cycles of "relatively pacific feeling," followed by "rising bellicosity and war," followed by "postwar nationalism," and then back to "relatively pacific feeling."[58] Getting even more specific, a behaviorally inclined political scientist, Frank L. Klingberg, using such indicators as naval expenditures, annexations, armed expeditions, diplomatic pressures, and attention paid to foreign matters in presidential speeches and party platforms, discovered alternating phases of "introversion" (averaging twenty-one years) and "extroversion" (averaging twenty-seven years). Klingberg added: "If America's fourth phase of extroversion (which began around 1940) should last as long as the previous extrovert phases, it would not end until well into the 1960s."[59] As social scientists, of course, we do not accept the notion that God plays numbers games with United States foreign policy. The most fruitful approach to this cyclical phenomenon, the author believes, is the generationally linked paradigm, which helps explain both the changes in orientation and their spacing in time.

Other writers have found a roughly generational interval of about twenty-five years between upsurges of world violence. (Klingberg too mentioned generations as one possible explanation for his foreign-policy cycles.) Denton and Phillips suggest what we might term a "forgetting" theory to explain their twenty-five-year cycles of violence: That generation, and particularly its decision makers, that experienced an intensive war tends to remember its horrors and avoid similar conflicts. The following generation of decision makers may forget the horrors and remember the heroism; this generation is more likely to engage in violence.[60] This explanation helps account for our Versailles paradigm, but it is flatly at odds with our Pearl Harbor paradigm, during which a generation, virtually all of whom experienced World War II firsthand, displayed little reluctance to apply force overseas. This generation was of course repelled by the violence of World War II but used it to explain why aggression must be "nipped in the bud" to prevent another large conflagration. Walt Rostow, for example, continued to insist that Vietnam *prevented* a large war. "If we had walked away from Asia or if we walk away from Asia now, the consequences will not be peace," said Rostow in 1971. "The consequence will be a larger war and quite possibly a nuclear war."[61]

This author subscribes to a cyclical theory of United States foreign policy only in the most general terms—namely, that if there are alternating orientations of interventionism and noninterventionism, then logically the former will produce more "action" and this will show up as intermittent peaks in statistical tabulations. The question of cycles falls behind the question of the conventional wisdom of foreign-policy thinkers.

In searching for explanations of any cyclical theory, of course, we cannot rule out purely external factors such as threats or challenges from abroad. It may be that such external forces have impinged upon the United States at roughly generational intervals and that we have merely reacted to them. This then dumps the generation question onto the offending land across the sea. The problem here is that during one epoch American foreign-policy thinkers may largely ignore threats and in another epoch they may take threats very seriously. As we have already considered, the Cuban uprising of the 1870s elicited relatively little response from the United States compared to our response to the Cuban uprising of the 1890s. America paid little attention to East Europe in the 1930s and a great deal of attention in the 1940s and 1950s. In 1948 the Soviet-Yugoslav split was seen as an anomaly; in the 1970s the Sino-Soviet dispute is seen as natural, the almost inevitable collision of two nationalisms. *Quisquid recipitur recipitur secundum modum recipiensis.* The world changes, of course, but it takes a changed set of American attitudes to perceive the new situation.

The problem is one of perception catching up with reality not on a continual and incremental basis, but delayed and in spurts. May we hazard that Vietnam will leave behind it a continuation of this pattern? The immediate impact of Vietnam on United States foreign policy is already apparent: the Senate's restorative revolt, demoralized armed forces, international economic difficulties, and skeptical allies. The longer-term effects may be far deeper. If the above generational-paradigm hypothesis is even approximately correct, we can expect persons who witnessed Vietnam while they were in their twenties to retain a noninterventionist orientation. As the elite of this generation gradually surfaces into policy-relevant positions, we can expect them to implement their views. The most important reactions to Vietnam, then, may be yet to come. We might remember in this regard that the depths of interwar isolationism did not come immediately after Versailles but rather a full decade and a half later, with the Neutrality Acts. Will the foreign-policy elite of the 1980s and 1990s still be slaying their long-dead foes?

NOTES

1. This formulation owes something to John Kenneth Galbraith's 1962 query to President Kennedy apropos of Vietnam: "Incidentally, who is the man in your administration who decides what countries are strategic?" Galbraith, *Ambassador's Journal* (Boston, 1969), p. 311.
2. Thomas S. Kuhn, *The Structure of Scientific Revolutions*, 2d ed. (Chicago, 1970), p. viii.
3. *Ibid.*, pp. 19–20.

4. *Ibid.*, p. 90.

5. *Ibid.*, p. 148.

6. *Ibid.*, p. 153.

7. *Ibid.*, p. 166.

8. *Ibid.*, p. 159.

9. The role of the elite in foreign policy should need little elaboration here. See Gabriel A. Almond, *The American People and Foreign Policy,* 2d ed. (New York, 1960), pp. 138–139; James N. Rosenau, *Public Opinion and Foreign Policy* (New York, 1961), pp. 35–36; James N. Rosenau, *National Leadership and Foreign Policy* (Princeton, N.J., 1963), pp. 6–10.

10. Herbert McCloskey, "Personality and Attitude Correlates of Foreign Policy Orientation," in James N. Rosenau (ed.), *Domestic Sources of Foreign Policy* (New York, 1967), pp. 51–109. As Almond put it: "There is some value in recognizing that an overtly interventionist and 'responsible' United States hides a covertly isolationist longing." Almond, *The American People,* p. 67. An attempt to refute Almond's "instability of mood" theory was marred by having all its data drawn from the peak years of the cold war. William R. Caspary, "The 'Mood Theory': A Study of Public Opinion and Foreign Policy," *American Political Science Review,* LXIV (June 1970), 536–647.

11. Nicholas John Spykman, *America's Strategy in World Politics* (New York, 1942), pp. 5, 7.

12. Karl Mannheim, *Essays on the Sociology of Knowledge,* ed. by Paul Kecskemeti (London, 1952), p. 291. Samuel P. Huntington has recently stressed the importance of generations in American political change. See "Paradigms of American Politics: Beyond the One, the Two, and the Many," *Political Science Quarterly,* 89, no. 1 (March 1974).

13. Arthur H. Vandenburg, Jr. (ed.), *The Private Papers of Senator Vandenburg* (Boston, 1952), p. 1.

14. Paul Seabury and Alvin Drischler called it "the Manchurian assumption" and saw it as the basis for our postwar alliances. Seabury and Drischler, "How to Decommit without Withdrawal Symptoms," *Foreign Policy,* 1 (Winter 1970–1971), 51.

15. It is surprising to learn, for example, that liberal internationalist Chester Bowles served on the national committee of America First. See Wayne S. Cole, *America First: The Battle Against Intervention* (Madison, Wis., 1953), p. 22.

16. Historian Norman Graebner poses the following as the key question in the debate over the origins of the cold war: "Why did the United States after 1939 permit the conquest of eastern Europe by Nazi forces, presumably forever, with scarcely a stir, but refused after 1944 to acknowledge any primary Russian interest or right of hegemony in the same region on the heels of a closely won Russian victory against the German invader?" The shift of foreign-policy paradigms helps answer this question. Graebner, "Cold War Origins and the Continuing Debate: A Review of the Literature," *Journal of Conflict Resolution,* 13 (March 1969), 131.

17. U.S., *Congressional Record,* 89th Cong., 1st Sess. (1965), CXI, Pt. 3, 3350–3351.

18. *New York Times,* October 3, 1965 (supplement), p. 5.

19. U.S., President, *Public Papers of the Presidents of the United States* (Washington, D.C.: Office of the *Federal Register,* National Archives and Records Service, 1945–19), Lyndon B. Johnson, 1965, p. 395.

20. U.S., Congress, Senate, Committee on Foreign Relations and Committee on Armed Services, *United States Troops in Europe,* Report, 90th Cong., 2d Sess. October 15, 1968 (Washington, D.C., 1968), p. 18.

21. *Public Papers of the Presidents,* Johnson, 1966, Book II, p. 861.

22. *The Pentagon Papers, as Published by the New York Times* (New York, 1971, paper ed.), p. 499.

23. A parallel figure in the field of journalism was Kennedy's friend Joseph Alsop, who also published a book in 1940 that established his views for decades. See Joseph Alsop and Robert Kintner, *American White Paper* (New York, 1940).

24. Such items raise the possibility that some of the paradigm shift may be explicable in terms of father-son conflict on the psychoanalytic plane. But that approach tends to minimize the substantive issue of strategic assumptions, which is the one that concerns us here. The elder Kennedy's isolationism is from Arthur Schlesinger, Jr., *A Thousand Days: John F. Kennedy in the White House* (Greenwich, Conn., 1967, paper ed.), pp. 85, 125.

25. John F. Kennedy, *Why England Slept*, 2d ed. (New York, 1961), p. 222.

26. *Ibid.*, p. 186.

27. *Ibid.*, p. 223.

28. *Ibid.*, p. 171.

29. *Ibid.*, pp. 169–170.

30. *Ibid.*, pp. 229–230.

31. John F. Kennedy, *The Strategy of Peace*, ed. by Allan Nevins (New York, 1960), p. 193.

32. U.S., *Congressional Record*, 85th Cong., 2d Sess. (1958), CIV, 17571.

33. Kennedy, *Strategy of Peace*, p. 213.

34. *Public Papers of the Presidents*, Kennedy, 1962, p. 807.

35. *Pentagon Papers*, p. 128.

36. *Ibid.*, pp. 27, 35–36, 148–149, 284.

37. For a good exposition of this "age-cohort hypothesis," in this case on the attitudes of European youth toward regional integration, see Ronald Inglehart, "An End to European Integration?" *American Political Science Review*, LXI (March 1967), 94–99.

38. See, for example, G. F. Hudson, Richard Lowenthal, and Roderick MacFarquhar, *The Sino-Soviet Dispute* (New York, 1961); Donald S. Zagoria, *The Sino-Soviet Conflict, 1956–1961* (Princeton, N.J., 1962); and Leopold Labedz and G. R. Urban (eds), *The Sino-Soviet Conflict* (London, 1964).

39. The Nixon doctrine was first enunciated on Guam, July 25, 1969, to this effect. See *Public Papers of the Presidents*, Nixon, 1969, p. 552.

40. John Kenneth Galbraith, "The Decline of American Powers," *Esquire*, March 1972, p. 163.

41. Arthur Schlesinger, Jr., "Vietnam and the End of the Age of Superpowers," *Harper's*, March 1969, p. 48.

42. Graham Allison came up with a similar but longer comparison of his foreign-policy "axioms" from interviews with more than a hundred elite young Americans. Allison, "Cool It: The Foreign Policy of Young America," *Foreign Policy*, 1 (Winter 1970–1971), 150–154.

43. Jean-Baptiste Duroselle, *From Wilson to Roosevelt: Foreign Policy of the United States, 1913–1945* (New York, 1968), p. 260.

44. Cordell Hull, *The Memoirs of Cordell Hull* (New York, 1948), Vol. 1, pp. 650–651.

45. Selig Adler, *The Isolationist Impulse: Its Twentieth Century Reaction* (New York, 1966), pp. 28–29.

46. Duroselle, *From Wilson to Roosevelt*, pp. 8–9.

47. Harley Notter, *The Origins of the Foreign Policy of Woodrow Wilson* (New York, 1965), pp. 106–129.

48. Thomas A. Bailey, *A Diplomatic History of American People*, 8th ed. (New York, 1969), p. 553.

49. Hull, *Memoirs*, pp. 33–36.

50. Kenneth N. Waltz, *Man, the State and War: A Theoretical Analysis* (New York, 1959), pp. 95–114.

51. Robert L. Beisner, *From the Old to the New Diplomacy, 1865–1900* (New York, forthcoming 1975).
52. Robert L. Beisner, *Twelve Against Empire: The Anti-Imperialists, 1898–1900* (New York, 1968), pp. 139–164, 203–211.
53. Robert L. Beisner, "1898 and 1968: the Anti-Imperialists and the Doves," *Political Science Quarterly*, LXXXV, no. 2 (June 1970).
54. See, for example, Stephen E. Ambrose, *Rise to Globalism: American Foreign Policy 1938–1970* (Baltimore, 1971); and Gary Porter, "Globalism—The Ideology of Total World Involvement," in Marcus G. Raskin and Bernard B. Fall (eds.), *The Vietnam Reader* (New York, 1965), pp. 322–327.
55. Wayne S. Cole, *An Interpretive History of American Foreign Relations* (Homewood, Ill., 1968), p. 443.
56. Stanley Hoffmann, *Gulliver's Troubles, Or the Setting of American Foreign Policy* (New York, 1969), p. 19.
57. Hans J. Morgenthau, *A New Foreign Policy for the United States* (New York, 1969), p. 15.
58. Dexter Perkins, *The American Approach to Foreign Policy*, 2d ed. (Cambridge, Mass., 1962), pp. 146–147.
59. Frank L. Klingberg, "The Historical Alternation of Moods in American Foreign Policy," *World Politics*, IV (January 1952).
60. Frank H. Denton and Warren Phillips, "Some Patterns in the History of Violence," *Journal of Conflict Resolution*, XII (June 1968), 193.
61. *Washington Post*, July 12, 1971, p. A14.

Domestic Constraints on Regime Change in U.S. Foreign Policy: The Need for Policy Legitimacy

Alexander L. George

> The acid test of a policy . . . is its ability to obtain domestic support. This has two aspects: the problem of legitimizing a policy within the governmental apparatus . . . and that of harmonizing it with the national experience.[1]

The study of change in the international system must include, of course, attention to the efforts of national actors to create new regimes or to modify existing ones. This chapter focuses upon the role of domestic constraints on the ability of

Alexander L. George, "Domestic Constraints on Regime Change in U.S. Foreign Policy: The Need for Policy Legitimacy,"in Ole Holsti, et al., *Change in the International System*, Boulder, CO: Westview Press, copyright © 1980. Reprinted by permission of Westview Press, Inc. and Alexander L. George.

governments to pursue goals of this kind in their foreign policy. The primary objective of the chapter will be to develop an analytical framework suitable for this purpose. The framework will be applied to an analysis of two historical cases in which the United States has attempted to develop a cooperative U.S.-Soviet relationship: first, Franklin D. Roosevelt's effort during World War II to develop a postwar international security system based on cooperation with the Soviet Union; second, the Nixon-Kissinger détente policy of attempting to develop a more constructive relationship with the Soviet Union.

The analysis of these historical cases will be selective and provisional; it is designed to illustrate the utility of the framework for assessing the impact of domestic constraints rather than to produce a definitive scholarly interpretation. For this reason documentation will be minimal.[2]

THE PROBLEM OF DEMOCRATIC CONTROL OF FOREIGN POLICY

No one who reviews the history of U.S. foreign policy since the end of World War II can fail to be impressed with the importance of domestic constraints in the shaping and conduct of that policy. Democratic control of foreign policy is of course indispensable in the U.S. political system. But the forces of public opinion, Congress, the media, and powerful interest groups often make themselves felt in ways that seriously complicate the ability of the president and his advisers to pursue long-range foreign policy objectives in a coherent, consistent manner. It is not surprising that presidents have reacted to these domestic pressures at times by trying to manipulate and control public opinion—as well as to inform and educate the public as best they can.

While efforts to manipulate public opinion cannot be condoned, nonetheless this unhappy experience does point to a fundamental problem that Roosevelt and every president since has faced. This is the problem of obtaining enough legitimacy for his policy towards the Soviet Union in the eyes of Congress and public opinion so that the forces of democratic control and domestic pressures do not hobble him and prevent him from conducting a coherent, consistent, and reasonably effective long-range policy.

To be able to do so, the president must achieve a fundamental and stable national consensus, one that encompasses enough members of his own administration, of Congress and of the interested public. It is contended here that such a consensus can *not* be achieved and maintained simply by the president adhering scrupulously to constitutional-legal requirements for the conduct of foreign policy, *or* by his following the customary norms for consultation of Congress, *or* by conducting an "open" foreign policy that avoids undue secrecy and deceptive practices, *or* by attempting to play the role of broker mediating and balancing the competing demands and claims on foreign policy advanced by the numerous domestic interest groups.

Neither can the president develop such a consensus merely by invoking "national interest" nor the requirements of "national security." In principle, of course, the criterion of "national interest" should assist the policy maker to cut through the complex, multivalued nature of foreign policy issues and to improve his judgment of the relative importance of different objectives. In practice, however, "national interest" has become so elastic and ambiguous a concept that its role as a guide to foreign policy is highly problematical and controversial. Most thoughtful observers of U.S. foreign policy have long since concluded that the "national interest" concept unfortunately lends itself more readily to being used by our leaders as political rhetoric for *justifying* their decisions and gaining support rather than as an exact, well-defined criterion that enables them to determine what actions and decisions to take. It is symptomatic of the deep crisis of U.S. foreign policy in the past decade that large elements of the public and of Congress are no longer persuaded that foreign policy actions are appropriate merely by the president's invocation of the symbol of "national interest." These skeptical sectors of the public and of Congress have come to view "the national interest" phrase as part of the shopworn political rhetoric that every administration in recent times has employed in order to justify questionable or arbitrary policies and decisions.

If "national interest" does not endow policy with legitimacy, what about a "bipartisan" foreign policy—is that not the way in which a basic consensus on foreign policy can be achieved in a democracy such as the United States? There have been times, it is true, when policy legitimacy has been associated with a bipartisan foreign policy, but it is important not to confuse cause and effect. Bipartisanship is the result, not the cause, of policy legitimacy. If enough members of both parties do not share a sense of the legitimacy of a particular foreign policy, calls for a bipartisan policy and appeals that politics should stop at the water's edge will have little effect except in crisis situations.

How, then, can a broad and stable consensus on behalf of a long-range foreign policy be achieved? The concept of "policy legitimacy" is relevant and useful in this context.[3] A president can achieve legitimacy for his policy only if he succeeds in convincing enough members of his administration, Congress, and the public that he indeed does have a policy and that it is soundly conceived. This requires two things: first, he must convince them that the objectives and goals of his policy are desirable and worth pursuing—in other words that his policy is consistent with fundamental national values and contributes to their enhancement. This is the *normative* or moral component of policy legitimacy.

Second, the president must convince people that he knows how to achieve these desirable long-range objectives. In other words, he must convince them that he understands other national actors and the evolving world situation well enough to enable him to influence the course of events in the desired direction with the means and resources at his disposal. This is the *cognitive* (or knowledge) basis for policy legitimacy.

Thus, policy legitimacy has both a normative-moral component and a cognitive basis. The normative component establishes the *desirability* of the policy; the cognitive component its *feasibility*.

Policy legitimacy is invaluable for the conduct of a long-range foreign policy. If the president gains this kind of understanding and acceptance of his effort to create a new international regime, then the day-to-day actions he takes on behalf of it will become less vulnerable to the many pressures and constraints the various manifestations of "democratic control" would otherwise impose on his ability to pursue that policy in a coherent, consistent manner. In the absence of the fundamental consensus that policy legitimacy creates, it becomes necessary for the president to justify each action to implement the long-range policy on its own merits rather than as part of a larger policy design and strategy. The necessity for ad hoc day-to-day building of consensus under these circumstances makes it virtually impossible for the president to conduct a long-range foreign policy in a coherent, effective manner.

Thus far we have identified the requirements for policy legitimacy in very general terms. In fact, however, the specific operational requirements of normative and cognitive legitimacy will be affected by the marked differences in level of interest and sophistication among individuals and groups. Policy legitimacy must encompass a variety of individuals and groups. Foremost among them are the president and his top foreign policy advisers and officials. It is difficult to imagine them pursuing foreign policy goals that they do not regard as possessing normative and cognitive legitimacy. The bases for their beliefs, however, will not necessarily be communicated fully to all other political actors. In general, as one moves from the highest level of policy making to the mass public, one expects to find a considerable simplification of the set of assertions and beliefs that lend support to the legitimacy of foreign policy. (This important refinement of the analytical framework will not be developed further here, since it will not be utilized in the case studies that follow.)

THE "ARCHITECTURE" OF FOREIGN POLICY

It was noted that in order to establish cognitive legitimacy for his policy, a president must be able to plausibly claim that he and his advisers possess the relevant knowledge and competence needed to choose correct policies and can carry them out effectively. Upon closer examination it is seen that the knowledge evoked in support of a policy consists of several sets of beliefs, each of which supports a different component of the policy in question. It is useful, therefore, to refine the analytical framework that we have presented thus far in order to understand better the policy maker's task of developing policy legitimacy.

Foreign policy that aims at establishing a new international system or regime generally has an internal structure—a set of interrelated components. These are (1) the *design objective* of the policy; (2) the *strategy* employed to achieve it; and (3) the *tactics* utilized in implementing that strategy. The choice of each of these components of the policy must be supported by claims that it is grounded in relevant knowledge. A set of plausible cognitive beliefs must support each of these three components of the policy if it is to acquire what we have been calling "cognitive legitimacy."

By taking the internal structure of policy explicitly into account we add a useful dimension to the concept of policy legitimacy. Now the cognitive component of policy legitimacy is analytically differentiated in a way that permits a more refined understanding of the task of achieving and maintaining policy legitimacy.

The "Internal Structure" of Foreign Policy	Supporting Cognitive Assertions and Beliefs
Choice of (1) Design objective	a,b,c,...n
Choice of (2) Strategy	a,b,c...n
Choice of (3) Tactics	a,b,c...n

Figure 14.1 The Problem of Cognitive Legitimacy: The "Internal Structure" of Foreign Policy and Supporting Cognitive Assertions and Beliefs

The analytical structure of the problem of achieving cognitive legitimacy is depicted in Figure 14.1.

By differentiating in this manner the *functional role* that different cognitive assertions and beliefs play in supporting different parts of the internal structure or "architecture" of a policy, the investigator is in a position to do a number of useful things. First, he can understand better the nature of the task a policy maker faces in attempting to achieve legitimacy for his policy. Thus in order for the policy maker himself to believe that his policy is feasible and to argue this plausibly to others, he has to articulate a set of cognitive beliefs about other national actors whose behavior he seeks to influence and about causal relationships in the issue area in question that will lend support not only to his choice of the design objectives of that policy but also to the strategy and tactics that he employs on its behalf.

Second, the specification of beliefs supporting the internal structure of a complex foreign policy enables the analyst, either at that time or later, to compare these beliefs with the state of scholarly knowledge on these matters. This permits a sharper, better focused evaluation of the validity of the cognitive premises on which different components of a given foreign policy are based.

Third, by keeping in mind the differentiated functional role of cognitive premises, the investigator can more easily refine the description and explanation of pressures for changes in foreign policy that are brought about by interpretations of events that are held to challenge the validity of some of these cognitive premises.

ROOSEVELT'S "GREAT DESIGN," STRATEGY, AND TACTICS

We shall now utilize the analytical framework outlined above to describe the substance of Roosevelt's postwar policy and to indicate how domestic opinion—and the related need for achieving as much policy legitimacy as possible—constrained Roosevelt's policy choices and his ability to achieve them.

We shall consider first Roosevelt's design objective for a postwar security system, what he himself called his Great Design.

To begin with, the very close connection between Roosevelt's wartime policy and his postwar plans should be recalled. Both were quite self-consciously based on Roosevelt's perception—widely shared by his generation—of the "lessons of the past," more specifically the explanations attributed to the various failures of policy after World War I that had led to the rise of totalitarianism and to World War II.[4] Thus, in contrast to the way in which World War I had ended, Roosevelt believed it to be essential this time to completely defeat, disarm, and occupy those aggressor nations that had started World War II. It was also necessary in Roosevelt's view to promote national self-determination more effectively and to prevent future depressions. But above all Roosevelt's planning was dominated by the belief that it was necessary to forestall the possibility that once the war was over, the United States would once again return to an isolationist foreign policy, as it had after World War I.

Thus the postwar objective to which Roosevelt gave the highest priority was to ensure and to legitimize an *internationalist* U.S. postwar foreign policy. We wanted the United States to participate fully, and in fact, to take the lead in efforts to create a workable postwar security system.

To gain public support for his war objectives and to prepare the ground for an internationalist foreign policy thereafter, Roosevelt invoked the nation's traditional idealist impulses and principles. They were written into the Atlantic Charter that he and Churchill agreed to in August 1941 (even before the United States formally entered the conflict) and to which the Russians gave qualified support later.

Thus the principles of the Atlantic Charter provided *normative* legitimacy for Roosevelt's war arms and his hopes for peace. Among the traditional ideals that Roosevelt invoked, one in particular is of interest here. This was the principle of self-determination and independence for all nations. It was this aspect of the normative legitimacy for his policies that was to severely complicate Roosevelt's problems with U.S. public opinion—and President Harry S. Truman's problems later on—when he had to deal with the Russians on matters of territorial settlements and control over Eastern Europe. (We shall return to this later.)

Isolationism had been strong in the United States in the 1930s *before* Pearl Harbor. But once the United States got into the war, U.S. opinion developed strong support for the idea that it should not return to an isolationist position. This shift in public opinion was helpful to Roosevelt's postwar plans, but only up to a point, for in fact those who opposed a return to isolationism were sharply divided over what type of internationalist policy the United States should pursue after the war. Woodrow Wilson's concept of collective security was revived and its supporters, strong in numbers and influence, wanted the United States to take the lead in establishing a new and stronger League of Nations.

Roosevelt himself, however, rejected this idealist approach as impractical and inadequate. He favored an approach that would take power realities into account. In his view it was important that the great powers use their military resources to preserve the peace. This would provide a more reliable way than a league for dealing with any new aggressive states that might emerge after the war. Roosevelt also wanted to establish a more effective postwar system than a new league could provide for preventing dangerous rivalries and conflicts from erupting among Britain, Russia, and the United States once the common enemy had been defeated. But Roosevelt did not wish to risk a battle with the Wilsonian idealists, and so he did not publicly articulate his disagreement with their views. Instead he attempted, with partial success, to use their internationalist viewpoint to help legitimate his own quite different version of an internationalist postwar policy.

Roosevelt's thinking about the requirements of a postwar security system was deeply influenced by his awareness of the situation that would confront the peace-makers once the war against the enemy powers was successfully concluded. The defeat of Nazi Germany and its allies would create an important power vacuum in Central Europe. The question of who and what would fill this vacuum would pose the most serious implications for the vital interests of both the Soviets and the Western powers. If the two sides could not cooperate fairly quickly in finding a mutually acceptable approach for dealing with the vacuum in Europe, then they would inevitably enter into the sharpest competition for control of Central Europe.

The resulting dangers to the peace, it could be foreseen, could be dealt with only within the framework of the existing alliance between the Western powers and the Soviet Union. There would be no other international forums or institu-tions to bring into play to regulate competition among the victorious powers over Central Europe. Whatever semblance of an international system that had existed in the period between the two world wars had collapsed. What is more, the mili-tary alliance between the Western powers and the Soviet Union had been forced on them by circumstances—the common danger of defeat and domination by Nazi Germany and its allies. Once the enemy powers were defeated, all of the long-standing differences in ideology and the historic lack of trust and mutual sus-piciousness between the West and the Soviet Union would have an opportunity to emerge once again.

Roosevelt was aware that once the wartime alliance achieved its purpose of defeating Hitler, there would remain only victors and vanquished and no interna-tional system that could provide an institutionalized structure and procedures by means of which the Western powers and the Russians could work out a solution to the power vacuum in the center of Europe. Roosevelt, then, was faced with two important and difficult postwar tasks: the need to create the beginnings of a new international system and the necessity of finding a way to prevent dangerous com-petition to fill the vacuum in Central Europe.

What were the various possibilities available for dealing with these closely related tasks? One possibility was to try to recreate a new balance-of-power system. But the question was, what kind of a balance-of-power system? The history of the last few centuries had seen several significantly different variants of a balance-of-power system.

Roosevelt rejected the kind of balance-of-power system marked by a great deal of competition and conflict among the major powers—the kind of system that had existed during the eighteenth century, that had failed to deter Napoleon from attempting to achieve hegemony, and that had also failed for a number of years to form the kind of coalition needed to bring him down. In Roosevelt's view a highly competitive balance-of-power system of this type for the postwar period would be neither desirable nor feasible. Britain would be too weak by itself to provide a military counterweight to Russia on the European continent. The United States, even with its enormous military power, would not want to or be able to bolster England for the purpose of balancing Soviet pressure in Europe. It must be remembered that Roosevelt operated on the premise—which seemed completely justified at the time—that U.S. public opinion would not tolerate leaving large U.S. military forces in Europe very long once the war ended. So the grim prospect Roosevelt had to contend with, and to avoid if possible, was that the Soviet Union could end up dominating Europe unless the Russians could be brought into a different kind of balance-of-power system.

One way to avoid this dilemma, of course, would have been for the United States and Britain to forego the war objective of inflicting total defeat on Germany and Italy and to settle instead for a negotiated compromise peace with Hitler and Mussolini. But it was most unlikely that this alternative could be made acceptable to U.S. (or British) public opinion. Besides, since the Russians too could have played this game, it would have quickly led to a race between the Western powers and the Russians to see who could first make a separate peace with Hitler in order to bring Germany in on its side of the newly emerging balance of power.

Possibly there was another way of avoiding the dangers that a power vacuum in Europe would pose to a new balance-of-power system. These dangers might be minimized or avoided if the Western powers and the Soviet Union got together and worked out a political division of Europe before the total defeat and occupation of Germany and Italy. But it is difficult to imagine how a political division of Europe between the Russians and the West could be successfully implemented during or immediately after the war, or be made acceptable to the U.S. people. If the thought occurred to Roosevelt, there is little indication that he regarded it as at all a feasible or desirable option. The most that could be done, and was done, was to agree on zones of occupation into which the military forces of the Soviet Union, Britain, and the United States would regroup after the defeat of Nazi Germany. This agreement on military zones of occupation reduced the immediate danger of conflict, but it was neither intended nor expected to eventuate in a political division of Europe; it was not part of a "spheres-of-influence" agreement at that time, even though spheres of influence would emerge later on, based on the occupation zones.

There was still another possibility. If a complete division of Europe between the Western powers and the Soviet Union was deemed impractical or undesirable, the two sides might at least agree to grant each other spheres of influence in parts of Europe, with Germany itself being placed under their joint military occupation. Something of the kind—a partial spheres-of-influence agreement covering Rumania, Hungary, Bulgaria, Italy, Greece, and Yugoslavia—was proposed by Churchill to Stalin at their private meeting in Moscow in October 1944 and accepted by Stalin. But Roosevelt, although initially sympathetic, felt he could not approve such an arrangement.

Roosevelt rejected the model of a highly competitive balance-of-power system and also the idea of attempting to reduce its conflict potential by creating spheres of influence for several reasons. First of all, he doubted—and in this he was undoubtedly right—that U.S. public opinion would agree to U.S. participation in such arrangements, given its historic antipathy to the European balance-of-power system. Besides, for Roosevelt to endorse or participate in a spheres-of-influence agreement would have directly contradicted the principle of self-determination and independence that he had written into the Atlantic Charter. That declaration was the major statement of Allied war aims and major means by which Roosevelt had secured public support for an internationalist post-war foreign policy. For this reason, while Roosevelt was indeed prepared to accept predominant Soviet influence in Eastern Europe, such an outcome had to be legit-imized through procedures consistent with the Atlantic Charter.

Besides, Roosevelt did not believe that a competitive balance-of-power sys-tem, even one moderated by spheres of influence in Europe, would eliminate rivalry for very long. Any such arrangements would prove to be unstable, and the world would soon become divided into two armed camps—a Western democratic one and a Soviet-led one. An arms race would ensue which at best would result in a dangerous armed truce, and at worst it would lead to another world war. In brief, Roosevelt foresaw the possibility that something like the cold war would emerge—that is, unless some alternative could be devised.

The only alternative, as Roosevelt saw it, was a version of the balance of power modeled on some aspects of the Concert System set up by the European powers in 1815 after defeating Napoleon. To this end Roosevelt hoped that the unity and cooperation of the Allies could be maintained after the defeat of the totalitarian states. This was the option Roosevelt favored from an early stage in the war. He called it his Great Design, and he succeeded in getting Churchill and Stalin to agree to it and to cooperate in trying to bring it about.

The Great Design called for the establishment of a postwar security system in which the United States, Great Britain, the Soviet Union—and hopefully eventu-ally China—would form a consortium of overwhelming power with which to keep the peace. These major powers, forming an executive committee, would consult and cooperate with each other to meet any threat to the peace, either from the defeated powers or any others that might arise to threaten the peace. These four powers would have a virtual monopoly of military power; all other states would be prevented from having military forces that could pose a serious threat to others. Quite appropriately, Roosevelt called this concept the "Four Policemen." It must be noticed that such a system would have violated the principle of the sovereign equality of all states, great or small, and hence it could not be reconciled with the Atlantic Charter.

Turning now to Roosevelt's "Grand Strategy" for achieving his Great Design, the first thing to be noted is that it called for the United States, Great Britain, and the Soviet Union to work out mutually acceptable settlements of the impor-tant territorial issues and political problems in Europe. These settlements would be reached through joint consultation and agreement; in other words, through a system of *collective* decision making, not unilateral action by either side. In this respect Roosevelt's Great Design was influenced by the recollection that in 1815, after the European powers finally succeeded in defeating Napoleon, they then formed a Concert System which relied upon frequent meetings of foreign ministers to make joint decisions with regard to keeping the peace, dealing with any threats to it, and resolving any disagreements that might arise among themselves.

Instead of a new balance-of-power system, therefore, Roosevelt sought to create a new Concert System that would maintain the unity and effective cooperation of the victorious Allies after the war as well. And instead of secret agreements and spheres-of-influence, he hoped that new governments would emerge in the occupied states of Europe through procedures and policies that were consistent with the principle of national self-determination and independence.

To this fundamental strategic concept Roosevelt added other elements: reliance on high-level personal diplomacy, confidence-building measures, and conciliation and appeasement of the Soviet Union's legitimate security needs.

As for Roosevelt's *tactics,* the emphasis was on the need to minimize conflict and disagreement in day-to-day relations, the importance of leaning over backwards not to give offense, and the avoidance of behavior that might be interpreted by the Soviets as indicating hostility or lack of sympathy.

Particularly at the level of tactics, but to some extent also at the level of strategy, there were some alternatives to the choices Roosevelt made. Generally speaking, the choice of a design objective—a particular Grand Design for policy—does of course constrain the choice of strategy; and the choice of a particular strategy constrains in turn the choice of tactics. One strategy may be more appropriate for pursuing a given design objective than another, and one set of tactics may be more effective than another. These choices of strategy and tactics are likely to be influenced by the policy maker's beliefs as to the relative efficacy of alternative strategies and tactics. It is entirely possible, therefore, as experience accumulates in attempting to achieve a long-range design-objective, that policy makers will be led to question their initial choice of tactics and/or strategy but without questioning—initially at least—the correctness and legitimacy of the design objective itself.

We have now identified Roosevelt's Grand Design, his Grand Strategy, and his tactics. *Each of them was supported by a set of cognitive beliefs having to do with the characteristics of the Soviets.* These beliefs constituted the knowledge base on which Roosevelt could draw in attempting to gain cognitive legitimacy for his overall postwar plans from members of his administration, Congress, and the public. From available historical materials it is relatively easy to identify the various cognitive beliefs about the Soviets that supported each component of the overall policy.[5]

How well founded were these beliefs about the Soviets on which Roosevelt's postwar policy rested? It must be recognized that the exigencies and pressures of the wartime situation—the need to get along with the Russians in order to ensure the defeat of the enemy powers—no doubt powerfully motivated Roosevelt to develop a somewhat benign, optimistic image of the Soviets. But was that image therefore naive? Was it simply wishful thinking to believe that the Soviets might participate in a cooperative postwar system of some kind?

Roosevelt's hopes and beliefs regarding the Soviets cannot be dismissed so easily as naive. The content of some of Roosevelt's policies and his judgment of the Soviet Union were indeed criticized by some persons at the time. But suffice it to say that the naivete regarding the Soviet Union that Roosevelt has been charged with was much more apparent *after* the failure of his hopes for postwar cooperation with the Russians than before. During the war itself, while Roosevelt was alive and even for a while thereafter, many specialists on the Soviet Union (for example, Charles Bohlen) and other foreign-policy experts, were not at all sure that his policy would fail. Many of the beliefs about the Soviet Union that supported Roosevelt's Grand Design enjoyed a considerable measure of plausibility and support. His policies and the beliefs that supported them were not a hasty improvisation but reflected careful deliberation on his part and on the part of quite a few advisers. Even skeptics about the Soviet Union thought that there was a chance that Soviet leaders would cooperate out of self-interest with Roosevelt's Grand Design. The generally successful wartime collaboration with the Soviets reinforced these hopes, and they were further strengthened by Roosevelt's assessment of Stalin's postwar intentions and the general endorsement he obtained from Stalin of the concept of a cooperative postwar security system.

It should be noted further that despite his generally optimistic personality and outlook, Roosevelt did not hide from himself or others close to him that his image of the Soviets might prove to be defective and that his hopes for postwar cooperation might eventually prove to be unfounded. He realized, in other words, that he was taking a calculated risk, and he remained sensitive to any Soviet actions that threatened the success of his postwar plans or appeared to call into question the validity of the premises on which it was based. Roosevelt was also quick to undertake remedial measures to bring Stalin back into line whenever necessary.

DOMESTIC CONSTRAINTS AFFECTING THE IMPLEMENTATION OF ROOSEVELT'S POSTWAR POLICIES

In addition to the constraints already noted on Roosevelt's choice of a "realist" oriented postwar security system, domestic pressures also hampered his effort to secure and maintain strong legitimacy for his policy. Although he strongly favored the Four Policemen concept, Roosevelt was most cautious in publicizing it. He did not seriously attempt to inform and educate public opinion on the matter because he feared that such an effort would shatter the domestic consensus for an internationalist postwar foreign policy. Roosevelt felt he had to blur the difference between his realistic approach to power and security and the Wilsonian idealists' desire for a system of collective security based on the creation of another stronger League of Nations. Roosevelt did speak about his Four Policemen concept privately with a number of influential opinion leaders. But when he attempted to float a trial balloon to publicize the idea in an interview with a journalist,[6] it triggered a sharply negative reaction at home from the idealists. As a result Roosevelt backed away from further efforts to educate public opinion in order to gain understanding and legitimacy for his Four Policemen concept.

From an early stage in World War II Roosevelt had strongly opposed setting up a new League of Nations after the war. He felt that the task of enforcing the peace would have to be left to the Four Policemen for a number of years. However, once again to avoid political troubles at home, Roosevelt bowed to the pressure of the idealists who wanted the United Nations set up before the war was over. Roosevelt therefore acquiesced when Secretary of State Cordell Hull, who himself was closely identified with the Wilsonian idealists, gradually transformed the Four Policemen idea into what became the Security Council of the United Nations. Roosevelt consoled himself with the thought that it was not the early establishment of the United Nations and the format of the Security Council that were critical but rather that the United States and the Soviet Union should preserve a friendly and cooperative relationship and that they should settle all important issues between them outside the Security Council and work together to maintain peace.

Roosevelt, as suggested earlier, could not approve an old-fashioned spheres-of-influence arrangement in Europe. He feared that it would be perceived by U.S. opinion as another example of how the cynical, immoral European powers periodically got together to make secret agreements to divide up the spoils at the expense of weaker states; and hence as a violation of the principle of national self-determination and independence. Such a development in U.S. opinion, Roosevelt foresaw, could jeopardize his postwar plans right from the beginning. But at the same time Roosevelt recognized that the Soviet Union's legitimate security needs in Eastern Europe would have to be satisfied. Since the Red Army was occupying Eastern Europe and would likely move into Central Europe as well, the Soviet Union could do as it wished there in any case. The United States would not employ force or threats of force to prevent or to dissuade the Soviets from creating friendly regimes and making territorial changes in Eastern Europe. This was understood and accepted even by those of Roosevelt's advisers—including Soviet experts in the State Department—who were most negative in their view of Soviet communism.[7]

From the standpoint of maintaining the U.S. public's support for his postwar policy it was terribly important for Roosevelt first that the Soviet Union should define its security needs in Eastern Europe in *minimal* terms and second that it should go about securing friendly regimes in Eastern Europe in ways that the United States and Britain could agree to and that would not flagrantly conflict with the principles of the Atlantic Charter. What was at stake for Roosevelt was the legitimacy in the eyes of the U.S. public of his entire plan for a postwar security system based on cooperation with the Soviet Union. If Soviet behavior in Eastern Europe was seen by the U.S. public as flagrantly conflicting with the principle of national self-determination and independence, it would create the image of an expansionist Soviet Union—one that could not be trusted.

Roosevelt hoped—perhaps somewhat naively—that the potential conflict between the Soviet Union's security requirements and the principles of the Atlantic Charter could be avoided or minimized in a number of ways. During the war he attempted to persuade Stalin that the complete defeat and disarming of Germany and the arrangements being made to weaken and control postwar Germany would do more to guarantee Soviet security than would Soviet territorial gains and the imposition of tightfisted Soviet control over Eastern Europe

Roosevelt also attempted to get Stalin to understand the difficulties with U.S. public opinion that would be created should the Soviet Union fail to cooperate in working out territorial settlements and political arrangements in Eastern Europe that did not flagrantly conflict with the commitment to uphold the principle of national self-determination and independence. In effect, Roosevelt was pleading for Stalin to show self-restraint; he hoped that Stalin would cooperate at least to the extent of providing a "cosmetic" facade to the creation of pro-Soviet regimes in Poland and other Eastern European countries. Stalin in fact was disposed to cooperate. Cosmetic solutions were in fact patched up several times. Thus Roosevelt and most of his advisers thought they had achieved that goal at the Yalta Conference in early 1945. But their optimism was quickly shaken by new difficulties with the Russians over interpretation of the Yalta agreements regarding Poland. Within a few months of becoming president, Truman too succeeded in patching up the disagreement over Poland, but once the war was over distrust of Soviet intentions mounted in Congress and among the public. People increasingly interpreted Soviet behavior in Eastern Europe as a harbinger of more ambitious expansionist aims, and it became more difficult to arrest the drift into the cold war.

Roosevelt died before these developments made themselves felt so acutely as to force major changes in his policy towards the Soviet Union. Among the many disadvantages Truman labored under in his effort to make a success of Roosevelt's policy was the reassertion by Congress, once the war ended in the summer of 1945, of its role in foreign policy. Truman was genuinely committed to trying to achieve Roosevelt's Great Design—that is, as best he could given the fact that Roosevelt never took Truman into his confidence and also given the fact that Roosevelt's advisers had various opinions as to how best to deal with the Russians.

Pressures and circumstances of this kind hampered Truman's ability to continue efforts to make Roosevelt's policy succeed, though he certainly tried to do so for a while; eventually, however, Truman was led to move step by step away from that policy to the policy of containment and balance of power associated with the cold war. But only gradually, and it should be noted, with considerable reluctance did Truman replace the image of the Soviets that supported Roosevelt's postwar policy with the quite different set of beliefs about the Soviet Union associated with the cold war.

Several hypotheses help to explain why the transition to containment and cold war was slow and difficult. First, as already noted, the exigencies and situational pressures of the wartime situation provided strong, indeed compelling, incentives for giving credence to evidence that supported the benign, optimistic image of the Soviets. And the generally successful wartime collaboration with the Soviets reinforced hopes that this image was sound and would prove to be stable. But to recognize this fact is by no means to imply that Roosevelt and later Truman were engaged in biased information processing of incoming data on Soviet behavior in order to confirm an existing optimistic image of the Russians. Rather the record shows that incoming information of new Soviet actions was interpreted sometimes as undermining some of the optimistic beliefs on which Roosevelt's policy rested but at other times as reinforcing them, so that there were ups and downs rather than a straight-line steady erosion of the optimistic image of the Soviets.

A second hypothesis helping to account for the gradualness of the transition to the cold war is to be found in the very nature of policy legitimacy. Once a foreign policy is established and achieves a degree of policy legitimacy—both normative and cognitive legitimacy—in the eyes of top policy makers themselves and enough other influential political actors, it is difficult for policy makers to contemplate replacing that policy with one that is radically different. An entirely new foreign policy will require new normative and/or cognitive legitimation. The uncertainty and expected difficulty of achieving adequate legitimation for a different policy reduces incentives for engaging in policy innovation and strengthens incentives to "save" the existing policy if only via modifications at the margins. *Substantial* erosion in public support for the existing policy and/or effective political pressure by influential critics would appear to be a necessary condition for overcoming the momentum of an established policy and for motivating top policy makers to address seriously the need for a basic overhauling of existing policy.

What this suggests, more specifically in the case at hand, is that disavowal of Roosevelt's policy of cooperation with the Soviet Union carried with it the risk of undermining the basic legitimation of *any* internationalist foreign policy, thereby encouraging a return to isolationism. The two alternative "realist" internationalist foreign policies which Roosevelt had rejected had, as noted earlier, severe disadvantages with regard to public acceptability. In the end Truman rejected both the spheres-of-influence and balance-of-power alternative, choosing instead a somewhat vaguely defined "containment" strategy which he coupled with support for the United Nations. (That the containment strategy and the ensuing cold war could take on some of the characteristics of a balance-of-power system—though bipolar rather than multipolar as in the eighteenth and nineteenth centuries—and eventually lead to a de facto spheres-of-influence arrangement was not clearly foreseen.)

The transition from Roosevelt's policy to containment and the cold war was, as noted earlier, a gradual one. Its relationship to the architecture of Roosevelt's policy is of particular interest. Thus the change started at the level of tactics, worked upwards to strategy, and finally extended to the level of design objectives.

Dissatisfaction with the way in which Roosevelt's policy was working emerged quite early, well before his death, and it focused initially and for some time on the tactics that were being employed. The "kid-gloves" treatment of the Russians was rejected as counterproductive by some advisers and officials, among them Averell Harriman, who was to become particularly influential with Truman's administration. It is true that Truman, quite soon after replacing Roosevelt, adopted a "get-tough" approach to the Russians. But as John Gaddis[8] and others have noted, "getting tough" was initially meant to apply only to a change in tactics in dealing with the Russians. This tactical innovation was to remain for some months part of an effort not to change Roosevelt's Great Design and his strategy but to achieve them more effectively.[9]

In effect Truman *improvised* an alternative to Roosevelt's Great Design over a period of time, working as it were from the bottom up—from tactics to strategy to design objectives—rather than deductively, as Roosevelt had done, from design objectives to strategy to tactics.[10]

As it evolved, the new cold war policy encountered serious difficulties in its ability to gain acceptance both from the standpoint of desirability and feasibility. In striving to attain policy legitimacy with Congress and the public for its cold war policies the Truman administration was led into a considerable rhetorical oversimplification and exaggeration of the Soviet threat, one that rested on a new "devil image" of the Soviets and a new premise to the effect that the U.S.-Soviet conflict was a zero-sum contest. The struggle to maintain policy legitimacy for the cold war led in time to considerable rigidification in the supporting beliefs and an unwillingness of U.S. policy makers to subject them to continual testing that stands in sharp contrast to Roosevelt's and Truman's initial willingness to reassess the policy premises of the earlier policy on the basis of new information.

By way of conclusion several points emerge from this analysis of the difficulties Roosevelt experienced in his efforts to obtain policy legitimacy for his postwar plans. First, U.S. isolationist sentiment was not powerful enough, once the United States got into the war, to prevent or hamper Roosevelt's ability to commit the country to an internationalist postwar policy. Roosevelt, however, was definitely hampered in pursuing the particular internationalist security plan that he favored by the strong idealist wing of the prointernationalist forces in the United States. The idealists felt that World War II provided a second chance to realize Woodrow Wilson's shattered dreams for collective security through a strong League of Nations. Roosevelt, on the other hand, believed this idealist approach to postwar security was naive and that it would not be effective. But in order not to jeopardize domestic support for the war and in order not to risk shattering the internationalist coalition that favored U.S. participation in some kind of postwar security system, Roosevelt shied away from trying to educate public opinion to understand and support his hard-boiled realist approach. Roosevelt felt he could not afford a direct confrontation with the Wilsonian idealists. To consolidate opinion behind U.S. war aims he issued the Atlantic Charter, which restated the country's historic idealist aspirations for national self-determination and equality of nations. And to avoid divisive controversy with the idealists, Roosevelt gradually diluted and modified his Four Policemen concept for postwar security and accepted instead the creation of the United Nations organization much earlier than he had thought desirable.

Thus Roosevelt did secure normative legitimation for an internationalist postwar foreign policy. *But* the means he employed for this purpose—the principles embodied in the Atlantic Charter—severely hampered his ability to design and pursue the particular kind of postwar security system he favored. One is struck, therefore, by the fundamental internal policy contradiction that plagued Roosevelt's efforts to put his Great Design for postwar cooperation with the Soviet Union into practice. For in fact the very national values and aspirations that he appealed to effectively to secure normative legitimation for an internationalist foreign policy served at the same time to impose severe constraints on the strategic flexibility he needed in order to deal with Eastern European issues.

Roosevelt's Grand Strategy called for accommodating the security needs of the Soviet Union in Eastern Europe; but the moral legitimation of his overall policy stood in the way. Roosevelt—and Truman later—found it very difficult to work out arrangements in Eastern Europe that would at the same time satisfy the Russians and not alienate idealist U.S. opinion that thought that thereby the principles of national self-determination and independence were being jeopardized. Roosevelt and for a while Truman as well continued to try to patch up arrangements in Eastern Europe (even "cosmetic" solutions) that would be acceptable to both Russian leaders and U.S. idealists. Their efforts eventually failed as time ran out; the U.S. image of the Soviets hardened and Truman began to improvise an alternative policy toward the Soviets.

The lesson that emerges from this experience is that a foreign policy is vulnerable if, as in this case, the means employed to secure normative legitimation of the policy at home conflict with the requirements of the grand strategy for achieving the design objectives of that policy.

THE NIXON-KISSINGER EFFORT TO SECURE POLICY LEGITIMACY FOR THE DÉTENTE POLICY

We turn now to our second case study, which we shall deal with even more briefly since it is more recent in time and there is less historical data and scholarship on which to draw. After many years of the cold war it is not surprising that the détente policy should be particularly difficult to legitimate well enough to provide U.S. policy makers with a stable fundamental national consensus to enable them to pursue the difficult long-range objectives of détente in a consistent, coherent manner. Such legitimacy as détente enjoyed was brittle to begin with. Moreover, some of the means Nixon and Kissinger employed to strengthen public support for the détente process, even though successful in the short run, as will be noted, entailed special risks. For a variety of reasons, such legitimacy and support as Nixon and Kissinger managed to acquire for the more ambitious of their détente objectives eroded badly well before the end of the two Nixon-Ford administrations.

An answer to the question of why the détente policy was difficult to legitimate and why such legitimacy as it acquired eroded so badly suggests itself if we compare its complex objectives and strategy with the stark simplicity of the cold war. During the cold war the U.S. objective was simply to contain the Soviet Union, without World War III, until some day hopefully the force of Soviet ideology and the forward thrust of Soviet foreign policy would moderate and spend themselves to achieve this long-range objective.

Détente policy, on the other hand, was more ambitious in its objectives and more complicated in its strategy. It aimed at persuading the Russians to mend their ways and to enter into a new "constructive relationship" with the United States. This was what might be called the long-range "grand design objective" of Nixon's détente policy. The development of a new constructive relationship between the two super nuclear powers was to serve as the foundation for a new international system—what Nixon vaguely referred to as "a stable structure of peace." Admittedly, as many commentators noted, what Nixon and Kissinger had in mind in these respects was not clearly conceptualized or spelled out, but it is clear that their détente policy did include the creation of a new U.S.-Soviet regime (or regimes) for security and economic issue areas. In other words, as with

Roosevelt's postwar plans, détente too had a long-range system-creating objective which required the development of a friendly, cooperative relationship between the two powers. And once again as in the case of Roosevelt's policy, the image of the Soviets that underlay the détente policy was that of a limited adversary, not that of an implacably hostile foe, as in the cold war image of the Soviets.

The cold war had been easier to legitimate domestically in the United States because it rested on a simple negative stereotype—a devil image of the Soviet leaders. Détente policy, on the other hand, had the more difficult task of getting people to view the Soviets as a limited adversary; but just what that was—neither friend nor foe, something in between—was not easy for many people to understand.

The Grand Strategy for achieving the long-range objectives of détente combined the use of deterrence strategy—a holdover from the cold war era—with various measures of conciliation-accommodation; in other words, a carrot-and-stick approach. The conciliation-accommodation component of deterrence strategy recalled important aspects of Roosevelt's strategy for winning the Soviet leaders over to cooperation in his postwar security system, but some of the underlying cognitive beliefs were different.

The conciliation-accommodation component of détente strategy consisted of various activities that were supposed to weave an increasingly complex and tighter web of incentives and penalties into the evolving U.S.-Soviet relationship. To this end Nixon and Kissinger held out to the Soviets the prospect of a variety of important benefits from détente:

1. Nixon and Kissinger attempted to turn to account Moscow's interest in trade, access to Western credits, grain, and technology.
2. They also indulged the Soviet Union's desire for enhanced international status and recognition as a superpower equal to the United States.
3. They held out the possibility of agreeing to the Soviets' long-standing desire for formal recognition of the territorial changes in Eastern Europe and of the dominant position the Soviet Union had acquired in Eastern Europe.
4. They hoped to further entangle the Soviets in their "web of incentives" and penalties by concluding a détente with Communist China. This, they expected, would strike fear into the hearts of Soviet leaders and motivate them to adopt more moderate and cooperative policies toward the United States.
5. Last but not least in importance, Nixon and Kissinger's web of incentives included negotiations for limiting the arms race and the danger of war.

The strategy of creating a web of incentives had as one of its underlying cognitive premises the belief that it would give the Soviets a strong and continuing stake in the détente process which would lead them to act with restraint in the Third World lest they jeopardize its benefits. As one writer aptly put it, "the strategy was to evolve détente into a new form of containment of the Soviet Union— or better still, *self-containment* on the part of the Russians."[11]

The Nixon-Kissinger strategy included other means as well to promote a new, U.S.-Soviet regime of a more constructive kind. Thus, U.S. leaders urged upon the Russians the necessity of adhering to a new set of norms and rules of conduct for restraining competition and conflict between the two superpowers throughout the world. (The underlying cognitive premise was that a set of norms of sufficient relevance and specificity could be formulated over time. That Soviet and U.S. leaders would not merely pay lip-service to them but also come to constrain their behavior accordingly in order to avoid conflict and promote the longer-range goals and benefits of détente.) These efforts to formulate a set of norms, encouraged by Soviet leaders, culminated in the Basic Principles Agreement signed by Nixon and Brezhnev at their summit meeting in May 1972. This document, which Kissinger heralded at the time as marking the end of the cold war, laid out general rules of conduct: Both governments agreed to cooperate to prevent "the development of situations capable of causing a dangerous exacerbation of their relations" and the possibility of wars into which they might be drawn; to forego efforts to obtain "unilateral advantage" at each other's expense; and to exercise mutual restraint in their relations. Cooperation to prevent the onset of dangerous crises into which they might be drawn was further emphasized in the Agreement on the Prevention of Nuclear War that the two leaders signed the following year. (The multilateral Helsinki Agreement of 1975, it may be noted, also included general crisis-prevention principles.)

This strategy was increasingly denigrated by U.S. critics of détente, who questioned its underlying premise and doubted its practicality. They argued that the Nixon administration was giving Moscow many tangible benefits in return for vague promises of good behavior and that it could offer no more than pious and naive hopes that the Soviets could be bribed into limiting their ambitions and their meddling in the Third World.

What this criticism overlooked was that Nixon and Kissinger did not rely solely on offering bribes and rewards for good behavior. In fact, as already noted, their strategy for inducing restraint on Soviet behavior relied upon continued use of deterrence threats as necessary, as well as positive incentives. If and when the Soviets did not act with restraint in the Third World, Nixon and Kissinger believed and often insisted that the United States must react firmly. And there were quite a few occasions when the Nixon-Ford administrations attempted to do so—i.e., in response to the Syrian tank invasion of Jordan in September 1970, in the Indian-Pakistani war in December 1971, in the case of the construction of a possible Soviet submarine base in Cuba in late 1970, in the Arab-Israeli War of 1973, and in Angola in 1975. In other words, when the "self-containment" Kissinger hoped to induce in Soviet leaders via the détente strategy did not suffice, he felt it was necessary to reinforce it with measures of the kind associated with traditional containment policy and deterrence strategy.

At first glance the strategy of rewards and punishments employed by Nixon and Kissinger bears a striking resemblance to what psychologists call "behavior modification." The Nixon administration in fact was using a carrot-and-stick policy in its effort to induce Soviet leaders to modify certain of their foreign policy behaviors and to resocialize them into new patterns of behavior that would be more consistent with the objectives and modalities of a new regime in U.S.-Soviet relations.

Several questions can be raised about the validity of the cognitive premises that underlay this strategy. In the first place, the effort to resocialize Russian leaders appears to have violated two basic principles of behavior modification. This technique works best when the therapist singles out *specific* items of behavior that are to be changed and indicates the *specific* approved behaviors that are to replace them. Nixon and Kissinger, however, described the behaviors to be eliminated from Soviet foreign policy in general terms and used generalities also to identify the hoped-for changes in Soviet behavior (as in the general principles contained in the Basic Principles Agreement).

Another important principle of behavior modification not sufficiently adhered to in détente strategy has to do with the timing of the reward to the subject. Just when the therapist rewards the subject may be critical in influencing him to modify a particular behavior in the desired direction. In behavior modification a reward is supposed to come *after* the subject behaves as desired; the function of the reward is to reinforce the new behavior. But Kissinger often gave benefits to the Soviets beforehand, i.e, as a bribe to induce Soviet leaders to behave in a generally desired direction.

In any case, whether or not Kissinger applied behavior modification principles correctly in his strategy, what he was trying to accomplish was very ambitious, and this raises another question regarding the feasibility of the strategy and whether still other premises on which it was based were justified. The strategy assumed that the rewards and punishments available to U.S. leaders for modifying Soviet behavior were sufficiently potent for the purpose. But this premise may be questioned. Rather, as some critics of détente held, it may be that Kissinger overestimated the leverage available to him for accomplishing so difficult and ambitious an objective. Perhaps it was overly optimistic to believe—and dangerous to encourage the U.S. public to believe, so as to gain legitimacy for the policy—that the web of incentives and penalties realistically available to the Nixon administration would suffice to create a stake in détente so valuable to Soviet leaders that they would give up opportunities to display their increased power and their efforts to extend their influence in the world. Interestingly, this was among the aspects of détente policy that was most sharply challenged by critics in levying the charge that Kissinger had "oversold" détente.

The legitimacy of détente strategy suffered also because its implementation confused the public. It was perhaps predictable that many members of Congress and the public would fail to grasp the subtleties of a strategy that combined deterrence threats and penalties with efforts at conciliation and bestowal of benefits. If the Soviets behaved so badly on some occasions so as to warrant threats or penalties, why then reward them in other respects? Should there not be more explicit quid pro quos whereby the Soviets would give up something concrete for each benefit we gave them? Criticism of this kind not only eroded the legitimacy of détente policy; it brought increasing pressure to bear on the administration to abandon or at least make significant changes in the strategy employed. The domestic politics of détente within the United States, magnified by Reagan's unexpectedly strong challenge in the Republican presidential primaries, forced the Ford administration to drive harder bargains with Moscow and to apply more exacting standards for acceptable agreements. (And this constraint has applied equally thus far to President Carter's approach to the Soviets.)

But perhaps the worst consequence of the way in which Kissinger applied the complex strategy of conciliation and deterrence was that it tended over time to polarize U.S. public opinion. Both the anti-Soviet hawks and the antiwar doves in this country became dissatisfied with the détente policy for different reasons. And with the passage of time both hawk and dove critics of the détente policy became stronger politically. Thus, when Kissinger bestowed benefits on the Soviets, the anti-Soviet hawks protested. And whenever Kissinger confronted the Soviets—as in the Arab-Israeli War of 1973 and over Angola—the doves sounded the alarm that the administration was about to start down the slippery slope into another Vietnam.

As a result Kissinger found himself caught in an increasingly severe whiplash between hawk and dove critics of his policy. Those members of Congress and the public who did understand and sympathize with the intricate logic and rationale of the dual strategy of conciliation and deterrence and who made up the centrist constituency whose support Kissinger so badly needed to maintain the momentum of the détente process were gradually neutralized by the growing strength and louder voices of hawk and dove critics.

Kissinger's difficulties with his hawkish critics were compounded by other adverse developments that he was unable to control and to which he inadvertently contributed on occasion. These developments included the Soviet leaders' repeated insistence—in part no doubt to quiet the opposition to détente from their own hawks—that détente did not mean that they were betraying their communist ideology and would forego support for "national liberation" movements. U.S. hawks interpreted such Soviet statements as exposing the fallacy of the cognitive premises on which were based Kissinger's aspirations for developing a new constructive relationship with the Soviets. Soviet insistence on defining détente in terms of their own concept of "peaceful coexistence" also revived concern over Soviet intentions. And this concern over the premises of the détente policy was much strengthened by the continuing buildup of Soviet strategic and other military capabilities coupled with the failure of the Strategic Arms Limitations Talks (SALT) negotiations to limit the arms race. Thus the question of Soviet intentions, which has periodically agitated American foreign policy experts and public opinion since the end of World War II, emerged once again as a highly salient and controversial issue.

Uneasiness about Kissinger's conduct of détente strategy was aggravated by the way in which he sometimes expressed his views about growing Soviet power and influence in the world. Kissinger's statements sometimes included unfortunate innuendoes to the effect that the Soviet Union was now the ascendant power and the United States a descending power. This theme was implicit rather than explicit in what Kissinger said, but it struck a highly sensitive chord among Americans who were suffering the many evidences of the decline of U.S. power and hegemony. Kissinger was charged with holding a Spenglerian view of the decline of the West, which of course he denied. But more than one critic detected evidences of pessimism in some of Kissinger's philosophical reflections on the state of the world with regard to the possibility that the West's will to resist expansion of Soviet power and influence was on the decline.

The attribution of such beliefs and predispositions to Kissinger made it all the more plausible to charge him with pursuing détente in a one-sided way, as if he were driven by the feeling that it was imperative for the United States to work out the best deal possible with its mighty adversary before the West grew even weaker. In this regard Kissinger's critics felt that he was underestimating the Soviet Union's economic and political weaknesses, its problems with its Eastern European client states and with Communist parties in the West, and the fact that the Soviet system was not really an appealing model for many developing countries.

For all of these reasons the legitimacy of the détente policy eroded badly, a development that enormously strengthened those various domestic constraints associated with "democratic control" of foreign policy mentioned at the beginning of this chapter. As a result Kissinger's ability to conduct a coherent, effective foreign policy on behalf of the laudable objectives of détente was shattered well before the end of the Ford administration. With the erosion of the stable domestic consensus on behalf of détente, Kissinger could no longer count on minimal public acceptance of the variety of actions that implementation of his détente strategy required. Not only was he no longer given the benefit of the doubt, some of his activities engendered suspicion that they were designed to serve his personal interests or the political fortunes of his administration. His secretive approach to decision making and his diplomatic style did much, of course, to enhance the distrust.

No doubt Kissinger believed that his détente policy fell victim to the public's impatience for quick results and its unreasonable demands for frequent concrete indications that the policy was succeeding. Kissinger might complain with some justification that critics of détente were not justified in expecting that each transaction with the Soviets should give reciprocal advantages to each side; or that the balance sheet should show a profit every month.

Given the ambitious character of the détente objective, which required resocialization of Soviet leaders and their acceptance of the norms of a new regime in U.S.-Soviet relations, it would be only reasonable to assume that considerable time and repeated efforts would be needed to accomplish that goal. In the meantime, before Dr. Kissinger's behavior modification therapy took full effect, one had to expect that the Soviets would occasionally misbehave. But if so, then how could one evaluate whether the strategy was succeeding? Kissinger's critics pointed to instances of Soviet meddling in Third Areas as evidence of the failure and unsound character of the strategy. Kissinger himself could only retort that Soviet behavior would have been perhaps even more aggressive and the confrontations more dangerous had it not been for détente. Neither side could prove its case; but the possibility must be entertained that the critics pronounced the strategy of inducing self-restraints in Soviet foreign policy a failure prematurely.

PUBLIC OPINION AND THE PROBLEM OF EVALUATING FOREIGN POLICY

Any complex long-range foreign policy such as Roosevelt's Grand Design or the Nixon-Kissinger détente policy needs considerable time to achieve its objectives. Such politics cannot be achieved overnight: one summit meeting between the heads of state will not do it; neither will one overall agreement or one decisive action. Nor can one even expect steady progress toward the long-range objective. It is more reasonable to expect occasional ups and downs.

Any long-range policy needs to be evaluated along the way. We expect a president and his administration to engage in objective, well-informed evaluations of the policies they are pursuing. Policy evaluation of Roosevelt's approach to the Russians—and of Nixon's détente policy—involve questions such as the following: Is the long-range concept of a "cooperative" U.S.-Soviet relationship clearly enough defined—that is, does the administration have a clear enough notion of what it is striving to accomplish? Is the *general strategy* the administration is employing to achieve that long-range objective a sound one; and is the strategy working well enough or does it need to be changed in some way? Are the day-to-day *tactics* that are being utilized to implement that strategy well conceived? Are they working or do they need to be changed?

These questions associated with policy evaluation, it may be noted, have to do with the "cognitive legitimacy" of a policy—i.e., the basis for the president's claim that he knows what he is doing; that he understands well enough the nature of the opponent and the forces at work in the world situation, and that he knows how to use the means available to him in order to achieve the long-range objectives of his policy.

The evaluation of an ongoing policy is difficult to begin with from a purely intellectual and analytical standpoint. It is all the more difficult if the monitoring and evaluation of a current policy is unduly influenced by the play of domestic politics.

A president who pursues a long-range foreign policy in a democracy such as ours runs into some formidable problems. In the absence of policy legitimacy the character of U.S. politics, the role of the modern mass media in our political life, and the volatile nature of public opinion combine to subject the president's pursuit of long-range foreign-policy objectives to constant scrutiny and evaluation. As a result the president finds himself forced to defend his long-range policy on a month-to-month—if not also a day-to-day—basis. When this happens, a shortened and often distorted time perspective is then introduced into the already difficult task of evaluating the policy and the related task of deciding whether changes in strategy and tactics are necessary.

One of the characteristics of the U.S. public is its impatience for quick results and its demand for frequent reassurances that a policy is succeeding. This impatience is often fed by and exploited by the mass media and by political opponents of the administration's policy. The result of these domestic political factors is to complicate the ability of a president to pursue a long-range policy with the patience and persistence that is needed. The play of public opinion and politics can distort the difficult task of evaluating the policy; it can erode its legitimacy; it can force changes in that policy before it has had a chance to prove itself.

Faced with the volatile tendencies of U.S. public opinion, a president and his advisers must attempt to carefully control the public's impatience for quick results. They must also offer meaningful assurances that the cognitive premises of their policy goals and of the strategy and tactics employed on their behalf are being subjected to careful, objective evaluation. They must also control their own tendency to pander to the public's demand for quick, dramatic results as a way of making up for the inadequate legitimacy that their policy enjoys. On this score Kissinger and Nixon can be criticized for having pandered to the public's impatience for quick results and its tendency to be impressed by dramatic achievements of a symbolic rather than substantive import. In the early years of détente, Nixon and Kissinger were able to come up with spectacular events that seemed to offer assurance that détente was working—the trips to Peking, the summits with Soviet leaders in Moscow and Washington, the multitude of agreements.[12] But thereby Nixon and Kissinger helped to create a frame of mind and a set of expectations in the public which worked against them later on, when they had no more rabbits to pull out of the hat for the time being. Day-to-day "successes"—whether real successes or contrived public-relations-type successes—are not only a poor substitute for genuine policy legitimacy; they can easily end up helping erode whatever legitimacy has been achieved for a complex, long-range policy such as détente.

ACKNOWLEDGMENTS

Research for this chapter was supported by a grant (number SOC 75–14079) from the National Science Foundation and by the Center for Advanced Study in the Behavioral Sciences, at which the author was a Fellow in 1976–1977. Parts of the chapter were presented earlier in a paper delivered to the Symposium on U.S. Foreign Policy in the Next Decade at the University of Missouri-Saint Louis, April 1977, and in a paper for a conference on approaches to the study of decision making at the Norwegian Institute of International Affairs, Oslo, Norway, August 1977.

NOTES

1. Henry Kissinger, *A World Restored,* (Boston:Houghton Mifflin Co., 1957).
2. In preparing this interpretative essay the author has relied mostly upon secondary sources describing Roosevelt's plans for a postwar security system and the Nixon-Kissinger détente policy.

    Roosevelt's "Great Design" for the postwar period was conveyed by him most explicitly in background interviews with Forrest Davis, who published detailed accounts of Roosevelt's plans and the beliefs supporting them in several articles appearing in the *Saturday Evening Post* "Roosevelt's World Blueprint,"10 April 1943; "What Really Happened at Teheran—I," 13 May 1944; "What Really Happened at Teheran—II," 20 May 1944. [For background and evidence of Roosevelt's later acknowledgment that Davis's articles accurately reflected his views, see John Lewis Gaddis, *The United States and the Origins of the Cold War* (New York:Columbia University Press, 1972), pp. 6, 153.] Detailed secondary accounts of Roosevelt's thinking and plans are to be found in Willard Range, *Franklin D. Roosevelt's World Order* (Athens:University of Georgia Press, 1959); Roland N. Stromberg, *Collective Security and American Foreign Policy* (New York: Praeger Publishers, 1963), see esp. chap. 8; Robert A. Divine, *Roosevelt and World War II* (Baltimore, Md.: Johns Hopkins University Press, 1969); John Lewis Gaddis, *Origins of the Cold War,* Daniel Yergin, *Shattered Peace* (Boston:Houghton Mifflin Co., 1977), esp. chap 2; and Robert Garson, "The Atlantic Alliance, Eastern Europe and the Origins of the Cold War From Pearl Harbor to Yalta," in H. C. Allen and Roger Thompson, eds, *Contrast and Connection* (Columbus: Ohio State University Press, 1976), pp. 296–319.

    For various reasons the Nixon-Kissinger policy of détente is more difficult to reconstruct in terms of the analytical framework ("design objective," "strategy," "tactics") employed in the essay. While Nixon and Kissinger often spoke in general terms regarding their long-range goal of a "new constructive relationship" with the Soviet Union and made cryptic references to a new balance-of-power system, they never disclosed (and perhaps never formulated) a more specific design concept for the international system they hoped to create. The term *détente* itself was a misnomer, since quite obviously the Nixon administration's objectives and strategy went well beyond securing merely a "relaxation of tensions" (which is the traditional definition of détentes and embraced a willingness to engage in substantial "appeasement" (in the pre 1930s nonpejorative sense of the term) and "accommodation" of the Soviet Union in the interest of inducing and socializing this "revolutionary" power into becoming a responsible member of a new, stable international system.

Perhaps the fullest statement—really, by that time a defense—of the détente policy was provided by Kissinger in his testimony before the U.S. Senate Committee on Foreign Relations, 19 September 1974 ["Détente with the Soviet Union: The Reality of Competition and the Imperative of Cooperation," reprinted in Robert J. Pranger, ed., *Détente and Defense* (Washington, D.C.: American Enterprise Institute for Public Policy Research, 1976), pp. 153–178]. See also earlier statements and speeches by Nixon and Kissinger and in particular the annual reports to the nation: Richard M. Nixon, *U.S. Foreign Policy for the 1970s,* (Washington, D.C.: U.S. Government Printing Office, 1970, 1971, 1972, and 1973); see also Helmut Sonnenfeldt, "The meaning of Détente," *Naval War College Review* 28:1 (Summer 1975).

Among the many published commentaries and critical appraisals of the détente policy, the most useful for present purposes is Stanley Hoffmann, *Primacy or World Order* (New York: McGraw-Hill Book Co., 1978), pp. 33–100, which contains observations regarding the difficulty of gaining legitimacy for the détente policy similar to those offered in the present essay. An important detailed study is the as yet unpublished dissertation by Dan Caldwell, "American-Soviet Détente and the Nixon-Kissinger Grand Design and Grand Strategy" (Ph.D. diss., Department of Political Science, Stanford University, 1978). Among the many other useful commentaries on the Nixon-Kissinger détente policy, see Stephen A. Garrett, "Nixonian Foreign policy: A New Balance of Power—or a Revived Concert?" *Polity* 8 (Spring 1976); Robert Osgood, ed., *America and the World,* vol. 2, *Retreat from Empire? The First Nixon Administration* (Baltimore, Md.: Johns Hopkins University Press, 1973); and B. Thomas Trout, "Legitimating Containment and Détente: A Comparative Analysis: (Paper presented to the Midwest Political Science Association, Chicago, Ill., 19–21 April 1979).

3. The concept of "policy legitimacy" (versus "regime legitimacy") is discussed in a stimulating and insightful way by B. Thomas Trout, "Rhetoric Revisited: Political Legitimation and the Cold War," *International Studies Quarterly* 19:3 (September 1975).

4. For a fuller account see for example John L. Gaddis, *Origins of the Cold War,* chaps. 1, 2.

5. A detailed listing is available from the author upon request.

6. Forrest Davis, "Roosevelt's World Blueprint," *Saturday Evening Post,* 10 April 1943.

7. That the State Department was not an "ideological monolith" in its attitude toward the Soviet Union during and immediately after World War II has been persuasively argued and documented in recent studies. [Cf., for example, Robert L. Messer, "Paths Not Taken: The United States Department of State and Alternatives to Containment, 1945–1946,"*Diplomatic History* 1 (Fall 1977).] Moreover, as Eduard Mark demonstrates, Charles Bohlen and other State Department specialists did not operate on the assumption that there was an ineluctable conflict between the principle of self-determination in Eastern Europe and legitimate Soviet security interests in that area. Instead, they distinguished between different kinds of spheres of influence, arguing that an "open" (versus an "exclusive") Soviet sphere of influence in Eastern Europe was acceptable to and consistent with U.S. interests. See "Charles E. Bohlen and The Acceptable Limits of Soviet Hegemony in Eastern Europe: A Memorandum of

18 October 1945," *Diplomatic History* 2 (Spring 1979). On this point see also Thomas G. Patterson, *On Every Front: The Making of the Cold War* (New York: W. W. Norton & Co., 1979), chap. 3.

8. Gaddis, *Origins of the Cold War*, pp. 198–205.

9. Important changes in Roosevelt's strategy took place later. They included a shift from appeasement to insistence on quid pro quos, and probably of greater significance, a willingness on Truman's part to make important exceptions to Roosevelt's practice of seeking joint decision making among the Great Powers on the major political and territorial questions affecting post-war Europe. Thus Truman, confronted by urgent problems—particularly economic—of governing occupied Germany, which the mechanisms for four-power control could not deal with to his satisfaction, gradually moved toward making unilateral decisions without the Russians and the creation of separate mechanisms for governing the three Western zones of Germany.

10. As John L. Gaddis notes in commenting on Truman's stormy interview with Soviet Foreign Minister Molotov on 23 April 1945, soon after Roosevelt's death—which was perhaps the first example of Truman's new "get-tough" tactics: "to view the new President's confrontation with Molotov as the opening move in a well-planned long-range strategy for dealing with the Soviet Union is to presume a degree of foresight and consistency which simply was not present during the early days of the Truman administration." (*Origins of the Cold War*, pp. 205–206)

11. Leslie Gelb, "The Kissinger Legacy," *N.Y. Times Magazine*, 31 October 1976, italics supplied.

12. The *timing* of the Nixon-Kissinger "spectaculars" may also have opened them to the criticism that détente moves were being used to gain partisan political advantage. For example, the China trip seemed timed to coincide with the 1972 primaries; the SALT Treaty was advantageously signed during the summer of 1972; and the wheat deal, too, coincided with 1972 presidential nomination conventions. (Source: Ole R. Holsti in a personal communication.)

↬

Business Versus Public Influence in U.S. Foreign Policy

Lawrence R. Jacobs and Benjamin I. Page

Some of the most important debates over U.S. foreign policy focus on who influences government decisions. According to the realist account, government officials design foreign policy to advance the nation's interests in competition with other states in the international system. The process of identifying the national

An earlier version of this paper was presented at the "Inequality and American Democracy Conference," November 7–8, 2003, Princeton, New Jersey.

interest is aided, some argue, by experts or "epistemic communities" that possess the specialization to objectively analyze an increasingly complex global environment. An alternative account argues that U.S. foreign policy is driven not by the national interest but rather by organized pressure groups and, especially, businesses in order to advance their own narrow interests. A third account insists that the pressure to win election motivates government officials to tailor foreign policy to the preferences of the mass public.

This chapter examines the relative influence of public opinion, experts, and critical interest groups—organized labor and, especially, business. We begin by reviewing the competing accounts of U.S. foreign policy and then discuss and analyze an unusual body of evidence for evaluating them.

I. ALTERNATIVE ACCOUNTS OF U.S. FOREIGN POLICY

Three prominent, empirically-based interpretations of U.S. foreign policy and what influences it offer what appear to be sharply different predictions.

NEOLIBERALISM AND ORGANIZED GROUPS   Many scholars who take a neoliberal approach to international politics emphasize the decisive influence of organized interest groups on foreign policy (e.g. Keohane, 1984). The assumption is that foreign policy is a function of shifting coalitions of multiple and competing political and societal actors. Executive and legislative officials with foreign policy authority bargain with domestic groups that use their members' votes, campaign contributions, threatened or actual capital flight, labor strikes, and other tools to affect the electoral benefits and costs to elected officials of choosing alternative policies (Gourevitch, 1986; Milner, 1988; Rogowski, 1989; Frieden, 1991). For instance, Keohane and Milner (1996) trace targeted government subsidies and trade protections to the influence of well-organized and financed groups; Snyder (1991) attributes defense policy to logrolling coalitions.

Organized labor, and perhaps even more so business corporations, possess critical resources for pressuring policy makers. The ability of labor to strike and to support research and experts on manpower issues as well as its political money, volunteers, millions of voters, and roots in many congressional districts make it a potentially significant voice in debates about foreign policy. Given its mission to protect the jobs and benefits of its members, "[labor] leaders have spoken out often on foreign affairs" (Galenson, 1986, 62). In addition to addressing foreign policies that affected its bread and butter interests at home, organized labor in the United States was a stalwart supporter of Washington's policies for challenging communism during the Cold War. Labor backed the Vietnam War, increases in defense spending, and various confrontations with the Soviet Union and China. Since the 1980s, labor's support for defense spending waned as the cold war ended and the AFL-CIO saw the influx of civil service and other unions representing white collar, professional and service occupations, challenging the dominance of unions representing blue-collar occupations in building and manufacturing (Lipset, 1986). But it is not clear how much impact labor has actually had. Some analyses of comparative public policy and U.S. foreign policy indicate that labor's influence on American government officials and foreign policy is not significant (e.g. Esping-Anderson, 1990).

Some neoliberal analysts of international politics have singled out business corporations and groups as particularly influential in American foreign policy because of businesses' effects on the economy and their capacity to prompt voters to punish the incumbent political party. "Since political leaders' electoral prospects depend on the state of the economy," Milner (1997) observes, "they must be concerned with those groups that can directly affect the economy" (62). A number of studies have reported the influence of business on specific types of foreign policy: Rogowski (1989) traces government economic policy to powerful domestic economic interests; Trubowitz (1998) points to uneven economic growth and struggles for regional economic advantage to explain U.S. foreign affairs; and Grossman and Helpman (1994 and 1995) link industry lobbying and campaign contributions to international trade relations and, specifically, increased tariffs for politically organized industries. Some argue that pressures on governments to tailor foreign policy to please business have increased over the past three decades with the emergence of an open world economy characterized by rapid international movement of capital and greater exposure to global economic competition (Bates and Lien, 1985; Winters, 1996).

The research suggests that different policy making institutions may vary in their susceptibility to organized pressures. Executive branch officials, who play an especially strong part in foreign policy (particularly national security policy), have been said to focus on identifying collective gains in pursuing the "national interest" and therefore to be somewhat more resistant to organized pressure (Krasner, 1978 and 1972; Art, 1973; Wildavsky, 1991). Organized groups may have been especially influential with Congress, where senators and, especially, Representatives (who are elected in relatively small districts) are acutely responsive to intense demands for concentrated benefits from narrowly-based groups representing constituents and campaign donors (Milner, 1997).

In short, interest-group-oriented scholars suggest that labor and, especially, business, should exert strong influence on U.S. foreign policy.

EPISTEMIC COMMUNITIES AND KNOWLEDGE-BASED EXPERTS   Research on "epistemic communities" has found that the growing complexity and uncertainty of global problems has "led policy makers to turn to new and different channels of advice" and, specifically, to a new "knowledge elite" that is recognized as possessing the technocratic expertise and competence to articulate the objective causes of international problems, the "real" stakes or interests of states affected by those problems, and appropriate policy remedies (Haas, 1992, 12; Nelkin, 1979; Adler and Haas, 1992; Hall, 1989). In the introduction to an influential special volume of *International Organization*, Peter Haas (1992) explained that the "epistemic community members' professional training, prestige, and reputation for expertise. . . accord them access to the political system and. . . . influence over policy debates" (17). Research in that volume and elsewhere (e.g. Hall, 1989; Nelkin, 1979) suggests that epistemic communities are the intermediaries which transmit the ideas of "networks of knowledge-based experts" into government institutions and influence the substantive content of foreign policies by setting agendas and formulating policy alternatives (Haas, 1992, 2–3; Adler and Haas, 1992).

Epistemic communities exist outside formal government institutions and are drawn from professionals and experts in the academy, think tanks, and other bodies of highly trained specialists in subjects as diverse as economic theory and military technology. These specialists provide critical technical expertise for government officials in the legislative and executive branches to define problems and help form their preferences regarding particular policies.

Research on epistemic communities has two important implications. First, it suggests that experts equip government officials to conduct analyses and reach decisions that can be independent of direct pressures from organized groups or citizens. The scholarship on epistemic communities predicts, then, that business and labor exert at best modest direct influence upon the foreign policy decisions of government officials.

Second, epistemic communities may serve as concrete mechanisms for identifying and addressing a state's objective interests, in the complex global power struggles that classical and structural realists emphasize. Even if objective interests related to inter-state competition, the structure of the international system, and a state's position in that system do constrain states (Waltz, 1959, 1979; Walt, 1987), the definition and identification of such interests in concrete terms is a practical challenge for government officials.[1] Students of epistemic communities argue that realists incorrectly "assume that a state's interests are clear and that the ways in which its interests may be most efficaciously pursued are equally clear" (Haas, 1992, 13–14; Adler and Haas, 1992, 367–9). Instead, they maintain, technical experts are the vehicle for the interpretation of international structures, the identification of the "imperatives" facing the state, and the articulation of state interests in international politics: "[H]uman agency lies at the interstices between systemic conditions, knowledge, and national actions" (Haas, 1992, 2). In short, research on epistemic communities suggests that conditions of uncertainty produce strong incentives for government officials charged with making foreign policy to respond to experts from think tanks, the academy and other reservoirs of highly trained specialists and professionals.

MEDIAN VOTER THEORY AND THE INFLUENCE OF PUBLIC OPINION   The median voter theory predicts that vote-seeking policy makers will respond strongly to the policy preferences of the mass public. Competition among officeholders and candidates to win elections is expected to motivate them to minimize the distance between their policy stands and the preferences of voters. In the case of unidimensional, two-party competition, both parties should converge at the midpoint of public opinion (Downs, 1957).[2] Empirical evidence of influences by public opinion upon foreign policy has been reported in a large and growing body of research by students of public opinion and policy (Bartels, 1991; Russett, 1990; Wittkopf, 1990; Holsti, 1996; Ostrom and Marra, 1986; Hartley and Russett, 1992; Sobel, 2001; Page and Shapiro, 1983; Monroe, 1979, 1998), as well as by some international relations scholars with broader interests (e.g. Putnam, 1988, 432, 436).

Theory suggests that the general public should have the most impact on highly salient issues that draw intense attention from the media and voters and thereby pose the most direct threat of electoral punishment for unresponsiveness. Presumably, as E.E. Schattschneider (1960) suggests, greater public attention to an issue expands the "scope of conflict" and heightens the risk for government officials who defy their constituents' views. In contrast, narrow, well-organized interests may dominate less visible issues. Some empirical evidence (e.g. Page and Shapiro, 1983, 181) seems to support the prediction of greater public influence with higher salience.

The assumption of government responsiveness to public opinion in median voter theory has informed research on the "democratic peace," which has found a tendency for individual democratic states and, especially, pairs of democratic states to be more pacific on average than non-democratic states (Russett and Oneal, 2001; for review see Elman, 1997, pp. 10–20). One aspect of democratic peace research argues that competitive elections "makes democratic leaders. . . sensitive to public opinion" because politicians either anticipate electoral punishment or they are thrown out of office for being unresponsive: "citizens in a democratic state can influence governmental policy directly, through public opinion, or indirectly, though their representatives."[3]

Tending to confirm the median voter theoretical prediction, quantitative analyses by students of public opinion have found, for example, that 62 percent of U.S. foreign policies *changed* in the same direction as public opinion (Page and Shapiro, 1983, 182), and that congressional-district-level public support for military spending was related to Congress members' votes on military spending bills during the presidency of Ronald Reagan (Bartels, 1991; also see Bartels 2002a and 2002b). Moreover, research based on case studies has reported that public opinion influences U.S. foreign policy by constraining government officials to a range of policies that voters support, removing from consideration broad policy directions that are opposed by the mass public (Sobel, 1991; Russett, 1990).

An ample body of quantitative and qualitative research, then, indicates that U.S. foreign policy and the policy preferences of government officials are substantially influenced by public opinion. Apparently accepting such influence as an empirical fact, a long line of observers including classical realists has urged policy makers *not* to respond to citizens' preferences because of concerns that the general public engaged in "simple moralistic and legalistic" thinking, was detached from the reality of international politics, exhibited unstable shifting "moods," and hungered for "quick results" (Morgenthau, 1973, pp. 135, 146–148; cf. Almond, 1950; Kennan, 1951). Walter Lippmann (1955) warned that following public opinion would create a "morbid derangement of the true functions of power" and produce policies "deadly to the very survival of the state as a free society" (15, 20, 26–27).

PROBLEMS WITH PAST RESEARCH   Previous research concerning the impact of organized groups, epistemic communities, and public opinion on U.S. foreign policy has produced an impressive body of results that invite diverse expectations regarding who influences government officials. This research also suggests that the characteristics of different government institutions may produce different patterns of influence. For example, members of the House of Representatives, which the Federalist Papers labeled the "people's House" due to their frequent election in small and decentralized districts, were expected to be especially sensitive to public opinion, while officials in the executive branch and Senate were expected to be less responsive due to their insulation from the public by indirect elections and longer terms in office.

Past research has not, however, definitely sorted out the relative impact of different factors upon U.S. foreign policy. This has resulted, at least in part, from two problems related to the scholarly division of labor: omitted variables and lack of comparative testing. Understandably, each of the three main approaches we have reviewed has focused on a set of variables of particular interest to it, rarely investigating and testing competing explanations at the same time. Most studies of public opinion and foreign policy, for example, (including those by the present authors) have failed to include any independent variables *other* than public opinion.

However understandable this strategy may be, it runs the risk that other important influences may be neglected. It may lead each approach to overestimate the importance of its own favorite factors and to offer little or no estimate of the *relative* impact of different possible influences. Also, even excellent case studies that disentangle causal mechanisms and trace processes of policy-making usually leave open the issue of how well they generalize beyond those particular cases.

What is needed, we believe, is *comparative* analysis (based on a large number of diverse cases) of the relative influence upon U.S. foreign policy of these key factors: organized groups (especially business and labor); epistemic communities from think tanks and the academy; and mass public opinion. The present paper offers a first step in that direction.

II. DATA AND METHODS

We have analyzed a set of data that are uniquely well suited to this purpose, based on eight quadrennial pairs of surveys—conducted from 1974 through 2002—that were sponsored by the Chicago Council on Foreign Relations or CCFR (and, in 2002, also by the German Marshall Fund of the United States) and implemented by the Gallup Organization and Louis Harris and Associates or its later incarnation, Harris Interactive.[4] These surveys provide data on a wide and diverse set of foreign policy preferences of two distinct groups: the general public, and a set of "foreign policy leaders" including important actors that make American policy (government officials in the executive branch, the House of Representatives, and the Senate), members of critical interest groups (especially business and labor), and members of epistemic communities (namely, educators and leaders of private foreign policy organizations or think tanks).[5] Our data come from paired surveys conducted at 8 different time points, for a total of 16 separate surveys.

The paired surveys of the mass public and foreign policy leaders have both strengths and limitations. The government officials and other elites were not randomly selected for interviews; they were chosen from institutional positions involving foreign policy responsibilities or expertise.[6] Nor were the numbers of elites interviewed in any single year very large.[7] The surveys of the general public, though, were based on random, relatively large samples of about 1,550 respondents each.[8]

Despite their limitations, the CCFR data make it possible to conduct what is, so far as we know, the first systematic examination of the relative influences of ordinary citizens, interest groups, and epistemic communities on American government officials across a wide range of foreign policy issues over a lengthy period of time. Data on large numbers of key policy makers are very difficult to obtain (but cf. Holsti and Rosenau, 1984), especially from samples that are comparable over multiple years.[9]

Pooling the Chicago Council surveys for cross-sectional analysis is a promising approach. The samples add up across surveys to 2,916 respondents from all groups of elites and 1,901 respondents from the theoretically crucial groups of leaders from government, business, labor, and experts. The elite samples have the advantage of being drawn in a consistent manner across years, because of continuity in survey organizations and research teams as well as conscious efforts to produce comparable data. In addition, the private and confidential nature of the interviews with respected survey organizations helped to discourage public posturing and encourage relatively candid expression of views.

A crucial advantage of using these survey data is that they permit us to analyze relationships using precise, directly comparable measures between the policy preferences of policy makers and those of the public, members of interest groups, and experts. These measures are based on responses to identical questions asked of the various groups at the same time. Previous researchers have generally lacked such comparable measures and have had to struggle with the question of exactly how close a given policy came to the wishes of particular actors.

Our analyses rest on the assumption that the expressed policy preferences of government officials are reasonable indicators of the foreign policies that they enact or pursue. Although we do not suppose that our data on policy makers' expressed preferences invariably and without exception correspond with actual policy, scrutiny of the data indicates that policy makers' responses have usually reflected the positions and actions of the institutions in which they held office. We believe that the problem of possible slippage between these survey responses and actual foreign policy is outweighed by the enormous advantage of being able to obtain precise, comparable, quantitative measures of the positions of government officials, organized groups, experts, and the public.[10]

Our dependent variables are measured in a simple fashion: the percentage of policy makers (that is, the percentage of all policy makers, or of a subset of policy makers from the administration, the House, or the Senate) who favored or opposed a particular policy alternative in a given survey.[11] We believe that these percentage measures generally reflect the position of the average policy maker on an underlying policy continuum. The percentage that "favors" a particular type of foreign aid, for example, may reflect the *amount* of aid that the average respondent favors.[12]

Our independent variables are measured in the same way: percentages of the general public, or of relevant subsets of elite respondents (of business people, labor leaders, or experts, for example) who favored or opposed the same policy alternative that the policy makers were asked about. Because "Don't know" and "Refuse to answer" responses are more common among the general public than among policy makers, we excluded those responses from the mass public surveys and recomputed percentages without them. This gave us comparable measures of the views of *those with opinions* among elites and the mass public.

The scope and duration of the Chicago Council's parallel studies of elites and the general public enabled us to analyze variations across different institutions (comparing subsets of policy makers from the administration, the House, and the Senate), and variations in levels of issue salience to the public. In addition, we separately examined three broad, exhaustive, and mutually exclusive policy domains: Diplomatic Policy (e.g. relations with other countries and international organizations); Defense Policy (including the recruitment and deployment of troops, military aid, and the development, procurement, and transfer to other countries of military hardware); and Economic Policy (e.g. issues related to trade, tariffs, and the protection and promotion of American jobs and businesses). Diplomatic and Defense policies were asked about most frequently (214 and 209 common items, respectively), followed by Economic policy (144 common items).

Since our aim is to sort out the *independent* impact of each factor and to compare them with each other, we relied primarily upon multivariate regression analyses. The meaningful and intuitively understandable units of measurement involved (percentage points on the familiar zero to 100 scale) led us to focus on unstandardized OLS regression coefficients, which can tell us how many percentage points of change in policy makers' support for a policy are typically associated (controlling for all other factors) with a one-percentage-point increase in support by (for instance) business respondents. A coefficient near zero would signal no influence at all upon policy makers by business, whereas a coefficient near 1.0 would signal very great influence. We conducted these regression analyses for all years combined (the most stable and reliable set of estimates) and for each separate year; for all policy makers combined and for each separate institutional subgroup of policy makers; for all issues together and for each of the three issue categories separately; and for issues grouped according to varying degrees of salience.

We employed three general types of regression models. First, we pooled the data across all eight pairs of surveys into a single cross section and regressed the preferences of policy makers at a given time on those of business people, experts, labor leaders, and ordinary citizens at the same time. The eight surveys of the mass public and eight parallel surveys of foreign policy leaders produced a total of 567 common survey items ascertaining preferences about foreign policy: that is, 567 questions about policy preferences that were asked in the same year, with identical wording, of both citizens and elites.[13] The number of common items varied from a high of 112 in 2002 to a low of 48 in 1986. For each of the 567 common items, then, we obtained measures of the policy preferences of policy makers, the general public, business people, labor leaders, and foreign policy experts, as well as other groups of leaders less relevant to the analysis. This pooled cross-sectional analysis allowed us to estimate the contemporaneous impact on policy makers by members of organized groups (business and labor), experts, and public opinion.

Although the cross-sectional analysis is valuable, we also wanted to examine possible complicating dynamics and causal ambiguities by including one or more variables measured over time. One possible complication is that past government decisions may structure or "lock in" the positions of current government officials. The views of foreign policy makers may be bound or conditioned by past government positions or commitments in treaties or agreements. This kind of self-reinforcing process has been found in the incrementalism of government budget making (Wildavsky, 1975). In short, we needed to design a regression model to incorporate the "inertial" forces of foreign affairs and, to the extent possible, control for them.

Our second type of regression model therefore addresses the potential for incremental, self-reinforcing dynamics by lagging the dependent variable to get at the effects of prior preferences of foreign policy decision makers. What we need are data on the past history of our dependent variables. Fortunately, our data set does allow us to identify many "two-time-period" cases—that is, pairs of identical survey items that were asked in two sequential surveys of both the mass public and elites. We identified 252 sequential pairs, which allow us to conduct regression analyses that lag the dependent variable for one period—using responses to the same policy preference question when it was asked in the survey four years earlier. In such regressions, policy makers' 1978 support for economic foreign aid (for example) is predicted by the policy makers' 1974 views on aid, together with the 1978 preferences of the mass public, business and labor leaders, and experts. This model allows us to examine the impact on policy makers of contemporaneous views of the general public, business and labor leaders, and experts, while taking account of the effects of the past policy preferences of government officials.

Another complicating factor concerns causality. Statistically disentangling whether public opinion and non-governmental elites affect policy makers, or whether the reverse happens—whether policy makers influence the preferences of others—is a daunting challenge. The tracking of temporal sequences (i.e., whether changes in hypothesized independent variables actually precede changes in the dependent variable) and the logic of "Granger causality" (i.e., whether the history of hypothesized independent variables actually adds explanatory power to that of the history of dependent variables) are valuable approaches for assessing the determinants of political phenomenon (see Freeman, 1983).

Our third type of regression model uses the data from sequential pairs of survey questions to conduct two-observation time series analyses. Although the restriction to two time points prevents us from conducting full-scale time series analyses, we can at least begin to get at the logic of causal time asymmetries and Granger causality. For example, in such a regression the 1978 preferences of policy makers concerning foreign economic aid are predicted by the 1974 preferences concerning aid of the public, experts, labor and business leaders, and the policy makers themselves. Since causes generally precede rather than follow effects, this time asymmetry adds to our confidence about causal inferences and indicates whether or not various factors have an impact over time. Incorporating the most recent past history of the independent and dependent variables begins to get at Granger causal logic.

The two-observation time series analyses maximize the potential of our data but are not without limitations. First, because of the four-year intervals between surveys, our lags are relatively long and may not allow us to distinguish the different speeds and effectiveness with which certain groups may exercise influence. For instance, major, internationally oriented business leaders may be able to exercise influence especially quickly because they are highly attuned to policy impacts and have privileged access to policy makers. By contrast, labor leaders may tend to have only delayed influence due to reliance on building up pressure in congressional districts or a national mass constituency. Second, we lack a full account of the history of the independent and dependent variables and therefore cannot conduct full Granger tests. We can only lag our variables one period. Finally, our use of two-observation cases reduces the number of cases available for analysis, which can make it difficult to find statistically significant results.

III.   ANALYZING INFLUENCES ON FOREIGN POLICY MAKERS

We began our analysis by examining bivariate relationships at one point in time between the preferences of all policy makers taken together, and those of the mass public as well as each of the seven distinct clusters of "foreign policy leaders" that the Chicago Council surveys repeatedly interviewed (from business, labor, educators, private foreign policy organizations or think tanks, editors and journalists from the media, special interest groups relevant to foreign policy, and religious officials). All these bivariate relationships were highly significant (at the .01 level) and quite large. The percentage of policy makers preferring a specific policy was most strongly correlated with the percentage preferring the same policy among respondents from the media (r=.94), business (r=.91), foreign policy organizations and think tanks (r=.90), and educators (r=.90). Religious leaders (r=.85) and labor leaders (r=.84) came not far behind, with the general public (r=.77) taking up the rear.

The current preferences of policy makers were almost as strongly correlated (and highly significantly so) with preferences from the *previous time period* for the media (r=.86), business (r=.85), foreign policy organizations and think tanks (r=.84), and educators (r=.83). Religious leaders (r=.78) and labor leaders (r=.81) again came not far behind, while the general public (r=.71) continued to trail the others.

The results for business are consistent with previous research on organized groups, and the findings for think tanks and educators are in line with the analysis of epistemic communities. The relatively low figures for the public are surprising given previous research findings that policy makers are highly responsive. On the other hand, a correlation in the .7 or .8 range cannot be sneered at. It could leave room for an estimate of substantial impact in the context of multivariate analysis.

The high correlations for religious leaders and the media are puzzling. In both cases, there is reason to doubt whether they really have a major, direct impact upon the making of U.S. foreign policy. Few scholars have asserted that they do, and in theoretical terms, any such influence would presumably be primarily channeled through the public. It seems possible that the high correlations are spurious or result from reciprocal relationships. The media, for example, have not often been identified by researchers as a direct influence on policy making, but considerable research does suggest the opposite causal connection—

i.e. the influence of government officials upon media that rely upon the officials as news sources (e.g. Sigal, 1973; Gans, 1979; Hallin, 1986; Bennett, 1990 and 1994; Herman and Chomsky, 1988; Nacos et al, 2000, Part I). And the media are often thought of as being affected by, as well as themselves influencing, their audiences, which consist largely of the general public and businesses that take out advertisements.

Not only do the preferences of all the elite groups surveyed by the Chicago Council correlate highly with the preferences of policymakers: they also correlate very highly with each other. Contemporaneous correlations were in the r=.90 to .92 range, and sometimes (as in the case of educators and the media) reached the near-astronomical level (for survey data) of .96; correlations with preferences at the previous time point were also quite high, though generally about a tenth of a point weaker. Substantively, this suggests the existence of something like a "foreign policy establishment," in which policy preferences are largely shared across several different categories of elites engaged in foreign policy, while the general public stands somewhat to the side. (Contemporaneous correlations between the preferences of the public and those of the various elite groups range from .82 and .83—for labor and religious leaders respectively—down to .68 for private foreign policy organizations and think tanks; correlations with responses from the previous time period are similar, though a bit lower.)

The policy preferences of members of this "foreign policy establishment"—especially experts, business people, and policy makers—have consistently differed from those of the general public in some respects. Ordinary Americans, for example, have repeatedly expressed stronger support for multilateral, cooperative foreign policy. The public, more than policy makers and other elites, has favored strengthening the United Nations, working closely with allies, and participating in international treaties and agreements like the Kyoto Agreement on global warming, the International Criminal Court, and the Comprehensive Nuclear Test Ban Treaty. Ordinary Americans have also regularly put a higher priority than elites on domestic-impact aspects of foreign policy, such as protecting Americans' jobs, stopping the inflow of illegal drugs, and reducing illegal immigration (see Rielly 1975, 1979, 1983, 1987, 1991, 1995, and 1999, and Boutin and Page, 2002.)

Methodologically, the high intercorrelations among elite groups augur possible trouble with multicollinearity. Sorting out distinct effects in a precise and reliable fashion is a difficult challenge. In any case, bivariate correlation coefficients are clearly inadequate for estimating the independent impacts of the public and various elite groups upon government officials. To test the hypotheses of interest requires multivariate analyses. We now turn to our three types of regression models: pooled cross-sectional analyses (what we refer to as Model 1); cross-sectional analyses that include a lagged dependent variable (Model 2); and time series analyses that regress the current preferences of policy makers on the preferences of policy makers, public, and non-governmental elites from the previous survey (Model 3).

The Dominance of Business and Experts

Our first step in the cross-sectional multivariate analysis (Model 1) was to estimate what could uncharitably be called a "garbage can" model, with policy makers' foreign policy preferences as the dependent variable and with the preferences of the general public and of each of the CCFR's seven distinct clusters of elites as independent variables. This regression revealed a pattern already hinted at by the bivariate correlations: rather substantial and highly significant coefficients for business (b=.31) and think tanks (b=.22), but a second-tier status for labor (b=.09, significant at only p<.05) and especially the public, which had a near-zero coefficient and apparently no statistically significant effect at all.[14]

Our additional regression models generally confirmed the impression of dominant influence by business. Model 2, which consists of mostly cross-sectional analysis but includes the lagged dependent variable (policy makers at t–1), showed large and highly significant coefficients for business (b=.29). The effects of labor and think tanks about half as strong, and the coefficient for the public failed to reach statistical significance. The estimated effect of the lagged dependent variable was statistically significant, though weak (b=.18). The implication is that, after taking account of policy makers' previous preferences, business continued to exert a substantial contemporaneous effect on government officials: business leaders apparently exert an influence that breaks through the self-reinforcing inertial process of foreign policy making.

Model 3 (which is the time series model that regresses the current preferences of policy makers on the preferences of the public and non-governmental elites from a prior survey) offers some evidence regarding causality that largely fits our earlier findings, but with a new wrinkle. Even with the unusually long lag of four years and the absence of fuller histories of the dependent variables, this model did confirm the influence of business (b=.27) and added new evidence of labor's effect (b=.36). The lagged dependent variable remained significant and substantial (b=.35) and the coefficients for the public, educators, think tanks, the media, and religious groups did not reach statistical significance. According to the logic of time asymmetries and Granger causality, this indicates that business and labor actually do influence the foreign policy preferences of policy makers. These initial results appear to support the notion that business access and resources may facilitate relatively quick impact, while labor exerts pressures over time as it works through decentralized congressional districts.

The "garbage can" models, however, produced, some very odd coefficients,[15] presumably because they ran afoul of two serious methodological problems. First, the cohesiveness of the "foreign policy establishment" did indeed produce extremely high levels of multicollinearity, with VIF coefficients of above 20 for the media and 15 for educators in the cross sectional analysis (a VIF coefficient above 10 is generally considered troubling: see Chatterjee and Price, 1991). Second, the theoretical rationale for the causal structure of the "garbage can" model is highly questionable. For example, this model treats the preferences of media figures as a purely independent variable that directly influences government officials, even though previous research (as noted above) suggests the opposite causal connection, casting a pall of causal ambiguity over the media coefficient. Direct impact by religious leaders is also questionable.

In order to address the methodological flaws of the "garbage can" model we refined the analysis to include only a theoretically solid core of independent variables. We dropped from analysis the media variable (which suffered from high multicollinearity and causal ambiguity), religious leaders (also causally ambiguous), and "special interest groups" (poorly defined and showing little estimated impact).[16] Further, we combined educators with respondents from private foreign policy organizations and think tanks, whose preferences were highly correlated with each other (r=.92) and played essentially the same roles in regressions when entered separately. The result is a single variable for the policy preferences of "experts," which is consistent with research on epistemic communities.

Subsequent regression analyses using refined, parsimonious models yielded results that were considerably more satisfying both substantively and methodologically.

In our first and most important set of refined analyses, the dependent variables were the foreign policy preferences of all policy makers combined, as well as those of the three distinct clusters of government officials in the House of Representatives, the Senate, and the Administration. These analyses included only the four independent variables needed to test the principal theoretical expectations we have discussed: the preferences of the general public, business, labor, and foreign policy experts. Each of these variables, with the possible exceptions of experts and the mass public, can reasonably be treated as exogenous with respect to government decision makers. The policy preferences of business and labor leaders are arguably rooted in economic interests and in well-developed values; they are not likely to vacillate with the particular officials currently holding office. "Experts," on the other hand, may be cultivated and even selected by officials. The foreign policy preferences of the mass public may be influenced by government officials as well; this would lend ambiguity to the interpretation of large coefficients for the public, but (as we will see) no such coefficients have been found. (Estimates of a *lack* of influence are largely free of causal ambiguity.)

As Table 1 indicates, our three regression models were rather effective in accounting for the variation in policy makers' preferences: adjusted R-squared values were all high, ranging from .70 to .90. Taken together, the preferences of business, experts, labor and the public account for the bulk of variation in the foreign policy preferences of policy makers, both contemporaneously and over time. This is particularly true for all policy makers together, but nearly as much so for the separate groups.

The strongest and most consistent results in Table 1 are the coefficients for business, which suggests that business corporations and associations have a strong—even dominant—impact upon the making of U.S. foreign policy. According to cross sectional analysis (Model 1), when business people change their preferences for a given foreign policy by 10 percentage points, policy makers (taken together) respond by changing their preferences about 5 points in the same direction. Business preferences were the strongest predictor within each of the three separate institutional arenas, peaking at a .71 coefficient for administration officials (more than double the only other significant coefficient, that of experts). This result is consistent with the expectations of many international relations scholars who focus on interest groups, but not with the expectations of those who envision an autonomous executive. To the extent that the executive dominates foreign policy, this is especially striking.

Taking account of possible inertial forces in policy making by lagging the dependent variable, Model 2 produces a similar story of business dominance

Table 1 INFLUENCES UPON THE FOREIGN POLICY PREFERENCES OF GOVERNMENT OFFICIALS (BASIC MODELS)

Independent Variables	Dependent Variables			
	All Policy Makers	House	Senate	Adm
Model 1: Pooled Cross Sectional Analysis				
Public$_t$	.03	.10*	.03	-.08
Business$_t$	.52**	.43**	.43**	.71**
Labor$_t$	.16**	.19**	.21**	.04
Experts$_t$	.30**	.28**	.31**	.31**
Model 2: Analysis with Lagged Dependent Variable				
Public$_t$	-.03	.03	.05	-.10
Business$_t$	.44**	.29**	.39**	.58**
Labor$_t$	.16**	.17**	.10	.03
Experts$_t$	.24**	.31**	.25*	.26**
Govt Officials$_{t-1}$ #	.19**	.22**	.24**	.23**
Model 3: Analysis with Independent and Dependent Variables Lagged				
Public$_{t-1}$	-.14	-.13	-.12	-.22*
Business$_{t-1}$	.24*	.18	.37**	.46**
Labor$_{t-1}$	.34**	.40**	.33**	.33**
Experts$_{t-1}$	.07	.11	.01	.04
Govt Officials$_{t-1}$ #	.39**	.34**	.21**	.28**
Adjusted R^2	.80	.79	.70	.72
N	212	212	212	212

Note: Entries are unstandardized coefficients from OLS regressions, with the percentage of government officials who take a given position as the dependent variable and the percentages of members of each of the listed groups who take that same position as independent variables.

 # We lagged the preferences of the government officials when they were the dependent variable. For instance, when we used all policy makers in the dependent variable, the preferences of this group of government officials in the previous survey were included as an independent variable.

Level of Significance: * p<.05 level, 2-tailed test; ** p<.01, 2-tailed test among all policy makers and, especially, administration officials (Table 1). The consistently significant and moderately strong coefficients for policy makers lagged one period indicate that the contemporary views of policy makers are indeed influenced or conditioned by the history of already established perspectives. Business leaders are exerting an effect on government officials, then, that is quite apart from whatever influence they had on past policy that carried forward through the self-reinforcing quality of previous decisions.

The Model 3 time series analysis in Table 1 provides a critical test of whether the views of business "cause" changes in the foreign policy preferences of policy makers, according to the logic of Granger models. Regressing the preferences of all policy makers (as well as each separate group of officials) on the independent and dependent variables from the prior survey largely confirmed the dominance of business, with one wrinkle. The logic of Granger causality suggests that business leaders are most influential on officials in the Senate and especially the administration, while not exerting any meaningful impact at all on officials in the House of Representatives. This institutional differentiation of business influence is supported by previous research in international relations, which stresses the responsiveness of administration officials to business in order to improve the performance of the economy and the prospects that voters will reward (rather than punish) the president and his party as the electorate retrospectively evaluates incumbent's term in office. The absence of significant business influence on officials in the House seems to contradict expectations, but it may simply mean than the House is more responsive to local, parochial groups than to the major multinational firms included in the CCFR surveys.

Experts appear to be the second strongest contemporaneous influence on policy makers' preferences (Table 1, Models 1 and 2). This result, which (to some extent, at least) fits the expectations of researchers on epistemic communities, applied with nearly identical magnitude to all policy makers combined and to those in each of the three institutional settings. But experts did not exert any significant influence at all according to the time series analysis (Model 3), suggesting that their effects are relatively quick and decay quickly—or possibly that the cross-sectional estimates are artifacts of specification error, and experts' preferences are results rather than causes of policy makers' stands.

Labor is estimated to exert contemporaneous influence on foreign policy decision makers, but only weakly (b=.16 for all policy makers in Models 1 and 2), and not consistently across the different clusters of officials. Research on the role of interest groups in the making of U.S. foreign policy generally anticipates just such a modest role for organized labor. What is surprising, though, is that Labor emerges as the second strongest influence in the time series analysis (Model 3), especially among government officials in the House of Representatives. These results offer substantial evidence regarding causal direction: Labor, despite its limited contemporaneous influence, is apparently able—possibly owing to its active presence in states and localities—to apply delayed pressure on government officials and, especially, House members who are particularly sensitive to organized pressure within their decentralized districts.

Perhaps the most surprising finding in this whole set of analyses is the failure of public opinion, even within these reduced and refined models, to show any substantial or consistent influence upon policy makers. The public's preferences had no significant positive coefficient anywhere except for the contemporaneous estimate for officials in the House of Representatives, and even there the estimated impact was quite weak (b=.10) (Model 1). The negative coefficients in the time series analysis (Model 3), if taken seriously, actually indicate that—controlling for the past views of governmental and non-governmental elites—officials tend perversely to move *away* from public opinion. But a more plausible interpretation is that the public simply has no effect at all.

These findings hint at partial confirmation of the Founders' expectations about the House as "the people's" chamber. More importantly, however, they run against the thrust of much past research that has found a substantial impact of public opinion.

The analyses in Table 1 are the bedrock of our empirical investigation, but we also used the same set of three regression models to explore possible variations over time and across three different domains of foreign policy—Defense, Diplomacy, and Economic issues. The separate analyses of each of the eight survey years produced results that generally paralleled those for all years combined (as shown in Table 1), with some apparently random variation in coefficients due to the small numbers of cases.[17] For the different issue domains, too, the general pattern held: business dominance, contemporaneous but not lagged effects of experts, and delayed effects by labor, with little impact from the public. In the Economic realm, where foreign policy cuts close to home, public opinion appeared to have significant contemporaneous influence on policy makers: a modest coefficient of .17 in Model 1 but a more substantial .36 in Model 2. With regard to Defense policy, Model 1 indicated that business had a particularly strong effect (b=.77) consistent with some previous literature (e.g., Snyder, 1991). But according to Model 2, experts (b=.58) roughly equaled business (b=.49) in effects on Defense policy. Because of the limited number of cases, we are cautious in interpreting these or other issue-specific results.

Searching for Public Influence on Government Officials

Given the surprisingly weak estimates of influence by public opinion (with the partial exception of influence on House members and in economic policy), we were concerned that real public influence might be masked by the inclusion in the analysis of labor leaders, whom we found to have moderate influence on policy makers and whose preferences are fairly strongly correlated with those of the public (r=.82.) In order to give public opinion the best possible opportunity to display effects, we dropped the labor variable and regressed the preferences of policy makers only on the preferences of the general public, business, and experts.

The amount of variance accounted for was virtually the same as in the earlier models, suggesting that the public and labor can indeed be substituted for each other without having much effect on predictive power. But even with these rather generous—and in fact implausible—causal assumptions (namely, that labor leaders have *no* independent impact upon foreign policy at all but are merely proxies for the general public), the estimated influence of public opinion upon the preference of government officials remained, at best, quite modest.

The Model 1 cross sectional analysis that excluded labor produced coefficients for public influence on all policymakers (b=.11), officials in the House (.21) and Senate officials (.12) that were statistically significant and larger than in the earlier analysis. But these remained much smaller than the comparable coefficients for business (.50 for all policy makers, .40 for House officials, .40 for Senate officials) or experts (.40, .41, .34., respectively) And in Model 2 they mostly vanished, with only a small coefficient for public influence on the "people's House" (.12) remaining statistically significant. In Model 3 (our touchstone for "real," over time influence), public opinion had no significant effects at all. Of particular importance, none of the three models indicated any significant public influence upon the administration, the main center for foreign policy decision making.

Analyses across the three different policy domains mostly continued to show the public as a minor influence, with less impact than experts or, especially, business. For diplomatic policies the public had a cross-sectional (Model 1) coefficient of .18, statistically significant but still well behind business' .40; the results were much the same with Model 2; the coefficient for the public was not statistically significant in Model 3. For economic policy, the public matched business (though trailed experts) with a .27 coefficient for Model 1, nearly matched experts with a .41 coefficient in Model 2 (which included the lagged dependent variable), and exerted no significant effect in Model 3 (time series analysis). Again, the public appears to have a somewhat more effective (though still secondary) voice on close-to-home, economic issues.

One additional context in which these generous, labor-excluded models produced estimates of significant influence by the general public involves highly salient issues. We used the percentage of respondents who gave "don't know" survey responses as a measure of *lack* of salience: the higher the level of "don't knows," the lower the salience. We divided our issue cases into four similarly sized groups with varying degrees of salience, and performed the three types of regression analysis separately on each. For none of the three regression models were there significant public coefficients with any of the three lower-salience groups of issues. For the cross-sectional Model 1, however, and for the very highest-salience group of issues (with only 0% to 4% "don't knows,") the public's coefficient was .21, significant at the p<.001 level. These findings are consistent with Schattschneider's (1960) framework; the public has little or no influence on issues that are out of the public eye, but some influence when salience is high.

Yet even under the ideal conditions for maximal public influence (a public-friendly model specification and the most salient issues with 4% or less "don't knows"), business was estimated to exert twice as much influence as public opinion (b=.44). Indeed, the estimated influence of the public evaporated altogether (i.e. it became non-significant) when we incorporated the history of policy makers' preferences or the past views of the public, business, experts, and government officials, using Models 2 and 3.

In short, in spite of generous model specifications, the effect of public opinion upon the preferences of foreign policy makers appears to be—at best—quite modest, when critical competing variables are controlled for.[18] These results challenge research that has suggested a strong public impact on foreign policy.

Of course our results do not completely rule out any influence by the general public on U.S. foreign policy. In addition to the effects on the House, highly salient issues, and economic policy that we have noted, the public may have substantial impact on particular foreign policy decisions, such as the highly salient questions of war and peace analyzed in Sobel (2001). We have not explored public effects upon agenda setting, or on the rhetorical packaging policy choices, or on decision makers' anticipations of later, *retrospective* public opinion. (The makers of foreign policy may, for example, work hard to avoid military casualties that tend to provoke electoral punishment; see Mueller, 1973.) It is possible that our use of policy makers' expressed preferences rather than actual policies as dependent variables may lead us to miss some "delegate"-style behavior in which policy makers act against their own inclinations in order to please the public. Finally, methodological factors may conceivably have deflated our estimates of public impact. But it is worth emphasizing that our measurements of public opinion (based on large surveys) are quite good; any attenuation of coefficients due to measurement error should affect elite groups more than the public. And causal ambiguity in model specification is not likely to be a problem: an erroneous finding of *non*-influence by the public is considerably less likely to result from specification bias than is an excessively large estimate of its influence.[19]

All in all, the implications of our findings for previous research connecting public opinion and policy making are sobering.

Indirect Business and Labor Influence through Experts?

The substantial influence of experts suggested by our cross-sectional models, though in line with past analyses of epistemic communities, is subject to doubt about its causal status. Even if one rules out (as our analyses do) the possibility of a consistent reciprocal influence of officials upon experts that may inflate their apparent impact on officials, there remains the question whether the preferences of experts are a truly independent variable or whether they function in an intervening role. In other words, experts might themselves be influenced by business or labor, and in turn transmit the preferences of those groups to officials.

Researchers on epistemic communities sometimes assume that independent, objective analysis by new "knowledge-based elites" guides policy makers; experts are not merely vehicles for pressing officials on behalf of organized interests or others. Yet the widespread funding of think tanks by business—and, to a much lesser extent, by organized labor through such organizations as the Economic Policy Institute (or EPI)—suggests that organized interest groups may sometimes affect who becomes a recognized expert and what such experts say. Thus experts might not be autonomous influences upon policy makers, but instead might—in whole or in part—convey the preferences of others to officials.

Without additional data we cannot hope to definitively untangle these causal complexities. But we already know, from our discussion of the "foreign policy establishment," that the policy preferences of experts are not statistically independent of the preferences of business or labor. They are quite highly correlated: the preferences of think tank respondents, for example, were correlated at $r=.90$ with the contemporaneous preferences of business and .80 with those of labor.

If we assume one-way causation from business and labor to experts,[20] we can go further and estimate the independent effects of each, through regressions in which experts' preferences are the dependent variable. The results, shown in

Table 2, are quite striking. The cross-sectional (Model 1) analysis indicates that business had a highly significant and quite large coefficient (b=.61, p<.001), and labor was not far behind (b=.42, p<.001).[21] After taking into account the reinforcing quality of experts' previous views (Model 2), business' estimated effect was nearly twice the magnitude of labor's (b=.48 versus .27). The four-year lag of business views, though, showed no significant effect (Model 3), which suggests that business's influence (if any) is felt relatively quickly.

The results in Table 2 suggest that organized groups influence experts, and that this impact is quite substantial. If we set aside the time series findings of no expert effects on policy makers, and accept the cross-sectional estimates of substantial contemporaneous effects, we can go on to estimate indirect effects that business and labor may have upon public officials through their influence on experts. For example, if (as the cross sectional analysis in Table 2 indicates) a 1 percentage point increase in business support for some policy generally leads to a .61 percentage point increase in experts' support for that policy, and if (as the cross-sectional analysis in Table 1 indicates) such a .61 percentage point increase for experts would then lead to a .183 ($.30 \times .61$) percentage point increase in officials' support, business would obtain a small but not irrelevant increment of indirect clout. This indirect impact of .183 can be added to the

Table 2 EFFECTS OF BUSINESS AND LABOR UPON THE FOREIGN POLICY PREFERENCES OF EXPERTS

Independent Variables	Experts as Dependent Variable		
Model 1: Pooled Cross Sectional Analysis			
Labor$_t$	.42**		
Business$_t$	.61**		
Model 2: Analysis with Lagged Dependent Variable			
Labor$_t$		.27**	
Business$_t$		.48**	
Experts$_{t-1}$		.28**	
Model 3: Analysis with Independent and Dependent Variables Lagged			
Labor$_{t-1}$			.19**
Business$_{t-1}$			.03
Experts$_{t-1}$			.70**
Adjusted R^2	.87	.92	.82
N	567	212	212

Note: Entries are unstandardized coefficients from OLS regressions, with the independent and dependent variables measured as the percentage taking the same position on a given issue.

Level of Significance: * p<.05 level, 2-tailed test, ** p<.01, 2-tailed test direct impact of business upon policy makers (estimated at .52 points in Table 1's cross sectional analysis), yielding a total business impact of slightly over .70. That is to say, a 10 percentage point increase in business support for a given policy may lead to a 7 point, rather than 5 point, increase in officials' support for that policy.[22] Similar calculations for labor based on the cross-sectional analysis indicate a .126 indirect effect of labor on officials. Adding that to the direct effect of .16 given in Table 1, the total impact of labor (in the cross sectional analysis) is about .29.[23] This suggests that labor may influence foreign policy almost as much by indirect means as it does directly, which underscores its surprising sway in foreign policy given its reputation for ineffectiveness in American politics. Labor's total effect combined with its modest over time role (Table 2, Model 3) suggests that it exercises a long-term national influence through experts. Even so, the estimated total effect upon foreign policy of business is more than twice that of labor.

Methodological uncertainties mean that we should not take the magnitudes of these estimates as gospel. Still, they pose a challenge for those who consider the views of experts to be altogether autonomous.

IV. FOREIGN POLICY, THE NATIONAL INTEREST, AND DEMOCRACY

Our analysis using three distinct types of statistical models indicates that business has a strong, consistent, and, at times, lopsided influence upon U.S. foreign policy. The estimates of strong business influence hold up under different statistical models and different political and institutional conditions, and are generally consistent over time. They hold for high- as well as low-salience issues, for a variety of substantive issue areas, and with respect to different institutional groups of policy makers (though especially among administration and Senate officials). They tend to confirm the theoretical expectations and case study research of the organized interest group literature in international relations.

The estimated impacts of experts upon policy makers do not generally match those of business, but they, too, are quite substantial, at least in the cross-sectional rather than time series data. This lends some credence to claims by the analysts of epistemic communities. Our further investigation of who influences experts, however, suggests that organized groups—not just independent, objective evaluations of complex international realities—may color the views of experts. These findings suggest that the foreign policy clout of business and labor may be augmented by an indirect influence upon policy makers that works through experts.

Labor, even taking into account its possible indirect influence, appears to have less impact on U.S. foreign policy than business does. This finding, too, fits with previous work by international relations scholars who focus on organized interest groups. Nonetheless, labor leaders do exert a surprisingly consistently (if secondary) influence on policy makers, especially among members of the House of Representatives and on particular policy areas.

The findings from our cross-sectional analyses as contrasted with the time series analyses (using lagged independent variables) suggest that the influence of business tends to be fairly quick, while labor's influence tends to be delayed and exerted over time as it makes its presence in congressional districts felt. Although labor's effect on foreign policy has been minimized among international relations scholars, our evidence of labor's impact is consistent with recent reevaluations of its nested impact on U.S. social welfare policy (Gottschaulk, 2001).

To our surprise, public opinion—the foreign policy preferences of ordinary citizens—was repeatedly estimated to exert little or no significant influence on government officials. Where the effect of public opinion emerged (namely, very high-salience issues, economic issues, and the House of Representatives), the absolute and relative magnitude of its influence was generally modest. The pattern of *non*-influence by public opinion is generally immune to issues of model specification and causal ambiguity that might affect some of our other results. It seems to contradict the expectations of a large body of previous research.

These findings have several implications for research on international affairs. First, they support the perennial plea (e.g., by Keohane, 1989, and Putnam, 1988) for international relations scholarship to move from mono-causal explanations to multi-causal explanations. Although our evidence suggests that business may exert the most influence on government officials, experts and, to a lesser extent, labor and (occasionally) public opinion also appear to help shape policy makers' views. These results suggest that three of the most prominent lines of analysis of foreign policy—the interest group, epistemic community, and public opinion approaches— each have some merit. But at the same time, each tends to omit critical variables and to avoid systematically examining the relative impact of competing influences. The danger of omitting alternative factors from consideration is that assessments of the importance of particular factors of interest may be inflated. This hazard seems particularly serious for quantitative analyses of the effect of public opinion on foreign policy (cf., however, Ostrom and Marra [1986] and Hartley and Russett [1992], which take steps to be multivariate.)

Second, our results have some troubling normative implications. The apparently weak influence of the public should disappoint those adherents of democratic theory (e.g. Dahl, 1989) who advocate substantial government responsiveness to citizens' preferences. It might initially please classical realist critics of public influence like Lippmann (1955), Morgenthau (1973) and Kennan (1951), who have urged policy makers to resist pressures from what they see as an ill-informed and capricious public. Yet those same critics—and many other observers—would also like to see policy makers rise above the politics of organized interest groups in order to pursue the "national interest," perhaps as identified by independent, objective experts. Our finding of substantial impact upon foreign policy by business—generally greater impact than by experts—suggests that purely technocratic determination of foreign policy does not usually occur. Competing political interests continue to fight over the national interest. Our results suggest that business often wins that competition.

BIBLIOGRAPHY

Adler, Emanuel and Peter Haas. 1992. "Conclusion: Epistemic Communities, World Order, and the Creation of a Reflective Research Program." *International Organization*. 46 (Winter): 367–390.

Almond, Gabriel. 1950. *The American People and Foreign Policy*. New York: Harcourt, Brace.

Art, Robert. 1973. "Bureaucratic Politics and American Foreign Policy: A Critique." *Policy Sciences* 4: 467–90.

Bartels, Larry. 1991. "Constituency Opinion and Congressional Policy Making: The Reagan Defense Buildup." *American Political Science Review* 85: 457–74.

Bartels, Larry. 2002a. "Partisan Politics and the U.S. Income Distribution, 1948–2000." Prepared for presentation at the Annual Meeting of the American Political Science Association, Boston, August 2002.

Bartels, Larry. 2002b. "Partisan Politics and the U.S. Income Distribution, 1948–2000." Paper prepared for the Russell Sage Foundation.

Bates, Robert, and Da-Hsiang Lien. 1985. "A Note on Taxation, Development, and Representative Government." *Politics and Society.* 14: 53–70.

Bennett, W. Lance. 1994. "The Media and the Foreign Policy Process" in *The New politics of American foreign policy* ed. by David Deese. New York: St. Martin's Press.

_____. 1990. "Toward a Theory of Press-State Relations in the United States." *Journal of Communications.* 40 (Spring): 103–25.

Bouton, Marshall M., and Benjamin I. Page (eds). 2002. *Worldviews 2002: American Public Opinion and Foreign Policy.* Chicago: Chicago Council on Foreign Relations.

Burke, Edmund. 1949. "Speech to the Electors of Bristol" in *Burke's Politics, Selected Writings and Speeches* ed. by R. Hoffmann and P Levack. New York: Alfred Knopf.

Chatterjee, Samprit, and Bertram Price. 1991. *Regression Analysis by Example.* 2nd Ed. New York: John Wiley.

Dahl, Robert A. 1989. *Democracy and its Critics.* New Haven: Yale University Press.

_____. 1961. *Who governs? Democracy and power in an American city.* New Haven: Yale University Press.

Doyle, Michael. 1983. "Kant, Liberal Legacies, and Foreign Affairs." *Philosophy and Public Affairs.* 12, no. 3 (Summer): 205–235, and 12, no. 4 (Fall): 323–53.

Downs, Anthony. 1957. *An Economic Theory of Democracy.* New York: Harper and Row.

Elman, Mariam Fendius. 1997. "Introduction: The Need for a Qualitative Test of the Democratic Peace Theory" in *Paths to Peace: Is Democracy the Answer?* Edited by M.F. Elman. Cambridge, MA: MIT Press.

Esping-Andersen, Gøsta. 1990. The Three Worlds of Welfare Capitalism. Princeton, N.J.: Princeton University Press.

Freeman, John. 1983. "Granger Causality and the Time Series Analysis of Political Relationships." *American Journal of Political Science.* 27 (May): 327–58.

Frieden, Jeffry. 1991. "Invested Interests: The Politics of National Economic Policies in a World of Global Finance." *International Organization.* 45: 425–51.

Galenson, Walter. 1986. "The Historical Role of American Trade Unionism" in *Unions in Transition: Entering the Second Century* ed. by Seymour Martin Lipset. San Francisco: Institute for Contemporary Studies.

Gans, Herbert J. 1979. *Deciding What's News.* New York: Random House.

Gottschalk, Marie. 2001. *In the Shadow of the Welfare State* (Ithaca, N.Y.: Cornell University Press).

Gourevitch, Peter. 1986. *Politics in Hard Times.* Ithaca, N.Y: Cornell University Press.

Grossman, Gene, and Ehhanan Helpman. 1995. "Trade Wars and Trade Talks." *Journal of Political Economy.* 103 (August): 675–708.

_____. 1994. "Protection for Sale." *American Economic Review.* 84 (September): 833–850.

Haas, Peter. 1992. "Introduction: Epistemic Communities and International Policy Coordination." *International Organization.* 46 (Winter): 1–35.

Hall, Peter. 1989. *The Political power of economic ideas: Keynesianism across nations.* Princeton: Princeton University Press.

Hallin, Daniel C. 1986. *The "Uncensored War": The Media and Vietnam.* New York: Oxford University Press.

Hartley, Thomas, and Bruce Russett. 1992. "Public Opinion and the Common Defense: Who Governs Military Spending in the United States?" *American Political Science Review.* 86 (December): 905–915.

Herman, Edward and Noam Chomsky. 1988. *Manufacturing consent: The Political Economy of the Mass Media.* New York: Pantheon Books.

Holsti, Oli. 1996. *Public Opinion and American Foreign Policy.* Ann Arbor: University of Michigan Press.

Holsti, Oli, and James N. Rosenau. 1984. *American Leadership in World Affairs: Vietnam and the Breakdown of Consensus.* London: Allen and Unwin.

Kennan, George. 1951. *American Diplomacy, 1900–1950.* (Chicago: University of Chicago Press).

Keohane, Robert. 1989. *International Institutions and State Power.* Boulder, Co: Westview Press.

_____. 1984. *After Hegemony: Cooperation and Discord in the World Political Economy.* Princeton: Princeton University Press.

Keohane, Robert, and Helen Milner, eds. 1996. *Internationalization and Domestic Politics.* Cambridge: Cambridge University Press.

Krasner, Stephen. 1978. *In Defense of the National Interest: Raw Materials, Investments, and U.S. Foreign Policy.* Princeton: Princeton University Press.

_____. 1972. "Are Bureaucracies Important? (Or Allison Wonderland)." *Foreign Policy* 7 (Summer): 159–179.

Lippmann, Walter. 1955. *Essays in the Public Philosophy.* Boston: Little, Brown & Co.

Lipset, Seymour Martin. 1986. *Unions in Transition: Entering the Second Century.* San Francisco: Institute for Contemporary Studies.

Milner, Helen. 1997. *Interests, Institutions, and Information: Domestic Politics and International Relations.* (Princeton, N.J.: Princeton University Press).

_____. 1988. *Resisting Protectionism.* Princeton: Princeton University Press.

Monroe, Alan D. 1979. "Consistency between Public Preferences and National Policy Decisions." *American Politics Quarterly* 7: 3–19.

_____. 1998. "American Public Opinion and Public Policy 1980–1993." *Public Opinion Quarterly* 62: 6–28.

Moravcsik, Andy. 1997. "Taking Preferences Seriously: A Liberal Theory of International Politics." *International Organization.* 51 (Autumn): 513–53.

Morgenthau, Hans. 1973. *Politics Among Nations.* New York: Knopf.

Mueller, John E. 1973. *War, Presidents and Public Opinion.* New York: Wiley.

Nacos, Brigette, Robert Shapiro, and Pierangelo Isernia. 2000. *Decision Making in a Glass House: Mass Media, Public Opinion, and American and European Foreign Policy in the 21ˢᵗ Century.* New York: Rowan and Littlefield Publishers.

Nelkin, Dorothy. 1979. "Scientific Knowledge, Public Policy, and Democracy." *Knowledge, Creation, Diffusion, Utilization.* 1 (September).

Ostrom, Charles W., Jr., and Robin E. Marra. 1986. "U.S. Defense Spending and the Soviet Estimate." *American Political Science Review* 80: 819–41.

Owen, John. 1994. "How Liberalism Produces Democratic Peace." *International Security.* 19 (Fall): 87–125.

Page, Benjamin I., and Robert Y. Shapiro. 1992. *The Rational Public: Fifty Years of Trends in Americans' Policy Preferences.* Chicago: University of Chicago Press.

_____. 1983. "Effects of Public Opinion on Policy." *American Political Science Review.* 77: 175–90.

Peterson, Susan. 1995. "How Democracies Differ: Public Opinion, State Structure, and the Lessons of the Fashoda Crisis." *Security Studies.* 5 (Autumn): 3–37.

Putnam, Robert. 1988. "Diplomacy and Domestic Politics: The Logic of Two-Level Games." *International Organization.* 42 (Summer): 427–60.

Rielly, John. 1975. *American Public Opinion and U.S. Foreign Policy, 1975.* Chicago: Chicago Council on Foreign Relations. Corresponding studies published in 1979, 1983, 1987, 1991, 1995, and 1999.

Rogowski, Ronald. 1989. *Commerce and Coalitions.* Princeton: Princeton University Press.

Rose, Gideon. 1998. "Neoclassical Realism and Theories of Foreign Policy." *World Politics.* 51: 144–72.

Russett, Bruce. 1990. *Controlling the Sword: The Democratic Governance of National Security.* Cambridge: Harvard University Press.

Russett, Bruce. 1996. "Why Democratic Peace?" in *Debating the Democratic Peace* ed. by M. Brown, S. Lynn-Jones, and S. Miller. Cambridge, MA: MIT Press, pp. 82–115.

Russett, Bruce and John Oneal. 2001. *Triangulating Peace: Democracy, Interdependence, and International Organizations.* New York: W.W. Norton & Co.

Sartori, Giovanni. 1987. *The Theory of Democracy Revisited.* Chatham, NJ: Chatham House.

Schattschneider, E.E. 1960. *The Semi-Sovereign People: A Realist's View of Democracy in America.* New York: Holt, Rinehart, and Winston.

Schumpeter, Joseph. 1950. *Capitalism, Socialism, and Democracy.* New York: Harper.

Sigal, Leon V. 1973. *Reporters and Officials: The Organization and Politics of Newsmaking.* Lexington, Mass.: D.C. Heath.

Snyder, Jack. 1991. *Myths of Empire: Domestic Politics and International Ambition.* Ithaca: Cornell University Press.

Sobel, Richard. 2001. *The Impact of Public Opinion on U.S. Foreign Policy Since Vietnam.* New York: Oxford University Press.

Trubowitz, Peter. 1998. *Defining the National Interest: Conflict and Change in American Foreign Policy.* Chicago: University of Chicago Press.

Walt, Stephen M. 1987. *The Origins of Alliances.* Ithaca, N.Y.: Cornell University Press.

Waltz, Kenneth. 1979. *Theory of International Politics.* Reading, MA: Addison-Wesley.

_____. 1959. *Man, the State, and War: A Theoretical Analysis.* New York: Columbia University Press.

Wildavsky, Aaron. 1991. "The Two Presidencies." In *The Two Presidencies: A Quarter Century Assessment.* ed. Steven Shull, 11–25. Chicago: Nelson-Hall Publishers.

_____. 1975. Budgeting: A comparative theory of budgetary processes. Boston: Little, Brown.

Winters, Jeffrey A. 1996. *Power in Motion.* Ithaca: Cornell University Press.

Wittkopf, E. 1990. *Faces of Internationalism: Public Opinion and American Foreign Policy.* Durham, N.C.: Duke University Press.

NOTES

1. Neo-realists devote more attention to the internal effects of domestic politics in the making of foreign policy choices and therefore examine more closely how state policy is formed (cf. Rose, 1998).

2. A number of technical issues affect this prediction. It does not generally hold for competition by more than two parties or in multidimensional issue spaces, and it may be upset if citizens with extreme opinions abstain from voting due to "alienation" from centrist parties.

3. Russett and Oneal, 2001, 274; Peterson, 1995, 10–11; also cf. Russett, 1996, 100. The democratic peace has been attributed not only to the impact of political representation but also to liberal norms that promote non-violent resolution of conflict, international law and shared membership in intergovernmental organizations, and economic interdependence that puts a premium on stable, ongoing commercial relations (Doyle, 1983; Russett and Oneal, 2001; Owen, 1994; Elman, 1997).

4. Gallup conducted the surveys in 1978, 1982, 1986, 1990, 1994, and 1998; Harris conducted them in 1974, and Harris Interactive did so in 2002.

5. Of less interest to the present analysis, the surveys of foreign policy leaders also included respondents from the media, religious leaders, special interest groups relevant to foreign policy, and (in 1974) leaders of minority groups. Moreover, as we discuss below, we created one category of "experts" by combining the distinct groups of "educators" (i.e. faculty who teach in the area of foreign affairs and presidents and chancellors of major universities), "special foreign policy organizations" (i.e. think tanks), and "private foreign policy groups" (i.e. presidents from major foreign policy organizations). In addition to analyzing the impact of this aggregated measure of "experts," we also investigated the separate impact of each of these distinct groups.

6. Senators and Representatives, for example, were chosen (at least through 1990) from the membership of committees and subcommittees related to foreign policy. Administration officials came from the Department of State and from internationally-oriented units of the Commerce, Treasury, Agriculture, and other departments, though rarely from the Department of Defense or the National Security Council. Business respondents were sampled mainly from corporate vice presidents for international affairs, and labor respondents from high level union officials oriented toward foreign affairs. Experts, as we later analyze them, include "educators" (academics specializing in foreign policy or international relations, as well as some high-level college administrators) and leaders or members of private foreign policy associations and think tanks.

7. The average number interviewed each year was about 76 for government officials, 58 for business, 28 for labor, and 79 for experts, which combines educators with individuals from think tanks. Although the categories of respondents are generally quite stable, the 1974 survey combined officials from the House, Senate, and Administration together, and did not survey think tank members. For the surveys from 1978 to 2002, the average number of government officials from the separate government institutions was the following: 19 from the Senate, 36 from the House, and 23 from the administration.

8. In 2002, 2,862 respondents were interviewed by telephone and 400 were interviewed in person, which made it possible to ensure comparability with the previous in-person surveys. We use the combined telephone and in-person data set. The interviews with

the public and leaders were typically conducted in the fall but in 2002 were carried out in June.

9. Holsti and Rosenau (1984) reports an outstanding study of a wide range of U.S. decision makers and foreign policy leaders, including high military officers (unfortunately excluded from the Chicago Council surveys).

10. Even if the correspondence between actual foreign policy and decision makers' expressed preferences is likely to be imperfect, ascertaining the determinants of policy makers' preferences is still of considerable interest so long as those preferences have any substantial impact at all upon policy.

Another possible concern in using these survey data is that some elite respondents undoubtedly delegated answering the CCFR questionnaires to staff members. We believe that subordinates' responses are generally likely to reflect the views of the superiors who hire, promote, and supervise them.

11. All items were dichotomized, using a quasi-random dichotomizing scheme that alternated the polarity of the responses we tabulated—i.e., whether we tabulated the percentage in "favor," the percentage "oppose[d]," or one of those percentages in some combination with neutral responses. The percentage of relevant respondents making that response or combination of responses was then recorded as the value of the dependent variable on that issue for that given year.

This randomizing scheme means that the polarity or direction of preferences on different issues does not have a common intuitive meaning. It is not always the case, for example, that higher percentages signal more "liberal" or more "internationalist" responses. But the randomization was necessary in order to ensure substantial variance and to avoid certain statistical biases in the analyses.

12. The precise relationship between (for example) the percentage of respondents favoring an "increase" in foreign aid, and the amount of aid increase favored by the average respondent, is likely to be complex and related to aspects of survey responses and underlying preferences about which we have little information. But our general point is that the percentage of policy makers "favoring" alternative X is likely to track the *amount* of X favored by the average respondent, which is more directly applicable to actual policy and of more central interest.

13. We necessarily deal only with questions asked of both elites and the general public. The public was asked a number of additional questions. We excluded non-policy survey items (that is, questions not related to preferences about future government action), such as those concerning past performance, or U.S. "vital interests," or "feeling thermometer" ratings of American and world leaders.

14. The unstandardized coefficient for the public was −.005, not significant at even the p<.10 level.

15. For instance, the Model 1 cross-sectional analysis produced coefficient for educators that was (implausibly) negative: −.22; the coefficient for the media was (also implausibly) a positive .63, higher than that for any other group. Models 2 and 3 produced substantially negative coefficients for educators (−.18) and special interest groups (−.22).

16. The preferences of "special interest groups" (for which we could find no definition in the survey documentation) had a non-significant coefficient of .02 in the cross-sectional analysis of the garbage can model.

17. In most years the coefficient for the public was close to zero, but in 1986 (with particularly few cases) it was an implausibly *negative* −.42. Coefficients for business hovered around .50. Those for labor and experts fluctuated around their combined-years values with no apparent pattern.

18. Given the surprisingly strong findings for labor's influence in Table 1 and the possibility that including public opinion may have underestimated its effect, we conducted our

3 regression models for equations that focused on labor, business, and experts as independent variables. The results parallel our earlier findings.

19. Reciprocal effects of government officials upon public opinion, for example, would bias our cross-sectional estimates of the public's influence on officials *upward* rather than downward.

20. We consider the assumption of one-way causation from business and labor to experts to be fairly plausible, because the deeply rooted economic interests of business and labor are likely to make them resistant to others' influence on their foreign policy preferences. Still, groups and individuals may provide financial support for experts in order to get serious advice (i.e. not only to persuade other audiences)—and may therefore sometimes be influenced by them to some degree. To the extent that this occurs, our estimates of effects upon experts will be biased upward.

21. A similar regression of experts' preferences on those of the public as well as business and labor yielded quite similar coefficients for business and labor, but a rather substantial *negative* coefficient (b=−.25) for the public. This casts considerable doubt on the proposition that public preferences positively influence experts' (or that experts' preferences positively affect the publics'). But multicollineary problems preclude taking either the negative sign or the magnitude of the coefficient very seriously.

22. The inclusion of a lagged dependent variable (Model 2) produced estimates of a substantial total business impact upon policy makers of .56: the indirect impact through experts is .115 (.24 × .48) and the direct impact of business upon policy makers is .44 (Table 1).

23. In the analysis with a lagged dependent variable (Model 2), labor has a slightly smaller total impact of .22: .06 indirect effect through experts (.24 [Table 1] × .27 [Table 2]), combined with a direct effect of .16.

$\mathcal{Z}$

Political Conflict and Foreign Policy in the United States: A Geographical Interpretation

Peter Trubowitz

INTRODUCTION

During the quarter-century that followed World War II, American leaders were able to mobilize broad domestic support for their foreign policies. While the conventional wisdom that 'politics stopped at the water's edge' was at best a half-truth, the fact remains that political leaders enjoyed considerable latitude in the making of foreign policy. No one would characterize more recent American foreign

Peter Trubowitz, "Political Conflict and Foreign Policy in the United States: A Geographical Interpretation," *Political Geography*, 12, 2 (March 1993): 121–135. Copyright © 1993, with permission from Elsevier.

policy-making in these terms. From the early 1970s onward, America's leaders experienced great difficulty in articulating a vision of the national interest that inspired broad support in Congress and the polity at large. The foreign policy consensus gave way to bitter and politically divisive conflicts over America's role in the world. Debates took on strongly emotional and symbolic overtones. The Cold War ended, but deep divisions over the ends and means of foreign policy persist. At a time when America's leaders need to make wise choices about the future, doubts remain about their ability to resolve the conflicts that have produced political gridlock and paralysis.

Practitioners, commentators and scholars recognize that American leaders no longer enjoy the freedom or autonomy in managing the nation's foreign policy that they once did. Disagreements arise when it comes to explaining this change. Some analysts locate the source of the problem in the electoral arena, and attribute the change to partisan politics and divided party government (McCormick and Wittkopf, 1990; Winik, 1991). Other observers stress the impact that the dispersion of power in Congress in the 1970s has had on the foreign policy-making process (Destler, 1981; Huntington, 1988; Warburg, 1989). They argue that the breakdown of the seniority system, the proliferation of subcommittees, and the expansion in staff and research resources has made it easier for individual members to pursue their own paths on foreign-policy matters and more difficult for the White House to control Congress. Still others emphasize divisions in élite and mass opinion (Holsti and Rosenau, 1984; Schneider, 1992). Such fragmentation, they contend, makes it harder for national leaders to mobilize consent and act strategically in the international arena.

This paper offers an alternative argument about why consensus-building in the area of foreign policy became more difficult. It is argued that since the early 1970s, conflict over foreign policy has been part-and-parcel of a larger, regionally-based struggle for national wealth and power. For over two decades, the fight over America's overseas ambitions and objectives has split the nation along regional lines, pitting the Northeast against the South. Support for the expansive and expensive foreign policy agenda that crystallized after World War II has remained strongest in the South where state and local economies benefit disproportionately from policies that require large federal defense outlays. In the Northeast, where the domestic costs of an expansionist foreign policy now outweigh the benefits, politicians have favored a more restrained and cost-conscious approach to foreign policy. The seemingly intractable divisions over foreign policy are the result of this competition between two regionally-based coalitions which have distinct—and often conflicting—interests.

This argument has two implications for understanding contemporary debates over American foreign policy. The first is that place matters. Sectionalism remains a fundamental feature of American politics, and the politics of foreign policy is no exception. Like other periods in American history when ideological conflicts over foreign policy were shaped by deeper conflicts of interests, today's conflicts between 'liberals' and 'conservatives' over the purposes of American power are fueled by conflicting sectional political imperatives. The second implication follows from this: there is no single national interest. Analysts who assume that America has a unique and discernible national interest, and that this interest should or can determine its relations with other nations, are unable to explain the persistent failure to achieve domestic consensus on international objectives. A regional framework which focuses on the struggle among domestic coalitions for control over the foreign policy agenda reveals how politically-contingent competing definitions of 'the' national interest actually are.

This argument is developed through an analysis of the patterns of regional conflict in the House of Representatives. Using Congress as a proxy for the national polity, the patterns of political alignment over foreign policy are reconstructed from 'key' legislative roll-call votes. The primary empirical task is to demonstrate that the conflicts over foreign policy that first arose in the late 1960s and early 1970s—when the Cold War consensus collapsed—are grounded in a regionally-based struggle that has split the nation's oldest and newest industrial regions into opposing camps. A full explanation of this pattern of regional alignment lies beyond the scope of this paper. For present purposes, a large literature on America's changing geography is drawn on to interpret and explain the pattern of regional competition over foreign policy that is revealed by the data analysis. The conclusion comprises a discussion of the broader implications of the analysis for American foreign policy in the post-Cold War era.

REGIONAL INTERESTS AND FOREIGN POLICY

The geographical diversity of the national economy and the spatially decentralized nature of political representation have made regionalism a distinctive and enduring feature of American political life. Geographical disparities in sectoral concentration, technological advancement and international competitiveness mean that the costs and benefits of public policies are often distributed unequally across the nation. The extreme localism of political representation in the US ensures that these regional differences find political expression at the national level. At the national level, the dispersal of decision-making power and competition between the national parties for regional electoral advantage magnifies the role of regional interests, economic needs and political imperatives in shaping the national agenda. Institutional decentralization provides various channels for elected officials to levy claims on the federal government's resources, initiate or obstruct policy change, and build policy coalitions with political élites from other parts of the country through logrolling, vote-trading, ideological appeals and the like. Regional political competition is the result. This is well understood by political geographers who study the regional bases of political conflict over domestic policy matters.

Regionalism also emerges as a consistent dimension of political competition over foreign policy. Often depicted as contests between competing visions of America's role in the world, conflicts over foreign policy are also conflicts of interest. They have a geographical dimension. To a large extent, this reflects the regionally uneven nature of American involvement in the world economy. During the 1890s, for example, the great debate between the 'imperialists' and the 'continentalists' over overseas expansion pitted the industrial and commercial Northeast against the agrarian South (Hays, 1957; Bensel, 1984; Baack and Ray, 1988). The West played a decisive swing role in the conflict. The Northeast favored a neomercantile strategy combining maritime power, territorial expansion and the bargaining tariff to penetrate and 'capture' underdeveloped markets in Latin America and Asia. The South, in many respects still a colonial appendage of the North, supported a less expansive, *laissez-faire* approach to commercial expansion. Southern interests stressed the advantages of free trade with industrialized nations in Europe and did not require overseas holdings or a large military establishment to achieve its commercial objectives.

A quarter of a century later, conflicting regional imperatives once again shaped debates over foreign policy. At issue this time were the causes of the Great Depression and how America should respond to it. The key question was whether America should assume an active role in promoting global economic recovery and preventing the emergence of closed spheres of influence in Europe and Asia. Politicians who came from parts of the country that had the most to gain from an open, interdependent world economy—the Northeast and South—generally favored policies designed to promote commercial liberalization, global monetary co-operation and collective security (Grassmuck, 1951; Schatz, 1972; Cole, 1983; Frieden, 1988). These 'internationalists' waged a fierce battle against their 'nationalist' rivals from the West. The nationalists, who represented areas of the country that were less competitive in the world economy, called for renewed trade protection and opposed attempts to stabilize global commercial and monetary relations, arguing that such policies granted the White House too much authority in the area of foreign policy and threatened republican ideals at home.

In each of these periods, politicians from different parts of the country sought to equate regional interests with the national interest. Foreign policy issues were debated in terms of their immediate impact on regional prosperity and their longer-range consequences for the social and political arrangements which sustained regional economies. The choices politicians made over foreign policy reflected the fact that decisions over the nation's strategic objectives, market orientation and military posture were not geographically neutral. There were regional winners and regional losers. In each period, politicians who championed a 'strong state' were those best-placed to exercise influence over and benefit from the centralization of power and authority that would accompany an active foreign policy. Competing foreign policy agendas were grounded in interests, and the institutional conflicts that arose between the executive and legislative branches reflected patterns of competition that were grounded in these broader societal conflicts.

Explaining deep and persistent conflict over US foreign policy requires some mapping of the nation's economic geography. Functional position alone, however, is too blunt an instrument to explain fully how regional competition over foreign policy is played out in the national political arena. Party politics also plays a role. American party leaders have a long if inglorious record of playing politics with the national interest (Varg, 1963; Terrill, 1973; Divine, 1974; Nincic, 1992). Within the structures of a two-party system, they have often used foreign policies to mobilize electoral support and marginalize political opponents. During the 1890s, Republican leaders used the lure of new markets in Latin America and Asia to attract agrarian interests in the West to their cause and thus to consolidate Republican hegemony at the national level. In the 1930s, the Democrats used tariff reform to exploit regional tensions within the Republican party and broaden the regional base of the New Deal coalition. These cases underscore the fact that regional foreign policy coalitions are forged in the electoral arena. This means that alternative visions of the national interest are shaped by partisan struggles for political advantage.

SPATIAL ANALYSIS OF HOUSE VOTING

The kind of sectional strife that structured the foreign policy debates of the 1890s and 1930s has not disappeared with time. This paper claims that today's foreign policy conflicts are also structured along regional lines. This proposition is tested by examining how members of the House of Representatives vote on key foreign policy issues from the Nixon through Reagan years. The analysis is based on roll-call votes defined as 'key' votes by groups that monitor political activity in the Congress. These groups are: Americans for Democratic Action, Americans for Constitutional Action, and *Congressional Quarterly*.[1] Each group publishes an annual list of votes on important national issues, foreign as well as domestic. These votes constitute a test of members' policy preferences and their positions on issues whose political significance is unlikely to be lost on elected officials. The data set includes all of the major foreign policy initiatives undertaken by a President that required approval by the House, and votes on all major foreign policy issues that reached the House floor. All of the votes included in the analysis were weighted equally.

The data set was broken down and organized by presidency.[2] For each of the presidencies from Nixon through Reagan, voting similarity or agreement scores were calculated for all pairs of state delegations using a modified version of the pairwise agreement index where state delegations (not individual members) are the unit of analysis.[3] Each state delegation's position on a vote was based on the majority position in the delegation voting yea or nay.[4] The voting index measures the percentage of agreement between state delegations on all of the key foreign policy votes during a presidency. The score is 100 when there is perfect agreement between the majority position of two state delegations; it is 0 if there is perfect disagreement. The number of key votes used to compute the agreement index between delegations varied across presidencies. In part, this reflects differences in the numbers of years Presidents were in office. It also reflects variations in the number of votes selected annually by the various organizations.

Multi-dimensional scaling (MDS) was used to capture the political geography of voting over foreign policy. The basic goal of MDS is to describe the empirical relationships between some set of objects in a space of fixed dimensionality. Others have used this technique to recover patterns in congressional voting (MacRae, 1970; Hoadley, 1980; Easterling, 1987). Here, the simplest, non-metric version is used to provide a spatial display of the voting alignments among congressional or state delegations over foreign policy at different points in time. The states (i.e. state delegations) are represented as points in the space, and distance is an analog for similarity (or dissimilarity). The goal is to find the configuration of interpoint distances between state delegations that corresponds as closely as possible to the similarities among the voting behavior of these delegations. Those state delegations which agree most often in voting are closest to each other in the resulting configuration of points. Those which disagree most are farthest apart in the space.

The most important and difficult stage in MDS analysis involves interpretation. First, the quality of a solution, or the fit between the data and the spatial configuration, must be determined. In the program used here, ALSCAL, the quality of a solution is defined by RSQ. Second, the appropriate dimensionality must be determined with respect to RSQ. In principle, a solution can be derived in any number of dimensions, and RSQ will always be higher when a higher dimensionality is allowed. Since MDS works in a space of fixed dimensionality, it is necessary to determine the most appropriate dimensionality, recognizing that there is a trade-off between the quality of fit (high RSQ) and parsimony (a small number of dimensions). Finally, the interpretation involves searching for meaningful patterns, usually defined as clusters or dimensions. While dimensional structure is often emphasized by analysts, it is equally valid to focus on clusters and search for areas or neighborhoods of the space that have meaning associated with other shared characteristics.[5] This is the approach adopted here.

MDS Results

The results of the scaling analysis are summarized in Table 16.1. Configurations were generated in one, two and three dimensions using ALSCAL. The two-dimensional configuration was selected as the best representation of voting patterns in each of the four presidencies. On average, the two-dimensional solutions account for 94.6 percent of the variance. A third dimension improves the fit by only 1.9 percent on average. (ALSCAL also generates a 'badness of fit' function, known as STRESS, which is also presented in Table 16.1.) The configurations are presented in Figures 16.1–4. The vertical and horizontal axes are not labelled and should not be interpreted in terms of two linear, orthogonal dimensions. The configurations should be interpreted as clusterings of states in a two-dimensional space. A closely grouped cluster of states indicates a cohesive voting bloc. States from the Northeast are underlined. Those from the South are in italics. States from the West are in regular typeface. See the Appendix for a listing of the states in each section.

Table 16.1 SUMMARY OF MULTI-DIMENSIONAL SCALING SOLUTIONS

Presidency	RSQ dimensions			STRESS dimensions		
	1	2	3	1	2	3
Nixon	0.843	0.928	0.957	0.233	0.130	0.090
Ford	0.944	0.966	0.979	0.142	0.094	0.067
Carter	0.854	0.924	0.948	0.221	0.133	0.099
Reagan	0.929	0.966	0.974	0.156	0.097	0.077

Source: Derived from recorded roll-call votes in US Congress.

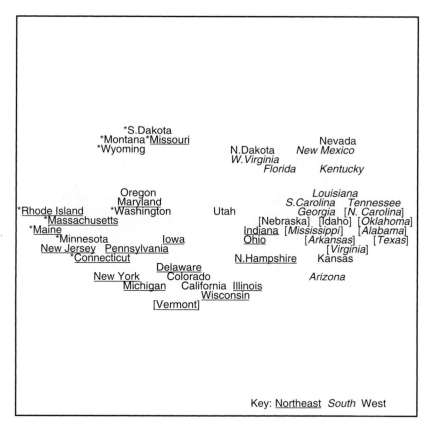

Figure 16.1 Foreign policy alignment during Nixon years. *Source:* derived from multi-dimensional scaling of key roll-call votes in US Congress.

A visual examination of the MDS configurations reveals that the voting align-ment is regional in nature. In each of the spatial maps, the pattern of alignment is defined by discrete clusters or blocs of states. While the cohesion of these voting blocks varies over time, it is apparent that a large proportion of the states consis-tently cluster on opposite sides of the configurations. During each of the four administrations, the pattern of alignment breaks down along north–south lines and falls along lines others have defined as rustbelt–sunbelt, snowbelt–sunbelt, or core–periphery (Phillips, 1969; Sale, 1975; Weinstein and Firestine, 1978; Bensel, 1984). States from the Northeast tend to cluster together on the left side of the voting spaces. Most of those from the South coalesce on the right side of the con-figurations. By contrast, the pattern of voting among states from the West is much more mixed. Some states—like California, Oregon and Washington—cluster with those from the Northeast. Others—like Idaho, Kansas and Nebraska—generally align with states from the South. The analysis indicates that there is little consen-sus over foreign policy.

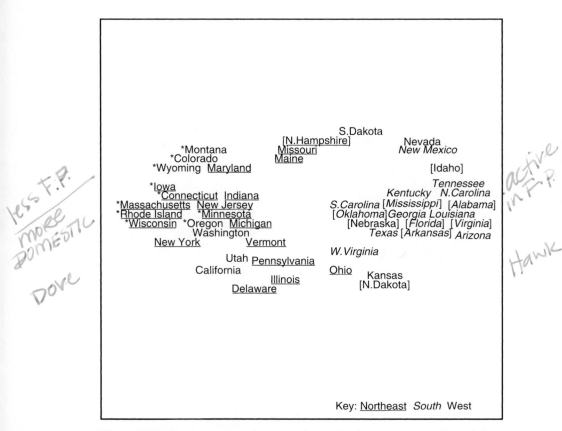

Figure 16.2 Foreign policy alignment during Ford years. *Source:* derived from multi-dimensional scaling of key roll-call votes in US Congress.

Since the Nixon years, the foreign policy agenda in Congress has been dominated by national security issues. While foreign economic policy issues became increasingly important during the Reagan years, the vast majority of the votes in the 1970s and 1980s concerned issues such as defense spending, arms control, war powers, covert operations, military aid, arms sales and overseas alliances. The common and divisive theme that linked these issues was the rising domestic opportunity cost of the *Pax Americana* built after World War II. Critics challenged the *status quo* on two fronts. First, they argued that the ends of American foreign policy outstripped the country's means. Collective energies and resources were being spent unwisely on an expansionist and sometimes misguided foreign policy at the expense of urgent domestic needs and problems. Second, they argued that the method used by national leaders to promote American power overseas threatened republican ideals at home by concentrating political power in the White House.

A number of methods may be used to determine how place-specific these political sentiments are. For present purposes, an index measuring state support for 'strategic retrenchment' was constructed using the votes described above. A vote

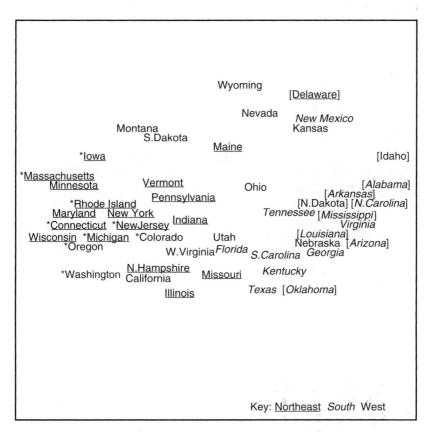

Figure 16.3 Foreign policy alignment during Carter years. *Source:* derived from multi-dimensional scaling of key roll-call votes in US Congress.

against any of the following was considered a vote in favor of strategic retrenchment: defense spending, foreign aid, arms sales, military bases, overseas alliances, military intervention, international institutions and presidential prerogative in the making of foreign policy. Votes for arms control were treated as a vote in favor of a policy of strategic retrenchment. The position of each member of Congress on these votes was identified. A mean support score for a strategy of retrenchment was calculated by averaging across the votes during each of the four administrations. A state mean was then formed by averaging the scores for all members of a congressional delegation.

In each of the figures, the 10 state delegations that scored highest on the index are marked with an asterisk. The 10 congressional delegations that scored lowest on the index are in brackets. Support for a policy of strategic retrenchment is clearly strongest among states that cluster on the left side of the voting space. Since the early 1970s, this coalition has lobbied for cuts in the defense budget, reductions in America's military presence overseas, and limits on presidential prerogative in the making of foreign policy (e.g war powers, covert operations, executive agreements). Many of these states are located in the Northeast. A few are from the West. By

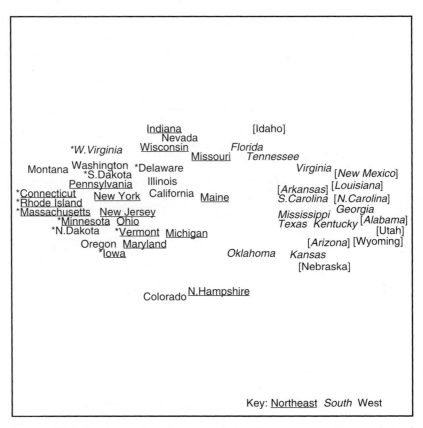

Figure 16.4 Foreign policy alignment during Reagan years. *Source:* derived from multi-dimensional scaling of key roll-call votes in US Congress.

contrast, states that cluster on the right side of the voting spaces have favored a more expansive and expensive conception of the nation's strategic interests, one that has placed a premium on military power. Most of those states that have strongly opposed efforts to scale-back America's role in world affairs are from the South.

THE RUSTBELT VERSUS THE SUNBELT

Why did the foreign policy debates of the 1970s and 1980s divide the nation along regional lines? Why did the pattern of regional cleavage that arose in the 1970s persist into the 1980s? This section provides an interpretation that locates the source of this conflict in America's changing geography. Drawing on the work of political and economic geographers, it is argued that the conflicts over foreign policy cannot be viewed in isolation from regionally-based struggles over domestic policy. The declining economic fortunes of the Northeast led politicians from this region to seek ways of reducing the costs of the nation's foreign policies in order to devote greater resources to domestic problems and needs. These efforts to redefine the nation's political priorities intensified existing tensions between the Northeast and

South over domestic policy and provided fertile ground for political leaders who sought to exploit this regional cleavage for electoral gain. The failure of American leaders to forge a broad and stable foreign policy consensus is one consequence.

It has been apparent for some time that the national political economy is undergoing a process of regional restructuring. Older centers of industrial production in the Northeast have been losing much of their economic base to other parts of the country (Agnew, 1987; Markusen, 1987). The migration of industries, jobs and people from the manufacturing belt to the sunbelt since the 1960s is one indication of this shift in economic activity. While many states located in the industrial core experienced sluggish growth rates and economic stagnation, many in the South and West became more prosperous and diversified (Rostow, 1977; Norton and Rees, 1979). The process of regional restructuring is reflected in the political arena. Shifts in regional populations have led to shifts in political power at the national level as the Northeast has lost congressional seats to the South and West through reapportionment (Stanley and Niemi, 1990). At the same time, the growing strength of the South and West in the electoral college has made these regions decisive battle grounds in national electoral campaigns.

Analysts identify a number of factors that have contributed to this process. The relative decline of the manufacturing belt has been linked to reductions in transport costs, the diffusion of large-scale, high-technology production, and regional disparities in labor costs, energy prices and local tax rates (Weinstein and Firestine, 1978; Rees, 1983). No less important are the uneven consequences of the erosion of American commercial power in the international economy (Glickman and Glasmeier, 1989; Markusen and Carlson, 1989). Since the 1960s, the manufacturing belt has suffered disproportionately from the migration of American firms overseas and the rise of Western Europe and Japan as industrial competitors. Spatial disparities in federal spending and federal tax policies have also played a role in accelerating, if not encouraging, regional restructuring (Advisory Commission on Intergovernmental Relations, 1980). Federal expenditures and tax policies are often cited as forces that have spurred the growth of sunbelt states while exacerbating economic difficulties in the manufacturing belt.

The erosion of the manufacturing belt's position in both the national economy and the world economy contributed decisively to the emergence of a new and intense debate over the nation's priorities. At the center of this debate lie questions of regional equity or fairness, and specifically, the issue of purported transfers of economic wealth and power from the manufacturing belt to the sunbelt (Dilger, 1982; Bensel, 1984; Markusen, 1987).[6] In the domestic arena, the re-emergence of sectional strife has colored a broad range of issues. In most accounts, the 1960s mark the beginning of this process, when regional divisions found expression in debates over civil rights, entitlement programs and unionization. By the 1970s, the scope of these debates expanded and gained notoriety as politicians from these regions locked horns over rising energy costs, capital flight to the sunbelt, and regional bias in federal tax and spending policies. The pattern of conflict between the manufacturing belt and the sunbelt continued through the 1980s, finding expression in a wide variety of issues ranging from 'deregulation' to 'industrial policy' to the 'Reagan deficit'.

The struggle between the manufacturing belt and the sunbelt was not limited to domestic policy matters. The widespread belief in the Northeast that federal spending and tax policies favored the South and West made the military budget an attractive target for criticism in the 1970s (Bensel, 1984; Malecki and Stark, 1988). In an era when much of the Northeast was experiencing hard economic times, elected officials and interest groups found it politically advantageous to emphasize the domestic opportunity costs of military intervention, military spending and military aid to the Third World (McCormick, 1989). Such concerns figured prominently in the debates over the Vietnam War. In the 1980s, this 'guns versus butter' controversy grew even sharper in response to the Reagan military build-up (Trubowitz and Roberts, 1992; Wirls, 1992). Many of those who opposed the military build-up believed that it disproportionately benefited the South and West. What some viewed as an unintended consequence of the administration's efforts to make America's military presence overseas more visible, others saw as an industrial policy veiled in the garb of national security.

Similar tensions surfaced in the area of foreign economic policy. The growing vulnerability of many of America's key industrial sectors to global competition in the 1970s led to growing disenchantment with free-trade policies in the Northeast. Free trade has proven to be a more attractive economic strategy in the South and West (Sanders, 1986; Wade and Gates, 1990). Conflicting regional interests also appear to have shaped political attitudes toward overseas investment. The rapid expansion of American firms overseas in the 1960s and 1970s penalized areas in the manufacturing belt where a disproportionate share of the nation's unionized work force resided (Gilpin, 1975; Bluestone and Harrison 1982). As early as 1970, labor unions like the AFL–CIO and the UAW began sending out distress signals, pointing to the consequences of 'capital flight' for the nation's traditional manufacturing sectors. In an effort to protect jobs, labor pursued a dual strategy: lobbying for common wage standards at home and tighter controls on the outflow of capital abroad. This strategy has struck a far more responsive chord in the Northeast than it has in the South.

The decline of America's industrial core does not fully explain these conflicts over foreign policy. Sectionally-based conflicts over foreign policy have also been fueled by partisan competition. In the 1970s, as northern Democrats gained greater control over the party's national agenda, party leaders pressed for cuts in the military budget, a larger role for Congress in foreign policy-making, and reductions in the size of US forces overseas. These efforts helped the Democratic party expand its political base in the Northeast. At the same time, however, they exacerbated tensions between the northern and southern wings of the party that had arisen over issues such as civil rights, social welfare and the Vietnam War (Sundquist, 1983; Bensel, 1984; Gillon, 1987; Black and Black, 1987). The emergence of this fault line in the Democratic party became increasingly difficult to paper over as a growing number of political organizations, like the Americans for Democratic Action and the Northeast–Midwest Institute, began to mobilize political and economic interests in the manufacturing belt to redress perceived regional inequities in federal spending, labor costs and energy prices.

This regional schism within the Democratic party provided new political opportunities for a Republican party that was also undergoing change. Over the course of the 1970s, the center of political gravity in the Republican party moved from East to West. The rise of the 'Reagan Right' in the late 1970s and early 1980s marked the culmination of a process that began in the 1960s with the divisive nomination of Goldwater for President. This process gradually eroded the power of the 'eastern' wing of the Republican party (Reinhard, 1983; Rae, 1989; Himmelstein, 1990). Touting the virtues of *'laissez-faire'*, 'law and order', and a 'strong national defense', the Republican party began to penetrate the once-solid Democratic South. This tactical shift is evident in the so-called southern strategy embraced by every Republican candidate for the White House since Nixon. Like Republicans in the 1890s who used the issue of tariff reform to divide the South and West, Republican party leaders in the current era have used defense policy to exploit regional tensions between the Northeast and South.

CONCLUSION

Since the early 1970s, the conflicts between the manufacturing belt and the sunbelt over national priorities have made it extremely difficult for national leaders to mobilize broad national support for their foreign policies. Like other eras in American history marked by protracted domestic struggles over 'the national interest', issues of foreign policy have been defined and debated in terms of their impact on regional growth, stability and power. This fundamental fact is obscured by accounts which identify ideological or institutional cleavages at the national level as the source of domestic political competition and conflict over the foreign policy agenda. What recedes from view are the regional political imperatives that structure the possibilities for building the clearly dominant and stable coalitions that give political leaders wide latitude in conducting foreign policy. The sectional cleavages of the 1970s and 1980s did not afford national leaders this possibility.

The present study suggests that sectionalism remains a persistent force in American political life, and in the foreign policy arena in particular. Contrary to what is now conventional wisdom among foreign policy analysts, sectionalism is not a relic of the past. The findings also speak to debates among political geographers. Some analysts now argue that the political salience of large macro-level cleavages—North versus South, core versus periphery—is fading (Garreau, 1981; Agnew, 1988; Martis, 1988). This study, however, follows the work of others (Bensel, 1984; Archer, 1988; Earle, 1992) in underscoring the enduring significance of macro-level or sectional cleavages in explaining political behavior (e.g. national elections, congressional voting, social movements) in the American context. Sectionalism may not be as salient a political force today as it was a century ago, but it continues to exert a powerful influence on how politicians interpret and respond to changes in America's position in the world.

This means that sectionalism will shape the politics of American foreign policy in the post-Cold War era. Such forces are already at play in the current debate over the 'peace dividend'. Like the debate over the Reagan military build-up in the

1980s, the debate over the 'military build-down' in the 1990s is breaking down along familiar regional lines. At issue is not just how much to cut the Pentagon's budget but perhaps more importantly, how the savings should be spent (Trubowitz, 1992). The stakes are high. The choices politicians face raise fundamental questions about the distribution of national resources, the locus of political power at the federal level and, last but not least, who will benefit and who will not. At a time when there is little consensus over how to revitalize the American economy, and where foreign policy issues are increasingly entering the political arena as economic issues, domestic political competition over foreign policy is likely to intensify. If the recent past is any guide to the future, debates over foreign policy will continue to be shaped by conflicting sectional interests.

ACKNOWLEDGMENTS

I wish to thank Catherine Boone, John O'Loughlin and anonymous reviewers of *Political Geography* for their comments and suggestions. Erik Devereux provided valuable assistance in the data collection and data analysis. The study was supported by a research fellowship from the Center for International Studies at Princeton University. The roll-call data were provided by the Inter-University Consortium for Political and Social Research. An earlier version of this paper was presented at Princeton's Center for International Studies.

NOTES

1. The author was unable to obtain key votes for the 99th Congress (1985–86) from the Americans for Constitutional Action. For this Congress, the list of votes from *Congressional Quarterly* and the Americans for Democratic Action was supplemented by those used by the *National Journal* in rating legislators.
2. The following time-frames were used to classify the votes by presidency: Nixon (1969–74); Ford (1975–76); Carter (1977–80); Reagan (1981–86). The voting records for the House during the 100th Congress (1987–88) were not available in time for this study.
3. The historical scope of the analysis makes it necessary to use a unit of analysis that is stable over time. States are a logical choice for such purposes. The boundaries of legislative districts change; state boundaries do not. Alaska and Hawaii were not included in the data analysis.
4. Following convention, paired votes and announced positions were treated as formal votes.
5. For a good discussion of this issue see Kruskal and Wish (1978).
6. This controversy gained notoriety in the mid–1970s with the publication of articles in the *New York Times*, *Business Week* and the *National Journal* on the regional flow of federal funds.

REFERENCES

Advisory Commission on Intergovernmental Relations (1980). *Regional Growth: Historic Perspective*. Washington, DC: ACIR.

Agnew, J. (1987). *The United States in the World-Economy: A Regional Geography.* Cambridge: Cambridge University Press.

Agnew, J. (1988). Beyond core and periphery: the myth of regional political-economic restructuring and sectionalism in contemporary American politics. *Political Geography Quarterly* 7, 127–139.

Archer, J. C. (1988). Macrogeographical versus microgeographical cleavages in American presidential elections: 1940–1984. *Political Geography Quarterly* 7, 111–125.

Baack, B. and Ray, E. (1988). Special interests and the nineteenth-century roots of the US military-industrial complex. *Research in Economic History* 11, 153–169.

Bensel, R. F. (1984). *Sectionalism and American Political Development: 1880–1980.* Madison, WI: University of Wisconsin Press.

Black, E. and Black, M. (1987). *Politics and Society in the South.* Cambridge, MA: Harvard University Press.

Bluestone, B. and Harrison, B. (1982). *The Deindustrialization of America: Plant Closings, Community Abandonment, and the Dismantling of Basic Industry.* New York: Basic Books.

Cole, W. S. (1983). *Roosevelt and the Isolationists: 1932–45.* Lincoln, NE: University of Nebraska Press.

Destler, I. M. (1981). Executive–congressional conflict in foreign policy. In *Congress Reconsidered,* 2nd edn. (L. C. Dodd and B. I. Oppenheimer eds.) pp. 342–363. Washington, DC: Congressional Quarterly Press.

Dilger, R. (1982). *The Sunbelt/Snowbelt Controversy: The War Over Federal Funds.* New York: New York University Press.

Divine, R. A. (1974). *Foreign Policy and US Presidential Elections, 1940–1948.* New York: New Viewpoints.

Earle, C. (1992). *Geographical Inquiry and American Historical Problems.* Stanford, CA: Stanford University Press.

Easterling, D. (1987). Political science: using the general Euclidean model to study ideological shifts in the US Senate. In *Multidimensional Scaling: History, Theory, and Applications* (F. Young and R. Hamer eds.) pp. 221–256. London: Lawrence Erlbaum Associates.

Frieden, J. (1988). Sectoral conflict and US foreign economic policy, 1914–1940. *International Organization* 42, 59–90.

Garreau, J. (1981). *The Nine Nations of North America.* Boston, MA: Houghton Mifflin.

Gillon, S. M. (1987). *Politics and Vision: The ADA and American Liberalism, 1947–1985.* Oxford: Oxford University Press.

Gilpin, R. (1975). *US Power and the Multinational Corporation: The Political Economy of Foreign Direct Investment.* New York: Basic Books.

Glickman, N. J. and Glasmeier, A. K. (1989). The international economy and the American South. In *Deindustrialization and Regional Economic Transformation: The Experience of the United States* (L. Rodwin and H. Sazanami eds.) pp. 60–80. Boston, MA: Unwin Hyman.

Grassmuck, G. L. (1951). *Sectional Biases in Congress on Foreign Policy.* Baltimore, MD: Johns Hopkins Press.

Hays, S. P. (1957). *The Response to Industrialism: 1885–1914.* Chicago, IL: University of Chicago Press.

Himmelstein, J. L. (1990). *To the Right: The Transformation of American Conservatism.* Berkeley, CA: University of California Press.

Hoadley, J. (1980). The emergence of political parties in Congress, 1789–1803. *American Political Science Review* 74, 757–779.

Holsti, O. R. and Rosenau, J. N. (1984). *American Leadership in World Affairs: Vietnam and the Breakdown of Consensus.* Boston, MA: Allen and Unwin.

Huntington, S. P. (1988). Foreign policy and the constitution. In *Crisis and Innovation: Constitutional Democracy in America* (F. Krinsky ed.) pp. 77–87. Oxford: Basil Blackwell.

Kruskal, J. B. and Wish, M. (1978). *Multidimensional Scaling*. Beverly Hills, CA: Sage Publications.

MacRae, D., Jr. (1970). *Issues and Parties in Legislative Voting*. New York: Harper and Row.

McCormick, J. M. and Wittkopf, E. R. (1990). Bipartisanship, partisanship, and ideology in congressional–executive foreign policy relations, 1947–1988. *Journal of Politics* 52, 1077–1100.

McCormick, T. J. (1989). *America's Half-Century: United States Foreign Policy in the Cold War*. Baltimore, MD: The Johns Hopkins University Press.

Malecki, E. J. and Stark, L. M. (1988). Regional and industrial variation in defence spending: some American evidence. In *Defence Expenditure and Regional Development* (M. J. Breheny ed.) pp. 67–101. London: Mansell Publishing Ltd.

Markusen, A. R. (1987). *Regions: The Economics and Politics of Territory*. Totowa, NJ: Rowman and Littlefield.

Markusen, A. R. and Carlson, V. (1989). Deindustrialization in the American Midwest: causes and responses. In *Deindustrialization and Regional Economic Transformation: The Experience of the United States* (L. Rodwin and H. Sazanami eds.) pp. 29–59. Boston, MA: Unwin Hyman.

Martis, K. C. (1988). Sectionalism and the United States Congress. *Political Geography Quarterly* 7, 99–109.

Nincic, M. (1992). Democracy and Foreign Policy: The Fallacy of Political Realism. New York: Columbia University Press.

Norton, R. D. and Rees, J. (1979). The product cycle and the spatial decentralization of American manufacturing. *Regional Studies* 13, 141–151.

Phillips, K. (1969). *The Emerging Republican Majority*. New York: Doubleday.

Rae, N. (1989). *The Decline of Liberal Republicans from 1952 to the Present*. Oxford: Oxford University Press.

Rees, J. (1983). Regional economic decentralization processes in the United States and their policy implications. In *Contemporary Studies in Sociology*, 2 (D. A. Hicks and N. Glickman eds.) pp. 241–278. Greenwich, CT: JAI Press.

Reinhard, D. W. (1983). *The Republican Right Since 1945*. Lexington, KY: The University Press of Kentucky.

Rostow, W. W. (1977). Regional change in the fifth Kondratieff upswing. In *The Rise of the Sunbelt Cities* (D. C. Perry and A. J. Watkins eds.) pp. 83–103. Beverly Hills, CA: Sage Publications.

Sale, K. (1975). *Power Shift: The Rise of the Southern Rim and its Challenge to the Eastern Establishment*. New York: Vintage Books.

Sanders, E. (1986). The regulatory surge of the 1970s in historical perspective. In *Public Regulation: New Perspectives on Institutions and Policies* (E. E. Bailey ed.) pp. 117–150. Cambridge; MA: The MIT Press.

Schatz, A. W. (1972). The reciprocal trade agreements program and the 'farm vote': 1934–1940. *Agricultural History* 46, 498–514.

Schneider, W. (1992). The old politics and the new world order. In *Eagle in a New World: American Grand Strategy in the Post-Cold War Era* (K. Oye, R. J. Lieber and D. Rothchild eds.) pp. 35–68. New York: HarperCollins.

Stanley, H. W. and Niemi, R. G. (1990). *Vital Statistics on American Politics,* 2nd edn. Washington, DC: Congressional Quarterly Press.

Sundquist, J. L. (1983). *Dynamics of the Party System: Alignment and Realignment of Political Parties in the United States.* Washington, DC: Brookings Institution.

Terrill, T. E. (1973). *The Tariff, Politics, and American Foreign Policy: 1874–1901.* Westport, CT: Greenwood Press.

Trubowitz, P. (1992). Déjà vu all over again: regional struggles over America's foreign policy agenda. Paper presented at the American Political Science Association, Chicago, Illinois.

Trubowitz, P. and Roberts, B. E.(1992). Regional interests and the Reagan military build-up. *Regional Studies* 26, 555–567.

Varg, P. A. (1963). *Foreign Policies of the Founding Fathers.* Lansing, MI: Michigan State University Press.

Wade, L. L. and Gates, J. B. (1990). A new tariff map of the United States (House of Representatives). *Political Geography Quarterly* 9, 284–304.

Warburg, G. F. (1989). *Conflict and Consensus: The Struggle between Congress and the President over Foreign Policymaking.* New York: Harper and Row.

Weinstein, B. L. and Firestine, R. E. (1978). *Regional Growth and Decline in the United States.* New York: Praeger.

Winik, J. (1991). The quest for bipartisanship: a new beginning for a new world order. *The Washington Quarterly* 14, 115–130.

Wirls, D. (1992). *Build-up: The Politics of Defense in the Reagan Era.* Ithaca, NY: Cornell University Press.

APPENDIX

Sectional division of states

NORTHEAST: Connecticut, Delaware, Illinois, Indiana, Iowa, Maine, Maryland, Massachusetts, Michigan, Minnesota, Missouri, New Hampshire, New Jersey, New York, Ohio, Pennsylvania, Rhode Island, Vermont, Wisconsin.

SOUTH: Alabama, Arizona, Arkansas, Florida, Georgia, Kentucky, Louisiana, Mississippi, New Mexico, North Carolina, Oklahoma, South Carolina, Tennessee, Texas, Virginia, West Virginia.

WEST: California, Colorado, Idaho, Kansas, Montana, Oregon, Nebraska, Nevada, North Dakota, South Dakota, Utah, Washington, Wyoming.

✧ PART SIX ✧

Bureaucratic Politics and Organizational Culture

During the 1970s the role of bureaucracy and organizational process was brought squarely into the study of American foreign policy. The basic insight is straightforward: foreign-policy officials sit atop huge bureaucracies, and the organizational politics and processes that produce decisions often color those decisions. The study of policy, in other words, cannot be separated from the process of creating it. A huge literature has emerged that extends and critiques the claims of this tradition.

The seminal contribution to this approach is Graham T. Allison's study of the Cuban missile crisis. Most studies of foreign policy, Allison argues, are based on rational models of decision making. Scholars attempt to understand policy in terms of the purposive actions of government; explanation involves reconstructing the rationality of the decision. Alongside this model, Allison places two additional models: bureaucratic politics and organizational process. These models highlight the bureaucratic operations within the black box of government. In using these models to reconstruct decision making during the Cuban missile crisis, Allison argues that the additional models help reveal decisions less explicable in terms of the rational model.

Stephen Krasner presents an important critique of the literature on bureaucratic politics, questioning the argument that the president is simply a victim of the huge organizations he commands. When the issues are sufficiently important, Krasner argues, top officials can overcome the vagaries of parochial bureaucratic interests and politics. Determining when the president cares enough about a particular policy and has the capacity to act as commander and when he lets bureaucratic politics and culture shape policy is an important task.

Conceptual Models and the Cuban Missile Crisis

Graham T. Allison

The Cuban missile crisis is a seminal event. For thirteen days of October 1962 there was a higher probability that more human lives would end suddenly than ever before in history. Had the worst occurred, the death of 100 million Americans, over 100 million Russians, and millions of Europeans as well would make previous natural calamities and inhumanities appear insignificant. Given the probability of disaster—which President Kennedy estimated as "between 1 out of 3 and even"—our escape seems awesome.[1] This event symbolizes a central if only partially thinkable fact about our existence. That such consequences could follow from the choices and actions of national governments obliges students of government as well as participants in governance to think hard about these problems.

Improved understanding of this crisis depends in part on more information and more probing analyses of available evidence. To contribute to these efforts is part of the purpose of this study. But here the missile crisis serves primarily as grist for a more general investigation. This study proceeds from the premise that marked improvement in our understanding of such events depends critically on more self-consciousness about what observers bring to the analysis. What each analyst sees and judges to be important is a function not only of the evidence about what happened but also of the "conceptual lenses" through which he looks at the evidence. The principal purpose of this essay is to explore some of the fundamental assumptions and categories employed by analysts in thinking about problems of governmental behavior, especially in foreign and military affairs.

The general argument can be summarized in three propositions:

1. Analysts think about problems of foreign and military policy in terms of largely implicit conceptual models that have significant consequences for the content of their thought.[2]

Though the present product of foreign policy analysis is neither systematic nor powerful, if one carefully examines explanations produced by analysts, a number of fundamental similarities emerge. Explanations produced by particular analysts display quite regular, predictable features. This predictability suggests a substructure. These regularities reflect an analyst's assumptions about the charac-

Graham T. Allison, "Conceptual Models and the Cuban Missile Crisis," *American Political Science Review*, 63, No. 3 (September 1969): 689–718. Reprinted with permission of the American Political Science Association.

ter of puzzles, the categories in which problems should be considered, the types of evidence that are relevant, and the determinants of occurrences. The first proposition is that clusters of such related assumptions constitute basic frames of reference or conceptual models in terms of which analysts both ask and answer the question: What happened? Why did the event happen? What will happen?[3] Such assumptions are central to the activities of explanation and prediction, for in attempting to explain a particular event, the analyst cannot simply describe the full state of the world leading up to that event. The logic of explanation requires that he single out the relevant, important determinants of the occurrence.[4] Moreover, as the logic of prediction underscores, the analyst must summarize the various determinants as they bear on the event in question. Conceptual models both fix the mesh of the nets that the analyst drags through the material in order to explain a particular action or decision and direct him to cast his net in select ponds, at certain depths, in order to catch the fish he is after.

> **2.** Most analysts explain (and predict) the behavior of national governments in terms of various forms of one basic conceptual model, here entitled the rational policy model (model I).[5]

In terms of this conceptual model, analysts attempt to understand happenings as the more or less purposive acts of unified national governments. For these analysts the point of an explanation is to show how the nation or government could have chosen the action in question, given the strategic problem that it faced. For example in confronting the problem posed by the Soviet installation of missiles in Cuba, rational-policy-model analysts attempt to show how this was a reasonable act from the point of view of the Soviet Union, given Soviet strategic objectives.

> **3.** Two "alternative" conceptual models, here labeled an organizational-process model (model II) and a bureaucratic-politics model (model III) provide a base for improved explanation and prediction.

Although the standard frame of reference has proved useful for many purposes, there is powerful evidence that it must be supplemented, if not supplanted, by frames of reference which focus upon the large organizations and political actors involved in the policy process. Model I's implication that important events have important causes, i.e., that monoliths perform large actions for big reasons, must be balanced by an appreciation of the facts (a) that monoliths are black boxes covering various gears and levers in a highly differentiated decision-making structure, and (b) that large acts are the consequences of innumerable and often conflicting smaller actions by individuals at various levels of bureaucratic organizations in the service of a variety of only partially compatible conceptions of national goals, organizational goals, and political objectives. Recent developments in the field of organization theory provide the foundation for the second model. According to this organizational-process model, what model I categorizes as "acts" and "choices" are instead *outputs* of large organizations functioning according to certain regular patterns of behavior. Faced with the problem of Soviet missiles in Cuba, a model II analyst identifies the relevant organizations and displays the patterns of organizational behavior from which this action emerged. The third model focuses on the internal politics of a government. Happenings in foreign affairs are understood, according to the bureaucratic-politics model, neither as choices nor as outputs. Instead, what happens is categorized as *outcomes* of various overlapping bargaining games among players arranged hierarchically in the national government. In confronting the problem posed by Soviet missiles in Cuba, a model III analyst displays the perceptions, motivations, positions, power, and maneuvers of principal players from which the outcome emerged.[6]

A central metaphor illuminates differences among these models. Foreign policy has often been compared to moves, sequences of moves, and games of chess. If one were limited to observations on a screen upon which moves in the chess game were projected without information as to how the pieces came to be moved, he would assume—as model I does—that an individual chess player was moving the pieces with reference to plans and maneuvers toward the goal of winning the game. But a pattern of moves can be imagined that would lead the serious observer, after watching several games, to consider the hypothesis that the chess player was not a single individual but rather a loose alliance of semi-independent organizations, each of which moved its set of pieces according to standard operating procedures. For example, movement of separate sets of pieces might proceed in turn, each according to a routine, the king's rook, bishop, and their pawns repeatedly attacking the opponent according to a fixed plan. Furthermore, it is conceivable that the pattern of play would suggest to an observer that a number of distinct players, with distinct objectives but shared power over the pieces, were determining the moves as the resultant of collegial bargaining. For example, the black rook's move might contribute to the loss of a black knight with no comparable gain for the black team, but with the black rook becoming the principal guardian of the "palace" on that side of the board.

The space available does not permit full development and support of such a general argument.[7] Rather, the sections that follow simply sketch each conceptual model, articulate it as an analytic paradigm, and apply it to produce an explanation. But each model is applied to the same event: the U.S. blockade of Cuba during the missile crisis. These "alternative explanations" of the same happening illustrate differences among the models—*at work*.[8] A crisis decision by a small group of men in the context of ultimate threat, this is a case of the rational policy model par excellence. The dimensions and factors that models II and III uncover in this case are therefore particularly suggestive. The concluding section of this paper suggests how the three models may be related and how they can be extended to generate predictions.

MODEL I: RATIONAL POLICY
Rational-Policy Model Illustrated

Where is the pinch of the puzzle raised by the *New York Times* over Soviet deployment of an antiballistic missile system?[9] The question, as the *Times* states it, concerns the Soviet Union's objective in allocating such large sums of money for this weapon system while at the same time seeming to pursue a policy of increasing détente. In former President Johnson's words, "the paradox is that this [Soviet deployment of an antiballistic missile system] should be happening at a time when there is abundant evidence that our mutual antagonism is beginning to ease."[10] This question troubles people primarily because Soviet antiballistic missile deployment, and evidence of Soviet actions towards détente, when juxtaposed in our implicit model, produce a question. With reference to what objective could the Soviet government have rationally chosen the simultaneous pursuit of these two courses of actions? This question arises only when the analyst attempts to structure events as purposive choices of consistent actors.

How do analysts attempt to explain the Soviet emplacement of missiles in Cuba? The most widely cited explanation of this occurrence has been produced by two RAND sovietologists, Arnold Horelick and Myron Rush.[11] They conclude that "the introduction of strategic missiles into Cuba was motivated chiefly by the Soviet leaders' desire to overcome . . . the existing large margin of U.S. strategic superiority."[12] How do they reach this conclusion? In Sherlock Holmes' style, they seize several salient characteristics of this action and use these features as criteria against which to test alternative hypotheses about Soviet objectives. For example, the size of the Soviet deployment and the simultaneous emplacement of more expensive, more visible intermediate-range missiles as well as medium-range missiles, it is argued, exclude an explanation of the action in terms of Cuban defense—since that objective could have been secured with a much smaller number of medium-range missiles alone. Their explanation presents an argument for one objective that permits interpretation of the details of Soviet behavior as a value-maximizing choice.

How do analysts account for the coming of the First World War? According to Hans Morgenthau, "the first World War had its origin exclusively in the fear of a disturbance of the European balance of power."[13] In the period preceding World War I, the Triple Alliance precariously balanced the Triple Entente. If either power combination could gain a decisive advantage in the Balkans, it would achieve a decisive advantage in the balance of power. "It was this fear," Morgenthau asserts, "that motivated Austria in July 1914 to settle its accounts with Serbia once and for all, and that induced Germany to support Austria unconditionally. It was the same fear that brought Russia to the support of Serbia, and France to the support of Russia."[14] How is Morgenthau able to resolve this problem so confidently? By imposing on the data a "rational outline."[15] The value of this method, according to Morgenthau, is that "it provides for rational discipline in action and creates astounding continuity in foreign policy which makes American, British, or Russian foreign policy appear as an intelligent, rational continuum . . . regardless of the different motives, preferences, and intellectual and moral qualities of successive statesmen."[16]

Stanley Hoffmann's essay "Restraints and Choices in American Foreign Policy" concentrates, characteristically, on "deep forces": the international system, ideology, and national character—which constitute restraints, limits, and blinders.[17] Only secondarily does he consider decisions. But when explaining particular occurrences, though emphasizing relevant constraints, he focuses on the choices of nations. American behavior in Southeast Asia is explained as a reasonable choice of "downgrading this particular alliance (SEATO) in favor of direct U.S.

involvement," given the constraint: "one is bound by one's commitments; one is committed by one's mistakes."[18] More frequently Hoffmann uncovers confusion or contradiction in the nation's choice. For example, U.S. policy towards under-developed countries is explained as "schizophrenic."[19] The method employed by Hoffman in producing these explanations as rational (or irrational) decisions, he terms "imaginative reconstruction."[20]

Deterrence is the cardinal problem of the contemporary strategic literature. Thomas Schelling's *Strategy of Conflict* formulates a number of propositions focused upon the dynamics of deterrence in the nuclear age. One of the major propositions concerns the stability of the balance of terror: in a situation of mutual deterrence the probability of nuclear war is reduced not by the "balance" (the sheer equality of the situation) but rather by the *stability* of the balance, i.e., the fact that neither opponent in striking first can destroy the other's ability to strike back.[21] How does Schelling support this proposition? Confidence in the contention stems not from an inductive canvass of a large number of previous cases, but rather from two calculations. In a situation of "balance" but vulnerability, there are values for which a rational opponent could choose to strike first, e.g., to destroy enemy capabilities to retaliate. In a "stable balance," where no matter who strikes first, each has an assured capability to retaliate with unacceptable damage, no rational agent could choose such a course of action (since that choice is effectively equivalent to choos-ing mutual homicide). Whereas most contemporary strategic thinking is driven *implicitly* by the motor upon which this calculation depends, Schelling explicitly recognizes that strategic theory does assume a model. The foundation of a theory of strategy is, he asserts: "the assumption of rational behavior—not just of intelligent behavior, but of behavior motivated by conscious calculation of advantages, calcula-tion that in turn is based on an explicit and internally consistent value system."[22]

What is striking about these examples from the literature of foreign policy and international relations are the similarities among analysts of various styles when they are called upon to produce explanations. Each assumes that what must be explained is an action, i.e., the realization of some purpose or intention. Each assumes that the actor is the national government. Each assumes that the action is chosen as a calculated response to a strategic problem. For each, explanation consists of showing what goal the government was pursuing in committing the act and how this action was a reasonable choice, given the nation's objectives. This set of assumptions characterizes the rational-policy model. The assertion that model I is the standard frame of reference implies no denial of highly visible differences among the interests of sovietologists, diplomatic historians, international relations theorists, and strategists. Indeed, in most respects differences among the work of Hans Morgenthau, Stanley Hoffmann, and Thomas Schelling could not be more pointed. Appreciation of the extent to which each relies predominantly on model I, however, reveals basic similarities among Morgenthau's method of "rational reenactment," Hoffmann's "imaginative reconstruction," and Schelling's "vicarious problem solving;" family resemblances among Morgenthau's "rational statesman," Hoffmann's "roulette player," and Schelling's "game theorist."[23]

Most contemporary analysts (as well as laymen) proceed predominantly— albeit most often implicitly—in terms of this model when attempting to explain happenings in foreign affairs. Indeed, that occurrences in foreign affairs are the *acts of nations* seems so fundamental to thinking about such problems that this underlying model has rarely been recognized: to explain an occurrence in foreign policy simply means to show how the government could have rationally chosen that action.[24] These brief examples illustrate five uses of the model. To prove that most analysts think largely in terms of the rational policy model is not possible. In this limited space it is not even possible to illustrate the range of employment of the framework. Rather my purpose is to convey to the reader a grasp of the model and a challenge: let the reader examine the literature with which he is most familiar and make his judgment.

The general characterization can be sharpened by articulating the rational-policy model as an "analytic paradigm" in the technical sense developed by Robert K. Merton for sociological analyses.[25] Systematic statement of basic assumptions, concepts, and propositions employed by model I analysts highlights the distinctive thrust of this style of analysis. To articulate a largely implicit framework is of necessity to caricature. But caricature can be instructive.

Rational Policy Paradigm

I. *Basic Unit of Analysis: Policy as National Choice*

Happenings in foreign affairs are conceived as actions chosen by the nation or national government.[26] Governments select the action that will maximize strategic goals and objectives. These "solutions" to strategic problems are the fundamental categories in terms of which the analyst perceives what is to be explained.

II. *Organizing Concepts*

A. National Actor   The nation or government, conceived as a rational unitary decision maker, is the agent. This actor has one set of specified goals (the equivalent of a consistent utility function), one set of perceived options, and a single estimate of the consequences that follow from each alternative.

B. The Problem   Action is chosen in response to the strategic problem which the nation faces. Threats and opportunities arising in the "international strategic marketplace" move the nation to act.

C. Static Selection   The sum of activity of representatives of the government relevant to a problem constitutes what the nation has chosen as its "solution." Thus the action is conceived as a steady-state choice among alternative outcomes (rather than, for example, a large number of partial choices in a dynamic stream).

D. Action as Rational Choice   The components include:

1. Goals and Objectives   National security and national interests are the principal categories in which strategic goals are conceived. Nations seek security and a range of further objectives. (Analysts rarely translate strategic goals and objectives into an explicit utility function; nevertheless, analysts do focus on major goals and objectives and trade off side effects in an intuitive fashion.)

2. Options   Various courses of action relevant to a strategic problem provide the spectrum of options.

3. Consequences   Enactment of each alternative course of action will produce a series of consequences. The relevant consequences constitute benefits and costs in terms of strategic goals and objectives.

4. Choice   Rational choice is value-maximizing. The rational agent selects the alternative whose consequences rank highest in terms of his goals and objectives.

III. Dominant Inference Pattern

This paradigm leads analysts to rely on the following pattern of inference: if a nation performed a particular action, that nation must have had ends towards which the action constituted an optimal means. The rational policy model's explanatory power stems from this inference pattern. Puzzlement is relieved by revealing the purposive pattern within which the occurrence can be located as a value-maximizing means.

IV. General Propositions

The disgrace of political science is the infrequency with which propositions of any generality are formulated and tested. "Paradigmatic analysis" argues for explicitness about the terms in which analysis proceeds and seriousness about the logic of explanation. Simply to illustrate the kind of propositions on which analysts who employ this model rely, the formulation includes several.

The basic assumption of value-maximizing behavior produces propositions central to most explanations. The general principle can be formulated as follows: the likelihood of any particular action results from a combination of the nation's (1) relevant values and objectives, (2) perceived alternative courses of action, (3) estimates of various sets of consequences (which will follow from each alternative), and (4) net valuation of each set of consequences. This yields two propositions.

a. An increase in the cost of an alternative, i.e., a reduction in the value of the set of consequences which will follow from that action, or a reduction in the probability of attaining fixed consequences, reduces the likelihood of that alternative being chosen.

b. A decrease in the costs of an alternative, i.e., an increase in the value of the set of consequences which will follow from that alternative, or an increase in the probability of attaining fixed consequences, increases the likelihood of that action being chosen.[27]

V. Specific Propositions

A. Deterrence   The likelihood of any particular attack results from the factors specified in the general proposition. Combined with factual assertions, this general proposition yields the propositions of the subtheory of deterrence.

 1. A stable nuclear balance reduces the likelihood of nuclear attack. This proposition is derived from the general proposition plus the asserted fact that a second-strike capability affects the potential attacker's calculations by increasing the likelihood and the costs of one particular set of consequences which might follow from attack—namely, retaliation.

2. A stable nuclear balance increases the probability of limited war. This proposition is derived from the general proposition plus the asserted fact that though increasing the costs of a nuclear exchange, a stable nuclear balance nevertheless produces a more significant reduction in the probability that such consequences would be chosen in response to a limited war. Thus this set of consequences weighs less heavily in the calculus.

B. SOVIET FORCE POSTURE   The Soviet Union chooses its force posture (i.e., its weapons and their deployment) as a value-maximizing means of implementing Soviet strategic objectives and military doctrine. A proposition of this sort underlies Secretary of Defense Laird's inference from the fact of two hundred SS-9s (large intercontinental missiles) to the assertion that "the Soviets are going for a first-strike capability, and there's no question about it."[28]

Variants of the Rational-Policy Model

This paradigm exhibits the characteristics of the most refined version of the rational model. The modern literature of strategy employs a model of this sort. Problems and pressures in the "international strategic marketplace" yield probabilities of occurrence. The international actor, which could be any national actor, is simply a value-maximizing mechanism for getting from the strategic problem to the logical solution. But the explanations and predictions produced by most analysts of foreign affairs depend primarily on variants of this "pure" model. The point of each is the same: to place the action within a value-maximizing framework, given certain constraints. Nevertheless, it may be helpful to identify several variants, each of which might be exhibited similarly as a paradigm. The first focuses upon the national actor and his choice in a particular situation, leading analysts to further constrain the goals, alternatives, and consequences considered. Thus, (1) national propensities or personality traits reflected in an "operational code," (2) concern with certain objectives, or (3) special principles of action narrow the "goals" or "alternatives" or "consequences" of the paradigm. For example, the Soviet deployment of ABMs is sometimes explained by reference to the Soviet's "defense-mindedness." Or a particular Soviet action is explained as an instance of a special rule of action in the Bolshevik operational code.[29] A second related cluster of variants focuses on the individual leader or leadership group as the actor whose preference function is maximized and whose personal (or group) characteristics are allowed to modify the alternatives, consequences, and rules of choice. Explanations of the U.S. involvement in Vietnam as a natural consequence of the Kennedy-Johnson administration's axioms of foreign policy rely on this variant. A third more complex variant of the basic model recognizes the existence of several actors within a government, for example, hawks and doves or military and civilians, but attempts to explain (or predict) an occurrence by reference to the objectives of the victorious actor. Thus, for example, some revisionist histories of the cold war recognize the forces of light and the forces of darkness within the U.S. government but explain American actions as a result of goals and perceptions of the victorious forces of darkness.

Each of these forms of the basic paradigm constitutes a formalization of what analysts typically rely upon implicitly. In the transition from implicit conceptual model to explicit paradigm much of the richness of the best employments of this model has been lost. But the purpose in raising loose, implicit conceptual models to an explicit level is to reveal the basic logic of analysts' activity. Perhaps some of the remaining artificiality that surrounds the statement of the paradigm can be erased by noting a number of the standard additions and modifications employed by analysts who proceed *predominantly* within the rational policy model. First, in the course of a document analysts shift from one variant of the basic model to another, occasionally appropriating in an ad hoc fashion aspects of a situation which are logically incompatible with the basic model. Second, in the course of explaining a number of occurrences, analysts sometimes pause over a particular event about which they have a great deal of information and unfold it in such detail that an impression of randomness is created. Third, having employed other assumptions and categories in deriving an explanation or prediction, analysts will present their product in a neat, convincing rational policy model package. (This accommodation is a favorite of members of the intelligence community whose association with the details of a process is considerable but who feel that by putting an occurrence in a larger rational framework, it will be more comprehensible to their audience.) Fourth, in attempting to offer an explanation—particularly in cases where a prediction derived from the basic model has failed—the notion of a "mistake" is invoked. Thus, the failure in the prediction of a "missile gap" is written off as a Soviet mistake in not taking advantage of their opportunity. Both these and other modifications permit model I analysts considerably more variety than the paradigm might suggest. But such accommodations are essentially appendages to the basic logic of these analyses.

The U.S. Blockade of Cuba: A First Cut[30]

The U.S. response to the Soviet Union's emplacement of missiles in Cuba must be understood in strategic terms as simple value-maximizing escalation. American nuclear superiority could be counted on to paralyze Soviet nuclear power; Soviet transgression of the nuclear threshold in response to an American use of lower levels of violence would be wildly irrational, since it would mean virtual destruction of the Soviet Communist system and Russian nation. American local superiority was overwhelming: it could be initiated at a low level while threatening with high credibility an ascending sequence of steps short of the nuclear threshold. All that was required was for the United States to bring to bear its strategic and local superiority in such a way that American determination to see the missiles removed would be demonstrated, while at the same time allowing Moscow time and room to retreat without humiliation. The naval blockade—euphemistically named a quarantine in order to circumvent the niceties of international law—did just that.

The U.S. government's selection of the blockade followed this logic. Apprised of the presence of Soviet missiles in Cuba, the president assembled an executive committee (ExCom) of the National Security Council and directed them to "set aside all other tasks to make a prompt and intense survey of the dangers and all possible courses of action."[31] This group functioned as "fifteen individuals on our own, representing the President and not different departments."[32] As one of the participants recalls, "The remarkable aspect of those meetings was a sense of complete equality."[33] Most of the time during the week that followed was spent canvassing all the possible tracks and weighing the arguments for and against each. Six major categories of action were considered.

1. Do Nothing   U.S. vulnerability to Soviet missiles was no new thing. Since the U.S. already lived under the gun of missiles based in Russia, a Soviet capability to strike from Cuba too made little real difference. The real danger stemmed from the possibility of U.S. overreaction. The U.S. should announce the Soviet action in a calm, casual manner, thereby deflating whatever political capital Khrushchev hoped to make of the missiles.

This argument fails on two counts. First, it grossly underestimates the military importance of the Soviet move. Not only would the Soviet Union's missile capability be doubled and the U.S. early warning system outflanked, the Soviet Union would have an opportunity to reverse the strategic balance by further installations, and indeed, in the longer run, to invest in cheaper, shorter-range rather than more expensive longer-range missiles. Second, the political importance of this move was undeniable. The Soviet Union's act challenged the American president's most solemn warning. If the U.S. failed to respond, no American commitment would be credible.

2. Diplomatic Pressures   Several forms were considered: an appeal to the U.N. or OAS for an inspection team, a secret approach to Khrushchev, and a direct approach to Khrushchev, perhaps at a summit meeting. The United States would demand that the missiles be removed, but the final settlement might include neutralization of Cuba, U.S. withdrawal from the Guantanamo base, and withdrawal of U.S. Jupiter missiles from Turkey or Italy.

Each form of the diplomatic approach had its own drawbacks. To arraign the Soviet Union before the U.N. Security Council held little promise, since the Russians could veto any proposed action. While the diplomats argued, the missiles would become operational. To send a secret emissary to Khrushchev demanding that the missiles be withdrawn would be to pose untenable alternatives. On the one hand, this would invite Khrushchev to seize the diplomatic initiative, perhaps committing himself to strategic retaliation in response to an attack on Cuba. On the other hand, this would tender an ultimatum that no great power could accept. To confront Khrushchev at a summit would guarantee demands for U.S. concessions, and the analogy between U.S. missiles in Turkey and Russian missiles in Cuba could not be erased.

But why not trade U.S. Jupiters in Turkey and Italy, which the president had previously ordered withdrawn, for the missiles in Cuba? The U.S. had chosen to withdraw these missiles in order to replace them with superior, less vulnerable Mediterranean Polaris submarines. But the middle of the crisis was no time for concessions. The offer of such a deal might suggest to the Soviets that the West would yield and thus tempt them to demand more. It would certainly confirm European suspicions about American willingness to sacrifice European interests when the chips were down. Finally, the basic issue should be kept clear. As the president stated in reply to Bertrand Russell, "I think your attention might well be directed to the burglars rather than to those who have caught the burglars."[34]

3. A SECRET APPROACH TO CASTRO   The crisis provided an opportunity to separate Cuba and Soviet Communism by offering Castro the alternatives, "split or fall." But Soviet troops transported, constructed, guarded, and controlled the missiles. Their removal would thus depend on a Soviet decision.

4. INVASION   The United States could take this occasion not only to remove the missiles but also to rid itself of Castro. A navy exercise had long been scheduled in which Marines, ferried from Florida in naval vessels, would liberate the imaginary island of Vieques.[35] Why not simply shift the point of disembarkment? (The Pentagon's foresight in planning this operation would be an appropriate antidote to the CIA's Bay of Pigs!)

Preparations were made for an invasion, but as a last resort. American troops would be forced to confront twenty thousand Soviets in the first cold war case of direct contact between the troops of the super powers. Such brinksmanship courted nuclear disaster, practically guaranteeing an equivalent Soviet move against Berlin.

5. SURGICAL AIR STRIKE   The missile sites should be removed by a clean, swift conventional attack. This was the effective counteraction which the attempted deception deserved. A surgical strike would remove the missiles and thus eliminate both the danger that the missiles might become operational and the fear that the Soviets would discover the American discovery and act first.

The initial attractiveness of this alternative was dulled by several difficulties. First, could the strike really be "surgical"? The air force could not guarantee destruction of all the missiles.[36] Some might be fired during the attack; some might not have been identified. In order to assure destruction of Soviet and Cuban means of retaliating, what was required was not a surgical but rather a massive attack—of at least five hundred sorties. Second, a surprise air attack would of course kill Russians at the missile sites. Pressures on the Soviet Union to retaliate would be so strong that an attack on Berlin or Turkey was highly probable. Third, the key problem with this program was that of advance warning. Could the President of the United States, with his memory of Pearl Harbor and his vision of future U.S. responsibility, order a "Pearl Harbor in reverse"? For 175 years unannounced Sunday morning attacks had been an anathema to our tradition.[37]

6. BLOCKADE   Indirect military action in the form of a blockade became more attractive as the ExCom dissected the other alternatives. An embargo on military shipments to Cuba enforced by a naval blockade was not without flaws, however.

Could the U.S. blockade Cuba without inviting Soviet reprisal in Berlin? The likely solution to joint blockades would be the lifting of both blockades, restoring the new status quo, and allowing the Soviets additional time to complete the missiles. Second, the possible consequences of the blockade resembled the drawbacks which disqualified the air strike. If Soviet ships did not stop, the United States would be forced to fire the first shot, inviting retaliation. Third, a blockade would deny the traditional freedom of the seas demanded by several of our close allies and might be held illegal, in violation of the U.N. charter and international law, unless the United States could obtain a two-thirds vote in the OAS. Finally, how could a blockade be related to the problem, namely, some seventy-five missiles on the island of Cuba, approaching operational readiness daily? A blockade offered the Soviets a spectrum of delaying tactics with which to buy time to complete the missile installations. Was a fait accompli not required?

In spite of these enormous difficulties the blockade had comparative advantages: (1) It was a middle course between inaction and attack, aggressive enough to communicate firmness of intention but nevertheless not so precipitous as a strike. (2) It placed on Khrushchev the burden of choice concerning the next step. He could avoid a direct military clash by keeping his ships away. His was the last clear chance. (3) No possible military confrontation could be more acceptable to the U.S. than a naval engagement in the Caribbean. (4) This move permitted the U.S., by flexing its conventional muscle, to exploit the threat of subsequent non-nuclear steps in each of which the U.S. would have significant superiority.

Particular arguments about advantages and disadvantages were powerful. The explanation of the American choice of the blockade lies in a more general principle, however. As President Kennedy stated in drawing the moral of the crisis:

> Above all, while defending our own vital interests, nuclear powers must avert those confrontations which bring an adversary to a choice of either a humiliating retreat or a nuclear war. To adopt that kind of course in the nuclear age would be evidence only of the bankruptcy of our policy—of a collective death wish for the world.[38]

The blockade was the United States' only real option.

MODEL II: ORGANIZATIONAL PROCESS

For some purposes governmental behavior can be usefully summarized as action chosen by a unitary rational decision maker: centrally controlled, completely informed, and value-maximizing. But this simplification must not be allowed to conceal the fact that a "government" consists of a conglomerate of semifeudal loosely allied organizations, each with a substantial life of its own. Government leaders do sit formally and to some extent in fact on top of this conglomerate. But governments perceive problems through organizational sensors. Governments define alternatives and estimate consequences as organizations process information. Governments act as these organizations enact routines. Government behavior can therefore be understood according to a second conceptual model, less as deliberate choices of leaders and more as *outputs* of large organizations functioning according to standard patterns of behavior.

To be responsive to a broad spectrum of problems, governments consist of large organizations among which primary responsibility for particular areas is divided. Each organization attends to a special set of problems and acts in quasi independence on these problems. But few important problems fall exclusively within the domain of a single organization. Thus government behavior relevant to any important problem reflects the independent output of several organizations, partially coordinated by government leaders. Government leaders can substantially disturb but not substantially control the behavior of these organizations.

To perform complex routines the behavior of large numbers of individuals must be coordinated. Coordination requires standard operating procedures: rules according to which things are done. Assured capability for reliable performance of action that depends upon the behavior of hundreds of persons requires established "programs." Indeed, if the eleven members of a football team are to perform adequately on any particular down, each player must not "do what he thinks needs to be done" or "do what the quarterback tells him to do." Rather each player must perform the maneuvers specified by a previously established play which the quarterback has simply called in this situation.

At any given time a government consists of *existing* organizations, each with a *fixed* set of standard operating procedures and programs. The behavior of these organizations—and consequently of the government—relevant to an issue in any particular instance is therefore determined primarily by routines established in these organizations prior to that instance. But organizations do change. Learning occurs gradually, over time. Dramatic organizational change occurs in response to major crises. Both learning and change are influenced by existing organizational capabilities.

Borrowed from studies of organizations, these loosely formulated propositions amount simply to *tendencies*. Each must be hedged by modifiers like "other things being equal" and "under certain conditions." In particular instances tendencies hold—more or less. In specific situations the relevant question is: more or less? But this is as it should be. For on the one hand, "organizations" are no more homogeneous a class than "solids." When scientists tried to generalize about "solids," they achieved similar results. Solids tend to expand when heated, but some do and some don't. More adequate categorization of the various elements now lumped under the rubric *organizations* is thus required. On the other hand, the behavior of particular organizations seems considerably more complex than the behavior of solids. Additional information about a particular organization is required for further specification of the tendency statements. In spite of these two caveats, the characterization of government action as organizational output differs distinctly from model I. Attempts to understand problems of foreign affairs in terms of this frame of reference should produce quite different explanations.[39]

Organizational Process Paradigm[40]

I. *Basic Unit of Analysis: Policy as Organizational Output*

The happenings of international politics are in three critical senses outputs of organizational processes. First, the actual occurrences are organizational outputs. For example, Chinese entry into the Korean War—that is, the fact that Chinese soldiers were firing at U.N. soldiers south of the Yalu in 1950—is an organizational action: the action of men who are soldiers in platoons which are in companies, which in turn are in armies, responding as privates to lieutenants who are responsible to captains and so on to the commander, moving into Korea, advancing against enemy troops, and firing according to fixed routines of the Chinese army. Government leaders' decisions trigger organizational routines. Government leaders can trim the edges of this output and exercise some choice in combining outputs. But the mass of behavior is determined by previously established procedures. Second, existing organizational routines for employing present physical capabilities constitute the effective options open to government leaders confronted with any problem. Only the existence of men, equipped and trained as armies and capable of being transported to North Korea, made entry into the Korean War a live option for the Chinese leaders. The fact that fixed programs (equipment, men, and routines which exist at the particular time) exhaust the range of buttons that leaders can push is not always perceived by these leaders. But in every case it is critical for an understanding of what is actually done. Third, organizational outputs structure the situation within the narrow constraints of which leaders must contribute their "decision" concerning an issue. Outputs raise the problem, provide the information, and make the initial moves that color the face of the issue that is turned to the leaders. As Theodore Sorensen has observed: "Presidents rarely, if ever, make decisions—particularly in foreign affairs—in the sense of writing their conclusions on a clean slate . . . The basic decisions, which confine their choices, have all too often been previously made."[41] If one understands the structure of the situation and the face of the issue—which are determined by the organizational outputs—the formal choice of the leaders is frequently anticlimactic.

II. *Organizing Concepts*

A. ORGANIZATIONAL ACTORS   The actor is not a monolithic nation or government but rather a constellation of loosely allied organizations on top of which government leaders sit. This constellation acts only as component organizations perform routines.[42]

B. FACTORED PROBLEMS AND FRACTIONATED POWER   Surveillance of the multiple facets of foreign affairs requires that problems be cut up and parceled out to various organizations. To avoid paralysis, primary power must accompany primary responsibility. But if organizations are permitted to do anything, a large part of what they do will be determined within the organization. Thus each organization perceives problems, processes information, and performs a range of actions in quasi independence (within broad guidelines of national policy). Factored problems and fractionated power are two edges of the same sword. Factoring permits more specialized attention to particular facets of problems than would be possible if government leaders tried to cope with these problems by themselves. But this additional attention must be paid for in the coin of discretion for *what* an organization attends to and *how* organizational responses are programmed.

C. PAROCHIAL PRIORITIES, PERCEPTIONS, AND ISSUES   Primary responsibility for a narrow set of problems encourages organizational parochialism. These tendencies are enhanced by a number of additional factors: (1) selective information available to the organization, (2) recruitment of personnel into the organization, (3) tenure of individuals in the organization, (4) small group pressures within the organization, and (5) distribution of rewards by the organization. Clients (e.g., interest groups), government allies (e.g., congressional committees), and extranational counterparts (e.g., the British Ministry of Defense for the Department of Defense, ISA, or the British Foreign Office for the Department of State, EUR) galvanize this parochialism. Thus organizations develop relatively stable propensities concerning operational priorities, perceptions, and issues.

D. Action as Organizational Output   The preeminent feature of organizational activity is its programmed character: the extent to which behavior in any particular case is an enactment of preestablished routines. In producing outputs the activity of each organization is characterized by:

1. Goals: Constraints, Defining Acceptable Performance   The operational goals of an organization are seldom revealed by formal mandates. Rather each organization's operational goals emerge as a set of constraints defining acceptable performance. Central among these constraints is organizational health, defined usually in terms of bodies assigned and dollars appropriated. The set of constraints emerges from a mix of expectations and demands of other organizations in the government, statutory authority, demands from citizens and special interest groups, and bargaining within the organization. These constraints represent a quasi resolution of conflict—the constraints are relatively stable, so there is some resolution. But conflict among alternative goals is always latent; hence it is a quasi resolution. Typically the constraints are formulated as imperatives to avoid roughly specified discomforts and disasters.[43]

2. Sequential Attention to Goals   The existence of conflict among operational constraints is resolved by the device of sequential attention. As a problem arises, the subunits of the organization most concerned with that problem deal with it in terms of the constraints they take to be most important. When the next problem arises, another cluster of subunits deals with it, focusing on a different set of constraints.

3. Standard Operating Procedures   Organizations perform their "higher" functions, such as attending to problem areas, monitoring information, and preparing relevant responses for likely contingencies, by doing "lower" tasks, for example, preparing budgets, producing reports, and developing hardware. Reliable performance of these tasks requires standard operating procedures (hereafter SOPs). Since procedures are "standard," they do not change quickly or easily. Without these standard procedures, it would not be possible to perform certain concerted tasks. But because of standard procedures, organizational behavior in particular instances often appears unduly formalized, sluggish, or inappropriate.

4. Programs and Repertoires   Organizations must be capable of performing actions in which the behavior of large numbers of individuals is carefully coordinated. Assured performance requires clusters of rehearsed SOPs for producing specific actions, e.g., fighting enemy units or answering an embassy's cable. Each cluster comprises a "program" (in the terms both of drama and computers) which the organization has available for dealing with a situation. The list of programs relevant to a type of activity, e.g., fighting, constitutes an organizational repertoire. The number of programs in a repertoire is always quite limited. When properly triggered, organizations execute programs; programs cannot be substantially changed in a particular situation. The more complex the action and the greater the number of individuals involved, the more important are programs and repertoires as determinants of organizational behavior.

5. UNCERTAINTY AVOIDANCE   Organizations do not attempt to estimate the probability distribution of future occurrences. Rather, organizations avoid uncertainty. By arranging a *negotiated environment,* organizations regularize the reactions of other actors with whom they have to deal. The primary environment, relations with other organizations that comprise the government, is stabilized by such arrangements as agreed budgetary splits, accepted areas of responsibility, and established conventional practices. The secondary environment, relations with the international world, is stabilized between allies by the establishment of contracts (alliances) and "club relations" (U.S. State and U.K. Foreign Office or U.S. Treasury and U.K. Treasury). Between enemies contracts and accepted conventional practices perform a similar function, for example the rules of the "precarious status quo" which President Kennedy referred to in the missile crisis. Where the international environment cannot be negotiated, organizations deal with remaining uncertainties by establishing a set of *standard scenarios* that constitute the contingencies for which they prepare. For example, the standard scenario for Tactical Air Command of the U.S. air force involves combat with enemy aircraft. Planes are designed and pilots trained to meet this problem. That these preparations are less relevant to more probable contingencies, e.g., provision of close-in ground support in limited wars like Vietnam, has had little impact on the scenario.

6. PROBLEM-DIRECTED SEARCH   Where situations cannot be construed as standard, organizations engage in search. The style of search and the solution are largely determined by existing routines. Organizational search for alternative courses of action is problem-oriented: it focuses on the atypical discomfort that must be avoided. It is simple-minded: the neighborhood of the symptom is searched first; then the neighborhood of the current alternative. Patterns of search reveal biases which in turn reflect such factors as specialized training or experience and patterns of communication.

7. ORGANIZATIONAL LEARNING AND CHANGE   The parameters of organizational behavior mostly persist. In response to nonstandard problems organizations search and routines evolve, assimilating new situations. Thus learning and change follow in large part from existing procedures. But marked changes in organizations do sometimes occur. Conditions in which dramatic changes are more likely include: (1) Periods of budgetary feast. Typically, organizations devour budgetary feasts by purchasing additional items on the existing shopping list. Nevertheless, if committed to change, leaders who control the budget can use extra funds to effect changes. (2) Periods of prolonged budgetary famine. Though a single year's famine typically results in few changes in organizational structure but a loss of

effectiveness in performing some programs, prolonged famine forces major retrenchment. (3) Dramatic performance failures. Dramatic change occurs (mostly) in response to major disasters. Confronted with an undeniable failure of procedures and repertoires, authorities outside the organization demand change, existing personnel are less resistant to change, and critical members of the organization are replaced by individuals committed to change.

E. CENTRAL COORDINATION AND CONTROL Action requires decentralization of responsibility and power. But problems lap over the jurisdictions of several organizations. Thus the necessity for decentralization runs headlong into the requirement for coordination. (Advocates of one horn or the other of this dilemma—responsive action entails decentralized power vs. coordinated action requires central control—account for a considerable part of the persistent demand for government reorganization.) Both the necessity for coordination and the centrality of foreign policy to national welfare guarantee the involvement of government leaders in the procedures of the organizations among which problems are divided and power shared. Each organization's propensities and routines can be disturbed by government leaders' intervention. Central direction and persistent control of organizational activity, however, is not possible. The relation among organizations and between organizations and the government leaders depends critically on a number of structural variables, including: (1) the nature of the job, (2) the measures and information available to government leaders, (3) the system of rewards and punishments for organizational members, and (4) the procedures by which human and material resources get committed. For example, to the extent that rewards and punishments for the members of an organization are distributed by higher authorities, these authorities can exercise some control by specifying criteria in terms of which organizational output is to be evaluated. These criteria become constraints within which organizational activity proceeds. But constraint is a crude instrument of control.

Intervention by government leaders does sometimes change the activity of an organization in an intended direction. But instances are fewer than might be expected. As Franklin Roosevelt, the master manipulator of government organizations, remarked:

> The Treasury is so large and far-flung and ingrained in its practices that I find it is almost impossible to get the action and results I want. . . . But the Treasury is not to be compared with the State Department. You should go through the experience of trying to get any changes in the thinking, policy, and action of the career diplomats and then you'd know what a real problem was. But the Treasury and the State Department put together are nothing compared with the na-a-vy . . . To change anything in the na-a-vy is like punching a feather bed. You punch it with your right and you punch it with your left until you are finally exhausted, and then you find the damn bed just as it was before you started punching.[44]

John Kennedy's experience seems to have been similar: "The State Department," he asserted, "is a bowl full of jelly."[45] And lest the McNamara revolution in the Defense Department seem too striking a counterexample, the navy's recent rejection of McNamara's major intervention in naval weapons procurement, the F-111B, should be studied as an antidote.

F. DECISIONS OF GOVERNMENT LEADERS   Organizational persistence does not exclude shifts in governmental behavior. For government leaders sit atop the conglomerate of organizations. Many important issues of governmental action require that these leaders decide what organizations will play out which programs where. Thus stability in the parochialisms and SOPs of individual organizations is consistent with some important shifts in the behavior of governments. The range of these shifts is defined by existing organizational programs.

III. Dominant Inference Pattern

If a nation performs an action of this type today, its organizational components must yesterday have been performing (or have had established routines for performing) an action only marginally different from this action. At any specific point in time, a government consists of an established conglomerate of organizations, each with existing goals, programs, and repertoires. The characteristics of a government's action in any instance follows from those established routines and from the choice of government leaders—on the basis of information and estimates provided by existing routines—among existing programs. The best explanation of an organization's behavior at t is $t - 1$; the prediction of $t + 1$ is t. Model II's explanatory power is achieved by uncovering the organizational routines and repertoires that produced the outputs that comprise the puzzling occurrence.

IV. General Propositions

A number of general propositions have been stated above. In order to illustrate clearly the type of proposition employed by model II analysts, this section formulates several more precisely.

A. ORGANIZATIONAL ACTION   Activity according to SOPs and programs does not constitute far-sighted, flexible adaptation to "the issue" (as it is conceived by the analyst). Detail and nuance of actions by organizations are determined predominantly by organizational routines, not government leaders' directions.

1. SOPs constitute routines for dealing with *standard* situations. Routines allow large numbers of ordinary individuals to deal with numerous instances, day after day, without considerable thought, by responding to basic stimuli. But this regularized capability for adequate performance is purchased at the price of standardization. If the SOPs are appropriate, average performance, i.e., performance averaged over the range of cases, is better than it would be if each instance were approached individually (given fixed talent, timing, and resource constraints). But specific instances, particularly critical instances that typically do not have "standard" characteristics, are often handled sluggishly or inappropriately.

2. A program, i.e., a complex action chosen from a short list of programs in a repertoire, is rarely tailored to the specific situation in which it is executed. Rather, the program is (at best) the most appropriate of the programs in a previously developed repertoire.
3. Since repertoires are developed by parochial organizations for standard scenarios defined by that organization, programs available for dealing with a particular situation are often ill-suited.

B. LIMITED FLEXIBILITY AND INCREMENTAL CHANGE   Major lines of organizational action are straight, i.e., behavior at one time is marginally different from that behavior at $t - 1$. Simple-minded predictions work best: Behavior at $t + 1$ will be marginally different from behavior at the present time.

1. Organizational budgets change incrementally—both with respect to totals and with respect to intraorganizational splits. Though organizations could divide the money available each year by carving up the pie anew (in the light of changes in objectives or environment), in practice, organizations take last year's budget as a base and adjust incrementally. Predictions that require large budgetary shifts in a single year between organizations or between units within an organization should be hedged.
2. Once undertaken, an organizational investment is not dropped at the point where "objective" costs outweigh benefits. Organizational stakes in adopted projects carry them quite beyond the loss point.

C. ADMINISTRATIVE FEASIBILITY   Adequate explanation, analysis, and prediction must include administrative feasibility as a major dimension. A considerable gap separates what leaders choose (or might rationally have chosen) and what organizations implement.

1. Organizations are blunt instruments. Projects that require several organizations to act with high degrees of precision and coordination are not likely to succeed.
2. Projects that demand that existing organization units depart from their accustomed functions and perform previously unprogrammed tasks are rarely accomplished in their designed form.
3. Government leaders can expect that each organization will do its part in terms of what the organization knows how to do.
4. Government leaders can expect incomplete and distorted information from each organization concerning its part of the problem.
5. Where an assigned piece of a problem is contrary to the existing goals of an organization, resistance to implementation of that piece will be encountered.

V. *Specific Propositions*

A. DETERRENCE   The probability of nuclear attack is less sensitive to balance and imbalance or stability and instability (as these concepts are employed by model I strategists) than it is to a number of organizational factors. Except for the special case in which the Soviet Union acquires a credible capability to destroy the U.S. with a disarming blow, U.S. superiority or inferiority affects the probability of a nuclear attack less than do a number of organizational factors.

First, if a nuclear attack occurs, it will result from organizational activity: the firing of rockets by members of a missile group. The enemy's *control system,* i.e., physical mechanisms and standard procedures which determine who can launch rockets when, is critical. Second, the enemy's programs for bringing his strategic forces to *alert status* determine probabilities of accidental firing and momentum. At the outbreak of World War I, if the Russian tsar had understood the organizational processes which his order of full mobilization triggered, he would have realized that he had chosen war. Third, organizational repertoires fix the range of effective choice open to enemy leaders. The menu available to Tsar Nicholas in 1914 has two entrees: full mobilization and no mobilization. Partial mobilization was not an organizational option. Fourth, since organizational routines set the chessboard, the training and deployment of troops and nuclear weapons is crucial. Given that the outbreak of hostilities in Berlin is more probable than most scenarios for nuclear war, facts about deployment, training, and tactical nuclear equipment of Soviet troops stationed in East Germany—which will influence the face of the issue seen by Soviet leaders at the outbreak of hostilities and the manner in which choice is implemented—are as critical as the question of "balance."

B. SOVIET FORCE POSTURE   Soviet force posture, i.e., the fact that certain weapons rather than others are procured and deployed, is determined by organizational factors such as the goals and procedures of existing military services and the goals and processes of research and design labs, within budgetary constraints that emerge from the government leader's choices. The frailty of the Soviet air force within the Soviet military establishment seems to have been a crucial element in the Soviet failure to acquire a large bomber force in the 1950s (thereby faulting American intelligence predictions of a "bomber gap"). The fact that missiles were controlled until 1960 in the Soviet Union by the Soviet ground forces, whose goals and procedures reflected no interest in an intercontinental mission, was not irrelevant to the slow Soviet buildup of ICBMs (thereby faulting U.S. intelligence predictions of a "missile gap"). These organizational factors (Soviet ground forces' control of missiles and that service's fixation with European scenarios) make the Soviet deployment of so many MRBMs that European targets could be destroyed three times over more understandable. Recent weapon developments, e.g., the testing of a fractional orbital bombardment system (FOBS) and multiple warheads for the SS-9, very likely reflect the activity and interests of a cluster of Soviet research and development organizations rather than a decision by Soviet leaders to acquire a first-strike weapon system. Careful attention to the organizational components of the Soviet military establishment (strategic rocket forces, navy, air force, ground forces, and national air defense), the missions and weapons systems to which each component is wedded (an independent weapon system assists survival as an independent service), and existing budgetary splits (which probably are relatively stable in the Soviet Union as they tend to be everywhere) offer potential improvements in medium- and longer-term predictions.

The U.S. Blockade of Cuba: A Second Cut

Organizational Intelligence

At 7:00 P.M. on October 22, 1962, President Kennedy disclosed the American discovery of the presence of Soviet strategic missiles in Cuba, declared a "strict quarantine on all offensive military equipment under shipment to Cuba," and demanded that "Chairman Khrushchev halt and eliminate this clandestine, reckless, and provocative threat to world peace."[46] This decision was reached at the pinnacle of the U.S. government after a critical week of deliberation. What initiated that precious week were photographs of Soviet missile sites in Cuba taken on October 14. These pictures might not have been taken until a week later. In that case, the President speculated, "I don't think probably we would have chosen as prudently as we finally did."[47] U.S. leaders might have received this information three weeks earlier—if a U-2 had flown over San Cristobal in the last week of September.[48] What determined the context in which American leaders came to choose the blockade was the discovery of missiles on October 14.

There has been considerable debate over alleged American intelligence failures in the Cuban missile crisis.[49] But what both critics and defenders have neglected is the fact that the discovery took place on October 14, rather than three weeks earlier or a week later, as a consequence of the established routines and procedures of the organizations which constitute the U.S. intelligence community. These organizations were neither more nor less successful than they had been the previous month or were to be in the months to follow.[50]

The notorious "September estimate," approved by the United States Intelligence Board (USIB) on September 19, concluded that the Soviet Union would not introduce offensive missiles into Cuba.[51] No U-2 flight was directed over the western end of Cuba (after September 5) before October 4.[52] No U-2 flew over the western end of Cuba until the flight that discovered the Soviet missiles on October 14.[53] Can these "failures" be accounted for in organizational terms?

On September 19, when USIB met to consider the question of Cuba, the "system" contained the following information: (1) shipping intelligence had noted the arrival in Cuba of two large-hatch Soviet lumber ships, which were riding high in the water; (2) refugee reports of countless sightings of missiles, but also a report that Castro's private pilot, after a night of drinking in Havana, had boasted: "We will fight to the death and perhaps we can win because we have everything, including atomic weapons"; (3) a sighting by a CIA agent of the rear profile of a strategic missile; (4) U-2 photos produced by flights of August 29, September 5, and 17 showing the construction of a number of SAM sites and other defensive missiles.[54] Not all of this information was on the desk of the estimators, however. Shipping intelligence experts noted the fact that large-hatch ships were riding high in the water and spelled out the inference: the ships must be carrying "space-consuming" cargo.[55] These facts were carefully included in the catalogue of intelligence concerning shipping. For experts sensitive to the Soviets' shortage of ships, however, these facts carried no special signal. The refugee report of Castro's private pilot's remark had been received at Opa Locka, Florida, along with vast reams of inaccurate reports generated by the refugee community. This report and a thousand others had to be checked and compared before being sent to Washington. The two weeks required for initial processing could have been shortened by a large increase in resources, but the yield of this source was already quite marginal. The CIA agent's sighting of the rear profile of a strategic missile had occurred on September 12; transmission time from agent sighting to arrival in Washington typically took nine to twelve days. Shortening this transmission time would impose severe cost in terms of danger to subagents, agents, and communication networks.

On the information available, the intelligence chiefs who predicted that the Soviet Union would not introduce offensive missiles into Cuba made a reasonable and defensible judgment.[56] Moreover, in the light of the fact that these organizations were gathering intelligence not only about Cuba but about potential occurrences in all parts of the world, the informational base available to the estimators involved nothing out of the ordinary. Nor, from an organizational perspective, is there anything startling about the gradual accumulation of evidence that led to the formulation of the hypothesis that the Soviets were installing missiles in Cuba and the decision on October 4 to direct a special flight over western Cuba.

The ten-day delay between that decision and the flight is another organizational story.[57] At the October 4 meeting the Defense Department took the opportunity to raise an issue important to its concerns. Given the increased danger that a U-2 would be downed, it would be better if the pilot were an officer in uniform rather than a CIA agent. Thus the air force should assume responsibility for U-2 flights over Cuba. To the contrary the CIA argued that this was an intelligence operation and thus within the CIA's jurisdiction. Moreover, CIA U-2s had been modified in certain ways which gave them advantages over Air Force U-2s in averting Soviet SAMs. Five days passed while the State Department pressed for less risky alternatives such as drones and the air force (in Department of Defense guise) and CIA engaged in territorial disputes. On October 9 a flight plan over San Cristobal was approved by COMOR, but to the CIA's dismay, air force pilots rather than CIA agents would take charge of the mission. At this point details become sketchy, but several members of the intelligence community have speculated that an air force pilot in an air force U-2 attempted a high-altitude overflight on October 9 that "flamed out", i.e., lost power, and thus had to descend in order to restart its engine. A second round between air force and CIA followed, as a result of which air force pilots were trained to fly CIA U-2s. A successful overflight took place on October 14.

This ten-day delay constitutes some form of "failure." In the face of well-founded suspicions concerning offensive Soviet missiles in Cuba that posed a critical threat to the United States's most vital interest, squabbling between organizations whose job it is to produce this information seems entirely inappropriate.

But for each of these organizations, the question involved the issue: "*Whose* job was it to be?" Moreover, the issue was not simply which organization would control U-2 flights over Cuba, but rather the broader issue of ownership of U-2 intelligence activities—a very long-standing territorial dispute. Thus though this delay was in one sense a "failure," it was also a nearly inevitable consequence of two facts: many jobs do not fall neatly into precisely defined organizational jurisdictions; and vigorous organizations are imperialistic.

Organizational Options

Deliberations of leaders in ExCom meetings produced broad outlines of alternatives. Details of these alternatives and blueprints for their implementation had to be specified by the organizations that would perform these tasks. These organizational outputs answered the question: What, specifically, *could* be done?

Discussion in the ExCom quickly narrowed the live options to two: an air strike and a blockade. The choice of the blockade instead of the air strike turned on two points: (1) the argument from morality and tradition that the United States could not perpetrate a "Pearl Harbor in reverse"; (2) the belief that a "surgical" air strike was impossible.[58] Whether the United States *might* strike first was a question not of capability but of morality. Whether the United States *could* perform the surgical strike was a factual question concerning capabilities. The majority of the members of the ExCom, including the president, initially preferred the air strike.[59] What effectively foreclosed this option, however, was the fact that the air strike they wanted could not be chosen with high confidence of success.[60] After having tentatively chosen the course of prudence—given that the surgical air strike was not an option—Kennedy reconsidered. On Sunday morning, October 21, he called the air force experts to a special meeting in his living quarters, where he probed once more for the option of a "surgical" air strike.[61] General Walter C. Sweeny, Commander of Tactical Air Forces, asserted again that the air force could guarantee no higher than 90 percent effectiveness in a surgical air strike.[62] That "fact" was false.

The air strike alternative provides a classic case of military estimates. One of the alternatives outlined by the ExCom was named *air strike*. Specification of the details of this alternative was delegated to the air force. Starting from an existing plan for massive U.S. military action against Cuba (prepared for contingencies like a response to a Soviet Berlin grab), air force estimators produced an attack to guarantee success.[63] This plan called for extensive bombardment of all missile sites, storage depots, airports, and in deference to the navy, the artillery batteries opposite the naval base at Guantanamo.[64] Members of the ExCom repeatedly expressed bewilderment at military estimates of the number of sorties required, likely casualties, and collateral damage. But the "surgical" air strike that the political leaders had in mind was never carefully examined during the first week of the crisis. Rather this option was simply excluded on the grounds that since the Soviet MRBMs in Cuba were classified "mobile" in U.S. manuals, extensive bombing was required. During the second week of the crisis careful examination revealed that the missiles were mobile in the sense that small houses are mobile: that is, they could be moved and reassembled in six days. After the missiles were reclassified "movable" and detailed plans for surgical air strikes specified, this action was added to the list of live options for the end of the second week.

Organizational Implementation

ExCom members separated several types of blockade: offensive weapons only, all armaments, and all strategic goods including POL (petroleum, oil, and lubricants). But the "details" of the operation were left to the navy. Before the president announced the blockade on Monday evening, the first stage of the navy's blueprint was in motion, and a problem loomed on the horizon.[65] The navy had a detailed plan for the blockade. The president had several less precise but equally determined notions concerning what should be done, when, and how. For the navy the issue was one of effective implementation of the navy's blockade—without the meddling and interference of political leaders. For the president the problem was to pace and manage events in such a way that the Soviet leaders would have time to see, think, and blink.

A careful reading of available sources uncovers an instructive incident. On Tuesday the British ambassador, Ormsby-Gore, after having attended a briefing on the details of the blockade, suggested to the president that the plan for intercepting Soviet ships far out of reach of Cuban jets did not facilitate Khrushchev's hard decision.[66] Why not make the interception much closer to Cuba and thus give the Russian leader more time? According to the public account and the recollection of a number of individuals involved, Kennedy "agreed immediately, called McNamara, and over emotional navy protest, issued the appropriate instructions."[67] As Sorensen records, "in a sharp clash with the Navy, he made certain his will prevailed."[68] The navy's plan for the blockade was thus changed by drawing the blockade much closer to Cuba.

A serious organizational orientation makes one suspicious of this account. More careful examination of the available evidence confirms these suspicions, though alternative accounts must be somewhat speculative. According to the public chronology, a quarantine drawn close to Cuba became effective on Wednesday morning, the first Soviet ship was contacted on Thursday morning, and the first boarding of a ship occurred on Friday. According to the statement by the Department of Defense, boarding of the *Marcula* by a party from the *John R. Pierce* "took place at 7:50 A.M., E.D.T., 180 miles northeast of Nassau."[69] The *Marcula* had been trailed since about 10:30 the previous evening.[70] Simple calculations suggest that the *Pierce* must have been stationed along the navy's original arc, which extended five hundred miles out to sea from Cape Magsi, Cuba's easternmost tip.[71] The blockade line was *not* moved as the president ordered and the accounts report.

What happened is not entirely clear. One can be certain, however, that Soviet ships passed through the line along which American destroyers had posted themselves before the official "first contact" with the Soviet ship. On October 26 a Soviet tanker arrived in Havana and was honored by a dockside rally for "running the blockade." Photographs of this vessel show the name *Vinnitsa* on the side of the vessel in Cyrillic letters.[72] But according to the official U.S. position, the first tanker to pass through the blockade was the *Bucharest,* which was hailed by the navy on the morning of October 25. Again simple mathematical calculation excludes the possibility that the *Bucharest* and the *Vinnitsa* were the same ship. It seems probable that the navy's resistance to the president's order that the blockade be drawn in closer to Cuba forced him to allow one or several Soviet ships to pass through the blockade after it was officially operative.[73]

This attempt to leash the navy's blockade had a price. On Wednesday morning, October 24, what the president had been awaiting occurred. The eighteen dry cargo ships heading towards the quarantine stopped dead in the water. This was the occasion of Dean Rusk's remark, "We are eyeball to eyeball and I think the other fellow just blinked."[74] But the navy had another interpretation. The ships had simply stopped to pick up Soviet submarine escorts. The president became quite concerned lest the navy—already riled because of presidential meddling in its affairs—blunder into an incident. Sensing the president's fears, McNamara became suspicious of the navy's procedures and routines for making the first interception. Calling on the Chief of Naval Operations in the navy's inner sanctum, the navy flag plot, McNamara put his questions harshly.[75] Who would make the first interception? Were Russian-speaking officers on board? How would submarines be dealt with? At one point McNamara asked Anderson what he would do if a Soviet ship's captain refused to answer questions about his cargo. Picking up the Manual of Navy Regulations, the navy man waved it in McNamara's face and shouted, "It's all in there." To which McNamara replied, "I don't give a damn what John Paul Jones would have done; I want to know what you are going to do, now."[76] The encounter ended on Anderson's remark: "Now, Mr. Secretary, if you and your deputy will go back to your office, the navy will run the blockade."[77]

MODEL III: BUREAUCRATIC POLITICS

The leaders who sit on top of organizations are not a monolithic group. Rather each is in his own right a player in a central competitive game. The name of the game is bureaucratic politics: bargaining along regularized channels among players positioned hierarchically within the government. Government behavior can thus be understood according to a third conceptual model not as organizational outputs but as outcomes of bargaining games. In contrast with model I, the bureaucratic politics model sees no unitary actor but rather many actors as players, who focus not on a single strategic issue but on many diverse intranational problems as well, in terms of no consistent set of strategic objectives but rather according to various conceptions of national, organizational, and personal goals, making government decisions not by rational choice but by the pulling and hauling that is politics.

The apparatus of each national government constitutes a complex arena for the intranational game. Political leaders at the top of this apparatus plus the men who occupy positions on top of the critical organizations form the circle of central players. Ascendancy to this circle assures some independent standing. The necessary decentralization of decisions required for action on the broad range of foreign policy problems guarantees that each player has considerable discretion. Thus power is shared.

The nature of problems of foreign policy permits fundamental disagreement among reasonable men concerning what ought to be done. Analyses yield conflicting recommendations. Separate responsibilities laid on the shoulders of individual personalities encourage differences in perceptions and priorities. But the issues are of first-order importance. What the nation does really matters. A wrong choice could mean irreparable damage. Thus responsible men are obliged to fight for what they are convinced is right.

Men share power. Men differ concerning what must be done. The differences matter. This milieu necessitates that policy be resolved by politics. What the nation does is sometimes the result of the triumph of one group over others. More often, however, different groups pulling in different directions yield a resultant distinct from what anyone intended. What moves the chess pieces is not simply the reasons which support a course of action, nor the routines of organizations which enact an alternative, but the power and skill of proponents and opponents of the action in question.

This characterization captures the thrust of the bureaucratic-politics orientation. If problems of foreign policy arose as discrete issues and decisions were determined one game at a time, this account would suffice. But most issues, e.g., Vietnam or the proliferation of nuclear weapons, emerge piecemeal, over time, one lump in one context, a second in another. Hundreds of issues compete for players' attention every day. Each player is forced to fix upon his issues for that day, fight them on their own terms, and rush on to the next. Thus the character of emerging issues and the pace at which the game is played converge to yield government "decisions" and "actions" as collages. Choices by one player, outcomes of minor games, outcomes of central games, and "foul-ups"—these pieces, when stuck to the same canvas, constitute government behavior relevant to an issue.

The concept of national security policy as political outcome contradicts both public imagery and academic orthodoxy. Issues vital to national security, it is said, are too important to be settled by political games. They must be "above" politics. To accuse someone of "playing politics with national security" is a most serious charge. What public conviction demands, the academic penchant for intellectual elegance reinforces. Internal politics is messy; moreover, according to prevailing doctrine, politicking lacks intellectual content. As such, it constitutes gossip for journalists rather than a subject for serious investigation. Occasional memoirs, anecdotes in historical accounts, and several detailed case studies to the contrary, most of the literature of foreign policy avoids bureaucratic politics. The gap between academic literature and the experience of participants in government is nowhere wider than at this point.

Bureaucratic Politics Paradigm[78]

I.   *Basic Unit of Analysis: Policy as Political Outcome*

The decisions and actions of governments are essentially intranational political outcomes: outcomes in the sense that what happens is not chosen as a solution to a problem but rather results from compromise, coalition, competition, and confusion among government officials who see different faces of an issue; political in the sense that the activity from which the outcomes emerge is best characterized as bargaining. Following Wittgenstein's use of the concept of a "game," national behavior in international affairs can be conceived as outcomes of intricate and subtle, simultaneous, overlapping games among players located in positions the hierarchical arrangement of which constitutes the government.[79] These games proceed neither at random nor at leisure. Regular channels structure the game. Deadlines force issues to the attention of busy players. The moves in the chess game are thus to be explained in terms of the bargaining among players with separate and unequal power over particular pieces and with separable objectives in distinguishable subgames.

II. *Organizing Concepts*

A. PLAYERS IN POSITIONS   The actor is neither a unitary nation nor a conglomerate of organizations, but rather a number of individual players. Groups of these players constitute the agent for particular government decisions and actions. Players are men in jobs.

Individuals become players in the national security policy game by occupying a critical position in an administration. For example, in the U.S. government the players include "Chiefs": the President, Secretaries of State, Defense, and Treasury, Director of the CIA, Joint Chiefs of Staff, and, since 1961, the Special Assistant for National Security Affairs;[80] "Staffers": the immediate staff of each Chief; "Indians": the political appointees and permanent government officials within each of the departments and agencies; and *Ad Hoc* Players": actors in the wider government game (especially "Congressional Influentials"), members of the press, spokesmen for important interest groups (especially the "bipartisan foreign policy establishment" in and out of Congress), and surrogates for each of these groups. Other members of the Congress, press, interest groups, and public form concentric circles around the central arena—circles which demarcate the permissive limits within which the game is played.

Positions define what players both may and must do. The advantages and handicaps with which each player can enter and play in various games stems from his position. So does a cluster of obligations for the performance of certain tasks. The two sides of this coin are illustrated by the position of the modern Secretary of State. First, in form and usually in fact, he is the primary repository of political judgment on the political-military issues that are the stuff of contemporary foreign policy; consequently, he is a senior personal advisor to the President. Second, he is the colleague of the President's other senior advisers on the problems of foreign policy, the Secretaries of Defense and Treasury, and the Special Assistant for National Security Affairs. Third, he is the ranking U.S. diplomat for serious negotiation. Fourth, he serves as an Administration voice to Congress, the country, and the world. Finally, he is "Mr. State Department" or "Mr. Foreign Office," "leader of officials, spokesman for their causes, guardian of their interests, judge of their disputes, superintendent of their work, master of their careers."[81] But he is not first one, and then the other. All of these obligations are his simultaneously. His performance in one affects his credit and power in the others. The perspective stemming from the daily work which he must oversee—the cable traffic by which his department maintains relations with other foreign offices—conflicts with the president's requirement that he serve as a generalist and coordinator of contrasting perspectives. The necessity that he be close to the President restricts the extent to which, and the force with which, he can front for his department. When he defers to the Secretary of Defense rather than fighting for his department's position—as he often must—he strains the loyalty of his officialdom. The Secretary's resolution of these conflicts depends not only upon the position, but also upon the player who occupies the position.

For players are also people. Men's metabolisms differ. The core of the bureaucratic politics mix is personality. (How each man manages to stand the heat in his kitchen, each player's basic operating style, and the complementarity or contradiction among personalities and styles in the inner circles are irreducible pieces of the policy blend.) Moreover, each person comes to his position with baggage in tow, including sensitivities to certain issues, commitments to various programs, and personal standing and debts with groups in the society.

B. PAROCHIAL PRIORITIES, PERCEPTIONS, AND ISSUES   Answers to the questions: "What is the issue?" and "What must be done?" are colored by the position from which the questions are considered. For the factors which encourage organizational parochialism also influence the players who occupy positions on top of (or within) these organizations. To motivate members of his organization, a player must be sensitive to the organization's orientation. The games into which the player can enter and the advantages with which he plays enhance these pressures. Thus propensities of perception stemming from position permit reliable prediction about a player's stances in many cases. But these propensities are filtered through the baggage which players bring to positions. Sensitivity to both the pressures and the baggage is thus required for many predictions.

C. INTERESTS, STAKES, AND POWER   Games are played to determine outcomes. But outcomes advance and impede each player's conception of the national interest, specific programs to which he is committed, the welfare of his friends, and his personal interests. These overlapping interests constitute the stakes for which games are played. Each player's ability to play successfully depends upon his power. Power, i.e., effective influence on policy outcomes, is an elusive blend of at least three elements: bargaining advantages (drawn from formal authority and obligations, institutional backing, constituents, expertise, and status), skill and will in using bargaining advantages, and other players' perceptions of the first two ingredients. Power wisely invested yields an enhanced reputation for effectiveness. Unsuccessful investment depletes both the stock of capital and the reputation. Thus each player must pick the issues on which he can play with a reasonable probability of success. But no player's power is sufficient to guarantee satisfactory outcomes. Each player's needs and fears run to many other players. What ensues is the most intricate and subtle of games known to man.

D. THE PROBLEM AND THE PROBLEMS   "Solutions" to strategic problems are not derived by detached analysts focusing coolly on *the* problem. Instead deadlines and events raise issues in games and demand decisions of busy players in contexts that influence the face the issue wears. The problems for the players are both narrower and broader than *the* strategic problem. For each player focuses not on the total strategic problem but rather on the decision that must be made now. But each decision has critical consequences not only for the strategic problem but for each player's organizational, reputational, and personal stakes. Thus the gap between the problems the player was solving and the problem upon which the analyst focuses is often very wide.

E. ACTION-CHANNELS   Bargaining games do not proceed randomly. Action-channels, i.e., regularized ways of producing action concerning types of issues, structure the game by preselecting the major players, determining their points of entrance into the game, and distributing particular advantages and disadvantages for each game. Most critically, channels determine "who's got the action," that is, which department's Indians actually do whatever is chosen. Weapon procurement decisions are made within the annual budgeting process; embassies' demands for action cables are answered according to routines of consultation and clearance from State to Defense and White House; requests for instructions from military groups (concerning assistance all the time, concerning operations during war) are composed by the military in consultation with the Office of the Secretary of Defense, State, and White House; crisis responses are debated among White House, State, Defense, CIA, and ad hoc players; major political speeches, especially by the president but also by other chiefs, are cleared through established channels.

F. ACTION AS POLITICS   Government decisions are made and government actions emerge neither as the calculated choice of a unified group nor as a formal summary of leaders' preferences. Rather the context of shared power but separate judgments concerning important choices determines that politics is the mechanism of choice. Note the *environment* in which the game is played: inordinate uncertainty about what must be done, the necessity that something be done, and crucial consequences of whatever is done. These features force responsible men to become active players. The *pace of the game*—hundreds of issues, numerous games, and multiple channels—compels players to fight to "get others' attention," to make them "see the facts," to assure that they "take the time to think seriously about the broader issue." The *structure of the game*—power shared by individuals with separate responsibilities—validates each player's feeling that "others don't see my problem," and "others must be persuaded to look at the issue from a less parochial perspective." The *rules of the game*—he who hesitates loses his chance to play at that point, and he who is uncertain about his recommendation is overpowered by others who are sure—pressures players to come down on one side of a 51:49 issue and play. The *rewards of the game*—effectiveness, i.e., impact on outcomes, as the immediate measure of performance—encourages hard play. Thus, most players come to fight to "make the government do what is right." The strategies and tactics employed are quite similar to those formalized by theorists of international relations.

G. STREAMS OF OUTCOMES   Important government decisions or actions emerge as collages composed of individual acts, outcomes of minor and major games, and foul-ups. Outcomes which could never have been chosen by an actor and would never have emerged from bargaining in a single game over the issue are fabricated piece by piece. Understanding of the outcome requires that it be disaggregated.

III. Dominant Inference Pattern

If a nation performed an action, that action was the *outcome* of bargaining among individuals and groups within the government. That outcome included *results* achieved by groups committed to a decision or action, *resultants* which emerged from bargaining among groups with quite different positions and *foul-ups*. Model III's explanatory power is achieved by revealing the pulling and hauling of various players, with different perceptions and priorities, focusing on separate problems, which yielded the outcomes that constitute the action in question.

IV. General Propositions

1. ACTION AND INTENTION   Action does not presuppose intention. The sum of behavior of representatives of a government relevant to an issue was rarely intended by any individual or group. Rather, separate individuals with different intentions contributed pieces which compose an outcome distinct from what anyone would have chosen.

2. WHERE YOU STAND DEPENDS ON WHERE YOU SIT[82]   Horizontally, the diverse demands upon each player shape his priorities, perceptions, and issues. For large classes of issues, e.g., budgets and procurement decisions, the stance of a particular player can be predicted with high reliability from information concerning his seat. In the notorious B-36 controversy, no one was surprised by Admiral Radford's testimony that "the B-36 under any theory of war is a bad gamble with national security," as opposed to Air Force Secretary Symington's claim that "a B-36 with an A-bomb can destroy distant objectives which might require ground armies years to take."[83]

3. CHIEFS AND INDIANS   The aphorism "where you stand depends on where you sit" has vertical as well as horizontal application. Vertically, the demands upon the president, chiefs, staffers, and Indians are quite distinct.

The foreign policy issues with which the president can deal are limited primarily by his crowded schedule: the necessity of dealing first with what comes next. His problem is to probe the special face worn by issues that come to his attention, to preserve his leeway until time has clarified the uncertainties, and to assess the relevant risks.

Foreign-policy chiefs deal most often with the hottest issue *de jour,* though they can get the attention of the president and other members of the government for other issues which they judge important. What they cannot guarantee is that "the president will pay the price" or that "the others will get on board." They must build a coalition of the relevant powers that be. They must "give the president confidence" in the right course of action.

Most problems are framed, alternatives specified, and proposals pushed, however, by Indians. Indians fight with Indians of other departments; for example, struggles between International Security Affairs of the Department of Defense and Political-Military of the State Department are a microcosm of the action at higher levels. But the Indian's major problem is how to get the *attention* of chiefs, how to get an issue decided, how to get the government "to do what is right."

In policy making then, the issue looking *down* is options: how to preserve my leeway until time clarifies uncertainties. The issue looking *sideways* is commitment: how to get others committed to my coalition. The issue looking *upwards* is confidence: how to give the boss confidence in doing what must be done. To paraphrase one of Neustadt's assertions which can be applied down the length of the ladder, the essence of a responsible official's task is to induce others to see that what needs to be done is what their own appraisal of their own responsibilities requires them to do in their own interests.

V. *Specific Propositions*

1. DETERRENCE   The probability of nuclear attack depends primarily on the probability of attack emerging as an outcome of the bureaucratic politics of the attacking government. First, which players can decide to launch an attack? Whether the effective power over action is controlled by an individual, a minor game, or the central game is critical. Second, though model I's confidence in nuclear deterrence stems from an assertion that in the end governments will not commit suicide, model III recalls historical precedents. Admiral Yamamoto, who designed the Japanese attack on Pearl Harbor, estimated accurately: "In the first six months to a year of war against the U.S. and England I will run wild, and I will show you an uninterrupted succession of victories; I must also tell you that, should the war be prolonged for two or three years, I have no confidence in our ultimate victory."[84] But Japan attacked. Thus, three questions might be considered. One: could any member of the government solve his problem by attack? What patterns of bargaining could yield attack as an outcome? The major difference between a stable balance of terror and a questionable balance may simply be that in the first case most members of the government appreciate fully the consequences of attack and are thus on guard against the emergence of this outcome. Two: what stream of outcomes might lead to an attack? At what point in that stream is the potential attacker's politics? If members of the U.S. government had been sensitive to the stream of decisions from which the Japanese attack on Pearl Harbor emerged, they would have been aware of a considerable probability of that attack. Three: how might miscalculation and confusion generate foul-ups that yield attack as an outcome? For example, in a crisis or after the beginning of conventional war, what happens to the information available to and the effective power of members of the central game?

The U.S. Blockade of Cuba: A Third Cut

The Politics of Discovery

A series of overlapping bargaining games determined both the date of the discovery of the Soviet missiles and the impact of this discovery on the administration. An explanation of the politics of the discovery is consequently a considerable piece of the explanation of the U.S. blockade.

Cuba was the Kennedy administration's "political Achilles' heel."[85] The months preceding the crisis were also months before the congressional elections, and the Republican Senatorial and Congressional Campaign Committee had announced that Cuba would be "the dominant issue of the 1962 campaign."[86] What the administration billed as a "more positive and indirect approach of isolating Castro from developing, democratic Latin America," Senators Keating, Goldwater, Capehart, Thurmond, and others attacked as a "do-nothing" policy.[87] In statements on the floor of the House and Senate, campaign speeches across the country, and interviews and articles carried by national news media, Cuba— particularly the Soviet program of increased arms aid—served as a stick for stirring the domestic political scene.[88]

These attacks drew blood. Prudence demanded a vigorous reaction. The president decided to meet the issue head on. The administration mounted a forceful campaign of denial designed to discredit critics' claims. The president himself manned the front line of this offensive, though almost all administration officials participated. In his news conference on August 19, President Kennedy attacked as "irresponsible" calls for an invasion of Cuba, stressing rather "the totality of our obligations" and promising to "watch what happens in Cuba with the closest attention."[89] On September 4 he issued a strong statement denying any provocative Soviet action in Cuba.[90] On September 13 he lashed out at "loose talk" calling for an invasion of Cuba.[91] The day before the flight of the U-2 which discovered the missiles, he campaigned in Capehart's Indiana against those "self-appointed generals and admirals who want to send someone else's sons to war."[92]

On Sunday, October 14, just as a U-2 was taking the first pictures of Soviet missiles, McGeorge Bundy was asserting:

> I *know* that there is no present evidence, and I think that there is no present likelihood that the Cuban government and the Soviet government would, in combination, attempt to install a major offensive capability.[93]

In this campaign to puncture the critics' charges, the administration discovered that the public needed positive slogans. Thus Kennedy fell into a tenuous semantic distinction between "offensive" and "defensive" weapons. This distinction originated in his September 4 statement that there was no evidence of "offensive ground to ground missiles" and warned "were it to be otherwise, the gravest issues would arise."[94] His September 13 statement turned on this distinction between "defensive" and "offensive" weapons and announced a firm commitment to action if the Soviet Union attempted to introduce the latter into Cuba.[95] Congressional committees elicited from administration officials testimony which read this distinction and the president's commitment into the *Congressional Record.*[96]

What the president least wanted to hear, the CIA was most hesitant to say plainly. On August 22 John McCone met privately with the president and voiced suspicions that the Soviets were preparing to introduce offensive missiles into Cuba.[97] Kennedy heard this as what it was: the suspicion of a hawk. McCone left Washington for a month's honeymoon on the Riviera. Fretting at Cap Ferrat, he bombarded his deputy, General Marshall Carter, with telegrams, but Carter, knowing that McCone had informed the president of his suspicions and received a cold reception, was reluctant to distribute these telegrams outside the CIA.[98] On September 9 a U-2 "on loan" to the Chinese Nationalists was downed over mainland China.[99] The Committee on Overhead Reconnaissance (COMOR) convened on September 10 with a sense of urgency.[100] Loss of another U-2 might incite world opinion to demand cancellation of U-2 flights. The president's campaign against those who asserted that the Soviets were acting provocatively in Cuba had begun. To risk downing a U-2 over Cuba was to risk chopping off the limb on which the president was sitting. That meeting decided to shy away from the western end of Cuba (where SAMs were becoming operational) and modify the flight pattern of the U-2s in order to reduce the probability that a U-2 would be lost.[101] USIB's unanimous approval of the September estimate reflects similar sensitivities. On September 13 the president had asserted that there were no Soviet offensive missiles in Cuba and committed his administration to act if offensive missiles were discovered. Before congressional committees, administration officials were denying that there was any evidence whatever of offensive missiles in Cuba. The implications of a national intelligence estimate which concluded that the Soviets were introducing offensive missiles into Cuba were not lost on the men who constituted America's highest intelligence assembly.

The October 4 COMOR decision to direct a flight over the western end of Cuba in effect "overturned" the September estimate, but without officially raising that issue. The decision represented McCone's victory, for which he had lobbied with the president before the September 10 decision, in telegrams before the September 19 estimate, and in person after his return to Washington. Though the politics of the intelligence community is closely guarded, several pieces of the story can be told.[102] By September 27 Colonel Wright and others in DIA believed that the Soviet Union was placing missiles in the San Cristobal area.[103] This area was marked suspicious by the CIA on September 29 and certified top priority on October 3. By October 4 McCone had the evidence required to raise the issue officially. The members of COMOR heard McCone's argument but were reluctant to make the hard decision he demanded. The significant probability that a U-2 would be downed made overflight of western Cuba a matter of real concern.[104]

The Politics of Issues

The U-2 photographs presented incontrovertible evidence of Soviet offensive missiles in Cuba. This revelation fell upon politicized players in a complex context. As one high official recalled, Khrushchev had caught us "with our pants down." What each of the central participants saw, and what each did to cover both his own and the administration's nakedness, created the spectrum of issues and answers.

At approximately 9:00 A.M. Tuesday morning, October 16, McGeorge Bundy went to the president's living quarters with the message: "Mr. President, there is now hard photographic evidence that the Russians have offensive missiles in Cuba."[105] Much has been made of Kennedy's "expression of surprise,"[106] but *"surprise"* fails to capture the character of his initial reaction. Rather it was one of startled anger, most adequately conveyed by the exclamation: "He can't do that to *me!"*[107] In terms of the president's attention and priorities at that moment,

Khrushchev had chosen the most unhelpful act of all. Kennedy had staked his full presidential authority on the assertion that the Soviets would not place offensive weapons in Cuba. Moreover, Khrushchev had assured the president through the most direct and personal channels that he was aware of the president's domestic political problem and that nothing would be done to exacerbate this problem. The chairman had *lied* to the president. Kennedy's initial reaction entailed action. The missiles must be removed.[108] The alternatives of "doing nothing" or "taking a diplomatic approach" could not have been less relevant to *his* problem.

These two tracks—doing nothing and taking a diplomatic approach—were the solutions advocated by two of his principal advisers. For Secretary of Defense McNamara the missiles raised the specter of nuclear war. He first framed the issue as a straightforward strategic problem. To understand the issue one had to grasp two obvious but difficult points. First, the missiles represented an inevitable occurrence: narrowing of the missile gap. It simply happened sooner rather than later. Second, the United States could accept this occurrence, since its consequences were minor: "seven-to-one missile 'superiority,' one-to-one missile 'equality,' one-to-seven missile 'inferiority'—the three postures are identical." McNamara's statement of this argument at the first meeting of the ExCom was summed up in the phrase "a missile is a missile."[109] "It makes no great difference," he maintained, "whether you are killed by a missile from the Soviet Union or Cuba."[110] The implication was clear. The United States should not initiate a crisis with the Soviet Union, risking a significant probability of nuclear war over an occurrence which had such small strategic implications.

The perceptions of McGeorge Bundy, the president's assistant for national security affairs, are the most difficult of all to reconstruct. There is no question that he initially argued for a diplomatic track.[111] But was Bundy laboring under his acknowledged burden of responsibility in Cuba I? Or was he playing the role of devil's advocate in order to make the president probe his own initial reaction and consider other options?

The president's brother, Robert Kennedy, saw most clearly the political wall against which Khrushchev had backed the president. But he, like McNamara, saw the prospect of nuclear doom. Was Khrushchev going to force the president to an insane act? At the first meeting of the ExCom he scribbled a note, "Now I know how Tojo felt when he was planning Pearl Harbor."[112] From the outset he searched for an alternative that would prevent the air strike.

The initial reaction of Theodore Sorensen, the president's special counsel and "alter ego," fell somewhere between that of the president and his brother. Like the president, Sorensen felt the poignancy of betrayal. If the president had been the architect of the policy which the missiles punctured, Sorensen was the draftsman. Khrushchev's deceitful move demanded a strong countermove. But like Robert Kennedy, Sorensen feared lest the shock and disgrace lead to disaster.

To the Joint Chiefs of Staff the issue was clear. *Now* was the time to do the job for which they had prepared contingency plans. Cuba I had been badly done; Cuba II would not be. The missiles provided the *occasion* to deal with the issue: cleansing the Western Hemisphere of Castro's communism. As the president recalled on the day the crisis ended, "An invasion would have been a mistake—a wrong use of our power. But the military are mad. They wanted to do this. It's lucky for us that we have McNamara over there."[113]

McCone's perceptions flowed from his confirmed prediction. As the Cassandra of the incident, he argued forcefully that the Soviets had installed the missiles in a daring political probe which the United States must meet with force. The time for an air strike was now.[114]

The Politics of Choice

The process by which the blockade emerged is a story of the most subtle and intricate probing, pulling, and hauling; leading, guiding, and spurring. Reconstruction of this process can only be tentative. Initially the president and most of his advisers wanted the clean surgical air strike. On the first day of the crisis, when informing Stevenson of the missiles, the president mentioned only two alternatives: "I suppose the alternatives are to go in by air and wipe them out or to take other steps to render them inoperable."[115] At the end of the week a sizable minority still favored an air strike. As Robert Kennedy recalled: "The fourteen people involved were very significant. . . . If six of them had been president of the U.S., I think that the world might have been blown up."[116] What prevented the air strike was a fortuitous coincidence of a number of factors—the absence of any one of which might have permitted that option to prevail.

First, McNamara's vision of holocaust set him firmly against the air strike. His initial attempt to frame the issue in strategic terms struck Kennedy as particularly inappropriate. Once McNamara realized that the name of the game was a strong response, however, he and his deputy Gilpatric chose the blockade as a fallback. When the Secretary of Defense—whose department had the action, whose reputation in the cabinet was unequaled, in whom the president demonstrated full confidence—marshalled the arguments for the blockade and refused to be moved, the blockade became a formidable alternative.

Second, Robert Kennedy—the president's closest confidant—was unwilling to see his brother become a "Tojo." His arguments against the air strike on moral grounds struck a chord in the president. Moreover, once his brother had stated these arguments so forcefully, the president could not have chosen his initially preferred course without in effect agreeing to become what RFK had condemned.

The president learned of the missiles on Tuesday morning. On Wednesday morning, in order to mask our discovery from the Russians, the president flew to Connecticut to keep a campaign commitment, leaving RFK as the unofficial chairman of the group. By the time the president returned on Wednesday evening, a critical third piece had been added to the picture. McNamara had presented his argument for the blockade. Robert Kennedy and Sorensen had joined McNamara. A powerful coalition of the advisers in whom the president had the greatest confidence, and with whom his style was most compatible, had emerged.

Fourth, the coalition that had formed behind the president's initial preference gave him reason to pause. *Who* supported the air strike—the Chiefs, McCone, Rusk, Nitze, and Acheson—as much as *how* they supported it, counted. Fifth, a piece of inaccurate information, which no one probed, permitted the blockade advocates to fuel (potential) uncertainties in the president's mind. When the president returned to Washington Wednesday evening, RFK and Sorensen met him at the airport. Sorensen gave the president a four-page memorandum outlining the areas of agreement and disagreement. The strongest argument was that the air strike simply could not be surgical.[117] After a day of prodding and questioning, the air force had asserted that it could not guarantee the success of a surgical air strike limited to the missiles alone.

Thursday evening, the president convened the ExCom at the White House. He declared his tentative choice of the blockade and directed that preparations be made to put it into effect by Monday morning.[118] Though he raised a question about the possibility of a surgical air strike subsequently, he seems to have accepted the experts' opinion that this was no live option.[119] (Acceptance of this estimate suggests that he may have learned the lesson of the Bay of Pigs—"Never rely on experts"—less well than he supposed.)[120] But this information was incorrect. That no one probed this estimate during the first week of the crisis poses an interesting question for further investigation.

A coalition, including the president, thus emerged from the president's initial decision that something had to be done; McNamara, Robert Kennedy, and Sorensen's resistance to the air strike; incompatibility between the president and the air strike advocates; and an inaccurate piece of information.[121]

CONCLUSION

This essay has obviously bitten off more than it has chewed. For further developments and synthesis of these arguments the reader is referred to the larger study.[122] In spite of the limits of space, however, it would be inappropriate to stop without spelling out several implications of the argument and addressing the question of relations among the models and extensions of them to activity beyond explanation.

At a minimum the intended implications of the argument presented here are four. First, formulation of alternative frames of reference and demonstration that different analysts, relying predominantly on different models, produce quite different explanations should encourage the analyst's self-consciousness about the nets he employs. The effect of these "spectacles" in sensitizing him to particular aspects of what is going on—framing the puzzle in one way rather than another, encouraging him to examine the problem in terms of certain categories rather than others, directing him to particular kinds of evidence, and relieving puzzlement by one procedure rather than another—must be recognized and explored.

Second, the argument implies a position on the problem of "the state of the art." While accepting the commonplace characterization of the present condition of foreign-policy analysis—personalistic, noncumulative, and sometimes insightful—this essay rejects both the counsel of despair's justification of this condition as a consequence of the character of the enterprise, and the "new frontiersmen's" demand for *a priori* theorizing on the frontiers and *ad hoc* appropriation of "new techniques."[123] What is required as a first step is noncasual examination of the present product: inspection of existing explanations, articulation of the conceptual models employed in producing them, formulation of the propositions relied upon, specification of the logic of the various intellectual enterprises, and reflection on the questions being asked. Though it is difficult to overemphasize the need for more systematic processing of more data, these preliminary matters of formulating questions with clarity and sensitivity to categories and assumptions so that fruitful acquisition of large quantities of data is possible are still a major hurdle in considering most important problems.

Third, the preliminary, partial paradigms presented here provide a basis for serious reexamination of many problems of foreign and military policy. Model II and model III cuts at problems typically treated in model I terms can permit significant improvements in explanation and prediction.[124] Full model II and III analyses require large amounts of information. But even in cases where the information base is severely limited, improvements are possible. Consider the problem of predicting Soviet strategic forces. In the mid–1950s, model I style calculations led to predictions that the Soviets would rapidly deploy large numbers of long-range bombers. From a model II perspective both the frailty of the air force within the Soviet military establishment and the budgetary implications of such a build-up would have led analysts to hedge this prediction. Moreover, model II would have pointed to a sure, visible indicator of such a build-up: noisy struggles among the services over major budgetary shifts. In the late 1950s and early 1960s model I calculations led to the prediction of immediate massive Soviet deployment of ICBMs. Again, a model II cut would have reduced this number because in the earlier period strategic rockets were controlled by the Soviet ground forces rather than an independent service, and in the later period this would have necessitated massive shifts in budgetary splits. Today, model I considerations lead many analysts both to recommend that an agreement not to deploy ABMs be a major American objective in upcoming strategic negotiations with the USSR and to predict success. From a model II vantage point the existence of an ongoing Soviet ABM program, the strength of the organization (National Air Defense) that controls ABMs, and the fact that an agreement to stop ABM deployment would force the virtual dismantling of this organization make a viable agreement of this sort much less likely. A model III cut suggests that (a) there must be significant differences among perceptions and priorities of Soviet leaders over strategic negotiations, (b) any agreement will affect some players' power bases, and (c) agreements that do not require extensive cuts in the sources of some major players' power will prove easier to negotiate and more viable.

Fourth, the present formulation of paradigms is simply an initial step. As such it leaves a long list of critical questions unanswered. Given any action, an imaginative analyst should always be able to construct some rationale for the government's choice. By imposing and relaxing constraints on the parameters of rational choice (as in variants of model I) analysts can construct a large number of accounts of any act as a rational choice. But does a statement of reasons why a rational actor would choose an action constitute an explanation of the *occurrence* of that action? How can model I analysis be forced to make more systematic contributions to the question of the determinants of occurrences? Model II's explanation of t in terms of $t - 1$ is explanation. The world is contiguous. But governments sometimes make sharp departures. Can an organizational process model be modified to suggest where change is likely? Attention to organizational change should afford greater understanding of why particular programs and SOPs are maintained by identifiable types of organizations and also how a manager can improve organizational performance. Model III tells a fascinating "story." But its complexity is enormous, the information requirements are often overwhelming, and many of the details of the bargaining may be superfluous. How can such a model be made parsimonious? The three models are obviously not exclusive alternatives. Indeed, the paradigms highlight the partial emphasis of the framework—what each emphasizes and what it leaves out. Each concentrates on one class of variables, in effect relegating other important factors to a ceteris parabus clause. Model I concentrates on "market factors:" pressures and incentives created by the "international strategic marketplace." Models II and III focus on the internal mechanism of the government that chooses in this environment. But can these relations be more fully specified? Adequate synthesis would require a typology of decisions and actions, some of which are more amenable to treatment in terms of one model and some to another. Government behavior is but one cluster of factors relevant to occurrences in foreign affairs. Most students of foreign policy adopt this focus (at least when explaining and predicting). Nevertheless, the dimensions of the chess board, the character of the pieces, and the rules of the game—factors considered by international systems theorists—constitute the context in which the pieces are moved. Can the major variables in the full function of determinants of foreign policy outcomes be identified?

Both the outline of a partial *ad hoc* working synthesis of the models and a sketch of their uses in activities other than explanation can be suggested by generating predictions in terms of each. Strategic surrender is an important problem of international relations and diplomatic history. War termination is a new, developing area of the strategic literature. Both of these interests lead scholars to address a central question: *Why* do nations surrender *when?* Whether implicit in explanations or more explicit in analysis, diplomatic historians and strategists rely upon propositions which can be turned forward to produce predictions. Thus at the risk of being timely—and in error—the present situation (August 1968) offers an interesting test case: Why will North Vietnam surrender when?[125]

In a nutshell, analysis according to model I asserts: nations quit when costs outweigh the benefits. North Vietnam will surrender when she realizes "that continued fighting can only generate additional costs without hope of compensating gains, this expectation being largely the consequence of the previous application of force by the dominant side."[126] U.S. actions can increase or decrease Hanoi's strategic costs. Bombing North Vietnam increases the pain and thus increases the probability of surrender. This proposition and prediction are not without meaning. That—"other things being equal"—nations are more likely to surrender when the strategic cost-benefit balance is negative is true. Nations rarely surrender when they are winning. The proposition specifies a range within which nations surrender. But over this broad range the relevant question is: why do nations surrender?

Models II and III focus upon the government machine through which this fact about the international strategic marketplace must be filtered to produce a surrender. These analysts are considerably less sanguine about the possibility of surrender *at the point* that the cost-benefit calculus turns negative. Never in history (i.e., in none of the five cases I have examined) have nations surrendered at that point. Surrender occurs sometime thereafter. *When* depends on process of organizations and politics of players within these governments—as they are affected by the opposing government. Moreover, the effects of the victorious power's action upon the surrendering nation cannot be adequately summarized as increasing or decreasing strategic costs. Imposing additional costs by bombing a nation may increase the probability of surrender. But it also may reduce it. An appreciation of the impact of the acts of one nation upon another thus requires some understanding of the machine which is being influenced. For more precise prediction, models II and III require considerably more information about the organizations and politics of North Vietnam than is publicly available. On the basis of the limited public information, however, these models can be suggestive.

Model II examines two subproblems. First, to have lost is not sufficient. The government must know that the strategic cost-benefit calculus is negative. But neither the categories nor the indicators of strategic costs and benefits are clear. And the sources of information about both are organizations whose parochial priorities and perceptions do not facilitate accurate information or estimation. Military evaluation of military performance, military estimates of factors like "enemy morale," and military predictions concerning when "the tide will turn" or "the corner will have been turned" are typically distorted. In cases of highly decentralized guerrilla operations, like Vietnam, these problems are exacerbated. Thus strategic costs will be underestimated. Only highly *visible* costs can have direct impact on leaders without being filtered through organizational channels. Second, since organizations define the details of options and execute actions, surrender (and negotiation) is likely to entail considerable bungling in the early stages. No organization can define options or prepare programs for this treasonous act. Thus, early overtures will be uncoordinated with the acts of other organizations, e.g., the fighting forces, creating contradictory "signals" to the victor.

Model III suggests that surrender will not come at the point that strategic costs outweigh benefits, but that it will not wait until the leadership group concludes that the war is lost. Rather the problem is better understood in terms of four additional propositions. First, strong advocates of the war effort, whose careers are closely identified with the war, rarely come to the conclusion that costs outweigh benefits. Second, quite often from the outset of a war, a number of members of the government (particularly those whose responsibilities sensitize them to problems other than war, e.g., economic planners or intelligence experts) are convinced that the war effort is futile. Third, surrender is likely to come as the result of a political shift that enhances the effective power of the latter group (and adds swing members to it). Fourth, the course of the war, particularly actions of the victor, can influence the advantages and disadvantages of players in the loser's government. Thus, North Vietnam will surrender not when its leaders have a change of heart, but when Hanoi has a change of leaders (or a change of effective power within the central circle). How U.S. bombing (or pause), threats, promises, or action in the South affect the game in Hanoi is subtle but nonetheless crucial.

That these three models could be applied to the surrender of governments other than North Vietnam should be obvious. But that exercise is left for the reader.

NOTES

1. Theodore Sorensen, *Kennedy* (New York, 1965), p. 705.
2. In attempting to understand problems of foreign affairs, analysts engage in a number of related, but logically separable enterprises: (a) description, (b) explanation, (c) prediction, (d) evaluation, and (e) recommendation. This essay focuses primarily on explanation (and by implication, prediction).
3. In arguing that explanations proceed in terms of implicit conceptual models, this essay makes no claim that foreign-policy analysts have developed any satisfactory empirically tested theory. In this essay the use of the term *model* without qualifiers should be read *conceptual scheme.*
4. For the purpose of this argument we shall accept Carl G. Hempel's characterization of the logic of explanation: an explanation "answers the question, 'Why did the explanadum-phenomenon occur?' by showing that the phenomenon resulted from particular circumstances, specified in C_1, C_2, ... C_k, in accordance with laws L_1, L_2, ... L_r. By pointing this out, the argument shows that given the particular circumstances and the laws in question, the occurrence of the phenomenon was to be *expected;* and it is in this sense that the explanation enables us to understand why the phenomenon occurred." *Aspects of Scientific Explanation* (New York, 1965), p. 337. While various patterns of explanation can be distinguished, *viz.*, Ernest Nagel, *The Structure of Science: Problems in the Logic of Scientific Explanation,* (New York, 1961), satisfactory scientific explanations exhibit this basic logic. Consequently prediction is the converse of explanation.
5. Earlier drafts of this argument have aroused heated arguments concerning proper names for these models. To choose names from ordinary language is to court confusion as well as familiarity. Perhaps it is best to think of these models as I, II, and III.
6. In strict terms the "outcomes" which these three models attempt to explain are essentially actions of national governments, i.e., the sum of activities of all individuals employed by a government relevant to an issue. These models focus not on a state of affairs, i.e., a full description of the world, but upon national decision and implementation. This distinction is stated clearly by Harold and Margaret Sprout, "Environmental Factors on the Study of International Politics," in James Rosenau (ed.), *International Politics and Foreign Policy* (Glencoe, Illinois, 1961), p. 116. This restriction excludes explanations offered principally in terms of international systems theories. Nevertheless, this restriction is not severe, since few interesting explanations of occurrences in foreign policy have been produced at that level of analysis. According to David Singer, "The nation state—our primary actor in international relations . . . is clearly the traditional focus among Western students and is the one which dominates all of the texts employed in English-speaking colleges and universities." David Singer, "The Level-of-Analysis Problem in International Relations," Klaus Knorr and Sidney Verba (eds.), *The International System* (Princeton, 1961). Similarly, Richard Brody's review of contemporary trends in the study of international relations finds that "scholars have come increasingly to focus on acts of nations. That is, they all focus on the behavior of nations in some respect. Having an interest in accounting for the behavior of nations in common, the prospects for a common frame of reference are enhanced."

7. For further development and support of these arguments see the author's larger study, *Bureaucracy and Policy: Conceptual Models and the Cuban Missile Crisis* (forthcoming). In its abbreviated form the argument must at some points appear overly stark. The limits of space have forced the omission of many reservations and refinements.

8. Each of the three "case snapshots" displays the work of a conceptual model as it is applied to explain the U.S. blockade of Cuba. But these three cuts are primarily exercises in hypothesis generation rather than hypothesis testing. Especially when separated from the larger study, these accounts may be misleading. The sources for these accounts include the full public record plus a large number of interviews with participants in the crisis.

9. *New York Times*, February 18, 1967.

10. *Ibid.*

11. Arnold Horelick and Myron Rush, *Strategic Power and Soviet Foreign Policy* (Chicago, 1965). Based on A. Horelick, "The Cuban Missile Crisis: An Analysis of Soviet Calculations and Behavior," *World Politics* (April 1964).

12. Horelick and Rush, *Strategic Power and Soviet Foreign Policy*, p. 154.

13. Hans Morgenthau, *Politics Among Nations* (3rd ed.; New York, 1960), p. 191.

14. *Ibid.*, p. 192.

15. *Ibid.*, p. 5.

16. *Ibid.*, pp. 5–6.

17. Stanley Hoffmann, *Daedalus* (Fall 1962); reprinted in *The State of War* (New York, 1965).

18. *Ibid.*, p. 171.

19. *Ibid.*, p. 189.

20. Following Robert MacIver; see Stanley Hoffmann, *Contemporary Theory in International Relations* (Englewood Cliffs, 1960), pp. 178–179.

21. Thomas Schelling, *The Strategy of Conflict* (New York, 1960), p. 232. This proposition was formulated earlier by A. Wohlstetter, "The Delicate Balance of Terror," *Foreign Affairs* (January 1959).

22. Schelling, *op. cit.*, p. 4.

23. See Morgenthau, *op. cit.*, p. 5; Hoffmann, *Contemporary Theory*, pp. 178–179; Hoffmann, "Roulette in the Cellar," *The State of War;* Schelling, *op. cit.*

24. The larger study examines several exceptions to this generalization. Sidney Verba's excellent essay "Assumptions of Rationality and Non-Rationality in Models of the International System" is less an exception than it is an approach to a somewhat different problem. Verba focuses upon models of rationality and irrationality of *individual* statesmen: in Knorr and Verba, *The International System.*

25. Robert K. Merton, *Social Theory and Social Structures* (Revised and Enlarged Edition; New York, 1957), pp. 12–16. Considerably weaker than a satisfactory theoretical model, paradigms nevertheless represent a short step in that direction from looser, implicit conceptual models. Neither the concepts nor the relations among the variables are sufficiently specified to yield propositions deductively. "Paradigmatic Analysis" nevertheless has considerable promise for clarifying and codifying styles of analysis in political science. Each of the paradigms stated here can be represented rigorously in mathematical terms. For example, model I lends itself to mathematical formulation along the lines of Herbert Simon's "Behavioral Theory of Rationality," *Models of Man* (New York, 1957). But this does not solve the most difficult problem of "measurement and estimation."

26. Though a variant of this model could easily be stochastic, this paradigm is stated in nonprobabilistic terms. In contemporary strategy a stochastic version of this model is sometimes used for predictions; but it is almost impossible to find an explanation of an occurrence in foreign affairs that is consistently probabilistic.

Analogies between model I and the concept of explanation developed by R. G. Collingwood, William Dray, and other revisionists among philosophers concerned with the critical philosophy of history are not accidental. For a summary of the revisionist position see Maurice Mandelbaum, "Historical Explanation: The Problem of Covering Laws," *History and Theory* (1960).

27. This model is an analogue of the theory of the rational entrepreneur which has been developed extensively in economic theories of the firm and the consumer. These two propositions specify the substitution effect. Refinement of this model and specification of additional general propositions by translating from the economic theory is straightforward.

28. *New York Times,* March 22, 1969.

29. See Nathan Leites, *A Study of Bolshevism* (Glencoe, Illinois, 1953).

30. As stated in the introduction, this "case snapshot" presents, without editorial commentary, a model I analyst's explanation of the U.S. blockade. The purpose is to illustrate a strong, characteristic rational policy model account. This account is (roughly) consistent with prevailing explanations of these events.

31. Theodore Sorensen, *op. cit.,* p. 675.

32. *Ibid.,* p. 679.

33. *Ibid.,* p. 679.

34. Elie Abel, *The Missile Crisis* (New York, 1966), p. 144.

35. *Ibid.,* p. 102.

36. Sorensen, *op. cit.,* p. 684.

37. *Ibid.,* p. 685. Though this was the formulation of the argument, the facts are not strictly accurate. Our tradition against surprise attack was rather younger than 175 years. For example President Theodore Roosevelt applauded Japan's attack on Russia in 1904.

38. *New York Times,* June, 1963.

39. The influence of organizational studies upon the present literature of foreign affairs is minimal. Specialists in international politics are not students of organization theory. Organization theory has only recently begun to study organizations as decision makers and has not yet produced behavioral studies of national security organizations from a decision-making perspective. It seems unlikely, however, that these gaps will remain unfilled much longer. Considerable progress has been made in the study of the business firm as an organization. Scholars have begun applying these insights to government organizations, and interest in an organizational perspective is spreading among institutions and individuals concerned with actual government operations. The "decision making" approach represented by Richard Snyder, R. Bruck, and B. Sapin, *Foreign Policy Decision-Making* (Glencoe, Illinois, 1962), incorporates a number of insights from organization theory.

40. The formulation of this paradigm is indebted both to the orientation and insights of Herbert Simon and to the behavioral model of the firm stated by Richard Cyert and James March, *A Behavioral Theory of the Firm* (Englewood Cliffs, 1963). Here, however, one is forced to grapple with the less routine, less quantified functions of the less differentiated elements in government organizations.

41. Theodore Sorensen, "You Get to Walk to Work," *New York Times Magazine,* March 19, 1967.

42. Organizations are not monolithic. The proper level of disaggregation depends upon the objectives of a piece of analysis. This paradigm is formulated with reference to the major organizations that constitute the U.S. government. Generalization to the major components of each department and agency should be relatively straightforward.

43. The stability of these constraints is dependent on such factors as rules for promotion and reward, budgeting and accounting procedures, and mundane operating procedures.

44. Marriner Eccles, *Beckoning Frontiers* (New York, 1951), p. 336.

45. Arthur Schlesinger, *A Thousand Days* (Boston, 1965), p. 406.

46. U.S. Department of State, *Bulletin,* XLVII, pp. 715–720.

47. Schlesinger, *op. cit.,* p. 803.

48. Theodore Sorensen, *Kennedy,* p. 675.

49. See U.S. Congress, Senate, Committee on Armed Services, Preparedness Investigation Subcommittee, *Interim Report on Cuban Military Build-up,* 88th Congress, 1st Session, 1963, p. 2; Hanson Baldwin, "Growing Risks of Bureaucratic Intelligence," *The Reporter* (August 15, 1963), 48–50; Roberta Wohlstetter, "Cuba and Pearl Harbor," *Foreign Affairs* (July, 1965), p. 706.

50. U.S. Congress, House of Representatives, Committee on Appropriations, Subcommittee on Department of Defense Appropriations, *Hearings,* 88th Congress, 1st Session, 1963, 25 ff.

51. R. Hilsman, *To Move a Nation* (New York, 1967), pp. 172–173.

52. Department of Defense Appropriations, *Hearings,* p. 67.

53. *Ibid.,* pp. 66–67.

54. For (1) Hilsman, *op. cit.,* p. 186; (2) Abel, *op. cit.,* p. 24; (3) Department of Defense Appropriations, *Hearings,* p. 64; Abel, *op. cit.,* p. 24; (4) Department of Defense Appropriations, *Hearings,* pp. 1–30.

55. The facts here are not entirely clear. This assertion is based on information from (1) "Department of Defense Briefing by the Honorable R. S. McNamara, Secretary of Defense, State Department Auditorium, 5:00 P.M., February 6, 1963." A verbatim transcript of a presentation actually made by General Carroll's assistant, John Hughes; and (2) Hilsman's statement, *op. cit.,* p. 186. But see R. Wohlstetter's interpretation, "Cuba and Pearl Harbor," p. 700.

56. See Hilsman, *op. cit.,* pp. 172–174.

57. Abel, *op. cit.,* pp. 26 ff; Weintal and Bartlett, *Facing the Brink* (New York, 1967), pp. 62 ff; *Cuban Military Build-up;* J. Daniel and J. Hubbell, *Strike in the West* (New York, 1963), pp. 15 ff.

58. Schlesinger, *op. cit.,* p. 804.

59. Sorensen, *Kennedy,* p. 684.

60. *Ibid.,* pp. 684 ff.

61. *Ibid.,* pp. 694–697.

62. *Ibid.,* p. 697; Abel, *op. cit.,* pp. 100–101.

63. Sorensen, *Kennedy,* p. 669.

64. Hilsman, *op. cit.,* p. 204.

65. See Abel, *op. cit.,* pp. 97 ff.

66. Schlesinger, *op. cit.,* p. 818.

67. *Ibid.*

68. Sorensen, *Kennedy,* p. 710.

69. *New York Times,* October 27, 1962.

70. Abel, *op. cit.,* p. 171.

71. For the location of the original arc see Abel, *op. cit.,* p. 141.

72. *Facts on File,* Vol. XXII, 1962, p. 376, published by Facts on File, Inc., New York, yearly.

73. This hypothesis would account for the mystery surrounding Kennedy's explosion at the leak of the stopping of the *Bucharest.* See Hilsman, *op. cit.,* p. 45.

74. Abel, *op. cit.,* p. 153.

75. See *ibid.,* pp. 154 ff.

76. *Ibid.,* p. 156.

77. *Ibid.*

78. This paradigm relies upon the small group of analysts who have begun to fill the gap. My primary source is the model implicit in the work of Richard E. Neustadt, though his concentration on presidential action has been generalized to a concern with policy as the outcome of political bargaining among a number of independent players, the president amounting to no more than a "superpower" among many lesser but considerable powers. As Warner Schilling argues, the substantive problems are of such inordinate difficulty that uncertainties and differences with regard to goals, alternatives, and consequences are inevitable. This necessitates what Roger Hilsman describes as the process of conflict and consensus building. The techniques employed in this process often resemble those used in legislative assemblies, though Samuel Huntington's characterization of the process as "legislative" overemphasizes the equality of participants as opposed to the hierarchy which structures the game. Moreover, whereas for Huntington foreign policy (in contrast to military policy) is set by the executive, this paradigm maintains that the activities which he describes as legislative are characteristic of the process by which foreign policy is made.

79. The theatrical metaphor of stage, roles, and actors is more common than this metaphor of games, positions, and players. Nevertheless, the rigidity connotated by the concept of *role* both in the theatrical sense of actors reciting fixed lines and in the sociological sense of fixed responses to specified social situations makes the concept of games, positions, and players more useful for this analysis of active participants in the determination of national policy. Objections to the terminology on the grounds that *game* connotes nonserious play overlook the concept's application to most serious problems both in Wittgenstein's philosophy and in contemporary game theory. Game theory typically treats more precisely structured games, but Wittgenstein's examination of the "language game" wherein men use words to communicate is quite analogous to this analysis of the less specified game of bureaucratic politics. See Ludwig Wittgenstein, *Philosophical Investigations,* and Thomas Schelling, "What is Game Theory?" in James Charlesworth, *Contemporary Political Analysis.*

80. Inclusion of the President's Special Assistant for National Security Affairs in the tier of "Chiefs" rather than among the "Staffers" involves a debatable choice. In fact he is both super-staffer and near-chief. His position has no statutory authority. He is especially de-pendent upon good relations with the President and the Secretaries of Defense and State. Nevertheless, he stands astride a genuine action-channel. The decision to include this position among the Chiefs reflects my judgment that the Bundy function is becoming institutionalized.

81. Richard E. Neustadt, Testimony, United States Senate, Committee on Government Operations, Subcommittee on National Security Staffing, *Administration of National Security,* March 26, 1963, pp. 82–83.

82. This aphorism was stated first, I think, by Don K. Price.

83. Paul Y. Hammond, "Super Carriers and B-36 Bombers," in Harold Stein (ed.), *American Civil-Military Decisions* (Birmingham, 1963).

84. Roberta Wohlstetter, *Pearl Harbor* (Stanford, 1962), p. 350.

85. Sorensen, *Kennedy,* p. 670.

86. *Ibid.*

87. *Ibid.,* pp. 670 ff.

88. *New York Times,* August, September, 1962.

89. *New York Times,* August 20, 1962.

90. *New York Times,* September 5, 1962.

91. *New York Times,* September 14, 1962.

92. *New York Times,* October 14, 1962.

93. Cited by Abel, *op. cit.*, p. 13.

94. *New York Times,* September 5, 1962.

95. *New York Times,* September 14, 1962.

96. Senate Foreign Relations Committee; Senate Armed Services Committee; House Committee on Appropriation; House Select Committee on Export Control.

97. Abel, *op. cit.*, pp. 17–18. According to McCone he told Kennedy, "The only construction I can put on the material going into Cuba is that the Russians are preparing to introduce offensive missiles." See also Weintal and Bartlett, *op. cit.*, pp. 60–61.

98. Abel, *op. cit.*, p. 23.

99. *New York Times,* September 10, 1962.

100. See Abel, *op. cit.*, pp. 25–26; and Hilsman, *op. cit.*, p. 174.

101. Department of Defense Appropriation, *Hearings,* 69.

102. A basic but somewhat contradictory account of parts of this story emerges in the Department of Defense Appropriations, *Hearings,* 1–70.

103. Department of Defense Appropriations, *Hearings,* 71.

104. The details of the ten days between the October 4 decision and the October 14 flight must be held in abeyance.

105. Abel, *op. cit.*, p. 44.

106. *Ibid.*, pp. 44 ff.

107. See Richard Neustadt, "Afterword," *Presidential Power* (New York, 1964).

108. Sorensen, *Kennedy,* p. 676; Schlesinger, *op. cit.*, p. 801.

109. Hilsman, *op. cit.*, p. 195.

110. *Ibid.*

111. Weintal and Bartlett, *op. cit.*, p. 67; Abel, *op. cit.*, p. 53.

112. Schlesinger, *op. cit.*, p. 803.

113. *Ibid.*, p. 831.

114. Abel, *op. cit.*, p. 186.

115. *Ibid.*, p. 49.

116. Interview, quoted by Ronald Steel, *New York Review of Books,* March 13, 1969, p. 22.

117. Sorensen, *Kennedy,* p. 686.

118. *Ibid.*, p. 691.

119. *Ibid.*, pp. 691–692.

120. Schlesinger, *op. cit.*, p. 296.

121. Space will not permit an account of the path from this coalition to the formal government decision on Saturday and action on Monday.

122. *Bureaucracy and Policy* (forthcoming, 1969).

123. Thus my position is quite distinct from both poles in the recent "great debate" about international relations. While many "traditionalists" of the sort Kaplan attacks adopt the first posture and many "scientists" of the sort attacked by Bull adopt the second, this third posture is relatively neutral with respect to whatever is in substantive dispute. See Hedly Bull, "International Theory: The Case for a Classical Approach," *World Politics* (April, 1966); and Morton Kaplan, "The New Great Debate: Traditionalism vs. Science in International Relations," *World Politics* (October, 1966).

124. A number of problems are now being examined in these terms both in the Bureaucracy Study Group on Bureaucracy and Policy of the Institute of Politics at Harvard University and at the Rand Corporation.

125. In response to several readers' recommendations, what follows is reproduced *verbatim* from the paper delivered at the September 1968 Association meetings (Rand P–3919). The discussion is heavily indebted to Ernest R. May.

126. Richard Snyder, *Deterrence and Defense* (Princeton, 1961), p. 11. For a more general presentation of this position see Paul Kecskemeti, *Strategic Surrender* (New York, 1964).

࣌ᔰ

Are Bureaucracies Important? (Or Allison Wonderland)

Stephen D. Krasner

Who and what shapes foreign policy? In recent years analyses have increasingly emphasized not rational calculations of the national interest or the political goals of national leaders but rather bureaucratic procedures and bureaucratic politics. Starting with Richard Neustadt's Presidential Power, a judicious study of leadership published in 1960, this approach has come to portray the American president as trapped by a permanent government more enemy than ally. Bureaucratic theorists imply that it is exceedingly difficult if not impossible for political leaders to control the organizational web which surrounds them. Important decisions result from numerous smaller actions taken by individuals at different levels in the bureaucracy who have partially incompatible national, bureaucratic, political, and personal objectives. They are not necessarily a reflection of the aims and values of high officials.

Presidential Power was well received by John Kennedy, who read it with interest, recommended it to his associates, and commissioned Neustadt to do a private study of the 1962 Skybolt incident. The approach has been developed and used by a number of scholars—Roger Hilsman, Morton Halperin, Arthur Schlesinger, Richard Barnet, and Graham Allison—some of whom held subcabinet positions during the 1960s. It was the subject of a special conference at the Rand Corporation, a main theme of a course at the Woodrow Wilson School at Princeton, and the subject of a faculty seminar at Harvard. It is the intellectual paradigm which guides the new public policy program in the John F. Kennedy School of Government at Harvard. Analyses of bureaucratic politics have been used to explain alliance behavior during the 1956 Suez crisis and the Skybolt incident, Truman's relations with MacArthur, American policy in Vietnam, and now most thoroughly the Cuban missile crisis in Graham Allison's *Essence of Decision: Explaining the Cuban Missile Crisis,* published in 1971 (Little, Brown & Company). Allison's volume is the elaboration of an earlier and influential article on this subject. With the publication of his book this approach to foreign policy now receives its definitive statement. The bureaucratic interpretation of foreign policy has become the conventional wisdom.

My argument here is that this vision is misleading, dangerous, and compelling: misleading because it obscures the power of the president; dangerous

Stephen D. Krasner, "Are Bureaucracies Important? (Or Allison Wonderland)," *Foreign Policy* 7 (Summer 1972): 159–179. Copyright © 1972 by the Carnegie Endowment for International Peace. Reprinted with permission.

because it undermines the assumptions of democratic politics by relieving high officials of responsibility; and compelling because it offers leaders an excuse for their failures and scholars an opportunity for innumerable reinterpretations and publications.

The contention that the chief executive is trammelled by the permanent government has disturbing implications for any effort to impute responsibility to public officials. A democratic political philosophy assumes that responsibility for the acts of governments can be attributed to elected officials. The charges of these men are embodied in legal statutes. The electorate punishes an erring official by rejecting him at the polls. Punishment is senseless unless high officials are responsible for the acts of government. Elections have some impact only if government, that most complex of modern organizations, can be controlled. If the bureaucratic machine escapes manipulation and direction even by the highest officials, then punishment is illogical. Elections are a farce not because the people suffer from false consciousness, but because public officials are impotent, enmeshed in a bureaucracy so large that the actions of government are not responsive to their will. What sense to vote a man out of office when his successor, regardless of his values, will be trapped in the same web of only incrementally mutable standard operating procedures?

THE RATIONAL-ACTOR MODEL

Conventional analyses that focus on the values and objectives of foreign policy, what Allison calls the rational-actor model, are perfectly coincident with the ethical assumptions of democratic politics. The state is viewed as a rational unified actor. The behavior of states is the outcome of a rational decision-making process. This process has three steps. The options for a given situation are spelled out. The consequences of each option are projected. A choice is made which maximizes the values held by decision makers. The analyst knows what the state did. His objective is to explain why by imputing to decision makers a set of values which are maximized by observed behavior. These values are his explanation of foreign policy.

The citizen, like the analyst, attributes error to either inappropriate values or lack of foresight. Ideally the electorate judges the officeholder by governmental performance, which is assumed to reflect the objectives and perspicacity of political leaders. Poor policy is made by leaders who fail to foresee accurately the consequences of their decisions or attempt to maximize values not held by the electorate. Political appeals, couched in terms of aims and values, are an appropriate guide for voters. For both the analyst who adheres to the rational-actor model and the citizen who decides elections, values are assumed to be the primary determinant of government behavior.

The bureaucratic-politics paradigm points to quite different determinants of policy. Political leaders can only with great difficulty overcome the inertia and self-serving interests of the permanent government. What counts is managerial skill. In *Essence of Decision* Graham Allison maintains that "the central questions of policy analysis are quite different from the kinds of questions analysts have traditionally asked. Indeed, the crucial questions seem to be matters of planning for management." Administrative feasibility, not substance, becomes the central concern.

The paradoxical conclusion—that bureaucratic analysis with its emphasis on policy guidance implies political nonresponsibility—has most clearly been brought out by discussions of American policy in Vietnam. Richard Neustadt on the concluding page of *Alliance Politics,* his most recent book, muses about a conversation he would have had with President Kennedy in the fall of 1963 had tragedy not intervened. "I considered asking whether, in the light of our machine's performance on a British problem, he conceived that it could cope with South Vietnam's. . . . [I]t was a good question, better than I knew. It haunts me still." For adherents of the bureaucratic-politics paradigm Vietnam was a failure of the "machine," a war in Arthur Schlesinger's words "which no president . . . desired or intended."[1] The machine dictated a policy which it could not successfully terminate. The machine, not the cold war ideology and hubris of Kennedy and Johnson, determined American behavior in Vietnam. Vietnam could hardly be a tragedy, for tragedies are made by choice and character, not fate. A knowing electorate would express sympathy, not levy blame. Machines cannot be held responsible for what they do, nor can the men caught in their workings.

The strength of the bureaucratic web has been attributed to two sources: organizational necessity and bureaucratic interest. The costs of coordination and search procedures are so high that complex organizations *must* settle for satisfactory rather than optimal solutions. Bureaucracies have interests defined in terms of budget allocation, autonomy, morale, and scope which they defend in a game of political bargaining and compromise within the executive branch.

The imperatives of organizational behavior limit flexibility. Without a division of labor and the establishment of standard operating procedures it would be impossible for large organizations to begin to fulfill their statutory objectives, that is to perform tasks designed to meet societal needs rather than merely to perpetuate the organization. A division of labor among and within organizations reduces the job of each particular division to manageable proportions. Once this division is made, the complexity confronting an organization or one of its parts is further reduced through the establishment of standard operating procedures. To deal with each problem as if it were *sui generis* would be impossible given limited resources and information-processing capacity and would make intraorganizational coordination extremely difficult. Bureaucracies are then unavoidably rigid; but without the rigidity imposed by division of labor and standard operating procedures, they could hardly begin to function at all.

However, this rigidity inevitably introduces distortions. All of the options to a given problem will not be presented with equal lucidity and conviction unless by some happenstance the organization has worked out its scenarios for that particular problem in advance. It is more likely that the organization will have addressed itself to something *like* the problem with which it is confronted. It has a set of options for such a hypothetical problem, and these options will be presented to deal with the actual issue at hand. Similarly, organizations cannot execute all policy suggestions with equal facility. The development of new standard operating procedures takes time. The procedures which would most faithfully execute a new policy are not likely to have been worked out. The clash between the rigidity of standard operating procedures which are absolutely necessary to achieve coordination among and within large organizations and the flexibility needed to spell out the options and their consequences for a new problem and to execute new policies is inevitable. It cannot be avoided even with the best of intentions of bureaucratic chiefs anxious to faithfully execute the desires of their leaders.

THE COSTS OF COORDINATION

The limitations imposed by the need to simplify and coordinate indicate that the great increase in governmental power accompanying industrialization has not been achieved without some costs in terms of control. Bureaucratic organizations and the material and symbolic resources which they direct have enormously increased the ability of the American president to influence the international environment. He operates, however, within limits set by organizational procedures.

A recognition of the limits imposed by bureaucratic necessities is a useful qualification of the assumption that states always maximize their interest. This does not, however, imply that the analyst should abandon a focus on values or assumptions of rationality. Standard operating procedures are rational given the costs of search procedures and need for coordination. The behavior of states is still determined by values, although foreign policy may reflect satisfactory rather than optimal outcomes.

An emphasis on the procedural limits of large organizations cannot explain nonincremental change. If government policy is an outcome of standard operating procedures, then behavior at time t is only incrementally different from behavior at time $t - 1$. The exceptions to this prediction leap out of events of even the last year—the Nixon visit to China and the new economic policy. Focusing on the needs dictated by organizational complexity is adequate only during periods when policy is altered very little or not at all. To reduce policy makers to nothing more than the caretakers and minor adjustors of standard operating procedures rings hollow in an era rife with debates and changes of the most fundamental kind in America's conception of its objectives and capabilities.

Bureaucratic analysts do not, however, place the burden of their argument on standard operating procedures but on bureaucratic politics. The objectives of officials are dictated by their bureaucratic position. Each bureau has its own interests. The interests which bureaucratic analysts emphasize are not clientalistic ties between government departments and societal groups or special relations with congressional committees. They are, rather, needs dictated by organizational survival and growth—budget allocations, internal morale, and autonomy. Conflicting objectives advocated by different bureau chiefs are reconciled by a political process. Policy results from compromises and bargaining. It does not necessarily reflect the values of the president, let alone of lesser actors.

The clearest expression of the motivational aspects of the bureaucratic politics approach is the by now well-known aphorism—where you stand depends upon where you sit. Decision makers, however, often do not stand where they sit. Sometimes they are not sitting anywhere. This is clearly illustrated by the positions taken by members of the ExCom during the Cuban missile crisis, which Allison elucidates at some length. While the military, in Pavlovian fashion, urged the use of arms, the secretary of defense took a much more pacific position. The wise old men such as Acheson, imported for the occasion, had no bureaucratic position to defend. Two of the most important members of the ExCom, Robert Kennedy and Theodore Sorensen, were loyal to the president, not to some bureaucratic barony. Similarly, in discussions of Vietnam in 1966 and 1967, it was the secretary of defense who advocated diplomacy and the secretary of state who defended the prerogatives of the military. During Skybolt McNamara was attuned to the president's budgetary concerns, not those of the air force.

Allison, the most recent expositor of the bureaucratic-politics approach, realizes the problems which these facts present. In describing motivation he backs off from an exclusive focus on bureaucratic position, arguing instead that decision makers are motivated by national, organizational, group, and personal interests. While maintaining that the "propensities and priorities stemming from position are sufficient to allow analysts to make reliable predictions about a player's stand" (a proposition violated by his own presentation), he also notes that "these propensities are filtered through the baggage that players bring to positions." For both the missile crisis and Vietnam it was the "baggage" of culture and values, not bureaucratic position, which determined the aims of high officials.

Bureaucratic analysis is also inadequate in its description of how policy is made. Its axiomatic assumption is that politics is a game with the preferences of players given and independent. This is not true. The president chooses most of the important players and sets the rules. He selects the men who head the large bureaucracies. These individuals must share his values. Certainly they identify with his beliefs to a greater extent than would a randomly chosen group of candidates. They also feel some personal fealty to the president who has elevated them from positions of corporate or legal to ones of historic significance. While bureau chiefs are undoubtedly torn by conflicting pressures arising either from their need to protect their own bureaucracies or from personal conviction, they must remain the president's men. At some point disagreement results in dismissal. The values which bureau chiefs assign to policy outcomes are not independent. They are related through a perspective shared with the president.

The president also structures the governmental environment in which he acts through his impact on what Allison calls "action-channels." These are decision-making processes which describe the participation of actors and their influence. The most important "action-channel" in the government is the president's ear. The president has a major role in determining who whispers into it. John Kennedy's reliance on his brother, whose bureaucratic position did not afford him any claim to a decision-making role in the missile crisis, is merely an extreme example. By allocating tasks, selecting the White House bureaucracy, and demonstrating special affections, the president also influences "action-channels" at lower levels of the government.

The president has an important impact on bureaucratic interests. Internal morale is partially determined by presidential behavior. The obscurity in which Secretary of State Rogers languished during the China trip affected both State

Department morale and recruitment prospects. Through the budget the president has a direct impact on that most vital of bureaucratic interests. While a bureau may use its societal clients and congressional allies to secure desired allocations, it is surely easier with the president's support than without it. The president can delimit or redefine the scope of an organization's activities by transferring tasks or establishing new agencies. Through public statements he can affect attitudes towards members of a particular bureaucracy and their functions.

THE PRESIDENT AS "KING"

The success a bureau enjoys in furthering its interests depends on maintaining the support and affection of the president. The implicit assumption of the bureaucratic-politics approach that departmental and presidential behavior are independent and comparably important is false. Allison, for instance, vacillates between describing the president as one "chief" among several and as a "king" standing above all other men. He describes in great detail the deliberations of the ExCom, implying that Kennedy's decision was in large part determined by its recommendations, and yet notes that during the crisis Kennedy vetoed an ExCom decision to bomb a SAM base after an American U-2 was shot down on October 27. In general bureaucratic analysts ignore the critical effect which the president has in choosing his advisers, establishing their access to decision making, and influencing bureaucratic interests.

All of this is not to deny that bureaucratic interests may sometimes be decisive in the formulation of foreign policy. Some policy options are never presented to the president. Others he deals with only cursorily, not going beyond options presented by the bureaucracy. This will only be the case if presidential interest and attention are absent. The failure of a chief executive to specify policy does not mean that the government takes no action. Individual bureaucracies may initiate policies which suit their own needs and objectives. The actions of different organizations may work at cross-purposes. The behavior of the state, that is, of some of its official organizations, in the international system appears confused or even contradictory. This is a situation which develops, however, not because of the independent power of government organizations but because of failures by decision makers to assert control.

The ability of bureaucracies to independently establish policies is a function of presidential attention. Presidential attention is a function of presidential values. The chief executive involves himself in those areas which he determines to be important. When the president does devote time and attention to an issue, he can compel the bureaucracy to present him with alternatives. He may do this, as Nixon apparently has, by establishing an organization under his special assistant for national security affairs, whose only bureaucratic interest is maintaining the president's confidence. The president may also rely upon several bureaucracies to secure proposals. The president may even resort to his own knowledge and sense of history to find options which his bureaucracy fails to present. Even when presidential attention is totally absent, bureaus are sensitive to his values. Policies which violate presidential objectives may bring presidential wrath.

While the president is undoubtedly constrained in the implementation of policy by existing bureaucratic procedures, he even has options in this area. As Allison points out, he can choose which agencies will perform what tasks. Programs are fungible and can be broken down into their individual standard operating procedures and recombined. Such exercises take time and effort, but the expenditure of such energies by the president is ultimately a reflection of his own values and not those of the bureaucracy. Within the structure which he has partially created himself he can, if he chooses, further manipulate both the options presented to him and the organizational tools for implementing them.

Neither organizational necessity nor bureaucratic interests are the fundamental determinants of policy. The limits imposed by standard operating procedures as well as the direction of policy are a function of the values of decision makers. The president creates much of the bureaucratic environment which surrounds him through his selection of bureau chiefs, determination of "action-channels," and statutory powers.

THE MISSILE CRISIS

Adherents of the bureaucratic-politics framework have not relied exclusively on general argument. They have attempted to substantiate their contentions with detailed investigations of particular historical events. The most painstaking is Graham Allison's analysis of the Cuban missile crisis in his *Essence of Decision.* In a superlative heuristic exercise Allison attempts to show that critical facts and relationships are ignored by conventional analysis that assumes states are unified rational actors. Only by examining the missile crisis in terms of organizational necessity and bureaucratic interests and politics can the formulation and implementation of policy be understood.

The missile crisis, as Allison notes, is a situation in which conventional analysis would appear most appropriate. The president devoted large amounts of time to policy formulation and implementation. Regular bureaucratic channels were short-circuited by the creation of an executive committee which included representatives of the bipartisan foreign-policy establishment, bureau chiefs, and the president's special aides. The president dealt with details which would normally be left to bureaucratic subordinates. If under such circumstances the president could not effectively control policy formulation and implementation, then the rational-actor model is gravely suspect.

In his analysis of the missile crisis Allison deals with three issues: the American choice of a blockade, the Soviet decision to place MRBMs and IRBMs on Cuba, and the Soviet decision to withdraw the missiles from Cuba. The American decision is given the most detailed attention. Allison notes three ways in which bureaucratic procedures and interests influenced the formulation of American policy: first in the elimination of the nonforcible alternatives; second through the collection of information; third through the standard operating procedures of the air force.

In formulating the U.S. response the ExCom considered six alternatives. These were:

1. Do nothing
2. Diplomatic pressure

3. A secret approach to Castro
4. Invasion
5. A surgical air strike
6. A naval blockade

The approach to Castro was abandoned because he did not have direct control of the missiles. An invasion was eliminated as a first step because it would not have been precluded by any of the other options. Bureaucratic factors were not involved.

The two nonmilitary options of doing nothing and lodging diplomatic protests were also abandoned from the outset because the president was not interested in them. In terms of both domestic and international politics this was the most important decision of the crisis. It was a decision which only the president had authority to make. Allison's case rests on proving that this decision was foreordained by bureaucratic roles. He lists several reasons for Kennedy's elimination of the nonforcible alternatives. Failure to act decisively would undermine the confidence of members of his administration, convince the permanent government that his administration lacked leadership, hurt the Democrats in the forthcoming election, destroy his reputation among members of Congress, create public distrust, encourage American allies and enemies to question American courage, invite a second Bay of Pigs, and feed his own doubts about himself. Allison quotes a statement by Kennedy that he feared impeachment and concludes that the "nonforcible paths—avoiding military measures, resorting instead to diplomacy—could not have been more irrelevant to *his* problems." Thus Allison argues that Kennedy had no choice.

Bureaucratic analysis, what Allison calls in his book the governmental-politics model, implies that any man in the same position would have had no choice. The elimination of passivity and diplomacy was ordained by the office and not by the man.

Such a judgment is essential to the governmental-politics model, for the resort to the "baggage" of values, culture, and psychology which the president carries with him undermines the explanatory and predictive power of the approach. To adopt, however, the view that the office determined Kennedy's action is both to underrate his power and to relieve him of responsibility. The president defines his own role. A different man could have chosen differently. Kennedy's *Profiles in Courage* had precisely dealt with men who had risked losing their political roles because of their "baggage" of values and culture.

Allison's use of the term *intragovernmental balance of power* to describe John Kennedy's elimination of diplomacy and passivity is misleading. The American government is not a balance-of-power system; at the very least it is a loose hierarchical one. Kennedy's judgments of the domestic, international, bureaucratic, and personal ramifications of his choice were determined by *who* he was as well as *what* he was. The central mystery of the crisis remains why Kennedy chose to risk nuclear war over missile placements which he knew did not dramatically alter the strategic balance. The answer to this puzzle can only be found through an examination of values, the central concern of conventional analysis.

The impact of bureaucratic interests and standard operating procedures is reduced then to the choice of the blockade instead of the surgical air strike. Allison places considerable emphasis on intelligence gathering in the determination of this choice. U-2 flights were the most important source of data about Cuba; their information was supplemented by refugee reports, analyses of shipping, and other kinds of intelligence. The timing of the U-2 flights, which Allison argues was determined primarily by bureaucratic struggles, was instrumental in determining Kennedy's decision:

> Had a U-2 flown over the western end of Cuba three weeks earlier, it could have discovered the missiles, giving the administration more time to consider alternatives and to act before the danger of operational missiles in Cuba became a major factor in the equation. Had the missiles not been discovered until two weeks later, the blockade would have been irrelevant, since the Soviet missile shipments would have been completed . . . An explanation of the politics of the discovery is consequently a considerable piece of the explanation of the U.S. blockade.

The delay, however, from September 15 to October 14, when the missiles were discovered reflected presidential values more than bureaucratic politics. The October 14 flight took place ten days after COMOR, the interdepartmental committee which directed the activity of the U-2s, had decided the flights should be made. "This ten-day delay constitutes some form of 'failure,'" Allison contends. It was the result, he argues, of a struggle between the Central Intelligence Agency and the air force over who would control the flights. The air force maintained that the flights over Cuba were sufficiently dangerous to warrant military supervision; the Central Intelligence Agency, anxious to guard its own prerogatives, maintained that its U-2s were technically superior.

However, the ten-day delay after the decision to make a flight over western Cuba was not entirely attributable to bureaucratic bickering. Allison reports an attempt to make a flight on October 9, which failed because the U-2 flamed out. Further delays resulted from bad weather. Thus the inactivity caused by bureaucratic infighting amounted to only five days (October 4 to October 9) once the general decision to make the flight was taken. The other five days' delay caused by engine failure and the weather must be attributed to some higher source than the machinations of the American bureaucracy.

However, there was also a long period of hesitation before October 4. John McCone, director of the Central Intelligence Agency, had indicated to the president on August 22 that he thought there was a strong possibility that the Soviets were preparing to put offensive missiles on Cuba. He did not have firm evidence, and his contentions were met with skepticism in the administration.

INCREASED RISKS

On September 10 COMOR had decided to restrict further U-2 flights over western Cuba. This decision was based upon factors which closely fit the rational-actor model of foreign policy formulation. COMOR decided to halt the flights because the recent installation of SAMs in western Cuba coupled with the loss of a Nationalist Chinese U-2 increased the probability and costs of a U-2 loss over Cuba. International opinion might force the cancellation of the flights altogether. The absence of information from U-2s would be a national, not simply a bureaucratic, cost. The president had been forcefully attacking the critics of his Cuba policy, arguing that patience and restraint were the best course of action. The loss of a U-2 over Cuba would tend to undermine the president's position. Thus, COMOR's decision on September 10 reflected a sensitivity to the needs and policies of the president rather than the parochial concerns of the permanent government.

The decision on October 4 to allow further flights was taken only after consultation with the president. The timing was determined largely by the wishes of the president. His actions were not circumscribed by decisions made at lower levels of the bureaucracy of which he was not aware. The flights were delayed because of conflicting pressures and risks confronting Kennedy. He was forced to weigh the potential benefits of additional knowledge against the possible losses if a U-2 were shot down.

What if the missiles had not been discovered until after October 14? Allison argues that had the missiles been discovered two weeks later, the blockade would have been irrelevant, since the missile shipments would have been completed. This is true, but only to a limited extent. The blockade was irrelevant even when it was put in place, for there were missiles already on the island. As Allison points out in his rational-actor cut at explaining the crisis, the blockade was both an act preventing the shipment of additional missiles and a signal of American firmness. The missiles already on Cuba were removed because of what the blockade meant and not because of what it did.

An inescapable dilemma confronted the United States. It could not retaliate until the missiles were on the island. Military threats or action required definitive proof. The United States could only justify actions with photographic evidence. It could only take photos after the missiles were on Cuba. The blockade could only be a demonstration of American firmness. Even if the missiles had not been discovered until they were operational, the United States might still have begun its response with a blockade.

Aside from the timing of the discovery of the missiles, Allison argues that the standard operating procedures of the air force affected the decision to blockade rather than to launch a surgical air strike. When the missiles were first discovered, the air force had no specific contingency plans for dealing with such a situation. They did, however, have a plan for a large-scale air strike carried out in conjunction with an invasion of Cuba. The plan called for the air bombardment of many targets. This led to some confusion during the first week of the ExCom's considerations because the air force was talking in terms of an air strike of some five hundred sorties, while there were only some forty known missile sites on Cuba. Before this confusion was clarified, a strong coalition of advisers was backing the blockade.

As a further example of the impact of standard operating procedures, Allison notes that the air force had classified the missiles as mobile. Because this classification assumed that the missiles might be moved immediately before an air strike, the commander of the air force would not guarantee that a surgical air strike would be completely effective. By the end of the first week of the ExCom's deliberations, when Kennedy made his decision for a blockade, the surgical air strike was presented as a "null option." The examination of the strike was not reopened until the following week, when civilian experts found that the missiles were not in fact mobile.

This incident suggests one caveat to Allison's assertion that the missile crisis is a case which discriminates against bureaucratic analysis. In crises, when time is short, the president may have to accept bureaucratic options which could be amended under more leisurely conditions.

NOT ANOTHER PEARL HARBOR

The impact of the air force's standard operating procedures on Kennedy's decision must, however, to some extent remain obscure. It is not likely that either McNamara, who initially called for a diplomatic response, or Robert Kennedy, who was partially concerned with the ethical implications of a surprise air strike, would have changed their recommendations even if the air force had estimated its capacities more optimistically. There were other reasons for choosing the blockade aside from the apparent infeasibility of the air strike. John Kennedy was not anxious to have the Pearl Harbor analogy and applied to the United States. At one of the early meetings of the ExCom his brother had passed a note saying, "I now know how Tojo felt when he was planning Pearl Harbor." The air strike could still be considered even if the blockade failed. A chief executive anxious to keep his options open would find a blockade a more prudent initial course of action.

Even if the air force had stated that a surgical air strike was feasible, this might have been discounted by the president. Kennedy had already experienced unrealistic military estimates. The Bay of Pigs was the most notable example. The United States did not use low-flying photographic reconnaissance until after the president had made his public announcement of the blockade. Prior to the president's speech on October 22, twenty high-altitude U-2 flights were made. After the speech there were eighty-five low-level missions, indicating that the intelligence community was not entirely confident that U-2 flights alone would reveal all of the missile sites. The Soviets might have been camouflaging some missiles on Cuba. Thus, even if the immobility of the missiles had been correctly estimated, it would have been rash to assume that an air strike would have extirpated all of the missiles. There were several reasons, aside from the air force's estimate, for rejecting the surgical strike.

Thus in terms of policy formulation it is not clear that the examples offered by Allison concerning the timing of discovery of the missiles and the standard operating procedures of the air force had a decisive impact on the choice of a blockade over a surgical air strike. The ultimate decisions did rest with the president. The elimination of the nonforcible options was a reflection of Kennedy's values. An explanation of the Cuban missile crisis which fails to explain policy in terms of the values of the chief decision maker must inevitably lose sight of the forest for the trees.

The most chilling passages in *Essence of Decision* are concerned not with the formulation of policy but with its implementation. In carrying out the blockade the limitations on the president's ability to control events become painfully clear.

Kennedy did keep extraordinarily close tabs on the workings of the blockade. The first Russian ship to reach the blockade was allowed to pass through without being intercepted on direct orders from the president. Kennedy felt it would be wise to allow Khrushchev more time. The president overrode the ExCom's decision to fire on a Cuban SAM base after a U-2 was shot down on October 27. A spy ship similar to the *Pueblo* was patrolling perilously close to Cuba and was ordered to move farther out to sea.

Despite concerted presidential attention coupled with an awareness of the necessity of watching minute details which would normally be left to lower levels of the bureaucracy, the president still had exceptional difficulty in controlling events. Kennedy personally ordered the navy to pull in the blockade from eight hundred miles to five hundred miles to give Khrushchev additional time in which to make his decision. Allison suggests that the ships were not drawn in. The navy, being both anxious to guard its prerogatives and confronted with the difficulty of moving large numbers of ships over millions of square miles of ocean, failed to promptly execute a presidential directive.

There were several random events which might have changed the outcome of the crisis. The navy used the blockade to test its antisubmarine operations. It was forcing Soviet submarines to surface at a time when the president and his advisers were unaware that contact with Russian ships had been made. A U-2 accidentally strayed over Siberia on October 22. Any one of these events, and perhaps others still unknown, could have triggered escalatory actions by the Russians.

Taken together, they strongly indicate how much caution is necessary when a random event may have costly consequences. A nation like a drunk staggering on a cliff should stay far from the edge. The only conclusion which can be drawn from the inability of the chief executive to fully control the implementation of a policy in which he was intensely interested and to which he devoted virtually all of his time for an extended period is that the risks were even greater than the president knew. Allison is more convincing on the problems concerned with policy implementation than on questions relating to policy formulation. Neither bureaucratic interests nor organizational procedures explain the positions taken by members of the ExCom, the elimination of passivity and diplomacy, or the choice of a blockade instead of an air strike.

CONCLUSION

A glimpse at almost any one of the major problems confronting American society indicates that a reformulation and clarification of objectives, not better control and direction of the bureaucracy, is critical. Conceptions of man and society long accepted are being undermined. The environmentalists present a fundamental challenge to the assumption that man can control and stand above nature, an assumption rooted both in the successes of technology and industrialization and Judeo-Christian assertions of man's exceptionalism. The nation's failure to formulate a consistent crime policy reflects in part an inability to decide whether criminals are freely willing rational men subject to determinations of guilt or innocence or the victims of socioeconomic conditions or psychological circumstances over which they have no control. The economy manages to defy accepted economic precepts by sustaining relatively high inflation and unemployment at the same time. Public officials and economists question the wisdom of economic growth. Conflicts exist over what the objectives of the nation should be and what its capacities are. On a whole range of social issues the society is torn between attributing problems to individual inadequacies and social injustice.

None of these issues can be decided just by improving managerial techniques. Before the niceties of bureaucratic implementation are investigated, it is necessary to know what objectives are being sought. Objectives are ultimately a reflection of values, of beliefs concerning what man and society ought to be. The failure of the American government to take decisive action in a number of critical areas reflects not so much the inertia of a large bureaucratic machine as a confusion over values which afflicts the society in general and its leaders in particular. It is in such circumstances too comforting to attribute failure to organizational inertia, although nothing could be more convenient for political leaders who having either not formulated any policy or advocated bad policies can blame their failures on the governmental structure. Both psychologically and politically, leaders may find it advantageous to have others think of them as ineffectual rather than evil. But the facts are otherwise—particularly in foreign policy. There the choices—and the responsibility—rest squarely with the president.

NOTE

1. Quoted in Daniel Ellsberg, "The Quagmire Myth and the Stalemate Machine," *Public Policy* (Spring 1971): 218.

✤ PART SEVEN ✤

Perceptions, Personality, and Social Psychology

These four essays are concerned with the cognitive and social psychological limitations and patterns of decision making in foreign policy. Rather than focus on societal or bureaucratic constraints on policy making, these writers focus on the role of the individual making choices. In a trail-blazing essay Robert Jervis presents a series of hypotheses that specify types of misperception in foreign-policy decision making. Decision makers tend to fit incoming information into existing theories and images. Decision makers tend to be closed to new information and to resist new theories or expectations. Jervis also explores the sources of these theories or images of other actors and the international system. Further hypotheses are developed about the way decision makers misperceive opposing actors and their processes of decision making. Taken together, Jervis presents a complex array of cognitive biases that decision makers are prone to exhibit and that constitute an interlocking web of misperceptions in foreign policy.

Philip Tetlock and Charles McGuire present a more general statement of the cognitive approach to foreign policy. What unites this approach is a set of assumptions about foreign policy decision makers and their environment: that the environment is overflowing with information and policy makers must inevitably deal with problems of incomplete and unreliable information. The central research question is to understand the cognitive strategies that policy makers rely on to make sense of their environment.

Yuen Foong Khong looks at one particularly powerful device that policy makers often use to make sense of the foreign policy circumstances they confront, the historical analogy. He argues that analogies are attractive to foreign policy officials for a variety of reasons: they make a new situation look familiar; they provide a normative assessment of the situation; they provide a convenient path to policy action; and they suggest what might happen in the future.

Winter and his associates explore the way political personalities can be described and predictions developed about the impact of personality on foreign policy. Former President George Bush and Soviet President Mikhail Gorbachev, who presided over the two superpowers at the end of the Cold War, provide the case studies for this type of analysis. The authors acknowledge that personality is not always a significant variable in the conduct of foreign policy—FDR's response to the Japanese attack on Pearl Harbor in 1941 had more to do with the structure of the situation than his own personality biases. But the authors argue that critical moments do occur when a leader's own personal history and psychological predispositions matter.

Hypotheses on Misperception

Robert Jervis

In determining how he will behave, an actor must try to predict how others will act and how their actions will affect his values. The actor must therefore develop an image of others and of their intentions. This image may, however, turn out to be an inaccurate one; the actor may for a number of reasons misperceive both others' actions and their intentions. In this research note I wish to discuss the types of misperceptions of other states' intentions which states tend to make. The concept of intention is complex, but here we can consider it to comprise the ways in which the state feels it will act in a wide range of future contingencies. These ways of acting usually are not specific and well developed plans. For many reasons a national or individual actor may not know how he will act under given conditions, but this problem cannot be dealt with here.

I. PREVIOUS TREATMENTS OF PERCEPTION IN INTERNATIONAL RELATIONS

Although diplomatic historians have discussed misperception in their treatments of specific events, students of international relations have generally ignored this topic. However, two sets of scholars have applied content analysis to the documents that flowed within and between governments in the six weeks preceding World War I. But the data have been put into quantitative form in a way that does not produce accurate measures of perceptions and intentions and that makes it impossible to gather useful evidence on misperception.[1]

The second group of theorists who have explicitly dealt with general questions of misperception in international relations consists of those, like Charles Osgood, Amitai Etzioni, and to a lesser extent Kenneth Boulding and J. David Singer, who have analyzed the cold war in terms of a spiral of misperception.[2] This approach

Robert Jervis, "Hypotheses on Misperception," *World Politics* 20, No. 3 (April 1968): 454–479.

grows partly out of the mathematical theories of L. F. Richardson[3] and partly out of findings of social and cognitive psychology, many of which will be discussed in this research note.

These authors state their case in general if not universal terms but do not provide many historical cases that are satisfactorily explained by their theories. Furthermore, they do not deal with any of the numerous instances that contradict their notion of the self-defeating aspects of the use of power. They ignore the fact that states are not individuals and that the findings of psychology can be applied to organizations only with great care. Most important, their theoretical analysis is for the most part of reduced value because it seems largely to be a product of their assumption that the Soviet Union is a basically status-quo power whose apparently aggressive behavior is a product of fear of the West. Yet they supply little or no evidence to support this view. Indeed, the explanation for the differences of opinion between the spiral theorists and the proponents of deterrence lies not in differing general views of international relations, differing values and morality,[4] or differing methods of analysis,[5] but in differing perceptions of Soviet intentions.

II. THEORIES—NECESSARY AND DANGEROUS

Despite the limitations of their approach, these writers have touched on a vital problem that has not been given systematic treatment by theorists of international relations. The evidence from both psychology and history overwhelmingly supports the view (which may be labeled hypothesis 1) that decision makers tend to fit incoming information into their existing theories and images. Indeed, their theories and images play a large part in determining what they notice. In other words, actors tend to perceive what they expect. Furthermore (hypothesis 1a), a theory will have greater impact on an actor's interpretation of data (a) the greater the ambiguity of the data and (b) the higher the degree of confidence with which the actor holds the theory.[6]

For many purposes we can use the concept of differing levels of perceptual thresholds to deal with the fact that it takes more, and more unambiguous, information for an actor to recognize an unexpected phenomenon than an expected one. An experiment by Bruner and Postman determined "that the recognition threshold for . . . incongruous playing cards (those with suits and colors reversed) is significantly higher than the threshold for normal cards."[7] Not only are people able to identify normal (and therefore expected) cards more quickly and easily than incongruous (and therefore unexpected) ones, but also they may at first take incongruous cards for normal ones.

However, we should not assume, as the spiral theorists often do, that it is necessarily irrational for actors to adjust incoming information to fit more closely their existing beliefs and images. (*Irrational* here describes acting under pressures that the actor would not admit as legitimate if he were conscious of them.) Abelson and Rosenberg label as "psycho-logic" the pressure to create a "balanced" cognitive structure—i.e., one in which "all relations among 'good elements' [in one's attitude structure] are positive (or null), all relations among 'bad elements' are positive (or null), and all relations between good and bad elements are negative (or null)." They correctly show that the "reasoning [this involves] would mortify a logician."[8] But those who have tried to apply this and similar cognitive theories to international relations have usually overlooked the fact that in many cases there are important logical links between the elements and the processes they describe which cannot be called "psycho-logic." (I am here using the term *logical* not in the narrow sense of drawing only those conclusions that follow necessarily from the premises, but rather in the sense of conforming to generally agreed-upon rules for the treating of evidence.) For example, Osgood claims that psycho-logic is displayed when the Soviets praise a man or a proposal and people in the West react by distrusting the object of this praise.[9] But if a person believes that the Russians are aggressive, it is logical for him to be suspicious of their moves. When we say that a decision maker "dislikes" another state, this usually means that he believes that that other state has policies conflicting with those of his nation. Reasoning and experience indicate to the decision maker that the "disliked" state is apt to harm his state's interests. Thus in these cases there is no need to invoke "psycho-logic," and it cannot be claimed that the cases demonstrate the substitution of "emotional consistency for rational consistency."[10]

The question of the relations among particular beliefs and cognitions can often be seen as part of the general topic of the relation of incoming bits of information to the receivers' already-established images. The need to fit data into a wider framework of beliefs, even if doing so does not seem to do justice to individual facts, is not, or at least is not only, a psychological drive that decreases the accuracy of our perceptions of the world, but is "essential to the logic of inquiry."[11] Facts can be interpreted and indeed identified only with the aid of hypotheses and theories. Pure empiricism is impossible, and it would be unwise to revise theories in the light of every bit of information that does not easily conform to them.[12] No hypothesis can be expected to account for all the evidence, and if a prevailing view is supported by many theories and by a large pool of findings, it should not be quickly altered. Too little rigidity can be as bad as too much.[13]

This is as true in the building of social and physical science as it is in policy making.[14] While it is terribly difficult to know when a finding throws serious doubt on accepted theories and should be followed up and when instead it was caused by experimental mistakes or minor errors in the theory, it is clear that scientists would make no progress if they followed Thomas Huxley's injunction to "sit down before fact as a mere child, be prepared to give up every preconceived notion, follow humbly wherever nature leads, or you will learn nothing."[15]

As Michael Polanyi explains, "It is true enough that the scientist must be prepared to submit at any moment to the adverse verdict of observational evidence. But not blindly. . . . There is always the possibility that as in [the cases of the periodic system of elements and the quantum theory of light], a deviation may not affect the essential correctness of a proposition. . . . The process of explaining away deviations is in fact quite indispensable to the daily routine of research," even though this may lead to the missing of a great discovery.[16] For example, in 1795 the astronomer Lalande did not follow up observations that contradicted the prevailing hypotheses and could have led him to discover the planet Neptune.[17]

Yet we should not be too quick to condemn such behavior. As Thomas Kuhn has noted, "There is no such thing as research without counterinstances."[18] If a set of basic theories—what Kuhn calls a paradigm—has been able to account for a mass of data, it should not be lightly trifled with. As Kuhn puts it: "Life-long resistance, particularly from those whose productive careers have committed them to an older tradition of normal science [i.e., science within the accepted paradigm], is not a violation of scientific standards but an index to the nature of scientific research itself. The source of resistance is the assurance that the older paradigm will ultimately solve all its problems, that nature can be shoved into the box the paradigm provides. Inevitably, at times of revolution, that assurance seems stubborn and pig-headed as indeed it sometimes becomes. But it is also something more. That same assurance is what makes normal science or puzzle-solving science possible."[19]

Thus it is important to see that the dilemma of how "open" to be to new information is one that inevitably plagues any attempt at understanding in any field. Instances in which evidence seems to be ignored or twisted to fit the existing theory can often be explained by this dilemma instead of by illogical or nonlogical psychological pressures toward consistency. This is especially true of decision makers' attempts to estimate the intentions of other states, since they must constantly take account of the danger that the other state is trying to deceive them.

The theoretical framework discussed thus far, together with an examination of many cases, suggests hypothesis 2: scholars and decision makers are apt to err by being too wedded to the established view and too closed to new information, as opposed to being too willing to alter their theories.[20] Another way of making this point is to argue that actors tend to establish their theories and expectations prematurely. In politics, of course, this is often necessary because of the need for action. But experimental evidence indicates that the same tendency also occurs on the unconscious level. Bruner and Postman found that "perhaps the greatest single barrier to the recognition of incongruous stimuli is the tendency for perceptual hypotheses to fixate after receiving a minimum of confirmation. . . . Once there had occurred in these cases a partial confirmation of the hypothesis . . . it seemed that nothing could change the subject's report."[21]

However, when we apply these and other findings to politics and discuss kinds of misperception, we should not quickly apply the label of cognitive distortion. We should proceed cautiously for two related reasons. The first is that the evidence available to decision makers almost always permits several interpretations. It should be noted that there are cases of visual perception in which different stimuli can produce exactly the same pattern on an observer's retina. Thus for an observer using one eye the same pattern would be produced by a sphere the size of a golf ball which was quite close to the observer, by a baseball-sized sphere that was further away, or by a basketball-sized sphere still further away. Without other clues the observer cannot possibly determine which of these stimuli he is presented with, and we would not want to call his incorrect perceptions examples of distortion. Such cases, relatively rare in visual perception, are frequent in international relations. The evidence available to decision makers is almost always very ambiguous, since accurate clues to others' intentions are surrounded by noise[22] and deception. In most cases, no matter how long, deeply, and "objectively" the evidence is analyzed, people can differ in their interpretations, and there are no general rules to indicate who is correct.

The second reason to avoid the label of cognitive distortion is that the distinction between perception and judgment, obscure enough in individual psychology, is almost absent in the making of inferences in international politics. Decision makers who reject information that contradicts their views—or who develop complex interpretations of it—often do so consciously and explicitly. Since the evidence available contains contradictory information, to make any inferences requires that much information be ignored or given interpretations that will seem tortuous to those who hold a different position.

Indeed, if we consider only the evidence available to a decision maker at the time of decision, the view later proved incorrect may be supported by as much evidence as the correct one—or even by more. Scholars have often been too unsympathetic with the people who were proved wrong. On closer examination it is frequently difficult to point to differences between those who were right and those who were wrong with respect to their openness to new information and willingness to modify their views. Winston Churchill, for example, did not open-mindedly view each Nazi action to see if the explanations provided by the appeasers accounted for the data better than his own beliefs. Instead, like Chamberlain, he fitted each bit of ambiguous information into his own hypotheses. That he was correct should not lead us to overlook the fact that his methods of analysis and use of theory to produce cognitive consistency did not basically differ from those of the appeasers.[23]

A consideration of the importance of expectations in influencing perception also indicates that the widespread belief in the prevalence of "wishful thinking" may be incorrect, or at least may be based on inadequate data. The psychological literature on the interaction between affect and perception is immense and cannot be treated here, but it should be noted that phenomena that at first were considered strong evidence for the impact of affect on perception often can be better treated as demonstrating the influence of expectations.[24] Thus, in international relations, cases like the United States' misestimation of the political climate in Cuba in April 1961, which may seem at first glance to have been instances of wishful thinking, may instead be more adequately explained by the theories held by the decision makers (e.g., Communist governments are unpopular). Of course desires may have an impact on perception by influencing expectations, but since so many other factors affect expectations, the net influence of desires may not be great.

There is evidence from both psychology[25] and international relations that when expectations and desires clash, expectations seem to be more important. The United States would like to believe that North Vietnam is about to negotiate or that the USSR is ready to give up what the United States believes is its goal of world domination, but ambiguous evidence is seen to confirm the opposite conclusion, which conforms to the United States' expectations. Actors are apt to be especially sensitive to evidence of grave danger if they think they can take action to protect themselves against the menace once it has been detected.

III. SAFEGUARDS

Can anything then be said to scholars and decision makers other than "Avoid being either too open or too closed, but be especially aware of the latter danger"? Although decision makers will always be faced with ambiguous and confusing evidence and will be forced to make inferences about others which will often be inaccurate, a number of safeguards may be suggested which could enable them to minimize their errors. First and most obvious, decision makers should be aware that they do not make "unbiased" interpretations of each new bit of incoming information, but rather are inevitably heavily influenced by the theories they expect to be verified. They should know that what may appear to them as a self-evident and unambiguous inference often seems so only because of their preexisting beliefs. To someone with a different theory the same data may appear to be unimportant or to support another explanation. Thus many events provide less independent support for the decision makers' images than they may at first realize. Knowledge of this should lead decision makers to examine more closely evidence that others believe contradicts their views.

Second, decision makers should see if their attitudes contain consistent or supporting beliefs that are not logically linked. These may be examples of true psycho-logic. While it is not logically surprising, nor is it evidence of psychological pressures, to find that people who believe that Russia is aggressive are very suspicious of any Soviet move, other kinds of consistency are more suspect. For example, most people who feel that it is important for the United States to win the war in Vietnam also feel that a meaningful victory is possible. And most people who feel defeat would neither endanger U.S. national security nor be costly in terms of other values also feel that we cannot win. Although there are important logical linkages between the two parts of each of these views (especially through theories of guerrilla warfare), they do not seem strong enough to explain the degree to which the opinions are correlated. Similarly, in Finland in the winter of 1939, those who felt that grave consequences would follow Finnish agreement to give Russia a military base also believed that the Soviets would withdraw their demand if Finland stood firm. And those who felt that concessions would not lead to loss of major values also believed that Russia would fight if need be.[26] In this country those who favored a nuclear test ban tended to argue that fallout was very harmful, that only limited improvements in technology would flow from further testing, and that a test ban would increase the chances for peace and security. Those who opposed the test ban were apt to disagree on all three points. This does not mean, of course, that the people holding such sets of supporting views were necessarily wrong in any one element. The Finns who wanted to make concessions to the USSR were probably correct in both parts of their argument. But decision makers should be suspicious if they hold a position in which elements that are not logically connected support the same conclusion. This condition is psychologically comfortable and makes decisions easier to reach (since competing values do not have to be balanced off against each other). The chances are thus considerable that at least part of the reason why a person holds some of these views is related to psychology and not to the substance of the evidence.

Decision makers should also be aware that actors who suddenly find themselves having an important shared interest with other actors have a tendency to overestimate the degree of common interest involved. This tendency is especially strong for those actors (e.g., the United States, at least before 1950) whose beliefs about international relations and morality imply that they can cooperate only with "good" states and that with those states there will be no major conflicts. On the other hand, states that have either a tradition of limited cooperation with others (e.g., Britain) or a strongly held theory that differentiates occasional from permanent allies[27] (e.g., the Soviet Union) find it easier to resist this tendency and need not devote special efforts to combating its danger.

A third safeguard for decision makers would be to make their assumptions, beliefs, and the predictions that follow from them as explicit as possible. An actor should try to determine, before events occur, what evidence would count for and against his theories. By knowing what to expect he would know what to be surprised by, and surprise could indicate to that actor that his beliefs needed reevaluation.[28]

A fourth safeguard is more complex. The decision maker should try to prevent individuals and organizations from letting their main task, political future, and identity become tied to specific theories and images of other actors.[29] If this occurs, subgoals originally sought for their contribution to higher ends will take on value of their own, and information indicating possible alternative routes to the original goals will not be carefully considered. For example, the U.S. Forest Service was unable to carry out its original purpose as effectively when it began to see its distinctive competence not in promoting the best use of lands and forests but rather in preventing all types of forest fires.[30]

Organizations that claim to be unbiased may not realize the extent to which their definition of their role has become involved with certain beliefs about the world. Allen Dulles is a victim of this lack of understanding when he says, "I grant that we are all creatures of prejudice, including CIA officials, but by entrusting intelligence coordination to our central intelligence service, which is excluded from policy making and is married to no particular military hardware, we can avoid to the greatest possible extent the bending of facts obtained through intelligence to suit a particular occupational viewpoint."[31] This statement overlooks the fact that the CIA has developed a certain view of international relations and of the cold war which maximizes the importance of its information gathering, espionage, and subversive activities. Since the CIA would lose its unique place in the government if it were decided that the "back alleys" of world politics were no longer vital to U.S. security, it is not surprising that the organization interprets information in a way that stresses the continued need for its techniques.

Fifth, decision makers should realize the validity and implications of Roberta Wohlstetter's argument that "a willingness to play with material from different angles and in the context of unpopular as well as popular hypotheses is an essential ingredient of a good detective, whether the end is the solution of a crime or an intelligence estimate."[32] However, it is often difficult psychologically and politically for any one person to do this. Since a decision maker usually cannot get "unbiased" treatments of data, he should instead seek to structure conflicting biases into the decision-making process. The decision maker, in other words, should have devil's advocates around. Just as, as Neustadt points out,[33] the decision maker will want to create conflicts among his subordinates in order to make appropriate choices, so he will also want to ensure that incoming information is examined from many different perspectives with many different hypotheses in mind. To some extent this kind of examination will be done automatically through the divergence of goals, training, experience, and information that exists in any large organization. But in many cases this divergence will not be sufficient. The views of those analyzing the data will still be too homogeneous, and the decision maker will have to go out of his way not only to cultivate but to create differing viewpoints.

While all that would be needed would be to have some people examining the data trying to validate unpopular hypotheses, it would probably be more effective if they actually believed and had a stake in the views they were trying to support. If in 1941 someone had had the task of proving the view that Japan would attack Pearl Harbor, the government might have been less surprised by the attack. And only a person who was out to show that Russia would take objectively great risks would have been apt to note that several ships with especially large hatches going to Cuba were riding high in the water, indicating the presence of a bulky but light cargo that was not likely to be anything other than strategic missiles. And many people who doubt the wisdom of the administration's Vietnam policy would be somewhat reassured if there were people in the government who searched the statements and actions of both sides in an effort to prove that North Vietnam was willing to negotiate and that the official interpretation of such moves as the communist activities during the Tet truce of 1967 was incorrect.

Of course all these safeguards involve costs. They would divert resources from other tasks and would increase internal dissension. Determining whether these costs would be worth the gains would depend on a detailed analysis of how the suggested safeguards might be implemented. Even if they were adopted by a government, of course, they would not eliminate the chance of misperception. However, the safeguards would make it more likely that national decision makers would make conscious choices about the way data were interpreted rather than merely assuming that they can be seen in only one way and can mean only one thing. Statesmen would thus be reminded of alternative images of others just as they are constantly reminded of alternative policies.

These safeguards are partly based on hypothesis 3: actors can more easily assimilate into their established image of another actor information contradicting that image if the information is transmitted and considered bit by bit than if it comes all at once. In the former case each piece of discrepant data can be coped with as it arrives and each of the conflicts with the prevailing view will be small enough to go unnoticed, to be dismissed as unimportant, or to necessitate at most a slight modification of the image (e.g., addition of exceptions to the rule). When the information arrives in a block, the contradiction between it and the prevailing view is apt to be much clearer and the probability of major cognitive reorganization will be higher.

IV.   SOURCES OF CONCEPTS

An actor's perceptual thresholds—and thus the images that ambiguous information is apt to produce—are influenced by what he has experienced and learned about.[34] If one actor is to perceive that another fits in a given category he must first have, or develop, a concept for that category. We can usefully distinguish three levels at which a concept can be present or absent. First, the concept can be completely missing. The actor's cognitive structure may not include anything corresponding to the phenomenon he is encountering. This situation can occur not only in science fiction but also in a world of rapid change or in the meeting of two dissimilar systems. Thus China's image of the Western world was extremely inaccurate in the mid-nineteenth century, her learning was very slow, and her responses were woefully inadequate. The West was spared a similar struggle only because it had the power to reshape the system it encountered. Once the actor clearly sees one instance of the new phenomenon, he is apt to recognize it much more quickly in the future.[35] Second, the actor can know about a concept but not believe that it reflects an actual phenomenon. Thus communist and Western decision makers are each aware of the other's explanation of how his system functions but do not think that the concept corresponds to reality. Communist elites, furthermore, deny that anything *could* correspond to the democracies' description of themselves. Third, the actor may hold a concept but not believe that another actor fills it at the present moment. Thus the British and French statesmen of the 1930s held a concept of states with unlimited ambitions. They realized that Napoleons were possible, but they did not think Hitler belonged in that category. Hypothesis 4 distinguishes these three cases: misperception is most difficult to correct in the case of a missing concept and least difficult to correct in the case of a recognized but presumably unfilled concept. All other things being equal (e.g., the degree to which the concept is central to the actor's cognitive structure), the first case requires more cognitive reorganization than does the second, and the second requires more reorganization than the third.

However, this hypothesis does not mean that learning will necessarily be slowest in the first case, for if the phenomena are totally new, the actor may make such grossly inappropriate responses that he will quickly acquire information clearly indicating that he is faced with something he does not understand. And the sooner the actor realizes that things are not—or may not be—what they seem, the sooner he is apt to correct his image.[36]

Three main sources contribute to decision makers' concepts of international relations and of other states and influence the level of their perceptual thresholds for various phenomena. First, an actor's beliefs about his own domestic political system are apt to be important. In some cases, like that of the USSR, the decision makers' concepts are tied to an ideology that explicitly provides a frame of reference for viewing foreign affairs. Even where this is not the case, experience with his own system will partly determine what the actor is familiar with and what he is apt to perceive in others. Louis Hartz claims, "It is the absence of the experience of social revolution which is at the heart of the whole American dilemma. . . . In a whole series of specific ways it enters into our difficulty of communication with the rest of the world. We find it difficult to understand Europe's 'social question.' . . . We are not familiar with the deeper social struggles of Asia and hence tend to interpret even reactionary regimes as 'democratic.'"[37] Similarly, George Kennan argues that in World War I the Allied powers, and especially America, could not understand the bitterness and violence of others' internal conflicts: ". . . The inability of the Allied statesmen to picture to themselves the passions of the Russian civil war [was partly caused by the fact that] we represent . . . a society in which the manifestations of evil have been carefully buried and sublimated in the social behavior of people, as in their very consciousness. For this reason, probably, despite our widely traveled and outwardly cosmopolitan lives, the mainsprings of political behavior in such a country as Russia tend to remain concealed from our vision."[38]

Second, concepts will be supplied by the actor's previous experiences. An experiment from another field illustrates this. Dearborn and Simon presented business executives from various divisions (e.g., sales, accounting, production) with the same hypothetical data and asked them for an analysis and recommendations from the standpoint of what would be best for the company as a whole. The executives' views heavily reflected their departmental perspectives.[39] William W. Kaufmann shows how the perceptions of Ambassador Joseph Kennedy were affected by his past: "As befitted a former chairman of the Securities Exchange and Maritime Commissions, his primary interest lay in economic matters. . . . The revolutionary character of the Nazi regime was not a phenomenon that he could easily grasp. . . . It was far simpler, and more in accord with his own premises, to explain German aggressiveness in economic terms. The Third Reich was dissatisfied, authoritarian, and expansive largely because her economy was unsound."[40] Similarly it has been argued that Chamberlain was slow to recognize Hitler's intentions partly because of the limiting nature of his personal background and business experiences.[41] The impact of training and experience seems to be demonstrated when the background of the appeasers is compared to that of their opponents. One difference stands out: "A substantially higher percentage of the anti-appeasers (irrespective of class origins) had the kind of knowledge which comes from close acquaintance, mainly professional, with foreign affairs."[42] Since members of the diplomatic corps are responsible for meeting threats to the nation's security before these grow to major proportions, and since they have learned about cases in which aggressive states were not recognized as such until very late, they may be prone to interpret ambiguous data as showing that others are aggressive. It should be stressed that we cannot say that the professionals of the 1930s were more apt to make accurate judgments of other states. Rather, they may have been more sensitive to the chance that others were aggressive. They would then rarely take an aggressor for a status-quo power, but would more often make the opposite error.[43] Thus in the years before World War I the permanent officials in the British Foreign Office overestimated German aggressiveness.[44]

A parallel demonstration in psychology of the impact of training on perception is presented by an experiment in which ambiguous pictures were shown to both advanced and beginning police-administration students. The advanced group perceived more violence in the pictures than did the beginners. The probable explanation is that "the law enforcer may come to accept crime as a familiar personal experience, one which he himself is not surprised to encounter. The acceptance of crime as a familiar experience in turn increases the ability or readiness to perceive violence where clues to it are potentially available."[45] This experiment lends weight to the view that the British diplomats' sensitivity to aggressive states was not totally a product of personnel selection procedures.

A third source of concepts, which frequently will be the most directly relevant to a decision maker's perception of international relations, is international history. As Henry Kissinger points out, one reason why statesmen were so slow to recognize the threat posed by Napoleon was that previous events had accustomed them only to actors who wanted to modify the existing system, not overthrow it.[46] The other side of the coin is even more striking: historical traumas can heavily influence future perceptions. They can either establish a state's image of the other state involved or can be used as analogies. An example of the former case is provided by the fact that for at least ten years after the Franco-Prussian War most of Europe's statesmen felt that Bismarck had aggressive plans when in fact his main goal was to protect the status quo. Of course the evidence was ambiguous. The post-1871 Bismarckian maneuvers, which were designed to keep peace, looked not unlike the pre-1871 maneuvers designed to set the stage for war. But that the post-1871 maneuvers were seen as indicating aggressive plans is largely attributable to the impact of Bismarck's earlier actions on the statemen's image of him.

A state's previous unfortunate experience with a type of danger can sensitize it to other examples of that danger. While this sensitivity may lead the state to avoid the mistake it committed in the past, it may also lead it mistakenly to believe that the present situation is like the past one. Santayana's maxim could be turned around: "Those who remember the past are condemned to make the opposite mistakes." As Paul Kecskemeti shows, both defenders and critics of the unconditional surrender plan of the Second World War thought in terms of the conditions of World War I.[47] Annette Baker Fox found that the Scandinavian countries' neutrality policies in World War II were strongly influenced by their experiences in the previous war, even though vital aspects of the two situations were different. Thus "Norway's success [during the First World War] in remaining nonbelligerent though pro-Allied gave the Norwegians confidence that their country could again stay out of war."[48] And the lesson drawn from the unfortunate results of this policy was an important factor in Norway's decision to join NATO.

The application of the Munich analogy to various contemporary events has been much commented on, and I do not wish to argue the substantive points at stake. But it seems clear that the probabilities that any state is facing an aggressor who has to be met by force are not altered by the career of Hitler and the history of the 1930s. Similarly the probability of an aggressor's announcing his plans is not increased (if anything, it is decreased) by the fact that Hitler wrote *Mein Kampf*. Yet decision makers are more sensitive to these possibilities, and thus more apt to perceive ambiguous evidence as indicating they apply to a given case, than they would have been had there been no Nazi Germany.

Historical analogies often precede, rather than follow, a careful analysis of a situation (e.g., Truman's initial reaction to the news of the invasion of South Korea was to think of the Japanese invasion of Manchuria). Noting this precedence, however, does not show us which of many analogies will come to a decision maker's mind. Truman could have thought of nineteenth-century European wars that were of no interest to the United States. Several factors having nothing to do with the event under consideration influence what analogies a decision maker is apt to make. One factor is the number of cases similar to the analogy with which the decision maker is familiar. Another is the importance of the past event to the political system of which the decision maker is a part. The more times such an event occurred and the greater its consequences were, the more a decision maker will be sensitive to the particular danger involved and the more he will be apt to see ambiguous stimuli as indicating another instance of this kind of event. A third factor is the degree of the decision maker's personal involvement in the past case—in time, energy, ego, and position. The last-mentioned variable will affect not only the event's impact on the decision maker's cognitive structure, but also the way he perceives the event and the lesson he draws. Someone who was involved in getting troops into South Korea after the attack will remember the Korean War differently from someone who was involved in considering the possible use of nuclear weapons or in deciding what messages should be sent to the Chinese. Greater personal involvement will usually give the event greater impact, especially if the decision maker's own views were validated by the event. One need not accept a total application of learning theory to nations to believe that "nothing fails like success."[49] It also seems likely that if many critics argued at the time that the decision maker was wrong, he will be even more apt to see other situations in terms of the original event. For example, because Anthony Eden left the government on account of his views and was later shown to have been correct, he probably was more apt to see as Hitlers other leaders with whom he had conflicts (e.g., Nasser). A fourth factor is the degree to which the analogy is compatible with the rest of his belief system. A fifth is the absence of alternative concepts and analogies. Individuals and states vary in the amount of direct or indirect political experience they have had which can provide different ways of interpreting data. Decision makers who are aware of multiple possibilities of states' intentions may be less likely to seize on an analogy prematurely. The perception of citizens of nations like the United States, which have relatively little history of international politics, may be more apt to be heavily influenced by the few major international events that have been important to their country.

The first three factors indicate that an event is more apt to shape present perceptions if it occurred in the recent rather than the remote past. If it occurred recently, the statesman will then know about it at first hand even if he was not involved in the making of policy at the time. Thus if generals are prepared to fight the last war, diplomats may be prepared to avoid the last war. Part of the Anglo-French reaction to Hitler can be explained by the prevailing beliefs that the First World War was to a large extent caused by misunderstandings and could have been avoided by farsighted and nonbelligerent diplomacy. And part of the Western perception of Russia and China can be explained by the view that appeasement was an inappropriate response to Hitler.[50]

V. THE EVOKED SET

The way people perceive data is influenced not only by their cognitive structure and theories about other actors but also by what they are concerned with at the time they receive the information. Information is evaluated in light of the small part of the person's memory that is presently active—the "evoked set." My perceptions of the dark streets I pass walking home from the movies will be different if the film I saw had dealt with spies than if it had been a comedy. If I am working on aiding a country's education system and I hear someone talk about the need for economic development in that state, I am apt to think he is concerned with education, whereas if I had been working on, say, trying to achieve political stability in that country, I would have placed his remarks in that framework.[51]

Thus hypothesis 5 states that when messages are sent from a different background of concerns and information than is possessed by the receiver, misunderstanding is likely. Person A and person B will read the same message quite differently if A has seen several related messages that B does not know about. This difference will be compounded if, as is frequently the case, A and B each assume that the other has the same background he does. This means that misperception can occur even when deception is neither intended nor expected. Thus Roberta Wohlstetter found not only that different parts of the United States government had different perceptions of data about Japan's intentions and messages partly because they saw the incoming information in very different contexts, but also that officers in the field misunderstood warnings from Washington: "Washington advised General Short [in Pearl Harbor] on November 27 to expect 'hostile action' at any moment, by which it meant 'attack on American possessions from without,' but General Short understood this phrase to mean 'sabotage.'"[52] Washington did not realize the extent to which Pearl Harbor considered the danger of sabotage to be primary, and furthermore it incorrectly believed that General Short had received the intercepts of the secret Japanese diplomatic messages available in Washington which indicated that surprise attack was a distinct possibility. Another implication of this hypothesis is that if important information is known to only part of the government of state A and part of the government of state B, international messages may be misunderstood by those parts of the receiver's government that do not match, in the information they have, the part of the sender's government that dispatched the message.[53]

Two additional hypotheses can be drawn from the problems of those sending messages. Hypothesis 6 states that when people spend a great deal of time drawing up a plan or making a decision, they tend to think that the message about it they wish to convey will be clear to the receiver.[54] Since they are aware of what is to them the important pattern in their actions, they often feel that the pattern will be equally obvious to others, and they overlook the degree to which the message is apparent to them only because they know what to look for. Those who have not participated in the endless meetings may not understand what information the sender is trying to convey. George Quester has shown how the German and to a lesser extent the British desire to maintain target limits on bombing in the first eighteen months of World War II was undermined partly by the fact that each side knew the limits it was seeking and its own reasons for any apparent "exceptions" (e.g., the German attack on Rotterdam) and incorrectly felt that these limits and reasons were equally clear to the other side.[55]

Hypothesis 7 holds that actors often do not realize that actions intended to project a given image may not have the desired effect because the actions themselves do not turn out as planned. Thus even without appreciable impact of different cognitive structures and backgrounds, an action may convey an unwanted message. For example, a country's representatives may not follow instructions and so may give others impressions contrary to those the home government wished to convey. The efforts of Washington and Berlin to settle their dispute over Samoa in the late 1880s were complicated by the provocative behavior of their agents on the spot. These agents not only increased the intensity of the local conflict but led the decision makers to become more suspicious of the other state because they tended to assume that their agents were obeying instructions and that the actions of the other side represented official policy. In such cases both sides will believe that the other is reading hostility into a policy of theirs which is friendly. Similarly, Quester's study shows that the attempt to limit bombing referred to above failed partly because neither side was able to bomb as accurately as it thought it could and thus did not realize the physical effects of its actions.[56]

VI.   FURTHER HYPOTHESES FROM THE PERSPECTIVE OF THE PERCEIVER

From the perspective of the perceiver several other hypotheses seem to hold. Hypothesis 8 is that there is an overall tendency for decision makers to see other states as more hostile than they are.[57] There seem to be more cases of statesmen incorrectly believing others are planning major acts against their interest than of statesmen being lulled by a potential aggressor. There are many reasons for this which are too complex to be treated here (e.g., some parts of the bureaucracy feel it is their responsibility to be suspicious of all other states; decision makers often feel they are "playing it safe" to believe and act as though the other state were hostile in questionable cases; and often, when people do not feel they are a threat to others, they find it difficult to believe that others may see them as a threat). It should be noted, however, that decision makers whose perceptions are described by this hypothesis would not necessarily further their own values by trying to correct for this tendency. The values of possible outcomes as well as their probabilities must be considered, and it may be that the probability of an unnecessary arms-tension cycle arising out of misperceptions, multiplied by the costs of such a cycle, may seem less to decision makers than the probability of incorrectly believing another state is friendly, multiplied by the costs of this eventuality.

Hypothesis 9 states that actors tend to see the behavior of others as more centralized, disciplined, and coordinated than it is. This hypothesis holds true in related ways. Frequently too many complex events are squeezed into a perceived pattern. Actors are hesitant to admit or even see that particular incidents cannot be explained by their theories.[58] Those events not caused by factors that are important parts of the perceiver's image are often seen as though they were. Further, actors see others as more internally united than they in fact are and generally overestimate the degree to which others are following a coherent policy. The degree to which the other side's policies are the product of internal bargaining,[59] internal misunderstandings, or subordinates' not following instructions is underestimated. This is the case partly because actors tend to be unfamiliar with the details of another state's policy-making processes. Seeing only the finished product, they find it simpler to try to construct a rational explanation for the policies, even though they know that such an analysis could not explain their own policies.[60]

Familiarity also accounts for hypothesis 10: because a state gets most of its information about the other state's policies from the other's foreign office, it tends to take the foreign office's position for the stand of the other government as a whole. In many cases this perception will be an accurate one, but when the other government is divided or when the other foreign office is acting without specific authorization, misperception may result. For example, part of the reason why in 1918 Allied governments incorrectly thought "that the Japanese were preparing to take action [in Siberia], if need be, with agreement with the British and French alone, disregarding the absence of American consent,"[61] was that Allied ambassadors had talked mostly with Foreign Minister Motono, who was among the minority of the Japanese favoring this policy. Similarly, America's NATO allies may have gained an inaccurate picture of the degree to which the American government was committed to the MLF because they had greatest contact with parts of the government that strongly favored the MLF. And states that tried to get information about Nazi foreign policy from German diplomats were often misled because these officials were generally ignorant of or out of sympathy with Hitler's plans. The Germans and the Japanese sometimes purposely misinformed their own ambassadors in order to deceive their enemies more effectively.

Hypothesis 11 states that actors tend to overestimate the degree to which others are acting in response to what they themselves do when the others behave in accordance with the actor's desires; but when the behavior of the other is undesired, it is usually seen as derived from internal forces. If the *effect* of another's action is to injure or threaten the first side, the first side is apt to believe that such was the other's *purpose*. An example of the first part of the hypothesis is provided by Kennan's account of the activities of official and unofficial American representatives who protested to the new Bolshevik government against several of its actions. When the Soviets changed their position, these representatives felt it was largely because of their influence.[62] This sort of interpretation can be explained not only by the fact that it is gratifying to the individual making it, but also, taking the other side of the coin mentioned in hypothesis 9, by the fact that the actor is most familiar with his own input into the other's decision and has less knowledge of other influences. The second part of hypothesis 11 is illustrated by the tendency of actors to believe that the hostile behavior of others is to be explained by the other side's motives and not by its reaction to the first side. Thus Chamberlain did not see that Hitler's behavior was related in part to his belief that the British were weak. More common is the failure to see that the other side is reacting out of fear of the first side, which can lead to self-fulfilling prophecies and spirals of misperception and hostility.

This difficulty is often compounded by an implication of hypothesis 12: when actors have intentions that they do not try to conceal from others, they tend to assume that others accurately perceive these intentions. Only rarely do they believe that others may be reacting to a much less favorable image of themselves than they think they are projecting.[63]

For state A to understand how state B perceives A's policy is often difficult because such understanding may involve a conflict with A's image of itself. Raymond Sontag argues that Anglo-German relations before World War I deteriorated partly because "the British did not like to think of themselves as selfish or unwilling to tolerate 'legitimate' German expansion. The Germans did not like to think of themselves as aggressive or unwilling to recognize 'legitimate' British vested interest."[64]

Hypothesis 13 suggests that if it is hard for an actor to believe that the other can see him as a menace, it is often even harder for him to see that issues important to him are not important to others. While he may know that another actor is on an opposing team, it may be more difficult for him to realize that the other is playing an entirely different game. This is especially true when the game he is playing seems vital to him.[65]

The final hypothesis, hypothesis 14, is as follows: actors tend to overlook the fact that evidence consistent with their theories may also be consistent with other views. When choosing between two theories, we have to pay attention only to data that cannot be accounted for by one of the theories. But it is common to find people claiming as proof of their theories data that could also support alternative views. This phenomenon is related to the point made earlier that any single bit of information can be interpreted only within a framework of hypotheses and theories. And while it is true that "we may without a vicious circularity accept some datum as a fact because it conforms to the very law for which it counts as another confirming instance, and reject an allegation of fact because it is already excluded by law,"[66] we should be careful lest we forget that a piece of information seems in many cases to confirm a certain hypothesis only because we already believe that hypothesis to be correct and that the information can with as much validity support a different hypothesis. For example, one of the reasons why the German attack on Norway took both that country and England by surprise, even though they had detected German ships moving toward Norway, was that they expected not an attack but an attempt by the Germans to break through the British blockade and reach the Atlantic. The initial course of the ships was consistent with either plan, but the British and Norwegians took this course to mean that their predictions were being borne out.[67] This is not to imply that the interpretation made was foolish, but only that the decision makers should have been aware that the evidence was also consistent with an invasion and should have had a bit less confidence in their views.

The longer the ships would have to travel the same route, whether they were going to one or another of two destinations, the more information would be needed to determine their plans. Taken as a metaphor, this incident applies generally to the treatment of evidence. Thus as long as Hitler made demands for control only of ethnically German areas, his actions could be explained either by the hypothesis that he had unlimited ambitions or by the hypothesis that he wanted to unite all the Germans. But actions against non-Germans (e.g., the takeover of Czechoslovakia in March 1938) could not be accounted for by the latter hypothesis. And it was this action that convinced the appeasers that Hitler had to be stopped. It is interesting to speculate on what the British reaction would have been had Hitler left Czechoslovakia alone for a while and instead made demands on Poland similar to those he eventually made in the summer of 1939. The two paths would then still not have diverged, and further misperception could have occurred.

NOTES

1. See for example Ole Holsti, Robert North, and Richard Brody, "Perception and Action in the 1914 Crisis," in J. David Singer, ed., *Quantitative International Politics* (New York, 1968). For a fuller discussion of the Stanford content analysis studies and the general problems of quantification, see my "The Costs of the Quantitative Study of International Relations," in Klaus Knorr and James N. Rosenau, eds., *Contending Approaches to International Politics* (forthcoming).
2. See, for example, Osgood, *An Alternative to War or Surrender* (Urbana, 1962); Etzioni, *The Hard Way to Peace* (New York, 1962); Boulding, "National Images and International Systems," *Journal of Conflict Resolution*, III (June 1959), 120–31; and Singer, *Deterrence, Arms Control, and Disarmament* (Columbus, 1962).
3. *Statistics of Deadly Quarrels* (Pittsburgh, 1960) and *Arms and Insecurity* (Chicago, 1960). For nonmathematicians a fine summary of Richardson's work is Anatol Rapoport's "L. F. Richardson's Mathematical Theory of War," *Journal of Conflict Resolution*, I (September 1957), 249–99.
4. See Philip Green, *Deadly Logic* (Columbus, 1966); Green, "Method and Substance in the Arms Debate," *World Politics*, XVI (July 1964), 642–67; and Robert A. Levine, "Fact and Morals in the Arms Debate," *World Politics*, XIV (January 1962), 239–58.
5. See Anatol Rapoport, *Strategy and Conscience* (New York, 1964).
6. Floyd Allport, *Theories of Perception and the Concept of Structure* (New York, 1955), 382; Ole Holsti, "Cognitive Dynamics and Images of the Enemy," in David Finlay, Ole Holsti, and Richard Fagen, *Enemies in Politics* (Chicago, 1967), 70.
7. Jerome Bruner and Leo Postman, "On the Perceptions of Incongruity: A Paradigm," in Jerome Bruner and David Krech, eds., *Perception and Personality* (Durham, N.C., 1949), 210.
8. Robert Abelson and Milton Rosenberg, "Symbolic Psycho-logic," *Behavioral Science*, III (January 1958), 4–5.
9. p. 27.
10. *Ibid.*, 26.
11. I have borrowed this phrase from Abraham Kaplan, who uses it in a different but related context in *The Conduct of Inquiry* (San Francisco, 1964), 86.
12. The spiral theorists are not the only ones to ignore the limits of empiricism. Roger Hilsman found that most consumers and producers of intelligence felt that intelligence should not deal with hypotheses but should only provide the policy makers with "all the facts" (*Strategic Intelligence and National Decisions* [Glencoe, 1956], 46). The close

interdependence between hypotheses and facts is overlooked partly because of the tendency to identify "hypotheses" with "policy preferences."

13. Karl Deutsch interestingly discusses a related question when he argues, "Autonomy . . . requires both intake from the present and recall from memory, and selfhood can be seen in just this continuous balancing of a limited present and a limited past. . . . No further self-determination is possible if either openness or memory is lost. . . . To the extent that [systems cease to be able to take in new information], they approach the behavior of a bullet or torpedo: their future action becomes almost completely determined by their past. On the other hand, a person without memory, an organization without values or policy . . . —all these no longer steer, but drift: their behavior depends little on their past and almost wholly on their present. Driftwood and the bullet are thus each the epitome of another kind of loss of self-control . . . " (*Nationalism and Social Communication* [Cambridge, Mass., 1954], 167–68). Also see Deutsch's *The Nerves of Government* (New York, 1963), 98–109, 200–256. A physicist makes a similar argument: "It is clear that if one is too attached to one's preconceived model, one will miss all radical discoveries. It is amazing to what degree one may fail to register mentally an observation which does not fit the initial image. . . . On the other hand, if one is too open-minded and pursues every hitherto-unknown phenomenon, one is almost certain to lose oneself in trivia" (Martin Deutsch, "Evidence and Inference in Nuclear Research," in Daniel Lerner, ed., *Evidence and Inference* [Glencoe, 1958], 102).

14. Raymond Bauer, "Problems of Perception and the Relations Between the U.S. and the Soviet Union," *Journal of Conflict Resolution*, V (September 1961), 223–29.

15. Quoted in W. I. B. Beveridge, *The Art of Scientific Investigation*, 3rd ed. (London, 1957), 50.

16. *Science, Faith, and Society* (Chicago, 1964), 31. For a further discussion of this problem, see *ibid.*, 16, 26–41, 90–94; Polanyi, *Personal Knowledge* (London, 1958), 8–15, 30, 143–68, 269–98, 310–11; Thomas Kuhn, *The Structure of Scientific Revolution* (Chicago, 1964); Kuhn, "The Function of Dogma in Scientific Research," in A. C. Crombie, ed., *Scientific Change* (New York, 1963), 344–69; the comments on Kuhn's paper by Hall, Polanyi, and Toulmin, and Kuhn's reply, *ibid.*, 370–95. For a related discussion of these points from a different perspective, see Norman Storer, *The Social System of Science* (New York, 1960), 116–22.

17. "He found that the position of one star relative to others . . . had shifted. Lalande was a good astronomer and knew that such a shift was unreasonable. He crossed out his first observation, put a question mark next to the second observation, and let the matter go" (Jerome Bruner, Jacqueline Goodnow, and George Austin, *A Study of Thinking* [New York, 1962], 105).

18. *The Structure of Scientific Revolution*, 79.

19. *Ibid.*, 150–51.

20. Requirements of effective political leadership may lead decision makers to voice fewer doubts than they have about existing policies and images, but this constraint can only partially explain this phenomenon. Similar calculations of political strategy may contribute to several of the hypotheses discussed below.

21. p. 221. Similarly, in experiments dealing with his subjects' perception of other people, Charles Dailey found that "premature judgment appears to make new data harder to assimilate than when the observer withholds judgment until all data are seen. It seems probable . . . that the observer mistakes his own inferences for facts" ("The Effects of Premature Conclusion Upon the Acquisition of Understanding of a Person," *Journal of Psychology*, XXX [January 1952], 149–50). For other theory and evidence on this point,

see Bruner, "On Perceptual Readiness," *Psychological Review*, LXIV (March 1957), 123–52; Gerald Davidson, "The Negative Effects of Early Exposure to Suboptimal Visual Stimuli," *Journal of Personality*, XXXII (June 1964), 278–95; Albert Myers, "An Experimental Analysis of a Tactical Blunder," *Journal of Abnormal and Social Psychology*, LXIX (November 1964), 493–98; and Dale Wyatt and Donald Campbell, "On the Liability of Stereotype or Hypothesis," *Journal of Abnormal and Social Psychology*, XLIV (October 1950), 496–500. It should be noted that this tendency makes "incremental" decision making more likely (David Braybrooke and Charles Lindblom, *A Strategy of Decision* [New York, 1963]), but the results of this process may lead the actor further from his goals.

22. For a use of this concept in political communication, see Roberta Wohlstetter, *Pearl Harbor* (Stanford, 1962).

23. Similarly, Robert Coulondre, the French ambassador to Berlin in 1939, was one of the few diplomats to appreciate the Nazi threat. Partly because of his earlier service in the USSR, "he was painfully sensitive to the threat of a Berlin-Moscow agreement. He noted with foreboding that Hitler had not attacked Russia in his *Reichstag* address of April 28. . . . So it went all spring and summer, the ambassador relaying each new evidence of the impending diplomatic revolution and adding to his admonitions his pleas for decisive counteraction" (Franklin Ford and Carl Schorske, "The Voice in the Wilderness: Robert Coulondre," in Gordon Craig and Felix Gilbert, eds., *The Diplomats*, Vol. III [New York, 1963] 573–74). His hypotheses were correct, but it is difficult to detect differences between the way he and those ambassadors who were incorrect, like Neville Henderson, selectively noted and interpreted information. However, to the extent that the fear of war influenced the appeasers' perceptions of Hitler's intentions, the appeasers' views did have an element of psycho-logic that was not present in their opponents' position.

24. See for example Donald Campbell, "Systematic Error on the Part of Human Links in Communications Systems," *Information and Control*, I (1958), 346–50; and Leo Postman, "The Experimental Analysis of Motivational Factors in Perception," in Judson S. Brown, ed., *Current Theory and Research in Motivation* (Lincoln, Neb., 1953), 59–108.

25. Dale Wyatt and Donald Campbell, "A Study of Interviewer Bias as Related to Interviewer's Expectations and Own Opinions," *International Journal of Opinion and Attitude Research*, IV (Spring 1950), 77–83.

26. Max Jacobson, *The Diplomacy of the Winter War* (Cambridge, Mass., 1961), 136–39.

27. Raymond Aron, *Peace and War* (Garden City, 1966), 29.

28. C. F. Kuhn, *The Structure of Scientific Revolution*, 65. A fairly high degree of knowledge is needed before one can state precise expectations. One indication of the lack of international-relations theory is that most of us are not sure what "naturally" flows from our theories and what constitutes either "puzzles" to be further explored with the paradigm or "anomalies" that cast doubt on the basic theories.

29. See Philip Selznick, *Leadership in Administration* (Evanston, 1957).

30. Ashley Schiff, *Fire and Water: Scientific Heresy in the Forest Service* (Cambridge, Mass., 1962). Despite its title, this book is a fascinating and valuable study.

31. *The Craft of Intelligence* (New York, 1963), 53.

32. p. 302. See Beveridge, 93, for a discussion of the idea that the scientist should keep in mind as many hypotheses as possible when conducting and analyzing experiments.

33. *Presidential Power* (New York, 1960).

34. Most psychologists argue that this influence also holds for perception of shapes. For data showing that people in different societies differ in respect to their predisposition

to experience certain optical illusions and for a convincing argument that this difference can be explained by the societies' different physical environments, which have led their people to develop different patterns of drawing inferences from ambiguous visual cues, see Marshall Segall, Donald Campbell, and Melville Herskovits, *The Influence of Culture on Visual Perceptions* (Indianapolis, 1966).

35. Thus when Bruner and Postman's subjects first were presented with incongruous playing cards (i.e., cards in which symbols and colors of the suits were not matching, producing red spades or black diamonds), long exposure times were necessary for correct identification. But once a subject correctly perceived the card and added this type of card to his repertoire of categories, he was able to identify other incongruous cards much more quickly. For an analogous example—in this case changes in the analysis of aerial reconnaissance photographs of an enemy's secret weapons-testing facilities produced by the belief that a previously unknown object may be present—see David Irving, *The Mare's Nest* (Boston, 1964), 66–67, 274–75.

36. Bruner and Postman, 220.

37. *The Liberal Tradition in America* (New York, 1955), 306.

38. *Russia and the West Under Lenin and Stalin* (New York, 1962), 142–43.

39. DeWitt Dearborn and Herbert Simon, "Selective Perception: A Note on the Departmental Identification of Executives," *Sociometry*, XXI (June 1958), 140–44.

40. "Two American Ambassadors: Bullitt and Kennedy," in Craig and Gilbert, 358–59.

41. Hugh Trevor-Roper puts this point well: "Brought up as a business man, successful in municipal politics, [Chamberlain's] outlook was entirely parochial. Educated Conservative aristocrats like Churchill, Eden, and Cranborne, whose families had long been used to political responsibility, had seen revolution and revolutionary leaders before, in their own history, and understood them correctly; but the Chamberlains, who had run from radical imperialism to timid conservatism in a generation of life in Birmingham, had no such understanding of history or the world: to them the scope of human politics was limited by their own parochial horizons, and Neville Chamberlain could not believe that Hitler was fundamentally different from himself. If Chamberlain wanted peace, so must Hitler" ("Munich—Its Lessons Ten Years Later," in Francis Loewenheim, ed., *Peace or Appeasement?* [Boston, 1965], 152–53). For a similar view see A. L. Rowse, *Appeasement* (New York, 1963), 117.

But Donald Lammers points out that the views of many prominent British public figures in the 1930s do not fit this generalization (*Explaining Munich* [Stanford, 1966], 13–140). Furthermore, arguments that stress the importance of the experiences and views of the actors' ancestors do not explain the links by which these influence the actors themselves. Presumably Churchill and Chamberlain read the same history books in school and had the same basic information about Britain's past role in the world. Thus what has to be demonstrated is that in their homes aristocrats like Churchill learned different things about politics and human nature than did middle-class people like Chamberlain and that these experiences had a significant impact. Alternatively, it could be argued that the patterns of child-rearing prevalent among the aristocracy influenced the children's personalities in a way that made them more likely to see others as aggressive.

42. *Ibid.*, 15.

43. During a debate on appeasement in the House of Commons, Harold Nicolson declared, "I know that those of us who believe in the traditions of our policy, . . . who believe that one great function of this country is to maintain moral standards in Europe, to maintain a settled pattern of international relations, not to make friends with people

who are demonstrably evil . . . —I know that those who hold such beliefs are accused of possessing the Foreign Office mind. I thank God that I possess the Foreign Office mind" (quoted in Martin Gilbert, *The Roots of Appeasement* [New York, 1966], 187). But the qualities Nicolson mentions and applauds may be related to a more basic attribute of "the Foreign Office mind"—suspiciousness.

44. George Monger, *The End of Isolation* (London, 1963). I am also indebted to Frederick Collignon for his unpublished manuscript and several conversations on this point.

45. Hans Toch and Richard Schulte, "Readiness to Perceive Violence as a Result of Police Training," *British Journal of Psychology*, LII (November 1961), 392 (original italics omitted). It should be stressed that one cannot say whether or not the advanced police students perceived the pictures "accurately." The point is that their training predisposed them to see violence in ambiguous situations. Whether on balance they would make fewer perceptual errors and better decisions is very hard to determine. For an experiment showing that training can lead people to "recognize" an expected stimulus even when that stimulus is in fact not shown, see Israel Goldiamond and William F. Hawkins, "Vexierversuch: The Log Relationship Between Word-Frequency and Recognition Obtained in the Absence of Stimulus Words," *Journal of Experimental Psychology*, LVI (December 1958), 457–63.

46. *A World Restored* (New York, 1964), 2–3.

47. *Strategic Surrender* (New York, 1964), 215–41.

48. *The Power of Small States* (Chicago, 1959), 81.

49. William Inge, *Outspoken Essays*, First Series (London, 1923), 88.

50. Of course, analogies themselves are not "unmoved movers." The interpretation of past events is not automatic and is informed by general views of international relations and complex judgments. And just as beliefs about the past influence the present, views about the present influence interpretations of history. It is difficult to determine the degree to which the United States' interpretation of the reasons it went to war in 1917 influenced American foreign policy in the 1920s and 1930s and how much the isolationism of that period influenced the histories of the war.

51. For some psychological experiments on this subject see Jerome Bruner and A. Leigh Minturn, "Perceptual Identification and Perceptual Organization," *Journal of General Psychology*, LIII (July 1955), 22–28; Seymour Feshbach and Robert Singer, "The Effects of Fear Arousal and Suppression of Fear Upon Social Perception," *Journal of Abnormal and Social Psychology*, LV (November 1957), 283–88; and Elsa Sippoal, "A Group Study of Some Effects of Preparatory Sets," *Psychology Monographs*, XLVI, No. 210 (1935), 27–28. For a general discussion of the importance of the perceiver's evoked set, see Postman, 87.

52. pp. 73–74.

53. For example, Roger Hilsman points out, "Those who knew of the peripheral reconnaissance flights that probed Soviet air defenses during the Eisenhower administration and the U-2 flights over the Soviet Union itself . . . were better able to understand some of the things the Soviets were saying and doing than people who did not know of these activities" (*To Move a Nation* [Garden City, 1967], 66). But it is also possible that those who knew about the U-2 flights at times misinterpreted Soviet messages by incorrectly believing that the sender was influenced by, or at least knew of, these flights.

54. I am grateful to Thomas Schelling for discussion on this point.

55. *Deterrence Before Hiroshima* (New York, 1966), 105–22.

56. *Ibid.*

57. For a slightly different formulation of this view, see Holsti, 27.

58. The Soviets consciously hold an extreme version of this view and seem to believe that nothing is accidental. See the discussion in Nathan Leites, *A Study of Bolshevism* (Glencoe, 1953), 67–73.

59. A. W. Marshall criticizes Western explanations of Soviet military posture for failing to take this into account. See his "Problems of Estimating Military Power," a paper presented at the 1966 Annual Meeting of the American Political Science Association, 16.

60. It has also been noted that in labor-management disputes both sides may be apt to believe incorrectly that the other is controlled from above, either from the international union office or from the company's central headquarters (Robert Blake, Herbert Shepard, and Jane Mouton, *Managing Intergroup Conflict in Industry* [Houston, 1964], 182). It has been further noted that both Democratic and Republican members of the House tend to see the other party as the one that is more disciplined and united (Charles Clapp, *The Congressman* [Washington, 1963], 17–19).

61. George Kennan, *Russia Leaves the War* (New York, 1967), 484.

62. *Ibid.*, 404, 408, 500.

63. Herbert Butterfield notes that these assumptions can contribute to the spiral of "Hobbesian fear. . . . You yourself may vividly feel the terrible fear that you have of the other party, but you cannot enter into the other man's counterfear or even understand why he should be particularly nervous. For you know that you yourself mean him no harm and that you want nothing from him save guarantees for your own safety; and it is never possible for you to realize or remember properly that since he cannot see the inside of your mind, he can never have the same assurance of your intentions that you have" (*History and Human Conflict* [London, 1951], 20).

64. *European Diplomatic History 1871–1932* (New York, 1933), 125. It takes great mental effort to realize that actions which seem only the natural consequence of defending your vital interests can look to others as though you are refusing them any chance of increasing their influence. In rebutting the famous Crowe "balance of power" memorandum of 1907, which justified a policy of "containing" Germany on the grounds that she was a threat to British national security, Sanderson, a former permanent undersecretary in the Foreign Office, wrote, "It has sometimes seemed to me that to a foreigner reading our press the British Empire must appear in the light of some huge giant sprawling all over the globe, with gouty fingers and toes stretching in every direction, which cannot be approached without eliciting a scream" (quoted in Monger, 315). But few other Englishmen could be convinced that others might see them this way.

65. George Kennan makes clear that in 1918 this kind of difficulty was partly responsible for the inability of either the Allies or the new Bolshevik government to understand the motivations of the other side: "There is . . . nothing in nature more egocentric than the embattled democracy. . . . It . . . tends to attach to its own cause an absolute value which distorts its own vision of everything else. . . . It will readily be seen that people who have got themselves into this frame of mind have little understanding for the issues of any contest other than the one in which they are involved. The idea of people wasting time and substance on any *other* issue seems to them preposterous" (*Russia and the West,* 11–12).

66. Kaplan, 89.

67. Johan Jorgen Holst, "Surprise, Signals, and Reaction: The Attack on Norway," *Cooperation and Conflict,* No. 1 (1966), 34. The Germans made a similar mistake in November 1942 when they interpreted the presence of an Allied convoy in the Mediterranean as confirming their belief that Malta would be resupplied. They thus were taken by surprise

when landings took place in North Africa (William Langer, *Our Vichy Gamble* [New York, 1966], 365).

☙

Cognitive Perspectives on Foreign Policy*

Philip E. Tetlock and Charles B. McGuire, Jr.

The last fifteen years have witnessed an impressive expansion of cognitive research on foreign policy—on both methodological and theoretical fronts. On the methodological front, investigators have shown skill in drawing insights from a variety of research techniques, including laboratory experiments (reviewed by Holsti and George, 1975; Jervis, 1976); historical case studies (George and Smoke, 1974; Janis, 1982; Lebow, 1981); content analyses of archival documents (Axelrod, 1976; Falkowski, 1979; Hermann, 1980a, 1980b; Tetlock, 1983c), interview and questionnaire studies (Bonham, Shapiro, and Trumble, 1979; Heradstveit, 1974, 1981); and computer simulations of belief systems (Abelson, 1968; Anderson and Thorson, 1982). There are, moreover, numerous examples of multimethod convergence in the research literature: investigators from different methodological traditions have often arrived at strikingly similar conclusions concerning the roles that cognitive variables play in the foreign policymaking process. The theoretical diversity is equally impressive and healthy. In developing hypotheses linking cognitive and foreign policy variables, investigators have drawn upon a variety of intellectual traditions, including work on attribution theory (Heradstveit, 1981; Jervis, 1976; Tetlock, 1983b); cognitive-consistency theory (Jervis, 1976); behavioral decision theory (Fischhoff, 1983; Jervis, 1982); the effects of stress on information processing (Holsti and George, 1975; Janis and Mann, 1977; Suedfeld and Tetlock, 1977), organizational principles underlying political belief systems (George, 1969; Holsti, 1977; Walker, 1983); and individual differences in cognitive styles (Bonham and Shapiro, 1977; Hermann, 1980a; Tetlock, 1981, 1983a, 1984). Each of these approaches has borne at least some empirical fruit.

We believe careful appraisal is now needed of what has been accomplished and of the directions in which theoretical and empirical work appears to be developing. We have divided our review chapter into four sections: "The Cognitive Research Program in Foreign Policy," "Representational Research," "Process Research," and "Conclusions."

---

*Philip E. Tetlock and Charles B. McGuire, Jr., "Cognitive Perspectives on Foreign Policy." Excerpted from S. Long, ed., *Political Behavior Annual* (Boulder, Colo.: Westview Press, 1985). Reprinted by permission of the author.

I. THE COGNITIVE RESEARCH PROGRAM IN FOREIGN POLICY

Cognitive research on foreign policy can be viewed as an incipient research program. The hard core of the cognitive research program is difficult to specify with confidence. (What fundamental assumptions do the overwhelming majority of investigators who work at this level of analysis share?) We believe, however, that the hard core consists of two key assumptions which deserve to be spelled out in detail:

1. The international environment imposes heavy information-processing demands upon policymakers. It is very difficult to identify the best or utility-maximizing solutions to most foreign policy problems. Policymakers must deal with incomplete and unreliable information on the intentions and capabilities of other states. The range of response options is indeterminate. The problem consequences of each option are shrouded in uncertainty. Policymakers must choose among options that vary on many, seemingly incommensurable value dimensions (e.g., economic interests, international prestige, domestic political advantages, human rights, even lives). Finally, to compound the difficulty of the task, policymakers must sometimes work under intense stress and time pressure.

2. Policymakers (like all human beings) are limited-capacity information processors who resort to simplifying strategies to deal with the complexity, uncertainty, and painful trade-offs with which the world confronts them (cf. Abelson and Levi, in press; Einhorn and Hogarth, 1981; George, 1980; Jervis, 1976; Nisbett and Ross, 1980; Simon, 1957; Taylor and Fiske, 1984). The foreign policy of a nation addresses itself, not to the external world per se, but to the simplified image of the external world constructed in the minds of those who make policy decisions (Axelrod, 1976; George, 1980; Holsti, 1976; Jervis, 1976). Policymakers may behave "rationally" (attempt to maximize expected utility) but only within the context of their simplified subjective representations of reality.

Implicit in these hard-core assumptions is the central research objective of the cognitive research program: to understand *the cognitive strategies that policymakers rely upon to construct and maintain their simplified images of the environment.* We find it useful to distinguish two basic types of cognitive strategies, both of which have received substantial attention: (a) reliance on cognitive or knowledge structures that provide frameworks for assimilating new information and choosing among policy options (belief systems, operational codes, cognitive maps, scripts); (b) reliance on low-effort judgmental and choice heuristics that permit policymakers to make up their minds quickly and with confidence in the correctness of their positions (e.g., "satisficing" decision rules, the availability, representativeness, and anchoring heuristics).

These two (by no means mutually exclusive) coping strategies correspond closely to the distinction cognitive psychologists have drawn between declarative knowledge (first category) and procedural knowledge (second category) of mental functioning (cf. Anderson, 1978, 1980). Research on declarative knowledge in the foreign policy domain—which we call representational research—is concerned with clarifying *what* policymakers think. What assumptions do they make about themselves, other states, the relationships among states, the goals or values underlying foreign policy, and the types of policies most instrumental to attaining those goals or values? Can typologies or taxonomies of foreign policy belief systems be developed? To what extent and in what ways do policymakers' initial beliefs or assumptions guide—even dominate—the interpretation of new evidence and the making of new decisions? The best-known examples of representational research are studies of the operational codes and cognitive maps of political elites (Axelrod, 1976; George, 1969, 1980; Heradstveit, 1981; Holsti, 1977). Research on procedural knowledge—which we call process research—is concerned with identifying abstract (content-free) laws of cognitive functioning that focus on *how* policymakers think about issues (the intellectual roots of process research can be directly traced to experimental cognitive and social psychology). The best-known examples of process research are studies of perception and misperception in international relations: the rules or heuristics that policymakers use in seeking causal explanations for the behavior of other states, in drawing lessons from history or in choosing among courses of action (cf. George, 1980; Jervis, 1976, 1982; Tetlock, 1983b).

Reasonable challenges can be raised to the hard-core premises of the program. One can question, for instance, the causal importance of policymakers' cognitions about the environment. Correlations between cognitions and actions are not sufficient to establish causality. The beliefs, perceptions, and values that people express may merely be justifications for policies they have already adopted as a result of other processes (e.g., psychodynamic needs and conflicts, bureaucratic role demands, domestic political pressures, international exigencies).

II.   REPRESENTATIONAL RESEARCH

Psychologists and political scientists have invented an intimidatingly long list of terms to describe the cognitive structures that perceivers rely upon in encoding new information. These terms include "scripts" (Abelson, 1981; Schank and Abelson, 1977); "operational codes" (George, 1969; Holsti, 1977); "cognitive maps" (Axelrod, 1976); "stereotypes" (Allport, 1954; Hamilton, 1979); "frames" (Minsky, 1975); "nuclear scenes" (Tompkins, 1979); "prototypes" (Cantor and Mischel, 1979); as well as the more traditional and inclusive term "schemas" (Nisbett and Ross, 1980). We do not propose a detailed classification of all possible cognitive structures in this chapter (for preliminary efforts in this area see Nisbett and Ross, 1980; Schank and Abelson, 1977; Taylor and Fiske, 1984). Our goals are more modest. We shall focus only on cognitive research specifically concerned with foreign policy. Within that domain, we further restrict our attention to two issues likely to be central to future theoretical developments in the field:

1. What theoretical and methodological tools are at our disposal to describe the cognitive structures that influence foreign policy?

2. To what extent is information processing in the foreign policy domain theory-driven (dominated by existing cognitive structures) as opposed to data-driven (responsive to external reality)?

Describing Foreign Policy Belief Systems

In principle, people can subscribe to an infinite variety of images of their own states, of other states, and of the relationships among states. We use the term "idiographic representational research" to describe case studies which present detailed descriptions of the foreign policy belief systems of individual decision makers. We use the term "nomothetic representational" research to describe studies in which the primary goal is the development and testing of general theoretical statements that apply to large populations of individuals. The focus thus shifts from the uniqueness of particular policymakers to underlying similarities or themes that permit cross-individual and cross-situational comparisons. We discuss three lines of nomothetic representational research: the work on operational codes, cognitive mapping, and personality correlates of foreign policy belief systems.

Operational Code Research

Operational codes impose badly needed cognitive order and stability on an ambiguous and complex international environment (George, 1969). They do so in multiple ways: by providing norms, standards, and guidelines that influence (but do not unilaterally determine) decision makers' choices of strategy and tactics in dealings with other nations. George proposed that the essence of an operational code can be captured in its answers to a number of "philosophical" questions concerning the "nature of the political universe" and a number of "instrumental" questions concerning the types of policies most likely to achieve important objectives (see also Holsti, 1977).

Operational codes are organized hierarchically such that central or core beliefs exert more influence on peripheral beliefs than vice versa. One strong "belief candidate" for a central organizing role in operational codes is whether the decision maker believes the political universe to be essentially one of conflict or one of harmony (Holsti, 1977). People who view the world in Hobbesian, zero-sum terms (a war of all against all) are likely to differ on a variety of belief dimensions from those who see the world as potentially harmonious. These two groups will tend to appraise the motives and goals of opponents differently and disagree on the best strategies for pursuing policy goals. Another strong candidate for a central organizing role in operational codes is the decision-maker's belief concerning the root causes of international conflict. People who attribute conflict to different root causes (e.g., human nature, attributes of nations, the international system) will tend to have different views on the likelihood of, and necessary conditions for, long-term peace.

Tetlock (1983b) notes that both sides seem to possess an unlimited capacity to view international events in ways that support their initial positions ("aggressive" Soviet acts can always be construed as defensive responses to external threats; "conciliatory" Soviet acts can always be construed as deceptive maneuvers designed to weaken Western resolve). This is consistent with the "principle of least resistance" in the attitude change literature (McGuire, in press). Those beliefs most likely to "give in" to contradictory evidence are beliefs that have the fewest connections to other beliefs in the cognitive system.

Cognitive Mapping

Cognitive mapping is a methodological technique for capturing the causal structure of policymakers' cognitive representations of policy domains (Axelrod, 1976). Cognitive maps consist of two key elements: concept variables, which are represented as points, and causal beliefs linking the concepts, represented as arrows between points. A concept variable is defined simply: something that can take on different values (e.g., defense spending, American national security, balance of trade). Causal beliefs exist whenever decision makers believe that change in one concept variable leads to change in another variable.

Axelrod and other investigators have constructed a number of cognitive maps based on detailed content analyses of archival documents (e.g., Hitler-Chamberlain negotiations at Munich, the British Far Eastern Committee deliberations on Persia) and interviews with policymakers (e.g., State Department officials, energy experts). These studies demonstrate, at minimum, that: (1) cognitive mapping can be done with acceptable levels of intercoder reliability; (2) policymaking deliberations are saturated with causal arguments and that maps of these deliberations tend to be large and elaborate (in the sense that many different concept variables are causally connected with each other). (See Axelrod, 1976; Bonham and Shapiro, 1976; Bonham, Shapiro, and Trumble, 1979; Levi and Tetlock, 1980; Ross, 1976.)

Systematic analysis of cognitive maps has, however, provided more than descriptive information; it has also deepened our understanding of the cognitive bases of foreign policy. For instance, although cognitive maps are large and causally elaborate, they also tend to be simple, in that maps do not usually include trade-off relationships. Preferred policies usually have only positive consequences; rejected policies, only negative ones (cf. Jervis, 1976). This obviously makes decision making much easier; competing, difficult-to-quantify values do not have to be weighed against each other. Maps also rarely include reciprocal causal relationships (feedback loops) among variables: causality flows in only one direction. Axelrod summarizes the cognitive portrait of the decision-maker that emerges from his work in this way:

> one who has more beliefs than he can handle, who employs a simplified image of the policy environment that is structurally easy to operate with, and who then acts rationally within the context of his simplified image. (1976)

Our confidence in this summary portrait is reinforced by the very similar conclusions that have emerged from laboratory research on judgment and decision making (Abelson and Levi, in press; Einhorn and Hogarth, 1981; Kahneman, Slovic, and Tversky, 1981).

Individual Difference Research on Belief Systems

Even the most prominent advocate of the realist school of international politics—Henry Kissinger—concedes that foreign policymakers "work in darkness"; they make choices not only without knowledge of the future but usually even without adequate knowledge of what is happening in the present (Kissinger, 1979). This "structural uncertainty" (Steinbruner, 1974) of foreign policy problems has led many analysts to propose an analogy between international politics and projective tests used in personality assessment: the international scene, in much the same way as a good projective test, evokes different psychologically important response themes from national leaders. Foreign policy belief systems do not emerge in a psychological vacuum; they emerge as plausible self-expressive responses to the situations in which policymakers find themselves (Etheredge, 1978). From this standpoint, it is essential to study the personality background or context out of which belief systems evolve.

Evidence on relations between personality and foreign policy preferences comes from the full range of methodological sources, including laboratory experiments, surveys, content analyses of archival documents, expert ratings of policymakers, and case studies (Christiansen, 1959; Eckhardt and Lentz, 1967; Etheredge, 1978; Lasswell, 1930; McClosky, 1967; Terhune, 1970; Tetlock, 1981; Tetlock, Crosby, and Crosby, 1981). The similarity in results across methodologies is, moreover, impressive.

These lines of research remind us that foreign policy belief systems do not exist in isolation from broader dimensions of individual differences in interpersonal style, cognitive style, and basic motivational variables. To paraphrase Lasswell (1930), foreign policy beliefs may sometimes serve as rationalizations for psychological needs and tendencies that have been displaced onto the international scene. A critical challenge for future theory will be to resolve the tension between purely cognitive analyses of foreign policy (which grant "functional autonomy" to belief systems) and motivational analyses of foreign policy (which view belief systems as subservient to other psychological variables and systems).

A Comment on Theory-Driven versus Data-Driven Processing

We turn from the nature of foreign policy belief systems to the impact of belief systems on the policymaking process. A casual reader of the literature might easily walk away with the impression that foreign policy is overwhelmingly "theory-driven" (i.e., that the preconceptions policymakers bring to decision-making situations are much more important determinants of the actions taken than is the objective evidence). Both experimental and case study evidence appear to support this conclusion. The laboratory evidence comes from multiple sources, including research on primary effects in impression formation, the resistance of political attitudes and stereotypes to change (Hamilton, 1979; Lord, Ross, and Lepper, 1979); rigidity or set effects in problem solving (Luchins, 1942); and the persistence of causal attributions even after the discrediting of the information on which the attributions were initially based (Nisbett and Ross, 1980). The evidence from actual foreign policy settings comes most importantly from the pioneering work of Jervis (1976). He notes that the historical record contains many references to government leaders who have treated belief-supportive information uncritically while simultaneously searching for all possible flaws in belief-challenging information.

We need to be careful, however, in discussing the theory-driven nature of foreign policy. Reliance on prior beliefs and expectations is not irrational per se (one would expect it from a "good Bayesian"); it becomes irrational only when perseverance and denial dominate openness and flexibility. Cognitive models of foreign policy—like cognitive models generally—must acknowledge the coexistence of theory-driven and data-driven processing. Each is necessary; neither will suffice alone (see Bennett, 1981).

III.   PROCESS RESEARCH

The previous section examined representational research on the beliefs and assumptions decision makers bring to policy problems and on the impact of those beliefs and assumptions on foreign policy. In this section, we focus on the rules or procedures that people may use in making policy decisions: the rules vary widely in form, in complexity, and in the "mental effort" required for their execution (Newell and Simon, 1972; Payne, 1982).

In practice, however, the laboratory and field evidence of the last ten years indicates that people do not rely equally on effort-demanding and top-of-the-head procedural rules. People appear to be "cognitive misers"—effort savers who show a marked preference for simple, low-effort heuristics that permit them to make up their minds quickly, easily, and with confidence in the correctness of the stands they have taken (see Abelson and Levi, in press; Einhorn and Hogarth, 1981; Fischhoff, 1981; Nisbett and Ross, 1980; Taylor and Fiske, 1984).

This "cognitive miser" theme helps to unify research on cognitive processes in foreign policy. We examine here five lines of research: work on the fundamental attribution error, extracting lessons from history, avoidance of value trade-offs, the policy-freezing effects of commitment, and crisis decision making. In each case, the cognitive miser image of the decision maker serves as leitmotif: policymakers often seem unwilling or unable to perform the demanding information-processing tasks required by normative models of judgment and choice.

The "Fundamental Attribution Error"

The fundamental attribution error has been described as a pervasive bias in social perception (Jones, 1979; Nisbett and Ross, 1980; Ross, 1977). Numerous experiments indicate that, in explaining the actions of others, people systematically underestimate the importance of external or situational causes of behavior and overestimate the importance of internal or dispositional causes (Kelley and Michela, 1980; Jones, 1979; Nisbett and Ross, 1980). The most influential explanation for the fundamental attribution error focuses on people's tendency to rely on low-effort judgmental heuristics (as opposed to more demanding procedural rules) in interpreting events. Jones (1979), for instance, argues that in many settings the most cognitively available (first-to-come-to-mind) explanation for behavior is some intrinsic property or disposition of the person who performed the behavior.

Do the laboratory studies describe judgmental processes that also operate in foreign policy settings? Our answer is a tentative yes. Two important qualifications should, however, be noted. First, the natural unit of causal analysis for foreign policymakers is often the nation-state, not the individual human actor used in laboratory experiments. With this caveat, though, much seems to fall into place. Jervis (1976) argues that policymakers tend to see the behavior of other states as more centralized, planned, and coordinated than it is. He notes, for instance, a number of historical situations in which national leaders have ascribed far too much significance to movements of military forces that were routine, accidental, or responses to immediate situational variables (e.g., the North Vietnamese interpretation of reduced American air attacks on Hanoi and Haiphong in 1966 as support for a peace initiative, not a reaction to inclement weather). Jervis also notes historical situations in which policymakers have seriously overestimated the internal coherence of the foreign policies of states. National policies are not always the result of long-term planning; sometimes they are reactions to immediate opportunities or setbacks or the products of miscalculation, miscommunication, bureaucratic infighting, or domestic political pressures. Observers often attribute Machiavellian intentions to policies that are the cumulative result of many unrelated causes (e.g., the Allies exaggerated the coordination among German, Italian, and Japanese moves in the late 1930s and early 1940s; the Soviets saw the failure of the Western powers to invade France in 1943 as part of a well-calculated effort to make the Soviet Union bear the brunt of the war against Nazi Germany).

A second qualification is also, however, necessary to our discussion of the fundamental attribution error. As with belief perseverance, we should refrain from strong normative judgments. We rarely know the true causes of the behavior of other states. In a world in which policymakers are motivated to make or misrepresent their intentions (Heuer, 1981), the truth tends to emerge slowly and rarely completely.

Extracting Lessons from History

Analogical reasoning can be defined as "the transfer of knowledge from one situation to another by a process of mapping—finding a set of one-to-one correspondences (often incomplete) between aspects of one body of information and other" (Gick and Holyoak, 1983, p. 2). Many psychologists regard analogical reasoning as fundamental to human intelligence and problem solving (e.g., Newell and Simon, 1972; Sternberg, 1982). People try to categorize and structure unfamiliar problems in terms of familiar ones.

Students of foreign policy have also paid attention to analogical reasoning—in particular, to how policymakers use historical precedents to justify current policies (George, 1980; Jervis, 1976; May, 1973). Case studies of foreign policy decisions are filled with references to policymakers who were determined to profit from what they think were the lessons of the past (e.g., Stanley Baldwin, Adolf Hitler, Harry Truman, Charles de Gaulle, John F. Kennedy, Lyndon Johnson). For instance, when the Korean War broke out unexpectedly in 1950, Harry Truman perceived parallels with totalitarian aggression in the 1930s and quickly concluded that the North Korean invasion had to be repelled (Paige, 1968). Similarly, Lyndon Johnson's fear of "another Castro" shaped his perceptions of the unrest in the Dominican Republic in 1965 and his judgment of the need for American intervention (Lowenthal, 1972).

There is nothing wrong with trying to learn from the past. Unfortunately, policymakers often draw simplistic, superficial, and biased lessons from history. Various lines of evidence are revealing in this connection:

1. One's political perspective heavily colors the conclusions one draws from history. In a survey of American opinion leaders, Holsti and Rosenau (1979) examined the lessons that supporters and opponents of American involvement drew from the Vietnam War. Prominent lessons for hawks were that the Soviet Union is expansionist and that the United States should avoid graduated escalation and honor alliance commitments. Prominent lessons for doves were that the United States should avoid guerrilla wars (e.g., Angola), that the press is more truthful on foreign policy than the administration, and the civilian leaders should be wary of military advice. Interestingly, *no one lesson* appeared on both the hawk and dove lists (cf. Zimmerman and Axelrod, 1981).

2. If contending states learn anything from one crisis experience to the next, it may be simply to become more belligerent in their dealings with adversaries. Lessons of history are often assimilated into Realpolitik belief systems that emphasize the importance of resolve and toughness when "vital interests" are at stake (Leng, 1983).

3. Policymakers rarely consider a broad range of historical analogies before deciding which one best fits the problem confronting them. They rely on the most salient or cognitively available precedent (usually a precedent that policymakers have experienced at firsthand or that occurred early in their adult lives).

4. Policymakers often draw sweeping generalizations from preferred historical analogies and are insensitive to differences between these analogies and current situations (history, after all, never repeats itself exactly). One rarely hears policymakers, privately or publicly, conceding the partial relevance of several analogies to a problem and then attempting to draw contingent rather than universal generalizations. For example, instead of "If a military buildup (or appeasement), then a nuclear holocaust," one could ask, "Under what conditions will one or the other policy increase or decrease the likelihood of war?"

Avoidance of Value Trade-Offs

In many decision-making situations, there are no clear right or wrong answers. Each policy option has both positive and negative features (e.g., lower inflation is accompanied by higher unemployment; greater military strength is accompanied by greater budget deficits). Available experimental and historical evidence indicates that decision makers find trade-offs unpleasant and tend to avoid them (Abelson and Levi, in press; Einhorn and Hogarth, 1981; Gallhofer and Saris, 1979; George, 1980; Jervis, 1976; Slovic, 1975; Steinbruner, 1974). Trade-offs are unpleasant for cognitive reasons (it is very difficult to "net out" the positive and negative features of alternatives—What common units can be used to compare the value of human lives and one's national credibility as an ally?) and for motivational reasons (it is very difficult to justify to oneself and to others that one has sacrificed one basic value in favor of another). To avoid trade-offs, decision makers rely on a variety of "noncompensatory choice heuristics" (Montgomery and Svenson, 1976). For instance, according to Tversky's (1972) elimination-by-aspects rule, people compare response alternatives on one value dimension at a time, with the values being selected with a probability proportional to their perceived importance. All alternatives not having satisfactory loadings on the first (most important) value are eliminated. A second value is then selected with a probability proportional to its importance, and the process continues until only one option remains.

Experimental data have repeatedly demonstrated the importance of noncompensatory choice heuristics in decision making (Bettman, 1979; Montgomery and Svenson, 1976; Payne, 1976; Tversky, 1972; Wallsten, 1980). In the words of Hammond and Mumpower (1979): "We are not accustomed to presenting the rationale for the choice between values. . . . When our values conflict, we retreat to a singular emphasis on our favorite value."

Research in foreign policy settings supports this generalization. As already noted, cognitive maps of policymaking deliberations make few references to value trade-offs (i.e., policy options typically are not seen as having contradictory effects on "utility"). Similarly, Jervis (1976) has used the term "belief system overkill" to describe the tendency of policymakers in historical situations to avoid trade-offs by generating a plethora of logically independent reasons in support of the stands they have taken. Jervis (1976, p. 137) describes the phenomenon in this way: "decision-makers do not simultaneously estimate how a policy will affect many values. Instead, they look at only one or two most salient values. As they come to favor a policy that seems best on these restricted dimensions, they alter their earlier beliefs and establish new ones so that as many reasons as possible support their choice." (See also George, 1980).

The Freezing Effects of Commitment

Once people have committed themselves to a course of action, they find it very difficult to retreat from that commitment. These "attitude-freezing" effects of commitment have been studied extensively in experimental social psychology and organizational behavior (e.g., Deutsch and Gerard, 1955; Helmreich and Collins, 1968; Janis and Mann, 1977; Kiesler, 1971; Staw, 1980). Public announcement of an attitudinal position increases later resistance to persuasive attacks on the attitude and motivates people to generate cognitions supportive of the attitude. The more irreversible the commitment, the stronger the effects tend to be (Janis and Mann, 1977; Staw, 1980). The most influential explanation for these findings is in terms of cognitive dissonance theory (Festinger, 1964). People seek to justify their commitments (and their self-images as rational, moral beings) by portraying actions they have freely chosen as reasonable and fair.

In addition to the laboratory evidence, many foreign policy examples exist of the "freezing" effects of commitment on the attitudes of national leaders. Jervis (1976) has offered the most comprehensive analysis of such effects. He identifies many plausible examples, including: the unwillingness of the pre-World War II Japanese government to compromise the gains achieved as a result of its large military losses in China, President Wilson's abandonment of his serious reservations about entering World War I after making the crucial decision, and the reluctance of American officials committed to the Diem regime in South Vietnam to acknowledge the regime's shortcomings. To some extent, such postcommitment bolstering of decisions is adaptive (little would be accomplished if we abandoned commitments in the face of the first setback). Postcommitment bolstering becomes "irrational" only when the desire of decision makers to justify their commitments (and to recoup "sunk costs"—Staw, 1980) blinds them to alternative policies with higher expected payoffs. Assessing exactly when postcommitment bolstering becomes irrational is, of course, a tricky judgment call.

Crisis Decision Making

Policymakers fall prey to the previously discussed biases and errors even under favorable information-processing conditions. Policymakers do not, however, always work under favorable conditions. They must sometimes function in highly stressful crisis environments in which they need to analyze large amounts of ambiguous and inconsistent evidence under severe time pressure, always with the knowledge that miscalculations may have serious consequences for their own careers and vital national interests (Brecher, 1979; C. Hermann, 1969; Holsti, Brody and North, 1969; Holsti and George, 1975; Lebow, 1981).

Converging evidence—from laboratory experiments and simulations, historical case studies, and content analyses of decision makers' statements—supports this "disruptive-stress" hypothesis. The experimental literature on the effects of stress is enormous (for reviews, see Janis and Mann, 1977; Staw, Sandelands, and Dutton, 1981). There is basic agreement, though, that high levels of stress reduce the complexity and quality of information processing. The impairment includes a lessened likelihood of accurately identifying and discriminating among unfamiliar stimuli (Postman and Bruner, 1948); rigid reliance on old, now inappropriate problem-solving strategies (Cowen, 1952); reduced search for new information (Schroder, Driver, and Streufert 1967); and heightened intolerance for inconsistent evidence (Streufert and Streufert, 1978).

Case studies and content analyses of historical records point to similar conclusions. As crises intensify, particularly crises that culminate in war, images of environment and policy options appear to simplify and rigidify. Policymakers are more likely to ignore alternative interpretations of events, to attend to a restricted range of options, and to view possible outcomes of the conflict in terms of absolute victory or defeat (C. Hermann, 1972; Holsti, 1972; Holsti and George, 1975; Lebow, 1981; Raphael, 1982; Suedfeld and Tetlock, 1977; Tetlock, 1979, 1983b, 1983c).

Simplification effects are not, however, an automatic reaction to international crises (see Tanter, 1978, for a detailed review). We need a theory—similar to the Janis and Mann (1977) conflict model of decision making—that allows for the possibility that threats to important values do not always disrupt, and sometimes even facilitate, complex information processing. The effects of crises may depend on many factors: individual difference variables (self-image as effective coper, track record of performance in previous crises) and situational variables (the reversibility and severity of existing threats).

IV. CONCLUDING REMARKS

How successful has the cognitive research program been? Many positive signs exist. There is no shortage of theoretical speculation and hypotheses on how cognitive variables influence foreign policy. Considerable research has been done. There are impressive indications of multimethod convergence in the work to date.

A cumulative body of knowledge appears to be developing. Perhaps most important, the research program continues to be "heuristically provocative" in the sense of suggesting new avenues of empirical and theoretical exploration.

But all is not well within the cognitive research program. Current theory is seriously fragmented. Consensus is lacking on the extent to which and the ways in which cognitive variables influence foreign policy. Contradictory examples can be identified for most, if not all, of the theoretical generalizations offered earlier on the role that cognitive variables play in foreign policy. Consider the following claims:

- Policymakers are too slow in revising their initial impressions of an event.
- Policymakers overestimate the importance of long-term planning and underestimate the importance of chance and immediate situational pressures as causes of the behavior of other states.
- Policymakers avoid difficult value trade-offs.
- Policymakers draw simple and biased lessons from history.
- Policymakers rigidly defend and bolster past commitments.
- Policymakers analyze information in especially simplistic and superficial ways under high-stress crisis conditions.

Although the preponderance of the evidence is consistent with the above generalizations, the exceptions cannot be glibly dismissed. One can point to laboratory and historical situations in which the generalizations do not hold up well (e.g., Abelson and Levi, in press; Janis, 1982; Jervis, 1976; Maoz, 1981; McAllister, Mitchell, and Beach, 1979; Payne, 1982; Tetlock, 1983b).

The cognitive research program must ultimately come to grips with these anomalies. We believe a viable cognitive theory will have to take the form of a "contingency theory" of political information processing—one that acknowledges the capacity of people to adopt different modes of information processing in response to changing circumstances. From a contingency theory perspective, the search for immutable laws of cognitive functioning is misguided (Jenkins, 1981; McAllister et al., 1979; Payne, 1982; Tetlock, 1984). The appropriate question is not "What kind of machine is the human information processor?" but rather "What kinds of machines do people become when confronted with particular types of tasks in particular types of environments?" No single cognitive portrait of the policymaker is possible. Under some conditions, people rely on complex information-processing rules that approximate those prescribed by normative models of judgment and choice. Under other conditions, policymakers rely on simple top-of-the-head rules that minimize mental effort and strain. The major objective of the positive heuristic of the research program should not be to arrive at a global characterization of the information processor; rather, it should be to identify the personality and situational boundary conditions for the applicability of different characterizations of the information processor.

REFERENCES

Abelson, R. P. (1968). "Psychological Implication." In R. P. Abelson et al., eds., *Theories of Cognitive Consistency: A Sourcebook*. Chicago: Rand-McNally.

——— (1973). "The Structure of Decision." In R. C. Schank, and K. M. Colby, eds., *Computer Models of Thought and Language*. San Francisco: Freeman.

———— (1981). "Psychological Status of the Script Concept." *American Psychologist* 36: 715–29.

Abelson, R. P., and Levi, A. (3d ed., in press). "Decision-Making and Decision Theory." In G. Lindzey and E. Aronson, eds., *Handbook of Social Psychology.* Reading, MA: Addison-Wesley.

Allison, G. (1972). *Essence of Decision.* Boston: Little, Brown.

Aliport, G. W. (1943). "The Ego in Contemporary Psychology," *Psychological Review* 50: 451–78.

———— (1954). *The Nature of Prejudice.* Garden City, NY: Doubleday/Anchor.

Anderson, J. (1976). *Language, Memory and Thought.* Hillsdale, NJ: Erlbaum.

———— (1978). "Arguments Concerning Representations for Mental Imagery." *Psychological Review* 85: 249–77.

———— (1980). *Cognitive Psychology and Its Implications.* San Francisco: Freeman.

Anderson, P. A., and Thorson, S. J. (1982). "Systems Simulation: Artificial Intelligence Based Simulations of Foreign Policy Decision Making." *Behavioral Science* 27: 176–93.

Axelrod, R. (1976). *Structure of Decision.* Princeton: Princeton University Press.

Bennett, W. L. (1981). "Perception and Cognition: An Information Processing Framework for Politics." In S. Long, ed., *Handbook of Political Behavior.* NY: Plenum.

Bellman, J. R. (1979). *An Information Processing Theory of Consumer Choice.* Reading, MA: Addison-Wesley.

Bonham, G. M., and Shapiro, M. J. (1976). "Explanation of the Unexpected: The Syrian Intervention in Jordan in 1970." In R. P. Axelrod, ed., *Structure of Decision.* Princeton: Princeton University Press.

———— (1977). "Foreign Policy Decision Making in Finland and Austria: The Application of a Cognitive Process Model." In G. M. Bonham and M. J. Shapiro, eds., *Thought and Action in Foreign Policy.* Basel: Birkhauser Verlag.

Bonham, G. M.; Shapiro, M.; and Trumble, T. (1979). "The October War: Changes in Cognitive Orientation Toward the Middle East Conflict." *International Studies Quarterly* 23: 3–44.

Brecher, M. (1979). "State Behavior in a Crisis: A Model." *Journal of Conflict Resolution* 23: 446–80.

Cantor, N., and Mischel, W. (1979). "Prototypes in Person Perception." In L. Berkowitz, ed., *Advances in Experimental Social Psychology.* Vol. 2, NY: Academic Press.

Cantril, H. (1967). *The Human Dimension: Experiences in Policy Research.* New Brunswick: Rutgers University Press.

Christiansen, B. (1959). *Attitudes Toward Foreign Affairs as a Function of Personality.* Oslo: Oslo University Press.

Converse, P. E. (1964). "The Nature of Belief Systems in Mass Publics." In D. Apter, ed., *Ideology and Discontent.* NY: The Free Press.

Cowen, E. L. (1952). "Stress Reduction and Problem Solving Rigidity." *Journal of Consulting Psychology* 16: 425–28.

Deutsch, M., and Gerard, H. (1955). "A Study of Normative and Informational Social Influences upon Individual Judgment." *Journal of Abnormal and Social Psychology* 15: 629–36.

Dollard, J.; Doob, L.; Miller, N.; Mowrer, O. H.; and Sears, R. (1939). *Frustration and Aggression.* New Haven: Yale University Press.

Eckhardt, W., and Lentz, T. (1967). "Factors of War/Peace Attitudes." *Peace Research Reviews* 1: 1–22.

Einhorn, H., and Hogarth, R. M. (1981). "Behavioral Decision Theory." *Annual Review of Psychology* 31: 53–88.

Etheredge, L. S. (1978). *A World of Men: The Private Sources of American Foreign Policy.* Cambridge: MIT Press.

——— (1981). "Government Learning: An Overview." In S. Long, ed., *Handbook of Political Behavior.* NY: Plenum.

Falkowski, L. S., ed. (1979). *Psychological Models in International Politics.* Boulder, CO: Westview Press.

Feifer, G. (February 1981). "Russian Disorders: The Sick Man of Europe." *Harpers.* pp. 41–55.

Festinger, L. (1964). *Conflict, Decision and Dissonance.* Stanford: Stanford University Press.

Fischhoff, B. (1975). "Hindsight and Foresight: The Effects of Outcome Knowledge on Judgment Under Uncertainty." *Journal of Experimental Psychology: Human Perception and Performance* 1: 288–99.

——— (1981). "For Those Condemned to Study the Past: Heuristics and Biases in Hindsight." In D. Kahneman, P. Slovic, and A. Tversky, eds., *Judgment Under Uncertainty.* Cambridge: Cambridge University Press.

——— (1983). "Strategic Policy Preferences: A Behavioral Decision Theory Perspective." *Journal of Social Issues* 39: 133–60.

Gallhofer, I. N., and Saris, W. E. (1979). "Strategy Choices of Foreign Policy-Makers." *Journal of Conflict Resolution* 23: 425–45.

George, A. L. (1969). "The 'Operational Code': A Neglected Approach to the Study of Political Leaders and Decision-Making." *International Studies Quarterly* 13: 190–222.

——— (1980). *Presidential Decisionmaking in Foreign Policy: The Effective Use of Information and Advice.* Boulder, CO: Westview Press.

George, A. L., and Smoke, R. (1974). *Deterrence in American Foreign Policy: Theory and Practice.* NY: Columbia University Press.

Gick, M., and Holyoak, K. (1983). "Schema Induction and Analogical Transfer." *Cognitive Psychology* 15: 1–38.

Hamilton, D. (1979). "A Cognitive-Attributional Analysis of Stereotyping." In L. Berkowitz, ed., *Advances in Experimental Social Psychology.* Vol. 12. NY: Academic Press.

Hammond, D., and Mumpower, J. (1979). "Risks and Safeguards in the Formation of Social Policy." *Knowledge: Creation, Diffusion, Utilization* 1: 245–58.

Helmreich, R., and Collins, B. (1968). "Studies in Forced Compliance: Commitment and Magnitude of Inducement to Comply as Determinants of Opinion Change." *Journal of Personality and Social Psychology* 10: 75–81.

Heradstveit, D. (1974). *Arab and Israeli Elite Perceptions.* Oslo: Universitatforlaget.

——— (1981). *The Arab-Israeli Conflict: Psychological Obstacles to Peace.* Oslo: Universitatforlaget.

Hermann, C. (1969). *Crises in Foreign Policy.* Indianapolis: Bobbs-Merrill.

——— (1972). *International Crises: Insights from Behavioral Research.* NY: The Free Press.

Hermann, M. G. (1980a). "Assessing the Personalities of Soviet Politburo Members." *Personality and Social Psychology Bulletin* 6: 332–52.

——— (1980b). "Explaining Foreign Policy Behavior Using the Personal Characteristics of Political Leaders." *International Studies Quarterly* 24: 7–46.

Heuer, R. (1981). "Strategic Deception and Counter-Deception." *International Studies Quarterly* 25: 294–327.

Hitch, C., and McKean, R. (1965). *The Economics of Defense in the Nuclear Age.* NY: Atheneum.

Holsti, O. R. (1972). *Crisis Escalation War.* Montreal: McGill-Queen's University Press.

——— (1976). "Foreign Policy Formation Viewed Cognitively." In R. Axelrod, ed., *Structure of Decision.* Princeton: Princeton University Press.

——— (1977). "The 'Operational Code' as an Approach to the Analysis of Belief Systems." *Final Report to the National Science Foundation.* Grant No. SOC 75–15368. Duke University.

Holsti, O. R.; Brody, R. A.; and North, R. C. (1969). "The Management of International Crisis: Affect and Action in American-Soviet Relations: " In D. G. Pruitt and R. C. Snyder, eds., *Theory and Research on the Causes of War.* Englewood Cliffs, NJ: Prentice-Hall.

Holsti, O. R., and George, A. L. (1975). "Effects of Stress Upon Foreign Policymaking." In C. P. Cotter, ed., *Political Science Annual.* Indianapolis: Bobbs-Merrill.

Holsti, O. R., and Rosenau, J. (1979). "Vietnam, Consensus, and the Belief Systems of American Leaders." *World Politics* 32: 1–56.

Janis, I. (2d ed., 1982), *Groupthink.* Boston: Houghton Mifflin.

Janis, I., and Mann, L. (1977). *Decision Making.* NY: The Free Press.

Jenkins, J. (1981). "Can We Have a Fruitful Cognitive Psychology?" In J. H. Flowers, ed., *Nebraska Symposium on Motivation.* Lincoln: University of Nebraska Press.

Jervis, R. (1976). *Perception and Misperception in International Politics.* Princeton: Princeton University Press.

——— (1982). "Perception and Misperception in International Politics: An Updating of the Analysis." Paper presented at the Annual Meeting of the International Society of Political Psychology, Washington, D.C., June 24–27, 1982.

Jones, E. E. (1979). "The Rocky Road from Acts to Dispositions." *American Psychologist* 34: 107–17.

Kahn, H. (1961). *On Thermonuclear War.* Princeton: Princeton University Press.

Kahneman, D.; Slovic, P.; and Tversky, A., eds. (1981). *Judgment Under Uncertainty: Heuristics and Biases.* Cambridge: Cambridge University Press.

Kaiser, R. (1981). "U.S.-Soviet Relations: Goodbye to Detente." *Foreign Affairs.* Special issue, "America and the World, 1980" 59 (3): 500–21.

Kelley, H. H., and Michela, J. (1980). "Attribution Theory and Research." *Annual Review of Psychology* 31: 457–501.

Kiesler, C., ed. (1971). *The Psychology of Commitment.* NY: Academic Press.

Kissinger, H. A. (1979). *White House Years.* NY: Knopf.

Lakatos, I. (1970). "Falsification and the Methodology of Scientific Research Programs." In I. Lakatos and A. Musgrave, eds., *Criticism and the Growth of Knowledge.* Cambridge: Cambridge University Press.

Lasswell, H. (1930). *Psychopathology and Politics.* Chicago: University of Chicago Press.

Lebow, R. N. (1981). *Between Peace and War.* Baltimore: Johns Hopkins University Press.

Leng, R. J. (1983). "When Will They Ever Learn?: Coercive Bargaining in Recurrent Crises." *Journal of Conflict Resolution* 27: 379–419.

Levi, A., and Tetlock, P. E. (1980). "A Cognitive Analysis of the Japanese Decision to Go to War." *Journal of Conflict Resolution* 24: 195–212.

Lord, C.; Ross, L.; and Lepper, M. (1979). "Biased Assimilation and Attitude Polarization: The Effects of Prior Theory on Subsequently Considered Evidence." *Journal of Personality and Social Psychology* 37: 2098–2108.

Lowenthal, A. F. (1972). *The Dominican Intervention.* Cambridge: Harvard University Press.

Luchins, A. S. (1942). "Mechanization in Problem-Solving: The Effects of Einstellung." *Psychological Monographs* 54: 1–95.

Lyons, E. (1954). *Our Secret Allies.* NY: Duell, Sloan and Pearce.

Maoz, Z. (1981). "The Decision to Raid Entebbe." *Journal of Conflict Resolution* 25: 677–707.

May, E. (1973). *Lessons of the Past.* NY: Oxford University Press.

McAllister, P. W.; Mitchell, T. R.; and Beach, L. R. (1979). "The Contingency Model for the Selection of Decision Strategies: An Empirical Test of the Effects of Significance, Accountability, and Reversibility." *Organizational Behavior and Human Performance* 24: 228–44.

McClosky, H. (1967). "Personality and Attitude Correlates of Foreign Policy Orientation." In J. N. Rosenau, ed., *Domestic Sources of Foreign Policy.* NY: The Free Press.

McGuire, W. J. (3d ed., in press). "The Nature of Attitudes and Attitude Change." In

G. Lindzey and E. Aronson, eds., *Handbook of Social Psychology.* Reading, MA: Addison-Wesley.

Minsky, M. (1975). "A Framework for Representing Knowledge." In P. H. Winston, ed., *Psychology of Computer Vision.* NY: McGraw-Hill.

Montgomery, H., and Svenson, O. (1976). "On Decision Rules and Information Processing Strategies for Choice Among Multiattribute Alternatives." *Scandinavian Journal of Psychology* 17: 283–91.

Newell, A., and Simon, H. A. (1972). *Human Problem Solving.* Englewood Cliffs, NJ: Prentice-Hall.

Niebuhr, R. (1960). *Moral Man and Immoral Society.* NY: Scribner's.

Nisbett, R., and Ross, L. (1980). *Human Inference: Strategies and Shortcomings of Social Judgment.* Englewood Cliffs, NJ: Prentice-Hall.

Paige, G. D. (1968). *The Korean Decision.* NY: The Free Press.

Payne, J. W. (1976). "Task Complexity and Contingent Processing in Decision-Making: An Information Search and Protocol Analysis." *Organizational Behavior and Human Performance* 16: 366–87.

——— (1982). "Contingent Decision Behavior." *Psychological Bulletin* 92: 382–402.

Postman, L., and Bruner, J. S. (1948). "Perception Under Stress." *Psychological Review* 55: 314–23.

Putnam, R. (1971). *The Beliefs of Politicians.* New Haven: Yale University Press.

Raphael, T. D. (1982). "Integrative Complexity Theory and Forecasting International Crises: Berlin 1946–1962." *Journal of Conflict Resolution* 26: 423–50.

Ross, L. (1977). "The Intuitive Psychologist and His Shortcomings: Distortions in the Attribution Process." In L. Berkowitz, ed., *Advances in Experimental Social Psychology.* Vol. 10, NY: Academic Press.

Ross, S. (1976). "Complexity and the Presidency: Gouverneur Morris in the Constitutional Convention." In R. Axelrod, ed., *Structure of Decision.* Princeton: Princeton University Press.

Schank, R. C., and Abelson, R. P. (1977). *Scripts, Plans, Goals and Understanding: An Inquiry into Human Knowledge Structures.* Hillsdale, NJ: Erlbaum.

Schelling, T. (1963). *The Strategy of Conflict.* Cambridge: Harvard University Press.

Schroder, H. M.; Driver, M.; and Streufert, S. (1967). *Human Information Processing.* NY: Holt, Rinehart and Winston.

Simon, H. A. (1957). *Models of Man: Social and Rational.* NY: Wiley.

Slovic, P. (1975). "Choice Between Equally Valued Alternatives." *Journal of Experimental Psychology: Human Perception and Performance* 1: 280–87.

Staw, B. M. (1980). "Rationality and Justification in Organizational Life." In B. M. Staw and L. Cummings, eds., *Research in Organizational Behavior.* Vol. 2. Greenwich, CT: JAI Press.

Staw, B. M.; Sandelands, L. E.; and Dutton, J. E. (1981). "Threat-Rigidity Effects in Organizational Behavior: A Multilevel Analysis." *Administrative Science Quarterly* 26: 501–24.

Steinbruner, J. (1974). *The Cybernetic Theory of Decision.* Princeton: Princeton University Press.

Steinbruner, J., and Carter, B. (1975). "The Organizational Dimension of the Strategic Posture: The Case for Reform." *Daedalus* (Summer) Issued as Vol. 4, No. 3, of *The Proceedings of the American Academy of Arts and Sciences.*

Sternberg, R. J. (1982). *Handbook of Human Intelligence.* NY: Cambridge University Press.

Streufert, S., and Streufert, S. (1978). *Behavior in the Complex Environment.* Washington, D.C.: Winston and Sons.

Suedfeld, P., and Tetlock, P. E. (1977). "Integrative Complexity of Communications in International Crises." *Journal of Conflict Resolution* 21: 168–78.

Tanter, R. (1978). "International Crisis Behavior: An Appraisal of the Literature." In M. Brecher, ed., *Studies of Crisis Behavior.* New Brunswick, NJ: Transaction.

Taylor, S., and Fiske, S. (1984). *Social Cognition.* Reading, MA: Addison-Wesley.

Terhune, K. (1970). "The Effects of Personality on Cooperation and Conflict." In R. G. Swingle, ed., *The Structure of Conflict.* NY: Academic Press.

Tetlock, P. E. (1979). "Identifying Victims of Groupthink from Public Statements of Decision Makers." *Journal of Personality and Social Psychology* 37: 1314–24.

———— (1981). "Personality and Isolationism: Content Analysis of Senatorial Speeches." *Journal of Personality and Social Psychology* 41: 737–43.

———— (1983a). "Accountability and Complexity of Thought." *Journal of Personality and Social Psychology* 45: 74–83.

———— (1983b). "Policy-Makers' Images of International Conflict." *Journal of Social Issues* 39: 67–86.

———— (1983c). "Psychological Research on Foreign Policy: A Methodological Overview." In L. Wheeler, ed., *Review of Personality and Social Psychology.* Vol. 4, Beverly Hills, CA: Sage.

———— (1984). "Accountability: The Neglected Social Context of Judgment and Choice." In B. Staw and L. Cummings, eds., *Research in Organizational Behavior.* Vol. 6, Greenwich, CT: JAI Press.

Tetlock, P. E.; Crosby, F.; and Crosby, T. (1981). "Political Psychobiography." *Micropolitics* 1: 193–213.

Tompkins, S. S. (1979). "Script Theory: Differential Magnification of Affects." In H. E. Howe and R. A. Dienstbier, eds., *Nebraska Symposium on Motivation.* Vol. 26. Lincoln: University of Nebraska Press.

Tuchman, B. (1962). *The Guns of August.* NY: Macmillan.

Tversky, A. (1972). "Elimination by Aspects: A Theory of Choice." *Psychological Review* 79: 281–99.

Walker, S. (1983). "The Motivational Foundations of Political Belief Systems: A Re-analysis of the Operational Code Construct." *International Studies Quarterly* 27: 179–201.

Wallsten, T. (1980). "Processes and Models to Describe Choice and Inference." In T. Wallsten, ed., *Cognitive Processes in Choice and Behavior.* Hillsdale, NJ: Erlbaum.

White, R. K. (1965). "Soviet Perceptions of the U.S. and the U.S.S.R." In H. C. Kelman, ed., *International Behavior.* NY: Holt, Rinehart and Winston.

——— (1969). "Three Not-so-Obvious Contributions of Psychology to Peace." Lewin Memorial Address, *Journal of Social Issues* 25 (4): 23–29.

——— (rev. ed., 1970). *Nobody Wanted War: Misperception in Vietnam and Other Wars.* NY: The Free Press.

——— (1977). "Misperception in the Arab-Israeli Conflict." *Journal of Social Issues* 33 (1): 190–221.

Wohlstetter, A. (1959). "The Delicate Balance of Terror." *Foreign Affairs* 37: 211–35.

Zimmerman, W., and Axelrod, R. P. (1981). "The Lessons of Vietnam and Soviet Foreign Policy." *World Politics* 34: 1–24.

Seduction by Analogy in Vietnam: The Malaya and Korea Analogies

Yuen Foong Khong

At the beginning of Herzog's *Aguirre the Wrath of God,* a troop of Spanish conquistadors is seen debating about whether to continue the dangerous search for El Dorado. The leader of the expedition urged the troop to turn back but lost out to his assistant Aguirre, who, through argument and intimidation, persuaded the entourage to continue. Aguirre invoked the Mexico analogy twice—Cortez founded Mexico against all odds and survived to reap the fortune—to bolster his argument. What he and his entourage did not know was that El Dorado, that "Lost City of Gold," was a fiction invented by the weak Peruvians to trick them. There was no El Dorado. Only death and destruction awaited them.

Analogies have not played quite so decisive a role in convincing America's leaders to fight communism in Greece, Korea or Vietnam. But they did inform the thinking of successive Presidents, Secretaries, Undersecretaries and others who formulated America's post-war foreign policy. As Paul Kattenburg, former chairman of the Interdepartmental Working Group on Vietnam in the early 1960's, puts it, "Reasoning by historical analogy became a virtual ritual in the United States under Secretaries of State Acheson (1949–52), Dulles (1953–58) and Rusk (1961–68). . . . " (1980, p. 98). Dean Acheson, for example, helped convince Congressional leaders to support Truman's request for $400 million in aid to Greece and Turkey in 1947 by emphasizing the drastic consequences of abdicating this responsibility: like apples in a barrel infected by one rotten one, he prophesized, the corruption of Greece would infect Iran and everything east. Truman's decision to defend South Korea in 1950 was strongly influenced by the lessons of the past. He saw North Korea's actions as analogous to those of Hitler's, Mussolini's and Japan's in the 1930s. These events taught that failure to check aggression early on only brought about a world war later (May, 1973, pp. 80–83). If the stakes were so high and the prevention of world war so worthy a goal, it should not come as a surprise that Truman approved MacArthur's march North to roll back totalitarianism (álá Germany and Japan) in the fall of 1950. Four years later, Eisenhower invoked the same analogies to persuade Churchill to join America to prevent the fall of Dien Bien Phu:

> If I may refer again to history; we failed to halt Hirohito, Mussolini and Hitler by not acting in unit and in time. That marked the beginning of many years of stark tragedy and desperate peril. May it not be that our nations have learned something from that lesson? . . . (cited in Pentagon Papers, 1971, v. 1, p. 99)

Churchill rejected the analogy; he feared that joint intervention by the United States and Britain "might well bring the world to the verge of a major war" (cited in Schlesinger, 1966, p.7). John F. Kennedy saw great similarities between Malaya and Vietnam—the New Villages of Malaya became Strategic Hamlets in Vietnam, the major difference being the New Villages worked whereas the Strategic Hamlets did not. In meetings with his advisers, Lyndon Johnson repeatedly voiced worries about Chinese intervention álá Korea if the United States pushed Hanoi too hard; United States intelligence then guessed and we now know that it was improbable that the Chinese would have intervened short of a United States invasion of North Vietnam (Pentagon Papers, v. 4, p. 63; Karnow, 1983, pp. 329, 452–53). More recent and even more dubious uses of analogies include seeing the Nicaraguan contras as the "moral equal of our Founding Fathers," as well as the claim that failure to aid the contras is tantamount to a Munich-like "self-defeating appeasement."

What makes historical analogies so attractive, despite their obvious limitations? I want to argue that historical analogies possess four properties which make them especially endearing to policy makers. One, they explain a new situation to us in terms we are familiar with. This is the "what is" or descriptive property of the analogy. Two, they provide a normative assessment of the situation. This is the "what ought to be" aspect. Three, analogies also prescribe a strategy to get from "what is" to "what ought to be." This is the prescriptive component of the analogy. Four, analogies also suggest what is likely to occur in the future. In other words, they also have predictive abilities. Not all historical analogies exhibit all four characteristics; when they do, however, they become especially potent, and perhaps in the last analysis, mischievous.

I hope to make the above points by examining two of the most important analogies used by policy makers in thinking about Vietnam: Malaya and Korea. Malaya and Korea have also been chosen because they succeed one another as the most important analogies: Malaya being especially relevant from 1961–63, Korea for the crucial years of 1964–66. The structural properties of these two analogies only partially illuminate why they were so popular despite being so imprecise; I am aware that there are cognitive, psychological and historical reasons which also account for their attractiveness. Cognitive explanations, for example, will stress the information processing value of analogies—they allow the policy maker to simplify and assess the vast amount of information out there. Historical-psychological explanations, on the other hand, will stress the degree to which direct experience with the events of the 1930s or 50s conditions policy makers to see future events along those lines. I deal with the cognitive and historical explanations in my research-in-progress; the focus in this paper shall be on the structural properties of analogies.

MALAYA AND THE NEW INSURGENCIES

John F. Kennedy and his New Frontiersmen came into office convinced that China and the Soviet Union formed a monolithic bloc bent on expanding the area under their control. Only containment by the United States—especially in Greece, Turkey and most of all, Korea—have kept the communists at bay. Despite the failure to "integrate" South Korea into the communist bloc, China and the Soviet Union remained inherently expansionist. Their new strategy, however, relied neither on missiles nor conventional troops. "Non-nuclear wars, and sub-limited or guerrilla warfare," Kennedy believed, "have since 1945 constituted the most active and constant threat to Free World security" (Public Papers, 1961, p. 229). National Security Action Memorandum 132, signed by Kennedy in February 1962, reiterated this theme. Kennedy directed Fowler Hamilton, the Administrator of the Agency for International Development, to "give utmost attention and emphasis to programs designed to counter Communist indirect aggression, which I regard as a grave threat during the 1960s" (Pentagon Papers, 1971, v. 2, p. 666). The key word here is indirect, for it was this new communist strategy which called for an appropriate U.S. response.

Kennedy's address to the graduating class of the U.S. Military Academy in the spring of 1962 is worth quoting at length because it spelled out his beliefs more concretely:

> Korea has not been the only battle ground since the end of the Second World War. Men have fought and died in Malaya, in Greece, in the Philippines, in Algeria and Cuba, and Cyprus and almost continuously on the Indo-China Peninsula. No nuclear weapons have been fired. No massive nuclear retaliation has been considered appropriate. This is another type of war, new in its intensity, ancient in its origin—war by guerrillas, subversives, insurgents, assassins, war by ambush instead of by combat; by infiltration, instead of aggression, seeking victory by eroding and exhausting the enemy instead of engaging him. It requires in those situations where we must counter it . . . a whole new kind of strategy, a wholly different kind of force, and therefore a new and wholly different kind of military training (Public Papers, 1962, p. 453).

Quite apart from the problem of telling the new graduates that their training might have been obsolete, this speech exemplified the thinking of the New Frontiersmen. The historian Ernest May found it surprising that documents of the Vietnam debate in 1961 contained few references to the Korean analogy whereas documents of 1964 contained many (May, 1973, p. 96). The diagnosis implied in the above speech explains this "surprise": Malaya, Greece, the Philippines, not Korea, were the models for thinking about Vietnam in the early 1960s. The Korea analogy illustrated the aggressive tendencies of communist regimes well but it had one shortcoming. In 1950, North Korea attempted a conventional invasion of the South; the U.S. U.N. response was also conventional. In 1961–62, the situation in Vietnam was different. Ngo Dinh Diem's South Vietnam was not threatened by an outright invasion of regular North Vietnamese units but by communist guerrillas who were mostly Southerners. Malaya and the other "indirect aggression" analogies were more useful in explaining the new kind of war brewing in South Vietnam and in thinking about the appropriate response to such threats.

The parallels between Malaya and Vietnam are striking. A British colony until 1957, Malaya was occupied by the Japanese during the Second World War. The Malayan Communist Party, reorganized as the Malayan People's Anti-Japanese Army (MPAJA) was the only domestic group to cooperate with the British to mount an armed resistance against the Japanese. MPAJA members, mostly ethnic Chinese, mounted guerrilla operations against the Japanese army. Although they succeeded in making life difficult for the Japanese, they were unable to dislodge them.

The MPAJA, however, attracted a substantial number of recruits and with their anti-imperialists credentials enhanced towards the end of the war, they emerged as a viable contender for power after Japan's surrender. Unlike Ho Chi Minh's Communist Party which took over Hanoi in the aftermath of Japan's defeat, the communists in Malaya did not or were unable to take over. While they did enjoy some support from Chinese peasants and workers, they did not really command the support of most Malays, the majority group in Malaya. When the British returned to Malaya, they quickly and ruthlessly surpressed the communist and the urban organizations (e.g. trade unions) controlled by them. Fighting for their political survival and also reasoning that they did not fight against an imperialist power only to bring back another, the Malayan Communist Party launched a major insurrection in 1948. The insurrection began with the ambush-murder of three European rubber estate managers; assassinations of government officials, terrorizing of uncooperative peasants—the kind of violence which Kennedy alluded to above—were common. The conflict dragged on for twelve years but in the end the guerrillas lost (Short, 1975).

Robert K. G. Thompson is the man most often credited for defeating the guerrillas in Malaya. Initially, the British saw the insurrection as a military problem. They launched large-scale military operations and bombed suspected jungle bases. Two years later, they were worse off than when they began (Hilsman, p. 429). Thompson concluded that so long as the guerrillas had the support—voluntary or involuntary—of the peasants, it was impossible to defeat them. He came up with the idea of "New Villages," secure hamlets where the peasants were isolated from the guerrillas. Civic action teams would visit to provide simple government services and the police would train the peasants in the use of firearms and win their confidence so that the communist sympathizers could be identified. The switch from a "search and destroy" strategy to a "clear and hold" strategy contributed greatly to the successful containment of communism in Malaya.

The Malaya analogy is helpful in making sense of the war in South Vietnam. Those familiar with the case of Malaya can identify similar forces at work: a legitimate government, supported by the majority, is threatened by local communist insurgents bent on seizing power at the behest of China and the Soviet Union. Related to, but distinct from, this description is a normative assessment of the parties in conflict in Malaya-South Vietnam: the cause of the guerrillas is unjust, as are the means—infiltration, assassination, terror—they employ. As such, the guerrillas ought to be defeated in South Vietnam as they were defeated in Malaya.

But the Malaya analogy does more than designate the end of defeating the communist guerrillas as good. It also prescribes a morally acceptable means of countering indirect aggression. By morally acceptable I mean a proportional response. In moral discourse, it is not enough to have a moral end, the means chosen to realize that end must also not incur disproportionate costs relative to the benefits conferred by achieving the end. In other words, a just end can be tarnished by unjust—i.e., disproportionate—means.

The proportional response suggested by the Malaya analogy is the construction of New Villages to physically isolate the guerrilla's potential supporters from the guerrillas. As conceived and executed by Robert K. G. Thompson in Malaya, this response to guerrilla insurgency passes the proportionality test because it leaves the rest of the population in peace and the costs of relocation are imposed on likely supporters. Weighed against the end of preserving a government supported by the majority, the costs do not appear disproportionate. The Kennedy administration encouraged Diem to follow this strategy and provided much of the material (Strategic Hamlet Kits) and money necessary to construct the Strategic Hamlets. It is of course not possible to say that Kennedy and his advisers (especially Roger Hilsman) believed in the Strategic Hamlet program because it was morally sound but it is possible to say that the Malaya analogy did not prescribe a strategy which might have exacted disproportionate costs. The idea of proportional response, with or without its moral dimension, would have appealed to the Kennedy administration. It fitted right in with the strategy of "flexible response," the attempt by Kennedy and his advisers to tailor the amount of force the U.S. should apply to the requirements of any given situation.

The Malaya analogy went beyond prescribing a proportional response, it also suggested that such a response could work. Again, in moral discourse, effectiveness is a critical consideration. Pursuing the most noble goal does not make one's actions morally sound if they are unlikely to achieve the goals. The Malaya analogy predicts a high probability of success: if the problem in Vietnam is like the problem in Malaya and if the New Villages worked in Malaya, then they or their equivalent—the Strategic Hamlets—are likely to work in South Vietnam as well. Thus Roger Hilsman, Assistant Secretary for Far Eastern Affairs, believed that the best way to "pull the teeth of the Viet Cong terrorist campaign" was not by killing them but by protecting the peasants in Strategic Hamlets. "[T]his technique," according to Hilsman, "was used successfully in Malaya against the Communist movement there" (*Department of State Bulletin,* July 8, 1963, p. 44). By suggesting that the prescribed means is able to attain the desired end (defeating the communist guerrillas), the predictive component of the Malaya analogy reinforces the normative weight of Kennedy's policy towards South Vietnam.

KOREA AND THE CHANGING CHARACTER OF THE VIETNAM WAR

By 1965 Malaya was no longer the dominant analogy. Its place was taken by the Korea analogy. The descriptive, normative, prescriptive and predictive elements found in the Malaya analogy are also present in the Korea analogy.

The Korea analogy was invoked primarily to show that the war in Vietnam was a war of aggression by the North against the South. This is in contrast to the Malaya analogy, which, while implying external support, saw the war primarily in terms of Southern guerrillas fighting against the army of South Vietnam (ARVN). The Korean analogy emphasized the more prominent role, if not the direct participation, of North Vietnamese soldiers. Thus Secretary of State Dean Rusk equated the infiltration of North Vietnamese material and men into South Vietnam with the overt aggression of North Korea against South Korea (*DOSB,* June 28, 1965, p. 1032). Lyndon Johnson did the same in his public speeches as well as his private conversations. Years after the he made the fateful decisions of 1965, Johnson admonished Doris Kearns, his biographer, for seeing the Vietnam conflict as a civil war:

> How . . . can you . . . say that South Vietnam is not a separate country with a tradition-ally recognized boundary? . . . Oh sure, there were some Koreans in both North and South Korea who believed their country was one country, yet was there any doubt that North Korean aggression took place? (Kearns, 1976, p. 328)

For William Bundy, perhaps the most consistent proponent of the Korea analogy, Korea forced the relearning of the lessons of the 1930s—"aggression of any sort must be met early and head-on or it will be met later and in tougher circumstances" (*DOSB,* February 8, 1965, p. 168). Adlai Stevenson's United Nation address titled "Aggression from the North" best captures the Johnson administration's position. Stevenson, reversing Kennedy's slighting of the Korea analogy, questioned the relevance of the Malaya, Greece and Philippine analogies and went on to emphasize the parallel between Vietnam and Korea: "North Vietnam's commitment to seize control of the South is no less total than was the commitment of the regime in North Korea in 1950" (*DOSB,* March 22 1965, p. 404).

What is interesting about the descriptive component of the Korea analogy is that it does provide a better description of "what is" in 1964–66. By the fall of 1964, the U.S. was finding "more and more 'bona fide' North Vietnamese soldiers among the infiltrees" (Pentagon Papers, v. 3, p. 207). An estimated ten thousand North Vietnamese troops went South in 1964 (Pentagon Papers, v. 3, p. 207; Cf.

Karnow, 1983, p. 334). As the perceived and actual nature of the war changed from guerrilla warfare to a mixture of guerrilla as well as conventional assaults, there was also a shift from reliance on the Malaya to the Korea analogy. Both the Malaya and Korea analogies explained the nature of the Vietnam conflict in terms we are familiar with; the Korea analogy, however, captured the changing nature of the conflict more successfully.

If one accepts the description of the North-South relationship—i.e., a case of the North trying to conquer the South—given by the Korea analogy, the actions of the North clearly become unjustifiable. Regardless of how it is put, the normative invocation is clear: aggression ought to be stopped, South Vietnam should not be allowed to fall, the United States ought to come to the help of the South.

The Korea analogy does more than merely invoke these normative ends, it also prescribes the means to realize them: through the introduction of U.S. troops. I am not claiming that when policy makers relied on the Korea analogy through-out 1965 in thinking about Vietnam, they were decisively influenced by the Korean strategy of using U.S. troops to halt aggression. However, if one believes that the problem in Vietnam is like the problem in Korea 1950, one is likely to consider quite seriously the ready-made answer supplied by the Korea analogy, namely, the introduction of U.S. troops. In this sense, the introduction of U.S. ground forces as the appropriate response is part and parcel of the Korea analogy.

Like the Malaya analogy, the Korea analogy also prescribed a proportional response. That is, if one accepts the description, provided by the Korea analogy, that the North was attacking the South. Introducing U.S. troops is proportional in the sense that it falls short of more drastic measures (e.g., invading North Vietnam or using nuclear weapons, see Pentagon Papers, v. 3, p. 623) and it is a step beyond merely advising and training the ARVN. If Kennedy's interest in not replying with overwhelming force had to do with the dictates of flexible response and the attempt to calibrate force to meet a given threat, Johnson's reluctance to consider a vastly disproportionate response had to do with the fear of bringing about a general war.

Evidence of Johnson's concern about proportionality can be found in a crucial meeting he had with his Joint Chiefs in July 1965, a few days before his decision to grant McNamara's request for 100 thousand combat troops. Johnson probed the JCS for North Vietnamese and Chinese reactions to the proposed U.S. action. The President was worried: "If we come in with hundreds of thousands of men and billions of dollars, won't this cause China and Russia to come in?" General Johnson, Army Chief of Staff, replied that they would not, to which Johnson retorted: "MacArthur didn't think they would come in either" (cited in Berman, 1982, pp. 117–18). It is well known that Johnson was always careful about not going beyond like MacArthur did. Consequently the use of nuclear weapons, the invasion of North Vietnam, destruction of the latter's dyke system and bombing the North Vietnamese civilians were never even proposed (Gelb and Betts, 1979, pp. 264–65).

Beyond proportionality is the issue of likelihood of success. Here again, the Korea analogy, like the Malaya and virtually all analogies used in thinking about Vietnam, predicts a high probability of success. If the problem in Korea and

Vietnam are essentially similar, it stands to reason that the strategy which proved ultimately successful in Korea, namely U.S. intervention, will also be successful in Vietnam. And probability of success, we have argued earlier, adds moral weight to the policy. By providing an optimistic prediction of the likely outcome of introducing U.S. troops, the Korea analogy makes this policy prescription all the more attractive.

MALAYA, KOREA AND VIETNAM: THE IGNORED DIFFERENCES

Having explored the features of the Malaya and Korea analogies which made them attractive to policy makers, it is necessary to point out that there were those who were suspicious of these analogies, in part and in whole. General L.L. Lemnitzer, Chairman of the Joint Chiefs of Staff in the first two years of Kennedy's administration, was highly skeptical of the Malaya analogy. In a memorandum to General Maxwell Taylor, Kennedy's handpicked personal adviser and soon-to-be successor to Lemnitzer, the latter complained that "The success of the counter-terrorist police organization in Malaya has had considerable impact" on the Kennedy administration's approach to Vietnam. Given the "considerable impact" of the Malaya analogy, General Lemnitzer felt obliged to point out its defects. He pointed to five "major differences between the situations in Malaya and South Vietnam." His analysis is prescient and important enough to be cited in full:

a. Malayan borders were far more controllable in that Thailand cooperated in refusing the Communists an operational safe haven.
b. The racial characteristics of the Chinese insurgents in Malaya made identification and segregation a relatively simple matter as compared to the situation in Vietnam where the Viet Cong cannot be distinguished from the loyal citizen.
c. The scarcity of food in Malaya versus the relative plenty in South Vietnam made the denial of food to the Communist guerrillas a far more important and readily usable weapon in Malaya.
d. Most importantly, in Malaya the British were in actual command, with all of the obvious advantages this entails, and used highly trained Commonwealth troops.
e. Finally, it took the British nearly 12 years to defeat an insurgency which was less strong than the one in South Vietnam. (Pentagon Papers, v. 2, p. 650).

Lemnitzer's critique of the Malaya analogy is interesting because it appreciated the on-the-ground differences between Malaya and South Vietnam. He took issue with the description, prescription and prediction provided by the Malaya analogy. The latter implied that sanctuaries for the guerrillas was not a major issue, Lemnitzer believed that such a description did not conform to the situation in South Vietnam, where the guerrillas could have "safe haven[s]" in Laos and Cambodia. Lemnitzer also found the prescription—emphasis on counter-terrorist police and hence political measures instead of emphasis on military measures— suggested the Malaya analogy wanting. He preferred the Philippine experience, where "the military framework used was highly successful" (Pentagon Papers, v. 2,

p. 650). Finally, Lemnitzer was less sanguine about the prediction of eventual success than Kennedy's civilian advisers. The implication of Lemnitzer's analysis was that the Vietnamese communists would be hard to beat.

History proved Lemnitzer right. Even with American troops and command, the National Liberation Front could not be subdued. Uncontrollable borders, namely sanctuaries and infiltration routes in Laos and Cambodia, also partially explain the difficulty. So does the difficulty of distinguishing loyal from disloyal peasants in Vietnam. There was also the character of the government being helped, a crucial difference omitted in Lemnitzer's analysis. Malaya had a relatively stable and popular government both as a British colony and as a newly independent country; it was apparent even by 1961 that the South Vietnamese government was neither popular nor stable. Within the Diem regime, there was constant infighting and jockeying for power, so much so that the only principals Diem could trust were his brothers and their wives; without, Diem did not encourage the setting up of institutions which could have channeled the political participation of the religious sects, nationalist political parties and students.

The other interesting point about Lemnitzer's critique is that it was ignored. The Kennedy administration continued to believe in the relevance of the Malaya analogy. Thus in April 1963, U. Alexis Johnson, Deputy Under Secretary of State suggested that the post war insurgencies in Burma, Indonesia, Malaya, Indochina and the Philippines were coordinated by China but singled out Malaya as the struggle which "provided valuable lessons which are now being applied in Viet-Nam" (*DOSB*, April 29, 1963, p. 636). Similarly, Roger Hilsman, Kennedy's major adviser on communist insurgencies, claimed that the best way to defeat the Viet Cong was not by killing them but by protecting them in strategic hamlets, a "technique used successfully in Malaya against the Communist movement there." (*DOSB*, July 8, 1963, p. 44).

The Strategic Hamlet program failed. Formally initiated as "Operation SUNRISE" in Bin Duong Province in early 1962, it died with the Ngos in late 1963. The failure of the strategic hamlet does not necessarily mean that the error lay in misapplying the lessons of Malaya to Vietnam but it does make the analogy suspect. It is, however, always necessary to point out the differences which account for the dissimilar outcomes. General Lemnitzer's memorandum—written in late 1961—is a first step in this direction. To be sure Lemnitzer was not addressing himself to the Strategic Hamlet program, but his observations, if correct, could help explain why a similar program was successful in Malaya but not in Vietnam.

The Korea analogy, on the other hand, found its antagonist in George Ball, Under Secretary of State. In an October 1964 memorandum to Dean Rusk, Robert McNamara and McGeorge Bundy, Ball sought to question "the assumptions of our Viet-Nam policy," before deciding in "the next few weeks" between a number of options, including bombing North Vietnam and introducing substantial U.S. ground forces in South Vietnam (Ball, Atlantic Monthly, July 1972, p. 36). Ball wrote:

> . . . I want to emphasize one key point at the outset: The problem of South Viet-Nam is *sui generis*. South Vietnam is not Korea, and in making fundamental decisions it would be a mistake for us to rely too heavily on the Korean analogy (Ball, 1972, p. 37).

Ball, like Lemnitzer, found five differences. Most of them, in this memorandum at least, dealt with the descriptive deficiencies of the Korean analogy: the U.S. had a clear United Nations mandate in Korea but not in South Vietnam; fifty-three other countries provided troops to fight in Korea while the U.S. was "going it alone" in Vietnam. More importantly, Syngman Rhee's government was stable and enjoyed wide support whereas South Vietnam was characterized by "governmental chaos." Perhaps the most important difference Ball identified was over the nature of the war: the Korean War was a classical case of invasion whereas in South Vietnam "there has been no invasion—only slow infiltration. . . . The Viet Cong insurgency does have substantial indigenous support" (Ball, 1972, p. 37). Whether Ball intended it or not, and I think he intended it, spelling out these differences raises questions about the normative assessment as well as the predictions provided by the Korean analogy. If the insurgency enjoyed substantial support and if the South Vietnamese government was incompetent, should and could the South Vietnamese regime be preserved?

Ball received better treatment from his superiors than Lemnitzer did from his. After reading the memorandum, Rusk, McNamara and Bundy debated the arguments with Ball on two successive Saturday afternoons (Atlantic Monthly, July 1972, p. 33). Ball failed to convince his superiors. The lessons of Korea continued to haunt the principal policy makers, almost to a man. Johnson could not forget "the withdrawal of our forces from South Korea and then our immediate reaction to the Communist aggression of 1950" and he worried about "repeating the same sharp reversal" in Vietnam (Johnson, 1971, p. 152). For Dean Rusk, the war in Vietnam, like Korea, was not a civil war but a case of aggression of one state against another across national boundaries. William Bundy argued that it took a war to beat back aggression in Korea and that it might take another to beat back the North Vietnamese and Chinese in Southeast Asia (*DOSB*, June 21, 1965).

If in retrospect some of Lyman Lemnitzer's and George Ball's objections to the Malaya and Korea analogy seem prescient and sound, one needs to remember that their advice was heard but not taken. This was so partly because the descriptive, normative, prescriptive and predictive components of the respective analogies combined to form an internally consistent and remarkably wholesome way to look at Vietnam. Together with the cognitive and historical-psychological reasons alluded to earlier but not discussed in this paper, these structural properties of historical analogies help explain why policy makers hold on to their analogies despite warnings about their limitations.

REFERENCES

Ball, George. "Top Secret: The Prophecy the President Rejected." *Atlantic Monthly*, July 1972.

Berman, Larry. *Planning A Tragedy.* New York: W. W. Norton, 1982.

Gelb, Leslie and Betts, Richard. *The Irony of Vietnam: The System Worked.* Washington D.C.: Brookings, 1979.

Hilsman, Roger. *To Move A Nation.* New York: Doubleday, 1967.

Karnow, Stanley. *Vietnam: A History.* New York: Viking, 1983.

Kattenburg, Paul. *The Vietnam Trauma.* New Jersey: Transaction, 1980.

Kearns, Doris. *Lyndon Johnson and the American Dream.* New York: Harper and Row, 1976.

May, Ernest. *Lessons of the Past: The Use and Misuse of History in American Foreign Policy.* New York: Oxford, 1973.

The Pentagon Papers: The Defense Department History of United States Decision Making on Vietnam. Senator Gravel edition. v. 1–4. Boston: Beacon Press, 1971.

Public Papers of the Presidents: John F. Kennedy.

Public Papers of the Presidents: Lyndon B. Johnson.

Schlesinger, Arthur. *The Bitter Heritage: Vietnam and American Democracy 1941–1966.* Boston: Houghton Mifflin, 1966.

Short, Anthony. *The Communist Insurrection in Malaya 1948–1960.* London: Frederick Muller, 1975.

United States Department of State. *Department of State Bulletin.* 1961–1966.

The Personalities of Bush and Gorbachev Measured at a Distance: Procedures, Portraits, and Policy

David G. Winter,[1] Margaret G. Hermann,[2]
Walter Weintraub,[3] and Stephen G. Walker[4]

INTRODUCTION

In recent months, internal developments within the Soviet Union, and between the Soviet Union and the United States, have raised the possibility of a new era in relations between the superpowers. In 1981, for example, who would have predicted that Ronald Reagan would cap his presidency, against the background of the Statue of Liberty, by exchanging smiles, handshakes, and waves with the leader of the Soviet Union? Or that newspaper headlines would speak of genuinely contested elections within the USSR (even mentioning the familiar democratic electoral paraphernalia of "exit polls"?) With the inauguration of George Bush, each country now has a leader of whom much is expected, yet about whom surprisingly little is known. What is George Bush really like? And who is the "real" Mikhail Gorbachev? How should we interpret their actions? What can we expect when they come together to negotiate?

Political Psychology, Vol.12, No. 2 (1991). Reprinted by permission of Blackwell Publishing.

ON STUDYING BUSH AND GORBACHEV
The Leader as "Projective Screen"

So far, each leader's actions, and even the "manifest" or policy content of their words, are an ambiguous stimulus (not unlike a Rorschach inkblot) in which different observers can read their own interpretations. With his hand initially extended to Congress in cooperation (after a negative campaign filled with innuendo), President Bush has confused liberal opponents and troubled his conservative supporters (Dionne, 1989). Yet in the first 18 months, Bush's administration seemed off to a slow start in terms of defining policy and filling positions, and echos of innuendo still emanated from the Republican National Committee. Events seem to confirm the words of *Time* magazine back during the campaign: "Many who know him find it difficult to imagine what he would do [as president]. . . . Could Bush show the decisiveness, the moral authority and necessary sense of command to guide the country . . . ?"

In the case of Gorbachev, opinion and analysis have been even more sharply divided. Many students of Soviet politics suggest that Gorbachev has chosen peace over socialism—"cooperation with the West over the search for unilateral advantage" (Holloway, 1989, pp. 67, 70); "not the struggle between classes but the common plight of man" (Legvold, 1989, p. 85). In sharp contrast, however, are the words of columnist William Safire (1989): "They're [Soviet leaders] all headed the same way—toward fixing the Soviet economy until it becomes strong enough to feed itself and afford the arms to dominate its neighbors." Richard Nixon's analysis runs along similar lines. Beneath the "fashionably tailored suits, the polished manners and the smooth touch in personal encounters," he suggests, the "new Gorbachev" is mainly motivated toward such familiar Soviet goals: "to erode the strength of the [NATO] alliance" and "to lull the West into a false sense of security," thus to create "a stronger Soviet Union and an expanding Soviet empire" (Nixon, 1989, pp. 207, 211, 218). Vice-President Quayle echos Nixon's doubts: "For although the Soviet leadership professes to adhere to 'new thinking,' it is still quite capable of 'old thinking,' as well" (1989, p. 6). One columnist reached even argued bluntly that "Gorbachev is on [a] power trip" (Charen, 1990). Finally, as we write, a respected authority on Soviet matters concluded that Gorbachev "is in truth a puzzling and enigmatic figure, and is becoming more so as his troubles deepen" (Shulman, 1990, p. 5).

Thus although Bush's career in government service spans several decades, and although Gorbachev has been in office for 6 years, we do not have consensus in the West about the "real" personalities of the two men—their motives, beliefs, operational codes, self-concept, and styles. (They are not unique in this respect. Previous behavior and the manifest content of campaign rhetoric are often of little use in forecasting American presidential behavior, as students of the surprising administrations of Chester Arthur, Harry Truman, and Lyndon Johnson can attest.)

The Importance of Leaders' Personalities

Are the answers to these questions important? Obviously personality is not the only predictor of political behavior, and sometimes it is not even a major predictor. (On December 8, 1941, for example, Franklin D. Roosevelt's personality was largely irrelevant to whether the United States declared war on Japan.) Whatever Bush's and Gorbachev's personalities, their political behavior will be strongly shaped and constrained by situational factors such as budget deficits and economic-organization difficulties, respectively. Still, conditions in both countries do embody many of Greenstein's (1969, chap. 2) classic criteria for identifying occasions when personalities of single actors can have an important influence on events: (1) First, Gorbachev and Bush occupy strategic locations in their respective political systems; (2) The present situation contains many new or ambiguous elements and is open to restructuring; (3) Internally and internationally, opposed forces are delicately balanced; (4) The important issues and problems demand active effort rather than routine role performance.

Thus in the 1990s we have, as it were, an equation in two unknowns. Perhaps psychological interpretations of the personalities of both leaders, drawing on systematic theory and research, could guide our understanding of events and even suggest answers to questions of policy. Yet we lack direct access to either leader, and so analysis and interpretation must be carried out at a distance. We intend this paper as a first step. Though drawn from diverse disciplines, each of the present authors is experienced in studying personality at a distance. We have applied our individual techniques to the study of Bush and Gorbachev, using both a common data set and individually selected additional materials. Drawing on the rather striking convergence of our separate results, we then construct personality profiles for both leaders. We conclude with some predictions and suggest a few broad policy implications.

We are acutely aware of the perils of prediction. What we write, during a time of nationalist ferment in the Baltic republics and negotiations for German unification, will appear in print only after many months. We run the risk of being dramatically wrong. [Indeed, the final draft of this paper was finished in June 1990, when the Iraqi invasion of Kuwait was only a gleam in Saddam Hussein's eye; and revisions were completed even as one columnist pronounced that "the Gorbachev era ends"; see Rosenthal (1990).] Yet if personality assessment at a distance is worth doing, it is worth doing boldly—suggesting answers that go beyond the obvious, to questions that are important.

ASSESSING PERSONALITY AT A DISTANCE

How can psychologists assess the motives of people whom they have never met and cannot study directly? In recent years, personality researchers have developed a variety of objective methods of measuring motives and other personality characteristics "at a distance," through systematic content analysis of speeches, interviews, and other spontaneous verbal material (Hermann, 1977, 1980a, 1980b, 1987; Walker, 1983; Weintraub, 1981, 1989; Winter, 1991; Winter and Stewart, 1977). These techniques have often been used in aggregate studies of political leaders—for example, in predicting foreign policy orientation or propensity for violence (Hermann, 1980a,b; Winter, 1980). Sometimes, though, at-a-distance techniques have been used to construct systematic portraits of particular leaders: Hermann assessed the motives and other personal characteristics of Ronald Reagan (1983) and Syrian leader Hafez Al-Assad (1988); Walker (1986) analyzed

Woodrow Wilson's operational code; Weintraub (1989) studied the verbal behavior of seven recent American presidents; and Winter and Carlson (1988) used the motive scores of Richard Nixon's first inaugural address to resolve several paradoxes of his political career, while seeking validation of these scores from a systematic review of Nixon's public and private life.

When prepared speeches and even "spontaneous" interview responses are scored for any psychological characteristic, skeptical readers often ask whether the resulting scores reflect the motives or other characteristics of the leader or of the speechwriters, or whether the scores are affected by efforts at positive self-presentation (even disinformation). Of course, speechwriters are generally selected for their ability to express what the leader wants to say, especially in the case of important speeches. In most cases, American presidents are involved in the preparation of important speeches [see Safire (1975, pp. 24, 25, 529, 530) and Price (1980, pp. 42–50) regarding Richard Nixon; and Noonan (1990, pp. 68–92, 186–200) regarding Reagan].

Using more spontaneous interview material may reduce (though it does not fully eliminate) this problem. Yet in a larger sense, it may not matter whether the source was the leader or a speechwriter, or whether the speeches reflect "real personality" or self-presentation. Whatever their status, they exist as, are taken as, and have effects as the leader's words.

The major assumption of the present at-a-distance study, then, is that a leader's words and the scores based on them are a reasonable guide to the speaker's personality. More specifically, we assume that the personality variables we have measured, using the procedures we have followed, are sufficiently robust to override any effects of authorship, impression management, disinformation, and ego defensiveness. We further assume that the effects of the particular topics discussed and the situation in which the leader speaks are adequately controlled by the comparison groups that we have used for interpreting the raw scores we obtained (see below). Obviously, these assumptions are debatable; but for us their usefulness rests on the pragmatic criterion of whether the scores are useful in predicting or interpreting interesting and significant political behavior and outcomes.

In the present paper, we apply our various techniques to a comparative study of Bush and Gorbachev. We then suggest some likely trends, opportunities, issues, problems, and pitfalls confronting each leader, both separately and in joint interaction.

PERSONALITY VARIABLES ASSESSED

Taken together, our methods cover quite a range of personality variables, including the major personality domains of motivation, cognition, styles, and traits and defenses, drawn from many different personality theories. In this section, we introduce each variable, describing its theoretical antecedents and how it is measured in verbal behavior, indicating who was responsible for its measurement in the present study, and noting the major references in the personality and political psychology literature. Table I summarizes this information.

Table I MAJOR PERSONALITY VARIABLES ASSESSED AT A DISTANCE
FOR BUSH AND GORBACHEV

Variable	Scoring description and major references
Motives (Hermann, 1987; Winter, 1991)	
Achievement	Concern with excellence, success in competition, or unique accomplishment.
Affiliation	Concern with warm, friendly relationships; friendly, convivial activity; nurturant help.
Power	Concern with impact or effect on others, prestige, or reputation.
Beliefs and styles (Hermann, 1980, 1987)	
Beliefs	
Nationalism	Identification with or favorable reference to own nation; nonidentification with or unfavorable reference to other nations.
Events controllable	Accepts responsibility for planning or initiating action.
Self-confidence	Self seen as instigator of activity, authority figure, or recipient of positive feedback.
Cognitive and interpersonal styles	
Conceptual complexity	Ratio of high complexity words to low complexity words.
Distrust	Doubts, misgivings, or expectation of harm from groups not identified with.
Task emphasis	Ratio of task words to interpersonal words.
Operational code (George, 1969; Walker, 1983, 1990)	
Self-attributions	
Friendly/hostile	Political life seen as harmonious vs. conflicted; relationship with opponents seen as friendly vs. hostile.
Optimistic/pessimistic	Optimism vs. pessimism about realizing values and aspirations.
High/low control	History seen as shaped by people vs. chance.
Comprehensive/limited goals	Articulates goals that are comprehensive and long-range vs. piecemeal and limited.
Self-scripts	
Methods of reaching goals	Verbal (promises, threats) versus action (reward, sanctions); politics (rewards, promises) vs. conflict (sanctions, threats); positive (appeals for support, gives support) vs. negative (resists, opposes).
Verbal style (reflecting traits and defenses) (Weintraub 1981, chap. 2; 1989, chap. 1)	
I/we ratio	Ratio of "I" pronouns to "we" pronouns.
Expression of feeling	Self-described as experiencing some feeling.
Evaluators	Judgments of good/bad, useful/useless, right/wrong, correct/incorrect, proper/improper, pleasant/unpleasant, and exclamations of opinion.
Direct references to audience	Direct references to the audience, the situation, or the physical surroundings.
Adverbial intensifiers	Adverbs that increase the force of a statement.
Rhetorical questions	Questions meant to arouse and engage the audience.
Retractors	Partial or complete retraction of an immediately preceeding statement.
Negatives	All negating words such as "not,""no,""never,""nobody," "nothing,"etc.
Explainers	Reasons or justifications for actions; causal connections.
Qualifiers	Expressions of uncertainty, modifiers that weaken assertions, and phrases contributing vagueness or looseness.
Creative expressions	Novel words or combinations of words; metaphors.

Motives

Motivation involves goals and goal-directed actions. Drawing on the classic theoretical insights of Freud (1915–1917/1961–1963), Jung (1910), and Murray (1938), personality psychologists have in recent decades developed methods of measuring several important human motives through content analysis of fantasy productions of other imaginative verbal material (see Atkinson, 1958). The *achievement motive* involves a concern for excellence and unique accomplishment, and is associated with restless activity, moderate risk-taking, using feedback or knowledge of results, and entrepreneurial activity (see McClelland, 1961). The *affiliation motive* involves a concern for close relations with others. Sometimes it predicts interpersonal warmth and self-disclosure, but under conditions of threat or stress, it can produce a "prickly," defensive orientation to others (see Boyatzis, 1973; McAdams, 1982). The *power motive,* a concern for impact and prestige, leads both to formal social power and also to profligate, impulsive actions such as aggression, drinking, and taking extreme risks (see Winter, 1973; Winter and Stewart, 1978). These three motives are selected from Murray's (1938) comprehensive taxonomy as involving some of the most common and important human goals and concerns. In the present study, power and affiliation motives were scored in two different ways: (a) by Hermann's computer-based adaptation of the original scoring systems, which focuses particularly on verb phrases, and (b) by Winter's (1991) integrated "running text" scoring system, which was also used to score achievement motivation.

Beliefs and Styles

These variables, scored by Hermann, reflect some of the most widely studied beliefs and dimensions of cognitive and interpersonal style, as emphasized in the personality theories of Kelly (1955), Rotter (1990), Rogers (1959) and others. *Nationalism* (or ethnocentrism), a belief in the superiority of one's own group or nation and the inferiority of others, and *distrust,* or suspicion of other people and institutions, are two key belief and stylistic components of authoritarianism, arguably the single most studied personality variable (see Adorno et al., 1950; Brown, 1965, chap. 10; Meloen et al., 1988; and Tucker, 1965).

Belief in the Controllability of Events

This belief captures the ancient distinction between will and fate as determinants of outcomes, as in the famous words of Cassius to Brutus, in Shakespeare's Julius Caesar (I, ii, 140–141):

> The fault, dear Brutus, is not in our stars
> But in ourselves, that we are underlings.

In modern personality research, this belief has been variously conceptualized as internal versus external locus of control (Strickland, 1977) and more recently as facilitating versus debilitating attributional style (Weiner, 1980; Zullow et al., 1989). Among leaders, the belief that events can be controlled is associated with effective action and adaptation.

Self-Confidence

The sense that one is both effective and loved reflects self-esteem and related aspects of the self-concept. Its theoretical roots go back to the psychoanalytic concept of narcissism. Ziller et al. (1977) have demonstrated its importance in leader behavior. Self-confident leaders tend to be active rather than reactive; however, leaders who are less self-confident may be better listeners and more responsive to others.

Conceptual Complexity

Conceptual complexity, or the ability to differentiate aspects or dimensions of the environment, derives from Kelly's theory of personality (1955; see also Bieri. 1961; and Ziller et al., 1977). As a cognitive style, it is negatively related to the "intolerance of ambiguity" (black-and-white thinking) component of authoritarianism. Among leaders, high nationalism and distrust and low conceptual complexity are associated with an aggressive, autocratic, and often simplistic political style.

Task Versus Social-Emotional Emphasis

This variable reflects two different kinds of leadership or interpersonal style, derived from early social psychological studies of experimental small groups [Bales (1958), see Byars (1973) for an extension of this distinction to specifically political material].[5] Task-focused leaders have an "agenda," whether relating to economic affairs or national security. Social-emotional leaders, lower in task emphasis, are more attuned to the subtle nuances, interpersonal structures, and shifting alignments of the political process.

Overall Personality Orientations

Recently Hermann (1987) has elaborated a series of six broad "orientations," each consisting of different combinations of the motivational and cognitive variables that she had previously studied as separate variables. For example, the "expansionist" orientation involves controlling more territory, resources, and people. It involves a combination of power motivation, nationalism and distrust, belief that events can be controlled, self-confidence, and a strong task emphasis. In contrast, the "developmental" orientation (composed of affiliation motivation, nationalism, cognitive complexity, self-confidence, and an interpersonal emphasis) involves improvement (with the help of other countries) rather than expansion. Table II lists these orientations along with their component variables.

Operational Codes and "Self-Scripts"

In contrast to the broad, abstract cognitive elements discussed above, which are drawn from psychological theories of personality, the concept of operational code was developed by political scientists to describe structures of specifically political beliefs. Originated by Leites (1951), the operational code construct has been developed by George (1969), Holsti (1970), and later Walker (1983, 1990). As reformulated by George, a political leader's operational code beliefs can be described as the "answers" (phrased as a choice from among two or more alternatives) to a series of philosophical and instrumental questions such as the following:

Table II PERSONALITY ORIENTATIONS AND THEIR COMPONENT VARIABLES[a]

Orientation	Definition	Component variables
Expansionist	Interest in gaining control over more territory, resources, or people	Power motivation Nationalism Belief in own ability to control events Self-confidence Distrust Task emphasis
Active independent	Interest in participating in the international community, but on one's own terms and without engendering a dependent relationship with another country	Affiliation motivation Nationalism Belief in own ability to control events Cognitive complexity Self-confidence Task emphasis
Influential	Interest in having an impact on other nations' foreign policy behavior, in playing a leadership role in regional or international affairs	Power Motivation Belief in own ability to control events Cognitive complexity Self-confidence Interpersonal emphasis
Mediator/Integrator	Concern with reconciling differences between other nations, with resolving problems in the international arena	Affiliation motivation Belief in own ability to control events Cognitive complexity Interpersonal emphasis
Opportunist	Interest in taking advantage of present circumstances, in dealing effectively with the demands and opportunities of the moment, in being expedient	Cognitive complexity Interpersonal emphasis
Developmental	Commitment to continued improvement of one's own nation with the best help available from other countries or international organizations	Affiliation motivation Nationalism Cognitive complexity Self-confidence Interpersonal emphasis

[a]Source: Adapted from Hermann (1987, pp. 170–173)

What is the essential nature of political life (friendly or hostile)? What are the prospects for realizing one's fundamental political aspirations? How much control can one have over history? How can political goals be pursued effectively? What is the best timing? What is the usefulness of different means?

In the present study, Walker conceptualized the answers to George's philosophical questions as a series of "self-attributions" describing the individual's relationship to the political universe (friendly versus hostile, optimistic versus pessimistic, high versus low control, and comprehensive versus limited goals), and conceptualized the answers to the instrumental questions as a series of "self-scripts" (promises, rewards, threats, sanctions, appeals, giving support, opposition and resistance). Specific self-attributions and self-scripts coded in the present study are shown in Table I. Taken together, these two kinds of codes act as cognitive heuristics, mediating or filtering the day-to-day flow of information about the situation and other political actors. Because the operational code construct is currently undergoing development and refinement (see Walker, 1990), the specific variables actually coded for Bush and Gorbachev are slightly different and the Gorbachev coding is more elaborate, as will be seen in Table VII. For example, the Bush coding emphasized his view of the political universe, while the later Gorbachev coding focused more on his view of self, or how the self was located in relation to that political universe.

Traits and Defenses

Traits are the everyday language of personality description: the enduring ways in which people interact with others and appear to them, as described in the writings of Jung (1921/1971), Eysenck (see Eysenck and Eysenck, 1985), and Allport (1961), among others. On the basis of numerous clinical experimental studies and at-a-distance research, Weintraub (1981, 1986, 1989) has measured several features of verbal style that are indicators of different traits and their characteristic defensive styles (as originally developed in the theoretical work of Anna Freud, 1946). Table III shows how the different verbal style measures, described in Table I, are combined to assess these traits and defenses (see Weintraub, 1989, pp. 95–102).

Recent personality research (see Eysenck and Eysenck, 1985; Norman, 1963) suggests that many of these traits can be further grouped into two major factors: introversion-extraversion and stability-neuroticism.

A Common Theoretical Conception of Personality

While we each have our own conceptions of personality, the present study reflects a shared theoretical view of personality that is eclectic and diverse, with special emphases on (a) motives or goals, (b) adaptive or defensive transformations of these goals, and (c) cognitive characteristics or "algorithms" that filter or process information from the environment.

SELECTING MATERIAL TO BE SCORED

All four methods of assessing personality at a distance are based on content analysis of verbal material, typically transcripts of speeches and press conference responses. In an effort to provide common databases for the present study, the second author assembled two collections of documents: (a) For Bush, there were transcripts of his "stump speech," several television interviews, and the New Hampshire Republican candidates' debate, all from the 1988 presidential election campaign. Comparison materials were available from the two other major candidates, Michael Dukakis and Jesse Jackson. (b) For Gorbachev, there were transcripts of 20 speeches and 27 interviews during the period December 10, 1984 through December 7, 1988. These two collections are referred to as the "standard samples."

Table III   COMPONENT VERBAL STYLE FEATURES OF TRAITS AND DEFENSE

Trait or Defense	Component Features of Verbal Behavior
Interpersonal style	
Engaging (vs. aloof)	Direct references
	Rhetorical questions
Passivity	Frequency of "me"
Oppositional	Negatives
Emotional style	
Emotional expressiveness	High I/we ratio
	Low nonpersonal references
	Expressions of feeling
	Evaluators
	Adverbial intensifiers
	Direct references
	Rhetorical questions
Anxiety	Negatives
	Explainers
	Qualifiers
Depression	High I/we ratio
	Low nonpersonal references
	Direct references
Anger	Negatives
	Frequency of "I" and "we"
Sensitivity to criticism	Adverbial intensifiers
	Negatives
	Evaluators
Decision-making style	
Decisiveness	High ratio of (I + we)/me
Dogmatic	Low qualifiers, low retractors
Impulsive	Low or moderate qualifiers, high retractors
Paranoid	High qualifiers, low retractors
Obsessive	High qualifiers, high retractors

The methods employed by each author, however, vary in the kinds and amounts of verbal material they customarily use, in the ways this material is analyzed, and in the nature and amount of material from other persons needed for making comparisons. Motive imagery scores, for example, are usually standardized within a sample of similar material from as many as 30 other people. In the present study, therefore, some authors selected from the standard samples and added extra material in ways that reflected their customary procedures. Table IV summarizes the materials used to score each category of personality variables.

In measuring Bush's motives, Winter used two sources: (a) scores from the October 12, 1987, speech announcing his candidacy for president, interpreted in comparison to similar speeches by 13 other major 1988 candidates (see Winter, 1988); and (b) his January 20, 1989 Inaugural Address, interpreted in comparison to all previous first inaugural addresses from George Washington through Ronald Reagan (see Winter, 1987, Table 1; 1990). Gorbachev's motive scores were also

Table IV   MATERIALS USED TO SCORE AND COMPARE PERSONALITY VARIABLES

	Material Used For	
Variable	Scoring	Comparison
Bush		
Motives	(a) Standard campaign sample (MGH)	(a) 1988 Standard campaign sample; also sample of 53 world leaders
	(b) Candidacy announcement speech (DGW)	(b) Other 1988 announcement speeches
	(c) Inaugural address (DGW)	(c) Other inaugurals
Beliefs and styles	Standard campaign sample	Standard campaign sample; also sample of 53 world leaders
Operational code	Foreign policy statements from standard campaign sample	Foreign policy statements from standard campaign sample
Traits and defenses	Selections from standard campaign sample	Selections from standard campaign sample; also selections from recent U.S. presidents
Gorbachev		
Motives	(a) Standard sample (MGH)	(a) Sample of 53 world leaders
	(b) Selected interviews from standard sample (DGW)	(b) Interviews from 22 world leaders
	(c) First "report" to CPSU Congress (DGW)	(c) Similar reports by Lenin through Brezhnev
Beliefs and styles	Standard sample	Sample of 53 world leaders
Operational code	Selected paragraphs from standard sample	No explicit comparison
Traits and defenses	Selections from standard sample	Selections from recent U.S. presidents; also (implicitly) selections from other Slavic leaders

based on two sources: (a) From the standard sample, four interviews from the period April–October 1985 (his first year in office), and two interviews from December 1987–June 1988, by which time the main lines of his policy were established, were scored. These were interpreted in comparison to scores from similar interviews with 22 world leaders (see Winter, 1990). (b) To compare Gorbachev with previous Soviet leaders, his first speech ("report") to a Congress of the Communist Party of the Soviet Union, after assuming the position of General Secretary, was scored along with equivalent speeches by Lenin, Stalin, Khrushchev, and Brezhnev.[6]

Hermann measured beliefs, cognitive and interpersonal styles, and affiliation and power motivation from the full standard samples. Bush's raw scores were interpreted in comparison with those of Dukakis and Jackson; Gorbachev's, in comparison with those of a sample of 53 world leaders. [See Hermann (1980b) for a detailed description of this sample.]

Walker measured Bush's operational code by examining campaign statements on foreign policy topics such as the Middle East, South Africa, U.S.-Soviet relations and arms control, and communist insurgency in the Western Hemisphere; as compared to similar statements by Dukakis and Jackson (providing at least an ordinal comparison). For Gorbachev, he examined a random subset of 107 paragraphs (stratified by occasion and topic) from the standard sample. Gorbachev's scores were directly interpreted without comparisons to others because at the time this latter coding was done each element of self-attribution or self-script had been elaborated into a pair of binary alternatives (see Walker, 1990).

Weintraub scored traits and defenses from a 6000–word subset of the standard sample for Bush, and from six interviews of the standard sample for Gorbachev. In both cases, scores were interpreted by comparison with those of seven postwar U.S. presidents (see Weintraub, 1989); Bush was also compared with Dukakis and Jackson, and Gorbachev with a sample of Slavic political leaders.

Methodological Issues

We intend this study as an approach to the goal of a standardized taxonomy for describing personality at a distance. Obviously the variation in materials used across (and sometimes within) each of the authors of this study means that this goal is not yet realized. While such variation creates a certain methodological "looseness" and possible difficulties, we believe that the convergence of results across methods and materials is sufficiently robust in the present case.

Two more specific methodological issues need to be addressed. Procedures for assessing interscorer reliability vary across the different techniques (see the references listed in Table I for details). For the motive, belief, and style variables, category agreement between scorers and experts and among scorers is usually calculated formally, with a standard of 0.85 or higher required for all variables [see Winter (1973, p. 248) for details of category agreement calculation]. While the verbal-style measures of traits are objectively defined (see Weintraub, 1989, pp. 11–16), formal measures of interscorer agreement are not routinely calculated. Operational code analysis involves more holistic interpretation of the speaker's entire line of argument. No formal measures of inter-scorer agreement are calculated.

The Gorbachev material, of course, had been translated from Russian into English (in some interviews, by way of some other intermediate language). Previous research (Hermann, 1980a, p. 352, n. 2; Winter, 1973, pp. 92–93) suggests that little bias on these scoring systems is introduced by this translation process.

RESULTS

Tables V through VIII present the results of the scoring and analysis of data for each of the main domains and variables of personality described in Tables I through IV. For each variable, the tables give scores both in raw form and then in comparison to the appropriate other groups, as discussed above. We will proceed domain by domain, presenting results, drawing conclusions and making predictions on the basis of previous research. In the final selection, we will bring all of

Table V MOTIVES OF BUSH AND GORBACHEV

		Bush			Gorbachev		
		Speech or Comp[a]	Score		Speech or Comp[a]	Score	
Motive	Study		Raw[b]	Comparison[c]		Raw[b]	Comparison[c]
Achievement	DGW	ACS	8.76	61	SS	3.82	59
	DGW	IA	7.85	58	CPSU	5.45	60
Mean				60 H			60 H
SD				1.5			0.5
Affiliation	MGH	WL	0.18	66	WL	0.20	68
		C88		53	PBM		58
	DGW	ACS	4.04	62	SS	3.91	69
		IA	10.81	83	CPSU	1.27	50
Mean				66 H			61 H
SD				10.9			7.8
Power	MGH	WL	0.44	72	WL	0.50	77
		C88		48	BPM		38
	DGW	ACS	8.76	51	SS	5.15	47
		IA	6.92	53	CPSU	1.88	39
Mean				56 M			50 M
SD				9.4			15.8

[a] Speech and/or comparison group for this score: For MGH analysis: SS = Standard sample; WL = Compared to 53 world leaders; BPM = Compared to Brezhnev-era Politburo members; C88 = compared to 1988 candidates. For DGW analysis: ACS = Announcement of candidacy speech (compared to other 1988 candidates); IA = Inaugural address (compared to other first inaugural addresses); SS = Standard sample (compared to 22 other world leaders); CPSU = First report after assuming leadershp to a Communist Party Congress (compared to first reports of other leaders).

[b] Proportion of verb phrases scored for imagery in MGH analysis; images per 1000 words in DGW analysis.

[c] Standard score (based on comparison group as in note a); M = 50, SD = 10. For averaged scores, H = high (one SD or more above comparison mean); M = medium (within SD of comparison mean).

our results, conclusions, and predictions together into integrated personality portraits of Bush and Gorbachev.

Motives

Table V presents motive scores for Bush and Gorbachev. Affiliation and power motives were measured in two different ways (Hermann's and Winter's procedures), using different samples of interviews and speeches, and making comparisons to several different groups of other political leaders. To facilitate comparisons of these different estimates, Table V presents the means and standard deviations for all estimates of each motive. Despite the differences of method, the results suggest reasonably clear and consistent motive profiles for each leader. Bush scores high in the achievement and affiliation motives, but only a little above average in power. (Compared with other Americans—1988 candidates or previous presidents—he is average; compared with leaders from other countries, he is high.) Gorbachev's motive profile—high achievement, high affiliation, and average power—is remarkably similar. As with Bush, the power comparison score depends on the comparison group used. Compared with other Soviet leaders, Gorbachev is low in power motivation; but compared with other world leaders, he is average (Winter) or high (Hermann).[7] This suggests that as a group, Soviet and American leaders may be more power-motivated than the world average.

Comparison to Other United States Presidents and Other World Leaders

Winter (1976, 1988) suggested that achievement, affiliation, and power motives could be conceptualized as three orthogonal dimensions, and that the more similar the motive profiles of any two leaders, the less the Pythagorean distance between the two "points" representing the motive scores of those leaders. By this criterion,[8] Bush and Gorbachev are very similar to each other, and each is more similar to Richard Nixon than to any other United States president. Compared to other world leaders (see Winter, 1990), Gorbachev most closely resembles King Hussein of Jordan, Enrico Berlinguer (leader of the Italian Communist party from 1972 until his death in 1984), Argentine general (later president from 1976 to 1981) Jorge Videla, and Brazilian general (later president from 1974 to 1979) Ernesto Giesel. He is *least* like Ayatollah Khomeini and SWAPO leader Sam Nujoma.

What is the use of such comparisons? Characterizing Bush as a "preppy Nixon" or Mikhail Gorbachev as a "socialist Nixon" may be an entertaining statistical game, but do these comparisons have any broader practical purpose? Similarities of motive profile may draw our attention to deeper similarities of style and performance. Thus Gorbachev, like Nixon, extricated his country from a disastrous "third world" war, and sought rapprochement with long-standing enemies. Like Hussein and Berlinguer, and in contrast to Khomeini, Gorbachev is charting a pragmatic course of realistic compromise through the minefields of militant ideological-theological dispute. Like Nixon, Bush reacts negatively to personalized criticism; also like Nixon, he walks a narrow line between suspicion and the desire to negotiate arms reduction.

These comparisons may also alert us to possible problems and dangers. Would Bush and Gorbachev, like Nixon, be vulnerable to scandal? And if their remarkable flexibility ever fails them, would they rigidly dig in to support a failing line of policy? Thus generals Videla and Geisel both set out to dismantle constricting bureaucracies and expand economic growth; but intractable problems, dissatisfaction, and opposition eventually led them toward authoritarian solutions—"dirty wars" against their own people if not outright attacks on a foreign enemy.

Predictions Based on Motive Scores

In terms of previous at-a-distance research on motives (see Terhune, 1968a, 1968b; Winter, 1980, 1991), the motive profiles of Bush and Gorbachev suggest that they will be *rationally cooperative* (high achievement and affiliation), interested in maximizing joint outcomes rather than exploiting the other (low power). They will *seek arms limitation agreements* (high affiliation) and will be *unlikely or use aggression* in the pursuit of policy (average power). On the other hand, they are sensitive to the nuances of friendship-versus-rejection (high affiliation). Under stress they may become prickly and defensive, especially if they perceive the other side as threatening or exploitative. If backed into an extreme corner in this way, they might even strike out with ill-conceived and inchoate hostility.

Beliefs and Styles

Table VI presents scores for the cognitive variables measured by Hermann's techniques. Again, the results vary somewhat according to which comparison groups are used. Considering the world leaders' comparison scores (which are based on the larger sample), Bush and Gorbachev both score high in nationalism, distrust, and conceptual complexity.[9] Their high complexity scores suggest that Bush and Gorbachev are both able to differentiate among alternative principles, policies, and points of view, and then to integrate these disparate elements into complex higher-order generalizations. Bush and Gorbachev both have strongly nationalist orientations and tend to distrust others. (This distrust may be a sign of the prickly defensiveness that affiliation-motivated people display when they are in uncomfortable situations). In most people, suspicious nationalism goes along with simplistic, black-or-white thinking [see Brown (1963, chap. 10) on these cognitions as features of the authoritarian personality]. In Bush and Gorbachev, however, these tendencies should be mitigated by their high conceptual complexity. Thus they may be able to defuse competitive, "patriotic" issues by making subtle distinctions and complex integrations—in short, by intellectualization.

Gorbachev's average scores on the belief that events are controllable, self-confidence, and task emphasis all suggest a leader who is reasonably capable of sustained, optimistic work. (For a Soviet leader, however, Gorbachev gives much

Table VI   BELIEFS AND STYLES OF BUSH AND GORBACHEV

	Bush			Gorbachev		
		Comparison Scores[b]			Comparison Scores[b]	
Variable	Raw score[a]	World leaders	1988 candidates	Raw score[a]	World leaders	Brezhnev Politburo members
Beliefs						
Nationalism	0.40	76 H	50 M	0.38	74 H	37 L
Events controllable	0.33	35 L	48 M	0.42	41 M	42 M
Self-confidence	0.60	31 L	48 M	0.84	48 M	75 H
Styles						
Conceptual complexity	0.54	64 H	48 M	0.54	64 H	74 H
Distrust	0.29	59 M	49 M	0.39	66 H	69 H
Task emphasis	0.47	37 L	47 M	0.61	48 M	20 L

[a] Proportion of time during which a characteristic that could have been exhibited was in fact exhibited.

[b] Standardized score (based on comparison group noted at the top of the column); M = 50, SD = 10. H = relatively high (one SD or more above comparison mean; M = medium (within one SD of comparison mean); L = relatively low (one SD or more below comparison mean).

greater emphasis to the interpersonal dimension of leadership than to task issues.) Bush's low scores on these three variables, in contrast, suggest a slightly more interpersonally focused leader, who is vulnerable to fatalistic drift (or distraction through affiliative conviviality), at least under stress.

Overall Personality Orientations

Scores on these cognitive variables (as well as scores on their affiliation and power motives) combine to suggest that Gorbachev has a *developmental orientation* to the political process. Previous research (see Hermann, 1987) shows that leaders with this orientation are intent on improving their nations, either economically or militarily, or both. But because they are uncertain that they or their nations can govern events, they are constantly trying to see what others can do to help them and through persuasion to get these others to be of aid. With constant vigilance, such leaders seek out those who appear able to shape events; indeed, they often seem aware of potentially rewarding relationships before most other actors in the international or domestic political system become aware.

Developmentally oriented leaders engage in "controlled dependence": they use others but do not become symbiotic with these others, nor do they try to control or dominate others. Through an attitude of friendliness and collaboration, they make others feel good but do so while committing only a moderate amount of their own resources. By taking the initiative, leaders with this orientation perceive they can work with others to create opportunities for themselves. The ultimate goal is improvement of the condition of the nation, and like a "dog with a bone," these leaders keep maneuvering their governments toward actions that will have some payoff toward that goal. They are not very tolerant of problems or events that take away from this ultimate goal, or of people who do not "pull their weight" in working toward the regime's goal.

Bush also has many aspects of the developmental orientation; but his primary political orientation is that of *integrator* or consensus-builder, concerned with morale and the cohesiveness of the groups with which he works (see Hermann, 1989). Leaders with this orientation see themselves as agents of the people, reflecting their needs and wishes, reconciling differences, and minimizing conflict. They are reactive, working on the policies and programs that their followers want addressed. As an integrator or mediator, Bush would seek to forge compromise and consensus among his constituents, letting them define the agenda rather than imposing one himself. For this orientation, the "best" policy is that which brings together the broadest base of support. Thus these leaders are driven by popularity ratings. For developmental leaders, in contrast, the "best" policy is whatever will solve the problem and improve the condition of the nation. They are driven by vision, thus, in the process, by the need for information, and finally by results.

Operational Codes

Table VII gives the operational code characterizations of each leader. As an incrementalist with limited goals, Bush sees the world as potentially dangerous, calling for a variety of responses but initially emphasizing the paths of conflict (threats,

Table VII   OPERATIONAL CODES OF BUSH AND GORBACHEV[a]

Component	Bush Characterization	Gorbachev Characterization
Self-attributions		
Friendly/hostile	Dangerous (potentially hostile relations with others; varied kinds of opponents)	Friendly (13:0)[b]
Optimistic/pessimistic	Optimistic	Optimistic (9:1)
High/low control	High control	Moderately high control (5:2)
Comprehensive/limited	Limited goals	Comprehensive goals (8:0)
Self-script		
Methods of reaching goals	Conflict	Mixed politics/conflict (9:8); Positive vs. negative (15:5); Verbal vs. action (12:5)

[a] *Note:* The conceptualizations and measurement of some variables were slightly different for Bush and Gorbachev; see text.

[b] Ratio of frequency of first alternative to frequency of second alternative.

sanctions), In a world perceived to be less dangerous and more friendly, Gorbachev has a comprehensive perspective and goals. While he can take either the path of politics (praise, reward) or the path of conflict, his choice of response emphasizes positive reactions rather than negative ones and words rather than action. In simplest terms, Bush employs *specific threats*, while Gorbachev is more likely to make broader *exhortations to virtue*. Both leaders express an optimistic sense of being able to control foreign policy outcomes.

Traits

Table VIII presents the scores on the verbal characteristics that Weintraub (1981, 1989) uses to construct trait ratings. Both Bush and Gorbachev have an engaging interpersonal style (high direct references and rhetorical questions). Bush's higher scores on negatives and "me" pronouns, however, suggest that his engaging style is tinged with oppositional and passive tendencies. In terms of emotional style, Bush and Gorbachev are both highly expressive, but in different ways. Bush shows personally expressive verbal characteristics (high I/we ratio, expressions of feeling, and low nonpersonal references). Gorbachev's expressivity, in contrast, is based on less personal verbal characteristics that suggest intensification and thus perhaps calculation (evaluators, adverbial intensifiers, direct references, and rhetorical questions). Gorbachev thus appears to engage in controlled expression of feelings; he is, in short, an accomplished actor-politician.

Neither Bush nor Gorbachev is especially high in anxiety (average negatives, explainers, and qualifiers), but Bush is perhaps prone to depression (high I/we ratio, direct references, low nonpersonal references). Both leaders are especially sensitive to criticism (high negatives and evaluators, and for Gorbachev, high adverbial

Table VIII   TRAITS AND DEFENSES OF BUSH AND GORBACHEV

Variable	Postwar U.S. Presidents Raw score[a]	Bush Raw score[a]	Comparisons[b] C88	USP	Gorbachev Raw score[a]	Comparison[b] USP
Use of "I"	25.0	47.8	H	H	11.8	L
Use of "we"	18.0	10.4	L	L	19.3	M
I/we ratio	1.4	4.6	H	H	0.6	L
Use of "me"	2.0	3.5	H	H	0.9	L
Expressions of feeling	3.0	4.0	H	M	1.8	L
Evaluators	9.0	15.0	M	H	12.4	H
Direct references to audience	2.0	4.2	H	H	3.1	M
Adverbial intensifiers	13.0	12.9	M	M	21.4	H
Rhetorical questions	1.0	2.5	H	H	2.5	H
Retractors	7.0	10.9	H	M	7.4	M
Negatives	12.0	1.52	M	M	13.1	M
Explainers	5.0	3.5	L	L	5.1	M
Qualifiers	11.0	9.0	M	M	6.3	L
Nonpersonal references	750.0	543.5	L	L	854.1	L
Creative expressions	2.0	4.0	M	M	1.3	L

[a]Frequency per 1000 words.

[b]Comparison groups: C88 = 1988 candidates; USP = postwar U.S. presidents.

intensifiers). In such cases, Bush is especially likely to show anger (high I, we, and negatives), while Gorbachev, in contrast, tends to take control of the challenge (frequent interruptions and direct engagement).

In terms of decision style, Bush appears rather impulsive (low qualifiers and high retractors). Sometimes leaders with this pattern can become paralyzed with indecision in crisis situations. Gorbachev shows a more balanced flexibility (moderate retractors). His low qualifiers score may suggest impulsive tendencies, although this may be in part an artifact of using some interviews in which he answered previously submitted questions. Bush scores moderate on creativity, while Gorbachev scores low. This suggests that Gorbachev draws on others for new ideas and solutions to problems.

Overall, both leaders are engaging, expressive, and perhaps impulsive and prone to anger. Neither is anxious, although Bush may be depressed on occasion. In terms of the broader factors of introversion-extraversion and neuroticism-stability, each leader could therefore be classified as a stable extravert, with Gorbachev a little more so and Bush a little less so on both dimensions.

DISCUSSION: PERSONALITY PORTRAITS, PREDICTIONS, AND POLICY

Personality Portraits of Bush and Gorbachev

Table IX draws together the scores presented in the last section into brief personality portraits of Bush and Gorbachev. Both are motivated primarily for achievement and affiliation—for standards of excellence, improvement, and innovation, as well as for friendly cooperation—rather than for impact, power, and exploitation. At heart, both are somewhat suspicious and nationalistic, characteristics which under threat could be defensively exacerbated by their high affiliation motives. Under most circumstances, however, both are able to recognize and deal with complexity, which keeps their suspicious nationalism under control.

Bush expresses his own emotions openly. He may be somewhat unpredictable, with episodes of impulsive behavior alternating with periods of depression and drift. In these circumstances, his conflict self-script may be engaged. Gorbachev is also expressive, but in a more calculated way. With greater emotional control, he is optimistic and capable of sustained effort, involving mostly positive verbal self-scripts that balance politics and conflict. Both leaders are reasonably stable extraverts.

Table IX   PERSONALITY PORTRAITS OF BUSH AND GORBACHEV

Personality Domain	Bush	Gorbachev
Motives	Achievement and affiliation; only moderate power	Achievement and affiliation; low to moderate power
Beliefs	Distrustful nationalist, but high on cognitive complexity	Distrustful nationalist, but high on cognitive complexity
	Events only seen as partly controllable	Events seen as controllable
	Low self-confidence	High self-confidence
Style	Tends to emphasize people rather than task	Tends to emphasize people and task
Operational code	Sees world as dangerous	Sees world as friendly
	Sets limited goals	Sets comprehensive goals
	Uses conflict	Uses politics (positive words) as well as conflict
Traits	Emotionally expressive	Emotionally expressive, in a calculated way
	Not anxious	Not anxious
	Vulnerable to depression, indecision	Not vulnerable to depression
	Sensitive to criticism	Sensitive to criticism
	Reacts with anger	Reacts by taking control of situation
	Impulsive	Somewhat impulsive
	Reasonably stable extravert	Stable extravert
Overall	*Integrator/mediator orientation* (with secondary developmental/ improvement orientation)	*Developmental/improvement orientation*

Gorbachev, with his developmental orientation, is concerned with solving national problems and seeking national improvement; to accomplish this he would seek out information and approach others for help. While Bush shares some of the characteristics of this developmental orientation, his stronger integrator/mediator orientation would lead him more to reconciling the feelings and opinions of others than to shaping his own agenda.

Predicting Political Outcomes

Cooperation

Considering these portraits in the light of previous at-a-distance research on political leaders, we can characterize both Bush and Gorbachev as leaders who want to be *peacemakers, concerned with development and not prone to seek political ends through violence and war.* They are likely to pursue interdependent rather than independent foreign policies. This conclusion is supported by their motive profiles, their cognitions or beliefs, and their patterns of traits.

With respect to Gorbachev, this analysis supports the "cooperative" view put forward by Holloway (1989) and Legvold (1989), rather than the traditionalist interpretations by Nixon, Quayle, and others quoted at the beginning of this paper.

Much of the Bush presidential record supports a similarly cooperative view. An apparent exception, such as the December 1989 invasion of Panama, would on this interpretation be understood as an expression of Bush's impulsivity rather than any enduring desire for power and conquest. Actually, the whole sequence of Bush's inaction during the October 1989 attempted coup in Panama and his invasion two months later may reflect his alternating tendencies toward passive drift and impulsive action. Our results are also consistent with phrases used by Duffy (1989, pp. 16, 22) to describe Bush's style: "very loyal to people, more than to ideas" and "reactive" (high affiliation motive) "gambles . . . only after carefully researching the odds," "lack of ideological conviction," and "regards almost anything . . . as negotiable" (high achievement motive); and "working his will among fellow [leaders] rather than through appeals to pubic opinion" (high affiliation motive, only moderate power motive).

Negotiation

Given this predisposition toward cooperation, what will happen when Bush and Gorbachev actually negotiate with each other? Of course, high-level negotiations are carefully orchestrated by policy planning staffs, with only limited scope for any effects of leaders' personalities. Nevertheless, it is interesting to extrapolate from several laboratory studies of motivation and negotiation behavior (see Schnackers and Kleinbeck, 1975; Terhune, 1968a, b) in order to estimate what these limited, marginal effects might be.

Under almost all bargaining conditions, achievement-motivated people are consistently the most cooperative negotiators. In international-relations simulation games, they have the highest ratio of cooperative acts to conflict acts. They are low in "military effort"; and while they may lie in simulation game "newspapers," they are likely to tell the truth in direct messages. These tendencies would be reinforced by their overall "developmental" orientations. (Power-motivated people, in contrast, are the most exploitative and conflict-prone.) Extrapolating (perhaps excessively) from these laboratory studies, then, we may expect that *Bush and Gorbachev will be predisposed by their personality dispositions toward coopera- tive negotiations for mutual advantage and toward maximizing joint outcomes.* Affiliation motivation, on the other hand, plays a much more variable role in nego- tiation, depending on the degree of threat in the "payoff matrix" and the perceived similarity of the counterplayer. Under low threat, and when surrounding others are similar in attitude and friendly in style (i.e., "friends"), affiliation-motivated people are genuinely warm and cooperative. Under higher threat, or when faced with strangers or dissimilar, unfriendly others ("enemies"), they can become sus- picious and defensive, perhaps reflecting their fear of rejection, as well as their nationalistic distrust and sensitivity to criticism.

Achievement and affiliation-motivated negotiators tend to articulate "strategic" and "mutual" reasons (rather than "greed") for their choices. They tend to view their partner as a "cooperator" or "fellow worker" rather than a "competitor," "yielder," or "gambler"—but with also occasional negative overtones of "opportunist."

Finally, their overall orientations of developmental (Gorbachev) and mediator (Bush) seem almost perfect foils for each other: Bush seeks a broader consensus; Gorbachev is willing to give that consensus in exchange for developmental help.

Change and Reform

Both leaders are faced with rapidly changing international and (for Gorbachev especially) domestic situations, creating a need for reforms and new policies. Their high achievement motive scores suggest both an opportunity and a possible problem. First, the evidence from laboratory and field studies suggests that people high in achievement motivation are more *likely to change policies that are not working.* For example, achievement-motivated people are more likely to pick up new information and, as a result, to modify their performance on the basis of results [Sinha and Mehta (1972); see also the general discussion in McClelland (1961, pp. 231–233, and 1985, pp. 237–238, 247–249)]. An earlier political example would be the dramatic changes introduced by achievement motivated Richard Nixon in American foreign policy (the opening to China and detente with the Soviet Union) and domestic policy (the "New Economic Policy" of 1971). This *capacity for conceptual breakthrough* seems evident in Gorbachev's words and deeds since 1985.

Among 20th-century American presidents, however, achievement motivation is significantly correlated with Barber's (1977) classification of "active-negative"[10]— that is, showing *under stress a self-defeating "rigidification"* or reluctance to give up an obviously failing policy. Barber's examples include Wilson, Hoover, Johnson, and Nixon, each of whom scored high in achievement motivation. Jimmy Carter, also high in achievement motivation, showed a similar pattern of rigidification and "malaise." These five leaders certainly did not lack the capacity for vision—that is, the ability to size up situations and forecast consequences.

Yet if these five leaders had the vision associated with achievement motivation, why did they sometimes ignore the gathering signs of failure, rigidly pursuing dis- credited policies? 1 suggest that their rigidity can be explained by their *sense of limited control over policy implementation.* Actual policy change involves the political process: compromising on a "less-than-the-best" alternative (in Simon's terms, "satisficing" rather than "optimizing"); repeated negotiating to secure approval from diffuse and decentralized groups; and delegating authority to people of doubtful competence, whom one did not choose and may not trust. Taken together, these steps all reflect the leader's limited control over policy implementation.

To leaders high in achievement motivation but low in power motivation, such lack of personal control over the achievement process would be aversive because they naturally tend to assume personal responsibility for outcomes.[11] To preserve a sense of personal control over outcomes, therefore, they may do one of three things: (1) make demagogic appeals to "the people" over the heads of "the politicians" (as did Wilson), (2) take ethical shortcuts (as did Nixon), or (3) become too deeply involved in minor details or "micromanaging" (as did Carter). Their perspective becomes foreshortened, their frustration mounts, and they become trapped. On the basis of their motive scores, *the problems of frustration and the temptations to popular demagoguery, shortcuts or micromanagement* might be potential problems for Bush and Gorbachev.

Political visions, once articulated, can only be achieved through the political process, success at which is likely to call for power motivation. To a power-motivated leader, building alliances through compromise, negotiating, calculating support, and careful monitoring of delegated authority are the very stuff of power—pleasures in themselves rather than painful distractions from a larger vision. If leaders scoring low or average in power motivation cannot be expected to enjoy these necessary functions, perhaps they can delegate them to a more power-motivated lieutenant. In that case, it becomes important to assess the motives of those around Bush and Gorbachev—people such as James Baker and Aleksandr Yakovlev, whom Legvold has termed "Gorbachev's alter ego" (1989, p. 85).

Another part of the political process involves articulating a political vision to the people. Initially, this involves arousing popular enthusiasm. But no vision is achieved overnight; and so leaders must sustain popular energy, bridging the inevitable times of deprivation and difficulty with continued commitment and sacrifice. These are the situations that call for charismatic leaders—Franklin Roosevelt and Churchill are vivid historical examples—whose high power motives lead them to seek impact on others, as part of "expansionist" or "influential" orientations (see Table II).

Considering the situations and leadership orientations of Bush and Gorbachev, then, we might speculate that any serious future erosion of consensus, or continuing difficulty and failure of development goals, could set the conditions for the emergence of alternative, power-motivated leaders who are better able to articulate (in Bush's words) "the vision thing" and thereby arouse popular enthusiasm and kindle popular energy. In history, the danger of charisma is that enthusiasm, once aroused, often overflows its visionary channels and spills over into aggression toward others.

Policy Implications

Perhaps it is always important to structure negotiations so that both parties like each other. *In negotiations between two affiliation-motivated leaders (each prone to distrust and nationalism), however, it becomes especially critical to insure that initial impressions are favorable:* (1) that the other is perceived as similar, and (2) that agreements on minor matters be used to build the impression of broader underlying agreement that will generate further momentum. For this reason it is probably wise to proceed slowly and cautiously. On each side, the reason for caution is not so much the question of whether the other side is "really" trustworthy, but rather whether they will be *perceived* as trustworthy. Ironically, these policy prescriptions for affiliation-motivated leaders in negotiation are aptly reflected in the advisory words of Richard Nixon—another leader very high in the affiliation motive, and known for being prickly and defensive in the presence of his "enemies"—whose doubts about Gorbachev were quoted at the beginning of this paper:

> The people of the United States and the people of the Soviet Union can be friends. *Because of our profound differences, the governments of our two nations cannot be friends....* Gorbachev's historic challenge is to implement reforms that will *remove those differences* (1989, p. 219, emphasis added).

Given the importance of these symbolic first steps, and the constant mutual potential for prickly defensiveness, some early 1989 exchanges in the U.S. Soviet dialogue seem unfortunate. In May, for example, defense secretary Cheney predicted, on television, that Gorbachev "would ultimately fail; that is to say, that he will not be able to reform the Soviet economy.... And when that happens, he's likely to be replaced by somebody who will be far more hostile...." ("Rethinking a gloomy view," 1989.) Two weeks later, presidential spokesperson Fitzwater described a Gorbachev weapons reduction proposal as "throwing out, in a kind of drugstore cowboy fashion, one arms control proposal after another" (Hoffman, 1989, p. A30).

On the other hand, an incident from the 1989 Malta summit meeting illustrates a more positive way of dealing with sensitivities of this sort (see Maynes, 1990). On the first day of the summit, Gorbachev complained about Bush's repeated statements that changes within the Soviet Union represented an acceptance of "western" democratic values. Democracy, Gorbachev argued, is a "universal" value; Bush's use of "western" had overtones that were humiliating both to himself and to the Soviet people. Bush replied that he had never thought about this; since that time, he has omitted the adjective "western" when speaking of "democratic values."

Since both leaders have the capacity for conceptualizing and articulating change, but also have possible problems with implementing that change, each leader would do well to cultivate implementation "back-up," in the form of associates whose power motivation would enable them to enjoy the political process in its own terms and for its own sake. Ideally, these associates should be immune from distrustful nationalism, be deliberative instead of impulsive, and be decisive (for Bush) and creative (for Gorbachev).

SUMMARY

Based on previous research with other political leaders and laboratory studies of ordinary people, there is reason to be optimistic about the impact of the personalities of Bush and Gorbachev on world peace and international cooperation, at least between the superpowers. Their motives seem benign. Their political orientations seem complementary—almost ideally so. To get the reconciliation, integration and wider consensus that he seeks, Bush seems willing to give the development help that Gorbachev wants and needs. Their beliefs and operational codes are largely compatible, with any problems (such as nationalism, or a low sense that events are controllable) being overcome by their traits and cognitive and interpersonal styles.

The biggest problem for both leaders is likely to be a sense of frustration and possible malaise if new ideas, structural reforms, and emerging reconciliations become bogged down in the mire of political opposition. Given the situation of the Soviet economy and nationalities, these are likely to be especially acute problems for Gorbachev, although long-term United States economic vulnerabilities could pose the same problem for Bush. In those circumstances, their personalities could make them vulnerable to frustration and depression; in an extreme case, even to impulsive and inchoate violence. Moreover, their low power motivation, in combination with latent sensitivity and distrust, could jeopardize their continuation in office.

So far at least, the 1989 and 1990 summit meetings between Bush and Gorbachev support the analyses suggested in this paper, demonstrating that with a positive start and especially strong efforts to minimize the mutual sense of threat, negotiations can proceed cooperatively toward a new structure of superpower peace.

ACKNOWLEDGMENTS

This paper is based on two symposia in which all four authors participated: "Assessing the personality characteristics of the current presidential candidates," at the July 1988 annual meeting of the International Society of Political Psychology, and "How Gorbachev's personality shapes Soviet foreign policy behavior," at the March 1989 annual meeting of the International Studies Association.

REFERENCES

Adorno, T. W., Frenkel-Brunswik, E., Levinson, D. J., and Sanford, R. N. (1950). *The authoritarian personality.* New York: Harper.

Allport, G. W. (1961). *Pattern and growth in personality.* New York: Holt, Rinehart, & Winston.

Atkinson, J. W. (Ed.). (1958). *Motives in fantasy, action, and society.* Princeton, NJ: Van Nostrand.

Bales, R. E (1958). Task roles and social roles in problem-solving groups. In E. E. Maccoby, T. M. Newcomb, and E. L. Hartley (Eds.), *Readings in social psychology* (3rd ed., pp. 437–447). New York: Holt, Rinehart, & Winston.

Barber, J. D. (1977). *Presidential character: Predicting Performance in the White House.* 2nd ed. Englewood Cliffs, NJ: Prentice-Hall.

Bieri, J. (1961). Complexity-simplicity as a personality variable in cognitive and preferential behavior. In D. W. Fiske and S. R. Maddi (Eds.), *Functions of varied experience* (pp. 355–379). Homewood, IL: Dorsey.

Boyatzis, R. (1973). Affiliation motivation. In D. C. McClelland & R. S. Steele (Eds.), *Human motivation* (pp. 252–276). Morristown, NJ: General Learning Press.

Brown, R. W. (1965). *Social psychology.* New York: Free Press.

Byars, R. S. (1973). Small-group theory and shifting styles of political leadership. *Comparative Political Studies,* 5, 443–469.

Charen, M. (1990, February 13). Gorbachev is on power trip. *Ann Arbor News,* p. All.

Dionne, E. J., Jr. (1989, May 14). Conservatives find Bush troubling. *New York Times,* section I, p. 24.

Duffy, M. (1989, August 21). Mr. Consensus. *Time,* 134, 16–22.

Eysenck, H. J., and Eysenck, M. W. (1985). *Personality and individual differences: A natural science approach.* New York: Plenum.

Freud, A. (1946). *The ego and the mechanisms of defense.* New York: International Universities Press.

Freud, S. (1961–1963). *Introductory lectures on psychoanalysis.* In J. Strachey (Ed.), *Standard edition of the complete psychological works of Sigmund Freud* (Vol. 15,16). London: Hogarth Press. (Original work published 1915–1917)

George, A. L. (1969). The "operational code: " A neglected approach to the study of political leaders and decision-making. *International Studies Quarterly* 13, 190–222.

Greenstein, F. 1. (1969). *Personality and politics.* Chicago: Markham.

Hermann, M. G. (Ed.) (1977). *A psychological examination of political leaders.* New York: Free Press.

Hermann, M. G. (1980a). Assessing the personalities of Soviet Politburo members. *Personality and Social Psychology Bulletin,* 6, 332–352.

Hermann, M. G. (1980b). Explaining foreign policy behavior using the personal characteristics of political leaders. *International Studies Quarterly,* 24, 7–46.

Hermann, M. G. (1983). Assessing personality at a distance: A portrait of Ronald Reagan. *Mershon Center Quarterly Report,* 7(6). Columbus, OH: Mershon Center of the Ohio State University.

Hermann, M. G. (1987). Assessing the foreign policy role orientations of sub-Saharan African leaders. In S. G. Walker (Ed.), *Role theory and foreign policy analysis* (pp. 161–198). Durham, NC: Duke University Press.

Hermann, M. G. (1988). Syria's Hafez Al-Assad. In B. Kellerman and J. Rubin (Eds.), *Leadership and negotiation in the Middle East* (pp. 70–95). New York: Praeger.

Hermann, M. G. (1989, Spring). Defining the Bush presidential style. *Mershon Memo.* Columbus OH: Ohio State University.

Hoffman, D. (1989, May 17). Gorbachev's gambits challenged. *Washington Post,* p. A1, A30.

Holloway, D. (1989). Gorbachev's new thinking. *Foreign Affairs,* 68(1), 66–81.

Holsti, O. (1970). The "Operational Code" approach to the study of political leaders: John Foster Dulles's philosophical and instrumental beliefs. *Canadian Journal of Political Science,* 3, 123–157.

Jervis, R. (1976). *Perception and misperception in international politics.* Princeton, NJ: Princeton University Press.

Jung, C. J. (1910). The association method. *American Journal of Psychology,* 21, 219–240.

Jung, C. J. (1971). *Psychological types.* In *The connected works of. C. J. Jung* (Vol. 6). Princeton, NJ: Princeton University Press. (Original work published 1921)

Kelly, G. A. (1955). *A theory of personality.* New York: Norton.

Legvold, R. (1989). The revolution in Soviet foreign policy. *Foreign Affairs.* 68, 82–98.

Leites, N. (1951). *The operational code of the Politburo.* New York: McGraw-Hill.

McAdams, D. P. (1982). Intimacy motivation. In A. 1. Stewart, (Ed.), *Motivation and society* (pp. 133–171). San Francisco: Jossey-Bass.

McClelland, D. C. (1961). *The achieving society.* Princeton, NJ: Van Nostrand.

Maynes, C. W. (1990). America without the Cold War. *Foreign Policy, 78,* 3–26.

Meloen, J. D., Hagendoom, L., Raaijmakers, Q., and Visser, L. (1988). Authoritarianism and the revival of political racism: Reassessment in the Netherlands of the reliability and validity of the concept of authoritarianism by Adorno *et al., Political Psychology,* 9, 413–429.

Murray, H. A. (1938). *Explorations in personality.* New York: Oxford University Press.

Nixon, R. M. (1989). American foreign policy: The Bush agenda. *Foreign Affairs.* 68, 199–219.

Noonan, P. (1990). *Present at the revolution.* New York: Random House.

Norman, W. (1963). Toward an adequate taxonomy of personality attributes: Replicated factor structure in peer nomination personality ratings. *Journal of Abnormal and Social Psychology,* 60, 574–583.

Parsons, T., and Bales, R. F. (1955). *Family: Socialization and interaction process.* Glencoe, IL: Free Press.

Price, R. (1977). *With Nixon.* New York: Viking Press.

Quayle, J. D. (1989, June 9). Text of remarks by the Vice President at the Conference on Atlantic Community. Washington, DC: Office of the Vice President.

Rethinking a gloomy view on perestroika. (1989, May 2). *New York Times,* p. I.

Rogers, C. R. (1959). A theory of therapy, personality, and interpersonal relationships, as developed in the client-centered framework. In S. Koch (Ed.), *Psychology: A study of a science,* Vol. 3. (pp. 184–256). New York: McGraw-Hill.

Rosenthal, A. M. (1990, September 21). The Gorbachev era ends. *New York Times,* p. A13.

Rotter, J. B. (1990). Internal versus external control of reinforcement: A case history of a variable. *American Psychologist,* 45, 489–493.

Safire, W. (1975). *Before the fall: An inside view of the pre-Watergate White House.* New York: Belmont Tower Books.

Safire, W. (1989, March 27). *Taking the crabby view of the grinning Russkies. New York Times,* section I, p. 17.

Schmitt, D. (1990, July). *Measuring the motives of Soviet leaders and Soviet society: Congruence created or congruence reflected?* Paper presented at the annual meeting of the International Society of Political Psychology, Washington. D.C.

Schnackers, U., and Kleinbeck, U. (1975). Machmotiv und machtthematisches Verhalten in einem Verhandlungsspiel [Power motivation and power-related behavior in a bargaining game]. *Archiv für Psychologie,* 127, 300–319.

Shulman, M. D. (1990, June 17). How well do we know this man? Review of D. Doder and L. Branson, *Gorbochev: Heretic in the Kremlin. New York Times Book Review,* p. 5.

Sinha, B. P., and Mehta, P. (1972). Farmers' need for achievement and change-proneness in acquisition of information from a farm telecast. *Rural Sociology,* 37, 417–427.

Strickland, B. (1977). Internal-external control of reinforcement. In T. Blass. (Ed.), *Personality variables in social behavior* (pp. 219–279). Hillsdale, NJ: Erlbaum.

Terhune, K. W. (1968a). Motives, situation, and interpersonal conflict within prisoners' dilemma. *Journal of Personality and Social Psychology Monograph Supplement,* 8, part 2.

Terhune, K. W. (1968b). Studies of motives, cooperation, and conflict within laboratory microcosms. *Buffalo Studies, 4,* 29–58.

Tetlock, P. E., and Boettger, R. (1989). Cognitive and rhetorical styles of traditionalist and reformist Soviet politicians: A content analysis study. *Political Psychology,* 10, 209–232.

Tucker, R. C. (1965). The dictator and totalitarianism. *World Politics,* 17, 55–83.

Walker, S. (1983). The motivational foundations of political belief systems: A re-analysis of the operational code construct. *International Studies Quarterly,* 27, 179–201.

Walker, S. (1986, July). *Woodrow Wilson's operational code.* Paper presented at the meeting of the International Society of Political Psychology, Amsterdam.

Walker, S. (1990). The evolution of operational code analysis. *Political Psychology,* 11. 403–418.

Weiner, B. (1980). *Human motivation.* New York: Holt, Rinehart and Winston.

Weintraub, W. (1981). *Verbal behavior: Adaptation and psychopathology.* New York: Springer.

Weintraub, W. (1986). Personality profiles of American presidents as revealed in their public statements: The presidential news conferences of Jimmy Carter and Ronald Reagan. *Political Psychology,* 7, 285–295.

Weintraub, W. (1989). *Verbal behavior in everyday life.* New York: Springer.

Winter, D. G. (1973). *The power motive.* New York: Free Press.

Winter, D. G. (1979). *Psychological characteristics of selected world leaders assessed at a distance.* Unpublished paper, Wesleyan University.

Winter, D. G. (1980). Measuring the motive patterns of southern Africa political leaders at a distance. *Political Psychology,* 2, 75–85.

Winter, D. G. (1987). Leader appeal, leader performance, and the motive profiles of leaders and followers: A study of American presidents and elections. *Journal of Personality and Social Psychology,* 52, 196–202.

Winter, D. G. (1988, July). What makes Jesse run? [Motives of the 1988 candidates]. *Psychology Today,* pp. 20ff.

Winter, D. G. (1990). *Inventory of motive scores of persons, groups, and societies measured at a distance.* Ann Arbor: University of Michigan Department of Psychology.

Winter, D. G. (1991). Measuring personality at a distance: Development of an integrated system for scoring motives in running text. In A. J. Stewart, J. M. Healy, Jr., and D. J. Ozer, (Eds.), *Perspectives in personality: Approaches to understanding lives.* London: Jessica Kingsley.

Winter, D. G., and Carlson, L. (1988). Using motive scores in the psychobiographical study of an individual: The case of Richard Nixon. *Journal of Personality,* 56, 75–102.

Winter, D. G., and Stewart, A. J. (1977). Content analysis as a method of studying political leaders. In M. G. Hermann (Ed.), *A psychological examination of political leaders* (pp. 27–61). New York: Free Press.

Winter, D. G., and Stewart, A. J (1978). The power motive. In H. London, and J. Exner (Eds.), *Dimensions of personality* (pp. 391–447). New York: Wiley.

Ziller, R. C., Stone, W. F., Jackson, R. M., and Terbovic, N. J. (1977). Self-other orientations and political behavior. In M. G. Hermann (Ed.), *A psychological examination of political leaders* (pp. 176–204). New York: Free Press.

Zullow, H. M., Oettingen, G., Peterson, C., and Seligman, M. E. P. (1988). Pessimistic explanatory style in the historical record: CAVing LBJ, presidential candidates, and East versus West Berlin. *American Psychologist,* 43, 673–682.

NOTES

1. Department of Psychology. University of Michigan. Ann Arbor, Michigan 48109.
2. Mershon Center, Ohio State University. Columbus, Ohio 43201.
3. Department of Psychiatry, University of Maryland School of Medicine. Baltimore, Maryland 21201.
4. Department of Political Science. Arizona State University. Tempe, Arizona 85281.
5. Parsons and Bales (1955) suggest that these two kinds of leaders reflect the even more basic distinction between "instrumental" and "expressive" functions.
6. We are grateful to David Schmidt (1990) for assembling this speech material, and to Janet E. Malley for scoring it. Malenkov, Andropov, and Chernenko were not included because they did not, as party leaders, give such a speech to a CPSU Congress. It is difficult to know whether Stalin's 1924 "Organizational Report," and even more, Lenin's 1918 "Political Report," can be properly compared with the later reports, which were given in a much different organizational setting and political climate. For standardization purposes, however. they were included because it was desirable to use as large a sample as possible.
7. One final source of data can be used to estimate Gorbachev's motive profile. His December 7, 1988, speech to the United Nations, when compared with the average of John F. Kennedy's two United Nations addresses, shows similar achievement and affiliation motivation levels, and a much lower power motive. Compared with other American presidents, Kennedy's Inaugural Address was about average in achievement and very high in affiliation and power (see Winter, 1987). Assuming that Kennedy's UN speeches were really similar to his inaugural (for which we have standardized scores), this would at least suggest that Gorbachev is relatively high in affiliation and low in power.
8. These comparisons were made using Bush's inaugural scores and Gorbachev's interview scores ("IA" and "SS," respectively, in Table IV).
9. Tetlock and Boettger (1989) found that Gorbachev scores high on a different but related measure of integrative complexity. Tetlock also found (personal communication) that Bush scored low during his vice-presidential years, but has increased to moderate as president.
10. Barber (1977) argues the reverse: that active-negative presidents are power-driven, while active-positives want to achieve. Since his analysis refers to manifest actions and results, rather than to latent motives, there is no necessary conflict with the present results. In addition, Barber's use of "achievement" and "power" motives is probably different from the scoring definitions.
11. To illustrate: In response to the disarmingly simple question, "Why not the best?" that Jimmy Carter used as the title of his campaign autobiography, a seasoned politician can suggest several "realpolitik" answers: (1) because members of Congress, foreign leaders, and others with veto power may have different ideas about what is "best;" (2) because "the best" might not benefit powerful constituencies; (3) because getting to "the best" may involve delays and detours—a "Pilgrim's Progress" through the quagmire of politics; (4) because "the best" costs too much; and (5) because reaching "the best" requires reliance on lower-level officials who are themselves far from being "the best."

ᘒ PART EIGHT ᘒ

American Foreign Policy
After the Cold War and 911

W hat should American foreign policy be after the Cold War? That is the question that has occupied scholars and pundits in the years since the fall of the Berlin Wall. The debate continues. There is agreement that the Cold War was a very unique period for American foreign policy—the overriding character of the Soviet threat gave a certain coherence and elegance to America's grand vision of foreign policy. Containment, bipolarity, and deterrence were the defining features of this long postwar era. Today it is more difficult to determine the interests, objectives, and strategies of American foreign policy.

A decade after the end of the Cold War, the most remarkable, and to some writers the most problematic characteristic of the international system, is the overwhelming power of the United States. A debate is unfolding among scholars and pundits about the stability of this unipolar system and about the strategies that the United States should pursue at this unusual historical moment. This debate about American foreign policy after the Cold War reflects a diversity of assumptions about the way the world works and the particular limits, capacities, legacies, and interests that the United States brings to foreign policy.

Samuel Huntington argues that the world is not as unipolar as American foreign policy officials think. The United States is the only superpower but other states are not easily dominated. These great powers in Europe and Asia will increasingly attempt to resist American hegemony and push the system in the direction of shared and balanced power. There is a deep and growing gap between the American view of its own power and the view of other countries of that power. To Americans it is benign and enlightened but to other countries it is worrisome and even threatening. The era of great power rivalry will return.

Twelve years after first introducing the idea of American unipolarity, Charles Krauthammer returns to revisit and assess his earlier position. Krauthammer finds that his argument has strengthened rather than weakened over the years: the United States is now more powerful than any other power in history but this world is unlikely to be safer, however, as new threats emerge from rogue states armed with weapons of mass destruction. Krauthammer argues for a new strategy to cope with this challenge, a strategy that should include sophisticated defenses, the option of preemptive action, and, above all, a willingness to pursue a policy of enlightened unilateralism. This last element is a critical necessity because America's unique responsibilities as a global hegemon mean that its needs may differ from those perceived as necessary by other countries.

According to G. John Ikenberry, radical new ideas are circulating about U.S. grand strategy, a development prompted by the twin characteristics of our age: catastrophic terrorism and American unipolar power. One vision, dominant within the Bush administration, amounts to a neo-imperial grand strategy that would radically transform the existing American-led international order, an order that is multilateral in character. The neo-imperial grand strategy abrogates all international constraints on American action, reserves to itself alone the right to act preemptively against sovereign states, and attaches little value to stability. Advocates of this strategy justify it as necessary to cope with the new security challenges posed by terrorists and rogue states. However, neo-imperialism may actually make America less secure because it is unsustainable, unmanageable, and cannot generate the cooperation necessary to solve the pressing challenges facing the United States.

In a far-reaching analysis of the Bush doctrine, Robert Jervis argues that the United States is imbued with a mission to remake international politics and is, therefore, no longer a status quo power. This doctrine has four distinct elements: it is liberal in character, sees vigorous policies including preventive war as the only way to tackle new threats, provides for unilateral action, and intends to preserve American primacy for the sake of peace and stability in international affairs. This radical departure in U.S. foreign policy is made possible by unusual circumstances, most important of which perhaps is the great power peace. Other states are likely to react with trepidation, not because the United States is particularly threatening but because hegemonic power, no matter how benign, is always viewed warily.

༈

The Lonely Superpower

Samuel P. Huntington

THE NEW DIMENSION OF POWER

During the past decade global politics has changed fundamentally in two ways. First, it has been substantially reconfigured along cultural and civilizational lines, as I have highlighted in the pages of this journal and documented at length in *The Clash of Civilizations and the Remaking of World Order*. Second, as argued in that book, global politics is also always about power and the struggle for power, and

Samuel P. Huntington, "The Lonely Superpower," *Foreign Affairs*, Vol 78, No. 2, (March–April 1999) pp. 35–50. Copyright © 1999 by the Council on Foreign Relations, Inc. Reprinted by permission.

today international relations is changing along that crucial dimension. The global structure of power in the Cold War was basically bipolar; the emerging structure is very different.

There is now only one superpower. But that does not mean that the world is *unipolar*. A unipolar system would have one superpower, no significant major powers, and many minor powers. As a result, the superpower could effectively resolve important international issues alone, and no combination of other states would have the power to prevent it from doing so. For several centuries the classical world under Rome, and at times East Asia under China, approximated this model. A *bipolar* system like the Cold War has two superpowers, and the relations between them are central to international politics. Each superpower dominates a coalition of allied states and competes with the other superpower for influence among nonaligned countries. A *multipolar* system has several major powers of comparable strength that cooperate and compete with each other in shifting patterns. A coalition of major states is necessary to resolve important international issues. European politics approximated this model for several centuries.

Contemporary international politics does not fit any of these three models. It is instead a strange hybrid, a *uni-multipolar* system with one superpower and several major powers. The settlement of key international issues requires action by the single superpower but always with some combination of other major states; the single superpower can, however, veto action on key issues by combinations of other states. The United States, of course, is the sole state with preeminence in every domain of power—economic, military, diplomatic, ideological, technological, and cultural—with the reach and capabilities to promote its interests in virtually every part of the world. At a second level are major regional powers that are preeminent in areas of the world without being able to extend their interests and capabilities as globally as the United States. They include the German-French condominium in Europe, Russia in Eurasia, China and potentially Japan in East Asia, India in South Asia, Iran in Southwest Asia, Brazil in Latin America, and South Africa and Nigeria in Africa. At a third level are secondary regional powers whose interests often conflict with the more powerful regional states. These include Britain in relation to the German-French combination, Ukraine in relation to Russia, Japan in relation to China, South Korea in relation to Japan, Pakistan in relation to India, Saudi Arabia in relation to Iran, and Argentina in relation to Brazil.

The superpower or hegemon in a unipolar system, lacking any major powers challenging it, is normally able to maintain its dominance over minor states for a long time until it is weakened by internal decay or by forces from outside the system, both of which happened to fifth-century Rome and nineteenth-century China. In a multipolar system, each state might prefer a unipolar system with itself as the single dominant power but the other major states will act to prevent that from happening, as was often the case in European politics. In the Cold War, each superpower quite explicitly preferred a unipolar system under its hegemony. However, the dynamics of the competition and their early awareness that an effort to create a unipolar system by armed force would be disastrous for both enabled bipolarity to endure for four decades until one state no longer could sustain the rivalry.

In each of these systems, the most powerful actors had an interest in maintaining the system. In a uni-multipolar system, this is less true. The United States would clearly prefer a unipolar system in which it would be the hegemon and often acts as if such a system existed. The major powers, on the other hand, would prefer a multipolar system in which they could pursue their interests, unilaterally and collectively, without being subject to constraints, coercion, and pressure by the stronger superpower. They feel threatened by what they see as the American pursuit of global hegemony. American officials feel frustrated by their failure to achieve that hegemony. None of the principal power-wielders in world affairs is happy with the status quo.

The superpower's efforts to create a unipolar system stimulate greater effort by the major powers to move toward a multipolar one. Virtually all major regional powers are increasingly asserting themselves to promote their own distinct interests, which often conflict with those of the United States. Global politics has thus moved from the bipolar system of the Cold War through a unipolar moment—highlighted by the Gulf War and is now passing through one or two uni-multipolar decades before it enters a truly multipolar 21st century. The United States, as Zbigniav Brzezinski has said, will be the first, last, and only global superpower.

NOT SO BENIGN

American officials quite naturally tend to act as if the world were unipolar. They boast of American power and American virtue, hailing the United States as a benevolent hegemon. They lecture other countries on the universal validity of American principles, practices, and institutions. At the 1997 G-7 summit in Denver, President Clinton boasted about the success of the American economy as a model for others. Secretary of State Madeleine K. Albright has called the United States "the indispensable nation" and said that "we stand tall and hence see further than other nations." This statement is true in the narrow sense that the United States is an indispensable participant in any effort to tackle major global problems. It is false in also implying that other nations are dispensable—the United States needs the cooperation of some major countries in handling any issue—and that American indispensability is the source of wisdom.

Addressing the problem of foreign perceptions of American "hegemonism," Deputy Secretary of State Strobe Talbott set forth this rationale: "In a fashion and to an extent that is unique in the history of Great Powers, the United States defines its strength—indeed, its very greatness—not in terms of its ability to achieve or maintain dominance over others, but in terms of its ability to work *with* others in the interests of the international community as a whole. . . . American foreign policy is consciously intended to advance *universal* values [his italics]." The most concise statement of the "benign hegemon" syndrome was made by Deputy Secretary of the Treasury Lawrence H. Summers when he called the United States the "first nonimperialist superpower"—a claim that manages in three words to exalt American uniqueness, American virtue, and American power.

American foreign policy is in considerable measure driven by such beliefs. In the past few years the United States has, among other things, attempted or been perceived as attempting more or less unilaterally to do the following: pressure other countries to adopt American values and practices regarding human rights and democracy; prevent other countries from acquiring military capabilities that could counter American conventional superiority; enforce American law extraterritorially in other societies; grade countries according to their adherence to American standards on human rights, drugs, terrorism, nuclear proliferation, missile proliferation, and now religious freedom; apply sanctions against countries that do not meet American standards on these issues; promote American corporate interests under the slogans of free trade and open markets; shape World Bank and International Monetary Fund policies to serve those same corporate interests; intervene in local conflicts in which it has relatively little direct interest; bludgeon other countries to adopt economic policies and social policies that will benefit American economic interests; promote American arms sales abroad while attempting to prevent comparable sales by other countries; force out one U.N. secretary-general and dictate the appointment of his successor; expand NATO initially to include Poland, Hungary, and the Czech Republic and no one else; undertake military action against Iraq and later maintain harsh economic sanctions against the regime; and categorize certain countries as "rogue states," excluding them from global institutions because they refuse to kowtow to American wishes.

In the unipolar moment at the end of the Cold War and the collapse of the Soviet Union, the United States was often able to impose its will on other countries. That moment has passed. The two principal tools of coercion that the United States now attempts to use are economic sanctions and military intervention. Sanctions work, however, only when other countries also support them, and that is decreasingly the case. Hence, the United States either applies them unilaterally to the detriment of its economic interests and its relations with its allies, or it does not enforce them, in which case they become symbols of American weakness.

At relatively low cost the United States can launch bombing or cruise missile attacks against its enemies. By themselves, however, such actions achieve little. More serious military interventions have to meet three conditions: They have to be legitimated through some international organization, such as the United Nations where they are subject to Russian, Chinese, or French veto; they also require the participation of allied forces, which may or may not be forthcoming, and they have to involve no American casualties and virtually no "collateral" casualties. Even if the United States meets all three conditions, it risks stirring up not only criticism at home but widespread political and popular backlash abroad.

American officials seem peculiarly blind to the fact that often the more the United States attacks a foreign leader, the more his popularity soars among his countrymen who applaud him for standing tall against the greatest power on earth. The demonizing of leaders has so far failed to shorten their tenure in power, from Fidel Castro (who has survived eight American presidents) to Slobodan Milošević and Saddam Hussein. Indeed, the best way for a dictator of a small country to prolong his tenure in power may be to provoke the United States into denouncing him as the leader of a "rogue regime" and a threat to global peace.

Neither the Clinton administration nor Congress nor the public is willing to pay the costs and accept the risks of unilateral global leadership. Some advocates of American leadership argue for increasing defense expenditures by 50 percent, but that is a nonstarter. The American public clearly sees no need to expend effort and resources to achieve American hegemony. In one 1997 poll, only 13 percent said they preferred a preeminent role for the United States in world affairs, while 74 percent said they wanted the United States to share power with other countries. Other polls have produced similar results. Public disinterest in international affairs is pervasive, abetted by the drastically shrinking media coverage of foreign events. Majorities of 55 to 66 percent of the public say that what happens in western Europe, Asia, Mexico, and Canada has little or no impact on their lives. However much foreign policy elites may ignore or deplore it, the United States lacks the domestic political base to create a unipolar world. American leaders repeatedly make threats, promise action, and fail to deliver. The result is a foreign policy of "rhetoric and retreat" and a growing reputation as a "hollow hegemon."

THE ROGUE SUPERPOWER

In acting as if this were a unipolar world, the United States is also becoming increasingly alone in the world. American leaders constantly claim to be speaking on behalf of "the international community." But whom do they have in mind? China? Russia? India? Pakistan? Iran? The Arab world? The Association of Southeast Asian Nations? Africa? Latin America? France? Do any of these countries or regions see the United States as the spokesman for a community of which they are a part? The community for which the United States speaks includes, at best, its Anglo-Saxon cousins (Britain, Canada, Australia, New Zealand) on most issues, Germany and some smaller European democracies on many issues, Israel on some Middle Eastern questions, and Japan on the implementation of U.N. resolutions. These are important states, but they fall far short of being the global international community.

On issue after issue, the Untied States has found itself increasingly alone, with one or a few partners, opposing most of the rest of the world's states and peoples. These issues include U.N. dues; sanctions against Cuba, Iran, Iraq, and Libya; the land mines treaty; global warming; an international war crimes tribunal; the Middle East; the use of force against Iraq and Yugoslavia; and the targeting of 35 countries with new economic sanctions between 1993 and 1996. On these and other issues, much of the international community is on one side and the United States is on the other. The circle of governments who see their interests coinciding with American interest is shrinking. This is manifest among other ways, in the central lineup among the permanent members of the U.N. Security Council. During the first decades of the Cold War, it was 4:1—the United States, the United Kingdom, France, and China against the Soviet Union. After Mao's communist government took China's seat, the lineup became 3:1:1, with China in a shifting middle position. Now it is 2:1:2, with the United States and the United Kingdom opposing China and Russia, and France in the middle spot.

While the United States regularly denounces various countries as "rogue states," in the eyes of many countries it is becoming the rogue superpower. One of

Japan's most distinguished diplomats, Ambassador Hisashi Owada, has argued that after World War II, the United States pursued a policy of "unilateral globalism," providing public goods in the form of security, opposition to communism, an open global economy, aid for economic development, and stronger international institutions. Now it is pursuing a policy of "global unilateralism," promoting its own particular interests with little reference to those of others. The United States is unlikely to become an isolationist country, withdrawing from the world. But it could become an isolated country, out of step with much of the world.

If a unipolar world were unavoidable, many countries might prefer the United States as the hegemon. But this is mostly because it is distant from them and hence unlikely to attempt to acquire any of their territory. American power is also valued by the secondary regional states as a constraint on the dominance of other major regional states. Benign hegemony, however, is in the eye of the hegemon. "One reads about the world's desire for American leadership only in the United States," one British diplomat observed. "Everywhere else one reads about American arrogance and unilateralism."

Political and intellectual leaders in most countries strongly resist the prospect of a unipolar world and favor the emergence of true multi-polarity. At a 1997 Harvard conference scholars reported that the elites of countries comprising at least two-thirds of the world's people—Chinese, Russians, Indians, Arabs, Muslims, and Africans—see the United States as the single greatest external threat to their societies. They do not regard America as a military threat but as a menace to their integrity, autonomy, prosperity, and freedom of action. They view the United States as intrusive, interventionist, exploitative, unilateralist, hegemonic, hypocritical, and applying double standards, engaging in what they label "financial imperialism" and "intellectual colonialism," with a foreign policy driven overwhelmingly by domestic politics. For Indian elites, an Indian scholar reported, "the United States represents the major diplomatic and political threat. On virtually every issue of concern to India, the United States has 'veto' or mobilizational power, whether it is on nuclear, technological, economic, environmental, or political matters. That is, the United States can deny India its objectives and can rally others to join it in punishing India." Its sins are "power, hubris, and greed." From the Russian perspective, a Moscow participant said, the United States pursues a policy of "coercive cooperation." All Russians oppose "a world based on a dominant U.S. leadership which would border on hegemony." In similar terms, the Beijing participant said Chinese leaders believe that the principal threats to peace, stability, and China are "hegemonism and power politics," meaning U.S. policies, which they say are designed to undermine and create disunity in the socialist states and developing countries. Arab elites see the United States as an evil force in world affairs, while the Japanese public rated in 1997 the United States as a threat to Japan second only to North Korea.

Such reactions are to be expected. American leaders believe that the world's business is their business. Other countries believe that what happens in their part of the world is their business, not America's, and quite explicitly respond. As Nelson Mandela said, his country rejects another state's having "the arrogance to tell us where we should go or which countries should be our friends. . . . We cannot accept that a state assumes the role of the world's policeman." In a bipolar world, many countries welcomed the United States as their protector against the other superpower. In a uni-multipolar world, in contrast, the world's only superpower is automatically a threat to other major powers. One by one, the major regional powers are making it clear that they do not want the United States messing around in regions where their interests are predominant. Iran, for instance, strongly opposes the U.S. military presence in the Persian Gulf. The current bad relations between the United States and Iran are the product of the Iranian revolution. If, however, the Shah or his son now ruled Iran, those relations would probably be deteriorating because Iran would see the American presence in the Gulf as a threat to its own hegemony there.

FLEXIBLE RESPONSES

Countries respond in various ways to American superpowerdom. At a relatively low level are widespread feelings of fear, resentment, and envy. These ensure that when at some point the United States suffers a humiliating rebuff from a Saddam or a Milošević, many countries will think, "They finally got what they had coming to them!" At a somewhat higher level, resentment may turn into dissent, with other countries, including allies, refusing to cooperate with the United States on the Persian Gulf, Cuba, Libya, Iran, extraterritoriality, nuclear proliferation, human rights, trade policies, and other issues. In a few cases, dissent has turned into outright opposition as countries attempt to defeat U.S. policy. The highest level of response would be the formation of an antihegemonic coalition involving several major powers. Such a grouping is impossible in a unipolar world because the other states are too weak to mount it. It appears in a multipolar world only when one state begins to become strong and troublesome enough to provoke it. It would, however, appear to be a natural phenomenon in a uni-multipolar world. Throughout history, major powers have tended to balance against the attempted domination by the strongest among them.

Some antihegemonic cooperation has occurred. Relations among non-Western societies are in general improving. Gatherings occur from which the United States is conspicuously absent, ranging from the Moscow meeting of the leaders of Germany, France, and Russia (which also excluded America's closest ally, Britain) to the bilateral meetings of China and Russia and of China and India. There have been recent rapprochements between Iran and Saudi Arabia and Iran and Iraq. The highly successful meeting of the Organization of the Islamic Conference hosted by Iran coincided with the disastrous Qatar meeting on Middle Eastern economic development sponsored by the United States. Russian Prime Minister Yevgeni Primakov has promoted Russia, China, and India as a "strategic triangle" to counterbalance the United States, and the "Primakov doctrine" reportedly enjoys substantial support across the entire Russian political spectrum.

Undoubtedly the single most important move toward an antihegemonic coalition, however, antedates the end of the Cold War: the formation of the European

Union and the creation of a common European currency. As French Foreign Minister Hubert Védrine has said, Europe must come together on its own and create a counterweight to stop the United States from dominating a multipolar world. Clearly the euro could pose an important challenge to the hegemony of the dollar in global finance.

Despite all these antihegemonic rumblings, however, a more broad-based, active, and formal anti-American coalition has yet to emerge. Several possible explanations come to mind.

First, it may be too soon. Over time the response to American hegemony may escalate from resentment and dissent to opposition and collective counteraction. The American hegemonic threat is less immediate and more diffuse than the prospect of imminent military conquest posed by European hegemons in the past. Hence, other powers can be more relaxed about forming a coalition to counter American dominance.

Second, while countries may resent U.S. power and wealth, they also want to benefit from them. The United States rewards countries that follow its leadership with access to the American market, foreign aid, military assistance, exemption from sanctions, silence about deviations from U.S. norms (as with Saudi human rights abuses and Israeli nuclear weapons), support for membership in international organizations, and bribes and White House visits for political leaders. Each major regional power also has an interest in securing U.S. support in conflicts with other regional powers. Given the benefits that the United States can distribute, the sensible course for other countries may well be, in international-relations lingo, not to "balance" against the United States but to "bandwagon" with it. Over time, however, as U.S. power declines, the benefits to be gained by cooperating with the United States will also decline, as will the costs of opposing it. Hence, this factor reinforces the possibility that an antihegemonic coalition could emerge in the future.

Third, the international-relations theory that predicts balancing under the current circumstances is a theory developed in the context of the European Westphalian system established in 1648. All the countries in that system shared a common European culture that distinguished them sharply from the Ottoman Turks and other peoples. They also took the nation-state as the basic unit in international relations and accepted the legal and theoretical equality of states despite their obvious differences in size, wealth, and power. Cultural commonality and legal equality thus facilitated the operation of a balance-of-power system to counter the emergence of a single hegemon, and even then it often operated quite imperfectly.

Global politics is now multicivilizational. France, Russia, and China may well have common interests in challenging U.S. hegemony, but their very different cultures are likely to make it difficult for them to organize an effective coalition. In addition, the idea of the sovereign legal equality of nation-states has not played a significant role in relations among non-Western societies, which see hierarchy rather than equality as the natural relation among peoples. The central questions in a relationship are: who is number one? who is number two? At least one factor that led to the breakup of the Sino-Soviet alliance at the end of the 1950s was Mao Zedong's unwillingness to play second fiddle to Stalin's successors in the Kremlin. Similarly, an obstacle to an anti-U.S. coalition between China and Russia now is Russian reluctance to be the junior partner of a much more populous and economically dynamic China. Cultural differences, jealousies, and rivalries may thwart the major powers from coalescing against the superpower.

Fourth, the principal source of contention between the superpower and the major regional powers is the former's intervention to limit, counter, or shape the actions of the latter. For the secondary regional powers, on the other hand, superpower intervention is a resource that they potentially can mobilize against their region's major power. The superpower and the secondary regional powers will thus often, although not always, share converging interests against major regional powers, and secondary regional powers will have little incentive to join in a coalition against the superpower.

THE LONELY SHERIFF

The interplay of power and culture will decisively mold patterns of alliance and antagonism among states in the coming years. In terms of culture, cooperation is more likely between countries with cultural commonalties; antagonism is more likely between countries with widely different cultures. In terms of power, the United States and the secondary regional powers have common interests in limiting the dominance of the major states in their regions. Thus the United States has warned China by strengthening its military alliance with Japan and supporting the modest extension of Japanese military capabilities. The U.S. special relationship with Britain provides leverage against the emerging power of a united Europe. America is working to develop close relations with Ukraine to counter any expansion of Russian power. With the emergence of Brazil as the dominant state in Latin America, U.S. relations with Argentina have greatly improved and the United States has designated Argentina a non-NATO military ally. The United States cooperates closely with Saudi Arabia to counter Iran's power in the Gulf and, less successfully, has worked with Pakistan to balance India in South Asia. In all these cases, cooperation serves mutual interests in containing the influence of the major regional power.

This interplay of power and culture suggests that the United States is likely to have difficult relations with the major regional powers, though less so with the European Union and Brazil than with the others. On the other hand, the United States should have reasonably cooperative relations with all the secondary regional powers, but have closer relations with the secondary regional powers that have similar cultures (Britain, Argentina, and possibly Ukraine) than those that have different cultures (Japan, South Korea, Saudi Arabia, Pakistan). Finally, relations between major and secondary regional powers of the same civilization (the EU and Britain, Russia and Ukraine, Brazil and Argentina, Iran and Saudi Arabia) should be less antagonistic than those between countries of different civilizations (China and Japan; Japan and Korea; India and Pakistan; Israel and the Arab states).

What are the implications of a uni-multipolar world for American policy?

First, it would behoove Americans to stop acting and talking as if this were a unipolar world. It is not. To deal with any major global issue, the United States needs the cooperation of at least some major powers. Unilateral sanctions and interventions are recipes for foreign policy disasters. Second, American leaders should abandon the benign hegemon illusion that a natural congruity exists between their interests and values and those of the rest of the world. It does not. At times, American actions may promote public goods and serve more widely accepted ends. But often they will not, in part because of the unique moralistic component in American policy but also simply because America is the only super-power, and hence its interests necessarily differ from those of other countries. This makes America unique but not benign in the eyes of those countries.

Third, while the United States cannot create a unipolar world, it is in U.S. interests to take advantage of its position as the only superpower in the existing international order and to use its resources to elicit cooperation from other coun-tries to deal with global issues in ways that satisfy American interests. This would essentially involve the Bismarckian strategy recommended by Josef Joffe, but it would also require Bismarckian talents to carry out, and, in any event, cannot be maintained indefinitely.

Fourth, the interaction of power and culture has special relevance for European-American relations. The dynamics of power encourage rivalry; cultural commonalities facilitate cooperation. The achievement of almost any major American goal depends on the triumph of the latter over the former. The relation with Europe is central to the success of American foreign policy, and given the pro- and anti-American outlooks of Britain and France, respectively, America's relations with Germany are central to its relations with Europe. Healthy cooperation with Europe is the prime antidote for the loneliness of American superpowerdom.

Richard N. Haass has argued that the United States should act as a global sher-iff, rounding up "posses" of other states to handle major international issues as they arise. Haass handled Persian Gulf matters at the White House in the Bush adminis-tration, and this proposal reflects the experience and success of that administration in putting together a heterogeneous global posse to force Saddam out of Kuwait. But that was then, in the unipolar moment. What happened then contrasts dramatically with the Iraqi crisis in the winter of 1998, when France, Russia, and China opposed the use of force and America assembled an Anglo-Saxon posse, not a global one. In December 1998 support for U.S. and British air strikes against Saddam was also lim-ited and criticism widespread. Most strikingly, no Arab government, including Kuwait, endorsed the action. Saudi Arabia refused to allow the United States to use its fighter planes based there. Efforts at rallying future posses are far more likely to resemble what happened in 1998 than what happened in 1990–91. Most of the world, as Mandela said, does not want the United States to be its policeman.

As a multipolar system emerges, the appropriate replacement for a global sheriff is community policing, with the major regional powers assuming primary responsibility for order in their own regions. Haass criticizes this suggestion on the grounds that the other states in a region, which I have called the secondary regional powers, will object to being policed by the leading regional powers. As I have indicated, their interests often do conflict. But the same tension is likely to hold in the relationship between the United States and major regional power. There is no reason why Americans should take responsibility for maintaining order if it can be done locally. While geography does not coincide exactly with culture, there is considerable overlap between regions and civilizations. For the reasons I set forth in my book, the core state of a civilization can better maintain order among the members of its extended family than can someone outside the family. There are also signs in some regions such as Africa, Southeast Asia, and perhaps even the Balkans that countries are beginning to develop collective means to maintain security. American intervention could then be restricted to those situations of potential violence, such as the Middle East and South Asia, involving major states of different civilizations.

In the multipolar world of the 21st century, the major powers will inevitably compete, clash, and coalesce with each other in various permutations and combinations. Such a world, however, will lack the tension and conflict between the superpower and the major regional powers that are the defining characteristic of a uni-multipolar world. For that reason, the United States could find life as a major power in a multipolar world less demanding, less contentious, and more rewarding than it was as the world's only superpower.

༄

The Unipolar Moment Revisited

Charles Krauthammer

> "It has been assumed that the old bipolar world would beget a multipolar world with power dispersed to new centers in Japan, Germany (and/or "Europe"), China and a diminished Soviet Union/Russia. [This is] mistaken. The immediate post-Cold War world is not multipolar. It is unipolar. The center of world power is an unchallenged superpower, the United States, attended by its Western allies."
>
> —The Unipolar Moment

In late 1990, shortly before the collapse of the Soviet Union, it was clear that the world we had known for half a century was disappearing. The question was what would succeed it. I suggested then that we had already entered the "unipolar moment." The gap in power between the leading nation and all the others was so unprecedented as to yield an international structure unique to modern history: unipolarity.

Charles Krauthammer, "The Unipolar Moment Revised," *National Interest,* No. 70, (Winter 2002/03) pp. 5–17. Reproduced with permission of the copyright owner. Further reproduction or distribution is prohibited without permission.

At the time, this thesis was generally seen as either wild optimism or simple American arrogance. The conventional wisdom was that with the demise of the Soviet empire the bipolarity of the second half of the 20th century would yield to multipolarity. The declinist school, led by Paul Kennedy, held that America, suffering from "imperial overstretch," was already in relative decline. The Asian enthusiasm, popularized by (among others) James Fallows, saw the second coming of the Rising Sun. The conventional wisdom was best captured by Senator Paul Tsongas: "The Cold War is over; Japan won."

They were wrong, and no one has put it more forcefully than Paul Kennedy himself in a classic recantation published earlier this year. "Nothing has ever existed like this disparity of power; nothing," he said of America's position today. "Charlemagne's empire was merely western European in its reach. The Roman empire stretched farther afield, but there was another great empire in Persia, and a larger one in China. There is, therefore, no comparison."[1] Not everyone is convinced. Samuel Huntington argued in 1999 that we had entered not a unipolar world but a "uni-multipolar world."[2] Tony Judt writes mockingly of the "loud boasts of unipolarity and hegemony" heard in Washington today.[3] But as Stephen Brooks and William Wohlforth argue in a recent review of the subject, those denying unipolarity can do so only by applying a ridiculous standard: that America be able to achieve all its goals everywhere all by itself. This is a standard not for unipolarity but for divinity. Among mortals, and in the context of the last half millennium of history, the current structure of the international system is clear: "If today's American primacy does not constitute unipolarity, then nothing ever will."[4]

A second feature of this new post-Cold War world, I ventured, would be a resurgent American isolationism. I was wrong. It turns out that the new norm for America is not post-World War I withdrawal but post-World War II engagement. In the 1990s, Pat Buchanan gave 1930s isolationism a run. He ended up carrying Palm Beach.

Finally, I suggested that a third feature of this new unipolar world would be an increase rather than a decrease in the threat of war, and that it would come from a new source: weapons of mass destruction wielded by rogue states. This would constitute a revolution in international relations, given that in the past it was great powers who presented the principal threats to world peace.

Where are we twelve years later? The two defining features of the new post-Cold War world remain: unipolarity and rogue states with weapons of mass destruction. Indeed, these characteristics have grown even more pronounced. Contrary to expectation, the United States has not regressed to the mean; rather, its dominance has dramatically increased. And during our holiday from history in the 1990s, the rogue state/WMD problem grew more acute. Indeed, we are now on the eve of history's first war over weapons of mass destruction.

> "The true geopolitical structure of the post-Cold War world . . . [is] a single pole of world power that consists of the United States at the apex of the industrial West. Perhaps it is more accurate to say the United States and behind it the West."—The Unipolar Moment

UNIPOLARITY AFTER SEPTEMBER 11, 2001

There is little need to rehearse the acceleration of unipolarity in the 1990s. Japan, whose claim to power rested exclusively on economics, went into economic decline. Germany stagnated. The Soviet Union ceased to exist, contracting into a smaller, radically weakened Russia. The European Union turned inward toward the great project of integration and built a strong social infrastructure at the expense of military capacity. Only China grew in strength, but coming from so far behind it will be decades before it can challenge American primacy—and that assumes that its current growth continues unabated.

The result is the dominance of a single power unlike anything ever seen. Even at its height Britain could always be seriously challenged by the next great-est powers. Britain had a smaller army than the land powers of Europe and its navy was equaled by the next two navies combined. Today, American military spending exceeds that of the next twenty countries combined. Its navy, air force and space power are unrivaled. Its technology is irresistible. It is dominant by every measure: military, economic, technological, diplomatic, cultural, even lin-guistic, with a myriad of countries trying to fend off the inexorable march of Internet-fueled MTV English.

American dominance has not gone unnoticed. During the 1990s, it was mainly China and Russia that denounced unipolarity in their occasional joint commu-niques. As the new century dawned it was on everyone's lips. A French foreign minister dubbed the United States not a superpower but a hyperpower. The dom-inant concern of foreign policy establishments everywhere became understanding and living with the 800-pound American gorilla.

And then September 11 heightened the asymmetry. It did so in three ways. First, and most obviously, it led to a demonstration of heretofore latent American military power. Kosovo, the first war ever fought and won exclusively from the air, had given a hint of America's quantum leap in military power (and the enormous gap that had developed between American and European military capabilities). But it took September 11 for the United States to unleash with concentrated fury a fuller display of its power in Afghanistan. Being a relatively pacific, commercial republic, the United States does not go around looking for demonstration wars. This one was thrust upon it. In response, America showed that at a range of 7,000 miles and with but a handful of losses, it could destroy within weeks a hardened, fanatical regime favored by geography and climate in the "graveyard of empires."

Such power might have been demonstrated earlier, but it was not. "I talked with the previous U.S. administration", said Vladimir Putin shortly after September 11, "and pointed out the bin Laden issue to them. They wrung their hands so helplessly and said, 'the Taliban are not turning him over, what can one do?' I remember I was surprised: If they are not turning him over, one has to think and do something."[5]

Nothing was done. President Clinton and others in his administration have protested that nothing could have been done, that even the 1998 African embassy bombings were not enough to mobilize the American people to strike back seri-ously against terrorism. The new Bush administration, too, did not give the prospect of mass-casualty terrorism (and the recommendations of the Hart-Rudman Commission) the priority it deserved. Without September 11, the giant would surely have slept longer. The world would have been aware of America's size and potential, but not its ferocity or its full capacities. (Paul Kennedy's homage to American power, for example, was offered in the wake of the Afghan campaign.)

Second, September 11 demonstrated a new form of American strength. The center of its economy was struck, its aviation shut down, Congress brought to a halt, the government sent underground, the country paralyzed and fearful. Yet within days the markets reopened, the economy began its recovery, the president mobilized the nation, and a united Congress immediately underwrote a huge new worldwide campaign against terror. The Pentagon started planning the U.S. military response even as its demolished western facade still smoldered.

America had long been perceived as invulnerable. That illusion was shattered on September 11, 2001. But with a demonstration of its recuperative powers—an economy and political system so deeply rooted and fundamentally sound that it could spring back to life within days—that sense of invulnerability assumed a new character. It was transmuted from impermeability to resilience, the product of unrivaled human, technological and political reserves.

The third effect of September 11 was to accelerate the realignment of the current great powers, such as they are, behind the United States. In 1990, America's principal ally was NATO. A decade later, its alliance base had grown to include former members of the Warsaw Pact. Some of the major powers, however, remained uncommitted. Russia and China flirted with the idea of an "anti-hegemonic alliance." Russian leaders made ostentatious visits to pieces of the old Soviet empire such as Cuba and North Korea. India and Pakistan, frozen out by the United States because of their nuclear testing, remained focused mainly on one another. But after September 11, the bystanders came calling. Pakistan made an immediate strategic decision to join the American camp. India enlisted with equal alacrity, offering the United States basing, overflight rights and a level of cooperation unheard of during its half century of Nehruist genuflection to anti-American non-alignment. Russia's Putin, seeing both a coincidence of interests in the fight against Islamic radicalism and an opportunity to gain acceptance in the Western camp, dramatically realigned Russian foreign policy toward the United States. (Russia has already been rewarded with a larger role in NATO and tacit American recognition of Russia's interests in its "near abroad.") China remains more distant but, also having a coincidence of interests with the United States in fighting Islamic radicalism, it has cooperated with the war on terror and muted its competition with America in the Pacific.

The realignment of the fence-sitters simply accentuates the historical anomaly of American unipolarity. Our experience with hegemony historically is that it inevitably creates a counterbalancing coalition of weaker powers, most recently against Napoleonic France and Germany (twice) in the 20th century. Nature abhors a vacuum; history abhors hegemony. Yet during the first decade of American unipolarity no such counterbalancing occurred. On the contrary, the great powers lined up behind the United States, all the more so after September 11.

"The most crucial new element in the post-Cold War world [is] the emergence of a new strategic environment marked by the proliferation of weapons of mass destruction. . . . The proliferation of weapons of mass destruction and their means of delivery will constitute the greatest single threat to world security for the rest of our lives. That is what makes a new international order not an imperial dream or a Wilsonian fantasy but a matter of the sheerest prudence. It is slowly dawning on the West that there is a need to establish some new regime to police these weapons and those who brandish them. . . . Iraq . . . is the prototype of this new strategic threat."

—The Unipolar Moment

The American hegemon has no great power enemies, an historical oddity of the first order. Yet it does face a serious threat to its dominance, indeed to its essential security. It comes from a source even more historically odd: an archipelago of rogue states (some connected with transnational terrorists) wielding weapons of mass destruction.

The threat is not trivial. It is the single greatest danger to the United States because, for all of America's dominance, and for all of its recently demonstrated resilience, there is one thing it might not survive: decapitation. The detonation of a dozen nuclear weapons in major American cities, or the spreading of smallpox or anthrax throughout the general population, is an existential threat. It is perhaps the only realistic threat to America as a functioning hegemon, perhaps even to America as a functioning modern society.

"It is of course banal to say that modern technology has shrunk the world. But the obvious corollary, that in a shrunken world the divide between regional superpowers and great powers is radically narrowed, is rarely drawn. Missiles shrink distance. Nuclear (or chemical or biological) devices multiply power. Both can be bought at market. Consequently the geopolitical map is irrevocably altered. Fifty years ago, Germany—centrally located, highly industrial and heavily populated—could pose a threat to world security and to the other great powers. It was inconceivable that a relatively small Middle Eastern state with an almost entirely imported industrial base could do anything more than threaten its neighbors. The central truth of the coming era is that this is no longer the case: relatively small, peripheral and backward states will be able to emerge rapidly as threats not only to regional, but to world, security."

—The Unipolar Moment

Like unipolarity, this is historically unique, WMD are not new, nor are rogue states. Their conjunction is. We have had fifty years of experience with nuclear weapons—but in the context of bipolarity, which gave the system a predictable, if perilous, stability. We have just now entered an era in which the capacity for inflicting mass death, and thus posing a threat both to world peace and to the dominant power, resides in small, peripheral states.

What does this conjunction of unique circumstances—unipolarity and the proliferation of terrible weapons—mean for American foreign policy? That the first and most urgent task is protection from these weapons. The catalyst for this realization was again September 11. Throughout the 1990s, it had been assumed that WMD posed no emergency because traditional concepts of deterrence would hold. September 11 revealed the possibility of future WMD—armed enemies both undeterrable and potentially undetectable. The 9/11 suicide bombers were undeterrable; the author of the subsequent anthrax attacks has proven undetectable.

The possible alliance of rogue states with such undeterrables and undetectables—and the possible transfer to them of weapons of mass destruction—presents a new strategic situation that demands a new strategic doctrine.

> "Any solution will have to include three elements: denying, disarming, and defending. First, we will have to develop a new regime, similar to COCOM (Coordinating Committee on Export Controls) to deny yet more high technology to such states. Second, those states that acquire such weapons anyway will have to submit to strict outside control or risk being physically disarmed. A final element must be the development of antiballistic missile and air defense systems to defend against those weapons that do escape Western control or preemption. . . . There is no alternative to confronting, deterring, and, if necessary, disarming states that brandish and use weapons of mass destruction. And there is no one to do that but the United States, backed by as many allies as will join the endeavor."
>
> —The Unipolar Moment

THE CRISIS OF UNIPOLARITY

Accordingly, not one but a host of new doctrines have come tumbling out since September 11. First came the with-us-or-against-us ultimatum to any state aiding, abetting or harboring terrorists. Then, pre-emptive attack on any enemy state developing weapons of mass destruction. And now, regime change in any such state.

The boldness of these policies—or, as much of the world contends, their arrogance—is breathtaking. The American anti-terrorism ultimatum, it is said, is high-handed and permits the arbitrary application of American power everywhere. Pre-emption is said to violate traditional doctrines of just war. And regime change, as Henry Kissinger has argued, threatens 350 years of post-Westphalian international practice. Taken together, they amount to an unprecedented assertion of American freedom of action and a definitive statement of a new American unilateralism.

To be sure, these are not the first instances of American unilateralism. Before September 11, the Bush administration had acted unilaterally, but on more minor matters, such as the Kyoto Protocol and the Biological Weapons Convention, and with less bluntness, as in its protracted negotiations with Russia over the ABM treaty. The "axis of evil" speech of January 29, however, took unilateralism to a new level. Latent resentments about American willfulness are latent no more. American dominance, which had been tolerated if not welcomed, is now producing such irritation and hostility in once friendly quarters, such as Europe, that some suggest we have arrived at the end of the opposition-free grace period that America had enjoyed during the unipolar moment.[6]

In short, post—9/11 U.S. unilateralism has produced the first crisis of unipolarity. It revolves around the central question of the unipolar age: Who will define the hegemon's ends?

The issue is not one of style but of purpose. Secretary of Defense Donald Rumsfeld gave the classic formulation of unilateralism when he said (regarding the Afghan war and the war on terrorism, but the principle is universal), "the mission determines the coalition." We take our friends where we find them, but only in order to help us in accomplishing the mission. The mission comes first, and we decide it.

Contrast this with the classic case study of multilateralism at work: the U.S. decision in February 1991 to conclude the Gulf War. As the Iraqi army was fleeing, the first Bush administration had to decide its final goal: the liberation of Kuwait or regime change in Iraq. It stopped at Kuwait. Why? Because, as Brent Scowcroft has explained, going further would have fractured the coalition, gone against our promises to allies and violated the UN resolutions under which we were acting. "Had we added occupation of Iraq and removal of Saddam Hussein to those objectives," wrote Scowcroft in the Washington Post on October 16, 2001, ". . . our Arab allies, refusing to countenance an invasion of an Arab colleague, would have deserted us." The coalition defined the mission.

Who should define American ends today? This is a question of agency but it leads directly to a fundamental question of policy. If the coalition—whether NATO, the wider Western alliance, ad hoc outfits such as the Gulf War alliance, the UN, or the "international community"—defines America's mission, we have one vision of America's role in the world. If, on the other hand, the mission defines the coalition, we have an entirely different vision.

> "A large segment of American opinion doubts the legitimacy of unilateral American action but accepts quite readily actions undertaken by the 'world community' acting in concert. Why it should matter to Americans that their actions get a Security Council nod from, say, Deng Xiaoping and the butchers of Tiananmen Square is beyond me. But to many Americans it matters. It is largely for domestic reasons, therefore, that American political leaders make sure to dress unilateral action in multilateral clothing. The danger, of course, is that they might come to believe their own pretense."
>
> —The Unipolar Moment

LIBERAL INTERNATIONALISM

For many Americans, multilateralism is no pretense. On the contrary: It has become the very core of the liberal internationalist school of American foreign policy. In the October 2002 debate authorizing the use of force in Iraq, the Democratic chairman of the Senate Armed Services Committee, Carl Levin, proposed authorizing the president to act only with prior approval from the UN Security Council. Senator Edward Kennedy put it succinctly while addressing the Johns Hopkins School of Advanced International Studies on September 27: "I'm waiting for the final recommendation of the Security Council before I'm going to say how I'm going to vote."

This logic is deeply puzzling. How exactly does the Security Council confer moral authority on American action? The Security Council is a committee of great powers, heirs to the victors in the Second World War. They manage the world in their own interest. The Security Council is, on the very rare occasions when it actually works, realpolitik by committee. But by what logic is it a repository of international morality? How does the approval of France and Russia, acting clearly and rationally in pursuit of their own interests in Iraq (largely oil and investment), confer legitimacy on an invasion?

That question was beyond me twelve years ago. It remains beyond me now. Yet this kind of logic utterly dominated the intervening Clinton years. The 1990s were marked by an obsession with "international legality" as expressed by this or that Security Council resolution. To take one long-forgotten example: After an Iraqi provocation in February 1998, President Clinton gave a speech at the Pentagon laying the foundation for an attack on Iraq (one of many that never came). He cited as justification for the use of force the need to enforce Iraqi promises made under post-Gulf War ceasefire conditions that "the United Nations demanded—not the United States—the United Nations." Note the formulation. Here is the president of the most powerful nation on earth stopping in mid-sentence to stress the primacy of commitments made to the UN over those made to the United States.

This was not surprising from a president whose first inaugural address pledged American action when "the will and conscience of the international community is defied." Early in the Clinton years, Madeleine Albright formulated the vision of the liberal internationalist school then in power as "assertive multilateralism." Its principal diplomatic activity was the pursuit of a dizzying array of universal treaties on chemical weapons, biological weapons, nuclear testing, global environment, land mines and the like. Its trademark was consultation: Clinton was famous for sending Secretary of State Warren Christopher on long trips (for example, through Europe on Balkan policy) or endless shuttles (uncountable pilgrimages to Damascus) to consult; he invariably returned home empty-handed and diminished. And its principal objective was good international citizenship: It was argued on myriad foreign policy issues that we could not do X because it would leave us "isolated." Thus in 1997 the Senate passed a chemical weapons convention that even some of its proponents admitted was unenforceable, largely because of the argument that everyone else had signed it and that failure to ratify would leave us isolated. Isolation, in and of itself, was seen as a diminished and even morally suspect condition.

A lesson in isolation occurred during the 1997 negotiations in Oslo over the land mine treaty. One of the rare holdouts, interestingly enough, was Finland. Finding himself scolded by his neighbors for opposing the land mine ban, the Finnish prime minister noted tartly that this was a "very convenient" pose for the "other Nordic countries" who "want Finland to be their land mine."

In many parts of the world, a thin line of American GIs is the land mine. The main reason we oppose the land mine treaty is that we need them in the DMZ in Korea. We man the lines there. Sweden and France and Canada do not have to worry about a North Korean invasion killing thousands of their soldiers. As the unipolar power and thus guarantor of peace in places where Swedes do not tread, we need weapons that others do not. Being uniquely situated in the world, we cannot afford the empty platitudes of allies not quite candid enough to admit that they live under the umbrella of American power. That often leaves us "isolated."

Multilateralism is the liberal internationalist's means of saving us from this shameful condition. But the point of the multilateralist imperative is not merely psychological. It has a clear and coherent geopolitical objective. It is a means that defines the ends. Its means—internationalism (the moral, legal and strategic primacy of international institutions over national interests) and legalism (the belief that the sinews of stability are laws, treaties and binding international contracts)—

are in service to a larger vision: remaking the international system in the image of domestic civil society. The multilateralist imperative seeks to establish an international order based not on sovereignty and power but on interdependence—a new order that, as Secretary of State Cordell Hull said upon returning from the Moscow Conference of 1943, abolishes the "need for spheres of influence, for alliances, for balance of power."

Liberal internationalism seeks through multilateralism to transcend power politics, narrow national interest and, ultimately, the nation—state itself. The nation-state is seen as some kind of archaic residue of an anarchic past, an affront to the vision of a domesticated international arena. This is why liberal thinkers embrace the erosion of sovereignty promised by the new information technologies and the easy movement of capital across borders. They welcome the decline of sovereignty as the road to the new globalism of a norm-driven, legally-bound international system broken to the mold of domestic society.[7]

The greatest sovereign, of course, is the American superpower, which is why liberal internationalists feel such acute discomfort with American dominance. To achieve their vision, America too—America especially—must be domesticated. Their project is thus to restrain America by building an entangling web of interdependence, tying down Gulliver with myriad strings that diminish his overweening power. Who, after all, was the ABM treaty or a land mine treaty going to restrain? North Korea?

This liberal internationalist vision—the multilateral handcuffing of American power—is, as Robert Kagan has pointed out, the dominant view in Europe.[8] That is to be expected, given Europe's weakness and America's power. But it is a mistake to see this as only a European view. The idea of a new international community with self-governing institutions and self-enforcing norms—the vision that requires the domestication of American power—is the view of the Democratic Party in the United States and of a large part of the American foreign policy establishment. They spent the last decade in power fashioning precisely those multilateral ties to restrain the American Gulliver and remake him into a tame international citizen.[9] The multilateralist project is to use—indeed, to use up-current American dominance to create a new international system in which new norms of legalism and interdependence rule in America's place—in short, a system that is no longer unipolar.

> "There is much pious talk about a new multilateral world and the promise of the United Nations as guarantor of a new post-Cold War order. But this is to mistake cause and effect, the United States and the United Nations. The United Nations is guarantor of nothing. Except in a formal sense, it can hardly be said to exist. Collective security? In the Gulf, without the United States leading and prodding, bribing and blackmailing, no one would have stirred. . . . The world would have written off Kuwait the way the last body pledged to collective security, the League of Nations, wrote off Abyssinia."
> —The Unipolar Moment

REALISM AND THE NEW UNILATERALISM

The basic division between the two major foreign policy schools in America centers on the question of what is, and what should be, the fundamental basis of international relations: paper or power. Liberal internationalism envisions a world order that, like domestic society, is governed by laws and not men. Realists see this vision as hopelessly Utopian. The history of paper treaties—from the prewar Kellogg-Briand Pact and Munich to the post-Cold War Oslo accords and the 1994 Agreed Framework with North Korea—is a history of naivete and cynicism, a combination both toxic and volatile that invariably ends badly. Trade agreements with Canada are one thing. Pieces of parchment to which existential enemies affix a signature are quite another. They are worse than worthless because they give a false sense of security and breed complacency. For the realist, the ultimate determinant of the most basic elements of international life—security, stability and peace—is power.

Which is why a realist would hardly forfeit the current unipolarity for the vain promise of goo-goo one-worldism. Nor, however, should a realist want to forfeit unipolarity for the familiarity of traditional multipolarity. Multipolarity is inherently fluid and unpredictable. Europe practiced multipolarity for centuries and found it so unstable and bloody, culminating in 1914 in the catastrophic collapse of delicately balanced alliance systems, that Europe sought its permanent abolition in political and economic union. Having abjured multipolarity for the region, it is odd in the extreme to then prefer multipolarity for the world.

Less can be said about the destiny of unipolarity. It is too new. Yet we do have the history of the last decade, our only modern experience with unipolarity, and it was a decade of unusual stability among all major powers. It would be foolish to project from just a ten-year experience, but that experience does call into question the basis for the claims that unipolarity is intrinsically unstable or impossible to sustain in a mass democracy.

I would argue that unipolarity, managed benignly, is far more likely to keep the peace. Benignity is, of course, in the eye of the beholder. But the American claim to benignity is not mere self-congratulation. We have a track record. Consider one of history's rare controlled experiments. In the 1940s, lines were drawn through three peoples—Germans, Koreans and Chinese—one side closely bound to the United States, the other to its adversary. It turned into a controlled experiment because both states in the divided lands shared a common culture. Fifty years later the results are in. Does anyone doubt the superiority, both moral and material, of West Germany vs. East Germany, South Korea vs. North Korea and Taiwan vs. China?[10]

Benignity is also manifest in the way others welcome our power. It is the reason, for example, that the Pacific Rim countries are loath to see our military presence diminished: They know that the United States is not an imperial power with a desire to rule other countries—which is why they so readily accept it as a balancer. It is the reason, too, why Europe, so seized with complaints about American high-handedness, nonetheless reacts with alarm to the occasional suggestion that America might withdraw its military presence. America came, but it did not come to rule. Unlike other hegemons and would-be hegemons, it does not entertain a grand vision of a new world. No Thousand Year Reich. No New Soviet Man. It has no great desire to remake human nature, to conquer for the extraction of natural resources, or to rule for the simple pleasure of dominion. Indeed, America is the first hegemonic power in history to be obsessed with "exit strategies." It could not wait to get out of Haiti and Somalia; it would get out of Kosovo and Bosnia today if it could. Its principal aim is to maintain the stability and relative tranquility of the current international system by enforcing, maintaining and extending the current peace.

The form of realism that I am arguing for—call it the new unilateralism—is clear in its determination to self-consciously and confidently deploy American power in pursuit of those global ends. Note: global ends. There is a form of unilateralism that is devoted only to narrow American self-interest and it has a name, too: It is called isolationism. Critics of the new unilateralism often confuse it with isolationism because both are prepared to unashamedly exercise American power. But isolationists oppose America acting as a unipolar power not because they disagree with the unilateral means, but because they deem the ends far too broad. Isolationists would abandon the larger world and use American power exclusively for the narrowest of American interests: manning Fortress America by defending the American homeland and putting up barriers to trade and immigration.

The new unilateralism defines American interests far beyond narrow self-defense. In particular, it identifies two other major interests, both global: extending the peace by advancing democracy and preserving the peace by acting as balancer of last resort. Britain was the balancer in Europe, joining the weaker coalition against the stronger to create equilibrium. America's unique global power allows it to be the balancer in every region. We balanced Iraq by supporting its weaker neighbors in the Gulf War. We balance China by supporting the ring of smaller states at its periphery (from South Korea to Taiwan, even to Vietnam). Our role in the Balkans was essentially to create a microbalance: to support the weaker Bosnian Muslims against their more dominant neighbors, and subsequently to support the weaker Albanian Kosovars against the Serbs.

Of course, both of these tasks often advance American national interests as well. The promotion of democracy multiplies the number of nations likely to be friendly to the United States, and regional equilibria produce stability that benefits a commercial republic like the United States. America's (intended) exertions on behalf of pre-emptive non-proliferation, too, are clearly in the interest of both the United States and the international system as a whole.

Critics find this paradoxical: acting unilaterally but for global ends. Why paradoxical? One can hardly argue that depriving Saddam (and potentially, terrorists) of WMD is not a global end. Unilateralism may be required to pursue this end. We may be left isolated in so doing, but we would be acting nevertheless in the name of global interests—larger than narrow American self-interest and larger, too, than the narrowly perceived self-interest of smaller, weaker powers (even great powers) that dare not confront the rising danger.

What is the essence of that larger interest? Most broadly defined, it is maintaining a stable, open and functioning unipolar system. Liberal internationalists disdain that goal as too selfish, as it makes paramount the preservation of both American power and independence. Isolationists reject the goal as too selfless, for defining American interests too globally and thus too generously.

A third critique comes from what might be called pragmatic realists, who see the new unilateralism 1 have outlined as hubristic, and whose objections are practical. They are prepared to engage in a pragmatic multilateralism. They value great power concert. They seek Security Council support not because it confers any moral authority, but because it spreads risk. In their view, a single hegemon risks far more violent resentment than would a power that consistently acts as primus inter pares, sharing rule-making functions with others.[11]

I have my doubts. The United States made an extraordinary effort in the Gulf War to get UN support, share decision-making, assemble a coalition and, as we have seen, deny itself the fruits of victory in order to honor coalition goals. Did that diminish the anti-American feeling in the region? Did it garner support for subsequent Iraq policy dictated by the original acquiescence to the coalition?

The attacks of September 11 were planned during the Clinton administration, an administration that made a fetish of consultation and did its utmost to subordinate American hegemony and smother unipolarity. The resentments were hardly assuaged. Why? Because the extremist rage against the United States is engendered by the very structure of the international system, not by the details of our management of it.

Pragmatic realists also value international support in the interest of sharing burdens, on the theory that sharing decision making enlists others in our own hegemonic enterprise and makes things less costly. If you are too vigorous in asserting yourself in the short-term, they argue, you are likely to injure yourself in the long-term when you encounter problems that require the full cooperation of other partners, such as counter-terrorism. As Brooks and Wohlforth put it, "Straining relationships now will lead only to a more challenging policy environment later on."[12]

If the concern about the new unilateralism is that American assertiveness be judiciously rationed, and that one needs to think long-term, it is hard to disagree. One does not go it alone or dictate terms on every issue. On some issues such as membership in and support of the WTO, where the long-term benefit both to the American national interest and global interests is demonstrable, one willingly constricts sovereignty. Trade agreements are easy calls, however, free trade being perhaps the only mathematically provable political good. Others require great skepticism. The Kyoto Protocol, for example, would have harmed the American economy while doing nothing for the global environment. (Increased emissions from China, India and Third World countries exempt from its provisions would have more than made up for American cuts.) Kyoto failed on its merits, but was nonetheless pushed because the rest of the world supported it. The same case was made for the chemical and biological weapons treaties—sure, they are useless or worse, but why not give in there in order to build good will for future needs? But appeasing multilateralism does not assuage it; appeasement merely legitimizes it. Repeated acquiescence to provisions that America deems injurious reinforces the notion that legitimacy derives from international consensus, thus undermining America's future freedom of action—and thus contradicting the pragmatic realists' own goals.

America must be guided by its independent judgement, both about its own interest and about the global interest. Especially on matters of national security, war-making and the deployment of power, America should neither defer nor contract out decision making, particularly when the concessions involve permanent structural constrictions such as those imposed by an International Criminal Court. Prudence, yes. No need to act the superpower in East Timor or Bosnia. But there is a need to do so in Afghanistan and in Iraq. No need to act the superpower on steel tariffs. But there is a need to do so on missile defense.

The prudent exercise of power allows, indeed calls for, occasional concessions on non-vital issues if only to maintain psychological good will. Arrogance and gratuitous high-handedness are counterproductive. But we should not delude ourselves as to what psychological good will buys. Countries will cooperate with us, first, out of their own self-interest and, second, out of the need and desire to cultivate good relations with the world's superpower. Warm and fuzzy feelings are a distant third. Take counterterrorism. After the attack on the U.S.S. Cole, Yemen did everything it could to stymie the American investigation. It lifted not a finger to suppress terrorism. This was under an American administration that was obsessively accommodating and multilateralist. Today, under the most unilateralist of administrations, Yemen has decided to assist in the war on terrorism. This was not a result of a sudden attack of good will toward America. It was a result of the war in Afghanistan, which concentrated the mind of heretofore recalcitrant states like Yemen on the costs of non-cooperation with the United States.[13] Coalitions are not made by superpowers going begging hat in hand. They are made by asserting a position and inviting others to join. What "pragmatic" realists often fail to realize is that unilateralism is the high road to multilateralism. When George Bush senior said of the Iraqi invasion of Kuwait, "this will not stand," and made it clear that he was prepared to act alone if necessary, that declaration—and the credibility of American determination to act unilaterally—in and of itself created a coalition. Hafez al-Assad did not join out of feelings of good will. He joined because no one wants to be left at the dock with the hegemon is sailing.

Unilateralism does not mean seeking to act alone. One acts in concert with others if possible. Unilateralism simply means that one does not allow oneself to be hostage to others. No unilateralist would, say, reject Security Council support for an attack on Iraq. The nontrivial question that separates unilateralism from mulilateralism—and that tests the "pragmatic realists"—is this: What do you do if, at the end of the day, the Security Council refuses to back you? Do you allow yourself to be dictated to on issues of vital national—and international—security?

When I first proposed the unipolar model in 1990, I suggested that we should accept both its burdens and opportunities and that, if America did not wreck its economy, unipolarity could last thirty or forty years. That seemed bold at the time. Today, it seems rather modest. The unipolar moment has become the unipolar era. It remains true, however, that its durability will be decided at home. It will depend largely on whether it is welcomed by Americans or seen as a burden to be shed—either because we are too good for the world (the isolationist critique) or because we are not worthy of it (the liberal internationalist critique).

The new unilateralism argues explicitly and unashamedly for maintaining unipolarity, for sustaining America's unrivaled dominance for the foreseeable future. It could be a long future, assuming we successfully manage the single greatest threat, namely, weapons of mass destruction in the hands of rogue states. This in itself will require the aggressive and confident application of unipolar power rather than falling back, as we did in the 1990s, on paralyzing multilateralism. The future of the unipolar era hinges on whether America is governed by those who wish to retain, augment and use unipolarity to advance not just American but global ends, or whether America is governed by those who wish to give it up—either by allowing unipolarity to decay as they retreat to Fortress America, or by passing on the burden by gradually transferring power to multilateral institutions as heirs to American hegemony. The challenge to unipolarity is not from the outside but from the inside. The choice is ours. To impiously paraphrase Benjamin Franklin: History has given you an empire, if you will keep it.

NOTES

1. Editor's note: This quotation, and all subsequent boxed quotations in this essay, are from Charles Krauthammer, "The Unipolar Moment", Foreign Affairs: America and the World (1990/91), which introduced the idea of American unipolarity. That essay was adapted from the first annual Henry M. Jackson Memorial Lecture, September 18, 1990.
2. Kennedy, "The Eagle has Landed", Financial Times, February 2, 2002.
3. Huntington, "The Lonely Superpower", Foreign Affairs (March/April 1999). By uni-multipolar Huntington means a system with a pre-eminent state whose sole participation is insufficient for the resolution of international issues. The superpower can still serve as a veto player, but requires other powers to achieve its ends.
4. Judt, "Its Own Worst Enemy", New York Review of Books, August 15, 2002.
5. Brooks and Wohlforth, "American Primacy in Perspective", Foreign Affairs (July/August 2002).
6. Interview with the German newspaper Bild, translated and reported in the Interfax News Bulletin, September 21, 2001.
7. A Sky News poll finds that even the British public considers George W. Bush a greater threat to world peace than Saddam Hussein. The poll was conducted September 26, 2002.
8. See my "A World Imagined", The New Republic, March 15, 1999, from which some of the foregoing discussion is drawn.
9. Kagan, "Power and Weakness", Policy Review (June 2002).
10. In "A World Imagined", I noted the oddity of an American governing elite adopting a goal-a constrained America-that is more logically the goal of foreigners: "The ultimate irony is that this is traditionally the vision of small nations. They wish to level the playing field with the big boys. For them, treaties, international institutions, and interdependence are the great equalizers. Leveling is fine for them. But for us? The greatest power in the world-the most dominant power relative to its rivals that the world has seen since the Roman empire—is led by people who seek to diminish that dominance and level the international arena."
11. This is not to claim, by any means, a perfect record of benignity. America has often made and continues to make alliances with unpleasant authoritarian regimes. As I argued recently in Time ("Dictatorships and Double Standards", September 23, 2002), such alliances are nonetheless justified so long as they are instrumental (meant to defeat the larger evil) and temporary (expire with the emergency). When Hitler was defeated, we stopped coddling Stalin. Forty years later, as the Soviet threat receded, the United States was instrumental in easing Pinochet out of power and overthrowing Marcos. We withdrew our support for these dictators once the two conditions that justified such alliances had disappeared: The global threat of Soviet communism had receded, and truly democratic domestic alternatives to these dictators had emerged.

12. This basic view is well-represented in The National Interest's Fall 2002 symposium, "September 1h One Year On: Power, Purpose and Strategy in U.S. Foreign Policy."
13. Brooks and Wohlforth, "American Primacy in Perspective."
14. The most recent and dramatic demonstration of this newfound cooperation was the CIA killing on November 4 of an Al-Qaeda leader in Yemen using a remotely operated Predator drone.

America's Imperial Ambition

G. John Ikenberry

THE LURES OF PREEMPTION

In the shadows of the Bush administration's war on terrorism, sweeping new ideas are circulating about U.S. grand strategy and the restructuring of today's unipolar world. They call for American unilateral and preemptive, even preventive, use of force, facilitated if possible by coalitions of the willing—but ultimately unconstrained by the rules and norms of the international community. At the extreme, these notions form a neoimperial vision in which the United States arrogates to itself the global role of setting standards, determining threats, using force, and meting out justice. It is a vision in which sovereignty becomes more absolute for America even as it becomes more conditional for countries that challenge Washington's standards of internal and external behavior. It is a vision made necessary—at least in the eyes of its advocates—by the new and apocalyptic character of contemporary terrorist threats and by America's unprecedented global dominance. These radical strategic ideas and impulses could transform today's world order in a way that the end of the Cold War, strangely enough, did not.

The exigencies of fighting terrorism in Afghanistan and the debate over intervening in Iraq obscure the profundity of this geopolitical challenge. Blueprints have not been produced, and Yalta-style summits have not been convened, but actions are afoot to dramatically alter the political order that the United States has built with its partners since the 1940s. The twin new realities of our age—catastrophic terrorism and American unipolar power—do necessitate a rethinking of the organizing principles of international order. America and the other major states do need a new consensus on terrorist threats, weapons of mass destruction (WMD), the use of force, and the global rules of the game. This imperative requires a better appreciation of the ideas coming out of the administration. But in turn, the administration should understand the virtues of the old order that it wishes to displace.

G. John Ikenberry, "America's Imperial Ambition," *Foreign Affairs*, Vol. 81, No. 5, (Sept–Oct 2002) pp. 44–60. Copyright © by the Council on Foreign Relations, Inc.

America's nascent neoimperial grand strategy threatens to rend the fabric of the international community and political partnerships precisely at a time when that community and those partnerships are urgently needed. It is an approach fraught with peril and likely to fail. It is not only politically unsustainable but diplomatically harmful. And if history is a guide, it will trigger antagonism and resistance that will leave America in a more hostile and divided world.

PROVEN LEGACIES

The mainstream of American foreign policy has been defined since the 1940s by two grand strategies that have built the modern international order. One is realist in orientation, organized around containment, deterrence, and the maintenance of the global balance of power. Facing a dangerous and expansive Soviet Union after 1945, the United States stepped forward to fill the vacuum left by a waning British Empire and a collapsing European order to provide a counter-weight to Stalin and his Red Army.

The touchstone of this strategy was containment, which sought to deny the Soviet Union the ability to expand its sphere of influence. Order was maintained by managing the bipolar balance between the American and Soviet camps. Stability was achieved through nuclear deterrence. For the first time, nuclear weapons and the doctrine of mutual assured destruction made war between the great powers irrational. But containment and global power-balancing ended with the collapse of the Soviet Union in 1991. Nuclear deterrence is no longer the defining logic of the existing order, although it remains a recessed feature that continues to impart stability in relations among China, Russia, and the West.

This strategy has yielded a bounty of institutions and partnerships for America. The most important have been the NATO and U.S.-Japan alliances, American-led security partnerships that have survived the end of the Cold War by providing a bulwark for stability through commitment and reassurance. The United States maintains a forward presence in Europe and East Asia; its alliance partners gain security protection as well as a measure of regularity in their relationship with the world's leading military power. But Cold War balancing has yielded more than a utilitarian alliance structure; it has generated a political order that has value in itself.

This grand strategy presupposes a loose framework of consultations and agreements to resolve differences: the great powers extend to each other the respect of equals, and they accommodate each other until vital interests come into play. The domestic affairs of these states remain precisely that—domestic. The great powers compete with each other, and although war is not unthinkable, sober statecraft and the balance of power offer the best hope for stability and peace.

George W. Bush ran for president emphasizing some of these themes, describing his approach to foreign policy as "new realism": the focus of American efforts should shift away from Clinton-era preoccupations with nation building, international social work, and the promiscuous use of force, and toward cultivating great-power relations and rebuilding the nation's military. Bush's efforts

to integrate Russia into the Western security order have been the most important manifestation of this realist grand strategy at work. The moderation in
Washington's confrontational rhetoric toward China also reflects this emphasis. If
the major European and Asian states play by the rules, the great-power order will
remain stable. (In a way, it is precisely because Europe is not a great power—or at
least seems to eschew the logic of great-power politics—that it is now generating
so much discord with the United States.)

The other grand strategy, forged during World War II as the United States
planned the reconstruction of the world economy, is liberal in orientation. It seeks
to build order around institutionalized political relations among integrated market
democracies, supported by an opening of economies. This agenda was not simply
an inspiration of American businessmen and economists, however. There have
always been geopolitical goals as well. Whereas America's realist grand strategy
was aimed at countering Soviet power, its liberal grand strategy was aimed at
avoiding a return to the 1930s, an era of regional blocs, trade conflict, and strategic rivalry. Open trade, democracy, and multilateral institutional relations went
together. Underlying this strategy was the view that a rule-based international
order, especially one in which the United States uses its political weight to derive
congenial rules, will most fully protect American interests, conserve its power, and
extend its influence.

This grand strategy has been pursued through an array of postwar initiatives
that look disarmingly like "low politics": the Bretton Woods institutions, the World
Trade Organization (WTO), and the Organization for Economic Cooperation and
Development are just a few examples. Together, they form a complex layer cake
of integrative initiatives that bind the democratic industrialized world together.
During the 1990s, the United States continued to pursue this liberal grand strategy. Both the first Bush and the Clinton administrations attempted to articulate a
vision of world order that was not dependent on an external threat or an explicit
policy of balance of power. Bush the elder talked about the importance of the
transatlantic community and articulated ideas about a more fully integrated Asia-
Pacific region. In both cases, the strategy offered a positive vision of alliance and
partnership built around common values, tradition, mutual self-interest, and the
preservation of stability. The Clinton administration likewise attempted to
describe the post-Cold War order in terms of the expansion of democracy and
open markets. In this vision, democracy provided the foundation for global and
regional community, and trade and capital flows were forces for political reform
and integration.

The current Bush administration is not eager to brandish this Clinton-looking
grand strategy, but it still invokes that strategy's ideas in various ways. Support
for Chinese entry into the WTO is based on the liberal anticipation that free
markets and integration into the Western economic order will create pressures
for Chinese political reform and discourage a belligerent foreign policy. Administration support for last year's multilateral trade-negotiating round in Doha,
Qatar, also was premised on the economic and political benefits of freer trade.
After September 11, U.S. Trade Representative Robert Zoellick even linked trade
expansion authority to the fight against terrorism: trade, growth, integration, and
political stability go together. Richard Haass, policy planning director at the State

Department, argued recently that "the principal aim of American foreign policy is to integrate other countries and organizations into arrangements that will sustain a world consistent with U.S. interests and values"—again, an echo of the liberal grand strategy. The administration's recent protectionist trade actions in steel and agriculture have triggered such a loud outcry around the world precisely because governments are worried that the United States might be retreating from this postwar liberal strategy.

AMERICA'S HISTORIC BARGAINS

These two grand strategies are rooted in divergent, even antagonistic, intellectual traditions. But over the last 50 years they have worked remarkably well together. The realist grand strategy created a political rationale for establishing major security commitments around the world. The liberal strategy created a positive agenda for American leadership. The United States could exercise its power and achieve its national interests, but it did so in a way that helped deepen the fabric of international community. American power did not destabilize world order; it helped create it. The development of rule-based agreements and political-security partnerships was good both for the United States and for much of the world. By the end of the 1990s, the result was an international political order of unprecedented size and success: a global coalition of democratic states tied together through markets, institutions, and security partnerships.

This international order was built on two historic bargains. One was the U.S. commitment to provide its European and Asian partners with security protection and access to American markets, technology, and supplies within an open world economy. In return, these countries agreed to be reliable partners providing diplomatic, economic, and logistical support for the United States as it led the wider Western postwar order. The other is the liberal bargain that addressed the uncertainties of American power. East Asian and European states agreed to accept American leadership and operate within an agreed-upon political-economic system. The United States, in response, opened itself up and bound itself to its partners. In effect, the United States built an institutionalized coalition of partners and reinforced the stability of these mutually beneficial relations by making itself more "user-friendly"—that is, by playing by the rules and creating ongoing political processes that facilitated consultation and joint decision making. The United States made its power safe for the world, and in return the world agreed to live within the U.S. system. These bargains date from the 1940s, but they continue to shore up the post-Cold War order. The result has been the most stable and prosperous international system in world history. But new ideas within the Bush administration—crystallized by September 11 and U.S. dominance—are unsettling this order and the political bargains behind it.

A NEW GRAND STRATEGY

For the first time since the dawn of the Cold War, a new grand strategy is taking shape in Washington. It is advanced most directly as a response to terrorism, but it also constitutes a broader view about how the United States should wield power and organize world order. According to this new paradigm, America is to be less bound to its partners and to global rules and institutions while it steps forward to play a more unilateral and anticipatory role in attacking terrorist threats and confronting rogue states seeking WMD. The United States will use its unrivaled military power to manage the global order.

This new grand strategy has seven elements. It begins with a fundamental commitment to maintaining a unipolar world in which the United States has no peer competitor. No coalition of great powers without the United States will be allowed to achieve hegemony. Bush made this point the centerpiece of American security policy in his West Point commencement address in June: "America has, and intends to keep, military strengths beyond challenges—thereby making the destabilizing arms races of other eras pointless, and limiting rivalries to trade and other pursuits of peace." The United States will not seek security through the more modest realist strategy of operating within a global system of power balancing, nor will it pursue a liberal strategy in which institutions, democracy, and integrated markets reduce the importance of power politics altogether. America will be so much more powerful than other major states that strategic rivalries and security competition among the great powers will disappear, leaving everyone—not just the United States—better off.

This goal made an unsettling early appearance at the end of the first Bush administration in a leaked Pentagon memorandum written by then Assistant Secretary of Defense Paul Wolfowitz. With the collapse of the Soviet Union, he wrote, the United States must act to prevent the rise of peer competitors in Europe and Asia. But the 1990s made this strategic aim moot. The United States grew faster than the other major states during the decade, it reduced military spending more slowly, and it dominated investment in the technological advancement of its forces. Today, however, the new goal is to make these advantages permanent—a fait accompli that will prompt other states to not even try to catch up. Some thinkers have described the strategy as "breakout," in which the United States moves so quickly to develop technological advantages (in robotics, lasers, satellites, precision munitions, etc.) that no state or coalition could ever challenge it as global leader, protector, and enforcer.

The second element is a dramatic new analysis of global threats and how they must be attacked. The grim new reality is that small groups of terrorists—perhaps aided by outlaw states—may soon acquire highly destructive nuclear, chemical, and biological weapons that can inflict catastrophic destruction. These terrorist groups cannot be appeased or deterred, the administration believes, so they must be eliminated. Secretary of Defense Donald Rumsfeld has articulated this frightening view with elegance: regarding the threats that confront the United States, he said, "There are things we know that we know. There are known unknowns. That is to say, there are things that we know we don't know. But there are also unknown unknowns. There are things we don't know we don't know. . . . Each year, we discover a few more of those unknown unknowns." In other words, there could exist groups of terrorists that no one knows about. They may have nuclear, chemical, or biological weapons that the United States did not know they could get, and they might be willing and able to attack without warning. In the age of terror, there is less room for error. Small networks of angry people can inflict unimaginable harm on the rest of the world. They are not nation-states, and they do not play by the accepted rules of the game.

The third element of the new strategy maintains that the Cold War concept of deterrence is outdated. Deterrence, sovereignty, and the balance of power work together. When deterrence is no longer viable, the larger realist edifice starts to crumble. The threat today is not other great powers that must be managed through second-strike nuclear capacity but the transnational terrorist networks that have no home address. They cannot be deterred because they are either willing to die for their cause or able to escape retaliation. The old defensive strategy of building missiles and other weapons that can survive a first strike and be used in a retaliatory strike to punish the attacker will no longer ensure security. The only option, then, is offense.

The use of force, this camp argues, will therefore need to be preemptive and perhaps even preventive—taking on potential threats before they can present a major problem. But this premise plays havoc with the old international rules of self-defense and United Nations norms about the proper use of force. Rumsfeld has articulated the justification for preemptive action by stating that the "absence of evidence is not evidence of absence of weapons of mass destruction." But such an approach renders international norms of self-defense—enshrined by Article 51 of the UN Charter—almost meaningless. The administration should remember that when Israeli jets bombed the Iraqi nuclear reactor at Osirak in 1981 in what Israel described as an act of self-defense, the world condemned it as an act of aggression. Even British Prime Minister Margaret Thatcher and the American ambassador to the UN, Jeane Kirkpatrick, criticized the action, and the United States joined in passing a UN resolution condemning it.

The Bush administration's security doctrine takes this country down the same slippery slope. Even without a clear threat, the United States now claims a right to use preemptive or preventive military force. At West Point, Bush put it succinctly when he stated that "the military must be ready to strike at a moment's notice in any dark corner of the world. All nations that decide for aggression and terror will pay a price." The administration defends this new doctrine as a necessary adjustment to a more uncertain and shifting threat environment. This policy of no regrets errs on the side of action—but it can also easily become national security by hunch or inference, leaving the world without clear-cut norms for justifying force.

As a result, the fourth element of this emerging grand strategy involves a recasting of the terms of sovereignty. Because these terrorist groups cannot be deterred, the United States must be prepared to intervene anywhere, anytime to preemptively destroy the threat. Terrorists do not respect borders, so neither can the United States. Moreover, countries that harbor terrorists, either by consent or because they are unable to enforce their laws within their territory, effectively forfeit their rights of sovereignty. Haass recently hinted at this notion in The New Yorker:

> What you are seeing in this administration is the emergence of a new principle or body of ideas . . . about what you might call the limits of sovereignty. Sovereignty entails obligations. One is not to massacre your own people. Another is not to support terrorism in any way. If a government fails to meet these obligations, then it forfeits some of the normal advantages of sovereignty, including the right to be left alone inside your

own territory. Other governments, including the United States, gain the right to intervene. In the case of terrorism, this can even lead to a right of preventive . . . self-defense. You essentially can act in anticipation if you have grounds to think it's a question of when, and not if, you're going to be attacked.

Here the war on terrorism and the problem of the proliferation of WMD get entangled. The worry is that a few despotic states—Iraq in particular, but also Iran and North Korea—will develop capabilities to produce weapons of mass destruction and put these weapons in the hands of terrorists. The regimes themselves may be deterred from using such capabilities, but they might pass along these weapons to terrorist networks that are not deterred. Thus another emerging principle within the Bush administration: the possession of WMD by unaccountable, unfriendly, despotic governments is itself a threat that must be countered. In the old era, despotic regimes were to be lamented but ultimately tolerated.

With the rise of terrorism and weapons of mass destruction, they are now unacceptable threats. Thus states that are not technically in violation of any existing international laws could nevertheless be targets of American force—if Washington determines that they have a prospective capacity to do harm.

The recasting of sovereignty is paradoxical. On the one hand, the new grand strategy reaffirms the importance of the territorial nation-state. After all, if all governments were accountable and capable of enforcing the rule of law within their sovereign territory, terrorists would find it very difficult to operate. The emerging Bush doctrine enshrines this idea: governments will be held responsible for what goes on inside their borders. On the other hand, sovereignty has been made newly conditional: governments that fail to act like respectable, law-abiding states will lose their sovereignty.

In one sense, such conditional sovereignty is not new. Great powers have willfully transgressed the norms of state sovereignty as far back as such norms have existed, particularly within their traditional spheres of influence, whenever the national interest dictated. The United States itself has done this within the western hemisphere since the nineteenth century. What is new and provocative in this notion today, however, is the Bush administration's inclination to apply it on a global basis, leaving to itself the authority to determine when sovereign rights have been forfeited, and doing so on an anticipatory basis.

The fifth element of this new grand strategy is a general depreciation of international rules, treaties, and security partnerships. This point relates to the new threats themselves: if the stakes are rising and the margins of error are shrinking in the war on terrorism, multilateral norms and agreements that sanction and limit the use of force are just annoying distractions. The critical task is to eliminate the threat. But the emerging unilateral strategy is also informed by a deeper suspicion about the value of international agreements themselves. Part of this view arises from a deeply felt and authentically American belief that the United States should not get entangled in the corrupting and constraining world of multilateral rules and institutions. For some Americans, the belief that American sovereignty is politically sacred leads to a preference for isolationism. But the more influential view—particularly after September 11—is not that the United States should withdraw from the world but that it should operate in the world on its own terms. The Bush administration's repudiation of a remarkable array of treaties and institutions—from the Kyoto Protocol on global warming to the International Criminal Court to the Biological Weapons Convention—reflects this new bias. Likewise, the United States signed a formal agreement with Russia on the reduction of deployed nuclear warheads only after Moscow's insistence; the Bush administration wanted only a "gentlemen's agreement." In other words, the United States has decided it is big enough, powerful enough, and remote enough to go it alone.

Sixth, the new grand strategy argues that the United States will need to play a direct and unconstrained role in responding to threats. This conviction is partially based on a judgment that no other country or coalition—even the European Union—has the force-projection capabilities to respond to terrorist and rogue states around the world. A decade of U.S. defense spending and modernization has left allies of the United States far behind.

In combat operations, alliance partners are increasingly finding it difficult to mesh with U.S. forces. This view is also based on the judgment that joint operations and the use of force through coalitions tend to hinder effective operations. To some observers, this lesson became clear in the allied bombing campaign over Kosovo. The sentiment was also expressed during the U.S. and allied military actions in Afghanistan. Rumsfeld explained this point earlier this year, when he said, "The mission must determine the coalition; the coalition must not determine the mission. If it does, the mission will be dumbed down to the lowest common denominator, and we can't afford that."

No one in the Bush administration argues that NATO or the U.S.-Japan alliance should be dismantled. Rather, these alliances are now seen as less useful to the United States as it confronts today's threats. Some officials argue that it is not that the United States chooses to depreciate alliance partnerships, but that the Europeans are unwilling to keep up. Whether that is true, the upgrading of the American military, along with its sheer size relative to the forces of the rest of the world, leaves the United States in a class by itself. In these circumstances, it is increasingly difficult to maintain the illusion of true alliance partnership. America's allies become merely strategic assets that are useful depending on the circumstance. The United States still finds attractive the logistical reach that its global alliance system provides, but the pacts with countries in Asia and Europe become more contingent and less premised on a vision of a common security community.

Finally, the new grand strategy attaches little value to international stability. There is an unsentimental view in the unilateralist camp that the traditions of the past must be shed. Whether it is withdrawal from the Anti-Ballistic Missile Treaty or the resistance to signing other formal arms-control treaties, policymakers are convinced that the United States needs to move beyond outmoded Cold War thinking. Administration officials have noted with some satisfaction that America's withdrawal from the ABM Treaty did not lead to a global arms race but actually paved the way for a historic arms-reduction agreement between the United States and Russia. This move is seen as a validation that moving beyond the old paradigm of great-power relations will not bring the international house down. The world can withstand radically new security approaches, and it will accommodate American unilateralism as well. But stability is not an end in itself. The administration's new hawkish policy toward North Korea, for example, might be destabilizing to the region, but such instability might be the necessary price for dislodging a dangerous and evil regime in Pyongyang.

In this brave new world, neoimperial thinkers contend that the older realist and liberal grand strategies are not very helpful. American security will not be ensured, as realist grand strategy assumes, by the preservation of deterrence and stable relations among the major powers. In a world of asymmetrical threats, the global balance of power is not the linchpin of war and peace. Likewise, liberal strategies of building order around open trade and democratic institutions might have some long-term impact on terrorism, but they do not address the immediacy of the threats. Apocalyptic violence is at our doorstep, so efforts at strengthening the rules and institutions of the international community are of little practical value. If we accept the worst-case imagining of "we don't know what we don't know," everything else is secondary: international rules, traditions of partnership, and standards of legitimacy. It is a war. And as Clausewitz famously remarked, "War is such a dangerous business that the mistakes which come from kindness are the very worst."

IMPERIAL DANGERS

Pitfalls accompany this neoimperial grand strategy, however. Unchecked U.S. power, shorn of legitimacy and disentangled from the postwar norms and institutions of the international order, will usher in a more hostile international system, making it far harder to achieve American interests. The secret of the United States' long brilliant run as the world's leading state was its ability and willingness to exercise power within alliance and multinational frameworks, which made its power and agenda more acceptable to allies and other key states around the world. This achievement has now been put at risk by the administration's new thinking.

The most immediate problem is that the neoimperialist approach is unsustainable. Going it alone might well succeed in removing Saddam Hussein from power, but it is far less certain that a strategy of counterproliferation, based on American willingness to use unilateral force to confront dangerous dictators, can work over the long term. An American policy that leaves the United States alone to decide which states are threats and how best to deny them weapons of mass destruction will lead to a diminishment of multilateral mechanisms—most important of which is the nonproliferation regime.

The Bush administration has elevated the threat of WMD to the top of its security agenda without investing its power or prestige in fostering, monitoring, and enforcing nonproliferation commitments. The tragedy of September 11 has given the Bush administration the authority and willingness to confront the Iraqs of the world. But that will not be enough when even more complicated cases come along—when it is not the use of force that is needed but concerted multilateral action to provide sanctions and inspections. Nor is it certain that a preemptive or preventive military intervention will go well; it might trigger a domestic political backlash to American-led and military-focused interventionism. America's well-meaning imperial strategy could undermine the principled multilateral agreements, institutional infrastructure, and cooperative spirit needed for the long-term success of nonproliferation goals.

The specific doctrine of preemptive action poses a related problem: once the United States feels it can take such a course, nothing will stop other countries from doing the same. Does the United States want this doctrine in the hands of Pakistan, or even China or Russia? After all, it would not require the intervening state to first provide evidence for its actions. The United States argues that to wait until all the evidence is in, or until authoritative international bodies support action, is to wait too long. Yet that approach is the only basis that the United States can use if it needs to appeal for restraint in the actions of others. Moreover, and quite paradoxically, overwhelming American conventional military might, combined with a policy of preemptive strikes, could lead hostile states to accelerate programs to acquire their only possible deterrent to the United States: WMD. This is another version of the security dilemma, but one made worse by a neoimperial grand strategy.

Another problem follows. The use of force to eliminate WMD capabilities or overturn dangerous regimes is never simple, whether it is pursued unilaterally or by a concert of major states. After the military intervention is over, the target country has to be put back together. Peacekeeping and state building are inevitably required, as are long-term strategies that bring the UN, the World Bank, and the major powers together to orchestrate aid and other forms of assistance. This is not heroic work, but it is utterly necessary. Peacekeeping troops may he required for many years, even after a new regime is built. Regional conflicts inflamed by outside military intervention must also be calmed. This is the "long tail" of burdens and commitments that comes with every major military action.

When these costs and obligations are added to America's imperial military role, it becomes even more doubtful that the neoimperial strategy can be sustained at home over the long haul—the classic problem of imperial overstretch. The United States could keep its military predominance for decades if it is supported by a growing and increasingly productive economy. But the indirect burdens of cleaning up the political mess in terrorist-prone failed states levy a hidden cost. Peacekeeping and state building will require coalitions of states and multilateral agencies that can be brought into the process only if the initial decisions about military intervention are hammered out in consultation with other major states. America's older realist and liberal grand strategies suddenly become relevant again.

A third problem with an imperial grand strategy is that it cannot generate the cooperation needed to solve practical problems at the heart of the U.S. foreign policy agenda. In the fight on terrorism, the United States needs cooperation from European and Asian countries in intelligence, law enforcement, and logistics. Outside the security sphere, realizing U.S. objectives depends even more on a continuous stream of amicable working relations with major states around the world. It needs partners for trade liberalization, global financial stabilization, environmental protection, deterring transnational organized crime, managing the rise of China, and a host of other thorny challenges. But it is impossible to expect would-be partners to acquiesce to America's self-appointed global security protectorate and then pursue business as usual in all other domains.

The key policy tool for states confronting a unipolar and unilateral America is to withhold cooperation in day-to-day relations with the United States. One obvious means is trade policy; the European response to the recent American decision to impose tariffs on imported steel is explicable in these terms. This particular struggle concerns specific trade issues, but it is also a struggle over how Washington exercises power. The United States may be a unipolar military power, but economic and political power is more evenly distributed across the globe. The major states may not have much leverage in directly restraining American military policy, but they can make the United States pay a price in other areas.

Finally, the neoimperial grand strategy poses a wider problem for the maintenance of American unipolar power. It steps into the oldest trap of powerful imperial states: self-encirclement. When the most powerful state in the world throws its weight around, unconstrained by rules or norms of legitimacy, it risks a backlash. Other countries will bridle at an international order in which the United States plays only by its own rules. The proponents of the new grand strategy have assumed that the United States can single-handedly deploy military power abroad and not suffer untoward consequences; relations will be coarser with friends and allies, they believe, but such are the costs of leadership. But history shows that powerful states tend to trigger self-encirclement by their own overestimation of their power. Charles V, Louis XIV, Napoleon, and the leaders of post-Bismarck Germany sought to expand their imperial domains and impose a coercive order on others. Their imperial orders were all brought down when other countries decided they were not prepared to live in a world dominated by an overweening coercive state. America's imperial goals and modus operandi are much more limited and benign than were those of age-old emperors. But a hard-line imperial grand strategy runs the risk that history will repeat itself.

BRING IN THE OLD

Wars change world politics, and so too will America's war on terrorism. How great states fight wars, how they define the stakes, how they make the peace in its aftermath—all give lasting shape to the international system that emerges after the guns fall silent. In mobilizing their societies for battle, wartime leaders have tended to describe the military struggle as more than simply the defeat of an enemy. Woodrow Wilson sent U.S. troops to Europe not only to stop the kaiser's army but to destroy militarism and usher in a worldwide democratic revolution. Franklin Roosevelt saw the war with Germany and Japan as a struggle to secure "four great freedoms." The Atlantic Charter was a statement of war aims that called no just for the defeat of fascism but for a new dedication to social welfare and human rights within an open and stable world system. To advance these visions, Wilson and Roosevelt proposed new international rules and mechanisms of cooperation. Their message was clear: If you bear the burdens of war, we, your leaders, will use this dreadful conflict to usher in a more peaceful and decent order among states. Fighting the war had as much to do with building global relations as it did with vanquishing an enemy.

Bush has not fully articulated a vision of postwar international order, aside from defining the struggle as one between freedom and evil. The world has seen Washington take determined steps to fight terrorism, but it does not yet have a sense of Bush's larger, positive agenda for a strengthened and more decent international order.

This failure explains why the sympathy and goodwill generated around the world for the United States after September 11 quickly disappeared. Newspapers that once proclaimed "We are all Americans," now express distrust toward America. The prevailing view is that the United States seems prepared to use its power to go after terrorists and evil regimes, but not to use it to help build a more stable and peaceful world order. The United States appears to be degrading the rules and institutions of international community, not enhancing them. To the rest of the world, neoimperial thinking has more to do with exercising power than with exercising leadership.

In contrast, America's older strategic orientations—balance-of-power realism and liberal multilateralism—suggest a mature world power that seeks stability and pursues its interests in ways that do not fundamentally threaten the positions of other states. They are strategies of co-option and reassurance. The new imperial grand strategy presents the United States very differently: a revisionist state seeking to parlay its momentary power advantages into a world order in which it runs the show. Unlike the hegemonic states of the past, the United States does not seek territory or outright political domination in Europe or Asia; "America has no empire to extend or utopia to establish," Bush noted in his West Point address. But the sheer power advantages that the United States possesses and the doctrines of preemption and counterterrorism that it is articulating do unsettle governments and people around the world, The costs could be high. The last thing the United States wants is for foreign diplomats and government leaders to ask, How can we work around, undermine, contain, and retaliate against U.S. power?

Rather than invent a new grand strategy, the United States should reinvigorate its older strategies, those based on the view that America's security partnerships are not simply instrumental tools but critical components of an American-led world political order that should be preserved. U.S. power is both leveraged and made more legitimate and user-friendly by these partnerships. The neoimperial thinkers are haunted by the specter of catastrophic terrorism and seek a radical reordering of America's role in the world. America's commanding unipolar power and the advent of frightening new terrorist threats feed this imperial temptation. But it is a grand strategic vision that, taken to the extreme, will leave the world more dangerous and divided—and the United States less secure.

Understanding the Bush Doctrine

Robert Jervis

The invasion of Iraq, although important in itself, is even more noteworthy as a manifestation of the Bush doctrine. In a sharp break from the President's pre-September 11 views that saw American leadership, and especially its use of force, restricted to defending narrow and traditional vital interests, he has enunciated a far-reaching program that calls for something very much like an empire.[1]

The doctrine has four elements: a strong belief in the importance of a state's domestic regime in determining its foreign policy and the related judgment that this is an opportune time to transform international politics; the perception of great threats that can be defeated only by new and vigorous policies, most notably preventive war; a willingness to act unilaterally when necessary; and, as both a cause and a summary of these beliefs, an overriding sense that peace and stability require the United States to assert its primacy in world politics. It is; of course, possible that I am exaggerating and that what we are seeing is mostly an elaborate rationale for the overthrow of Saddam Hussein that will have little relevance beyond that. I think the doctrine is real, however. It is quite articulate, and American policy since the end of the military campaign has been consistent with it. Furthermore, there is a tendency for people to act in accord with the explanations they have given for their own behavior, which means that the doctrine could guide behavior even if it were originally a rationalization.[2]

I will describe, explain, and evaluate the doctrine. These three tasks are hard to separate. Evaluation and explanation are particularly and perhaps disturbingly close. To see the doctrine as a response to an unusual external environment may verge on endorsing it, especially for Realists who both oppose the doctrine and see states as rational. In the end, I believe it to be the product of idiosyncratic and structural factors, both a normal reaction to an abnormal situation and a policy that is likely to bring grief to the world and the United States. The United States may be only the latest in a long line of countries that is unable to place sensible limits on its fears and aspirations.[3]

DEMOCRACY AND LIBERALISM

This is not to say that the doctrine is entirely consistent, and one component may not fit well with the rest despite receiving pride of place in the "The National Security Strategy of the U.S.," which starts thusly: "The great struggles of the

Robert Jervis, Adlai E. Stevenson Professor of International Politics at Columbia University, served as president of the American Political Science Association in 2000–01. He is the author of numerous books and articles on international politics. His most recent book is *System Effects: Complexity in Political and Social Life*. *Political Science Quarterly*, 118 (Fall 2003): 365–388. Reprinted by permission.

twentieth century between liberty and totalitarianism ended with a decisive victory for the forces of freedom—and a single sustainable model for national success: freedom, democracy, and free enterprise." The spread of these values opens the path to "make the world not just safer but better," a "path [that] is not America's alone. It is open to all."[4] This taps deep American beliefs and traditions enunciated by Woodrow Wilson and echoed by Bill Clinton, and it is linked to the belief, common among powerful states, that its values are universal and their spread will benefit the entire world. Just as Wilson sought to "teach [the countries of Latin America] "to elect good men," so Bush will bring free markets and free elections to countries without them. This agenda horrifies Realists (and perhaps realists).[5] Some mid-level officials think this is window dressing; by contrast, John Gaddis sees it as the heart of the doctrine,[6] a view that is endorsed by other officials.

The administration's argument is that strong measures to spread democracy are needed and will be efficacious. Liberating Iraq will not only produce democracy there, but it will also encourage democracy in the rest of the Middle East. There is no incompatibility between Islam or any other culture and democracy; the example of political pluralism in one country will be emulated. The implicit belief is that democracy can take hold when the artificial obstacles to it are removed. Far from being the product of unusually propitious circumstances, a free and pluralist system is the "natural order" that will prevail unless something special intervenes.[7] Furthermore, more democracies will mean greater stability, peaceful relations with neighbors, and less terrorism, comforting claims that evidence indicates is questionable at best.[8] Would a democratic Iraq be stable? Would an Iraq that reflected the will of its people recognize Israel or renounce all claims to Kuwait? Would a democratic Palestinian state be more willing to live at peace with Israel than an authoritarian one, especially if it did not gain all of the territory lost in 1967? Previous experience also calls into question the links between democracy and free markets, each of which can readily undermine the other. But such doubts do not cloud official pronouncements or even the off-the-record comments of top officials. The United States now appears to have a faith-based foreign policy.

This or any other administration may not act on it. No American government has been willing to sacrifice stability and support of U.S. policy to honor democracy in countries like Algeria, Egypt, Saudi Arabia, and Pakistan.[9] But the current view does parallel Ronald Reagan's policy of not accepting a detente with the Union of Soviet Socialist Republics (USSR) that was limited to arms control and insisting on a larger agenda that included human rights within the Soviet Union and, thus, implicitly called for a new domestic regime. The Bush administration is heir to this tradition when it declares that any agreement with North Korea would have to address a range a problems in addition to nuclear weapons, including "the abominable way [the North] treats its people."[10] The argument is that, as in Iraq, regime change is necessary because tyrannical governments will always be prone to disregard agreements and coerce their neighbors just as they mistreat their own citizens. Notwithstanding their being Realists in their views about how states influence one another, Bush and his colleagues are Liberals in their beliefs about the sources of foreign policy.

Consistent with liberalism, this perspective is highly optimistic in seeing the possibility of progress. A week after September 11, Bush is reported to have told one of his closest advisers: "We have an opportunity to restructure the world toward freedom, and we have to get it right." He expounded this theme in a formal speech marking the six-month anniversary of the attack: "When the terrorists are disrupted and scattered and discredited, . . . we will see then that the old and serious disputes can be settled within the bounds of reason, and goodwill, and mutual security. I see a peaceful world beyond the war on terror, and with courage and unity, we are building that world together."[11] In February 2002, the President responded to a reporter's question about the predictable French criticism of his policy by saying that "history has given us a unique opportunity to defend freedom. And we're going to seize the moment, and do it."[12] One month later, he declared, "We understand history has called us into action, and we are not going to miss that opportunity to make the world more peaceful and more free."[13]

The absence of any competing model for organizing societies noted at the start of the National Security document is part of the explanation for the optimism. Another is the expectation of a benign form of domino dynamics, as the replacement of the Iraqi regime is expected to embolden the forces of freedom and deter other potential disturbers of the peace. Before the war, Bush declared that when Saddam is overthrown "other regimes will be given a clear warning that support for terror will not be tolerated. Without this outside support for terrorism, Palestinians who are working for reform and long for democracy will be in a better position to choose new leaders—true leaders who strive for peace."[14] After the war, Bush reaffirmed his belief that "a free Iraq can be an example of reform and progress to all the Middle East."[15] Even some analysts like Thomas Friedman, who are skeptical of much of the administration's policy, believe that the demonstration effect of regime change in Iraq can be large and salutary.

The mechanisms by which these effects are expected to occur are not entirely clear. One involves establishing an American reputation for opposing tyranny. But the power of reputation is questioned by the Bush administration's skepticism toward deterrence, which works partly by this means. Another mechanism is the power of example: people will see that tyrants are not invulnerable and that democracy can provide a better life. But seeing one dictator overthrown (not an unusual occurrence) may not have much influence on others. The dynamics within the Soviet bloc in 1989–1991 were a product of special conditions, and while contagion, tipping, and positive feedback do occur, so does negative feedback. We may hope for the former, but it is unreasonable to expect it.

THREAT AND PREVENTIVE WAR

The second pillar of the Bush doctrine is that we live in a time not only of opportunity, but also of great threat posed primarily by terrorists and rogue states. Optimism and pessimism are linked in the belief that if the United States does not make the world better, it will grow more dangerous. As Bush said in his West Point address of 1 June 2002: "Today our enemies see weapons of mass destruction as weapons of choice. For rogue states these weapons are tools of intimidation and military aggression against their neighbors. These weapons may also allow these states to attempt to blackmail the U.S. and our allies to prevent us from deterring or repelling the aggressive behavior of rogue states. Such states also see these weapons as their best means of overcoming the conventional superiority of the U.S."[16]

These threats cannot be contained by deterrence. Terrorists are fanatics, and there is nothing that they value that we can hold at risk; rogues like Iraq are risk-acceptant and accident prone. The heightened sense of vulnerability increases the dissatisfaction with deterrence, but it is noteworthy that this stance taps into the longstanding Republican critique of many American Cold War policies. One wing of the party always sought defense rather than deterrence (or, to be more precise, deterrence by denial instead of deterrence by punishment), and this was reflected in the search for escalation dominance, multiple nuclear options, and defense against ballistic missiles.[17]

Because even defense may not be possible against terrorists or rogues, the United States must be ready to wage preventive wars and to act "against . . . emerging threats before they are fully formed," as Bush puts it.[18] Prevention is not a new element in world politics, although Dale Copeland's important treatment exaggerates its previous centrality.[19] Israel launched a preventive strike against the Iraqi nuclear program in 1981; during the Cold War, U.S. officials contemplated attacking the USSR and the Peoples' Republic of China (PRC) before they could develop robust nuclear capabilities.[20] The Monroe doctrine and westward expansion in the nineteenth century stemmed in part from the American desire to prevent any European power from establishing a presence that could menace the United States.

The United States was a weak country at that time; now the preventive war doctrine is based on strength and on the associated desire to ensure the maintenance of American dominance. Critics argue that preventive wars are rarely necessary because deterrence can be effective and many threats are exaggerated or can be met with strong but less militarized policies. Libya, for example, once the leading rogue, now seems to be outside of the axis of evil. Otto von Bismarck called preventive wars "suicide for fear of death," and, although the disparity of power between the United States and its adversaries means this is no longer the case, the argument for such wars implies a high degree of confidence that the future will be bleak unless they are undertaken or at least a belief that this world will be worse than the likely one produced by the war.

This policy faces three large obstacles. First, by definition, the relevant information is hard to obtain because it involves predictions about threats that reside sometime in the future. Thus, while in retrospect it is easy to say that the Western allies should have stopped Hitler long before 1939, at the time it was far from clear that he would turn out to be such a menace. No one who reads Neville Chamberlain's speeches can believe that he was a fool. In some cases, a well-placed spy might be able to provide solid evidence that the other had to be stopped, but in many other cases—perhaps including Nazi Germany—even this would not be sufficient, because leaders do not themselves know how they will act in the future. The Bush doctrine implies that the problem is not so difficult, because the state's foreign policy is shaped, if not determined, by its domestic political system. Thus, knowing that North Korea, Iran, and Syria are brutal dictatorships tells us that they will seek to dominate their neighbors, sponsor terrorism, and threaten the United States. But while the generalization that states that oppress their own people will disturb the international system fits many cases, it is far from universal, which means that such short-cuts to the assessment process are fallible. Second and relatedly, even information on capabilities and past behavior may be difficult to come by, as the case of Iraq shows. Saddam's links to terrorists were murky and remain subject to debate, and while much remains unclear, it seems that the United States and Britain not only publicly exaggerated, but also privately overestimated, the extent of his weapons of mass destruction (WMD) program.

Third, unless all challengers are deterred by the exercise of the doctrine in Iraq, preventive war will have to be repeated as other threats reach a similar threshold. Doing so will require sustained domestic, if not international, support, which is made less likely by the first two complications. The very nature of a preventive war means that the evidence is ambiguous and the supporting arguments are subject to rebuttal. If Britain and France had gone to war with Germany before 1939, large segments of the public would have believed that the war was not necessary. If it had gone badly, the public would have wanted to sue for peace; if it had gone well, public opinion would have questioned its wisdom. While it is too early to say how American opinion will view Saddam's overthrow (and opinion is likely to change over time), a degree of skepticism that will inhibit the repetition of this policy seems probable.

National leaders are aware of these difficulties and generally hesitate to take strong actions in the face of such uncertainty. While one common motive for war has been the belief that the situation will deteriorate unless the state acts strongly now, and indeed this kind of fear drives the security dilemma, leaders usually put off decisions if they can. They know that many potential threats will never eventuate or will be made worse by precipitous military action, and they are predisposed to postpone, to await further developments and information, to kick the can down the road. In rejecting this approach in Iraq, if not in North Korea, Bush and his colleagues are behaving unusually, although this does not mean they are wrong.

Part of the reason for their stance is the feeling of vulnerability and the consequent belief that the risks and costs of inaction are unacceptably high. Note one of the few lines that brought applause in Bush's Cincinnati speech of 7 October 2002 and that shows the powerful psychological link between September 11 and the drive to depose Saddam: "We will not live in fear." Taken literally, this makes no sense. Unfortunately, fear is often well founded. What it indicates is an understandable desire for a safer world, despite that fact that the United States did live in fear throughout the Cold War and survived quite well. But if the sentence has little logical meaning, the emotion it embodies is an understandable fear of fear, a drive to gain certainty, an impulse to assert control by acting.[21]

This reading of Bush's statement is consistent with my impression that many people who opposed invading Iraq before September 11, but altered their positions afterwards, had not taken terrorism terribly seriously before September 11, a category that includes George Bush.[22] Those who had studied the subject were, of course, surprised by the timing and method of the attacks, but not that they took place; they changed their beliefs only incrementally. But Bush frequently acknowledges, indeed stresses, that he was shocked by the assault, which greatly increased his feelings of danger and led him to feel that drastically different policies were necessary. As he put it in his Cincinnati speech: "On September 11th, 2001, America felt its vulnerability." It is no accident that this sentence comes between two paragraphs about the need to disarm Iraq. Three months later, in response to an accusation that he always wanted to invade Iraq, Bush replied: "prior to September 11, we were discussing smart sanctions. . . . After September 11, the doctrine of containment just doesn't hold any water. . . . My vision shifted dramatically after September 11, because I now realize the stakes, I realize the world has changed."[23] Secretary of Defense Donald Rumsfeld similarly explained that the United States "did not act in Iraq because dramatic new evidence of Iraq's pursuit of weapons of mass murder. We acted because we saw the existing evidence in a new light, through the prism of our experience on September 11,"[24] The claim that some possibilities are unlikely enough to be put aside lost plausibility in face of the obvious retort: "What could be less likely than terrorists flying airplanes into the World Trade Center and the Pentagon?" During the Cold War, Bernard Brodie expressed his exasperation with wild suggestions about military actions the USSR might undertake: "All sorts of notions and propositions are churned out, and often presented for consideration with the prefatory words: 'It is conceivable that. . . .' Such words establish their own truth, for the fact that someone has conceived of whatever proposition follows is enough to establish that it is conceivable. Whether it is worth a second thought, however, is another matter."[25] Worst-case analysis is now hard to dismiss.

The fact that no one can guarantee that an adversary with WMD will not use them means that fear cannot be banished. Although administration officials exaggerated the danger that Saddam posed, they also revealed their true fears when they talked about the possibility that he could use WMD against the United States or its allies. At least some of them may have been insensitive to the magnitude of this possibility; what mattered was its very existence. Psychology plays an important role here because people value certainty and are willing to pay a high price to decrease the probability of a danger from slight to none.[26] Bush's choice of words declaring a formal end to the organized combat in Iraq was telling: "this much is certain: No terrorist network will gain weapons of mass destruction from the Iraqi regime."[27] Concomitantly, people often feel that uncertainty can be best eliminated by taking the initiative. As Bush put it in his letter accompanying the submission of his National Security Strategy, "In the new world we have entered, the only path to peace and security is the path of action." The body of the document declared that "The greater the threat, the greater is the risk of inaction."[28] In the past, a state could let a potential threat grow because it might not turn into a major menace. Now, if one follows this cautious path and the worst case does arise, the price will be prohibitive. Thus, Senator Orrin Hatch dismissed the argument that since the threat from Iraq was not imminent the United States could afford to rely on diplomacy and deterrence by saying, "Imminence becomes murkier in the era of terrorism and weapons of mass destruction."[29] It then makes sense to strike much sooner and more often, even though in some cases doing so will not have been necessary.

UNILATERALISM

The perceived need for preventive wars is linked to the fundamental unilateralism of the Bush doctrine, since it is hard to get a consensus for such strong actions and other states have every reason to let the dominant power carry the full burden.[30] Unilateralism also has deep roots in the non-northeastern parts of the Republican party, was well represented in the Reagan administration, draws on long-standing American political traditions, and was part of Bush's outlook before September 11. Of course, assistance from others was needed in Afghanistan and Iraq. But these should not be mistaken for joint ventures, as the United States did not bend its policy to meet others' preferences. In stressing that the United States is building coalitions in the plural rather than an alliance (the mission determines the coalition, in Rumsfeld's phrase), American leaders have made it clear that they will forego the participation of any particular country rather than compromise.

The seeming exception of policy toward North Korea, in which the United States refuses to negotiate bilaterally and insists that the problem is one for the international community, is actually consistent with this approach. Others were not consulted on the policy and in fact resisted it. The obvious purpose of the American stance was to get others to apply pressure on the adversary. While this is a legitimate aim and, perhaps, the best policy, it is one the United States has selected on its own. Multilaterialism here is purely instrumental, a way to avoid giving what the United States regards as a concession to North Korea and a means of further weakening and isolating it, despite others believing this is unwise.

Even before September 11, Bush displayed little willingness to cater to world public opinion or to heed the cries of outrage from European countries as the United States interpreted its interests and the interests of the world in its own way. Thus, the Bush administration walked away from the Kyoto treaty, the International Criminal Court, and the protocol implementing the ban on biological weapons rather than try to work within these frameworks and modify them. The United States also ignored European criticisms of its Middle Eastern policy. On a smaller scale, it forced out the heads of the Organization for the Prohibition of Chemical Weapons and the Intergovernmental Panel on Climate Change. In response to this kind of behavior, European diplomats can only say: "Big partners should consult with smaller partners."[31] The operative word is "should." When in the wake of the overthrow of Saddam, Chirac declares: "We are no longer in an era where one or two countries control the fate of another country," he describes the world as he would like it to be, not as it is.[32]

The administration has defended each of its actions, but not its general stance. The most principled, persuasive, and perhaps correct defense is built around the difficulty in procuring public goods. As long as leadership is shared, very little will happen because no one actor will be willing to shoulder the costs and the responsibilities. "At this moment in history, if there is a problem, we're expected to deal with it," is how Bush explains it. "We are trying to lead the world," is what one administration official said when the United States blocked language in a UN declaration on child health that might be read as condoning abortion.[33] This is not entirely hypocritical: many of the countries that endorsed the Kyoto protocol had grave reservations but were unwilling to stand up to strongly committed domestic groups.

Real consultation is likely to produce inaction, as was true in 1993, when Clinton called for "lift and strike" in Yugoslavia (that is, lifting the arms embargo against Bosnia and striking Serbian forces). But because he believed in sharing power and was unwilling to move on his own, he sent Secretary of State Warren Christopher to ascertain European views. This multilateral and democratic procedure did not work because the Europeans did not want to be put on the spot; in the face of apparent American indecision, they refused to endorse such a strong policy. If the United States had informed the Europeans rather than consulted them, they probably would have complained, but gone along; what critics call unilateralism often is effective leadership. Could Yasir Arafat have been moved from his central position if the United States had sought consensus rather than staking out its own position? Bush could also argue that just as Reagan's ignoring the sophisticated European counsels to moderate his rhetoric led to the delegitimation of the Soviet system, so his insistence on confronting tyrants has slowly brought others around to his general perspective, if not to his particular policies.

In this context, the strong opposition of allies to overthrowing Saddam was an advantage as well as a disadvantage to Bush. While it exacted domestic costs, complicated the effort to rebuild Iraq, and perhaps fed Saddam's illusion that he could avoid a war, it gave the United States the opportunity to demonstrate that it would override strenuous objections from allies if this was necessary to reach its goals. While this horrified multilateralists, it showed that Bush was serious about his doctrine. When Kofi Annan declared that an American attack without Security Council endorsement "would not be in conformity with the [UN] charter," he may not have realized that for some members of the Bush administration this would be part of the point of the action.[34]

AMERICAN HEGEMONY

The final element of the doctrine, which draws together the others, is the establishment of American hegemony, primacy, or empire.[35] In the Bush doctrine, there are no universal norms or rules governing all states.[36] On the contrary, order can be maintained only if the dominant power behaves quite differently from the others. Thus the administration is not worried that its preventive war doctrine or attacking Iraq without Security Council endorsement will set a precedent for others because the dictates do not bind the United States. Similarly, the United States sees no contradiction between expanding the ambit of nuclear weapons to threaten their employment even if others have not used WMD first on the one hand and a vigorous antiproliferation policy on the other. American security, world stability, and the spread of liberalism require the United States to act in ways others cannot and must not. This is not a double standard, but is what world order requires.

Hegemony is implied when the Nuclear Posture Review talks of dissuading future military competitors. At first glance, this seems to refer to Russia and China. But the point applies to the countries of Western Europe as well, either individually or as a unit. This was clear in the draft defense guidance written by

Paul Wolfowitz for Dick Cheney at the end of the first Bush administration and also was implied by President George W. Bush when he declared to the graduating cadets at West Point: "America has, and intends to keep, military strengths beyond challenge—thereby making the destabilizing arms races of other eras pointless, and limiting rivalries to trade and other pursuits of peace."[37] This would mean not only sustaining such a high level of military spending that no other country or group of countries would be tempted to challenge it, but also using force on behalf of others so they will not need to develop potent military establishments of their own. In an implicit endorsement of hegemonic stability theory, the driving belief is that the world cannot afford to return to traditional multipolar balance of power politics, which would inevitably turn dangerous and destructive.[38]

Although many observers, myself included, were taken by surprise by this turn in American policy, we probably should not have been. It is consistent with standard patterns of international politics and with much previous American behavior in the Cold War. As early as the start of World War II, American leaders understood that the United States would emerge as the prime architect of the new international politics.[39] In the years before the Soviet Union was perceived as a deadly menace, American leaders understood that theirs would be the major role in maintaining peace and prosperity.

Even had the Soviet Union been more benign, instability, power vacuums, and the anticipation of future rivalries would have led the United States to use and increase the enormous power it had developed.[40] The task could not be done by the United States alone, however. The world was not strictly bipolar, especially because the United States sought to limit its defense spending, and the prime target of the conflict was the allegiance of West Europe. The United States knew that allied, and especially European, support was necessary to resist Soviet encroachments. Allies, fearing a return to American isolationism, reciprocally made great efforts to draw the United States in.[41] Although American power was central and consent often was forthcoming only because of veiled (or not so veiled) rewards and threats, on fundamental issues the United States had to take allied interests and views to heart. Thus, Charles Maier exaggerates only slightly when he refers to "consensual American hegemony" within the West.[42]

As Europe stabilized and the American deterrent force became concentrated in intercontinental bombers and missiles, the need for allies, although still considerable, diminished. The United States could rebuff Britain and France at Suez in a way that it could not have done five years earlier. Twenty-five years later, Reagan could pay even less heed to allied wishes than Eisenhower had. Of course, the United States could not do everything it wanted. Not only was it restrained by Soviet power, but to go it alone would have alienated domestic opinion, risked policy setbacks, and endangered an international economic system already under great pressure. But the degree to which the United States sought consensus and respected allied desires varied from issue to issue and president to president. Above a significant but limited minimum level, cooperation with allies had become a matter of choice, not necessity.

The required minimum level of cooperation decreased with the end of the Cold War and the emergence of unipolarity. The United States now has a greater share of world power than any state since the beginning of the state system, and it is not likely to lose this position in the foreseeable future.[43] Before the first Bush's presidency, the United States used a mixture of carrots and sticks and pursued sometimes narrower but often broader conceptions of its interest. Clinton, and Bush before him, cultivated allies and worked hard to maintain large coalitions. Most scholars approve of this mode of behavior, seeing it as the best if not the only way for the United States to secure desired behavior from others, minimize the costs to itself, and most smoothly manage a complex and contentious world.[44] But the choice of this approach was indeed a choice, revocable upon the appearance of changed circumstances and a different leader. The structure of world power meant that there was always a possibility that the United States would act on its own.

Until recently, however, it did not seem clear that the United States would in fact behave in a highly unilateral fashion and assert its primacy. The new American stance was precipitated, if not caused by, the interaction between the terrorist attacks and the election of George W. Bush, who brought to the office a more uni-lateral outlook than his predecessor and his domestic opponents. Bush's response to September 11 may parallel his earlier religious conversion and owe something to his religious beliefs, especially in his propensity to see the struggle as one between good and evil. There is reason to believe that just as his coming to Christ gave meaning to his previously aimless and dissolute personal life, so the war on terrorism has become, not only the defining characteristic of his foreign policy, but also his sacred mission. An associate of the President reports: "I believe the president was sincere, after 9/11, thinking 'This is what I was put on this earth for.'"[45] We can only specu-late on what President Al Gore would have done. My estimate is that he would have invaded Afghanistan, but not proceeded against Iraq; nor would he have moved away from treaties and other arrangements over a wide range of issues. To some extent, the current assertion of strong American hegemony may be an accident.

But it was an accident waiting to happen. To start with, there are structural reasons to have expected a large terrorist attack. Bin Laden had attacked American interests abroad and from early on sought to strike the homeland. His enmity stemmed primarily from the establishment of U.S. bases in Saudi Arabia, which was a product of America's worldwide responsibilities. Ironically, the over-throw of Saddam is likely to permit the United States to reduce its presence in Saudi Arabia, although I doubt if bin Laden expected this result to follow from his attack or that he will now be satisfied. Furthermore, al Qaeda was not the only group targeting the United States; as Richard Betts has argued, terrorism is the obvious weapon of weak actors against the leading state.[46]

Even without terrorism, both internal and structural factors predisposed the United States to assert its dominance. I think structural factors are more important, but it is almost a truism of the history of American foreign relations that the United States rarely if ever engages in deeply cooperative ventures with equals.[47] Unlike the European states who were surrounded by peers, once the United States had established its dominance first over its neighbors and then over the rest of the New World, it had great choice about the terms on which it would work with others. Thus, when the United States intervened in World War I, it insisted that the coali-tion be called the "Allied and Associated Powers"—that is, it was an associate with freedom of action, not an ally. The structure of the American government, its weak party system, its domestic diversity, and its political traditions, all make sustained cooperation difficult. It would be an exaggeration to say that unilateralism is the American way of foreign policy, but there certainly is a strong pull in this direction.

More importantly, the United States may be acting like a normal state that has gained a position of dominance.[48] There are four facets to this argument. First and most general is the core of the Realist outlook that power is checked most effectively and often only by counterbalancing power. It follows that states that are not subject to external restraints tend to feel few restraints at all. As Edmund Burke put it, in a position endorsed by Hans Morgenthau: "I dread our *own* power and our *own* ambition; I dread our being too much dreaded. It is ridiculous to say that we are not men, and that, as men, we shall never wish to aggrandize ourselves."[49] With this as one of his driving ideas, Kenneth Waltz saw the likelihood of current behavior from the start of the post-Cold War era:

> The powerful state may, and the United States does, think of itself as acting for the sake of peace, justice, and well-being in the world. But these terms will be defined to the liking of the powerful, which may conflict with the preferences and the interests of others. In international politics, overwhelming power repels and leads others to try to balance against it. With benign intent, the United States has behaved, and until its power is brought into a semblance of balance, will continue to behave in ways that annoy and frighten others.[50]

Parts of the Bush doctrine are unique to the circumstances, but it is the exception rather than the rule for states to stay on the path of moderation when others do not force them to do so.[51]

Second, states' definitions of their interests tend to expand as their power does.[52] It then becomes worth pursuing a whole host of objectives that were out of reach when the state's security was in doubt and all efforts had to be directed to primary objectives. Under the new circumstances, states seek what Arnold Wolfers called "milieu goals."[53] The hope of spreading democracy and liberalism throughout the world has always been an American goal, but the lack of a peer competitor now makes it more realistic—although perhaps not very realistic—to actively strive for it. Seen in this light, the administration's perception that this is a time of great opportunity in the Middle East is the product, not so much of the special circumstances in the region, but of the enormous resources at America's disposal.

More specifically, the quick American victory in Afghanistan probably contributed to the expansion of American goals. Likewise, the easy military victory in Iraq, providing the occupation can be brought to a successful conclusion, will encourage the pursuit of a wider agenda, if not threatening force against other tyrants ("moving down the list," in the current phrase). Bush's initial speech after September 11 declared war on terrorists "with a global reach." This was ambitious, but at least the restriction to these kinds of terrorists meant that many others were not of concern. The modifier was dropped in the wake of Afghanistan, however. Not only did rhetoric shift to seeing terrorism in general as a menace to civilization and "the new totalitarian threat,"[54] but the United States sent first military trainers and then a combat unit to the Philippines to attack guerrillas who posed only a minimal threat to

Americans and who have no significant links to al Qaeda. Furthermore, at least up until a point, the exercise of power can increase power as well as interests. I do not think that the desire to control a large supply of oil was significant motivation for the Iraqi war, but it will give the United States an additional instrument of influence.

A third structural explanation for American behavior is that increased relative power brings with it new fears. The reasons are both objective and subjective. As Wolfers notes in his classic essay on "National Security as Ambiguous Symbol," the latter can diverge from the former.[55] In one manifestation of this, as major threats disappear, people psychologically elevate ones that were previously seen as quite manageable.[56] People now seem to be as worried as they were during the height of the Cold War despite the fact that a terrorist or rogue attack, even with WMD, could cause only a small fraction of a possible World War III's devastation. But there is more to it than psychology. A dominant state acquires an enormous stake in the world order, and interests spread throughout the globe. Most countries are primarily concerned with what happens in their immediate neighborhoods; the world is the hegemon's neighborhood, and it is not only hubris that leads it to be concerned with anything that happens anywhere. The result is a fusion of narrow and broad self-interest. At a point when most analysts were worried about the decline of American power, not its excesses, Waltz noted that for the United States, "like some earlier great powers . . . the interest of the country in security came to be identified with the maintenance of a certain world order. For countries at the top, this is predictable behavior. . . . Once a state's interests reach a certain extent, they become self-reinforcing."[57]

The historian John S. Galbraith explored the related dynamic of the "turbulent frontier" that produced the unintended expansion of colonialism. As a European power gained an enclave in Africa or Asia, usually along the coast or river, it also gained an unpacified boundary that had to be policed. This led to further expansion of influence and often of settlement, and this in turn produced a new area that had to be protected and a new zone of threat.[58] There were few natural limits to this process. There are not likely to be many now. The wars in Afghanistan and Iraq have led to the establishment of U.S. bases and security commitments in central Asia, an area previously beyond reach. It is not hard to imagine how the United States could be drawn further into politics in the region and to find itself using force to oppose terrorist or guerrilla movements that arise there, perhaps in part in reaction to the American presence. The same dynamic could play out in Colombia.

The fourth facet can be seen as a broader conception of the previous point. As Realists stress, even states that find the status quo acceptable have to worry about the future.[59] The more an actor sees the current situation as satisfactory, the more it will expect the future to be worse. Psychology plays a role here too: prospect theory argues that actors are prone to accept great risks when they believe they will suffer losses unless they act boldly. The adoption of a preventive war doctrine may be a mistake, especially if taken too far, but is not foreign to normal state behavior. It appeals to states that have a valued position to maintain. However secure states are, only rarely can they be secure enough, and if they are currently very powerful, they will have strong reasons to act now to prevent a deterioration that could allow others to harm them in the future.[60]

All this means that under the Bush doctrine the United States is not a status quo power. Its motives may not be selfish, but the combination of power, fear, and perceived opportunity leads it to seek to reshape world politics and the societies of many of its members. This tracks with and extends traditional ideas in American foreign relations held by both liberals and conservatives who saw the United States as a revolutionary country. As the first modern democracy, the United States was founded on principles of equality, progress, and a government subordinate to civil society that, while initially being uniquely American, had universal applicability. Because a state's foreign policy is inseparable from its domestic regime, a safe and peaceful world required the spread of these arrangements.[61] Under current conditions of terrorism and WMD, tyrannical governments pose too much of a potential if not actual danger to be tolerated. The world cannot stand still. Without strong American intervention, the international environment will become more menacing to America and its values, but strong action can increase its security and produce a better world. In a process akin to the deep security dilemma,[62] in order to protect itself, the United States is impelled to act in a way that will increase, or at least bring to the surface, conflicts with others. Even if the prevailing situation is satisfactory, it cannot be maintained by purely defensive measures. Making the world safe for American democracy is believed to require that dictatorial regimes be banished, or at least kept from weapons of mass destruction. Although not mentioned in the pronouncements, the Bush doctrine is made possible by the existence of a security community among the world's most powerful and developed states—the United States, Western Europe, and Japan.[63] The lack of fears of war among these countries allows the United States to focus on other dangers and to pursue other goals. Furthermore, the development of the security community gives the United States a position that it now wants to preserve.

HEGEMONY, IRAQ, AND EUROPE

This perspective on the Bush doctrine helps explain international disagreements about Iraq. Most accounts of the French opposition stress its preoccupation with glory and its traditional jealousy and disdain for the United States. Europe's resistance to the war is attributed to the peaceful world view produced by its success in overcoming historical rivalries and creating a law-governed by society, summarized by the phrase "Americans are from Mars, the Europeans are from Venus."[64] Also frequently mentioned is the European aversion to the crude and bullying American style: "Bush is just a cowboy." There is something to these position, but are Europeans really so averse to force and wedded to law? When faced with domestic terrorism, Germany and other European countries did not hesitate to employ unrestrained state power that John Ashcroft would envy, and their current treatment of minorities, especially Muslims, does not strike these populations as liberal. The French continue to intervene in Africa unilaterally, disregarded legal rulings to drop their ban on British beef, and join other European states in playing as fast and loose with trade regulations as does the United States. Most European states favored the war in Kosovo and supported the United States in Afghanistan; had they been attacked on September 11, they might not have maintained their aversion to the use of force.

Even more glaringly, the claims for a deep cultural divided overlook the fundamental difference between how Europe and the United States are placed in the international system. The fact that the latter is hegemonic has three implications. First, only the United States has the power to do anything about problems like Iraq; the others have incentives to ride free. Second, the large European states have every reason to be concerned about American hegemony and sufficient resources to seek to constrain it. This is not traditional power balancing, which is driven by security fears; the French are not afraid of an American attack, and the German worry is that the United States will withdraw too many of its troops. But they do fear that a world dominated by the United States would be one in which their values and interests would be served only at American sufferance. It is hardly surprising that an April 2002 poll showed that overwhelming majorities within many European countries felt that American policy toward Iraq and the Middle East in general was based "mainly on its own interests."[65] The National Security Advisor, Condoleezza Rice, has forgotten her knowledge of basic international politics when she expresses her shock at discovering that "there were times that it appeared that American power was seen [by France and Germany] to be more dangerous than, perhaps, Saddam Hussein."[66] The United States may be correct that American dominance serves Europe and the world, but we should not be startled when others beg to differ. The United States probably is as benign a hegemon as the world has ever seen. Its large domestic market, relatively tolerant values, domestic diversity, and geographic isolation all are helpful. But a hegemon it remains, and by that very fact it must make others uneasy.

Third, the Europeans' stress on the need to go through the Security Council shows less their abstract attachment to law and world governance than their appreciation of power. France especially, but also Russia and China (two countries that are not from Venus), will gain enormously if they can establish the principle that large-scale force can be used only with the approval of the Council, of which they are permanent members. Security Council membership is one of the major resources at these countries' disposal. The statement of a Russian leader that "if someone tries to wage war on their own account . . . without an international mandate, it means all the world is confusion and a wild jungle"[67] would carry more moral weight if Russia did not have a veto in the mandate-granting body. If the Council were not central, French influence would be much diminished.

The United Kingdom does not readily fit this picture, of course. Structure always leaves room for choice, and Tony Blair told Parliament on 24 September 2002 that "it is an article of faith with me that the American relationship and our ability to partner [with] America in these difficult issues is of fundamental importance, not just to this country but to the wider world." Blair's personal views may be part of the explanation, but this has been the British stance ever since World War II, which resisted becoming too much a part of Europe and sought to maintain a major role in the world through supporting rather than opposing the United States. But only one ally can seek to have a "special relationship" with the hegemon, and Britain's having taken this role makes it harder for others to emulate it.

Structure also explains why many of the smaller European countries chose to support the United States in Iraq despite hostile public opinion. The dominance they fear most is not American, but Franco-German. The United States is more powerful, but France and Germany are closer and more likely to menace them.[68] Seeking a distant protector is a standard practice in international politics. That France and Germany resented the resulting opposition is no more surprising than the American dismissal of "old Europe," with the resulting parallel that while France and Germany bitterly decried the American effort to hustle them into line, they disparaged and bullied the East European states that sided with the United States—quite un-Venusian behavior.

CONCLUSION

Where we will go from here depends in part on unpredictable events such as economic shocks, the course of reconstruction in Iraq, the targets and success of future terrorist attacks, and the characteristics of the leaders that arise through diverse domestic processes. The war against Saddam, however, already marks out the path on which the United States is embarked and illuminates the links between preventive war and hegemony, which was much of the reason for the opposition at home and abroad. Bush's goals are extraordinarily ambitious, involving remaking not only international politics but recalcitrant societies as well, which is seen as an end in itself and a means to American security. For better or (and?) for worse, the United States has set itself tasks that prudent states would shun. As a result, it will be infringing on what adversaries, if not allies, see as their vital interests. Coercion and especially deterrence may be insufficient for these tasks because these instruments share with traditional diplomacy the desire to minimize conflict by limiting one's own claims to interests that others can afford to respect. States that seek more need to be highly assertive if not aggressive, which provides additional reasons to question the goals themselves. The beliefs of Bush and his colleagues that Saddam's regime would have been an unacceptable menace to American interests if it had been allowed to obtain nuclear weapons not only tell us about their fears for the limits of United States influence that might have been imposed, but also speak volumes about the expansive definition of United States interests that they hold.[69]

The war is hard to understand if the only objective was to disarm Saddam or even to remove him from power. Even had the inflated estimates of his WMD capability been accurate, the danger was simply too remote to justify the effort. But if changing the Iraqi regime was expected to bring democracy and stability to the Middle East, discourage tyrants and energize reformers throughout the world, and demonstrate the American willingness to provide a high degree of what it considers world order whether others like it or not, then as part of a larger project, the war makes sense. Those who find both the hopes and the fears excessive if not delusional agree with the great British statesman Lord Salisbury when he tried to bring some perspective to the Eastern Crisis of 1877–1878: "It has generally been acknowledged to be madness to go to war for an idea, but if anything is more unsatisfactory, it is to go to war against a nightmare."[70]

We can only speculate about the crucial question of whether the Bush doctrine will work. Contrary to the common impression, democracies, especially the United States, do not find it easy to sustain a clear line of policy when the external environment is not compelling. Domestic priorities ordinarily loom large, and few Americans think of their country as having an imperial mission. Wilsonianism may provide a substitute for the older European ideologies of a *mission civilisatrice* and the white man's burden, but since it rests on the assumption that its role will not only be noble but also popular, I am skeptical that it will endure if it meets much indigenous opposition from those who are supposed to benefit from it. Significant casualties will surely be corrosive, and when the going gets tough I think the United States will draw back.

Furthermore, while the United States is the strongest country in the world, its power is still subject to two familiar limitations: it is harder to build than to destroy, and success depends on others' decisions because their cooperation is necessary for the state to reach its goals. Of course, American military capability is not to be ignored, and I doubt whether countries like Iran, Syria, and North Korea will ignore it. They may well reason as Bush expects them to and limit their WMD programs and support for terrorism, if not reform domestically. But the prospects for long-run compliance are less bright. Although, a frontal assault on American interests is perhaps unlikely, highly motivated adversaries will not give up the quest to advance their interests as they see them. The war in Iraq has increased the risks of their pursuing nuclear weapons, but it has also increased their incentives to do so. Amid the debate about what these weapons can accomplish, everyone agrees that they can deter invasion, which makes them very attractive to states who fear they might be in the American gun sights. Both Waltz's argument that proliferation will produce stability and the contrary and more common claim that it would make the world more dangerous imply that the spread of nuclear weapons will reduce American influence because others will have less need of its security guarantees and will be able to fend off its threats to their vital interests.[71] The American attempt to minimize the ability of others to resist U.S. pressures is the mark of a country bent, not on maintaining the status quo, but on fashioning a new and better order.

Obviously, U.S. military capabilities matter less in relations with allies and probably with Russia. From them the United States wants wholehearted cooperation on issues such as sharing highly sensitive information on terrorism, rebuilding failed states, preventing proliferation, and, perhaps most importantly, managing the international economy. There is little danger or hope that Europe will form a united counterweight to the United States and try to thwart it by active opposition, let alone the use of force. But political resistance is quite possible and, even more than with adversaries, the fate of the American design for world order lies in the hands of its allies.[72] Although the United States governs many of the incentives that Europe and potential supporters face, what it needs from them cannot be coerced. It is possible that they will see themselves better off with the United States as an assertive hegemon, allowing them to gain the benefits of world order while being spared the costs, and they may conclude that any challenge would fail or bring with it dangerous rivalry. Without the war in Iraq, I doubt that the spring of 2003 would have seen the degree of cooperation that the United States obtained from Europe in combatting the Iranian nuclear program and from Japan and the PRC in containing North Korea.

But I suspect that much will depend on the allies' answers to several questions: Can the American domestic political system sustain the Bush doctrine over the long run? Will the United States be open to allied influence and values? Will it put pressure on Israel as well as on the Arabs to reach a settlement? More generally, will it seek to advance the broad interests of the diverse countries and people in the world, or will it exploit its power for its own narrower political, economic, and social interests? Bush's world gives little place for other states—even democracies—except as members of a supporting cast. Conflating broader with narrower interests and believing that one has a monopoly on wisdom are obvious ways that a hegemon can come to be seen as tyrannical.[73] Woodrow Wilson said that both nationalism and internationalism called for the United States to join the League of Nations: "The greatest nationalist is the man who wants his nation to be the greatest nation, and the greatest nation is the nation which penetrates to the heart of its duty and mission among the nations of the world. With every flash of insight into the great politics of mankind, the nation that has that vision is elevated to a place of influence and power which it cannot get by arms."[74] Wilson surely meant what he said, but his great certainty that he knew what was best for the world was troubling. In the presidential campaign, Bush said that the United States needed a "more humble foreign policy."[75] But its objectives and conceptions make the Bush doctrine quite the opposite. Avoiding this imperial temptation will be the greatest challenge that the United States faces.

NOTES

1. For somewhat similar analyses, but with quite different evaluations, see James Chace, "Imperial America and the Common Interest," *World Policy* 19 (Spring 2002): 1–9; Charles Krauthammer, "The Unipolar Moment Revisited," *National Interest* 70 (Winter 2002/03): 5–17; Stephen Peter Rosen, "An Empire, If You Can Keep It," ibid 71 (Spring 2003): 51–62; Robert Art, *A Grand Strategy for America* (Ithaca, NY: Cornell University Press, 2003), 87–92.

2. See Deborah Larson, *Origins of Containment: A Psychological Explanation* (Princeton: Princeton University Press, 1985), which draws on Bem's theory of self-perception. See Daryl Bem, "Self-Perception Theory" in Leonard Berkowitz, ed., *Advances in Experimental Social Psychology*, vol. 6 (New York: Academic Press, 1972), 1–62.

3. Paul Kennedy, *The Rise and Fall of the Great Powers: Economic Change and Military Conflict from 1500 to 2000* (New York: Random House, 1987); Robert Gilpin, *War and Change in World Politics* (New York: Cambridge University Press, 1981); Geoffrey Parker, *The Grand Strategy of Philip II* (New Haven: Yale University Press, 1998).

4. White House, "The National Security Strategy of the United States" (Washington, DC: September 2002), i, 1. Bush's West Point speech similarly declared: "Moral truth is the same in every culture, in every time, and in every place. . . . We are in a conflict between good and evil. . . . When it comes to the common rights and needs of men and women, there is no clash of civilizations." "Remarks by the President at 2002 Graduation Exercise of the Unites States Military Academy," White House Press Release, 1 June 2002, 3; Paul Allen, *Philip III and Pax Hispanica, 1598–1621: The Failure of Grand Strategy* (New Haven: Yale University Press, 2000).

5. Thus, Samuel Huntington, who agrees that a state's foreign policy is strongly influenced by its domestic regime, argues that conflict can be reduced only by not pushing Western values on other societies. See his *The Clash of Civilizations and the Remaking of the World Order* (New York: Simon and Schuster, 1996).

6. John Lewis Gaddis, "Bush's Security Strategy," *Foreign Policy* 133 (November/ December 2002): 50–57.

7. For the concept of natural order, see Stephen Toulmin, *Foresight and Understanding: An Enquiry into the Aims of Science* (Bloomington: Indiana University Press, 1961).

8. Edward Mansfield and Jack Snyder, *Democratization and War* (Cambridge, MA: MIT Press, forthcoming).

9. It can be argued that Carter's policy toward the shah's regime in Iran is an exception. There is something to this, but the conflict between his policy and stability is more apparent in retrospect than it was at the time.

10. Quoted in David Sanger, "U.S. to Withdraw From Arms Accord With North Korea," *New York Times*, 20 October 2002.

11. Quoted in Frank Bruni, "For President, a Mission and a Role in History," ibid. 22 September 2001; "President Thanks World Coalition for Anti-Terrorism Efforts," White House Press Release, 11 March 2002, 3–4; also see "Remarks by the President at 2002 Graduation Exercise," 4–5.

12. "President Bush, Prime Minister Koizumi Hold Press Conference," White House Press Release, 18 February 2002, 6.

13. "President, Vice President Discuss the Middle East," White House Press Release, 21 March 2002, 2.

14. Speech to the American Enterprise Institute, 26 February 2003. For a general discussion of the administration's optimism about the effects of overthrowing Saddam on the Middle East, see Philip Gordon, "Bush's Middle East Vision," *Survival* 45 (Spring 2003): 155–165.

15. Quoted in David Sanger and Thom Shanker, "Bush Says Regime in Iraq is No More; Syria is Penalized," *New York Times*, 16 April 2003.

16. Also see White House, *National Strategy to Combat Weapons of Mass Destruction* (Washington, DC: December 2002), 1.

17. It is no accident that the leading theorist of this school of thought, Albert Wohlstetter, trained and sponsored many of the driving figures of the Bush administration, such as Paul Wolfowitz and Richard Perle.

18. Letter accompanying "National Security Strategy of the United States," ii. Calling this aspect of the doctrine as our policy against Iraq "preemptive," as the Bush administration does, is to do violence to the English language. No one thought that Iraq was about to attack anyone; rather, the argument was that Iraq and perhaps others are terrible menaces that eventually will do the United States great harm and must be dealt with as soon as possible, before the harm has been inflicted and while prophylactic actions can be taken at reasonable cost. For a study of cases, see Robert Litwak, "The New Calculus of Pre-emption," *Survival* 44 (Winter 2002–03): 53–79.

19. Dale Copeland, *The Origins of Major War* (Ithaca, NY: Cornell University Press, 2000); also see John Mearsheimer, *Tragedy of Great Power Politics* (New York: Norton, 2001). For important conceptual distinctions and propositions, see Jack Levy, "Declining Power and the Preventive Motivation for War," *World Politics* 40 (October 1987): 82–107; for a study that is skeptical of the general prevalence of preventive wars but presents one example, Jack Levy and Joseph Gochal, "Democracy and Preventive War: Israel and the 1996 Sinai Campaign," *Security Studies* 11 (Winter 2001/2): 1–49. On the U.S. experience, see Art, *A Grand Strategy for America*, 181–197. Randall Schweller argues that democratic states fight preventively only under very restrictive circumstances: "Domestic Structure and Preventive War: Are Democracies More Pacific?" *World Politics* 44 (January 1992): 235–269; he notes the unusual nature of the Israeli cases. For the argument that states are generally well served resisting the temptation to fight preventively, see Richard Betts, "Striking First: A History of Thankfully Lost Opportunities," *Ethics and International Affairs*

17 (2003): 17–24. For a review of power transition theory, which in one interpretation is driven by preventive motivation, see Jacek Kugler and Douglas Lemke, *Parity and War: Evaluations and Extensions of The War Ledger* (Ann Arbor: University of Michigan Press, 1996).

20. Marc Trachtenberg, *History and Strategy* (Princeton: Princeton University Press, 1991), chap. 3; William Burr and Jeffrey Richelson, "Whether to 'Strangle the Baby in the Cradle': The United States and the Chinese Nuclear Program, 1960–64," *International Security* 25 (Winter 2000/01): 54–99. Gregory Mitrovich shows how much of American early Cold War policy was driven by the fear that it could not sustain a prolonged confrontation: *Undermining the Kremlin: America's Strategy to Subvert the Soviet Bloc, 1947–1956* (Ithaca, NY: Cornell University Press, 2000).

21. A minor illustration of the power of fear was the closing of a New York subway station when a first-year art student taped to the girders and walls thirty-seven black boxes with the word "fear" on them, an unlikely thing for a bomber to do. See Michael Kimmelman, "In New York, Art Is Crime, And Crime Becomes Art," *New York Times*, 18 December 2002. For a study of how people's willingness to sacrifice civil liberties are affected by their fear of a future attack, see Darren Davis and Brian Silver, "Civil Liberties vs. Security: Public Opinion in this Context of the Terrorist Attacks on America" (unpublished manuscript); Leonie Huddy, Stanley Feldman, Charles Taber, and Gallya Lahav, "The Politics of Threat: Cognitive and Affective Reactions to 9/11" (paper presented at the annual meeting of the American Political Science Association, Boston, 29 August–1 September 2002); Leonie Huddy, Stanley Feldman, Theresa Capelos, and Colin Provost, "The Consequences of Terrorism: Disentangling the Effects of Personal and National Threat," *Political Psychology* 23 (September 2002): 485–510. For a general theory of the impact of feelings of vulnerability on policy, see Charles Kupchan, *The Vulnerability of Empire* (Ithaca, NY: Cornell University Press, 1994),

22. According to Robert Woodward, George Tenet believed that "Bush had been the least prepared of all of [the administration leaders] for the terrorist attacks." See *Bush at War* (New York: Simon and Schuster, 2002), 318. Before then, his administration had concentrated on Russia and the PRC.

23. *New York Times*, 1 February 2003.

24. Quoted in James Risen, David Sanger, and Thom Shanker, "In Sketchy Data, Trying to Gauge Iraq Threat," ibid., 20 July 2003.

25. Bernard Brodie, "The Development of Nuclear Strategy," *International Security* 2 (Spring 1978): 83.

26. Daniel Kahneman and Amos Tversky, eds., *Choices, Values, and Frames* (New York: Cambridge University Press, 2000).

27. "Transcript of President Bush's Remarks on the End of Major Combat in Iraq," *New York Times*, 2 March 2003. (Emphasis added.) He used a similar formulation three months later: "President Meets with Small Business Owners in New Jersey," 16 June 2003, White House Press Release.

28. "National Security Strategy of the United States," ii, 15; also see "In President's Words: Free People Will Keep the Peace of the World," *New York Times*, 27 February 2003; "Bush's Speech on Iraq: 'Saddam Hussein and His Sons Must Leave," ibid., 18 March 2003; Tony Blair's statement quoted in Emma Daly, "Both Britain and Spain Dismiss Offer On Iraq Missiles," ibid., 1 March 2003.

29. Quoted in Carl Hulse, "Senate Republicans Back Bush's Iraq Policy, as Democrats Call it Rash and Bullying." ibid., 8 March 2003.

30. One of those outside the government who helped formulate the Bush doctrine denies that it is unilateralism. See Philip Zelikow, "The Transformation of National Security," *National Interest* 71 (Spring 2003): 24–25.

31. Quoted in Steven Erlanger, "Bush's Move On ABM Pact Gives Pause to Europeans," *New York Times*, 13 December 2001; also see Suzanne Daley, "Many in Europe Voice Worry that U.S. Will Not Consult Them," ibid., 31 January 2002; Erlanger, "Protests, and Friends Too, Await Bush in Europe," ibid., 22 May 2002; Elizabeth Becker, "U.S. Unilateralism Worries Trade Officials," ibid., 17 March 2003.

32. Quoted in Karen DeYoung, "Chirac Moves To Repair United States Ties," *Washington Post*, 16 April 2003.

33. Quoted in Bob Woodward interview with Bush in ibid., 19 November 2002; also see Woodward, *Bush at War*, 281; quoted in Somini Sengupta, "U.N. Forum Stalls on Sex Education and Abortion Rights," *New York Times*, 10 May 2002.

34. Patrick Tylor and Felicity Barringer, "Annan Says U.S. Will Violate Charter if It Acts Without Approval," ibid., 11 March 2003.

35. Paul Schroeder sharply differentiates hegemony from empire, arguing that the former is much more benign and rests on a high degree of consent and respect for diverse interests: "Empire or Hegemony?" address given to the American Historical Association meeting, Chicago, 3 January 2003. I agree that distinctions are needed, but at this point both the terms and the developing American policy are unclear. I have a soft spot in my heart for primacy because it has the fewest connotations. Ten years ago I argued that the United States did not need to seek primacy (at least I was sensible enough to avoid saying whether the United States would be sensible): Jervis, "The Future of World Politics: Will it Resemble the Past?" *International Security* 16 (Winter 1991/92): 39–73; "International Primacy: Is the Game Worth the Candle?" ibid., 17 (Spring 1993): 52–67. For discussions about what an empire means today, whether it necessarily involves territorial control and how it can be maintained, see Rosen, "An Empire if You Can Keep It"; also see Kurth, "Migration and the Dynamics of Empire," *National Interest* 71 (Spring 2003): 5–16; and Anna Simons, "The Death of Conquest," ibid., 41–49.

36. Only after World War I was lip-service paid to the concept that all states had equal rights. The current United States stance would be familiar to any nineteenth-century diplomat.

37. Remarks by the President at 2002 Graduation Exercise," 4. The Wolfowitz draft is summarized in stories in the *New York Times*. 8 March and 24 May 1992. Also see Zalmay Khalilzad, *From Containment to Global Leadership? America and the World After the Cold War* (Santa Monica, CA: RAND, 1995); and Robert Kagan and William Kristol, eds., *Present Dangers: Crisis and Opportunity in American Foreign and Defense Policy* (San Francisco: Encounter Books, 2000). This stance gives others incentives to develop asymmetric responses, of which terrorism is only the most obvious example. For possible PRC options, see Thomas Christensen, "Posing Problems Without Catching Up: China's Rise and Challenges for U.S. Security Policy," *International Security* 25 (Spring 2001): 5–40.

38. It is noteworthy that hegemonic stability theory comes with both a malign and a benign version. See Duncan Snidal, "The Limits of Hegemonic Stability Theory," *International Organization* 25 (Autumn 1985): 579–614; for the applicability of these theories to the pre-Bush post-Cold War world, see Michael Mastanduno, "Preserving the Unipolar Moment: Realist Theories and United States Grand Strategy after the Cold War," *International Security* 21 (Spring 1997): 49–88; see the exchange between Mark Sheetz and Mastanduno in ibid., 22 (Winter 1997/98): 168–174; Ethan Kapstein and Michael Mastanduno, eds., *Unipolar Politics: Realism and State Strategies After*

the Cold War (New York: Columbia University Press, 1999); G. John Ikenberry, ed., *America Unrivaled: The Future of the Balance of Power* (Ithaca, NY: Cornell University Press, 2002).

39. See, for example, David Reynolds, *From Munich to Pearl Harbor: Roosevelt's America and the Origins of the Second World War* (Chicago: Dee, 2001); Warren Kimball, *The Juggler: Franklin Roosevelt as Wartime Statesman* (Princeton: Princeton University Press, 1991).

40. Melvyn Leffler, *A Preponderance of Power: National Security, the Truman Administration, and the Cold War* (Stanford, CA: Stanford University Press, 1992); Thomas Christensen, *Useful Adversaries: Grand Strategy, Domestic Mobilization, and Sino-American Conflict, 1947–1958* (Princeton: Princeton University Press, 1996); for the domestically imposed limits on this process, sec Aaron Friedberg, *In the Shadow of the Garrison State: America's Anti-Statism and Its Cold War Grand Strategy* (Princeton: Princeton University Press, 2000); Michael Hogan, *A Cross of Iron: Harry S. Truman and the Origins of the National Security State, 1945–1954* (New York: Cambridge University Press, 1998).

41. Geir Lunstestad, "Empire by Invitation? The United States and Western Europe, 1945–1952," *Journal of Peace Research* 23 (September 1986): 263–277; James McAllister, *No Exit: America and the German Problem, 1943–1954* (Ithaca, NY: Cornell University Press, 2002).

42. Charles Maier, *In Search of Stability: Explorations in Historical Political Economy* (New York: Cambridge University Press, 1987), 148. Also see John Lewis Gaddis, *We Now Know: Rethinking Cold War History* (New York: Oxford University Press, 1997); and Thomas Risse-Kappen, *Cooperation Among Democracies: The European Influence on U.S. Foreign Policy* (Princeton: Princeton University Press, 1995).

43. William Wohlforth, "The Stability of a Unipolar World," *International Security* 24 (Summer 1999): 5–41; see also Kenneth Waltz, "Structural Realism After the Cold War," ibid. 25 (Summer 2000): 5–41. For a dissenting view, see Immanuel Wallerstein, "The Eagle Has Crash Landed," Foreign Policy 131 (July/August 2002): 60–68. The well-crafted argument by Robert Kudrle that the United States does not always gets its way even on some important issues is correct, but I think does not contradict the basic structural point: "Hegemony Strikes Out: The U.S. Global Role in Anti-Trust, Tax Evasion, and Illegal Immigration," *International Studies Perspectives* 4 (February 2003): 52–71.

44. See, for example, G. John Ikenberry, "After September 11: America's Grand Strategy and International Order in the Age of Terror," *Survival* 43 (Winter 2001–2002): 19–34; Ikenberry, *After Victory: Institutions, Strategic Restraint, and the Rebuilding of Order After Major War* (Princeton: Princeton University Press, 2000); John Gerard Ruggie, *Winning the Peace: America and the New World Order* (New York: Columbia University Press, 1996); Joseph Nye, *The Paradox of American Power: Why the World's Only Superpower Can't Go It Alone* (New York: Oxford University Press. 2002); John Steinbrunner, *Principles of Global Security* (Washington, DC: Brookings Institution, 2000). More popular treatments are Clyde Prestowitz, *Rogue Nation: American Unilateralism and the Failure of Good Intentions* (New York: Basic Books, 2003); and Michael Hirsh, *At War With Ourselves: Why America Is Squandering Its Chance to Build a Better World* (New York: Oxford University Press, 2003).

45. Quoted in James Harding, "Conflicting Views From Two Bush Camps," *Financial Times,* 20 March 2003; for a perceptive analysis, see Bruni, "For President, a Mission and a Role in History." Also see Woodward, *Bush at War,* 102, 205, 281.

46. Richard Betts, "The Soft Underbelly of American Primacy: Tactical Advantages of Terror," *Political Science Quarterly* 117 (Spring 2002): 19–36.

47. See, for example, Jesse Helms's defense of unilateralism as the only way consistent with American interests and traditions: "American Sovereignty and the UN," *National Interest* 62 (Winter 2000/ 01): 31–34. For a discussion of historical, sociological, and geographical sources of the moralistic outlook in American foreign policy, see Arnold Wolfers, *Discord and Collaboration* (Baltimore: Johns Hopkins University Press, 1962), chap. 15; and Louis Hartz, *The Liberal Tradition in America* (New York: Harcourt, Brace, 1955), chap. 11. For a discussion of current U.S. policy in terms of its self-image as an exceptional state, see Stanley Hoffmann, "The High and the Mighty," *American Prospect* 13 (January 2003): 28–31.

48. Thus, it is not entirely surprising that many of the beliefs mustered in support of United States policy toward Iraq parallel those held by European expansionists in earlier eras: Jack Snyder, "Imperial Temptations," *National Interest* 71 (Spring 2003): 29–40.

49. Quoted in Hans Morgenthau, *Politics Among Nations*, 5th ed. (New York: Knopf, 1978), 169–170. (Emphasis in the original.)

50. Kenneth Waltz, "America as a Model for the World? A Foreign Policy Perspective," *PS: Political Science and Politics* 24 (December 1991): 69; also see Waltz's discussion of the Gulf War: "A Necessary War?" in Harry Kriesler, ed., *Confrontation in the Gulf* (Berkeley, CA: Institute of International Studies, 1992), 59–65. Charles Krauthammer also expected this kind of behavior, but believed that it will serve the world as well as the American interests. Krauthammer, "The Unipolar Moment," *Foreign Affairs, America and the World, 1990–91* 70 (no. 1, 23–33); also see Krauthammer, "The Unipolar Moment Revisited." For a critical analysis, see Chace, "Imperial America and the Common Interest." As Waltz noted much earlier, even William Fulbright, while decrying the arrogance of American power, said that the United States could and should "lead the world in an effort to change the nature of its politics": quoted in *Theory of International Politics* (Reading, MA: Addison-Wesley, 1979), 201.

51. Alexander Wendt and, more persuasively, Paul Schroeder, would disagree or at least modify this generalization, arguing that prevailing ideas can and have led to more moderate and consensual behavior: Wendt, *Social Theory of International Politics* (New York: Cambridge University Press, 1999); Schroeder, *The Transformation of European Politics, 1762–1848* (New York: Oxford University Press, 1994); and "Does the History of International Politics Go Anywhere?" In David Wetzel and Theodore Hamerow, eds., *International Politics and German History* (Westport, CT: Praeger, 1997), 15–36. This is a central question of international politics and history that I cannot fully discuss here, but believe that at least the mild statement that unbalanced power is dangerous can easily be sustained.

52. See, for example, Fareed Zakaria, "Realism and Domestic Politics: A Review Essay," *International Security* 17 (Summer 1992): 177–198; Robert Tucker, "The Radical Critique Assessed" in Tucker, *The Radical Left and American Foreign Policy* (Baltimore: Johns Hopkins University Press, 1971), 69–77, 106–111. For a discussion of alternative possibilities suggested by American history, see Edward Rhodes, "The Imperial Logic of Bush's Liberal Agenda," *Survival* 45 (Spring 2003): 131–154.

53. Wolfers, *Discord and Collaboration*, chap. 5.

54. "President Thanks World Coalition for Anti-Terrorism Efforts"; David Sanger, "In Reichstag, Bush Condemns Terror as New Despotism," *New York Times*, 24 May 2002. Also see "Remarks by President at 2002 Graduation Exercise." The question of how broad the target should be was debated within the administration from the start, with Bush initially insisting on a focus on al Qaeda: Woodward, *Bush at War.*

55. Wolfers, *Discord and Collaboration*, chap. 10.

56. John Mueller, "The Catastrophe Quota: Trouble after the Cold War," *Journal of Conflict Resolution* 38 (September 1994): 355–375; also see Frederick Hartmann, *The Conservation of Enemies: A Study in Enmity* (Westport, CT: Greenwood Press, 1982).

57. Waltz, *Theory of International Politics*, 200.

58. John S. Galbraith, "The 'Turbulent Frontier' as a Factor in British Expansion," *Comparative Studies in Society and History* 2 (January 1960): 34–48; *Reluctant Empire: British Policy on the South African Frontier, 1834–1854* (Berkeley: University of California Press, 1963). Also see Ronald Robinson and John Gallager with Alice Denny, *Africa and the Victorians: The Official Mind of Imperialism* (London: Macmillan, 1961). A related imperial dynamic that is likely to recur is that turning a previously recalcitrant state into a client usually weakens it internally and requires further intervention.

59. See esp., Copeland, *Origins of Major War;* Mearsheimer, *Tragedy of Great Power Politics*.

60. Waltz (*Theory of International Politics*) sees this behavior as often self-defeating; Mearsheimer (*Tragedy of Great Power Politics*) implies that it is not; Copeland's position is somewhere in between.

61. George W. Bush would endorse Wilson's claim that America's goal must be "the destruction of every arbitrary power anywhere in the world that can separately, secretly, and of its single choice disturb the peace of the world" just as he would join Clinton in calling for "the spread of his revolt [i.e., the American revolution], this liberation, to the great stage of the world itself!" "An Address at Mount Vernon," 4 July 1918, in Arthur Link et al., eds., *The Papers of Woodrow Wilson,* vol. 48, *May 13–July 17, 1918* (Princeton: Princeton University Press, 1985), 516–517.

62. Robert Jervis, "Was the Cold War a Security Dilemma?" *Journal of Cold War History* 3 (Winter 2001): 36–60; also see Paul Roe, "Former Yugoslavia: The Security Dilemma That Never Was?" *European Journal of International Relations* 6 (September 2000): 373–393. The current combination of fear and hope that produces offensive actions for defensive motives resembles the combination that produced the pursuit of preponderance in the aftermath of World War II.

63. Robert Jervis, "Theories of War in an Era of Leading Power Peace," *American Political Science Review* 96 (March 2003): 1–14.

64. The best known statement of this position is Robert Kagan, *Of Paradise and Power: America and Europe in the New World Order* (New York: Knopf, 2003).

65. Adam Clymer, "European Poll Faults U.S. for its Policy in the Mid East," *New York Times,* 19 April 2002.

66. Quoted in David Sanger, "Witness to Auschwitz Evil, Bush Draws a Lesson," ibid., 1 June 2003.

67. Quoted in John Tagliabue, "France and Russia Ready to Use Veto Against Iraq War," ibid., 6 March 2003.

68. This is a version of Stephen Walt's argument that states balance against threat, not power: *The Origins of Alliances* (Ithaca, NY: Cornell University Press, 1987).

69. I have discussed how Bush's policy toward Iraq does and does not fit with deterrence thinking in "The Confrontation Between Iraq and the United States: Implications for the Theory and Practice of Deterrence," *European Journal of International Relations* 9 (June 2003): 315–337.

70. Quoted in R. W. Seton-Watson, *Disraeli, Gladstone, and the Eastern Question* (New York: Norton, 1972), 222.

71. Kenneth Waltz, *The Spread of Nuclear Weapons: More May Be Better* (London: IISS, Adelphi Paper No. 171, 1981); Scott Sagan and Kenneth Waltz, *The Spread of Nuclear Weapons: A Debate Renewed* (New York: Norton, 2003). For a range of views, see Marc

Trachtenberg, "Waltzing to Armgeddon?" *National Interest* 69 (Fall 2002): 144–155; Eric Herring, ed., *Preventing the Use of Weapons of Mass Destruction,* special issue of *Journal of Strategic Studies* 23 (March 2000); T. V. Paul, Richard Harknett, and James Wirtz, eds., *The Absolute Weapon Revisited: Nuclear Arms and the Emerging International Order* (Ann Arbor: University of Michigan Press, 1998).

72. For a discussion of possible forms of nonviolent opposition, see Robert Pape, "Soft Balancing Against the United States" (unpublished paper, University of Chicago, 2003).

73. See David Calleo, *The German Problem Reconsidered: Germany and the World Order, 1870 to the Present* (New York: Cambridge University Press, 1978) for a summary of relevant laboratory experiments;; see Robert Goodin, "How Amoral *Is* Hegemon," *Perspectives on Politics* 1 (March 2003): 123–126.

74. "A Luncheon Address to the St. Louis Chamber of Commerce," 5 September 1919 in Arthur Link et al., eds., *The Papers of Woodrow Wilson,* vol. 63, *September 4– November 5, 1919* (Princeton: Princeton University Press, 1990), 33.

75. Quoted in David Sanger, "A New View of Where America Fits in the World," *New York Times,* 18 February 2001.

°I am grateful for comments from Robert Art, Richard Betts, Jim Caraley, Dale Copeland, Peter Gourevitch, Chaim Kaufmann, Robert Lieber, Marc Trachtenberg, and Kenneth Waltz.